				Values of Words
16 Grammar	17 Usage	18 A Glossary of Usage (240 entries)	19	The Dictionary

REFERENCE RESOURCES

20 Units of Discourse: A Microgrammar	21 Nouns	22 Pronouns	23 Verbs and Verbals
24 Adjectives	25 Adverbs	26 Prepositions	27 Conjunctions
28 Interjections	29 Phrases	30 Subordinate Clauses	31 Sentences

32 Manuscript Form

32A Period	32B Ellipsis Points	32C Question Mark	32D Exclamation Point	32E Comma
32F Semicolon	32G Colon	32H Dash	32I Hyphen	32J Apo
32K Parentheses	32L Square Brackets	32M Quotation Marks	32N Slant	32O Cap
32P Italics	32Q Numbers	32R Spelling	32S Mechanics of Letter Form	

33 Glossary of Additional Linguistic, Literary, and Rhetorical Terms (220 entries)

ot Language

THE HOLT
GUIDE TO
ENGLISH

THE HOLT GUIDE TO ENGLISH

A Contemporary
Handbook of Rhetoric,
Language, and Literature

WILLIAM F. IRMSCHER
University of Washington

HOLT, RINEHART AND WINSTON, INC.
New York   Chicago   San Francisco   Atlanta
Dallas   Montreal   Toronto   London   Sydney

ACKNOWLEDGMENTS

For permission to reprint materials copyrighted by authors, publishers, and agents, I am indebted to the following:

"Ain't," from *The American Heritage Dictionary of the English Language.* © Copyright 1969, 1970 by American Heritage Publishing Co., Inc. Reprinted by permission.

"Beautiful," from *The American College Dictionary* (Random House, 1947). Reprinted by permission of Random House, Inc.

"My Sweet Old Etcetera" by E. E. Cummings. Copyright 1926, by Horace Liveright; renewed, 1954, by E. E. Cummings. Reprinted from *Poems 1923-1954* by E. E. Cummings by permission of Harcourt Brace Jovanovich, Inc. From *Complete Poems 1913-1935* by E. E. Cummings, by permission of MacGibbon & Kee Ltd.

Excerpts from *Murder in the Cathedral* by T. S. Eliot by permission of Harcourt Brace Jovanovich, Inc., and Faber and Faber Ltd.

Excerpt from *The Sound and the Fury* by William Faulkner, by permission of Random House, Inc., the Author's Literary Estate, and Chatto & Windus.

"Dust of Snow" and excerpt from "The Mending Wall" by Robert Frost. From *The Poetry of Robert Frost* edited by Edward Connery Lathem. Copyright 1923, 1930, 1939, © 1969 by Holt, Rinehart and Winston, Inc. Copyright 1951, © 1958 by Robert Frost. Copyright © 1967 by Lesley Frost Ballantine. Reprinted by permission of Holt, Rinehart and Winston, Inc., and Jonathan Cape Ltd.

Excerpt from *A Farewell to Arms* by Ernest Hemingway, by permission of Charles Scribner's Sons.

Excerpt from "The Windhover" by Gerard Manley Hopkins. From *Poems of Gerard Manley Hopkins* by Gerard Manley Hopkins, by permission of Oxford University Press.

Excerpt from "Reveille" from "A Shropshire Lad"—Authorised Edition—from *The Collected Poems of A. E. Housman.* Copyright 1939, 1940, © 1959 by Holt, Rinehart and Winston, Inc. Copyright © 1967, 1968 by Robert E. Symons. Reprinted by permission of Holt, Rinehart and Winston, Inc., and The Society of Authors as the literary representative of the Estate of A. E. Housman, and Jonathan Cape Ltd., publishers of A. E. Housman's *Collected Poems.*

"Inspire," from *The Random House Dictionary of the English Language* (1968), College Edition, by permission of Random House, Inc.

"Inspire," from *Webster's New World Dictionary* of the American Language, Second College Edition. Copyright © 1970 by The World Publishing Company, Cleveland and New York.

Excerpts from "The Bald Soprano" by Eugene Ionesco. From *Four Plays* by Eugene Ionesco. Reprinted by permission of Grove Press, Inc. Translated from the French by Donald M. Allen. Copyright © 1958 by Grove Press, Inc., and Calder and Boyars Ltd.

Excerpt from *Exit the King* by Eugene Ionesco, reprinted by permission of Grove Press, Inc. Translated from the French by Donald Watson. Copyright © 1963 by John Calder (Publishers) Ltd.

"The Death of the Ball Turret Gunner" by Randall Jarrell. Reprinted with the permission of Farrar, Straus & Giroux, Inc., from *The Complete Poems* by Randall Jarrell, copyright © 1945, 1969 by Mrs. Randall Jarrell.

Excerpt from "Araby" by James Joyce. From *Dubliners* by James Joyce, reprinted by permission of The Viking Press, Inc.

Excerpt from "Boots" by Rudyard Kipling. From *Kipling: A Selection of His Stories and Poems* by Rudyard Kipling. Reprinted by permission of Doubleday & Company, Inc.

Excerpt from "Come Live with Me and Be My Love" by C. Day Lewis. From *Collected Poems (1954)* by C. Day Lewis, copyright 1954 by C. Day Lewis, reprinted by permission of the Harold Matson Company, Inc., Chatto & Windus, and Jonathan Cape Ltd.

Excerpt from "The End of the World" by Archibald MacLeish. From *Collected Poems 1917–1952* by Archibald MacLeish, reprinted by permission of Houghton Mifflin Company.

Map from *The Pronunciation of English in the Atlantic States* by Hans Kurath and Raven I. McDavid, Jr. Reprinted by permission of The University of Michigan Press.

Map from *Dialects U.S.A.* by Jean Malmstrom. Copyright © 1963, by the National Council of Teachers of English.

Excerpt from "Portrait of the Artist as a Prematurely Old Man" by Ogden Nash. From *The Face Is Familiar* by Ogden Nash. Reprinted by permission of Curtis Brown, Ltd. Copyright © 1934 The Curtis Publishing Co., and by permission of Little, Brown and Co.

"Revolution: The Vicious Circle" by John Nist. From *College Composition and Communication*. Copyright © 1968 by the National Council of Teachers of English. Reprinted by permission of the publisher and John Nist.

Excerpt from "Arms and the Boy" by Wilfred Owen. From Wilfred Owen, *Collected Poems*. Copyright Chatto & Windus, Ltd. 1946 © 1963. Reprinted by permission of New Directions Publishing Corporation, Mr. Harold Owen, and Chatto & Windus.

Excerpt from *Pale Horse, Pale Rider* by Katherine Anne Porter. Reprinted by permission of Harcourt Brace Jovanovich, Inc., and by permission of Jonathan Cape Limited, publishers of *The Collected Stories of Katherine Anne Porter*.

Excerpt from "Dance Figure" by Ezra Pound, *Personae*. Copyright 1926 by Ezra Pound. Reprinted by permission of New Directions Publishing Corporation.

Excerpt from "Winter Remembered" by John Crowe Ransom. From *Selected Poems* by John Crowe Ransom. Reprinted by permission of Random House, Inc., and by permission of Laurence Pollinger Limited, and Eyre & Spottiswoode Ltd.

"Luke Havergal" by Edwin Arlington Robinson is reprinted by permission of Charles Scribner's Sons from *The Children of the Night* by Edwin Arlington Robinson (1897).

Excerpt from letter from Theodore Roethke to Kenneth Burke. From *Selected Letters of Theodore Roethke,* ed. Ralph J. Mills, Jr.: Reprinted by permission of the University of Washington Press.

"Septuagint," by permission. From *Webster's Seventh New Collegiate Dictionary* © 1970 by G. & C. Merriam Co., Publishers of the Merriam-Webster Dictionaries.

Excerpt from *Man and Superman* by George Bernard Shaw. Reprinted by permission of The Society of Authors, for the Bernard Shaw Estate.

Excerpt from "Aubade" by Edith Sitwell. From *Collected Poems of Edith Sitwell.* Reprinted by permission of Vanguard Press, Inc., and David Higham Associates, Ltd.

Excerpt from *Travels with Charley:* In Search of America by John Steinbeck. Copyright © 1961, 1962 by The Curtis Publishing Company, Inc. Copyright © 1962 by John Steinbeck. Reprinted by permission of The Viking Press, Inc., and McIntosh and Otis, Inc.

"Anecdote of the Jar" by Wallace Stevens. Copyright 1923 and renewed 1951 by Wallace Stevens. Reprinted from *The Collected Poems of Wallace Stevens* by permission of Alfred A. Knopf, Inc., and Faber and Faber Ltd.

Excerpts from "And Death Shall Have No Dominion" and "Do Not Go Gentle into that Good Night" by Dylan Thomas, *Collected Poems.* Copyright 1943 by New Directions Publishing Corporation. Reprinted by permission of New Directions Publishing Corporation. From *Collected Poems of Dylan Thomas.* Reprinted by permission of J. M. Dent & Sons Ltd.

"University Professors" through "Updike, John," from *The Readers' Guide to Periodical Literature,* (Vol. 26, p. 1246). Reprinted by permission of H. W. Wilson Company.

Excerpt from "First World War, October, 1939" in *One Man's Meat* by E. B. White. Copyright 1939 by E. B. White. By permission of Harper & Row, Publishers, Inc.

Excerpt from *The Glass Menagerie* by Tennessee Williams in *Six Modern American Plays.* Reprinted by permission of Random House, Inc. *The Glass Menagerie* copyright, 1945, 1948, by Tennessee Williams and Edwina D. Williams. New Directions.

Excerpt from *White Man Listen!* by Richard Wright. Copyright © 1957 by Richard Wright. Reprinted by permission of Doubleday & Company, Inc., and Paul R. Reynolds, Inc.

To Mildred

Preface

The purpose of this handbook is to provide a complete and flexible text which will serve both reference and teaching purposes. To this end, it gives full attention to rhetoric, language, literature, criticism, and composition. The ever-expanding nature of English studies makes it increasingly difficult to keep up with both past and current developments. Thus, this book attempts to assemble in one place a variety of background information for the study of English and to explain with a completeness that is adequate for most general purposes.

In order to achieve this comprehensiveness, certain arbitrary decisions have been made about space. For example, all study aids for the instructor and student have been included in a separate manual. As a result, the book is more flexible for those who prefer not to use them; for those who do, they are easily available. The study aids are keyed to the text and suggest the kinds of projects that students can undertake to reach their own conclusions concerning the qualities that produce good writers and good writing.

I have tried to achieve a number of specific objectives:

1. To set positive guidelines for the discussion of writing and to maintain a positive emphasis in the discussion of revision and usage by pointing out what a writer should *strive for* rather than what he should *avoid*.
2. To bring new thought and treatment to such topics as the writer's

attitudes, the audience, the drama of thinking, nonlinear logic, the paragraph bloc, variations of prose style, and, in specific terms, the characteristics that mark good writing.

3. To give background about the nature of literature and the genres of fiction, drama, and poetry as a means of understanding them, and to supply specific suggestions for writing on literary topics without inviting the stereotype of a student theme about literature instead of a personal, meaningful commentary.

4. To provide adequate information for the preparation of a reference paper without creating a special mystique about its difficulties.

5. To give a coverage of grammar that recognizes the contributions of several grammars without setting forth the complete description of any particular one, and to include material on the grammatical implications of the sound system.

6. To inform the reader about English usage on the assumption that flexible standards of usage do operate, subject to dialectal and individual variations; to leave appropriate choices, then, to the informed reader in terms of style and audience without imposing prescriptions or proscriptions.

7. To add interest to bare fact by including, where possible, brief historical material (on gender, for example) and explaining why certain distinctions are made (mass nouns and count nouns, for example).

8. To define terms so that they are understandable to the non-specialist, but not to avoid difficult terms like *dialectic* or *phoneme* or *tragedy,* despite the simplifications that a relatively brief definition demands.

9. To supply a full reference guide to manuscript form and to offer a workable approach to spelling problems.

10. To include in the final glossary concise explanations of terms that are frequently assumed by English professors but that are all too often unknown to students or too infrequently explained to them.

For a project of this magnitude, I have referred to more sources than I can possibly list. Some have been useful for major concepts, some for detail. But I fully recognize my deep sense of indebtedness to the scholarship of others that makes a book of this kind possible. For helpful criticism of the manuscript, I am particularly grateful to Professors Edward P. J. Corbett, Robert M. Gorrell, and Samuel R. Levin. Of inestimable help throughout the entire project has been the advice and commentary of Professor Richard Beal. For assistance in the planning, I am also indebted to my former colleague, Professor Paul Jenkins. My special thanks go to Phillip Leininger for initiating this project and providing the necessary encouragement and probing to keep it going.

The chief work on the manuscript has been done by my invaluable secretary, Mrs. Shirley Hanson; I am willing to gamble that she is one of the best in the nation.

All of these individuals have given the book strength; its limitations, to be sure, are my own.

Seattle, Washington   W.F.I.
September 1971

Contents

REFERENCE RESOURCES

THE
ELEMENTS
OF
RHETORIC

1

The Role
of Rhetoric

If the Age of Aquarius is to be a peaceful and just age, it will have to be an age of honest rhetoric. That will mean reclaiming rhetoric from many of the shoddy uses it has been put to. Today, it serves the advertiser, helping him to peddle health, ease, and happiness to the consumer who is led to believe he can buy them. It serves the politician, helping him to say impressively that something will be when many of us sense that it won't. It serves the propagandist, promoting causes with a gloss upon the facts. But rhetoric does not have to represent blandishment, bombast, or veneer. These are only the abuses of rhetoric. In its best sense, rhetoric seeks to draw men together, attempts to establish agreement by willing consent, and tries to create an identity of purpose among them to promote meaningful action. In these terms, rhetoric remains one of man's best hopes for a better day.

No one invented rhetoric. It sprang into being as soon as men saw the possibility of resolving their differences by speaking instead of fighting. Early rhetoric was concerned with the art of speaking in the law courts, the legislative assemblies, and councils of war. It was an art of persuading and exhorting. Ideally, it was designed to promote justice, to seek goodness, and to envision truth and beauty. As an art of persuasion, however, it was inevitable that rhetoric would be used by deceitful men for selfish purposes as well as by just men for virtuous causes. Thus, rhetoric has always had two implications. What we now call "mere rhetoric"—style without significance—need not obscure the fact that an-

3

other kind of rhetoric can be made to serve good causes in honest ways.

To speak of the need for an honest rhetoric in the twentieth century is therefore to reassert the ethical basis of rhetoric, to reclaim it as a force for justice. But in so doing we need also to consider the complications of our age in contrast to far simpler times when vast audiences were not accessible by means of mass communications. Publications, radio, and television now operate as inescapable influences upon our thinking—shaping our values, analyzing the current scene, making judgments for us, appealing for our acceptance and support. These are all concerns of rhetoric, but they are far more complex than at any time in the past because of the kind of world in which we live.

The extension of the ordinary man's world by means of mass media has made him dependent upon these influences as interpreters of the many things he can now experience. How is it possible for each man to think intelligently and make sound judgments about foreign wars, the population explosion, the pollution problem, the social revolution, the urban dilemma, spiraling costs, the prevailing morality, education in the schools, and so on and on—major issues brought to his attention in hourly newscasts, daily newspapers, and weekly digests. In this highly complex society, group after group seeks to win an audience. What are the factors that cause us to be persuaded, to accept, and to identify? How do we come to understand our responses except to know what rhetoric involves?

Recent thinking about rhetoric emphasizes that all rhetoric need not be verbal. Never has the word been so freely used in new contexts to suggest ways of appealing and influencing: the rhetoric of gesture, the rhetoric of the march, the rhetoric of the sit-in. True, in many instances actions have supplanted the spoken and written word. But everything spoken of in the name of rhetoric is not necessarily rhetoric. The "rhetoric of the nightstick," "the rhetoric of the twisted arm," and "the rhetoric of the hydrogen bomb" are distorted phrases because, though the nightstick and the twisted arm and the bomb may be ways to change men's actions, they leave the individual no choice, no willing assent, no voluntary involvement. Any means that deliberately forces or antagonizes or causes men to be divided fails to qualify as rhetoric.

It is wholly possible that the proliferation of groups to be heard in our time is responsible for a growing movement of anti-rhetoric—a non-rhetoric that does not seek to persuade but to demand, that has abandoned reason and emotional involvement in favor of intimidation; that depends upon shouts, threats, violence, and the exploitation of fear and anxiety rather than appeals to awareness, explanation, and willing acceptance. People ultimately scream who cannot otherwise be heard. They struggle when their screams are ignored. They may be justified in their struggle, but violence is not rhetoric. It may be an outward sign, however, that rhetoric has failed. If rhetoric does not fail, it then stands as a force against oppression, as a wedge against closed structures, as a force for freedom against tyranny. That is the importance of a vital and honest rhetoric in the twentieth century.

2

The Writer

In handbooks of this kind, the writer is often referred to as if he were a stereotype. Of course, he is not. He is a person; he is an individual. He has his own capabilities, his own temperament, his own stock of knowledge and experience, his own values, and his own limitations and inhibitions. All of these shape the writer. His system of values may at first seem irrelevant, but all we need to do is remind ourselves of the effect of personal attitudes upon writing. If an individual is motivated to learn only those things that have immediate or short-range cash value, he may be little interested in writing, which seems to him a long-term, poor-return investment or, at best, a concern of those who in his eyes are less practical-minded. Yet this shortsighted, utilitarian view overlooks what writing does for those who take it seriously.

Clearly, some people write better than others. They always will. But some people swim better than others too; some paint better, some read better, some speak better. The fact that a few people excel in a particular activity does not seem to discourage many others from trying, if they enjoy what they do and see benefits in it.

Even though every person who tries writing is an individual and may have his own way of going about the job, it is possible to set down a few generalizations about the process and an even more complete statement about qualities that are usually considered the marks of successful writing. Doing these two things draws a line of distinction between the act of writing and the product. What has been written may be of primary importance to the reader, but how to produce it is the writer's chief concern. And his personal views can exert a strong influence upon his writing before he ever does anything.

THE WRITER'S ATTITUDE TOWARD WRITING

Of first importance to the writer is his attitude toward writing itself. Some people dismiss it as something they can't do. What they usually mean is that it is something they don't want to do. Writing is something that any literate person can do, even without instruction. Everyone talks—another way of verbalizing thoughts—and that is background enough to begin to write.

No one can write for anyone else. If a teacher of writing takes the hand of a student and writes something with him, it is quite a different matter from the teacher of art who takes the hand of a student and helps him with the contour of a line. The teacher of writing is only going through the motions of penmanship, because what is being composed is the teacher's thinking and his words, not the student's. When the teacher of art helps a student, he is also doing something mechanical, but he is able to demonstrate a skill that is an important part of the process of drawing. Writing is not primarily a mechanical skill; it is a psychological act.

Because writing is a form of behavior, it cannot be made an exact science, and it is unfair to reduce it to rules that supposedly solve problems for everyone. Following somebody's system—step 1, step 2, step 3—gets results of a kind, but it may not be the kind that a writer does naturally, and it is not necessarily the kind that will meet every writing situation. The student who approaches each writing assignment with an equation (five arguments against capital punishment are . . . , three characteristics of today's youth are . . . , two predominant qualities of Picasso's paintings are . . .) will ultimately find himself locked in by his system, incapable of exploring a topic flexibly. Many skills can be taught in this lockstep fashion, but the invention and imagination needed for writing can be cultivated best in an environment that permits the writer first to be himself.

Writing, therefore, is not an act that needs to be postponed until all of the preliminaries have been mastered. It is a remarkably flexible and intuitive act that permits a writer to do many things well without always knowing precisely why he has made the right decisions. All he needs is the incentive to try. But he may not have a clear idea why he should try in the first place.

If one student insists that he is not likely to do more than write a few letters during the rest of his life, he may feel no great need to improve his writing ability. If another student thinks that someone else will always do his writing for him, that dictation will solve all of his needs, then he too may be poorly motivated. If someone else thinks he can get by in composition with the least possible effort because most people don't really care how something is written, then he also may be unenthusiastic about writing. These are all practical objections, to be sure, and they all contain an element of truth. However, they underestimate to a great extent what the demands for writing are upon the educated person, and they ignore the dependency, inconvenience, and frustration that occur when an individual lacks the capacity and confidence to do a job of writing on his own. The age of specialization has not diminished the need for written communication; it has increased it. Objections based on utility alone, however, underestimate the force of writing. The written document cannot be as easily forgotten as talk, which fades away immediately with the sound waves. And the writer who thinks that most people don't care about the quality of writing may misjudge what their reactions are to extremely poor writing. What he interprets as general indifference is more likely a widespread expectation that most published writing and personal communication will be both comprehensible and literate.

Yet to think of writing only in terms of its most obvious practical uses is to ignore a number of other benefits to be derived from writing. What does writing do for someone besides act as a means of communication with others?

First, it shows the individual what he actually knows and does not know or what he thinks he knows but cannot support. Talking does the same thing to a certain extent, but talking is ordinarily a dialogue. One speaker gets support from the other; they reinforce each other. Writing differs in that the writer has to carry the whole burden himself. It is a private act. If the writer is unable to push thoughts beyond generalizations, he can't very well carry on the act of writing. Writing, therefore, doesn't let anyone fool himself. It is visible proof of what an individual knows and what he is thinking.

Writing is also a means of organizing what we think. In early nonverbal stages, thinking occurs as a kind of gestalt. It is a total experience; ideas and emotions and sensations mix together. These are never completely separated, but writing can't be produced as an electronic flash like television. It has to be set down word after word in successive sentences and, in a sense, act like a thin wire channeling the mental charge of the mind. The linear form of words does not mean that ideas and feelings lose their force, but they are put under controls for useful purposes. Writing, therefore, helps to control and direct thinking and feeling.

Writing also helps us to weigh thought. The fact that we write slowly, in contrast to talking, is one of its strengths. We make discoveries as we write. We may suddenly see the limitations of our own thinking, or we may see relationships that we have not seen before. One thing suggests another. Setting down a thought helps us to reflect upon it. Once put down on paper, it is separated from the internal mechanism of our thinking, and we are sometimes able to see our own ideas and hear our own voices quite objectively, particularly if a period of time has intervened. To write clearly is to perceive clearly.

Finally, writing inescapably mirrors the self, no matter how plain and impersonal the style. Honest writing has to be an individual act, and as such it is a strong force for individualism against the massive pressures for conformity and system in our world. Because writing is a commitment of thoughts and feelings to paper, it requires some self-confidence. Clearly, if a writer has uncertainties about himself—who he is, where he is, what he knows, what his purposes are—he will have trouble writing. At the same time, however, writing is a way of working out those uncertainties and of finding an anchor. In *Soul on Ice,* Eldridge Cleaver makes an impressive comment to this point:

> I lost my self-respect. My pride as a man dissolved and my whole fragile moral structure seemed to collapse, completely shattered.
> That is why I started to write. To save myself.

Writing may not necessarily be easy, but it is a way for the individual to find himself. As in all creative acts, self has to be a part of the doing.

THE WRITER'S ATTITUDE TOWARD LANGUAGE

Of similar importance to the writer is his attitude toward language. Communication can be carried on with very limited resources, particularly in speech. Most people, whether they are educated or not, do not have much trouble making themselves understood in their daily affairs—but simple everyday acts of communication are not very complex. Occasions for writing are not only different but far more demanding in their use of language. If an individual operates on the assumption that he can get by with crude tools, he is sure to fall short of doing a craftsman's job. A craftsman has regard for his tools and pride in what he can produce with them. Good writing demands a craftsman's attitude toward language.

Further, if a person thinks that any kind of language will serve any purpose of writing, he limits the audience he can write for. The broader the audience he wants to address, the more inclusive the language needs to be. The furthest extension is a kind of national language, capable of being understood throughout the country. National magazines use a national language. All media that address a wide audience use a national language—essentially a standard dialect and standard usage. English is not different from French, German, or Italian in this respect, and the lack of a common national dialect in less developed countries, for example, China, India, and certain emerging African nations is universally accepted as a barrier to advancement. A standard dialect actually operates to everyone's advantage.

Acknowledging a standard dialect is not to say that other dialects are not effective and valuable. But, given the great diversity among English-speaking people, it is not true that all dialects are equal in reaching out to the total audience or in realizing the fullest capacity of the English language for expression. It stands to reason that the person with plentiful resources of language will find writing easier and more pleasurable. If he acquires a growing respect for the power of language to communicate, influence, and delight, he will come to see writing as something worth doing and worth doing well.

THE WRITER'S ATTITUDE TOWARD THE READER-CRITIC

The reluctance that many people show about writing can often be traced to an unexpressed view they hold about the reader-critic, particularly in a classroom situation. First, they see the reader as an enemy, not a friend. And, in truth, if an instructor consistently has only negative things to say about a student's writing, it is easy for the student to turn in routine work—writing that plays it safe, ventures nothing, and falls into dullness. Because all writing, no matter how good or bad it is, is a personal creation, the writer is naturally sensitive. The respect of a critic for the integrity of the writer and, in turn, the respect of the writer for his critic's intelligence and judgment are necessary conditions for criticism to function constructively.

A second common attitude toward the reader-critic that hinders writing is the view that the critic's comments are unfair because he does not understand what is down on the paper. And very often the reader does not understand. Even though the writer knows what his own prose says, he is frequently too close to his subject to be his own best critic. The impersonal view, the outside view, can sometimes reveal that in many instances the writer's mind was ahead of his pen, and the prose therefore has leaped over thoughts that only the writer can supply. Whether the writer likes it or not, the final judge of his prose is the reader. The enemy of the writer is not his reader but the chaos and confusion that both of them seek to overcome.

Finally, a good working relationship between a writer and his reader-critic depends upon the two of them seeing eye to eye on certain basic questions: What is the function of criticism? What essentially does improvement in writing mean? Does it mean proofreading? Eliminating errors in grammar, spelling, and punctuation? Does it mean learning the refinements of usage—what offends some people and what doesn't? Does it mean realizing the full potential of language by learning how to write things in varied and interesting ways? Does it mean being able to analyze more carefully, to be able to support opinions, and to put them down persuasively? All of these represent improvements of one kind or another, but they also represent a range of emphasis from matters of correctness to matters of appropriateness to matters of style to matters of substance. If a student says he wants to learn to write better, it all depends what he means and expects. If a writer and his reader-critic differ about what good writing is, then criticism is not apt to help, or it may even go so far as to harm if the writer firmly believes that the instructor is holding back from him a set of prescriptions that will provide all of the solutions to his writing problems. Hundreds of books about writing have been written, but even though a student could master all of them he would still have to make his own applications.

THE WRITER'S VOICE

Writing is capable of expressing both thoughts and feelings. The two can never be completely separated, but feelings can certainly be suppressed to the extent that some prose reads as if it were completely impersonal. Note the essentially bland tone of the following account of the living conditions of a family in Alabama:

Passage 1

George Gudger, 31-year old Alabama tenant farmer and his wife Annie Mae, 27, are no strangers to hard living. As a sharecropper with no land, no home, no mule, and no tools, Gudger is financially dependent on the landlord, who each Spring loans him equipment to work the land and rations money to support himself while the crop is growing. This debt is paid back, with interest, through the labor of Gudger and his family. The best the Gudgers have ever cleared after these annual transactions is $125. From this remaining sum they pay doctors' bills, repay any other debts plus interest, and make an attempt to clothe and feed four children under the age of ten until the following Spring.

This is an almost completely undramatized statement. There is no noticeable sign that the writer has personally observed the situation; these are all facts that he might have read in a book. In fact, their source is actually James Agee's *Now Let Us Praise Famous Men*. The account is sympathetic, but there is no special pleading. About the only sign of an attempt to influence the reader's feelings comes in the second sentence: "... with no land, no home, no mule, and no tools. ..." This brief piling up of phrases, which repeat the word "no," builds to a momentary climax and reveals a show of feeling. Otherwise, the facts are left to speak for themselves.

The relative objectivity of this passage may be compared with another view of the same scene:

Passage 2

In the midst of the hurried world of white collar workers, factory men, and the others who fill up spaces in the melange of today's metropolitan society, it is reassuring to stop for a moment to remember that to the south of our industrial cities lies a countryside of quaint sharecroppers, earning a living off nature's soil. A visit to this area will leave one with an understanding of the words "If I did not work, these worlds would perish," and of the important vision which inspired Markham's "Man with a Hoe." For here, a man's work is his life: from the moment he is old enough to pronounce the word until the last time he methodically returns his hatchet to its appropriate place among the other crude but highly valued tools, his life is spent in honest toil, the backbone of a great nation.

If we were not told that this is an account of the same situation in Passage 1, we would never know it from the prose. The viewpoint has changed completely; there are no hard facts. The writer looks upon the scene as if he were viewing a nineteenth-century landscape in an art museum. In fact, it would seem that the spirit of Millet's *The Angelus* has served as his model for interpreting the facts. This Alabama is a serene countryside dotted with "quaint sharecroppers," but we cannot get a close look at them because the wide-sweeping perspective diminishes them. The vast canvas also includes "white collar workers, factory men, and others who fill up spaces in the melange of today's metropolitan society. ..." At such a distance, the writer can romanticize. He makes pronouncements about the nobility of honest labor and moralizes with pious phrases. The passage expresses feeling, but it is feeling without involvement. The attitude is superficial; the tone sentimental; the style glossy. Writing of this kind tells us more about the writer than about the subject.

In a technical sense, these two passages use the same approach; that is, both are third person accounts, the writer is apart from his material, and the reader is an observer limited by what the writer tells. The treatment is quite different from that of still another writer who involves the reader by telling about herself and the kind of life she lives:

Passage 3

In two rooms of bare boards and a kitchen slapped up against the side of the house, six human beings sleep, eat, work, grow, and die in the midst of dirt, filth, and insects that they can't get away from. I can go running back to Spic and Span floors, Windex windows, Glade-filled rooms, and Blue Cheer clothes; but these people are stuck here, trapped by the life they lead, forced to stay on the land and forced to stay together.

This passage describes a personal reaction and intensifies the emotion by contrasting the living conditions of the sharecropper family with the writer's own style of living. It is written as if the author had seen with her own eyes. Each of these three passages, therefore, demonstrates how the writer's relation to his subject creates a different effect.

Almost any passage of prose can be characterized in terms of its voice. *Voice* is simply an analogy, a way of saying that the voice of the writer can be perceived in his prose as readily as if he had spoken the words. It is something partly under his control by the choices he makes about point of view and words and strategies; it is also something beyond his control because the personal voice, as Robert Frost has phrased it, gets "somehow entangled in the words and fastened to the page for the ear of the imagination." Frost thinks that voice is the only thing "that can save prose from itself."

When the writer is intentionally anonymous, the prose can be voiceless. The directions on a box of frozen vegetables, for example, are not intended to reveal anything about the writer. He is only an undifferentiated voice. He is supposed to write prose that is factual, precise, bland, controlled. Completely impersonal prose of this variety, however, is difficult to write for any extended space because essentially it requires the writer to mask himself completely. Even the author of Passage 1 does not completely obscure the personal voice. But, in general, that paragraph represents what is usually referred to as a plain style, a kind of writing whose main purpose is to provide facts without commentary or editorializing, prose that informs rather than persuades.

If a writer has no design to obscure himself, then the voices he can assume are as various as the attitudes he is capable of taking toward his material. He can be formal or informal, satiric, sentimental, ironic, or humorous. He can also be superficial, pompous, naive, or offensive. These are effects that are at times beyond his control, although any writer who respects criticism can learn about the bad effects he may unintentionally create.

The way we characterize a writer's voice is almost completely associational, based upon the things a writer does with language. Knowing him personally does not change what the prose itself conveys. Our responses are conditioned by a number of conventional devices. Exaggeration conveys emotion. Moderate words and simple, ordered sentences imply rational control. Punning and playing with sounds suggest informality and lightness of tone; ornateness is associated with the grandiose and formal. Relationships of this kind prevail in our thinking because they are true not only of the responses we have to writing but to other art forms as well. Agitated lines and sharp contrasts of color are the painter's ways of expressing strong feeling. A musician uses dynamics for emotional effects, or he can turn to the order and symmetry of a fugue for music that is intellectually appealing. One might add similar examples from architecture, dance, or landscape gardening. Only in terms of common techniques in the arts are we able to interpret an artist's intentions. It is questionable how far anyone can go to upset these normal expectations if he wants the tone of his writing to be properly interpreted.

THE WRITER'S POINT OF VIEW

The term "point of view" may be understood in a quite literal sense. It is the way a writer views his material. It is the stance he takes. He can be inside or outside, close or far away, beneath or above. These are figurative ways of saying that he can be a participant or an observer, close to his subject or removed from it, or looking at his subject from different angles. These perspectives also determine the degree of subjectivity or objectivity in a piece of writing. Another description of the sharecropper and his family will indicate what difference point of view makes. This passage takes the form of a personal letter by a young lady to her parents:

Passage 4

Well, I'm finally here. It seemed as if the train would never arrive, but I'm now situated in the backroom of a schoolhouse. I've even begun to meet the people I will work with during the coming months. All the knowledge of an expert could not have prepared me for the sickening conditions I find here! And in America too! One family, the Gudgers, lives in such a pathetic situation that I practically cried when I visited them. The six of them have a tiny shack, half of which is unusable. It is filthy and stinks from a combination of many, many odors. Their food is all but inedible, and the beds are overrun with a variety of bugs. I saw the baby scratch at some!

This is a highly subjective paragraph for two reasons: first, because the writer seems very close to the subject; and, second, because the writer cannot escape her own personal observations and feelings. The purpose of the writing is, of course, different from that in either Passages 1, 2, or 3. This is a personal letter. The writer is actually the subject of the letter—how she feels and why she feels as she does. There is no attempt to get beyond the self, as the writer of Passage 3 does, for example.

Objectivity is a capacity to assume other perspectives besides one's own. In an objective piece of writing, a writer can certainly come to his own conclusions, but objective consideration means simply that in the process of forming his own opinions he has considered and weighed other possible viewpoints. Objectivity is possible only when the writer attempts to get beyond the self and to gain some distance from his subject. It should by no means be assumed that subjectivity is bad and objectivity good. The relative merits of either depend upon the writer's purpose and his reader's expectations. The writer of Passage 4 seems too close and involved at the moment of writing to see beyond the things that upset her personally; the writer of Passage 2, by contrast, seems too far away to make any dependable observations. He ultimately falls back upon his way of thinking about the world in general. Both passages are subjective in their thinking, although they present the material differently.

THE PERSONAL PRONOUN AND POINT OF VIEW

Comparison of Passage 2, written in third person, and Passage 4, written in first person, indicates that subjectivity does not depend wholly upon the choice of pronouns. Ordinarily, anything written in first person singular tends to be more familiar and intimate than anything written in third person. Yet the writer should be aware, both in his reading and in his own writing, that pronouns shift in their uses. They may have a variety of implications, and the writer may use them to represent himself in different ways:

Uses of "I"

I—the writer by name, in his own right, with his own individual experience brought to bear upon the writing:

At the moment I am writing these words, I am distinctly depressed.
J. Middleton Murray

I—the writer as a representative of a group or spokesman for it:

What to the American slave is your Fourth of July? I answer: a day that reveals to him, more than all other days in the year, the gross injustice and cruelty to which he is the constant victim.
Frederick Douglass (1852)

I—the writer in some capacity as an official or as an authority upon a special subject:

> From the moment I examined the preliminary drawings I was disturbed and puzzled by its design, and I am still disturbed, though further reflection and observation have revealed a little of Wright's intentions and decisions.
>
> Lewis Mumford, as an authority on urban architecture, commenting on Frank Lloyd Wright's drawings for the Guggenheim Museum in New York

Frequently, the writer's role is implicit rather than expressed. He does not have to use obvious phrases like "as President of the United States" or "as an admirer of Gandhi" to make clear that he is writing in a special capacity and that his point of view restricts what he says. At times, however, a writer in conflict with his official position will add the qualification "but I personally think...."

I—the writer as a neutral, hypothetical subject:

> When I refuse to obey an unjust law, I do not contest the right of the majority to command, but I simply appeal from the sovereignty of the people to the sovereignty of mankind.
>
> Alexis de Tocqueville

I—the writer as an impersonal editorial guide:

> I have already suggested that our sexual uncertainties reflect a deep conflict we feel in areas other than those of our sexual emotions.
>
> Diana Trilling

Uses of "We"

We—a plural that embraces the writer and reader:

> Now comparing these instances together, we shall have no difficulty in determining the principle of this apparent variation in the application of the term which I am examining.
>
> John Henry Newman

We—spokesmen for a body; editorial "we":

> What we propose to do here, then, is to examine the word *antonym,* to determine the concept it involves, and to state its definition in as clear terms as possible.
>
> Introduction to *Webster's New Dictionary of Synonyms*

We—a disguised "I" (closely related to the editorial "we"):

We have already suggested a doubt whether indecent books or perform-ances in fact either alter people's natures for the worse or even stimulate them to immoral behaviour. . . .

> Unsigned article, *The* [London] *Times Literary Supplement,* August 4, 1961

When we write criticism we have to be continually on our guard against this sort of thing. If we honestly believe a work to be very bad we cannot help hating it.

> C. S. Lewis

We—representatives of a particular group, possibly excluding the reader:

Revolutions and civil wars are brutal and messy things, and the results are rarely satisfactory. At least, that was so with the Irish Revolu-tion. We had forced the English to come to terms and then had a civil war as to whether the terms were good enough.

> Frank O'Connor, an Irishman speaking for Irishmen

We—all mankind, including the writer and the reader:

The realist at last loses patience with ideals altogether, and sees in them only something to blind us, something to numb us, something to murder self in us, something whereby, instead of resisting death, we can disarm it by committing suicide.

> George Bernard Shaw

Uses of "One"

One—representing the writer and reader:

Remembering that, one sees what function these post cards, in their humble way, are performing.

> George Orwell

One—indefinite reference to all persons, including the writer:

Can we invent rituals? Can one artificially create collective art?

> Erich Fromm

One—an extended "I"; one of the speaker's kind:

I learned in New Jersey that to be a Negro meant, precisely, that one was never looked at but was simply at the mercy of the reflexes the color of one's skin caused in other people.

James Baldwin

One—a disguised "I":

One is finally driven to conclude that all Huxley's intellectual paraphernalia conceals an intelligence at war with itself, or struggling vainly for a clear position from which to attack. And while in this essay I am interested directly only in the early novels, it would be unrealistic not to bear in mind also the constant gropings and changes of position in his later work.

Sean O'Faolain

Use of "He" as Disguised "I":

Adams had looked at most of the accumulations of art in the storehouses called Art Museums; yet he did not know how to look at the art exhibits of 1900.

Henry Adams [writing about himself]

Other Indirect References to the Speaker or Writer:

The chair wishes to thank . . .
This writer was present when . . .
The editors have attempted to . . .

It should be apparent from the examples above that the ways in which a writer represents himself vary greatly in their formality and directness. The more indirect the form, the more it tends to be contrived. The simple use of "I" remains the writer's most natural and inconspicuous way of referring to himself. The use of "I" does not necessarily make prose egocentric. The element of subjectivity is much more affected by the writer's view of the world around him than by his choice of pronouns. If he has only one perspective—his own—he will find it difficult to escape the limitations of his own view. If he has a world of perspectives, he will be capable of broader vision and more perceptive analysis.

3

The Audience

The writer's view of his own material is closely related to the view he takes of his audience. It affects what he says and how he says it. A person in a discussion group can shift his position or alter his tone in response to the feedback he gets. Even a formal lecturer can change his tactics if he finds he is getting no response from his audience. Or a lawyer going into court can prepare for a fairly well-defined audience: he knows something about the judge, the jurors, and the setting. In instances like these, the speaker has an advantage over the writer because his listener is present and responding in some way, either favorably or indifferently. The writer, however, is his own audience, at least at the time of writing. He may have reaction later, but at the moment of composition he has to cope with an invisible and often unknown audience. He may know a few things about his potential readers, but these may provide him only general guidelines about the choices he has to make. A free-lance writer, for example, usually studies the magazine he intends to write for; the magazine has already carved out its audience by the choices it has made in the past. He has to infer, then, what qualities appeal to the "typical reader" of *Harper's* or *Playboy* or *Ebony*. A student writing for his professor and his peers also has a strong advantage. Because he knows precisely who the people in his classroom are, he may not fully realize what the absence of a clearly defined audience means until he has to write under other conditions. **19**

Because knowledge of an audience is often obscure, and trying to imagine a particular one can distract a writer from his thoughts, he may have to depend upon some inner sense of audience, something he determines before he begins to write. Whom is he writing for? Even if he cannot escape the fact that he may be writing for an audience of one, his professor, he still has to make certain decisions about that person. If he is writing about a work of literature, is his assumption then that he and his professor both share a common interest in the work and an intellectual curiosity about it? Or, if the topic concerns a current issue like the grading system, is then the assumption that he and his professor are divided—divided by their relationship as student and teacher or by their age or academic training? Once a writer internalizes several assumptions about the kind of audience he is writing for, a good number of decisions about language, selection of detail, and tone follow in due course. If he is aware of no assumptions that he makes, however, a writer cannot very well decide whether his choices are reasonable ones.

Even though a reader is only one person, an audience is many persons. The writer almost always has to depend upon generalizations about a collective audience, made up of individuals joined together in the writer's mind by some common bond. For a writer to say to himself that he will write for an "educated audience" is not very meaningful. That high-level generalization may decide a few things about grammar and usage, but not much else. In the abstract, the educated audience may be thought of as a unit, but, in actuality, it is highly fragmented. It can be subdivided by age, sex, educational differences, social status, and personal interests of all kinds. The treatment of any topic on politics, education, or morality would vary considerably in terms of one or more of these segments. In one sense, the fragmentation of the audience simplifies the problem of the writer. For example, it is simpler for a doctor to write an article on the dangers of heart disease for men over forty than for a student radical to write an article for all Americans about the evils of the university system. In each instance the writer may know his purpose very clearly, but in the first example the audience is well defined; in the second, the audience is diffuse and infinitely varied.

WRITER-AUDIENCE RELATIONSHIPS

In what ways, then, may the writer-audience relationship be considered? Basically, a writer first has to decide whether his audience is on a par with him, whether he must in some way defer to his audience, or whether they must defer to him. These relationships fall into several categories.

As Specialist to Specialist

Almost everybody is a specialist in something, whether it is commonplace like cooking and swimming or extraordinary like gyrostatics and Platonism. The term "specialist" is a relative term indicating that some people either know much more or have much greater experience than other people, who by comparison have only a general and somewhat superficial knowledge of that subject. On most topics, the great majority of people fall into the category of generalists; a few are specialists. Everyone is supposedly a specialist upon himself.

Specialization is by no means limited to scholarship. There are specialists on any subject or activity—jazz, football, drag racing, astrology. Specialists in a particular area usually represent an in-group. There may be differences of interpretation among them, but not great differences in their commitment to the subject. They speak the same language; they have mastered their own jargon. Their common interest bridges their differences and provides them shortcuts in communication. Specialists are demanding of one another, but a specialist writing for his peers has a considerably easier job than a specialist writing for generalists.

As Specialist to Generalist

The specialist-to-generalist is one of the most difficult of the relationships because it holds innumerable pitfalls for the writer. In a typical situation, the specialist-as-authority writes for an amateur audience—an audience supposedly interested in learning more, but not yet experienced enough to be members of the in-group. What can the writer assume this audience knows? Does he begin from zero? What terms need to be defined? What language will be completely unfamiliar? If he explains too much, will he be condescending? If he explains too little, will he be obscure? The basic problem, therefore, is one of accommodation—simplifying the concepts, at times giving generalizations without extensive support, and popularizing the language. The more specialized the topic, the more difficult the translation. In the Preface to *The Miracle of Language,* a popularization of scholarly approaches to the English language, Charlton Laird comments upon the dilemma of the specialist writing for a broad audience:

> In the belief that promoting the popular understanding of language is a worthy endeavor, I have tried to write so that a dogged person can understand me and a charitable reader can stay awake. Popularization has necessitated simplification; I hope it has not led me into downright error.

The popular magazines are, of course, expert in this kind of accommodation, but very often their writers are not true specialists; they are generalists writing for generalists.

As Generalist to Generalist

No writer-reader relationship exists on a completely equal basis, because the writer always has a temporary advantage over the reader, a moment of control as it were. The free-lance writer is a good example of the generalist who becomes a temporary expert. As a professional writer, he has to be a generalist or he will run out of magazines to submit to. Typically, a free-lance writer may read seven or eight books on a subject, interview several professionals, attend a number of performances or lectures if they are relevant, and with his newly acquired "expertness" write the kind of article that appeals to a wide audience. The extent of that audience, of course, depends upon the level of knowledge and language the writer chooses. In one of his well-known *nonlectures,* E. E. Cummings tells about the editor of the magazine "possessing the largest circulation on earth," whose first rule for writers supposedly was "eight to eighty"—every article had to appeal "to anybody, man woman or child, between the ages of eight and eighty years. . . ." The anecdote hits upon the idea of a common denominator, particularly the writer's decision how low his common denominator will be.

The generalist writing for the generalist can never assume he has a captive audience. A specialist often makes himself a captive reader because he feels an obligation to read everything in his field, whether it is poorly written or well written. The general reader, however, is more discriminating in this respect. Unless the writer lures him and sustains his interest, he gives up. General readers don't bore themselves unless they have to. In this large category of writing, therefore, rhetoric is a particularly strong factor. The audience cannot be ignored.

As Generalist to Specialist

At first thought, it might seem that there would be no need for the generalist to write for the specialist; yet almost all student-teacher writing falls into this category. It is not surprising, therefore, that students often approach this kind of "test" writing with a lack of confidence. What every generalist needs to realize, however, is that his lack of knowledge about a subject can be offset by fresh perception. If it were possible, many specialists would undoubtedly trade some of their knowledge for the completely unencumbered perspective of the newcomer. A beginning student in American literature can say something new about *Moby Dick.* In fact, he must take advantage of the unique position he has of experiencing something for the first time which to the specialist has become dulled by familiarity.

Another familiar generalist-to-specialist kind of writing is the open inquiry, common in the daily newspaper. It often takes the form of a letter. The writer seeks information or advice. He may write openly about himself or his situation, and then pose a question. Often the circumstances of the individual voluntarily looking to an authority affect the whole content and tone of the writing.

Having established categories of this kind, one might continue to subdivide and refine them—the generalist by sex and age or by education and social standing—but to do so would only complicate the writer's sense of audience. If a writer knows specifically he is writing for the Boy Scouts or teenage girls or middle-aged suburban women, then his job is clear. Otherwise a general category is better than none.

It should be added that student-teacher writing could conceivably fall into any of the four categories, although it seems to be concentrated in the last. As specialist to specialist, the student would have to know in advance that he and his instructor share a common specialty, perhaps photography, and that the student is as advanced and as experienced as the instructor. As specialist to generalist, the student's job would be to assess what he is a specialist in. If he were the expert photographer and the instructor only an amateur, the responsibility of accommodating the subject to the audience would be the same as that of any other authority writing for an interested reader. Age or sex or professional status would be irrelevant.

The student who writes a term paper, especially on a topic outside the instructor's specialty, becomes basically the generalist writing for the generalist, and his responsibilities to inform and to create interest are no less than those of the free-lance writer preparing an article for sale. Yet term papers, although they may be sound in their facts, frequently suggest that the writer feels no particular obligation to win his audience. Unfortunately, the student all too often takes his captive audience for granted.

For the classification and analysis of examples in terms of the audience, see pp. 146–157.

THE EXTENDED AUDIENCE

Besides thinking of an audience as a fairly well-defined group of readers at a particular time or as a kind of inward conscience that keeps the writer aware of his obligations to someone besides himself, it is also possible for a writer to address a situation rather than a particular audience. In such cases, the audience is, in an extended sense, everyone. One is reminded of public figures who use special occasions like after-dinner speeches, graduation addresses, and dedication ceremonies to address a national or world situation. They may be speaking to a particular group gathered to listen, but the speech has been written with the extended audience in mind. Because of the extended audience, the arguments are general and the tone impersonal.

Proclamations, manifestos, demands, and open letters are all forms of public writing. In that they are often declarations, they attempt to shape an audience, not let the audience influence what will be said or how it will be said. Such writing cannot be said to deny that an audience exists, but it can be said to ignore the audience and its preferences in order to change it. Essentially, all revolutionary writing—revolutionary in idea or technique—dares to intimidate and antagonize the audience. Experimental writers have grounds for thinking that an audience can be tyrannical. An audience in the most general sense is conventional. It likes predictable patterns and temperate expression. It prefers to be served meaning rather than to work for it. It is not surprising, therefore, that writers who have influenced prose style in the past have been those who were willing to forgo the favor of one audience in order to create a new one. It is also not surprising that the bulk of writers at any one time seek a common ground with their audience.

THE CONTINUING AUDIENCE

The great unknown is the continuing audience. Yet any published work has a potential audience beyond its writer's own lifetime. Every surviving work has had a history of its own—where it has been read, when it has been revived, for what purpose it has been used, who has been influenced by it. An established writer generally acquires a sense of his immortality, but in gaining a vision of future fame he may well lose the present.

Perhaps the greatest mistake a writer can make is to try to write for the future rather than for his own time. It is true that the purely topical work will pass away quickly, but it is also true that the universality of a work beyond its time is a judgment of the future, not a quality that the writer can inject. Big thoughts do not necessarily insure universal truths. It is difficult to imagine that the writer of the ancient tale of Joseph and his brothers thought that he was writing his story for future ages. He wrote with honest insight, and that quality has been recognized ever since. Every writer, no matter how modest, can attempt no less.

THE PERSONAL PRONOUNS AND THE AUDIENCE

The point of view and the corresponding pronouns a writer chooses reflect how he wants to involve his audience. Of course, in a third person account, the audience is not addressed; it is implicit. The audience is actively involved only when the writer uses first person plural ("we," "us," "our") or second person singular or plural ("you"). All of these pronouns invite an identity of the audience with the writer. The writer of a third person account, however, does not necessarily ignore his audience. He simply involves it in a different way by selection of detail, choice of words and images, and the tone of his remarks.

The use of "you" is a definite decision to address the audience directly, but it can be a formal or an informal "you," a specific or a general one. The implications will vary:

You—the immediate reader, addressed as an individual:

It is not the function of the dictionary-maker to tell you how to speak, any more than it is the function of the mapmaker to move rivers or rearrange mountains or fill in lakes.

Clarence L. Barnhart

You—an indefinite reference, essentially informal in tone:

It is a professional warning, not at all unlike what a golf professional means when he tells us to keep our eye on the ball. Once lift your eye from the actuality of the moment, he seems to say, and you are distracted, deceived, deflected, lose focus, strike without accuracy, and the next thing you know you are in the rough of the sentimental, or the bogus.

Sean O'Faolain

You—reference to a particular group, not necessarily including the reader:

That my first novel should win this most coveted prize [National Book Award] must certainly indicate that there is a crisis in the American novel. You as critics have told us so.

Ralph Ellison

You—the reader, but also in an extended sense all men:

If you look into your own mind, which are you, Don Quixote or Sancho Panza? Almost certainly you are both.

George Orwell

Thus, the decision to use second person "you" may not always add a personal note. And if it is overused, it can also tend to lose its effect as a personal address. A writer can show that he is aware of his audience no matter what point of view he adopts.

4

The Subject: Generating a Topic

The mind is constantly recording, responding, remembering, reflecting. Thinking is a free-ranging process, not bound by time or space. It can at times be concerned with fact or feeling or fantasy. It can come up with the completely unpredictable.

In considering the thinking process as background for writing, the problem seldom arises that nothing is going on in someone's mind. The problem is that there is much unfocused activity, even a great amount of wasted mental energy. The first thing a writing assignment does is bring the writer to a realization that his thoughts have to be brought under some kind of control. Writing, as it finally looks when it gets down on paper, is quite different from the form it has as thinking. For example, writing is linear: one word has to follow another. It can suggest only in limited ways the spontaneousness, instantaneousness, and wholeness of thought. It cannot even come as close to the complete experience of thought as a painting or a photograph, which can be experienced with an at-onceness. These art forms can be diagnosed and analyzed after they have been viewed, but the first experience is a total one. On the other hand, writing must be taken in parcels, and only after it has been read completely can it be viewed as a whole.

The second thing a writing assignment does is make the writer realize that he has to expand a thought for the reader so that he can come to understand what the writer thinks. It is this expansion of a topic that often causes the beginning writer his greatest problem. Are there **27** specific ways of helping a thought to grow? Clearly, there are many. Aristotle set down twenty-eight ways. Someone else might invent fewer or more, but the difficulty is that listing too many ways can hinder more than help. A multitude of road signs confuses the driver; a multitude of directions confuses the writer. The key, then, is whether there is some easy, simple device, applicable to any situation, that will help the writer to generate things to say.

The twentieth-century rhetorician Kenneth Burke has provided a formula which he thinks gives the thinker a set of blanket terms that will meet all of his needs. What follows is an adaptation and simplification of Burke's terms. These fifteen questions, divided into five categories, are capable of accumulating a mass of material. Trying to find answers is all a part of the prewriting stage. They are means of gathering resources. The process that follows may not occur at one sitting; thoughts occur to a writer constantly as he is preparing his topic, even after he begins to develop it. But once a writer begins to generate his topic, he has a specific advantage if he can go about his job in a disciplined way. Basically, however, prewriting is advance preparation for the stages that follow when the writer must then be concerned with focusing, selecting, organizing, and finally writing.

THE DRAMA OF THINKING

Burke says that if we think of anything as if it were a part of a drama, then we can use certain dramatic terms to help us see the whole thing. A drama has action, setting, actors, and various devices for projecting these, all usually enacted for a purpose. It follows, then, that one can ask a few very simple questions to find out about each of these: what was done, when and where was it done, who or what did it, how was it done, and why was it done? What is immediately apparent is that all of these overlap and depend upon one another. Given an action (*what*), the most important part of learning *why* might be explaining *who, when,* and *where.* Together they represent a complete statement. It is their interrelatedness that makes them generating principles, but only, of course, if they can be applied to any topic. The terms, therefore, need further expansion and explanation.

Action

An action is anything that has happened or is happening. In this general sense, an action can be either physical or mental. A boxing match is an action; so also is a personal thought like "I wonder why so and so didn't win." A poem, a story, or a play is an action. A scientific discovery, a space feat, an educational experiment, or a Supreme Court decision is an action. This sampling of actions will suggest that the act is very often the starting point of our thinking about writing. If an assignment is free choice, our first thought might be as big and general and vague as an urge to write about the generation gap or the military or the population explosion; or, conceivably, that first thought might be as limited and personal and specific as "I don't like Johnny Carson." Nevertheless, an action is often the starting point.

Often, however, writing assignments are not free choice. They may begin:

Consider the following quotation:

Compare *Six Characters in Search of an Author* and *The Zoo Story* in terms of . . .

Analyze the logic of censorship.

What each assignment does is provide the student with a specific kind of action—a literary work or a well-defined topic—and then leave him on his own. Where does he go from there?

If a writer wants to generate thoughts about an action, he has several basic questions to ask himself:

1. What happened?

The question applies to any past deed. Even though this may seem the simplest question of all to answer, it is often one of the most difficult. Immediately following an event, if ten people are asked, "What happened?" they may possibly give ten different answers, at least ten answers reflecting a different viewpoint and emphasis. The more distant the event, the more obscure the facts. Reporters and historians spend much of their time first trying to find out what happened. New histories now tell us that things did not happen during the Civil War exactly as old histories told us, or old histories did not tell us all that happened. Knowing what happened may make all the difference in answering other questions.

2. What is happening?

The question applies to any event occurring at the present, but also what is happening in any literary work we read or in any performance we see. It also includes the results, namely, the reaction. If the actions are obscure to the writer, the motives of the characters may be also. The media of the twentieth century have made us more and more aware of what is going on about us than would ever have been possible in the past. Yet our capacity to see does not always answer what is happening because we see only parts and are left to construct the whole. In current events, we do not always know what is happening. In fact, only rarely ever do we know *all* that is happening. The advantage in analyzing literature is that a writer often tells us what he wants us to know about what is happening, and we are at least limited to his clues, even though we may have to make inferences about the things he does not tell us.

3. What will happen?

The question applies to any speculation about an event or development that has not yet occurred. The answer is almost always based upon what has happened or is happening, but it represents the capacity of the thinker to generate ideas beyond the facts at hand. In what direction are things moving? On the basis of what we know now, what can we expect to happen? This kind of thinking is not prophecy, simply logical projection on the basis of known factors. It is often one of the interesting turns writing can take.

4. What is it?

The question applies to any act or thought that requires definition: What is existentialism? What is extrasensory perception? What is the twelve-tone technique? Often in order to say what something is, it is first necessary to sort it out from all others like it. In order to define Romanticism, it might be useful to make a specific identification: What kind of Romanticism? Which one of several possibilities?

Actor-Agent

One part of the drama of thinking logically leads to another. Action is, of course, inseparable from actors or the agents who are responsible for an action. In this sense, an agent does not necessarily need to be a person; it may be a cause or a force or a motivating influence. In one story, a storm may be used an an agent, as the storm in Shakespeare's *The Tempest* tosses a shipwrecked crew on to a strange island; in another, with a shift of emphasis, it may become the center of the action or the scene. Fear, malice, and greed may be depicted as consuming forces in such a way that people are only the victims of evil, not self-determining agents in their own right.

Given any agent, there is the possibility of both co-agents and counter-agents—friends and enemies, associates and antagonists, supporting forces and counterforces. Who are the co-agents of Antigone in

Sophocles' play? Are the gods on her side? In Thoreau's essay *Civil Disobedience,* the government is the antagonist of the individual; the majority is the enemy of the minority of one. The matter of the agent within a piece of writing is not the only matter of interest. The author himself is the agent of a book, and much interest of a biographical nature often revolves around him as a man. Who is the author? What kind of man is he? What about him throws light upon the internal structure of what he has written?

If a writer is going to generate thoughts that focus upon the agent, he has three basic questions to ask himself about the source of action:

1. Who did it? Who is doing it?

The questions apply to any situation in which the agent is unknown. People read hundreds of murder mysteries and detective stories to find out "who did it," but there the answer is always given. In other real life situations, the answer may be speculative. Arson in the cities. Who is responsible? War in Asia. Who are the co-agents? Racial oppression. Who is involved? Evil in general. Who originated it?

2. What did it?

The question applies to all the impersonal forces that act to bring about thoughts and actions. At times, these may be only abstract ways of referring to people in a collective sense: society, government, the military, the radical component, religious pressure. These are continuing agents; they persist after the men who represent them at a particular time pass from the scene. It is therefore not unusual for a writer to explain actions in terms of intangible forces—the conservative mood of the country—particularly when he is attempting to determine causes or trying to philosophize about the ongoing history of man.

3. What kind of agent is it?

This question applies to an agent who is known. It asks for full information concerning the active agents—details about one person or the qualities of individuals who act as a group. If individuals picket the White House, what do they share in common? If a new Secretary-General of the United Nations is appointed, who is he? If a first novel becomes a best seller, the public asks who the writer is—not his name but his identity. The description of an agent quickly overlaps all of the other questions because the writer may go on to explain the writer's family background, the influences upon him, his preoccupations, his techniques, and his purposes. Answers to all of the basic questions about a person would be capable of generating a complete biography.

Scene

Having considered the action and the agents, a writer may then turn to the scene. Anything that happens occurs in a setting. There is always a backdrop against which the action takes place; there is a location for the play of events. Anything that happens occurs at a particular time; it may be that it could not have happened at another time.

Time and place are therefore important to the scene. In an extended sense, the scene might be the environment in which something happens. We can think of specific ones like the urban ghetto or Miami Beach or the campus of the privately endowed college. In a more abstract way, we can speak of the moral climate or the temper of the 1970s or the age of affluence. These scenes are less concrete, but they can be meaningful if they are explained and illustrated.

Besides the immediate scene, events can be considered against the background of the past. History often attempts to interpret current happenings in terms of the past or even to set up a theory of history on the basis of recurrences. Criticism evaluates current literary works in terms of tradition and convention. What is happening in higher education may be better understood by reference to what has happened in the past. The fact that time is a continuum makes history relevant. What happens now is at least related to what has already happened, even if there has been a radical break. Reference to the total scene, past and present, is therefore a means of generating thoughts.

The questions about the scene of an action are simple and direct:

1. Where did it happen? Where is it happening?

Answering these questions does not mean merely naming the place but describing the conditions, going beyond surface appearances to determine the true circumstances. What was the atmosphere? The morale? The prevailing situation? Novelists do not always provide readers with an everyday environment. They may create unusual situations in unusual places in critical times in order to show how men act under extraordinary circumstances. The twentieth-century absurdist movement in the drama and in the novel depends to a great extent upon characters acting in grotesque settings and situations. To ignore the scene is to fail partly to understand the action.

2. When did it happen?

The *where* and the *when* are so closely connected that they are hardly separate considerations. We refer to the timelessness of things, but that is not to say that they are unrelated to a time, only that they persist beyond their time. Beethoven's music may be timeless, but it grew out of the special circumstances that characterized the late eighteenth and early nineteenth centuries.

A particular time is such a crucial factor in shaping actions that we sometimes refer to all of the diversity of a scene simply as "the times"—the times of Michelangelo, the times of Luther, the times of Malcolm X. What occurs at one particular time may not occur at another because circumstances have changed. The times, therefore, may be the main focus of a writer's attention.

3. What is the background?

This question applies to the background of an action—the historical scene. It therefore applies to actions that have occurred in the past as well as those that are happening. All actions have references to other actions, either evolving from them or reacting against them. All of the present acts before the backdrop of the past.

Means

In approaching a general subject, a writer needs to consider further that all actions require means. The agent needs tools to work, ways of achieving a purpose, methods of development, resources for implementing, instruments for operating. Agents are usually observable, but not always the means. The means, when known, often stir up controversy. The war machine uses guns, bombs, gases, tanks, and men as its wheels and cogs. The government depends upon laws, taxes, force, authority, and consent for its operation; higher education, upon requirements, examinations, grades, lectures, research, and experimentation. In the case of higher education, more and more students seem to be going to college—an approval of the action—but more and more seem to object to the procedures—a disapproval of the means.

Since the means of any action are constantly subject to change and experimentation, they often create disturbing reactions. Music that employs a new harmonics changes the action completely. Art that experiments with new media upsets traditional expectations. Writers who write plotless plays and stories obviously are attempting new means of expression, but readers resist change. In view of the vast implications of means in both concrete and abstract terms, the basic questions will generate an infinite number of other thoughts:

1. How did he do it?

The question applies mainly to actions in which the agent is a person. If he accomplishes something, if he effects a change, how did he do it? The interest in means can never be ignored, because men are always concerned whether the end justifies the means. In 1945,

President Harry Truman made a decision to drop two nuclear bombs upon cities in Japan. The vast destruction and loss of life are a matter of record, but a long war ended. Every thinking person weighed the end against the means.

2. What means were used?

The question applies mainly to processes and products. Heart transplants have become a fact of the 1970s. What means were used to achieve this successful operation? Were human beings used as guinea pigs in the early operations? European films have revolutionized the art of film-making. What means do they use? Immediately this question concerning *how* involves *who*—Bergman or Antonioni or Fellini? We read a newspaper editorial. What arguments does it use to support its position? A Broadway company produces a modern adaptation of Bizet's *Carmen*. What means does it use? In almost any example that might be cited, the means are the substance of the action because through them the action is realized.

Purpose

Finally, in the generative process, one should weigh the possibility of intention. It cannot be said that everything that happens has a purpose. Some things happen accidentally; some by chain reaction. All happenings may have a cause, but not all have a discernible purpose, because purpose presupposes an actor or agent who has designed an action with intent. Purpose appeals to man's intellectual curiosity. He is not satisfied with being only an observer. He wants to probe motivation. He wants explanations. He is endlessly plagued by the recurring thought that there must be a purpose, even when happenings appear purposeless.

The nature of the purpose may or may not justify an action. It is always intimately tied in with the means. In fact, means and ends over a period of time sometimes fuse: the means become an end. It happens with work. At one point in his career, a man may work to make money to do other things that satisfy him. But if he works and works so that he no longer has time for other pleasures, work becomes an end in itself. It may be the purpose and the end of all his efforts.

Many individuals and groups find it necessary to declare their purposes in advance. Without declared objectives, they can win no support; they can gain no resources to bring about an action. At times a writer concerns himself with investigating whether the stated purposes of an organization are its true purposes or whether purposes have changed in the course of action.

Even though a purpose may be apparent, a writer can always generate thoughts by reasking the basic question:

1. Why?

"Why did he do it?" questions personal motives. "Why was it done?" questions the objectives and purposes of any movement or institution or phenomenon whose agent is unknown. *Why* is an all-embracing question because it often can be answered only in terms of all of the other questions: *why* in terms of the person, *why* in terms of the time and place, *why* in terms of the means. What is answerable in terms of one is not always as clearly answerable in terms of the others.

Finally, *why* leads man to his most metaphysical speculations about the universe itself. Our knowledge of the universe is limited primarily to the scene—what we observe—and to some of the means—the principles by which it operates. But how it actually came into being—the means—is unknown, and its agent and purpose are likewise unknown. To provide answers, science theorizes about possibilities of origin; religion advances explanations about who and why. Thus, even in the most universal concerns of mankind, *who, what, where, when, how,* and *why* are the basic questions upon which all other thoughts rest.

In summary, then, the basic questions in terms of the drama of thinking may be set down as follows:

ACTION
>What happened?
>What is happening?
>What will happen?
>What is it?

ACTOR-AGENT
>Who did it?
>Who is doing it?
>What did it?
>What kind of agent is it?

SCENE
>Where did it happen?
>Where is it happening?
>When did it happen?
>What is the background?

MEANS
>How did he do it?
>What means were used?

PURPOSE
>Why?

RANDOM SEARCHING AND THINKING

These five topics subdivided into fifteen basic questions are capable of generating propositions or kernel thoughts. At the time of writing, they must be expanded, supported, and evaluated. For example, if someone wanted to write about student activism in 1968–1970, but did not know precisely what he wanted to write about, he might approach the subject as a complete drama and generate topics like these:

ACTION, STUDENT ACTIVISM

What happened? (overlaps Background)

Revolts and violence at Harvard, Berkeley, San Francisco State, Columbia, Kent State, Sorbonne, Free University of Berlin, University of Rome.
Spread of revolt into other colleges and lower schools

What is happening? (relative, of course, to the time since 1968–1970)

Continuing student agitation; increasing violence
Growing reaction among the American public
Punishment of protestors by schools and legislatures
Rapid measures of academic reform within the schools

What will happen?

Probability of further adjustments in the universities to meet student demands
Possibility that intense feelings will subside and conditions stabilize
Possibility that universities will be closed or destroyed
Possibility that the majority of students will react against violence
Certainty that nothing will be the same again
Hope that the end of the Vietnam war will change things

What is it? (overlaps Purpose)

Theories concerning activism as a movement:
1. Theory of "historical irrelevance"—students displaced in dehumanized, computerized society; no role
2. Theory of intensified Oedipal rebellion: generation gap; blind hatred of parents
3. Theory of international conspiracy
4. Theory of revolt as a continuation and extension of the egalitarian revolutions begun in the eighteenth century
5. Theory of post-Industrial Revolution: search for new values

6. Last gasp of Romanticism
7. Protest against irrelevance and impersonality of universities
8. Protest against collusion of universities with a militaristic government and other elements of the racist establishment
9. Manifestation of utopianism in a paradoxical age of poverty and affluence

ACTOR-AGENT

Who did [is doing] it?

Agents—students in high schools and colleges: radicals, militants, moderate reformers
Co-agents—outside agitators; moral support of leaders like Eugene McCarthy and Edward Kennedy; sympathetic faculty members
Counteragents—established middle class society over 30; non-college young people under 30; leaders like George Wallace; military men

What is responsible? (overlaps Scene)

What kind of agent is it?

Activist students
    Offspring of educated, liberal, and often affluent parents
    Intelligent, thoughtful, knowledgeable
    Resistant to authority; committed "to do their own thing"
    Idealistic; morally righteous
    Unconventional in dress, manners, and tactics
    Minority groups seeking equal rights

SCENE

Where did it happen?

First, in Europe and South America, chiefly in underdeveloped countries lacking a stable society

Where is it happening?

In the United States and abroad
In advanced nations of the world
In liberal, distinguished universities as well as numerous other schools. (A significant question also would be, Where is it *not* happening and why?)

When did it happen?

Conjunction of events: assassination of President Kennedy, challenge of Eugene McCarthy to President Johnson, assassination of Martin Luther King, Watts riots in Los Angeles, Democratic Convention of 1968 in Chicago, continuation of Vietnam war, assassination of Robert Kennedy, Kent State killings

What is the background?

New concept of mass higher education
Growth in size of the multiversity and corresponding depersonalization
Extended period of student life at more advanced stages of intellectual and emotional development
Unpopularity of Vietnam war; "peacetime" draft
Increased industrialization and intensified modernization; erosion of old values
Abroad: bad living conditions in universities and unemployability of graduates
Selection policies of universities discriminating against minority groups

MEANS

What means were used?

Violence, obstruction
Peaceful demonstrations; draftcard burning
Formal demands submitted to the universities
Discussion and speeches
Unconventional and sometimes illegal conduct
Unconventional dress and manners

PURPOSE (overlaps Action and Scene)

Why?

To revive an exhausted society
To extend the benefits of the egalitarian revolution begun in the eighteenth century to increasing numbers of people
To right the wrongs of society toward oppressed and deprived groups
To search for new values and a more meaningful existence

WHERE DO THE ANSWERS COME FROM?

These topics are by no means exhaustive; they only begin to suggest what thoughts can be generated by the questions. But where do the extensions of the answers come from, the modifications of the kernel thoughts?

First, every writer is strongly dependent upon personal observation. On a subject like student activism, any student knows what he sees and hears on campus, that is, if he bothers to look and listen. One of the problems of nonwriters is that they are often not very keen observers. They may even look but not see, hear but not perceive. The task of writing alerts the writer's senses to the things going on around him.

Television and movies now give the individual an expanded view of the events going on in the world. Even though the camera itself is a selector and censor, it cannot always black out all of the action. The observer can draw conclusions from his own observations. The media have extended the perspectives of people who are limited to one place and time.

Second, every writer is dependent upon reading. Everyone constantly needs new resources. One thought generates another, particularly when someone's thinking is quite different from our own. On a topic like student activism, a writer would have not only the daily newspaper accounts but the analytical and interpretive articles that appear in weekly and monthly magazines. Finally, he would have access to full-length treatments in books by writers who have concentrated on the topic. The notes above on student activism are drawn from material written by Lewis Feuer, Zbigniew Brzezinsky, Daniel Bell, Philippe Aries, and Kenneth Keniston. Men like these bring to bear their own learning and observation upon a current problem.

In like manner, any writer has his own educational background from which to draw. The significance of a liberal education is its scope. A student's knowledge outside his major may not be profound, but he at least has some idea what disciplines can be brought to bear meaningfully upon a problem. With a general educational background, he has a start toward pursuing any topic in depth. It is apparent that the student-activist movement is a complex amalgam of elements that permit any number of specialists to speak meaningfully upon some phase of it: the anthropologist, the historian, the political scientist, the psychologist, the sociologist, the humanist, the linguist, the man of religion, the educationist, and many other interested groups from administrators and parents to policemen and businessmen.

Finally, every writer has his own capacities for reflection. Having gathered his observations and his materials, he can himself view them from his own point of view and thinking. He can make inferences, make comparisons, and form opinions. What the complete drama of thinking does not include is a final value judgment: Is what is happening justified? Is it good in terms of immediate goals? Or long-range goals? Has it succeeded? Has it been worth the struggle? From answers to questions like these, opinions are formed. Once a writer has determined his opinions, he is ready to argue his case, to give his reasons, and to try to persuade others. At this point of reflection, thinking has moved close to the writing stage.

FOCUSING AND SELECTING

After a writer has let his thoughts explore a topic widely, he is confronted with the need to focus, particularly if he intends to give his subject any depth within a relatively small space. In terms of all of the things that might be written about student activism, the typical 500-word theme is a very brief space. It therefore demands a limited topic that can be treated briefly but adequately. Topics like the following begin to suggest the kind of selection that is necessary, although some of these are considerably broader than others:

Agent
1. What the student radical I know is like
2. Who the winners and losers were in the last demonstration on campus

Action
1. Student protest as mob action
2. What happens when violence begins

Scene
1. A particular situation on campus that needs reevaluation
2. Whether students hate their professors

Means
1. Role of the police in student demonstrations
2. The rhetoric of a radical

Purpose
1. What education is for
2. Cooperative and conflicting purposes of various independently organized student groups

These topics represent a selection from the complete drama, but none states a thesis. Assuming a position on any one of these narrows the subject even further. A writer might, for example, take the position that students do not hate their professors; that the relation is different even though the professors may be the same age as their parents. Or a student might argue that an example of protest writing is not rhetoric but anti-rhetoric, because in making demands and leaving the reader no choice it abandons one of the fundamental principles of honest rhetoric. Sharpening the focus makes a subject manageable. The more closely a student draws his topic to his own experience, the more likely he will be able to write easily and persuasively.

THE OPEN TOPIC

The open topic is an assignment that sets almost no limitations upon the writer. He is free to choose his own subject. In such instances, the key dramatic terms help the writer to reduce many possibilities to one or several related ones. The following theme, in response to a relatively open topic, will illustrate what choices this student made in his focus and selection of material.

ASSIGNMENT Choose a satiric cartoon from a newspaper or magazine. Without including the cartoon with your paper, describe and analyze it to make clear what commentary the artist makes upon his subject.

► STUDENT PAPER (written in class)

No One Does Anything

The general scene: a bit of background

No roofs ever get fixed. Who fixes a roof when it's raining, and who needs to when it isn't? That's human nature.

The immediate scene and action

I am looking at a cartoon by Mauldin that ridicules man's failure to work up a sense of urgency about a pressing issue, just as the bit of homely wisdom about roofs satirizes man's tendency to explain away his inactivity. The entire setting of this cartoon is filled with gray smoke from billowing smokestacks. A river runs black with pollution from the surrounding factories. The trees are dead from the poisonous air and water. But fresh rain pours from the sky. Two fish in the river look hopefully skyward, exclaiming, "Aahhh—Water!" No one else is around.

Means and purpose

Mauldin draws the scene with deliberate ugliness. It is meant to represent typical industries on a typical river in a typical city of the United States. The scene is familiar because every metropolitan center has one like it, but the ugliness of

Mauldin's picture makes us realize how desperate the situation is becoming. Negligent man may find himself in the same plight as the helpless fish.

The future scene: a bit of reflection

But then the time may come when people will no longer ignore the ugliness and threat of pollution and do something about it. When that time comes, the satirist will have done another job of showing men their all-too-human tendencies and turn his pen to another problem at hand.

In fewer than 250 words, this student manages in a very concise and concrete way to describe and explain a cartoon. The theme tells us what he sees, what he interprets to be the comment, what he sees as the function of the satirist. Someone else might give a different interpretation.

Because he is writing about a cartoon treating the contamination of nature, the student, like the cartoonist, concentrates upon the scene. He, like the cartoonist, also uses broad strokes, not documenting the discussion with specific illustrations. Facts about Mauldin as a cartoonist or about the history of pollution in world history are unnecessary here. What is said seems adequate for the assignment set forth. If the assignment had asked for a longer paper, clearly the theme would have had to take up other parts of the total drama and treat the subject of pollution in much greater detail. The paper, however, illustrates what focus and selectioin can do to accommodate a big topic to a small space.

THE LIMITED TOPIC

The limited topic is an assignment that provides a narrower focus for the student, leaving him to restrict it even further by selection of detail. In one sense, this is a more demanding kind of assignment because it cuts out an infinite number of possibilities. In another sense, it helps those students who find difficulty in narrowing subjects to manageable limits. The following theme illustrates what choices were made for the student and what choices were left open to him.

ASSIGNMENT   Read "The Odor of Chrysanthemums," "The Shadow in the Rose Garden," and "The White Stocking" by D. H. Lawrence in our anthology. What attitudes about love do these stories express? What part does abuse play in love? What part tenderness? What kinds of premises ought to govern love relations, according to Lawrence?

► STUDENT PAPER

Paradoxes of Love in D. H. Lawrence

Lawrence believes the heart of a man's existence is his subjective being. The characters in his stories are manifestations of the mysterious control of the emotion over life. Love is a strong force in his characters. Without understanding why, they battle each other in obscure, profound ways, abusing the ones they love, both physically and spiritually. Tenderness follows: after struggling against each other, a bond of unconscious understanding grows between them, making them gentle and respectful of each other.

The action: a thesis

In "The Odor of Chrysanthemums" Elizabeth Bates realizes she has abused her husband. When she looks at his lifeless body, she perceives exactly what their married life has been. Her husband's spirit had died long before his body. Elizabeth is terrified and humiliated to see that the gap between her and her husband is the same in death as it had been in life. She knows she had loved him falsely. The compassion she feels toward the dead man is a result of her confused, guilt-ridden emotions, not grief at his death.

Agents: Example 1

The people in "The Shadow in the Rose Garden" do not come to a conscious realization of their struggle. They argue, and the woman feels that she hates her husband. There is a wide gap between them, although neither of them is wholly aware what keeps them apart. They both feel the icy, clammy fog that divides them. The husband and wife hold an impersonal respect for each other. The husband, though puzzled, somehow intrinsically knows that he should leave his wife alone.

Agents: Example 2

Elsie and Ted in "The White Stocking" abuse each other more violently than the other two couples; yet they love each other more strongly. Elsie fights against her husband, deliberately trying to make him angry. She escapes from him by taking imaginary excursions. She always comes back to him, however, because she loves him. Ted is confused by Elsie. He doesn't understand how he can

Agents: Example 3

love her as he does and then become angry enough to destroy her. At the end of the story, they speak no words of conciliation. The violent struggle between them has resulted in an unconscious communication that brings them together tenderly.

The action: return to the thesis

These stories show Lawrence's ideas about human relations. One of these is that people should let their emotions rule them. Elizabeth Bates had stifled her feelings toward her husband so that finally she was shocked to find that she had no feelings for him. Lawrence also seems to think that emotional and physical relations are sufficient. The people in his stories do not know each other very well. The obvious idea is that a love relation is possible when people can communicate with the unconscious, emotional parts of their being. Love is the complete communication between the emotions.

This is an assignment that limits the writer to particular stories and calls for a thesis (what attitudes about love do these stories express?) and a conclusion (what kinds of premises ought to govern love relations, according to Lawrence?). The writer chooses to write in terms of the agents in the stories. He does not discuss all of the possible love relations—of a mother toward her children or of one friend's love for another; he selects only three parallel love relations that also involve abuse and tenderness, suggested by the assignment as a possible lead. Questions of the kind given by this instructor should be seen as guidelines for thinking about the stories, as means of selection, not as questions to be answered like an examination. In this theme, the writer does not go beyond the stories themselves to talk of Lawrence as a writer or of marriage as an institution or of the times in which these stories were written. He focuses and sticks to relevant material.

THE BASIC QUESTIONS AND THE FORMS OF DISCOURSE

Traditionally, narration, description, argumentation, and exposition have been spoken of as the basic modes of discourse. Each represents a shifting concern on the part of the writer. He must at times be concerned with setting forth facts (*exposition*), speaking of them in terms of space (*description*), writing about them in terms of time (*narration*), and resolving the conflict of facts (*argumentation*). The modes, however, seldom exist as pure forms. The writer shifts naturally from one to the other as he turns from one question to another. There is a definite correspondence between the basic questions one asks about a subject and the way he writes about them:

What happened?
What is happening?   ] Narration

What will happen?   Narration, exposition, argumentation

What is it?   Exposition, including definition, illustration, and process

Who did it?
Who is doing it?   Description and exposition, including
What did it?   definition, illustration, comparison
What kind of agent is it?   and contrast

Where did it happen?
Where is it happening?
When did it happen?   Description, narration, and exposition
What is the background?

How did he do it?
What means were used?   ] Description, narration, and exposition

Why?   Exposition and argumentation, including persuasive writing

Once the writer realizes that the modes of writing intuitively follow his own thoughts—or, to put it another way—once he realizes that thoughts have a way of shaping themselves, he will also have learned that prewriting is one of the most important parts of writing, because it is then that the course of writing is set.

5

Structure

By the time the writer reaches the point of composition, it is possible that his thoughts have begun to shape themselves as he sees the direction in which things are moving. It is then that he needs to determine more consciously what form his remarks will take. If the overall design is clear, however, the thoughts will often fall into place. Form is not an enemy of the writer; it is his way of keeping things under control. Neither is form an enemy of the reader; it is his means of following the writer's thoughts.

Form is a fact of all the arts as well as of nature. Yet there are significant differences. An architect designing a ten-story building has more rigid principles of form to follow than a potter shaping an urn on his wheel. Yet the potter's freedom might be more limited if he were shaping a vessel to be used for a set purpose, for example, making a pitcher. Practical considerations sometimes have a definite influence upon form. Basically, however, the creator is bound, first, by the principles of his craft and then strongly affected by the conventions of his art, whether he is a conformist or a rebel.

The primary fact about language, as we have noted, is that words have to be set down in linear sequence. Words must assume some grammatical form in order to communicate unambiguously, and the most conventional form is the sentence, divided into two parts. Once the subject has been stated, we expect the predicate. In similar ways, larger units of discourse are also ordered, but there are no set forms. They create their own expectations.

SET FORM AND DEVELOPING FORM

Set forms of discourse are conventional forms of language that can be described and imitated. They are almost all limited to imaginative literature. A variety of verse forms, such as the sonnet, the villanelle, and the closed couplet, can be described precisely. Others, like the epic and the classical tragedy, are longer and more flexible forms, but they are still bound by an orderly arrangement of parts that can be listed. On the other hand, the contemporary novel gives clear indication of another kind of form, best described as developing form.

The difference between set form and developing form becomes evident in terms of the reader's approach to each. It is possible for the reader to have expectations concerning set form before he ever begins. He simply has to know what a sonnet is, and he will know what to expect. On the other hand, it is not possible for him to have expectations concerning developing form before he starts to read. His expectations come only as the writer creates them in the course of his work. Form in this sense is not something that exists, like a map to be followed; it is something that happens along the way, like a hiker finding his path through the woods. But, in turn, a reader is entitled to criticize developing form as readily as he would set form if the writer fails to fulfill his own promises.

Thus, both set form and developing form operate on the basis of expectations—one in advance of reading, one in the course of reading. Kenneth Burke gives a covering definition of both varieties: "A work has form," he writes, "in so far as one part of it leads a reader to anticipate another part, to be gratified by the sequence." In the second part of his statement, Burke touches upon the fundamental appeal of form—not only does it bring order out of chaos, but it satisfies the preference of most people for shape rather than shapelessness.

THE ESSAY AS A DEVELOPING FORM

The modern essay is clearly a developing form. The writer is free to determine its destiny. Perhaps the most popular convention of the essay is a prevailing notion that it should fall into three parts, an introduction, main body, and conclusion. This kind of organization is not bad, unless the introduction and conclusion are thought of as if they were announcements before and after the main program and not as integral parts of it. In order to emphasize that the parts of an essay represent a unit, it is more helpful to think of the three parts simply as a beginning, a middle, and an end. These more flexible terms help the writer to avoid an obvious three-part pattern. It is known that several prolific opera composers of the nineteenth century, like Rossini and Donizetti, took overtures they had written for early failures and attached them to new operas written at a later period. The perfunctory introductions of many student themes sometimes suggest that they are also detachable beginnings that could be spliced to two or three other themes as well as the one at hand. If, however, a writer thinks of the first words of an essay as the beginning of the developing form of that essay, the beginning has to take on a different significance.

How to Begin: A Dozen Suggestions

There are two ways to think about beginning. One is in terms of effect; the other is in terms of structure. These are simple ways of saying that a beginning may have a rhetorical function or a logical function. On one basis or the other we can decide whether a beginning is effective or not. A few examples of student writing will indicate which beginnings are doing work and which are not. Four students, given limited writing topics upon Dickens' *Hard Times,* begin in the following ways:

> In *Hard Times,* Dickens compares Fact and Fancy as someone else would compare Good and Evil, Dark and Light, or Heaven and Hell. To him there is only one conclusion: Fact is bad, Fancy is good. Every believer of Fact, every follower of Gradgrindism, is defeated like a villain in a fairy tale. But every believer of Fancy, every member of the proletariat who is able to overcome human suffering, finds the Light of Happiness.
>
> Student 1

This opening is itself a good combination of factual statement and fanciful treatment. The writer very briefly summarizes the themes of the novel and states Dickens' preference, but he does this in the manner of a fairy tale in which the characters are sharp opposites. After this beginning, the writer focuses upon two characters who show factual and fanciful attitudes toward religion, but this development is not announced; it logically follows the beginning.

> Dickens uses striking contrasts in the characters of *Hard Times* to make his point and get it across to his audience. He does this by taking that which he is satirizing, in this case, fact, and placing it beside its opposite, in this case, fancy. An example of such a contrast is one of Sissy Jupe and Mr. Bounderby.
>
> Student 2

This student has almost precisely the same approach as Student 1; he is going to compare two characters to illustrate Dickens' commentary upon Fact and Fancy and indicates that he will proceed in that way. But this opening is ineffectual, chiefly because it is padded. The facts are lost in a mass of unnecessary words.

> The characters of *Hard Times* seem to be divided between the School of Fact and the Circus of Fancy. Bitzer, a colorless, mean, selfish individual, represents the Gradgrindian philosophy of Fact. His opposite is Sissy, the humble, loving, compassionate product of the Circus of Fancy. Dickens uses these two characters to show the dehumanizing influence of Fact and the humanizing power of Fancy.
>
> Student 3

This is yet another version of the same approach, starting with a generalization, quickly narrowed to two characters. The last sentence provides a logical guideline for the discussion to follow. The strength of this opening lies in its compactness and apt phrases.

> How important is fact in our own society? What role does fancy play? When Dickens wrote *Hard Times* in 1854, society was facing the same dilemma we face today. Is fantasy necessary? Dickens says yes. I would like to show how Dickens answers the question by looking at two female characters: Sissy Jupe and Louisa Gradgrind.
>
> Student 4

This opening starts further afield and uses a different strategy. The writer tries to involve his reader by a series of questions and using "we" to invite identity. The switch to first person in the last sentence is consistent with the sense of nearness this writer is trying to establish with his audience, but the last sentence is also an outline in miniature. This beginning has both a rhetorical and a logical purpose.

The first three openings employ no special device such as the questions in the fourth one. They are simple statements, which depend mainly upon generalizations, and they vary in their effectiveness with the writer's choice and arrangement of the words. A survey of the opening sentences and paragraphs by established writers in reputable magazines will indicate that most openings are straightforward statements of fact or opinion, usually wasting no words. Openings of this kind attempt to state the thesis briefly and establish the tone of the article; they provide a clue to both the ideas and the style, and a reader sometimes makes up his mind after the first paragraph whether he wants to continue to read. The importance of a good beginning cannot be overestimated.

The dozen examples of opening sentences given below are not beyond the capacities of any beginning writer. What the examples characteristically demonstrate is that these writers begin with confidence, even at times with daring. Established writers, however, do not limit themselves to one kind of opening. They begin in a number of different ways.

1. With an anecdote that leads into the main topic:

   A student editor, criticizing the draft of a catalogue for a new college, three times deleted the words "liberal education" from the draft. Coming upon it again, she circled the words and wrote in the margin: "What in the world is it?"

   Harris Wofford, "In Search of
   Liberal Education

2. With the setting as background for the exposition to follow:

   "When something starts to happen, groove with it; don't just sit there. You're not the audience; you're the oppressed. You're oppressed by the Modern Language Association."

   The speaker was an intense young thing, dressed in bell-bottom slacks and a lumberjack shirt. Her audience consisted of several hundred members of the professional association for college teachers of language and literature gathered at a "radical caucus" the evening before the annual meeting of the MLA in New York just before Christmas.

   Wallace Roberts, "Voices
   in the Classroom"

3. With narration, beginning in the middle of things, inviting further reading:

   They marched into the crystal-hung East Room of the White House together, the President and the tall, white-thatched man he had chosen to begin remaking the world's most powerful court in his image.

   "The Changing of the Guard,"
   Newsweek, June 2, 1969

4. With an apt quotation relevant to the thought:

   "I never made a mistake," Will Rogers once said of this wholly ceremonial role as the honorary "Mayor" of Beverly Hills, "partly because I never made a decision." It would be unfair to characterize President Nixon's first months in office with such sweeping irreverence. But it is true that he has not made either the number of mistakes his most fervent detractors expected or the number of decisions his most fervent admirers desired. The most visible hallmark of his first one hundred days in office has been caution.

   Theodore C. Sorensen, "The First
   Hundred Days of Richard M. Nixon"

5. With a firm statement of opinion, arousing the reader's feelings:

Our age has not wanted for authorized acts of madness and moral collapse, but it is doubtful if anything in recent history has produced greater feelings of disgust and horror than the recent protracted argument at Paris over the shape of the negotiating table.

Norman Cousins, "Send the
Astronauts to Paris"

6. With a prediction:

America is facing a manpower crisis of awesome and dangerous proportions. What is done, or not done, about it in the next few years will affect the quality of life in this country for generations. Nor is it any exaggeration to say that if the correct solutions for the problem are not conceived and carried out, the United States will be confronted with potential disaster.

John Tebbel, "People and Jobs"

7. With unusual or sensational detail:

One night a few weeks ago, the ten members of the cast and staff of an Off-Broadway play were arrested after the opening performance. They were charged with "consensual sodomy, public lewdness, and obscenity."

Goodman Ace, "The G-Whiz String"

8. With reflective questions:

If, indeed, it is true that taxes are as inevitable as death, what considerations determine whether we must pay more or less? Isn't it simply a matter of how much money "the government" needs to meet its responsibilities to the people? Why can't we take a good, hard look at what we want government to spend money on, set a price tag for these services, and then collect the money deemed necessary according to an ability-to-pay formula, or on some other equitable basis? Wouldn't this be a great deal simpler than our present system of exemptions, deductions, write-offs, and a thousand and one other opportunities for maneuvers that have made a national pastime of searching for "tax angles"? In other words, once we have agreed that, in one way or another, government must collect the tax revenue it needs to stay in business, doesn't it all boil down to finding the fairest means to raise the money?

Haig Babian, "Can Taxes Do More
Than Raise Revenue?"

9. With a definition:

> *Overlive* means that we have more than enough for everyone but not everyone gets his share. It's as simple as that.
>
> Charles J. Calitri, "Everybody Wants In"

10. With a figure of speech:

> Insomnia is my baby. We have been going steady for a good twenty years now, and there is no hint that the dull baggage is ready to break off the affair.
>
> Roger Angell, "Ainmosni"

11. With a play upon words:

> A sign over one section of the public library in my town reads "Young Adults Oversize." Although it refers to books too large for normal shelving, it might also stand as a metaphor for the college student who has outgrown the limits of his own collection of textbooks and "favorite" authors, who seeks to pin down the expanding world of ideas into which he is moving to something solid and permanent.
>
> David Dempsey, "Seventh Amy Loveman Award"

12. With humor:

> There's good news in the paper. America has its first drive-in funeral parlor. I had almost given up hope that the country could ever reach the goal that it is so obviously striving for—the day when we will be able to do everything without getting out of the car. But now I know that the impossible dream is possible.
>
> William Zinsser, "Time-Saver for Busy Mourners"

Because the beginning is an important element in establishing a good relation between writer and reader, several kinds of beginnings are therefore best avoided:

1. The apology, complaint, or personal dilemma:

> I have now read "Love Among the Ruins" for the third and, I hope, the last time. I notice one element which is used sporadically throughout the story. The topic of which I am speaking is the use of the word "State" in the place of God's name.
>
> Student theme

2. The panoramic beginning, typically a survey reaching back to the dim past:

War is a topic which has been handled admirably by poets throughout the course of history and man's conscious destruction of his fellow man. Homer first described "man's inhumanity to man" and the results that war can have in his epic poem *The Iliad.* In the intervening years, the poet has continued to use war as the subject of his poetry, for war begets sorrow, and expressing emotion is the poet's stock in trade. [Written as the opening of a theme asking the student to compare two contemporary war poems.]

3. The mystery opening, making the theme dependent upon material from an outside source known to the instructor but to no other reader:

The main thing that I noticed in the poem was the way the tone changed from stanza to stanza.

Student theme

4. The overworked beginning:

Webster's dictionary defines *love* as ...

In Book 1 of *Gulliver's Travels,* Swift says ...

5. The perfectly obvious statement:

Brave New World confronts man with a question that has in the past and will in the future most certainly be a human problem.

The utopian society has always been considered the ideal society.

Gulliver's Travels contains a very important thought which everyone should think about.

How to End: A Dozen Suggestions

Like the beginning of an essay, the ending may be thought of primarily in terms of structure or in terms of effect, but in either case the important thing about ending is to leave the reader with a sense of completeness. Isolated examples of final paragraphs demonstrate very little, because as endings they can be judged only in terms of what has gone before. Characteristically, however, writers end in a number of different ways:

1. With a final paragraph or sentence that completes the logical pattern that the essay has been developing.
2. With a rephrasing and reassertion of the main thesis.
3. With a concluding opinion supported by the previous discussion.
4. With a speculative question or statement that leaves the subject open for further thought.
5. With musing upon the broader implications of the topic.
6. With a return to the theme, question, or image in the opening paragraph so that the essay is rounded out.
7. With an ironic twist or unexpected turn of thought.
8. With a note of high persuasion or challenge, comparable to the peroration of the classical oration.
9. With an appropriate anecdote.
10. With a telling quotation.
11. With a descriptive passage, using the setting as a final commentary.
12. With a laugh.

Essentially these devices for ending an essay correspond to the kinds of intonations that occur at the end of a sentence, either falling, rising, or level. Those endings that come to a logical conclusion, just as we intuitively know the end of a sentence, are falling; those that end with a question or move to a persuasive climax are rising; those that are reflective or leave the subject as an open question tend to be level because the reader is left to resolve the problem in his own mind.

Ending seldom presents the same problem to a writer as beginning or developing the major portion of the essay. Once the beginning and middle are complete, the ending usually follows in natural sequence. Several kinds of endings, however, are best avoided:

1.   The unnecessary summary:

A theme of 500 words seldom requires a formal summary, one that restates in a full paragraph what has just been discussed in two or three previous ones. At times, it may be appropriate to draw together the thought of a short paper, but this can usually be done in one compact sentence. For the most part, summaries are necessary only in long works, where they perform a service to the reader by drawing together major points for his final consideration.

2.   The postscript:

A postscript is simply a thought that the author adds after the ending has already been reached. If the form of the essay has been fully developed, the reader knows where the ending is. A postscript may not necessarily be an irrelevant thought, but it is unsatisfying because it is misplaced in the development of the essay proper. An afterthought, therefore, is better dropped altogether or integrated into the total pattern of the essay.

3. The obvious ending:

The phrase "In conclusion" is the most obvious of endings. Characteristically, readers don't like to be told the obvious. If the organization of an essay has been thoughtfully developed, the ending is self-evident without a special announcement.

The Design of the Middle

In what terms does one think of developing the major portion of an essay? What are the organizational principles that apply to overall structure as opposed to the development of the individual paragraphs? Clearly, the answers to these questions must be stated in broad generalities that correspond to characteristic ways of thinking.

First, we should consider that our ways of thinking about things do not always correspond to our ways of experiencing them. We observe and feel and absorb. We think also, but not always logically in the formal sense of that term. Logical thinking is a special way of interpreting experience. For example, in our culture we think of time in terms of minutes, hours, days, months, and years; and these are logically laid out in a straight line. We refer to a man's lifespan as living from age one to age seventy, each year in sequence. A clock measures time. Yet neither time nor growing old is in actuality the kind of experience we talk about. In one way or another, time can be ignored, transcended, speeded up, turned backward or forward, even though measurements continue uniformly, falling bodies travel at 32 feet per second, and the alarm clock rings at 6:30 sharp. Time is a continuum, but whether it exists in the manner that we think about it is another matter. Aging is growth and change and has nothing much to do with marking off the passing years on a calendar. Some men of fifty are older than other men at sixty. Nevertheless, straight-line thinking has become our traditional standard for logical thought. It is a one-directional sequence of sentences, with parts connected link by link to form a chain of reasoning. When it is put down in writing, it is therefore fragmentary, connected, successive discourse. When the chain is broken, we try to supply the connection; or, being unable to, dismiss the line of reasoning as weak.

TRADITIONAL PATTERNS OF ORDER

One important demand that linear logic makes upon the writer is finding an overall pattern of order. The pattern will usually be determined by the subject matter itself, but the writer needs to be aware of the directions he can take. Most arrangements will fall into one of five patterns—time order, space order, grouping, moving from the particular to the general, or moving from the general to the particular.

Pattern 1: Time Order

The most obvious time order is historical—that which begins at the beginning and proceeds in an orderly sequence to the end. Historical time is closely associated with narration, but it is by no means limited to it. If a writer plans to review our present state of knowledge about the moon, intending to present a new theory about gravitational irregularities on that satellite, he can present his evidence in chronological order, from the earliest known relevant data to the latest. Or if a writer plans a process paper, telling how to do something, his most logical arrangement is a step-by-step order, beginning with step one and proceeding to the end. Any skipping of stages along the way will only confuse the explanation. In like manner, articles that treat a problem and a solution or a question and an answer usually proceed in that order because, in terms of time, problems and questions usually precede solutions and answers.

In addition to straight historical time, writing also uses what might be termed artistic time, that is, an arbitrary rearrangement of time for a special effect. Narrative lends itself best to this treatment. A story may begin at the end, flash back to the beginning, and then fill in events until the end is reached again. The advantage is that the reader is able to reflect upon every incident along the way in terms of what will ultimately happen. The reader's knowledge of what the outcome will be often gives him an ironic perspective of the things that occur.

In a similar way, a story may begin in the middle of a conflict, then narrate events leading up to that conflict, and proceed to carry the story to a conclusion. Thus, by various means, the writer can be a maker of his own time, unrestricted by clock, sun, or seasons.

Pattern 2: Space Order

Space order is usually associated with descriptive writing. Visualizing tends to be a total experience, a seeing of everything at once. It is only in telling about a setting or a scene that a writer must decide where to begin and where to go next. If he is describing a work of art—a painting, for instance—part of the decision has already been made for him by the artist. By line, by color, and by light an artist is able to create a focus in his painting—the object one sees first, that which calls attention to itself. A description of a painting, therefore, might logically begin with the central focus and proceed to the other things that relate to it. In like manner, any description might proceed on that basis. If a writer were trying to describe a confused scene—a mass demonstration, for example—he might choose to focus first upon the leader or possibly an anonymous person in the group to show the effect of the crowd upon an individual.

Any description, of course, depends upon the way things are arranged to begin with. If five people are seated in a row, they are likely to be viewed from left to right or from right to left. If we attempt to recall the contents of a room, we may find it helpful to proceed mentally around the perimeter. These are conventional scanning devices, and they have therefore become the standard for orderly space arrangement. Undoubtedly, the rapid shifting of scene that television and contemporary motion picture techniques have made familiar to all of us will continue to influence patterns of space order in writing because these techniques tend not to move in straight lines and circles but in flashes—back and forth, here and there.

Pattern 3: Grouping or Classification

Grouping is a pattern of order based upon selection. It is not limited by time order or space order because the writer is free to select those materials that relate to o: e another regardless of their time or place of origin. They must simply be able to fit a particular classification. For example, if a writer wants to characterize the New Left of the early 1970s in the United States, he might proceed by groupings: the New Left in terms of concepts of law, in terms of concepts of ethics, in terms of concepts of education, in terms of concepts of religion. Any one of these classifications might invite comparisons with the past—attitudes toward social reform in the 1930s as compared with attitudes in 1970—or with places—Oriental attitudes toward women as opposed to Western attitudes. The controlling theme will determine both the selection of subgroups and the relevance of material to be included in those categories.

Classification is a form of analysis, a breaking down of a broad topic into parts. The parts are variations upon a common theme. The principle of order, then, depends upon the connections between the parts and the whole and the support that they give to the controlling idea. Which comes first and which comes second may not make a great deal of difference in terms of the logic, but there might be considerable difference in terms of the effect. A writer who is defending a position naturally holds his strongest points to the last, but this is basically a rhetorical decision, not a logical one. Admittedly, the line of distinction between the two is very fine.

Pattern 4: Moving from the Particular to the General

Moving from the particular to the general is, of course, the pattern of inductive thinking. It is proceeding from known facts to a conclusion. What should be evident is that proceeding in this way is the writer's attempt to reproduce his own thinking process on paper, showing the way he has reached his conclusions. If the way is orderly, the reader may accept the writer's conclusion. But there is always the possibility that steps along the way are too big or that the final step is too much of a leap. The reader can test his reaction to the following student theme, which moves from particular personal observations to a final conclusion about race relations:

Ants in My Driveway

I have never really been a true lover of nature. That is, I have never stood and stared for any great length of time at a river or a forest, nor have I ever been interested in observing the journey of a caterpillar. Yet, one day last week I spent, I am almost ashamed to say, over an hour in my driveway entirely entranced by the activities of a colony of ants.

It had been a warm summer day, and after eight hours of hard work I decided to relax and at the same time give the lawn some much needed water. I grabbed a lawn chair out of the back yard and set it in the driveway facing the grass. After removing my shirt I picked up the hose, attached a nozzle to the end, turned on the water, and then settled down in the chair to bask in the last rays of the dying sun and give the grass a good soaking. I had not been watering ten minutes when I noticed a few ants scurrying to and fro on the cement. I observed three or four for quite some time before I realized that the entire area was overrun with them. I seemed almost hypnotized by the doings of these creatures.

There were quite clearly two different kinds of ants; yet the only visual difference between them was their color. The red ants looked and moved exactly as the black ants did. However, as I observed closer, I saw that there were many more red ants than black ones. At the time this did not strike me as significant because all the ants seemed to be doing some work, although the blacks were clearly doing most of the heavy jobs.

Suddenly my attention was drawn a little ways off to a very strange sight. Two ants who had been dragging a small crumb of bread to the entrance of their colony beneath the cement were savagely attacked and overwhelmed by a comparatively large spider. Almost immediately a regiment of ants retaliated. A fierce struggle took place, and the battle was nearly decided when I noticed a very odd fact: the black ants comprised the bulk of the attacking force. Outnumbered five to one in the colony, the blacks represented about 60 percent of the attackers. Soon the spider was overpowered by the ants and killed.

After the battle, the ants dispersed and headed for the shelter of their underground quarters. To my astonishment, I saw that the black and the red ants had separate entrances; the blacks funneled into a crack on the opposite side of the driveway. I then realized that all the food that had been carried earlier had been taken into the entrance of the red ants.

From these observations, I could draw no conclusion other than this: the black ants were a subjugated minority, not because they were inferior but because they were fewer in number and because they were black. Reflecting upon the things I had seen, I turned off the water, coiled up the hose, and went back into the house.

In this very simple statement, the reader has no reason to reject the particulars about the ants because they presumably are factual. Further, it is obvious that the conclusion is intended to comment upon people rather than ants. The writer reads his own thoughts into the events. What he says about race relations may be quite true, but the theme is only a way of reminding us; it is not proof. The reader who needs to be persuaded that the conclusion is true is not likely to be convinced by this particular argument because nothing in the analogy is binding—ants are ants and people are people. Obviously, in a paper built upon scientific facts or verifiable data, the final observation might be less easily rejected. Proceeding from the particular to the general, from experience to theory, is essentially the scientific method, and in such instances the conclusion changes only when new knowledge alters the evidence.

Pattern 5: Moving from the General to the Particular

The reverse procedure—from the general to the particular—is possibly the most common overall pattern of writing. It begins with a thesis statement, a conclusion, or a generalization and proceeds to support it or, in the case of syllogistic reasoning, to draw from the generalization a conclusion by a series of well-formulated premises. (See discussion of syllogisms, pp. 70–75.)

What the writer does in this kind of orderly procedure is to begin with a general statement that he has accepted in his own mind and that he wants the reader also to accept. It is therefore not unusual to find the starting premise often rephrased at the end of the essay after the support has been given. The opening of a student paper on one of the San Francisco poets will suggest one way this pattern can be set up:

> Gregory Corso, one of the San Francisco "beat" poets, is one of the fresher, more spontaneous writers of today. When you experience his poetry, you experience his mind. He has the vitality of a child's imagination and talks about pasting Tannu Tuva postage stamps all over a picket fence and leaving the milkman a note saying, "penguin dust, bring me penguin dust, I want penguin dust." Sometimes flippant and mischievous and sometimes lonely and bitter, Corso is constantly feeding us his energy.

This opening paragraph already begins to give its particulars, but the remainder of the paper is devoted to observations about particular poems by Corso supporting the writer's observations that he is fresh, spontaneous, and energetic, "sometimes flippant and mischievous and sometimes lonely and bitter." These qualities set up the reader's expectations. If the examples that follow do not fulfill these expectations, then the generalizations at the beginning have been overstated.

Basically, the pattern of proceeding from the general to the particular is a means of probing in depth, the kind of examination we do not often do in speaking. In conversation, we often state generalizations without support. In writing, these can be pursued in detail to the reader's own satisfaction. It is a demand the reader constantly makes of the big statement. Why is it true? What evidence is there to support it? In anticipating these questions, the writer must choose some pattern of order that supplies the evidence, either placed in first position as in Pattern 4 or in last position as in Pattern 5.

NONLINEAR LOGIC

More and more, however, any reader of current prose has to give recognition to another kind of logic. Marshall McLuhan calls it nonlinear logic. It is the kind of thinking and writing in which all of the details are not spelled out and linked together; the reader is given disconnected parts and left to make his own associations. It has been influenced by experimental novels and poetry, by abstract art, advertising, and television. It might be described as fluid, mosaic, or kaleidoscopic, whatever best conveys the notion of a multidimensional effect that does not so much lead the audience as a group in one direction and to one conclusion as it allows them to participate individually in their own way. It is still logical in the sense that it is based upon relations among the parts, but it is a logic that may jump instead of move step by step. It is a logic that does not provide all of the connections. Ultimately, the appeal of this new logic may be more emotional than intellectual, but as a way of thinking and writing it needs to be recognized.

Two paragraphs will illustrate both kinds of thinking:

> *EXPLOSION!* A great noise—perhaps a plane has crashed, or the earth opened—every day there are predictions of earthquakes. But staring down the chasm we see only another blown up Chronicle headline, with no news beneath it. We seem to be falling into the chasm, but it is not news; we slide down, a phrase unformed, a world unconceptualized . . . seeing ourselves, not through the media's transits, but only across the open air, have we any reality? We who have been raised by television, we have been robbed of the concrete. Earthquakes lead often to Oz (no, not in the Wizard, but in later works) or unsuspected wonders in mid-Earth caverns; but with no telephone lines to aid the transmission, will the cameramen demur, remain in Paris, coffee—please, no milk—and cordiality, the North Vietnamese representative is about to read his statement? The chasm is over us now, merely a slice defining the sky . . . it looks quite blue . . . we are quite lost . . . .

> Why did we come? We are a generation who believe, perhaps more strongly than any in centuries, that it is our job to save the world—and appropriately so, for the hour has come when only desperate measures will prevent the human race from stumbling into extinction. We are threatened not merely by the pride and fear and shortsightedness of president and premiers, and the power at their commands, but by centuries of gross negligence on the part of those who—through our own laziness—we have allowed to direct the activities of this species on this planet.

> Paul Williams,
> "The View from Now:
> A Symphony"

These two paragraphs make different demands upon the reader, and the first paragraph is clearly more demanding. It asks the reader to experience the prose; the second asks him to follow the thought. The second paragraph asks a question and answers it; it proceeds with all of the logical connections. Paragraph one leaves things out. We have a series of associations.

Typically, if two things occur together, we try to find a conventional association between them. If the words "baseball" and "fans" are put side by side, for example, we immediately think of "fans" as people who attend baseball games because that meaning puts both words into the single context of sports. There is a likeness. If it were explained that "fans" means electric fans, however, we would be pushed to find a context that would connect baseball and electric fans, something perhaps like electric fans for baseball parks.

Further, if "red" and "green" are put side by side, we make two conventional associations. They are alike because they are both colors; they are different because the words signify two hues.

Finally, if we hear a crash of window glass and see a baseball lying on the floor and a group of boys playing outside, we associate the two as cause and effect. One implies the other. In similar ways, an answer implies a question; a solution implies a problem; an action implies an agent.

In each of these relations, we try to associate the things put side by side by some likeness, difference, or implication. When one thought seems to have no conventional association with the thought preceding it, we call it a *non sequitur,* meaning quite literally, "it does not follow." Yet, in actual experience, it is possible to put two things side by side that seem to have none of the conventional associations. For example, we do not ordinarily associate a cup and a typewriter. But if we saw the two sitting next to one another on a table, we would be inclined to connect them in our thinking because of their nearness to one another in the same setting. Furthermore, we would probably find ourselves trying to make a connection between them, possibly explaining that the writer drank a cup of coffee and left it sitting next to his typewriter. But this inference would be filling in the gap between cup and type-writer, creating a context and making a conventional association.

In terms of this discussion of ways of thinking, a rereading of paragraph one of Paul Williams' prose on page 61 will reveal that his writing becomes difficult to understand in terms of conventional logic because two thoughts that seem to have no obvious connection are put side by side, and the reader is left to make something of the meaning. At that point, the reader has to help himself, because the writer has chosen not to help. The reader, therefore, becomes an active participant, not just an interested spectator. Nonlinear prose of this kind operates on a different principle from linear prose. Its effect is different. It is fast moving. It can create a total impression without explaining all of the details. It is a way of translating sensory experiences into writing. If a writer wants to explain his own ideas carefully or to present an argument, however, he needs to turn to linear prose because only in connected discourse of that kind do the writer's precise intentions come through clearly and unambiguously.

OUTLINING AS AN AID TO PLANNING

The outline has two functions: it can help the writer find an overall pattern for his thoughts, or it can help him analyze the structure of his essay after it has been written. A distinction needs to be made between outlines written in advance of writing and outlines written after at least the first draft has been completed.

Inasmuch as the writer often generates thoughts in the act of writing and even discovers new directions, an outline written in advance is most useful if it does not attempt to freeze the organization. Clearly, it should show the overall pattern and major topics, but these should be flexible. The chief advantage of making an outline at all is that it permits the writer to see if he actually does have a plan and purpose in mind. Like all writing, if the writer has nothing specific in mind, he can put nothing down.

The outline written after the essay has been written is primarily a testing device—a self-testing device. If the outline indicates an obviously illogical arrangement or a disproportionate treatment of one topic and neglect of others, the writer is still free to make adjustments. If an outline is thought of as planning and testing, then it is not merely an exercise. It is order visualized; it is structure diagramed. The writer can see what he is doing.

Working outlines, of course, may be merely notes or jottings, but beginning writers will learn that the demands of formal outlining are in part also the demands of controlled writing: order, proportion, and parallelism. Attempting to meet these demands is a means of cultivating an intuitive sense of order.

Formal outlines follow several conventions:

1. They frequently begin with a one-sentence thesis statement, designed to help the writer formulate his essential point.
2. They subdivide topics by a system of numbers and letters, followed by a period.

I.
   A.
   B.
      1.
      2.
         a.
         b.
II.

3. Dividing ordinarily implies a minimum of two parts: if I, then II; if A, then B. If the writer wants to discuss only one subcategory under a main heading, he may separate it from the main topic by a colon:

I. The Sound of the New Rock: Electronic Amplification

4. Introduction and conclusion, if listed at all, are not indicated as numbered parts. They are followed by brief statements of purpose and not subdivided:

Introduction: Circumstances leading up to the building of Resurrection City, June, 1968
[Discussion of what happened]
Conclusion: A final evaluation of the poor people's protest

5. Numbered topics are phrased consistently. If the outline is a sentence outline, topics are phrased as complete sentences. If the outline is a topic outline, parallel topics are phrased in parallel fashion: nouns with other nouns, adjectives with adjectives, phrases with phrases, and clauses with clauses:

Parallel phrasing with nouns
I. Effects of fluoridated water on tooth decay
II. Effects of fluoridated water on other parts of the body

or

Parallel phrasing with clauses
I. How fluoridated water affects tooth decay
II. How fluoridated water affects other parts of the body

Outlines, therefore, may assume slightly different forms, but the forms should not be mixed. The exception is that a thesis sentence is almost always phrased as a complete sentence whether the form is a topic outline or a sentence outline.

THE SENTENCE OUTLINE

Thesis: The nature of humor remains basically unchanged throughout life; it only grows more sophisticated.

    I. A child typically finds fun in antics.
       A. Clowns and pets appeal because of their silliness.
       B. Animated cartoons appeal because they are exaggerated and imaginative.
       C. Riddles and rhymes are amusing because of their sounds and suspense.
       D. Unexpected falls are funny.

    II. A teenager adds additional sources of amusement.
       A. Jokes, clean and dirty ones, play upon words and situations.
       B. Mockery provides cruel amusement.
       C. Practical jokes entertain because of one-upmanship.
       D. Unexpected falls are funny.

III. An adult typically adds other sources of amusement.
   A. Grotesque happenings are absurd.
   B. Slapstick is a form of release from inhibitions.
   C. Subtle jokes and ironic humor are intellectually delightful.
   D. Unexpected falls are funny.

IV. Humor at all levels depends upon incongruities, turns, twists—the unexpected.

THE TOPIC OUTLINE

Thesis: The nature of humor remains basically unchanged throughout life; it only grows more sophisticated.

   I. The appeal of antics to children
   A. Silly clowns and pets
   B. Exaggerated and imaginative movie cartoons
   C. Tricky riddles and rhymes
   D. Unexpected falls

   II. The added appeals to teenagers
   A. Verbal and situation humor in jokes
   B. Cruel mockery
   C. Surprising practical jokes
   D. Unexpected falls

   III. The further sources of amusement for adults
   A. Grotesque happenings as absurdities
   B. Slapstick as release of pressure
   C. Intellectually appealing jokes and irony
   D. Unexpected falls

   IV. Humor at all levels based upon incongruity and the unexpected

This particular outline shows balance in the subdivisions because each of three parts is divided in turn into four parts. But no such exact balance is necessary. What the outline suggests is that the writer is probably interested in giving proportionate treatment to the three stages of childhood, adolescence, and adulthood. Section IV might conceivably be listed as a conclusion. One would expect it to be briefer than the preceding sections because it is a drawing together of the evidence, a final commentary upon the nature of humor. This outline reveals that the writer has planned his essay by proceeding from the particular to the general in terms of an orderly time sequence.

6

Logic:
The Test
of Argument

Logic helps to shape the structure of an argument; it also acts as a test of argument. In this sense, logic is concerned with the form of an argument, not the truth of its premises. If an argument is properly constructed, the conclusion is valid because it must follow the premises; the conclusion is a logical necessity. The following syllogism is valid because it violates no basic principle of logic; it is logical but not true:

All Frenchmen are anti-American.
Jacques is a Frenchman.
Therefore, Jacques is anti-American.

But to say that an argument is valid is not to claim that it is either sound or effective. The soundness of an argument lies in both the truth and validity of its assertions and the extent to which it convinces on the basis of reasoning. An effective argument depends upon a writer's style and could be both false and invalid, even though highly persuasive.

It is therefore the intention of this section to speak of logic as both the test of the validity and the soundness of an argument, but not to comment upon style, for the style of an argument is ultimately a matter of individual temperament and strategy.

INDUCTIVE REASONING

Inductive reasoning is a way of thinking that enables us to make general statements on the basis of particular examples and evidence. It is therefore both a way of discovering (making an inductive leap) and a way of explaining. The generalization may take the form of a definite conclusion, an hypothesis, or a recommendation. On the basis of certain kinds of evidence, a generalization may be 100 percent true. For example, if a professor says, "No one in my 9:30 class received a failing grade," the generalization can be accepted as universally true, since it is based upon all possible examples. Any generalization based upon less than complete evidence is held to be generally true. In fact, most generalizations that we make are based upon high probability rather than absolute certainty, simply because generalizations about human behavior and attitudes cannot be made upon all possible cases, only upon representative samplings. Doctors prescribe on the basis of high probability, following certain hypotheses drawn from medical research and practice. For example, barbiturates are useful as sedatives, but they may also be fatal if mixed with alcohol. Neither of these facts is an absolute certainty, but each is a sufficiently authoritative generalization to deserve respect, and one fact does not necessarily contradict the other. It cannot be said that barbiturates are fatal drugs, because in most instances, properly used, they are not.

Judgments, recommendations, and predictions tend to be the most controversial kinds of conclusion, and their general acceptance depends upon the strength of given evidence. A jury's decision of "guilty" or "not guilty" is made after it weighs the evidence for and against the accused; but the more circumstantial the evidence, the less certain the decision. In a series of articles, a local newspaper may list reasons for the city to move as quickly as possible to implement rapid transit. If the arguments are convincing, the recommendation may get results. If they are not, it will fail.

Since inductive reasoning is ordinarily based upon conclusions drawn from evidence, the test of an argument based upon this approach therefore lies in key questions directed to the nature of the evidence and the nature of the conclusion:

1. Is the evidence reliable?

The reliability of evidence depends in part upon its source. For most of our generalizations, we depend mainly upon observing, experimenting, and reading. It is therefore relevant to consider whether what we have seen is representative, what we have done by experimentation is sound, and what we have read has been written by knowledgeable individuals with objectivity. It is obvious that differences of opinion exist because people see differently and accept different sources of authority.

A young teaching assistant who during his tenure taught about 700 students in freshman English out of approximately 20,000 students who took the course during the same period of time writes: "Freshman English competes with physical education for the distinction of being the most detested course offered at the University. Anyone who has not learned that from his students has made little use of the small class situation." Is his personal evidence reliable? Is it more reliable than student questionnaires taken during the same period of time which do not confirm this opinion? In what way did he determine student views? Did he ask students a direct question or merely make inferences from their reactions and motivations? The fact that he says he learned this information from his own students leads to the second question.

2. Is the evidence adequate?

If evidence gathered on the basis of fifty samples produces one conclusion and evidence gathered on the basis of a thousand samples produces contrary evidence, one might conclude that the first sampling is inadequate, provided both samples include approximately the same cross section of persons. If fifty Southern Baptists in Texas were questioned and a thousand Congregationalists in all fifty states were also asked if they believed in the literal interpretation of the Bible, the results from these two groups could obviously not be compared on the basis of adequacy. Neither would be a random sampling. If a statement were made that Southern Baptists in Texas tend to accept the literal interpretation of the Bible, then the sampling of the first group might be adequate to support that generalization. However, if the statement were made that most people in the United States do not accept the literal interpretation of the Bible and the generalization was based upon the sampling of Congregationalists, it would have to be rejected because the sample is biased. Adequate evidence depends upon a sufficient number of samples and a suitable representation within the sample.

Often a fair question is whether there is any evidence at all for a generalization or whether the statement was made on the basis of only one or two personal contacts or whether evidence exists but the writer has neglected to investigate it. A student writes, "Hemingway's *A Farewell to Arms* is a mixture of love, war, and even fantasy that has never before been written in a story of war. War has been the inspiration of many stories, but I doubt that anyone else has ever dug so deeply into its terrible meaning as Hemingway has." One wonders how many war stories from Homer to Hemingway this student has read to justify these generalizations. Or whether he has merely borrowed them from some knowledgeable person who has read extensively or whether he has simply written them with little or no evidence.

3. When several inferences are possible, which is the simplest and least forced?

Given a set of circumstances, we are often left to offer an explanation about what happened or what caused an incident. Several years ago, a small white private plane disappeared while flying from Seattle to Spokane over snow-covered mountains during bad weather. Days later, nothing had been seen or heard from the plane. The most natural assumption was that the plane crashed in a remote mountain region and could not be spotted by air because the white-on-white of the plane in the snow made the plane invisible. That is actually what had happened. At the time of disappearance, someone might also have theorized that the plane flew in the wrong direction and later crashed at sea, but such an inference would have substituted a less likely explanation for a more plausible one.

Consider another example: an old lady steps off a curb, begins to cross the street on a red light, and is killed by an automobile. In the absence of further information, it is simpler to assume that the woman absentmindedly wandered into the street against the light and was killed accidentally, not that she deliberately committed suicide. If, however, additional information revealed that she was in a desperate state of mind because of a fatal illness, that she had declared her intention to kill herself, and that she was quite alert when last seen, suicide might then seem a simpler and more likely explanation of her death than accident.

4. Are there obvious exceptions to the generalization? If so, does it still hold?

A conclusion that is generally true but not universally true naturally allows exceptions, but the exceptions need to be explained. Many people say that Arizona is a good place for asthmatics. Yet some individuals have to leave Arizona because they develop asthma in that region. The first generalization holds true for asthmatics who respond to a hot, dry climate. Others allergic to desert growth are able to live elsewhere more comfortably. In this instance, the truth of the generalization depends upon classifications of asthmatics. The generalization about Arizona as a good region for some asthmatics holds; other asthmatics simply fall into another group.

At times, we have to abandon old hypotheses and beliefs because they can no longer be maintained in view of new knowledge and discovery; the exceptions grow too numerous. Doctors no longer practice bleeding as a general cure-all. Inactivity is no longer considered the best postoperative program for patients. Tin is no longer considered the best metal for "tin cans"; mushrooms are not believed to be poisonous. Apart from generalizations and hypotheses that are changed by new scientific data, every thoughtful person finds himself adjusting his opinions as he tests them by new knowledge gained through increased awareness and observation. These may concern social prejudices or religious beliefs or moral convictions, but new evidence is always capable of challenging established ideas, even though changes may come slowly.

5. Is the cause an adequate explanation of the effect?

There is a tendency to hit upon the obvious as the cause of an effect, even though it may be a totally inadequate explanation. A person found unconscious in a diabetic coma in front of a bar at midnight is likely to be thought dead drunk. Or a perennial joker who has many times put on an act of drowning may be answered with a laugh in a real emergency. In such cases, the effect misleads observers into inferring the wrong cause and doing nothing to help.

In another category, causes may be given which fail to take into account other possible causes. The bombing of Pearl Harbor in World War II may have prompted America's declaration of war against Japan, but this explanation of the immediate cause is not sufficient to account for all of the complex causes that prompted the attack in the first place. A driver may appear to have run his car into a guard rail and killed himself, but an autopsy may reveal that the intervening cause was a heart attack.

Superstitions and popular lore survive upon coincidences and irrational associations of cause and effect. Someone kills a cricket in the house; someone else in the household dies. A superstitious person makes an inevitable connection between these two events, whereas none actually exists. Because of their outdoor life, Indians have always been thought to have keen eyesight. Studies show, however, that they actually have poorer eyesight than whites. Thus the obvious association of good eyesight and Indians is not necessarily an accurate one.

DEDUCTIVE REASONING

Deductive reasoning is a way of thinking that draws inferences from general statements or uses generalizations to apply what is true in one instance to what is true in another related instance. Deduction therefore has a certain predictive value in the sense that one statement can be used to imply another if the proper connections between the two can be made. Even though deductive reasoning is commonly explained as a movement from the general to the particular, it is wholly possible that reasoning of this kind will move only from one general statement to another general statement. The important thing, however, is that the generalization is prior to the conclusion, and the two are logically connected by certain terms. Deductive reasoning, therefore, operates on the basis of a complex system of rules and limitations which set the tests for validity.

In actual practice, emotional persuasion can obscure weaknesses in reasoning by providing distractions from the line of argument. Given time for sober analysis, however, a reader can subject an argument to careful scrutiny. For example, in a paper written about George Orwell's *Animal Farm,* a student expresses this judgment: "Orwell didn't ruin his story by going into too much detail." How can this opinion be weighed? Upon what assumption is it based? Has it been formed by a process of reasoning? We cannot know whether the student ever consciously reasoned out his judgment, but we can reconstruct a kind of thinking that may have occurred over a period of time. Possibly in his reading assignments the student found himself more and more bored by detail, particularly descriptive detail. Gradually, by a process of induction the idea grew in his mind that detail ruins stories—at least, so he thought. If he reached this conclusion, the application to Orwell's *Animal Farm* follows logically:

Major premise: Authors ruin stories by going into too much detail.

Minor premise: Orwell does not go into too much detail in his story *Animal Farm.*

Conclusion: Therefore, Orwell doesn't ruin *Animal Farm.*

This reduction of an argument to its essential premises and conclusion is called a *syllogism.*

Admittedly, the terms in this particular syllogism are not very precise, but the impreciseness of the language begins to test the reasoning. What kind of detail does the student refer to? How much is too much? "Ruin" in what sense? Nevertheless, these are the student's words, and he has come to a particular conclusion on the basis of a general operating principle, which is implicit, not expressed, in his sentence. When one of the premises of a syllogism is omitted in a written or oral statement, the telescoped version of the syllogism is called an *enthymeme.*

THE CATEGORICAL SYLLOGISM

The categorical syllogism may assume several forms, but a few principles are common to all of them.

1.   The syllogism is limited to three statements: a major premise, a minor premise, and a conclusion.

> **Major premise:** All men are mortal.
> **Minor premise:** Socrates is a man.
> **Conclusion:**   Socrates is mortal.

2.   The syllogism is also limited to three and only three terms. Every syllogism must include one term that is common to the major and minor premise but does not appear in the conclusion. This link is called the *middle term*. In the model syllogism, "man" is the middle term. The *major term* is the predicate of the conclusion ("mortal"); the *minor term* is the subject of the conclusion ("Socrates").

3.   The middle term must be distributed at least once. A distributed term is one that includes all members of its class. An undistributed term is one that is not all inclusive. In the model syllogism, "men" is distributed in the major premise. The reference to Socrates is also distributed because an individual by name is considered the only member of his class.

4.   If a particular term is distributed in the conclusion, it must also be distributed in the premises. If a term is undistributed in a premise, it cannot be distributed in the conclusion.

5.   If one premise is negative, the conclusion must be negative.

6.   If both premises are negative, no conclusion can be drawn.

7.   If both premises are qualified, that is, made particular by a word like "some" or "most," no conclusion can be drawn.

Syllogisms that violate these rules are invalid and, as arguments, are unsound.

Almost all propositions may assume one of four forms: universal affirmative, universal negative, particular affirmative, and particular negative. A statement that refers to all instances is called *universal;* a statement that is qualified is called *particular.*

> **Universal affirmative:** All mailboxes in this city are green.
> **Universal negative:**   No mailboxes in this city are red.
> **Particular affirmative:** Some mailboxes are indoors.
> **Particular negative:**   Some mailboxes are not outdoors.

Although other propositions may not be phrased in the exact words of the models, they may still be included in these four categories. For example, "a majority" may be interpreted as the equivalent of "some," since a qualified phrase is less than the universal "all."

Given these propositions and working rules, the validity of an argument can be tested. At the same time, reducing a statement to a syllogism may also be a way of showing the flimsiness of its premises. A student writes:

> Any interpretation a student writes is bound to be better than the professor's because it will come closer to the student's understanding than to the professor's.

Since this sentence expresses a comparative judgment, it seems to be based upon some principle of what a good interpretation is. In an attempt to penetrate the fuzziness of the thinking, we might attempt to formulate a syllogism:

Major premise: All interpretations that are close to a student's understanding are good.

Minor premise: All interpretations a student writes are close to his understanding.

Conclusion: Therefore, all interpretations a student writes are good.

In like manner, we might establish that a professor's interpretations which go beyond the student's understanding are bad, forming the basis for the comparative judgment in the original statement. What this kind of demonstration reveals is that we may disregard a person's valid conclusions if we reject any one of his premises. Given certain premises, many ridiculous things can be argued, but if we examine the premises and find them to be true, we are then obligated to accept the conclusion if it has been validly drawn from the true premises.

THE CONDITIONAL SYLLOGISM

Conditional syllogisms are those that can be phrased in terms of *if ... then*. One premise implies the other.

Premise 1: If the mathematics proficiency requirement is dropped, enrollment in Mathematics 101 will probably decrease.

Premise 2: The requirement will be dropped.

Conclusion: Then, enrollment in Mathematics 101 will probably decrease.

It should be noted that the parts of the first premise—the *if* clause, called the antecedent, and the *then* clause, called the consequent—are not reversible. It does not hold that if the enrollment in Mathematics 101 decreases, the requirement has been dropped. The decrease may be due to other causes. This conditional syllogism is based upon only one hypothesis; namely, if the requirement is dropped, a drop in enrollment is likely to follow. On the basis of this kind of predictive reasoning, we often make plans for the future. The negative, of course, also holds true: if the requirement is not dropped, enrollment in the course is not likely to decrease, unless, of course, new circumstances enter.

In other instances, however, the conditional syllogism expresses a necessary relation. These are the basis of mathematical proofs: if two angles are equal to a third angle, they are then equal to each other.

$$\text{If} \quad A = C$$
$$\text{If} \quad B = C$$
$$\text{Then} \quad A = B$$

The conditional syllogism is not limited to two premises and a single conclusion. It may have any number of premises. It therefore resembles very closely the kind of argument that occurs in written discourse when a writer tries to establish a point. The soundness of a conditional argument depends, of course, upon the relation between the conclusion and the conditions. Are the conditions true? Will the conclusion necessarily follow? If any number of variables can intervene between the *if* and the *then,* the argument tends to lose its force.

THE ALTERNATIVE SYLLOGISM

Alternative syllogisms are those that can be phrased in terms of *either ... or.* One premise excludes the other, although at times an *either ... or* relation means "perhaps both."

Premise 1: In order to arrive on time, you have to take either the 6:30 A.M. or 10:30 A.M. flight.
Premise 2: Not 6:30.
Conclusion: Therefore, 10:30.

This happens to be a syllogism in which both of the alternatives are possible. In other instances, however, the alternatives are exclusive:

Premise 1: Either we choose to meet once again this quarter, or we adjourn for the summer.
Premise 2: Decision not to adjourn.
Conclusion: Therefore, we meet once again this quarter.

One alternative may be true and the other false, leading to a faulty conclusion:

> **Premise 1:**   Either the judge is a Democrat, or he is against free enterprise.
> **Premise 2:**   He is not against free enterprise.
> **Conclusion:**   Therefore, he is a Democrat.

When both alternatives are true and possible, an inference cannot be made by simply affirming one; there is always the possibility that both will occur.

> **Premise 1:**   Either fees will have to be raised or the enrollment restricted.
> **Premise 2:**   Fees will be raised.
> **Invalid Conclusion:** Therefore, enrollment will not be restricted.

In this case, the conclusion is invalid because the decision to restrict the enrollment may depend upon other factors besides money. Space may be equally important. Only when an argument can deny one alternative in order to assert the other does it become valid.

The strength of argument based upon the alternative syllogism depends upon the sharpness of the options. Are there other alternatives that have not been considered? Is a choice necessary if both alternatives can be maintained? In arguing for a particular candidate in an election, the choice must be candidate A or candidate B. But in arguing how to solve the city's traffic problems, an argument based upon alternatives can be refuted if it can be shown that the best choice is not A *or* B, but A *and* B, in short, that they are not exclusive alternatives. An argument based upon alternatives can persuade only if the listeners believe that all of the alternatives are real ones in the first place, that they are exclusive of one another in the second, and, finally, that they consist of the genuinely possible alternatives. Only then is a clear choice possible.

REASONING BY ANALOGY

Reasoning by analogy is the weakest of all the forms of argument because no conclusion can be logically established by this method. The writer may state a conclusion, but the reader is not bound to accept it on the basis of the reasoning, simply because two contexts are brought into relation with one another which may involve quite different principles and values. Can the habit of wild male animals to roam in packs be used to justify a man's desire to spend one night a week away from home? Can the slaughter of animals for meat be used to justify the slaughter of human beings in warfare? These analogies are farfetched, but they show how comparison can give a distorted and oversimplified view of a situation.

Yet analogy is useful for purposes of illustration; and if the similarity between two things or two situations is close enough, readers may choose to ignore the lack of necessary connection and accept the conclusion of the argument. Often it is necessary to examine the language of an analogy carefully to determine whether the argument is misleading. For example, a student justifies his negative feelings toward blacks by drawing parallels between them and other minority groups:

> It is very true that we Americans, like many Europeans, brought African people to our country to be our slaves. But today they are on their own, a free people. They had a difficult time in America proving themselves to the rest of the Americans, but so have the Jews, the Japanese, and the Chinese. The fact is that the Jews, Japanese, and Chinese have succeeded in being accepted, and the Negroes have not. It seems to me that the answer is simply that these other people have helped themselves; they had initiative.

This paragraph is based upon a premise that those minority groups that prove themselves by self-initiative are accepted by Americans. This in itself is a shaky premise, but the writer goes on to assert that the Jews, Japanese, and Chinese have met this test; the Negroes have not. The analogy breaks down in at least two places. It first ignores the significant difference in the history of these groups. Only the Negroes came as slaves; the others did not. But the passage goes on: "But today they are on their own, a free people." In what sense are Negroes free? Constitutionally free? Economically free? Socially free? On this point, close parallels exist between all of the minority groups because they have all been subjected to restrictions of freedom, but even then the differences between them are perhaps greater than the similarities. What at first seems like a logical parallel turns out to be a flimsy comparison.

Comparison can be highly illuminating if it is not pushed to prove a point. It is interesting to draw analogies, as Plato did, between the government of the individual soul and the government of the city state, since, as he reasoned, the state is made up of individuals; but it is another matter to justify aristocracy over democracy as a form of government on the basis of such an analogy. It may be useful to consider what happened in Germany in the early 1930s in terms of what is happening in the United States in the 1960s and early 1970s if the comparison is not used to infer that we are moving inevitably toward a dictatorial state. Many historical analogies are instructive, but it is another thing to conclude that the pattern of the future follows precisely the pattern of the past. The more closely related two things are, the more sound an analogy based upon them will be, but close similarity then works against the advantage of an analogy to create a fresh perspective by bringing two quite different things in relation to one another.

COMMON FALLACIES

A fallacy is best described as a counterfeit argument, one that has market value because it passes as the real thing. Because arguments depend upon words, facts, and relations, fallacies arise from the ways these are handled. Unfortunately, people do not always know when they are being fooled; in fact, some writers and speakers are not aware that they themselves fall into errors of reasoning. Knowledge of fallacies is therefore important in preparing and responding to argument.

Many fallacies are self-evident. They spring from faulty kinds of reasoning: a hasty generalization unwarranted by the evidence, a forced analogy, a vague appeal to unnamed authorities, a substitution of simple extreme alternatives for a weighing of many possible choices. These are all false ways of arguing, although, as experience shows, at times very powerful ways. The number of fallacies are numerous, because for every principle of inference or deduction there is the possibility of a violation. These are considered formal fallacies. Three are particularly common in everyday reasoning.

1. Begging the question

The fallacy of "begging the question" occurs when the conclusion is essentially a rephrasing of the beginning assumption. The argument therefore is circular, getting nowhere in proving a point because it assumes to be true what should be proved. Someone might say, "Use of marijuana is bad because it is illegal." But why illegal? "It's illegal because it's immoral." The reply merely rephrases the original premise; it makes "bad," "illegal," and "immoral" synonymous terms. The reply begs the question.

2. The confusion of *all* and *some*

Reasoning that misleads the reader to substitute "all" for "some" is more formally known as the fallacy of the undistributed middle. The possible viciousness of this fallacy becomes obvious when we see it spelled out in syllogistic form:

Major premise: All Communists oppose the capitalist system.
Minor premise: Some who oppose the capitalist system are student protesters.
Conclusion: Therefore, some student protesters are Communists.

It is true that some student protesters are acknowledged Communists, but it is not proved by this particular syllogism. In both the major and minor premises, "those who oppose the capitalist system" is an undistributed term. It does not refer to everyone who opposes capitalism. Socialists may also oppose capitalism. Therefore, it is possible for many people to be opponents of capitalism and not be Communists.

Another conclusion of the same syllogism that would read "All student protesters are Communists" would be equally invalid because "student protesters" is an undistributed term in the minor premise and therefore cannot become universal in the conclusion.

Substituting "all" for "some" is an insidious way of incriminating innocent persons. The evacuation of Japanese-American civilians from the West Coast during World War II and their transfer to detention camps would seem to have grown from an assumption that all potential enemies of this nation had to be confined. Since all Japanese-American civilians were considered potential enemies, they were evacuated. Perhaps *some* Japanese-Americans were potential enemies, but *most* were responsible citizens who supported the war effort just as other Americans. The reasoning that was used was fallacious, and the fallacy caused undue hardship among a group of loyal citizens.

3. *Post hoc, ergo propter hoc*

Literally translated, the Latin words mean, "After this, therefore, on account of this." It is erroneous cause-and-effect reasoning: one thing happens, another follows; the first is inferred to be cause of the second. Of course, one thing that happens before another need not necessarily be its cause. The *post hoc* fallacy can be easily reduced to absurdity. A grandmother tells a young bride that, as soon as she knows she is pregnant, she can determine the sex of her child by sleeping on her left side if she wants a boy and sleeping on her right side if she wants a girl. In the course of years, the young lady, faithful to the practice, has two boys and two girls in exactly the order she wants them. She recommends the method to her friends because the results have been perfect. It should be noted that a *reductio ad absurdum* (reducing an argument to absurdity) can itself be a fallacy if it serves only to ridicule and fails to make clear the weakness of the position it is mocking.

Apart from formal fallacies that violate the rules of inference, there are a number of informal fallacies. These seem to function by confusing the argument, evading the issue, or substituting emotion for evidence.

1. Confusing the argument

An argument can be confused mainly by two methods: using ambiguous language or distorting the evidence. Sound argument rests upon clear and precise terms. Many arguments bog down because words are used vaguely or the terms shift in their meaning. In his book *The Hero,* Lord Raglan writes, "Since history depends upon written chronology, and the savage has no written chronology, the savage can have no history." Out of context the argument is confusing because it seems to be based upon an extremely limited definition of history. Yet reference to the book indicates that Lord Raglan defines history in precisely those terms: "History is the recital in chronological sequence of events that are known to have occurred." If we grant Lord Raglan his definition, his conclusion is probably true, but if we substitute a broader definition the conclusion does not hold.

A student writes, "A person who has compassion and understanding for everyone and hatred for none is Christlike. He is a Christian." This conclusion is based either upon the untenable assumption that all Christians are Christlike, or there has been an unconscious shift of terms in the last sentence from "Christlike" to "Christian." The two words cannot substitute for one another.

Confusion, whether deliberate or not, also arises from the manipulation of evidence, particularly statistical evidence. Figures can be made to prove almost anything, usually by suppressing some of the evidence. One store may advertise that its prices are lower, but suppress the fact that its interest rates are higher. A high school administration may publicize that its current graduating class has received more scholarships than any other class in the history of the school, but suppress the fact that the class is larger than any previous one and the percentage of scholarships is 5 percent lower than three other classes. A political incumbent may supply statistics indicating that his administration has brought unprecedented revenues to the state, but suppress information about unprecedented expenditures. The distortion of evidence is actually a device of oversimplification. Since the general reader seldom has access to complete statistical evidence, he is not to be blamed if he takes a skeptical attitude toward figures in general.

2. Evading the issue

Ignoring the question and introducing irrelevant issues are also common fallacies of everyday reasoning. Ignoring the question is usually a deliberate attempt to avoid controversial or unpleasant issues. In one sense, a reply that ignores the question is a total irrelevancy; yet it is particularly common in personal interviews involving direct questions. A diplomat asked to comment upon our present relations with Israel may begin with a review of our past relations, stopping short of the current situation. If further questions explore new issues, he manages to skirt the original question. The practice is also common among student writers who, asked to analyze some particular work, merely summarize and fail to come to grips with the question.

Irrelevant arguments are more subtle. They may appear to be related, particularly if they are wrapped in syllogistic phrasing. For example, a graduate student attempts to explain the unpopularity of a particular freshman course in this way:

> There are two possible explanations: something is wrong with the students, or something is wrong with the course. If something is wrong with the freshmen, then I don't see why the same things aren't wrong with graduate students. Therefore, the faculty ought to consider the desires of graduate students to the same extent that graduate students are willing to consider the desires of freshmen.

The argument begins logically by setting up an alternative, but it then turns quickly to graduate students. It is not clear what they have to do with the argument about freshmen, except that the writer wants to add a bit of special pleading that is totally irrelevant to his main point.

3. Substituting emotion for evidence

Arguments that substitute emotion for evidence are also irrelevancies, but they represent a special kind of fallacy in that they shove reasoning aside and appeal to feelings. In so doing, they actually cloud the issues. One of the most common is an *ad hominem* argument. In simplest terms, an *ad hominem* argument attacks the man instead of the issues. It is a common political practice, particularly when the issues are sticky or when the candidates are not sufficiently different in their views to represent opposing sides of an argument. In such cases, the contest may shift to personal grounds. Attacks can be forthright, but often they are couched in simplified language that condemns by association. One senator or another will be labeled a hawk, an isolationist, a left-winger, or a negativist. All of these words are intended to draw responses, but not rational ones.

Other appeals that play upon the emotions and prejudices of people but do not necessarily involve personalities are called *ad populum* arguments (literally, "to the people"). These appeals cover a wide range of feelings, but a few are more commonly exploited than others: blind patriotism (*American forces cannot be withdrawn. Has America ever lost a war?*); self-interest and bigotry (*Approval of the open housing law will ruin property values in the suburbs*); anti-intellectualism (*Draft dodgers have been encouraged by the weirdo professors of our universities*); suspicion and prudishness (*It should be quite clear by now that there is a nation-wide Communist-supported plot to encourage the moral decay of our youth through sex education in schools and lewd motion pictures featuring perversion and nudity*). Even though any of these positions might be argued on legitimate grounds, the *ad populum* approach shortcuts the process of careful support and takes advantage of the weakness of many people to jump to quick conclusions.

ARGUMENTATION AND REFUTATION

Argumentation, by definition, is dispute. It implies that there are opposing positions. Someone might claim that on the basis of such a definition anything in the world can be argued. Perhaps so, but some things are less arguable than others. It is hardly worth arguing whether newspapers should or should not have headlines if no issue is involved, or whether Hemingway should have written *A Farewell to Arms* before *Torrents of Spring,* since he didn't do it. Any viable issue, however, naturally lines up proponents and opponents.

Argumentation serves to consider pros and cons. A writer can argue in three different ways. First, he can take an affirmative position and set forth his own arguments. Second, he can give further evidence that will counterbalance the arguments of his opponents. If these arguments have not yet been advanced, he can try to anticipate them. (Aristotle thought that anyone who argues a case should know the opposing position as well as his own. Lawyers still seem to follow this advice.) As a third means of argumentation, he can point to fallacies in his opponents' arguments as a way of discrediting them. Strong argumentation, therefore, demands careful study of evidence, and it requires perceptive reasoning to detect flaws in all arguments, whether those of an opponent or one's own.

It would be reassuring to believe that the strongest and most infallible arguments always prevail. We know that does not always happen. When it does not, the blame rests with those people who are easy victims of their feelings and those who in their ignorance fail even to perceive the difference between sound and fallacious reasoning.

Preparation for Argumentation

One of the first considerations in argument is the need to find common ground. If two sides have irreconcilable positions, argumentation will accomplish nothing. It will be only confrontation, denial, and quarreling. Finding common ground means arguing within the same context. A laboratory worker who defends vivisection does so in terms of the ultimate knowledge that may be gained from experimentation. His arguments are scientific. A layman who opposes vivisection does so in terms of cruelty to innocent creatures. His arguments are humane. This particular issue continues to be debated. One thing seems apparent: the argument is not one of simple alternatives. It seems that vivisection will continue to be used as a scientific method of research. Vivisectionists who want to justify their position to the public emphasize that their work also has an ultimate humanitarian value. The choice is not a humane pursuit or an inhumane one. In turn, antivivisectionists, admitting the need for scientific experimentation, can continue to insist that it be done humanely. Once this common ground has been reached, once the common context of scientific necessity and humane values have been established and accepted, the opponents can move closer together.

The second consideration in argumentation is taking into account the opposing arguments. If these can be anticipated, they can be prepared for and parried. In order to do this, however, an individual must first concede that the opposition has justifications of its own, particularly if it represents an entrenched position. For example, if a student wants to prepare a careful argument advocating that the letter-grading system be abolished in colleges throughout the country, he might attempt to list as objectively as possible *Arguments for Change* and *Arguments against Change.* To say that there is no rational justification for grades is only an opinion. Unless the student is willing to examine what justifications have been given for grades and can prove that they are irrational, he has not advanced an argument.

A weighing of arguments on this particular question can be done in an orderly way.

Proposition: That letter-grades be abolished and replaced by a credit/no credit system, supplemented by written evaluations, sent to the student and made a part of his permanent record.

Arguments for Change	**Counterarguments to Be Anticipated**
1. Grades support the authority of professors; they undermine the self-autonomy of students. They impose upon students the judgment of superiors.	If professors were not authorities by virtue of what they know, there would be no point in a student coming to college. Self-autonomy must lie in the student's freedom to choose his own course of study.
2. Grades lead to grade grubbing. The grade is all that counts, not what a student learns.	This is what students make of grades. The professor knows that ability, knowledge, and motivation are what count, and he attempts to make the grade reflect how the student has used his abilities.

3. Grades represent a judgment by a particular professor in a particular course. Because standards vary among institutions, departments, and professors, they are relative and imperfect measures.

Because a grade does measure the extent to which a student performs in terms of specific demands, it comments upon his capacity to meet standards other than his own. What is finally important is not a single grade but the cumulative record. An institution, department, or professor gains a good or bad reputation over a period of time.

4. Grades are dehumanized symbols. They substitute a numerical value for a qualitative judgment. The substitution of a credit/no credit system with written evaluations will permit professors to analyze students, not label them. Students will be able to understand their strengths and weaknesses better when they are given the evaluations.

A grade is not a character sketch. It is a standardized symbol indicating comparative performance. Written evaluations would ultimately produce a standardized language of their own, permitting us no better self-appraisal than present grades. Note the jargon of elementary school report cards.

5. Grades are negative motivators. They make students work for artificial goals. They prevent a student from doing his best work because he is under pressure to get a grade. They create anxiety and fear of failure. A student is made to doubt his personal worth.

Granted that self-motivation is preferable to any forced learning, yet grades can promote initiative, particularly if a student is working for a professor he respects. No educational system will eliminate human anxieties. Almost any performer will testify that an element of tension puts him at his very best.

6. Grades encourage conformity. They reward plodders and penalize thinkers. They take away the student's freedom to learn in his own way and to pursue his own conclusions.

These consequences depend upon individual professors. A college program is disciplined and concentrated learning. Some highly inventive people drop out because they choose not to submit to any system. A plodder may be unimaginative, but he is not necessarily stupid.

7. Grades make students passive, leaving the professor to carry the active role. They protect bad teaching by stifling criticism.

An irrelevant argument. Improvement of teaching and teacher evaluation can be done without reform of the grading system.

8. Grades encourage unnecessary competition among students. Education should be devoted to the process of learning, not to the survival of the most competitive.

Competition, with or without grades, seems to be a human tendency, not limited to education. It bothers the first-year student more than advanced students because he approaches an unknown situation. Competition can promote excellence.

9. Grades have no correlation with success in later life. Graduate schools can do without them because they now depend upon supplementary information.

Grades may have no necessary correlation with success (however that is defined), but the records of many prominent citizens would suggest that they are a fairly reliable index.

Possible Additional Arguments by the Opposition

Counterarguments to These

1. Grades cannot very well be abolished at the college level without abolishing them in the lower schools as well. At present, students are grade-conditioned. If grades are withheld, they demand them.

The conditioning of students is exactly one of the evils of the system. What is definitely needed is a reform of the whole practice along the line, not just an adjustment in colleges where students have learned to speak for themselves.

2. Reform of the grading system ignores the administrative difficulties, bulky evaluation sheets, lack of standardized information to be exchanged with other schools and to be studied, increased workload for professors, unadaptability to computer systems.

Any change creates inconveniences, but these are usually solved in time. Evaluations, for example, could be put on small computerized microfiche. A revision of the system would require adjustments in the thinking of many people, but these are the very changes that are being urged.

3. The five levels of grading are approximate correspondences to the kind of "grading" that pervades our entire society. The college is therefore both realistic and relevant in the system it maintains.

The school grading system merely perpetuates the present way of thinking. A new system in the schools would ultimately produce a fairer system of evaluation in life.

These notes only begin to suggest how a self-dialogue can be carried on if an individual is first willing to place a temporary moratorium on his feelings and then begin to investigate both sides of a question as honestly as he can. Rational argument requires objectivity. It is carried on by statement and counterstatement. It degenerates only when the arguments are abandoned, and loaded language, accusations, and unsupported generalizations are substituted for sober reflection.

Argumentation, therefore, makes these demands upon a writer:

1. To accumulate strong, adequate, and verifiable evidence.
2. To define terms.
3. To group arguments.
4. To invent the arguments of the opposition.
5. To detect fallacies.
6. To argue in a clear, unconfused sequence.
7. To use precise and appropriate language in support of the arguments.

7

Paragraphing

THE PARAGRAPH BLOC

What writer ordinarily knows how many paragraphs he will write in an essay before he begins? If he plans his topic well, he may have several major points in mind, but each could take two or three or even more paragraphs to develop fully. What the writer is likely to know in advance is that his essay will have several parts, each developing a major topic. These organizational units consisting of several paragraphs traditionally have no name, but for purposes of discussion they may be referred to as a paragraph bloc.

The term "paragraph bloc" is a unit of discourse that has not been given adequate recognition or study until recently. Its meaning is closely related to the political use of the word "bloc." In politics, a bloc is a group of people who work together for some common cause. In discourse, a bloc is a group of paragraphs that work together to develop a major segment of thought. It is an important unit in terms of the logic of the essay as a whole. It closely resembles the major headings of an outline, for those sections do not necessarily correspond to the paragraphing of a paper but to the main points being discussed. The extent to which each is developed determines the number of paragraphs.

The paragraph bloc, therefore, cannot be defined arbitrarily in terms of length. In a short theme, it may consist of two paragraphs, or possibly the entire theme will be a single bloc of four or five paragraphs. In a book, a bloc may be eight or ten paragraphs or the equivalent of a numbered section within a chapter. In terms of structure, the paragraph bloc is a developing form; that is, the writer controls it; he limits it or extends it as he thinks necessary. It cannot be defined as a set pattern, but it can be clearly recognized. In Chapter II of *Patterns of Culture,* Ruth Benedict discusses the diversity of cultures. She begins with a narrative bloc of four paragraphs about a California Indian named Ramon, whose cultural values are quite different from those of most Californians. It is a story in itself. She then follows this with a bloc of three paragraphs developing the idea of selection as a prime factor in cultural life: each culture chooses to emphasize certain aspects of life and regard others lightly. Then extended illustrations follow. Fourteen paragraphs are given to a discussion of adolescence and adulthood. These represent one bloc. She signals a change to another topic by the opening sentence of a new bloc:

> Warfare is another social theme that may or may not be used in any culture.

This new bloc on warfare consists of four additional paragraphs, each beginning in the following way:

> There are even quainter notions, from our standpoint, associated with warfare in different parts of the world.

> On the other hand, it may be just as impossible for a people to conceive of the possibility of a state of war.

> I myself tried to talk of warfare to the Mission Indians of California, but it was impossible.

> War is, we have been forced to admit even in the face of its huge place in our civilization, an asocial trait.

When the next paragraph begins with the words "Warfare is not an isolated case" and moves to the subject of mating and marriage, we know that the warfare bloc has been completed. Thus each of the blocs throughout the chapter becomes an illustration of the cultural diversity indicated by the title of the chapter.

In an editorial in the *Saturday Review* entitled "Toward a New Language," Norman Cousins writes as follows:

> A black extremist breaks into church services, shouts his demands for race reparations, and later asserts that his action was justified because the white community understands only the language of force.
> A white teen-ager in Chicago shoots into a Negro home. He doesn't

know the occupants, but it makes no difference. The blacks must be taught a lesson, he says, in the only way they understand—force.

An Arab spokesman declares that violent reprisals against Israelis are necessary because this is the only language the Israelis understand.

An Israeli spokesman declares that violent reprisals against Arabs are necessary because this is the only language the Arabs understand.

A Pentagon spokesman, appearing before the Senate Foreign Relations Committee, calls for maximum bombing of North Vietnam because the direct application of force is the only language Hanoi understands.

A Hanoi spokesman calls on the North Vietnamese to redouble their efforts against the United States because force is the only language Washington understands.

What a man really says, of course, when he says that someone else can be persuaded only by force, is that he himself is incapable of more rational means of communication. The total effect, both on the small-level and the large—from the university campus to the international arena, from the tempers of the individual to the outbursts of large aggregations—is that life on this planet has become increasingly disfigured and hazardous. Men who insist on communicating through force in a nuclear age disqualify themselves for meaningful survival.

These seven paragraphs represent a single paragraph bloc. Considered as a unit they proceed from the particular to the general. It could be argued that they actually represent only one paragraph broken down into seven parts. It is true that they do represent one logical unit, but rhetorically they are discrete parts. If Cousins had put them all together as one paragraph he would have lost the force of each separate example; he would have obscured the pattern of three contrasting pairs and a conclusion at the end; and he would have disguised the parallel structure and almost equal length of the first six short paragraphs. What he does is to dramatize the effect by setting off the parts separately.

The Cousins selection suggests one further observation: Cousins does not appear to be as much interested in what some school texts say a paragraph should *be* as he is in what he can make paragraphing *do* for a special effect.

THE PARAGRAPH

What we should readily recognize is that paragraphing practices vary. Some writers paragraph solely on the basis of content. To them, a paragraph is a way of dividing the continuous flow of discourse into meaningful parts; it is primarily a logical unit, and each paragraph develops one point in some depth.

Other writers, however, operate upon wholly different premises. Some of their paragraphs are logical units; but others, like the ones written by Norman Cousins, are rhetorical, separated from one another for purposes of emphasis and variety. What is illogical about the divisions from one standpoint will be interpretive from the other. Rhetorical paragraphing, for the most part, uses the visual effect of short paragraphs to do in writing what a speaker can do by intonation and gesture. A student, asked to write about his notion of a modern-day Utopia, begins in this way:

> Temperamentally unsuited for safety and security, restless in stable circumstances—in short, as a human being preferring a roller-coaster's careening and lurching to the merry-go-round's even circling—I am perhaps unfit to design a Utopia pleasing to most men.
> But what would I wish if what I wish were possible?
> I would like men and women to be free.
> Free, not from the necessity of working, but from any need to work in any way at any task whose purpose is lost in the doing of it.
> I do not mean that every man's work would be a means of feeding his mind and body, or that everyone who did not work in this way would hurry home to read *Saturday Review*—there are more important things—but that no work of any man or woman would repudiate their human dignity by leaving their lives in the end cheap as a beast's, and that no one—whether because of extreme poverty or extreme greed—would be so caught up in the grind of getting and spending that he would lay waste his powers of joy and love and openness to beauty.

This particular theme continues with two more paragraphs of approximately one hundred words each, so that the short paragraphs—the question, the answer, and the elaboration in paragraphs two, three, and four—are not typical of a writer who does not know what he is doing. They can be taken as wholly intentional. In fact, they focus upon key ideas and provide a rhythmic contrast to customary even-flowing paragraphs of one or two hundred words each. Perhaps, in the writer's own words, these short paragraphs represent "careening and lurching," which he prefers to the "even circling" of longer ones.

Therefore, one standard of measurement cannot be applied to all paragraphs. They may be visual devices, as newspapers use them; they may be logical divisions, as we most commonly think of them; and they may also be rhetorical units, as individual writers use them for special effect. In all of these uses, however, the paragraph represents a relatively short unit of varying length that divides discourse for purposes of readability and better understanding.

Levels of Generality

The shaping of a paragraph may be best understood in terms of an ebbing and flowing of sentences between the general and the particular. If the relation between a writer and reader were completely intimate, so that they shared the same knowledge and the same background, generalities could possibly be written without support. But even when a writer and reader share the same knowledge and experience, detail is still necessary as a means of making perfectly clear what the writer has in mind. In an article written at the end of 1968, for example, Bruce Chapman begins a paragraph with the sentence: "Nobody is celebrating at the end of this political year; there is a pervasive malaise." He could have stopped at this point, and there would have been a good bit of implicit understanding on the part of his readers. But because he is an experienced writer, he does not take things for granted. He continues with particular explanations about his general statement:

> We are in the eighth winter of a vicious little war, where hope is dispensed chiefly as a foil for disappointment. We are haunted yet by the incubus of political assassination and the succubus of racial terrorism. The Democratic Convention was a riot; the Democratic campaign, as Disraeli would have said, an "organized hypocrisy." As for the Republicans, from Miami on they were willfully irrelevant, practicing the politics of blah.
>
> "Politics 68"

After these details, he returns to a restatement of his general observation at the beginning: "Nineteen sixty-four was an electoral emetic; 1968 is what came up." Thus, this paragraph begins on a general level, moves to the particulars, then returns to the general at the end. Particulars are the writer's way of earning the right to make generalizations. Generalizations, in turn, are the statements that give meaningful interpretations of particulars. Both are necessary parts of writing.

All paragraphs, of course, do not move on a simple two-level alternation of general and particular. Whenever detail needs further elaboration, a paragraph may move to further particulars:

> One of James's weaknesses, and it pervaded his government of the kingdom, was his penchant for the handsome young men he made his favorites, or minions. Among these was Robert Carr, whom he created Earl of Somerset before the Overbury affair. Sir Thomas Overbury, imprisoned by the king on a flimsy pretense, died mysteriously in the Tower of London in 1613, and three years later Carr was condemned to death for Overbury's murder. Carr strenuously maintained his innocence, but his wife, also condemned, confessed that she had sent poisoned jellies and tarts to the prisoner. It is this Countess of Somerset who is the ostensible subject of the present biography; she had earlier been Lady Essex.
>
> Harry T. Moore, "Fatal Frolics in the Tower of London"

This paragraph begins with a lead-in sentence, a generalization that merely sets up the discussion; the second sentence gives an example; then the two succeeding sentences explain what the Overbury affair was. The final sentence indicates that the paragraph has found its mooring. This is the point that the author has been leading up to. It may therefore be identified as the topic sentence of the paragraph. The topic sentence is the highest level of generality within a particular paragraph or within a paragraph bloc. Every paragraph may not have a topic sentence, since, as we have seen, paragraphs sometimes operate within a larger scheme of thought. In a paragraph bloc, the topic sentence is the organizing sentence of the whole group of paragraphs. A topic sentence is therefore important because it is a brief general statement of the main point being discussed. Whether it comes first, last, or in the middle is simply a matter of individual strategy, but without doubt the frequency of topic sentences at the beginning of paragraphs merely reflects a congenial way of beginning with the general and proceeding to the particular.

DEVELOPING PARAGRAPHS

What are the writer's resources for developing paragraphs? How does he add support? What form do various details take? In answer,

1. *He can qualify, elaborate, or restate in different words:*

> Lead-in sentence
> Elaboration
> Topic sentence
>
> This is the function of the clock. It will not retreat one second in all the millennia to come. It will cut you down, replace your future with a past, and put you under the sod. At the age of sixty, you will have spent twenty years sleeping, twenty more growing up, and twenty trying to leave your mark on our cave.
>
> Jim Bishop, "Time Is the Only True Enemy"

2. *He can define and give examples:*

> Topic sentence
> Definition
>
> Jewish jokes are not funny. They are not even jokes, but potted observations about Jewishness given anecdotal form and a punch line. The response is laughter, though not the sort of laughter that greets the regular (usually obscene) male-company story; it is ambiguous, it conceals, or fails to conceal, a ruefulness, a reflectiveness, a sense of resignation. How true that is, we are meant to feel, how wry, how inescapable, how

Example

Jewish. Cohen at the travel agency rejects ex-pro-Nazi Italy and Spain, not to speak of Germany and Austria, for his vacation trip; the busy clerk leaves him thoughtfully spinning a globe; when the clerk returns, Cohen

Restatement of topic sentence

says, "Maybe you got another globe?" That is the basic Jewish joke; hardly a joke at all.

Kingsley Amis, "Waxing Wroth"

3. *He can classify:*

Topic sentence

   There are rebels and rebels. Some conspire to overthrow their country's government. Some are terrorists, risking or sacrificing their lives in an effort to destroy a particularly hateful representative of the

Classifications

powers that be. Others become guerrillas. There are also those who are less temperamental and might be called radicals rather than rebels; they devote themselves to the propaganda of revolutionary ideas for the purpose of winning over the masses, or else use their literary talents to defend their specific doctrines.

Max Nomad, "A Radical's Real Reasons"

4. *He can summarize and analyze:*

Lead-in sentence

   Without any hope for a relief from human suffering in death, we may wonder what Kunitz' views on contemporary life are. This subject is best covered in

Summary and analysis

"The Fitting of the Mask." This poem says simply, "And everyone, you know, must wear a mask." The masks are used, says Kunitz, by modern men to represent their outward intentions while concealing themselves. But now, because of the many horrors of the twentieth century, the seller of the masks sings "There's nothing left that's decent in our stock." In the poem, modern man attempts to buy a mask, but there are none left, and he is forced to look in a mirror and see his true

Interpretation and topic sentence

self. Predictably, modern man finds that the worst possible face is the one of reality.

Student paragraph

5. *He can give reasons:*

Topic sentence

   The new regime will be very sparing of promises to alien societies. It will not repeat the mistake of

Example

President Kennedy, in his first official months, when he said that we would try to renovate the economies of Latin America in ten years' time, an implied promise that set some progress in motion, but excited expectation far more.

Restatement of topic sentence

Reasons

Mr. Nixon has refrained from promises of that kind even to our own people. He knows that we are in deep trouble at home not only because these social and racial problems are inherently very difficult to solve and the programs for solving them may have been hastily conceived, but also because progress itself has been outrun and discounted because of the impatient expectations stirred by the promises.

Eric Sevareid, "Richard Nixon's Mandate"

6. *He can present facts:*

Topic sentence

Various "in-depth" studies of campus attitudes are beginning to correct the impression that college students are the vanguard of a revolutionary generation bent upon ripping up society and letting the pieces fall where they may. The latest of these, a study by Elmo Roper, financed but not interfered with by Standard Oil of New Jersey and employing the pollsters' usual techniques, shows that the noisy militants one reads so much about in the newspapers and sees so much of on television constitute a less-than-10 per cent minority and that a majority consider American institutions "basically sound."

Illustration with facts

Return to the study in general

Continuation of facts

The study was conducted on 96 campuses, concentrating on senior men about to be graduated but including male freshmen and alumni of the Class of 1964. The attitudes of these groups were found to be similar. Members of all three were confident that they could find satisfactory places in an imperfect society; they thought they might improve it; only 9 percent of the seniors considered society so evil as to be proof against reform. Rating the nation's problems by priority of seriousness, they put race relations first, crime and lawlessness second, poverty and slum conditions third and avoidance of war fourth. The alumni were bothered, too, by inflated prices.

Kenneth Crawford, "Campus 'Revolution' "

7. *He can compare and contrast:*

Topic sentence

Comparison

The standard of American skiing is amazingly high. I find the average skill of American skiers higher than that of Europeans, even though skiing in the United States has been popular for a relatively short

Contrast

time. It must have something to do with the fact that Americans, when they start something new, want to do it well and therefore work hard at it. Europeans are inclined to take skiing more as relaxation and fun than as a sport. They are content with being just proficient enough to enjoy it.

> Henry Brandon, "Nixon Starts Down the Run"

8. *He can describe:*

Description of a Place:

Topic sentence

Support with illustrations

Description

Even the art of Greece is not so chaste as tradition has it. When Sorokin declares that until the third century B.C. Greek art contained 'nothing vulgar, coarse, or debasing,' nothing of the crudity of our own 'sensate' art, he has presumably forgotten Aristophanes, the satirists and polemists, the phallic images, the many-breasted Artemis of Ephesus, the celebrations of sexuality and homosexuality—all the Dionysian or Bacchic elements of Greek culture that led the barbarian Scythians (according to Herodotus) to deplore the Greek fondness for frenzy. But the Acropolis of Athens is the clearest illustration of the deceptive magic of time. Time has purified it; sweeping away the gaudy confusion, leaving only the stainless marble; the Parthenon stands alone in majestic simplicity, in the perfect proportions of its skeletal outlines. And so we forget that these temples were once painted in lively colors and decorated with gold leaf, in something like Oriental luxuriance. We forget the huge statues of the gods that were crowded into them, and about them, in utter disregard of harmony and proportion. We forget the astonishing clutter of slabs, statues, and monuments that filled the Acropolis—a hodge-podge that makes Radio City seem a model of architectual restraint.

> Herbert J. Muller, *The Uses of the Past*

Description of Events

Lead-in question

Detailed description

How can you explain to someone who was not there what it was like to live during the ghastly months just before Franklin D. Roosevelt took office for the first time? So many millions were out of work, some of them actually starving, that one American family in two was directly affected. Trade was as close to a complete standstill as trade can get, the United States as near economic collapse as a growing young country can become without actually being in physical revolution. With the economic and social motors groaning toward a breakdown, with banks closing in every state, and money gradually becoming a scarce and fearsome thing, with panic everywhere and hunger stalking the cities as Iowa farmers dumped their milk because there was no market for it at any price, the early days of 1933 were undeniably among the most difficult any American has ever lived through, an unforgettable moment of personal and national agony.

Conclusion and topic sentence

Richard L. Tobin,
"A Year to Remember"

9. *He can narrate:*

Topic sentence

Narration

He [the chronic convict] has to get back inside without letting it appear, to his colleagues or himself, that he wants to come back. One man was released, stole a bright red Jeep, parked in front of a finance company office, held up the finance company, drove down the block and parked in front of the nearest tavern, went inside and set his pistol and the finance company's money box on the bar in full sight of everyone, ordered drinks for the house—and complained about his bad luck when the police walked in a few minutes later. The type is not uncommon. He'll come back screaming, but no matter what gets in his way, he will come back: it's home.

Restatement of topic sentence

Bruce Jackson, "Who Goes to Prison:
Caste and Careerism in Crime"

10. *He can use an allusion and quote relevant material:*

Allusion with relevant quotation

Application of the anecdote and topic sentence

Elaboration

When Don Quixote interrupts Sancho Panza, complaining that a tale he is telling is too full of repetitions and diversions, the redoubtable Sancho defends his method simply. "The way I'm telling it," he says, "is the way all stories are told in my country. It isn't fair for your worship to ask me to get new habits." With as little fuss Jean Stafford has clung tenaciously for twenty-five years to her established short story strategies. It is as if, having long ago found her special country and habits, she too sees no use for newness.

Robert Maurer, "The Deceptive
Facade"

11. *He can catalog details:*

<table>
<tr>
<td>Topic sentence</td>
<td>The rush is on. Come and get it: Afro-Americanism, black studies, the Negro heritage. From Harvard to Ocean Hill, from Duke to Madison Avenue, they are trying, as they say, to restore the Negro to his rightful place in American history and culture; black (and white) intellectuals, scholars, teachers, politicians,</td>
</tr>
<tr>
<td>Cataloging of particulars</td>
<td>hustlers busy with black restoration. The spirit is upon them, the writers and publishers, the polemicists and pushers, and the implications are enormous. But the richest soil is education, the schools and colleges, and the processes of growing up in which they're involved.</td>
</tr>
</table>

Peter Schrag, "The New Black Myths"

12. *He can develop an analogy or figure of speech:*

<table>
<tr>
<td>Topic sentence</td>
<td>New York is a palimpsest.*Successive layers, never wholly erasing the earlier ones, have provided different</td>
</tr>
<tr>
<td>Development of the figure of speech</td>
<td>outlines for the profiles of New York. And each of these profiles has given a different character to New York, providing at successive historical periods a distinctive face whose traces, etched deeply, remain visible.</td>
</tr>
</table>

Daniel Bell, "The Forces Shaping the City: The Four Faces of New York"

A few of these techniques, like 10, 11, and 12, are fairly sophisticated ones, but all of the others are quite spontaneous ways of expanding a topic which everyone uses in both speaking and writing.

PARAGRAPH PATTERNS

The arrangement of sentences within a paragraph normally follows a limited number of patterns:

1. From general to particular
2. From particular to general
3. Alternating order
4. Order of time
5. Order of space
6. Order of climax

---

*palimpsest—"a parchment, tablet, etc. that has been written upon or inscribed two or three times, the previous text or texts having been imperfectly erased and remaining, therefore, still visible." *Webster's New World Dictionary.*

These ways of development are not independent of one another. In a paragraph which in its overall order may proceed from the general to the particular, the details may be arranged in chronological order or climactic order. These principles therefore are the directions of movement within a paragraph; they are intuitive ways of thinking and feeling about things. They are not special techniques peculiar to writers (there are comparable kinds of movement in music), although they may be brought under greater control by the writer.

1. From General to Particular

Paragraphs of this order will characteristically begin with a topic sentence and proceed to give support of some kind:

Topic sentence	Pier Francesco Caletti-Bruni (1602–1676), known as Francesco Cavalli, was the first very popular composer of operas. From 1639—when his first opera was
Support: Fact 1	staged at the Teatro San Cassiano, Venice—until 1659, one or another of the Venetian opera houses presented from one to four new operas by Cavalli every year but
Fact 2	two. Even more indicative of his popularity is the fact that many of his forty or so operas spread quickly to
Fact 3	other Italian cities and abroad. In 1660–61, he visited Paris, where at least two of his operas supplied elements of the festivities honoring the marriage of Louis XIV, one of them with interpolated ballet music by Lully.
Fact 4	Cavalli wrote his last stage work in 1669, and thereafter, having become *maestro di cappella* at St. Mark's, Venice, composed only religious works. After the death of Claudio Monteverdi in 1643, Cavalli's only major rival as purveyor of operas to opera-mad audiences was Marco Antonio Cesti.

Herbert Weinstock, "Venice 1644 (?), Glyndebourne 1967"

In this paragraph, the first sentence contains the generalization. The facts testifying to Cavalli's popularity are then chronologically arranged within the part of the paragraph that follows.

Narration and description can use this same order. The following paragraph, for example, begins with an overview and proceeds to give details:

	From a window of my apartment I have a view of a movie house on Manhattan's East Side, where, ever
The general scene	since last December, *The Graduate* has attracted long lines of patrons. During some of the coldest winter weekends, the lines extended around the corner all the

A particular scene

way down the block, much like those at Radio City Music Hall during holiday periods—except that the people waiting for the next showing were not family groups but mostly young people in their teens and early twenties. One night when it was eight degrees outside I passed the line and noticed how little they seemed to be bothered by the weather; they stomped their feet, they made cheerful chatter; it was as though they all knew they were going to see something good, something made for *them*. There were other cinemas nearby, but no one waited outside in the cold. *The Graduate* was the film to see.

Hollis Alpert, " 'The Graduate' Makes Out"

2. From Particular to General

Paragraphs of this order characteristically begin with details of some kind—possibly narrative, descriptive, or expository—and proceed to offer some general statement at the end.

Three particular theories

Elaboration

General observation

Galileo said that the earth moves and that the sun is fixed; the Inquisition said that the earth is fixed and the sun moves; and Newtonian astronomers, adopting an absolute theory of space, said that both the sun and the earth move. But now we say that any one of these three statements is equally true, provided that you have fixed your sense of "rest" and "motion" in the way required by the statement adopted. At the date of Galileo's controversy with the Inquisition, Galileo's way of stating the facts was, beyond question, the fruitful procedure for the sake of scientific research. But in itself it was not more true than the formulation of the Inquisition. But at that time the modern concepts of relative motion were in nobody's mind, so that the statements were made in ignorance of the qualifications required for their more perfect truth. Yet this question of the motions of the earth and the sun expresses a real fact in the universe, and all sides had got hold of important truths concerning it. But, with the knowledge of those times, the truths appeared to be inconsistent.

Alfred North Whitehead, "Religion and Science"

Since paragraphs of this kind often begin with the familiar and proceed to the unfamiliar, they reflect our natural way of learning. We explore known facts in order to arrive at new hypotheses; we proceed from particular details to theoretical principles; we put pieces together to reconstruct a whole. We also narrate and describe in these terms, first giving details which suggest some observation to be made later:

Descriptive details	Springtime, about to ripen into sultry summer in Charleston, was breathing its first in the North Carolina mountains. White dogwood blossoms blanketed the slopes, and azaleas were blushing into bloom. Maple, hickory, birch, and oak trees, not yet come to full leaf, spread a filmy green shadow across the land. On the drive from the airport to Asheville, I opened the window of the Austin-Healy and pushed my face into the cool gush of air, breathing it in like a transfusion. I ask:
Observation	Is there a sweeter affirmation of life than a cruise through the highlands in a sports car on a shining spring day?

David Butwin, "A Climate Fit for Weathermen"

3. Alternating Order

Alternating order is the natural movement of comparison and contrast or of pro and con discussion. The shifts may be frequent—back and forth from *a* to *b, a* to *b, a* to *b*—or the details may be presented in simple complementary order—*a,* then *b*. The following paragraph follows the simple *a* and *b* pattern:

Part A	The protagonists in the stories are generally poor, but well educated, having seen better days. They are patient and deserving, people of family, who have nice but run-down old houses with a few good antiques. They
Part B	are ladies and gentlemen in every sense. Crooks are easily identifiable, because they are vulgar, bad-tempered, and have an unfortunate tendency to raise their voices to people. They have red or coarse, bushy black hair, and nicknames like "Spike," "Red," "Snorky," or "Flip." They further identify themselves by their regrettable preference for checkered suits, yellow overcoats, elevator shoes, and (for the oilier, better-educated crook) striped pants, spats, and goatees. Criminals always have a physical oddity: a long nose, or a missing middle finger.

Arthur Prager, "The Secret of Nancy Drew—Pushing Forty and Going Strong"

The paragraph falls into two parts: details about the protagonists; then, by contrast, details about crooks.

In a more complex comparison, John W. Aldridge briefly describes two books in the introductory paragraph of a review and then in a second paragraph sets about to compare and contrast them, considering several points in terms of each of the books:

Book A	John Updike has now issued a collection of his stories about the writer Henry Bech, while Alice and Kenneth Hamilton, two Canadian academics who must surely be Updike's foremost disciples in the Northern
Book B	Hemisphere, have written the first full-length critical study of his work. The two books juxtapose in a way that is both symmetrical and altogether ominous.
Book A	In Henry Bech, Updike has created an imaginary writer who, in certain particulars of temperament and
Book B	career, is very much like himself. The Hamiltons have created a perhaps equally imaginary writer who in certain particulars is very much like Updike, but who resembles far more strikingly Kierkegaard, Karl Barth, St. John of the Cross, and the prophet Isaiah. Updike's
Book A	portrait of Bech is warm, humane, engaging, and, for the most part, wholly convincing as fiction. The Ham-
Book B	iltons' portrait of Updike is cold, pretentious, and wholly unconvincing whether taken as fiction or as fact. As they present him, Updike is seen to have none of
Book A	the attractive qualities of Bech, nor is he a writer in whose reality one can begin to believe. He emerges
Book B	rather, as a kind of monster symbolist and theological guru, a creation of higher Neo-New Critical necromancy, whose work is viewed not as literary art but as a repository of the major religious and mythological imagery underlying the thought of the Western World from the Greeks to Paul Tillich.

> John W. Aldridge, "An Askew Halo for John Updike"

4. Time Order

Time order is most closely associated with narrative, but any collection of material—for example, a body of information about submarine plant life—may be presented in the order that the findings were made. Any material, of course, can be simply enumerated as if the details were being given in a list from first to last:

Topic sentence	Our life in the sanatorium was like that of hogs,
Support arranged in	nothing but eating and sleeping. At seven a bell rang
time order	for breakfast. We had to bathe at eight and at nine we had to go back to sleep until eleven, which was

lunchtime. From twelve to three we had to sleep again. From three until four, which was dinner time, we were allowed to be awake, and after eating we had to sleep once more. They didn't allow us to walk around much, and an asthmatic like me needs to walk.

Oscar Lewis, "One Can Suffer Anywhere"

This paragraph is actually a description of sanatorium life ordered in terms of the events of a typical day.

The second example is not a description of actual events like the first one but a hypothetical reconstruction of the career of a developing novelist from his twenties to his forties. The writer divides the time sequence into two paragraphs. The first paragraph states the thesis and treats the early career.

Topic Sentence	Over the last fifty years in America, we've developed a bad habit of trying our young writers by fire and ice. In the beginning is the fire. A first novelist
The writer in his twenties	in his early twenties, filled with a delicate balance between confidence and insecurity—a balance that should be labeled DO NOT DISTURB—is suddenly thrust into the limelight, lionized, publicized, enriched, and adulated to gratify the machinery of publishing. If his head isn't turned, if the humble doggedness that took him successfully through his first novel isn't dissipated, if he isn't marginally corrupted by his first taste of love and money, then he must be an unusually strong and wise
Second stage of early career	young man. And after the fire, comes, in too many cases, the beginning of the ice: the sophomore jinx of a second novel, with mild reviews or bad reviews or no reviews at all.

L. E. Sissman, "John Updike: Midpoint and After"

In a long second paragraph, Sissman continues to trace the career of the novelist into his thirties and forties. At the end of these two introductory paragraphs, chronologically arranged, he then turns to John Updike as a particular case in point.

5. Space Order

Space order is most closely associated with description:

It is a "round" village, with the houses lining the edges of the perimeter lanes, but with shops, church, pub, school, chapel, spread along a central road following the bank of a creek officially known as the

Potsford River but called locally the "Black Ditch." The center of the village remains self-contained and quiet in spite of farm machines, motor-bikes, and the dull murmur of summer holiday traffic. Jets from the American base at Bentwaters occasionally ordain an immense sound and the place seems riven, splintered—yet it resumes its wholeness the second the plane vanishes. Nobody looks up . . .

> Ronald Blythe, "England's
> Cruel Earth"

This particular description is conceived in terms of a circle and its center. At first, the perspective looks downward, then shifts upward to the jets in the sky.

A second example makes us particularly aware of a road as the point from which a couple walking along look about them to see one thing, then another. The writer seems keenly aware of other linear forms: the "streaks of yellow wild flowers in the fields" and the rows of growing cabbages. The writer covers space much in the same manner that a movie camera would view it:

Shoshone and I walked back to the main road that cuts across the 320-acre ranch. The sun had burned through the fog, highlighting streaks of yellow wild flowers in the fields. Black Angus cows were grazing by the road. People in hillbilly clothes, with funny hats and sashes, were coming out of the bushes carrying musical instruments and sacks of rice and beans. About a mile from the front gate we came to the community garden, with a scarecrow made of rusty metal in the shape of a nude girl. Two children were chasing each other from row to row, shrieking with laughter, as their mother picked cabbage. A sign read, "Permit not required to settle here."

> Sara Davidson, "Open Land"

In addition to scenic description, space order may also be used as the basis for arranging expository details. An essay on archaeology, for example, might discuss findings in terms of their place of origin: discoveries at Corinth, discoveries at Athens, discoveries at Delos.

6. Climactic Order

Climactic order implies both a rising to a climax and a falling away from it. It depends upon an order of sentences from least important to most important, from the known to the unknown with a sense of suspense, from the lowest to the highest, or in any number of other ways that produce a cumulative effect. It therefore applies to any mode of writing, whether it is argument, narrative, description, or persuasion.

Description of James Brudenell, later Lord Cardigan, commander of the famous Light Brigade, which made its charge at the Battle of Balaclava:

Cumulative details

It was to be expected that his parents and sisters should be passionately attached to him, and natural affection and pride were immensely heightened by the circumstance of his extraordinary good looks. In him the Brudenell beauty had come to flower. He was tall, with wide shoulders tapering to a narrow waist, his hair was golden, his eyes flashing sapphire blue, his nose aristocratic, his bearing proud. If there was a fault it was that the lower part of his face was oddly long and narrow so that sometimes one was surprised to catch an obstinate, almost a foxy, look. But the boy had a dash and gallantry that were irresistible. He did not know what fear was. A superb and reckless horseman, he risked his neck on the most dangerous brutes. No

Climax

tree was too tall for him to climb, no tower too high to scale. He excelled in swordsmanship and promised to be a first-class shot. He had in addition to courage another characteristic which impressed itself on all who

Anticlimax

met him. He was, alas, unusually stupid; in fact, as Greville pronounced later, an ass. The melancholy truth was that his glorious golden head had nothing in it.

Cecil Woodham-Smith, *The Charge of the Light Brigade*

The rising and falling motion of this paragraph is so sharply defined that the reader cannot fail to respond to its effect.

In the following example, Martin Luther King achieves a cumulative effect by piling one fact upon another, repeating the same words at the beginning of each of six sentences. The final sentence ends with a sense of drama:

All of this represents disappointment lifted to astronomical proportions. It is disappointment with timid white moderates who feel that they can set the timetable for the Negro's freedom. It is disappointment with a federal administration that seems to be more concerned about winning an ill-considered war in Vietnam than about winning the war against poverty here at home. It is disappointment with white legislators who pass laws in behalf of Negro rights that they never intended to implement. It is disappointment with the Christian church that appears to be more white than Christian, and with many white clergymen who prefer to remain silent behind the security of stained-glass windows. It is disappointment with some Negro clergymen who are more concerned about the size of the wheel base on their automobiles than about the quality of their service to the Negro community. It is disappointment with the Negro middle class that has sailed or struggled out of the muddy ponds into the relatively fresh-flowing waters of the mainstream, and in the process has forgotten the stench of the backwaters where their brothers are still drowning.

Martin Luther King, *Where Do We Go from Here: Chaos or Community?*

THE TEST OF SUCCESSFUL PARAGRAPHS

Even though paragraphing is a highly flexible system, almost wholly controlled by the writer, the results are nevertheless more successful in some instances than in others. Because the paragraph is a conventional unit of discourse, certain expectations persist in the minds of readers. Successful paragraphs, therefore, must ultimately meet these tests:

1. Are they purposeful?

This question assumes that paragraphing aids the reader in various ways by making meaningful divisions in the development of the thought, by marking shifts of focus to new topics, by intentionally separating material for emphasis, by slowing or accelerating the pace of reading. An indifferent writer can defeat these purposes and actually confuse the reader by failing to paragraph when the sense of the content demands it. Most writers know that they discover paragraphs as they go along; they end them and indent just as naturally as they supply periods and capital letters to sentences. These writers treat paragraphing as if it were punctuation. They recognize it as a means of clarifying and interpreting subject matter in order to make their intentions precise.

2. Are they adequately developed?

The development of a paragraph, of course, depends upon its purpose. If a paragraph is transitional, it may be brief. In Chapter I of *The Decline and Fall of the Romantic Ideal,* F. L. Lucas pauses momentarily after eight pages of discussion to write:

What in fact is "Romanticism"? What, historically has it been? What can or should it be?

In terms of its purpose, this paragraph is adequately developed because it poses three questions which he intends to answer in the first three chapters of the book. His plan is laid out fully but briefly. The answers come later.

Adequate development means that a satisfactory paragraph is as long as it needs to be. If it provides a transition, it may be one sentence. If a writer wants to make a point and support it, however, the paragraph may be 200 words or more.

Yet it is possible to make judgments about inadequate paragraph development. We tend to think that a paragraph is inadequately developed if the writer supplies too little evidence and leaves the reader unfulfilled; if it poses a question and gives no answer; or, if it supplies a group of details without a conclusion. A sense of paragraph patterns helps a writer to know when he has reached an ending, at what point he can most effectively make a paragraph break.

3. Are they sufficiently varied?

Paragraphs set up a rhythmic effect in a composition just as variation of sentence length produces a stylistic effect within a paragraph. Many nineteenth-century prose writers are now difficult to read because we have become accustomed to more rapidly paced prose produced by shorter sentences and relatively shorter paragraphs. Prose reads rapidly or slowly in proportion to paragraph length. Narrative with frequent divisions for dialogue and separate actions reads quickly. Analysis with an intricate interweaving of sentences within lengthy paragraphs reads more slowly. Undoubtedly, the newspaper with its typically brief paragraphs designed for rapid reading has been a major influence upon the faster pace of twentieth-century prose. The short snatches of journalistic prose, however, are as unsatisfactory for most expository writing as long, ponderous segments. A variation of paragraph lengths serves to keep the pace moving while still allowing the writer occasion to expand fully upon his topics.

4. Are they unified?

The unity of a paragraph or paragraph bloc should not be thought to mean that it has only one idea. A paragraph contains many ideas, but taken together those ideas ought to have a singleness of purpose. They ought to hang together on one thread. That common thread is frequently expressed in the topic sentence, although the unifying theme may extend beyond a single paragraph. Unity, therefore, is a test of relevance. Do all of the sentences in a paragraph belong there? Has the writer allowed his thoughts to drift? Occasionally a writer digresses, that is, wanders aimlessly from the topic. It can be done purposefully to provide what the writer considers necessary background, but if he does so, it is usually advisable to declare his intention with a phrase like, "To digress momentarily to explain why. . . ." In this way, he shows that even his digression is actually relevant in an indirect way.

The unity of the parts in a paragraph can be judged only in terms of the purpose of the whole. In reading the following group of sentences, we are pushed to find a unifying theme:

> Cooking is more prefabricated. Few clothes are sewn. Fire and heat are not made. Among poor people there used to be more sweated domestic industry, which didn't do the adults any good but taught something to small children.

Even though these particular sentences do not seem to relate to one another, each of them relates to the common thesis of a paragraph written by Paul Goodman in *Growing Up Absurd:*

Lead-in example	People use machines that they do not understand and cannot repair. For instance, the electric motors: one cannot imagine anything more beautiful and edu-
Generalization and topic sentence	cative than such motors, yet there may be three or four in a house, cased and out of sight; and when they blow they are taken away to be repaired. Their influence is then retarding, for what the child sees is that compe-
Supporting details	tence does not exist in ordinary people, but in the system of interlocking specialties. This is unavailable to the child, it is too abstract. Children go shopping with Mama; but supermarket shopping for cellophane pack-ages is less knowledgeable and bargainable than the older shopping, as well as providing tasteless Texas fruit and vegetables bred for nonperishability and appearance rather than for eating. Cooking is more prefabricated. Few clothes are sewn. Fire and heat are not made. Among poor people there used to be more sweated domestic industry, which didn't do the adults any good but taught something to small children. Now, on the contrary, the man and perhaps the woman of the house work in distant offices and factories, increasingly on parts and processes that don't mean anything to a child. A child might not even know what work his daddy does.
Restatement of topic sentence in more specific terms	Shop talk will be, almost invariably, griping about in-terpersonal relations. If the kid has less confidence that he can make or fix anything, his parents can't either; and what they do work at is beyond his grasp.

With the total context available, we can see how the pieces fit together to form a whole. Submitting the paragraph to a rigid testing, one might question the relevance of the phrase "as well as providing tasteless Texas fruit and vegetables bred for nonperishability and appearance rather than for eating." It is not totally necessary, although it is clearly suggested by Goodman's total theme of the relations between youth and organized society.

Unity, therefore, depends upon the writer's capacity to keep his sentences under control. If they are allowed to take their own course, there is no telling where free association will lead them.

5. Are they coherent?

Unity and coherence are closely related. Whereas the first is a test of relevance, the second is a test of connectedness. Coherence is the way both the sentences in a paragraph and the paragraphs in an entire composition are interlocked. Anything within paragraphs or between paragraphs that links, draws together, or associates is a means of coherence. Some of these devices are more obvious than others.

The most obvious device of coherence is the use of transitional words and phrases, which indicate relationships clearly and signal the direction in which the prose is moving. In the following paragraph, the connecting links are italicized:

> The burning of draft cards or American flags involves direct violation of law. Laws forbidding the burning or desecration of the national flag have existed for many years, *and* it is hardly likely that anyone would seriously contest their constitutionality or legality. In the case of draft cards, *however,* it has been vigorously urged that the federal law prohibiting mutilation or burning of draft cards serves no real purpose and was recently enacted by the Congress merely to punish dissent. *For this reason,* it is said, the law is an unconstitutional burden on the right of free speech. *Therefore,* it is argued, the draft card burning should not be held to involve a violation of law. A case involving this question is awaiting decision by the Supreme Court *and* I cannot comment upon it. *But* the point that I make is that if the law forbidding the burning of a draft card is held to be constitutional and valid, the fact that the card is burned as a result of noble and constitutionally protected motives is no help to the offender.
>
> Abe Fortas, *Concerning Dissent and Civil Disobedience*

Even though Fortas depends heavily upon the formal device of transitional words, another factor is also working strongly to hold this paragraph together. In a tightly unified paragraph, we would normally expect a recurrence of certain words or equivalent terms. In this particular paragraph, repetition of words like "burning," "draft cards," and "constitutionality" acts as a thematic link.

Some paragraphs may depend almost wholly upon chains of words to hold them together rather than conventional function words. The following paragraph by Marshall McLuhan has only one formal phrase: "In a word" at the end introduces a brief summary. Otherwise the paragraph hangs together on its thematic associations and chains of equivalent words. Two of these interlinking chains are indicated by the circled words:

> A century ago the British craze for the (monocle) gave to the wearer the power of the (camera) to fix people in a superior stare, as if they were objects. Erich von Stroheim did a great job with the (monocle) in creating the haughty Prussian officer. Both (monocle and camera) tend to turn people into things, and the (photograph) extends and multiplies the human image to the proportions of (mass-produced merchandise.) The movie stars and matinee idols are put in the public domain by (photography.) They become dreams that (money can buy.) They can be (bought) and hugged and thumbed more easily than public (prostitutes.) (Mass-produced merchandise) has always made some people uneasy in its (prostitute) aspect. Jean Genet's *The Balcony* is a play on this theme of society as a (brothel) environed by violence and horror. The avid desire of mankind to (prostitute) itself stands up against the chaos of revolution. The (brothel) remains firm and permanent amidst the most furious changes. In a word, (photography) has inspired Genet with the theme of the world since (photography) as a (Brothel-without-Walls.)
>
> Marshall McLuhan, *Understanding Media*

Another analysis of the same paragraph indicates that other word connections are also operating. Of particular importance are pronouns that have their antecedents in previous sentences, words that refer to one another, and the repetition of particular words:

> A century ago the British craze for the monocle gave to the (wearer) the power of the camera to fix people in a superior stare, as if they were objects. (Erich von Stroheim) did a great job with the monocle in creating the (haughty Prussian officer.) Both monocle and camera tend to turn people into things, and the photograph extends and multiplies the human image to the proportions of mass-produced merchandise. The (movie stars and matinee idols) are put in the public domain by photography. (They) become dreams that money can buy. (They) can be bought and hugged and thumbed more easily than public prostitutes. Mass-produced merchandise has always made some people uneasy in its

prostitute aspect. (Jean Genet's) *The Balcony* is a play on this theme of society as a brothel environed by violence and horror. The avid desire of mankind to prostitute itself stands up against the chaos of revolution. The brothel remains firm and permanent amidst the most furious changes. In a word, photography has inspired (Genet) with the theme of the world since photography as a Brothel-without-Walls.

Marshall McLuhan, *Understanding Media*

Besides formal transitions and word associations, sentences and paragraphs are also linked to one another by rhetorical strategies: repetition, series, parallel structure, question and answer, and contrast. A variety of these is illustrated in a paragraph by Archibald MacLeish:

	But nevertheless the uneasiness remained and became more and more evident in our books, our paint-
Two questions repeated for emphasis	ing, our music—even the new directions of our medical sciences. Who were *we* in this strange new world? What part did *we* play in it? Someone had written a
Two sentences with parallel beginnings	new equation somewhere, pushed the doors of ignorance back a little, entered the darkened room of knowledge by one more step. Someone else had found a way to make use of that new knowledge, put it to work. Our
Repetition for emphasis	lives had changed but without *our* changing them, without our intending them to change. Improvements had appeared and we had accepted them. We had bought
Four sentences with common subject and parallel structure	Mr. Ford's machines by the hundreds of thousands. We had ordered radios by the millions and then installed TVs. And now we took to the air, flew from city to city, from continent to continent, from climate to climate, following summer up and down the earth like birds. We
Repetition for emphasis	were new men in a new life in a new world . . . but a world *we* had not made—had not, at least, intended to make.

Archibald MacLeish, "The Great American Frustration"

The marginal notations identify the strategies that connect these sentences, but the same kinds of repetitions and structural parallelism are also operating within sentences. The entire paragraph demonstrates an intensive use of repetition and parallelism as ways of tying thoughts together.

Coherence, therefore, cannot be reduced to the simple mechanical matter of inserting a few "therefores" and "yets" in the prose. These may help, but in the final analysis the essential ties are those that grow out of the thought and structure of the composition.

8

The Rhetoric
of the Sentence

The sentence is an extremely flexible unit, even though grammatically it has only two basic parts, the subject and the predicate. These parts can be reduced to a fragment, expanded to indefinite length, rearranged, interrupted, and transformed. The variations upon a kernel sentence allow such infinite variety that two writers seldom produce duplicate sentences, although they may write many sentences that use the same basic techniques. An awareness of sentence strategies gives the writer all of the resources he needs to develop an appealing prose style adequate to the expression of his thoughts and feelings. It should be noted, however, that such devices, to be successful, cannot be contrived; they must grow out of the writer's thought and inventiveness, consistent with his own sense of rhythm and natural way of thinking. They must be used unaffectedly to reinforce the content, not to ornament it. A deliberate display of rhetorical strategies may indicate virtuosity, like that of a pianist who is anxious to show off his skill, but ostentation can also doom writing to superficiality if that skill has nothing to do with the interpretation of the thought. The timeless principle that art disguises artfulness applies to writing as well as to other modes of expression.

SENTENCE LENGTH

There is no particular stylistic virtue in a long sentence, a short sentence, or one of moderate length. There is virtue, however, in enough variety to avoid the ponderousness of too many long sentences, the choppiness of too many short ones, and the monotony of too many medium-length ones. Sentence length is basically a matter of prose rhythm, and the writer who cannot sense the rhythms of his sentences will find little help in word counts and statistical analyses.

Sentence length is closely related to a writer's purpose. If he wants to accelerate the movement, to incorporate material rapidly, he can turn to short sentences. If he wants to slow the movement for probing and reflecting, he can lengthen them. Three paragraphs from John Steinbeck's *Travels with Charley,* a nonfiction work, will illustrate the adjustment of sentence length to his changing purposes. The number of words in each sentence in indicated by the superscripts.

And there are true secrets in the desert.[8] In the war of sun and dryness against living things, life has its secrets of survival.[16] Life, no matter on what level, must be moist or it will disappear.[13] I find most interesting the conspiracy of life in the desert to circumvent the death rays of the all-conquering sun.[20] The beaten earth appears defeated and dead, but it only appears so.[12] A vast and inventive organization of living matter survives by seeming to have lost.[14] The gray and dusty sage wears oily armor to protect its inward small moistness.[14] Some plants engorge themselves with water in the rare rainfall and store it for future use.[16] Animal life wears a hard, dry skin or an outer skeleton to defy the desiccation.[15] And every living thing has developed techniques for finding or creating shade.[12] Small reptiles and rodents burrow or slide below the surface or cling to the shaded side of an outcropping.[19] Movement is slow to preserve energy, and it is a rare animal which can or will defy the sun for long.[21] A rattlesnake will die in an hour of full sun.[10] Some insects of bolder inventiveness have devised personal refrigeration systems.[10] Those animals which must drink moisture get it at second hand—a rabbit from a leaf, a coyote from the blood of a rabbit.[24]

One may look in vain for living creatures in the daytime, but when the sun goes and the night gives consent, a world of creatures awakens and takes up its intricate patter.[32] Then the hunted come out and the hunters, and hunters of the hunters.[13] The night awakes to buzzing and to cries and barks.[10]

When, very late in the history of our planet, the incredible accident of life occurred, a balance of chemical factors, combined with temperature, in quantities and in kinds so delicate as to be unlikely all came together in the retort of time and a new thing emerged, soft and helpless and unprotected in the savage world of unlife.[58] Then processes of change and variation took place in the organisms, so that one kind became different from all others.[20] But one ingredient, perhaps the most important of all, is planted in every life form—the factor of survival.[19] No living thing is without it, nor could life exist without this magic formula.[14] Of course, each form developed its own machinery for survival, and some failed and disappeared while others people the earth.[20] The first life might easily have been snuffed out and the accident may never have happened again—but, once it existed, its first quality, its duty, preoccupation, direction, and end, shared by every living thing, is to go on living.[40] And so it does and it will until some other accident cancels it.[14] And the desert, the dry and sun-lashed desert, is a good school in which to observe the cleverness and the infinite variety of techniques of survival under pitiless opposition.[29] Life could not change the sun or water the desert, so it changed itself.[14]

If we arbitrarily accept 20 or 21 words as the length of an average sentence written by a professional writer, we will note that most of the sentences in the first paragraph quoted are shorter than average, and only the last sentence is slightly longer. Further, there is no subordination. The sentences move in quick linear succession. The movement is appropriate for the description and multiple illustrations that Steinbeck crowds into this paragraph. But Steinbeck does not limit himself to the short sentence. We note that in the second and third paragraphs he writes sentences of 32, 58, 40, and 29 words and that each of these long sentences is followed by one considerably more brief. The third paragraph as a whole turns to different sentence strategies from paragraph one and employs a more leisurely style for purposes of commentary and explanation.

Sentence averages tell little about a writer except as they hit the extremes. A consistently low average of 12 or 15 will suggest that the writer lacks the capacity to expand sentences beyond the most simple forms, or a preponderantly high average of 30 or 35 will imply that he lacks a sense of variety to break discourse into smaller units for movement and emphasis.

The sharp contrast of long and short is one of the most effective ways of making a point. The short sentence is climactic; it is forceful.

> The first and most evident of the conflicts is that between choosing, on the one hand, to publish whatever most easily interests the largest number of readers most quickly—that is to say, yellow journalism—and, on the other hand, to provide, even at a commercial loss, an adequate supply of what the public will in the longer run need to know. This is responsible journalism.
>
> Walter Lippman, "On the Importance of Being Free"

> To do battle man must give only his life, but to love he must give his soul. Battle is easier.
>
> Student sentence

The strength of these short sentences following longer ones grows out of the rhythmic contrast. The period following them speaks with strong finality. The point has been made.

PERIODIC SENTENCES

A periodic sentence is grammatically constructed so that the main thought is suspended until the end of the sentence. It therefore has a forward thrust. The reader must wait until the end for the meaning to emerge. It is a sentence that reserves its climax for the final position. It ends with a note of emphasis. The meaning of each of the following sentences would be completely altered by changing several words at the very end:

> It comes as a great shock to discover that the country which is your birthplace and to which you owe your life and identity has not, in its whole system of reality, evolved any place for you.
> James Baldwin, "The American Dream and the American Negro"

> For, in all this passionate protest, there is virtually no intimation, even in the loud negatives of what these young people are *for*.
> Philip Wylie, "Generation of Zeroes"

> Perhaps the greatest value of having roommates is that it provides what a professor of mine used to call a Cross-Cultural Experience.
> Joan Paulson, "Why Roommates Make the Best Wives"

> When you considered liquor harmless and fashionable, the fact that it was illegal seemed laughable.
> Richard Goldstein, "1 in 7: Drugs on Campus"

Examination of the structure of these sentences indicates that three of them depend upon the anticipation created by using "it" or "there"; the fourth uses the construction "the fact that . . . ," which has the same effect of postponing the completed thought until the final word has been added. The periodic sentence characteristically depends upon some structure that delays the completion of a sentence pattern until the last moment.

CUMULATIVE SENTENCES

A cumulative sentence is grammatically constructed so that the main thought is first stated and then added to by various phrases and clauses. It differs from the periodic sentence in that it might be terminated at any of several points beyond the basic pattern without altering the meaning. Detail is not worked into the basic sentence itself; it is added at the end.

The cumulative sentence is typically informal in its effect because the additions often suggest the kind of afterthoughts we tag on to a sentence when we speak but cannot go back to add. The result is a loosely structured sentence, but not a disorderly one. The cumulative sentence demands no regularity of structure, although a writer may use parallel phrasing if he wishes. The following sentences show a variety of ways in which detail can be added—by means of participial phrases, prepositional phrases, absolute phrases, noun phrases, and clauses; and these do not exhaust the possibilities:

> I used to park my car on a hill and sit silently observant, listening to the talk ringing out from neighbor to neighbor, seeing the inhabitants drowsing in their doorways, taking it all in with nostalgia—the sage smell on the wind, the sunlight without time, the village without destiny.
>
> Loren Eiseley, *The Immense Journey*

> We would sit round the long shiny table, made of some very pale-coloured, hard wood, with Sim goading, threatening, exhorting, sometimes joking, very occasionally praising, but always prodding, prodding away at one's mind to keep it up to the right pitch of concentration, as one might keep a sleepy person awake by sticking pins into him.
>
> George Orwell, "Such, Such Were the Joys ..."

> All marriage is a sort of gambling, like blackjack or poker, with a slight finality to it, a decision about eternity and forevers, with irrevocable implications; and losing is naturally a part of it.
>
> Student sentence

> He arrived on horseback, the reins loose, the stirrups tossing free.
>
> Student sentence

QUESTIONS

Strictly speaking, a rhetorical question is one to which no direct reply is expected. It is a device that makes the reader feel he is weighing the issues. Sometimes the writer may not even have an answer to his own question, or he may not care to offer one; but by posing a question he focuses upon a problem. In an essay on the poet Dylan Thomas, Richard Whittington-Egan stops at one point to question whether or not "Dylan-the-actor was playing the role which he had created for Dylan-the-poet":

> Was it really, then, all make-believe? Or was he a fringe alcoholic, stalwartly refusing to admit the fact even to himself?
>
> Richard Whittington-Egan, "The Tosspoet"

These particular questions are not answered directly in the essay, but they do suggest possible interpretations.

The rhetorical question can also function as an argumentative device if its answer appears completely self-evident:

> Who can argue on the side of poverty, or against justice, or against the idea of a Great Society?
>
> Norman Mailer, "Lyndon Johnson"

Here Mailer uses the question to make a concession, only to follow it in succeeding sentences by reservations about the Johnson Administration.

In a different way, a question may actually contain its answer and only invite assent. When Thoreau asks, "This American government,—what is it but a tradition, though a recent one, endeavoring to transmit itself unimpaired to posterity, but each instant losing some of its integrity?"—the form of the question is only a means of making a statement. In another passage, he uses questions to pose alternatives. His subject is military men:

> They have no doubt that it is a damnable business in which they are concerned; they are all peaceably inclined. Now, what are they? Men at all? or small movable forts and magazines, at the service of some unscrupulous man in power?
>
> *Civil Disobedience*

Other writers, however, use the question as if they were carrying on a dialogue with themselves. They pose a question, then answer it. The question becomes a structural device; it is a convenient way of introducing a new topic, particularly at the beginning of a paragraph. "How is the humanization of sex impeded?" asks a writer; then he offers two reasons. Other questions, however, are mere springboards: "What are the facts?" "How typical is all this?" "What consequences can we expect?" These are followed by answers, but the questions themselves, empty as they are of content, merely add variety to the majority of declarative sentences.

COORDINATION AND SUBORDINATION

Coordination links sentences and shorter units with conjunctions; subordination transforms sentences into dependent structures. The two processes produce different stylistic effects. Coordination tends to loosen the prose style; subordination, to tighten it. Coordination is expansive; subordination is economical. Coordination is common in speech because one thing merely follows another in sequence. Subordination predominates in writing because it requires forethought. We commonly speak sentences like this one:

> The baseball game has been postponed, so we have to find something else to do.

But in writing we would probably subordinate one of the sentences to get rid of an overused *so:*

> Since the baseball game has been postponed, we have to find something else to do.

Coordination may be said to have a horizontal, forward-moving effect; subordination, a vertical, in-depth one. (For a list of coordinating conjunctions and guidelines for their use, see pages 483 and 484. For principles of coordination, see pages 502–504.)

Studies of children's writing at various grade levels indicate rather consistently that the use of various kinds of subordinate structures increases with age. Subordinating, then, can be taken as a mark of mature style, although the experienced writer also knows that he can gain special effects by stringing together words or clauses or sentences with conjunctions:

> Out in the club the Epics, with four electric instruments going, are playing "Doing the Dog," and Misty is doing the Dog, and Janet is doing the Mashed Potatoes, and Jerrie Miller is doing the Monkey, with a few baroque emendations, but Marlene reflects a moment, as if upon her busy round of work with the churches, the benefit balls, the women's groups and the youth.
>
> Tom Wolfe, "The Peppermint Lounge
Revisited"

Above all, subordination permits a compactness and variety of expression that would otherwise be impossible if the language permitted no transformations of the basic patterns. It is one of the most important sentence strategies. (For a list of subordinating conjunctions, see page 483. For principles of subordination, see pages 504–505.)

PASSIVE VOICE CONSTRUCTIONS

Phrasing a sentence in passive voice is a means of transposing the doer of an action and the receiver of an action for a different stylistic effect. Subject and object are reversed by a change of the verb form:

A tornado hit Biloxi, Mississippi.

Biloxi, Mississippi, was hit by a tornado.

The difference between these two sentences is essentially one of emphasis, and the preference of one over the other would depend upon the writer's intentions. Newspaper reports commonly focus upon the object of a crime, particularly if the agent is yet unknown or unidentified:

The First National Bank was robbed by an unidentified group of teenagers at 2:30 this afternoon.

In other instances, however, passive voice tends to be a feeble way of expressing what can be said much more forcefully in active voice:

Passive construction: "We Shall Overcome" was sung by thousands of marchers in the street.

Active construction: Thousands of marchers in the street sang "We Shall Overcome."

Passive construction: It was known to me long before the teacher found out.

Active construction: I knew about it long before the teacher found out.

The use of passive voice is often used in technical, scientific, and other kinds of scholarly writing both as a means of establishing an impersonal tone and as an economical way of setting down thoughts when the actions and facts are of primary importance, not those who performed them or discovered them. Passive voice is particularly common in historical writing. In the following passage, it is used conveniently and unobtrusively:

How deep the hatred against the new Christians had become was demonstrated in 1449 when Toledo was called upon to contribute a million maravedis for the defence of the frontier. The community refused and tax-gatherers—most of them *marranos*—were sent into the city to enforce the collection. Not only were they assaulted, but the houses of all the new Christians were destroyed and those who attempted to defend them or their property were brutally beaten or killed. All of the king's attempts to restore order failed, and he was compelled to watch feebly as the council passed an edict forbidding new Christians to hold any public office. The envenomed wording of the edict, the *Sentencia Estatuto,* demonstrated clearly that the animosity sprang from more than a religious difference. It had become a genuine race-hatred.

Abram Leon Sachar, *A History of the Jews*

INVERSION AND TRANSPOSITION

Inversion is a device of reversing the customary word order of a basic sentence. As a strategy, it works because most sentences follow a regular pattern. Therefore, moving a word or phrase or clause from its usual position to a less obvious one gives it a special emphasis:

Regular word order: I may be hungry, but I'm not desperate yet.
Inversion: Hungry I may be, but I'm not desperate yet.

Regular word order: He was ready to sacrifice his money if necessary.

Inversion: His money he was ready to sacrifice if necessary.

In these examples, words like "yet" and "if necessary" can also be transposed. Of course, any movable part of a sentence can be rearranged for a slightly different effect:

Basic sentence: We find these facts to be unalterable: that war is inevitable; that pride, greed, and lust for power are weapons of destruction within man.

Other arrangements: These facts we find to be unalterable:

Unalterable we find these facts to be:

That war is inevitable; that pride, greed, and lust for power are weapons of destruction within man—these facts we find to be unalterable.

Inversion is a strategy that must be handled cautiously because it is as likely to be awkward as it is effective:

Regular word order: Alexander the Great was not only a great general but also a disseminator of Greek culture.

Awkward inversion: Not only a great general but also a disseminator of Greek culture was Alexander the Great.

Like most other strategies, inverted structures have to be tested in context, since they clearly tamper with rhythmic patterns that we normally expect. When aptly used, however, they can do exactly what they are intended to do.

> My point is that a very large proportion of the progress during those years must be attributed to the influence of Bentham. There can be no doubt that nine-tenths of the people living in England in the latter part of the last century were happier then they would have been if he had never lived. So shallow was his philosophy that he would have regarded this as a vindication of his activities. We, in our more enlightened age, can see that such a view is preposterous; but it may fortify us to review the grounds for rejecting a grovelling utilitarianism such as that of Bentham.
>
> Bertrand Russell, "The Harm That Good Men Do"

The inversion in the third sentence of this passage manages to be both unobtrusive and at the same time emphatic; it shores up the meaning but does not call attention to itself as a device. Effective inversion operates on that kind of paradoxical effect.

INTERRUPTED MOVEMENT

The interruption of a sentence to insert comment may be a deliberate strategy to call attention to an aside, a means of moving a word, phrase, or clause to a more emphatic position, or simply an effort to make the writing a little more informal. In tightly controlled prose, the incidental thoughts that pop into our minds are ordinarily censored out. In a freer style, these are included by means of some punctuation device—sometimes commas, sometimes dashes, sometimes parentheses or square brackets. Some writers are obviously more disposed to this kind of rearrangement and side discourse than others, but almost everyone comes upon some occasion that invites an interpolation. The chief caution is to avoid chopping up the discourse to such an extent that the reader is left without a clear line of thought.

The following sentences represent a variety of uses:

> The evidence, if reliable, is highly incriminating. [cp. If the evidence is reliable, it is highly incriminating.]
>
> Student sentence

> The party was, as they say, a bash.
>
> Student sentence

> Governments—ours as well as theirs—are responsible for the conditions
> that will permit open access to the major canals of the world.
>
> Student sentence

> Beauty devoid of responsibility might be a way of describing a familiar
> kind of female punk: the hollywood star who makes marriage a game
> of musical chairs (or beds) and love a five-star final.
>
> Marya Mannes, "Let's Stop
> Exalting Punks"

> My still inchoate but nevertheless clearly heretical sentiments about
> literature and my incipient rebellion against the academic life had been
> causing me a good deal of anxiety—was I turning into a "sellout"?—and
> I had feared that they might shock Trilling, who had, after all, followed
> the very course I was half-consciously proposing to desert on the ground
> —was it a rationalization?—that there was something false in such a life
> for someone like me.
>
> Norman Podhoretz, *Making It*

The last example illustrates the use of the interrupter as a stylistic
device for suggesting hesitation and uncertainty—something comparable
to a stream-of-consciousness technique that tries to catch vacillations
of the mind. The interruption, however, is not eccentric; it is common
in most conventional kinds of prose, representing only a break in rhythm
that keeps the reader alert to the meaning.

BALANCE AND PARALLELISM

Whereas interruption operates by breaking regular rhythmic patterns, balance operates on the principle of recurring pattern. Balance
within a sentence weighs one part evenly with another. Parallelism,
which refers simply to similarity of structure, frequently works hand
in hand with balance. Two parts alike in structure are possibly alike
in rhythm as well. But balance and parallelism do not necessarily imply
completely symmetrical phrasing:

> But individuals like students are by virtue of their stage in life changeable
> and changing, malleable yet often intransigent.
>
> Kenneth Keniston, "The Faces in the
> Lecture Room"

In this sentence, "malleable yet often intransigent" has the same 1–2
effect of balance as "changeable and changing," but when the two are
put together the result is something slightly asymmetrical because
the rhythms are different and the patterns are not exactly parallel.

Thus, balance and parallelism are closely tied with matters of symmetry and asymmetry. There is a tendency sometimes to think of symmetry as a righting of something that is wrong, an arranging of something that is crooked—therefore, a special artistic virtue. Yet we need to observe that the unbalanced and asymmetrical are as common in our experience as the balanced and symmetrical. Nature itself is filled with asymmetrical forms: trees, cloud formations, streams, and mountains. We may be less aware of asymmetrical forms, but they are wholly natural—all of which is to say that some writers reject balance and parallelism as contrived and artificial. Ultimately, the use of balanced and parallel structures is a private choice, a mark of individual style. Some writers cannot avoid them because these strategies satisfy a feeling. We can see this affinity operating in each of the following sentences:

Balance and parallelism	We are an active, ingenious, pragmatic race, concerned with production rather than enjoyment, with practicality rather than contemplation, with efficiency rather than understanding, and with information rather than wisdom.

Dwight Macdonald, "Howtoism"

Balance and parallelism Balance without parallelism	The moon was always measured in terms of hope and reassurance and the heart pangs of youth on such a night as this; it is now measured in terms of mileage and foot-pounds of rocket thrust. Children sent sharp, sweet wishes to the moon; now they dream of blunt-nosed missiles.

Eric Sevareid, "The Dark of the Moon"

Parallelism and imbalance	For in sports, as in gambling, and as in most of the activities that we think of as peculiarly masculine, the greater the risk, the more serious the play, the keener the fun.

George Stade, "Game Theory"

Exact balance and parallelism	The love of liberty is the love of others; the love of power is the love of ourselves.

William Hazlitt, "Political Essays"

The Hazlitt quotation illustrates a sentence that can be easily memorized, and dictionaries of famous quotations are filled with similar examples. It is one of the fringe benefits of balance and parallelism. But quotability sometimes raises the question whether an easy phrase does not also kill "analytical invigoration," a phrase once used by

William F. Buckley, Jr., in deploring the resounding but empty phrases of a political figure. Of course, balance and parallelism need not be either false or superficial. Their effectiveness is a matter of appropriateness; John Kennedy's words remain both memorable and meaningful:

> Ask not what your country can do for you—ask what you can do for your country.

REPETITION

Repetition is a device of subtle insinuation and wholly obvious emphasis. In prose, whole sentences are never repeated consecutively as speakers do occasionally for emphasis, but a sentence can be repeated intermittently to make a point. Undoubtedly, one of the best known examples is Iago's speech to Roderigo in Shakespeare's *Othello:*

> Come, be a man. Drown thyself? Drown cats, and blind puppies. I have professed me thy friend, and I confess me knit to thy deserving with cables of perdurable toughness. I could never better stead thee than now. Put money in thy purse; follow thou the wars; defeat thy favour with an usurped beard. I say, put money in thy purse. It cannot be that Desdemona should long continue her love to the Moor—put money in thy purse—nor he his to her. It was a violent commencement in her, and thou shalt see an answerable sequestration; put but money in thy purse. These Moors are changeable in their wills—fill thy purse with money. The food that to him now is as luscious as locusts shall be to him shortly as bitter as coloquintida. She must change for youth; when she is sated with his body she will find the error of her choice. Therefore put money in thy purse. If thou wilt needs damn thyself, do it a more delicate way than drowning. Make all the money thou canst. If sanctimony and a frail vow, betwixt an erring barbarian and a supersubtle Venetian be not too hard for my wits, and all the tribe of hell, thou shalt enjoy her—therefore make money. A pox of drowning thyself, it is clean out of the way. Seek thou rather to be hanged in compassing thy joy, than to be drowned, and go without her.
>
> I, iii

The effect of any repetition varies with the number of occurrences; that is, anything beyond two or three repetitions assumes emotional overtones rather than a calculated effect of stress. The first example below illustrates repetition used with restraint and emphasis:

> The Father in *Six Characters* expounds almost continually upon a philosophy of denial—denial that a man has a consistent identity, denial that one man has always been viewed the same by himself and those around him, even denial that philosophizing about anything will get anyone anywhere.
>
> Student sentence

The second example, by its repetition of five words and use of italics, shows greater intensity:

> There *must* be a language in which all but the most highly technical matters can be discussed without distortion or falsification or watering-down; there *must* be a language impartially free of all the various jargons through which the "disciplines" maintain their proud and debilitating isolation; there *must* be a language in which the kinship of these disciplines is expressed and revealed and reaffirmed.
>
> Norman Podhoretz, "In Defense of Editing"

The final example shows how completely devastating repetition can be. The passage is taken from Mary Campbell's newspaper review of Brian Bedford's performance as Hamlet:

> Bedford's Hamlet has no personality, no depth and no motivation. He shows no melancholy, no fears or turmoil, no antic humors, no dissembling, no "almost blunted purpose."

Repetition can hardly be considered apart from parallelism and cataloguing, because frequently they all work together to reinforce one another. Overused, they all become uneventful. As strategies, their effectiveness springs from contrast—their departure from the most customary arrangements.

SERIES

Like repetition, a series has a cumulative effect. A series of two we often take for granted. Sentences with compound subjects, compound verbs, or compound objects are extremely common:

> The fancy is a kaleidoscope; it shifts and lights a path into the world of everyday.
>
> Student sentence

> He loved the cutthroat and the steelhead with their brilliance and spirit.
>
> Student sentence

At times, the meanings of the words do not vary greatly from one another, but the preference for two rather than one seems to satisfy the writer's sense of balance. The tendency to write doublets constantly instead of a single word needs to be guarded against, because a habit of twoness can accumulate a good number of unnecessary words.

Series beyond two items are capable of a whole range of effects, and those effects are also conditioned by the use or absence of connectives. The right or wrong of using or not using conjunctions depends solely upon the reader's response to the rhythms that the writer sets up. The patterns of the following sentences seem to have a rightness about the way they read, but they vary in their use of conjunctions:

> It is worth noting that when individual nations can no longer trust their leaders they also cease to trust or believe or understand each other.
>
> Student sentence

> The makings of an all-American athlete are agility, courage, two strong legs, and a draft deferment.
>
> Student sentence

> Voices mingled in the auditorium—loud, raucous voices, excited voices, authoritative voices, laughing, directing, reverberating, augmenting each other—then diminishing gradually into silence.
>
> Student sentence

The ultimate in writing a series is the catalog, a device of overwhelming the reader with a list of representative examples that seem to be all-inclusive. The catalog is panoramic; it expresses scope, sweep, fullness. Tom Wolfe uses it often in his writing:

> Good old boys from all over the South roared together after the Stanchion—Speed! Guts!—pouring into Birmingham, Daytona Beach, Randleman, North Carolina; Atlanta, Hickory, Bristol, Tennessee; Augusta, Georgia; Richmond, Virginia; Asheville, North Carolina; Charlotte, Myrtle Beach—tens of thousands of them.
>
> "The Last American Hero"

A Truman Capote catalog pushes even further:

> Father is a world traveler. Cards arrive: he is in Seville, now Copenhagen, now Milan, next week Manchester, everywhere and all the while on a gaudy spending spree. Buying: blue crockery from a Danish castle. Pink apothecary jars from an old London pharmacy. English brass, Barcelona lamps, Battersea boxes, French paperweights, Italian witch balls, Greek icons, Venetian blackamoors, Spanish saints, Korean cabinets; and junk, glorious junk, a jumble of ragged dolls, broken buttons, a stuffed kangaroo, an aviary of owls under a great glass bell, the playing pieces of obsolete games, the paper moneys of defunct governments, an ivory umbrella cane *sans* umbrella, crested chamber pots and mustache mugs and irreparable clocks, cracked violins, a sundial that weighs seven

hundred pounds, skills, snake vertebrae, elephants' hoofs, sleigh bells and Eskimo carvings and mounted swordfish, medieval milkmaid stools, rusted firearms and flaking waltz-age mirrors.

"Brooklyn Heights: A Personal Memoir"

In such an example, the eccentricity of the extended catalog matches the eccentricity of the subject matter, but, no doubt fully aware of the length, the writer skillfully groups the items and varies the connectives. The final test of a catalog is its capacity to be exhaustive without being exhausting.

STRATEGIES OF SOUND

Just as words on a page cannot be separated from the rhythms they produce, so words cannot be separated from their sounds, whether they are spoken or not. The inner sense of sound is not necessarily dependent upon the ear, but the things that we hear and like no doubt affect the "sounds" that we see and like.

Phrasing that repeats words or plays upon homophones tends to attract attention. For that reason we see them frequently in advertisements and on bumper stickers and signs; they serve as repeatable slogans:

When guns are outlawed, only outlaws will have guns.

It's hard to keep your body in good physical shape; it may be even harder to keep your money in good fiscal shape.

In general, when sober communication is in order, this kind of playfulness, particularly punning, has no place because it often smacks of triviality and forced cleverness.

On the other hand, alliteration is both tasteful and pleasing when it acts as an unobtrusive link between the words of a sentence. It is not difficult to separate subtle examples from forced ones. In general, any use of alliteration becomes excessive when sound predominates over sense.

Subtle alliteration:

A vast and inventive organization of living matter survives by seeming to have lost.

John Steinbeck

> We are more and more conversant with the chemistry of that clod of clay on a speck of star-dust, that we call human life.
>
> Irwin Edman

Too deliberate alliteration:

> Traffic cannot untangle in Boise and Bozeman, as well as Boston and Bobo, Texas. All movement has ended in Seattle, Seaside, Secaucus, and Sand Flea, Fla. There is a national dragon, stretching everywhere. All commerce, all continuity, all congress has ceased.
>
> Lorenzo Milam

> It could be that this explosion of special levy nay-sayers results from the belated suspicion that, in the past, some legislators, proud and powerful legislators, "dressed in a little brief authority," have played such fantastic partisan pranks for possible personal political profit so persistently as to preclude passage of any program of tax reform.
>
> Letter to the Editor, *Seattle Post Intelligencer*

Clearly some alliteration is more obvious than others, but it is not too difficult to determine when the bounds of discreet use have been passed. Some writers have a more natural tendency to alliterate than others; they therefore need to be more cautious of the way sounds intrude upon meaning.

STRATEGY AND EMPHASIS

The rhetoric of the sentence, of course, finds extension in the paragraph and paragraph bloc. Sentence strategies such as climactic arrangement, variation of length, inversion, interruption, balance, parallelism, repetition, and sound devices operate on a larger scale as well as within the sentence. In actuality, they are the writer's substitutes for stress, intonation, and pause, the speaker's stock and trade for emphasis. The writer can also resort to mechanical devices like underlining, italics, capitals, boldface type, and large print, but composing strategies are more natural because they grow out of the writer's responses to his own material. Even though a writer may map out his thoughts with care, he cannot plot every sentence and paragraph in advance as if it were a bit of choreography. As composing takes place, the writer has to depend upon his ingenuity to arrange words in such ways that the reader will read them as the writer intends, without the use of artificial devices. Inasmuch as strategies reflect characteristic ways of thinking, a writer does not need to dwell on them, like a golfer planning his shots; they occur spontaneously as soon as he knows what he wants to say. Learning what writers do is one way to build writing confidence; if a writer is sure of his craft, he can concentrate upon the substance of his remarks, and he may even find himself choosing between a number of ways of putting them down in order to find the most suitable one.

A close examination of a passage of nonfiction by Richard Wright will indicate, first, that more things are happening in the prose to influence us as readers than we realize. Second, the analysis should show that these strategies are not additions or contrivances but an integral part of the prose. They reflect Wright's manner and feeling. In short, they are his natural way of writing.

Length
of
sentences

Series of six introductory phrases, varied in structure	Buttressed by their belief that their God had entrusted the earth into their keeping, drunk with power and possibility, waxing rich through trade in commodities, human and non-human, with awesome naval and merchant marines at their disposal, their countries filled with human debris anxious for any adventures, psychologically armed with new facts, white Western Christian civilization during the fourteenth, fifteenth,	
Transposition and interrupted movement	sixteenth, and seventeenth centuries, with a long, slow, and bloody explosion, hurled itself upon the sprawling masses of colored humanity in Asia and Africa.	84
	I say to you white men of the West: Don't be too proud of how easily you conquered and plundered	
Balance and parallelism	those Asians and Africans. You had unwitting allies in	24
Alliteration	your campaigns; you had Fifth Columns in the form of indigenous cultures to facilitate your military, missionary, and mercenary efforts. Your collaborators in	25
Repetition of "habits"	those regions consisted of the mental habits of the people, habits for which they were in no way responsible, no more than you were responsible for yours. Those	30
	habits constituted corps of saboteurs, of spies, if you will, that worked in the interests of European aggres-	
Balance and parallelism with inversion	sion. You must realize that it was not your courage or racial superiority that made you win, nor was it the racial inferiority or cowardice of the Asians and Africans	19
	that made them lose. This is an important point that you must grasp, or your concern with this problem will	33
Question with interrupted movement	be forever wide of the facts. How, then, did the West, numerically the minority, achieve, during the last four centuries, so many dazzling victories over the body of	22
	colored mankind? Frankly, it took you centuries to do	24

a job that could have been done in fifty years! You   17

Cataloging   had the motive, the fire power, the will, the religious

Single-word   spur, the superior organization, but you dallied. Why? 18–1

question   You were not aware exactly of what you were doing.   10

You didn't suspect your impersonal strength, or the

impersonal weakness on the other side. You were as   14

Inversion   unconscious, at bottom, as were your victims about

what was really taking place.   16

From *White Man, Listen!*

Average: 24

9

Style

It is not possible to write style. A writer writes thoughts and impressions in phrases and sentences and paragraphs as they occur to him. Style is the total effect of that writing. It depends in part upon the subject, the structure, the words, the strategies, and, of course, upon the writer and audience. Definitions of style tend usually to focus upon one of these to the exclusion of the others so that the definitions themselves seem contradictory or at least incomplete. Some theorists contend that style is one and pervasive, inseparable in its elements and inseparable from the writer who produces it. Others contend that the components can be isolated, in fact, that style is a kind of outward covering of inward meaning and can therefore be changed like a garment. On the other hand, Susan Sontag has commented that this particular metaphor might be more meaningful if we thought of style as something on the inside and matter on the outside—style as a continuing factor and subject matter as changing. However, metaphysical and aesthetic considerations of this kind have little practical value for the beginning writer. They may even be harmful if they lead him to think that style is a matter beyond his understanding and control. Matters of style are both accessible and controllable. Even though a writer cannot easily escape his most characteristic habits of mind and temperament, he can do many things to give substance to his thought, to develop vocabulary and techniques, and to cultivate taste and judgment. All of these can be accomplished through reading. If a writer becomes aware of stylistic effects in other people's writing, good or bad, he can begin to develop critical standards to apply to his own writing.

We have almost no set names or classifications for style, because terms tend to be descriptive and impressionistic rather than exact. Words like "flowing" or "rich" or "diffuse" or "mannered" characterize the effect of a particular work or passage. More precise description comes only in the analysis of style. Style, therefore, can be talked about impressionistically or analytically. The analytical approach tries to say how effects are created. It investigates causes. It reveals what a writer has to do if he wants to model his own style after another writer's or if he wants to develop a personal style that is compatible to him and readable to others. Sections of this handbook on the Writer's Voice, the Writer's Point of View, Structure, Paragraphing, and The Rhetoric of the Sentence discuss a number of features that affect style. Several others need to be commented upon in detail.

STYLE AND WORDS: DENOTATION AND CONNOTATION

Just as form is man's attack upon chaos and confusion, so words are his attempt to conquer inarticulateness. Speech and writing are kinds of codes—codes that depend mainly upon words. Writing, of course, is more exclusively dependent upon words than speech, because the speaker has many nonverbal means of influencing an audience. Mathematical symbols, musical notations, and line and color are also codes for articulating thoughts and feelings, and each code has its own basic principles which permit the system to operate. From time to time, codes are displaced because they have lost their efficiency or their magic. Marshall McLuhan has prophesized that, in an age of computer technology, writing will in time become as outmoded as smoke signals. What his bold prediction prompts us to ask is what efficiency and magic do words still have for us now.

Since words are our most common means of expressing ideas, it would be relevant to know how words function to convey meaning. The problem immediately suggests all kinds of philosophical speculations, but a writer has to come to grips with a few workable answers, even though they may oversimplify a highly complex problem.

First, great numbers of words in the language have a specific referent; that is, they refer to something specific in time and space, and that meaning is concrete in the mind of the user. "Fire" in its basic sense has reference to our common perception of burning and flame. It can be both seen and felt, and heat is as inseparably connected with it as light. Whether fire refers to the flame of a match, burning logs in a grate, or a conflagration, the word has a hard core of meaning which we understand. We know that "fire" is not the same as "rain" nor "wood" the same as "fur" because the referents cannot be very easily confused. It is true that each man chooses a particular referent from his own experience—everyone has not seen the same fire, for example—but the individual's capacity to communicate simple concepts lies in his ability to link the right word with the right referent. This definition of a word in terms of specific referable properties is its *denotation*. If meaning were only a matter of mastering the denotative properties of words, communication would be considerably more simple than it is.

The meanings of very few words of the language, however, are limited to a one-to-one relation between symbol and referent. Words may retain a simple, permanent nucleus of meaning, but they also acquire an ever-increasing number of satellite meanings. The collected associations of a word are its *connotations*. Many connotations are similar because many human experiences are similar. Standardized connotations, that is, associations which most people share, result in extended meanings of a word, as "fire" comes to mean "ardor" and "inspiration"; but other associations will be wholly personal and different. In general, personal connotations cannot be limited or defined, but their connection with basic meanings, like nerve fibers connected to the central brain center, open up all the emotional and imaginative possibilities of language.

STYLE AND WORDS: ABSTRACT AND CONCRETE

Do words divorce thought from feelings? Only in the sense that some words fail to touch nerve responses at all. We can think first of structure words like "that," "for," "whereas," and "however"; we can then think of abstract words like "result," "tendency," and "distribution." These are essentially unfeeling words. As a generalization, words that have concrete associations tend to be more capable of emotional expression than abstract words. In one sense, anything written is more abstract than the experience itself, because writing is a symbolic transcription of the experience. The word "fire" is more abstract than the actual burning, but among words themselves "fire" is less abstract than other words. Both "passion" and "zeal," as synonyms of "firiness," are more abstract than the word "fire" itself because they are further removed from the referent and more generalized. Further, words like "feeling" and "endeavor" seem even more abstract and generalized than "passion" and "zeal." An abstract word, therefore, functions as a kind of summary term; a concrete word, as a specific example. Only when abstract words are tied to experiences—like "resistance" to the French underground during World War II or a small boy's refusal to be bullied by a bigger one—can their meaning be made specific and ultimately viable. All the dictionary can say by way of definition is that "resistance" means "the opposition offered by one thing, force, etc., to another." This is an abstract definition devoid of specific meaning or feeling, although it is a covering definition. In writing, abstract words act similarly as ways of grouping and generalizing about individual experiences.

It is apparent that some subjects invite the use of more abstract words than others; or, to put the matter differently, some subjects invite more words with precise denotative value to the exclusion of words with expressive qualities. It is one thing to discuss death as man's inevitable fate; it is another to describe a fatal accident that takes the lives of three young men. One topic is by nature theoretical and generalized; the other, actual and specific. The first would probably be more abstract than the second, but it does not necessarily follow that the total effect of writing on an abstract subject has to be vague and unfeeling. Its effect is influenced by the balance of abstract and concrete words working together in a total context. An excess of abstract words invariably produces an impenetrable and dull style:

> The reason people exclude strange or "wrong" ideas is out of fear. But the same fear prompts them to use the same methods everyone else uses to obtain the same goals, spiritual or mental. The point is not that it is undesirable to want certain middle-class material things or to have a certain set of values. The most important part of life is to be free enough within one's own spirit so that other values and wants and methods of obtaining them can be seen and tolerated.
>
> Student paragraph

A paragraph of this kind causes the reader to wonder what the writer has in mind. Each of the following phrases lacks a sense of the specific: "strange or 'wrong' ideas," "the same fear," "the same methods," "the same goals," "certain middle-class material things," "certain set of values," and "other values and wants and methods." These indefinite references make the prose diffuse. Although each one need not be spelled out, a balance of abstractions and specific illustrations phrased in concrete terms will clarify and liven an abstract discussion. Concrete words have the capacity to act upon less vital words in a sentence. The stylistic effect of words, therefore, is largely a matter of words in context.

WORDS IN CONTEXT

The total context of discourse influences the use of words in three main ways: (1) it fixes a perspective by which we choose among several possible meanings of a word; (2) it extends the imaginative capability of words by allowing different perspectives to be brought in conjunction with one another; (3) it sets up rhythmic patterns and sound patterns that affect the choices of words.

1.   A word with multiple and extended meanings is capable of operating in different contexts without confusion. For example, we set aside the literal meaning of "head" as a biological term when it is used in new contexts such as "the head of a pin," "the head of a boil," "the head of a department," "the head on beer," "a river's head," "the head word of a phrase," or "bringing matters to a head." With varying degrees of generality, each of these uses has a carry-over meaning of "something at the top," but the context in each case determines a more specific meaning that does not permit us to mistake one for the other.

Context also permits us to interpret the meaning of idiomatic phrases and special expressions that otherwise would be quite meaningless. The expression "cheap is cheap" is circular and says nothing at all in a literal sense, but it is a kind of telegraphic way of saying in context that anything sold at a cheap price is probably inferior in quality. Likewise, "bread is bread" means that bread will sustain us if nothing more tasty is available. But these interpretations are not written into the words; readers attach them because the context invites them. The multiple meanings of counter words (see page 389) also get sorted out on the basis of context.

2.   Puns begin to move into the area of figurative language because they derive their effect from the operation of two contexts at the same time; we are subjected to a kind of double exposure. For example, shortly following the first orbital trip around the moon, a scientist, wanting to emphasize that exploring the depths of the sea was as important as probing the far reaches of space, chose to make his point by means of a *double entendre:* "The ocean's bottom," he said, "is infinitely more attractive than the moon's behind."

All metaphor, one of the major sources of expressiveness in the language, works on a comparable principle of using particular words in a context they do not literally refer to:

> I'm back from vacation. I didn't get a chance to wade back in. It has been the high dive in deep water from the first day.

Metaphor is a process of analogy, but the context usually makes clear if it is to be understood literally or figuratively. Some metaphors lose their power of analogy because they are absorbed into new contexts, no longer recalling previous ones. For example, clouds seem to have their own way of drifting; the use of "drifting" does not ordinarily recall water. Nor does "He jumped at the suggestion" conjure up an image of sudden physical action. Nor do "loud colors" or "piercing sounds" suggest a mixture of sense impressions. These all represent faded metaphors which have assumed literal denotations in new contexts.

All active figurative language, however, draws two perspectives into relation to one another. Metaphor is as close as writing can come to a musical duet in which two performers sing simultaneously, possibly with contrary feelings but with a single effect. One singer may voice feelings of intense hate and the other feelings of intense love, but the effect is a single one of intensity, even though it draws from two different sources. Metaphor functions by an interaction of two frames of reference. In expository writing, it is usually the interaction of the concrete and the abstract; that is, the concrete adds exactness and vigor to the abstract. Metaphor is a writer's attempt to find greater precision of meaning and, in finding it through metaphor, also to add vitality and imaginativeness to the prose. In a sentence trying to explain an abstract concept of language, Suzanne Langer adds a simile in order to clinch her point:

> As it is, however, all language has a form which requires us to string out our ideas even though their objects rest one within the other; as pieces of clothing that are actually worn one over the other have to be strung side by side on the clothesline.
>
> *Philosophy in a New Key*

With an intricate sense of intermeshing contexts, Norman Podhoretz writes this sentence:

> Yet if he [an editor] whores too avidly after strange gods, desiring this man's art and that man's scope, the magazine will avenge itself by refusing to assimilate the foreign substance.
>
> "In Defense of Editing"

Here the Biblical scene of God's avenging himself upon the children of Israel for "whoring after strange gods" is interspersed with a quotation from Shakespeare's Sonnet 29 and concluded with a phrase that seems to be drawn from biology. The whole mixture is applied to the problem of editing a current magazine. One might possibly argue that the Podhoretz sentence is more showy than functional, but there is no doubt that metaphor and allusion add interest to its literal meaning.

The concreteness of an analogy is capable of bringing an idea into focus. If the abstract is compared with the abstract, however, the effect is far less pointed, like "It quieted pain and sorrow like love overcoming strife." Because the statement and the comparison in this case are both generalities, the meaning is not greatly sharpened.

3.   Finally, context provides the measure for the rhythmic combinations and sound patterns of words in sequence. No single word is without either rhythm or sound, but all words do not combine with each other harmoniously any more than all colors do. Somerset Maugham writes, "Words have weight, sound and appearance; it is only by considering these that you can write a sentence that is good to look

at and good to listen to." Maugham's own very plain sentence falls easily into segments, offers no obstacles to the eye, reads with a continuous rhythm up to a point, and then ends with a pleasant balanced pattern. With the unobtrusive sounds and rhythms of his sentence, we can compare a sentence from an advertisement:

> X-bourbons are about the American-iest bourbons around. It's almost un-American for a bourbon-lover not to know 'em!

A coinage like "American-iest" is as troublesome to the eye as it is to the tongue, and the deliberate attempt at folksiness makes the sentence too obvious in its appeal. Rhythm and sound are as inescapably a fact of writing as they are of speech. The chief difference is that the writer has to depend upon his auditory imagination to substitute for the ear. Yet there is no reason why a writer cannot test his prose by reading it aloud until he can develop written ease as well as conversational ease.

Jonathan Swift defined style as "proper words in proper places." The definition implies that context determines what goes where properly. But Swift's comment may lead too easily to the conclusion that the choice of words is mechanical: all seems to depend upon knowing what is proper, and the rest will follow, like putting together a jigsaw puzzle. Yet lively prose requires far more than learning proprieties. Defining "lively prose" precisely is difficult, but Yurek Lazowski gets at the heart of the matter when he comments upon style in dance: "It is not enough in ballet just for the people to move in the right places at the right time. That is only the skeleton, but the heart doesn't beat yet. You have to give life to it." In like manner, the writer must give life to words by his involvement with them.

STYLE AND FEELING: TONE

A writer gives life to prose primarily by expressing feeling in writing, not telling about it but showing it by the choice and arrangement of words. What we as readers feel about prose is our response to its tone. It is in part a response to the writer's voice; it is also an awareness of the writer's purpose and attitude. At times, a particular tone—humorous, solemn, satiric—will grow out of the writer's concern with his material. Or the writer's voice may change in terms of his audience; he may assume a formal or familiar or learned manner. Since tone may vary with all the possible moods and attitudes of a writer and at times may show itself unintentionally, it remains to be seen how effects are transferred to a reader through writing. These can be discussed in terms of varying degrees of manner and method.

Variations of Informal and Formal

Informal and formal are the measures of distance between the writer and his audience. When the writer makes the audience feel close, the tone is informal. When the writer assumes an impersonal relation with his audience, the tone is formal. Either effect may or may not be appropriate to the situation. For example, a student being admitted to the graduate program of a large university failed to indicate on his application which degree he wanted to work for. When he was asked, he replied by mail:

> If this letter may be appended to my application, I hereby proclaim my intention to proceed to the Ph.D. degree after earning the MA.

In this case, the relation between the writer and the chairman of graduate studies was not a close one, but it hardly justified the tone of a public proclamation in the letter. The candidate might have responded in a simple, direct manner:

> After I finish the MA, I intend to study for the Ph.D.

This rewriting eliminates the verbiage of the unnecessary clause and the passive voice construction; it drops the pompous language of "hereby proclaim" and substitutes "finish" for "earning" and "study" for "proceed" to make the tone throughout less guarded.

Formal tone does not need to be either pompous or stiff, although it is characteristically temperate in its language and uses strategies that preserve an impression of full control:

> I am a man of the law. I have dedicated myself to uphold the law and to enforce its commands. I fully accept the principle that each of us is subject to law; that each of us is bound to obey the law enacted by his government.
>
> But if I had lived in Germany in Hitler's days, I hope I would have refused to wear an armband, to *Heil Hitler,* to submit to genocide. This I hope, although Hitler's edicts were law until allied weapons buried the Third Reich.
>
> Abe Fortas, *Concerning Dissent and Civil Disobedience*

These two paragraphs show some slight variation in formality. In the first, Mr. Fortas speaks as a judge, and the choice of words and the arrangement sound familiarly like a formal oath of office. In the second paragraph, Mr. Fortas speaks as a private citizen. The series of three infinitives—"to wear," "to Heil Hitler," and "to submit"—and the repetition of "I hope" give a somewhat more relaxed tone to the writing, but it is in no sense as open and free as the following prose:

> When I saw Planet of the Apes a couple of months ago, I liked it. I just plain liked it—an ingenious, adventurous, humorous, deliciously spooky example of one of my favorite popular genres, science fiction, that was smartly made and contained a useful moral or two. I should have trusted my instincts, stood up and proclaimed my affectionate regard for the things right off.
>
> Richard Schickel, "Second Thoughts on Ape-Men"

We can observe first that the subject matter of this writing is less weighty than that of Mr. Fortas, and Richard Schickel, as the movie reviewer of a popular magazine, occupies a position considerably less dignified than that of Associate Justice of the Supreme Court. Therefore, an easy manner is appropriate both to this writer and his audience. His phrasing is conversational—"I liked it. I just plain liked it"; he does not hesitate to throw in a bit of current jargon like "spooky." When he uses a word like "proclaimed," he follows it with an unstilted object: "my affectionate regard for the things right off." Yet the writing is not overly familiar; its variety of words is unforced. Even though Schickel mixes a few learned words and ordinary ones, there is no marked change in tone, as in the following sentence:

> In my growth from mushroomhood to "scholar" it was necessary for me to find a personal language which would give intelligible form to my own instincts and judgments in situations where intelligent critical reaction was called for.

This passage is taken from a statement of personal objectives written by a student applying for a graduate assistantship. Its playful phrasing at the beginning is hardly consistent with the density of the words that follow. It is an odd mixture of coyness and pomposity, and the writer seems clearly uneasy. Only when the writer and the reader are at ease with one another does informality result. A reader, however, can be put off either by chumminess (an abuse of informality) or aloofness (an abuse of formality).

Most student writing is informal and appropriately should be, because informality comes naturally to young people. Further, informality does not have to be taught. In many instances, however, it has to be encouraged, chiefly because many students have a mistaken notion that informality is inappropriate to serious writing. Informality in writing is seldom inappropriate if informality helps to make the prose spontaneous, flexible, and sincere.

Variations of Clear and Obscure

Everyone is capable of occasionally writing an awkward, ambiguous, illogical, or unduly elliptical sentence. But a single vague sentence does not produce an obscure style. Obscurity grows out of repeated habits in a writer's prose that leave the reader doubtful about his precise meanings. The following illustrations are brief, but they should be looked upon only as typical of many other passages throughout writing that is considered unclear. Obscurity results from

1. The tendency to use more words than necessary:

This acquired privilege to regulate the activities of the family invites the possibility and probability of censorship of conflicting opinions without further investigation into which side could be right.

Student sentence

2. The tendency to write unduly long sentences:

And even after it was done, the victim had no recourse whatever since, unlike sacrilege and obscenity, we have no laws against bad taste, perhaps because in a democracy the majority of the people who make the laws don't recognize bad taste when they see it, or perhaps because in our democracy bad taste has been converted into a marketable and therefore taxable and therefore lobbyable commodity by the merchandising federations which at the same simultaneous time create the market (not the appetite: that did not need creating: only pandering to) and the product to serve it, and bad taste by simple solvency was purified of bad taste and absolved.

William Faulkner, "On Privacy: The American Dream, What Happened to It?"

3. The tendency to use too many abstract polysyllables and circumlocutions:

The problem of modality leads directly and immediately to the problem of historicity. The talk-write pedagogy is essentially ahistorical on two different levels. Like all behavioral techniques, it is ahistorical with regard to the origin of scribal non-fluencies: it attacks the nonfluency-as-dysfunction, with no attention to originating cause. Much more to the point here, talk-write is philosophically ahistorical regarding the relationship between vocal and scribal activity: it handles both as equivalent modalities of verbal behavior. This places it in sharp contrast with the current think-write pedagogies, which exhibit an historicity which has been largely confirmed by linguistic research. Indeed, one of the great anomalies of the current compositional situation may be that the conceptual framework we have borrowed in part from linguistics is actually inhibitive of genuine progress in scribal pedagogy. The linguistic viewpoint is largely historico-descriptive. It is also, and as a consequence, pervasively hierarchic.

Robert Zoellner, "A Behavioral
Pedagogy for Composition"

4. The tendency to be abstruse:

What is reality, and what is pretense in Pirandello's *Six Characters?* Through the Father, one may feel that Pirandello is saying that the character is more real than the actor, since the character's personality does not change. On the contrary, while the character's personality may be more stable, the actor is real, and his personality is, at any instant, real. Like the characters in the play, reality knows no past or future, except what may be implied by the present. Pretense includes any influences of the past or thoughts of the future.

Student paragraph

5. The tendency to garble words and constructions:

Swift so cleverly approaches and attacks human deficiencies that even after the readers realize it is them that Gulliver is talking about they submit not only to Swift's veracity, but begin to, I feel, exhibit the same incensement Swift has in hope of finding a Utopian society.

Student sentence

6. The tendency to leave gaps in the development of a thought:

Some of the excesses in the current excursions into aural, oral, tactile, and kinetic experience may in fact be directly responsive to the sensory deprivation of the print culture. Nature abhors a vacuum. No one glories in the sight of kids totally out of control in reaction to the Beatles. Some say, "What are the Beatles doing to these kids?" Others say, "What have we done to these kids?" All the data isn't in on what it means to be a balanced human being.

Student paragraph

The ways of obscurity are many, but chief among them is redundancy. Even though piling up words and repeating the same thought in slightly different terms are standard ways of making ourselves understood when we speak, the same techniques in writing have almost the opposite effect. For the most part, profuseness and redundancy in writing tend to obscure thought; spareness and directness are assets to clear expression.

Fuzziness of meaning also results from too many private and obscure allusions, from the use of words known only to extremely restricted groups ("fugleman," "hyparistic," "ontogentically"), from ambiguous phrasing, and from general disorganization. A completely lucid style is so unusual that critics often mention clarity as a special mark of praise, like the following comment by Caskie Stinnett of *Holiday:*

> Lillian Hellman has written her memoirs, *An Unfinished Woman* (Little, Brown), and it's surprising how clear, intelligent writing can seize a reader and thrill him in a way no other medium can.

Similarly, critics seldom fail to condemn persistent fogginess. The smog of writing is often referred to as gobbledygook, a word that was coined in the 1940s to describe the impenetrable jargon and style of government documents, but a word that has stuck in the language because it seems to be needed as a label whenever and wherever writing is written.

Variations of Plain and Fancy

Plainness of style is a quality of restraint—an absence of excess and complication. One kind of plain style is purely utilitarian. Its chief purpose is clear communication. It therefore avoids irony, figurative language, and strategies that from the standpoint of pure practicality seem to divert interest from *what* is said to *how* it is said. Prose of this kind is factual and impersonal. It is efficient. It is the typical language of reporting and informing:

> **Zachary Taylor National Cemetery**—4701 Brownsboro Road—A monument marking the grave of the 12th President dominates the reservation. Taylor was less than a year old when he moved with his parents to Kentucky and settled in the home which is within sight of the cemetery.
>
> At the cemetery entrance, turn right and drive past one road to Blankenbaker Lane and turn right. A marker a quarter of a mile down Blankenbaker locates Springfield, the home of Taylor, now privately owned and not open to the public. Continue north to Locust Grove, the mansion where George Rogers Clark spent his last years.
>
> Tourist Guidebook

The plain style of the guidebook, textbook, manual, and communiqué is indispensable for factual communication—we encounter it constantly—but, as a style of writing, it also tends to be commonplace.

Nevertheless, *plain* and *prosaic* do not have to be accepted as counterparts of one another. A plain style is also capable of simple elegance:

> In the beginning, there was the land, stretching in majesty from ocean to ocean. The land was rich in its diversity—of mountains and valley, of deserts and grassy plains, of singing brooks and rushing, mighty rivers, of plant and animal life.
>
> Beneath the surface of the land, greater riches were hidden—life-giving water, fuel to fire man's industries, ore to build his cities of steel in a far distant time.
>
> And there were no people. The land was virgin; prostitution of the land was in the unknown future.
>
> Muriel Crosby, "English: New
Dimensions and New Demands"

The plainness here is the simplicity of words and structure. Yet, at the same time, there is a subtle intricacy of series, balanced constructions, and parallelism. The style recalls both the restraint and techniques of narrative passages of the Book of Genesis. In fact, the best description of the tone is Biblical. Yet the strategy that produces this stylistic effect does not degenerate into fanciness, if fanciness is understood to mean a purely ornamental device that actually disguises meaning because it calls too much attention to itself. A too conscious striving for effect can defeat the writer's purpose:

> Forgive! For forgiveness is the fragrance of a violet on the heel of the one who crushed it.
>
> Abigail van Buren

This brief sentence is both elaborate in language and profuse in feeling to the point of sentimentality. It is a fancy style, not because the words are extraordinary but because the total effect is excessive and the metaphor more decorative than functional.

Between stark simplicity and extravagance lies a whole range of effects. One extreme is not categorically good and the other bad. Plainness can be barren, and extravagance can be capable of grandeur. In the hands of another writer, plainness can be imaginative and extravagance gaudy. One effect or the other depends upon the writer's capacity to keep words and feelings under control. When a writer loses his control, he also loses control of his own style.

Variations of Exaggeration and Understatement

Exaggeration and understatement are opposite techniques, but they are not necessarily different in their purpose. Both are ways of trying to get an emphasis beyond simple factual statement. Exaggeration, or hyperbole, is the easier and more obvious of the two. It depends simply upon adding words, enlarging the scope, magnifying the idea, heightening the effect, or overstating the problem. As a writing technique, it deliberately distorts, but the distortion is not intended to falsify, only to intensify. For example, a writer may try to arouse strong feelings by exaggeration. When it is applied to personal attack, the result is invective—a particular kind of abuse Westbrook Pegler was capable of when he wrote about Franklin D. Roosevelt:

> That Mr. Roosevelt has his faults I would be among the first to admit under very little pressure, but as a social and political liver-shaker he has had no equal in our time in this country. Ornery, tricky, stubborn, wayward and strong as a bull, he has bucked, wheeled, kicked, walked on his hind legs, tried to mash us against the barn and scrape our heads off under the door in more than five years of continuous plunging, and he apparently isn't even breathing hard yet.
>
> Pull him out of one willful, pesky trick and he will stand there a minute with his head down, showing the whites of his eyes and then go tearing off across the yard hell-bent, rattling our teeth and every bone and joint in our body.
>
> "Rough Riding"

Paradoxically, the same technique can be employed to produce humor. The extent of exaggeration can produce anything from mild amusement to verbal slapstick. Broad comedy is the stock and trade of a columnist like Erma Bombeck:

> I have never taken household hints too seriously.
>
> Once I sent a suggestion to Good Housekeeping pointing out that dust balls stored under the bed throughout the year make wonderful, safe toys for the baby and were unique stocking stuffers.
>
> They cancelled my subscription.

Another writer exaggerates less and creates a wry kind of humor.

> 1968 was a rotten year—a succession of jolts, shocks, fingers in the eye, and knees in the groin for all of us. You could sit for the next five hours trying to think of something cheerful that happened during 1968, and every time you came up with something someone would point out that the good thing you recalled actually took place during 1967 or 1945 or 1066.
>
> Patrick Butler, "1968—And the Hell with It"

The alternative to adding and magnifying for a special effect is minimizing. It is a device of withholding rather than overwhelming, and its element of restraint seems to carry over emotionally to the reader. The reader knows when a controlled or casual statement is disproportionate to the writer's far more intense feelings. A student, commenting upon changes that take place in growing up, compresses a wealth of implication into a one-word metaphor:

> When a child finds the "moral answer" and incorporates it into his experience, he dies into adulthood.

In general, however, understatement remains a rare feature of student writing because the inexperienced writer, like the inexperienced actor, seems more inclined to overplay than underplay.

The disproportion between the writer's intention and the phrasing that produces understatement can also create an ironic tone, often with overtones of humor. There is no mistaking this quality in Swift's writing:

> Last week I saw a woman flayed, and you will hardly believe how much it altered her person for the worse.

In a more subtle, seemingly casual way, Carl Rowan writes:

> It has been said that, by nature, the American people love the underdog. It must be true, for we create so many of them.

Knowing that Carl Rowan is a black writer adds even further to the intensity of his statement.

Because understatement is a form of calm expression, it is probably a tone that some writers are incapable of. It would be difficult to imagine that the writer of the following sentence would be much disposed to understatement under any circumstances:

> I have had it with the continual effrontery of the bleeding-heart do-gooders, and their latest whine, urging investigation of a police officer for doing his duty.

In matters of feeling, the man and the style are likely to be one.

Hyperbole and understatement, of course, can be sustained at much greater length than these examples. One of the great challenges to editors and writers all over the world occurred in July 1969 when they were faced with the task of trying to write about the drama of the space voyage which would put man on the moon for the first time. Many writers attempted to match the magnitude of the event by inflated prose; adjectives like "great," "wonderful," "fantastic," and "fabulous" quickly became feeble resources. The descriptions began with the blast

off at Cape Kennedy on July 16; the departure of Apollo 11 invited
flamboyant kinds of prose like the following:

> Just before the emissaries left the cape, the morning star, Venus,
> fading in the early sunlight, seemed to wink down at Pad 39-A. It re-
> minded some that men were just inching into space by going to the moon.
> But no step would be tougher than this one, the first step.
>
> The launching to the moon came in a litany of thunder and light
> on Cape Kennedy's Pad 39-A.
>
> The sun-orange flame from the Saturn V rocket's mighty booster
> snaked out to sear the pad and blacken the palmetto scrub that struggles
> to exist on this sandy cape.
>
> The sound—a chest-thumping staccato—poured across the barren
> flats and pounded into the nearest observers more than three miles away.
>
> A few cruising pelicans dived for safety. Some men cried.
>
> The Mighty Boeing-Built booster agonizingly lifted its 6½ million-
> pound burden away from the pad. The booster was devouring fuel at
> a rate of 30,000 pounds a second, but the rocket seemed to only inch
> up and away from the launching tower.
>
> There was a moment of silence before the sound reached the ob-
> servers, then a whispered "Go, baby, go" and finally a wild cheer as the
> rocket cleared the tower and the thunder reached the viewing stands.
>
> William W. Prochnau, *The Seattle*
> *Times,* July 16, 1969

Much more rare among various reports was an attempt to get
the same effect by a relative kind of simplicity and understatement.
By comparison with the previous example, the following one shows
restraint:

> It is in many ways the most stunning of all the spectacles man
> has created, the sight not so much of a lifetime as of a millennium.
> You have to see this rising star in person. No one is going to tell you
> about it and make you understand.
>
> If the American republic should live for a thousand years, 9:32
> A.M. EDT July 16, 1969, may not be kept as its finest hour. But, in the
> last thousand years, man's world cannot have held a more exciting
> minute.
>
> A tongue of incandescent flame—so bright that it pained, so mystic
> in flow that it held one's eye on the symmetry of its slow arc—rode the
> Florida sky in the name of Apollo 11. At least one viewer among the
> thousands who stood watch this hazy day thought of the word apocalypse.
>
> The view of an Apollo ascent—given the portent of this one—can
> be a revelation, a striking visual disclosure, of what man has done at
> the tail end of his first million years as a definable entity.
>
> H. D. Quigg, *The Seattle Post-*
> *Intelligencer,* July 17, 1969

Significantly, however, the impact of the entire event was perhaps most remarkably expressed in the simple understated phrases of Neil Armstrong in his first words from the moon:

That's one small step for a man, one giant leap for mankind.

Variations of Tired and Vigorous

It is misleading to associate vigorous language with novelty. A writer does not need to be constantly inventing new words in order to give his writing a sense of freshness. It is mainly a matter of avoiding tired combinations.

Various free-association tests indicate that people respond to stimuli with a high degree of uniformity. When given a stimulus word like "color," they will most commonly say "red," or in response to "flower" they will say "rose." Most respondents will also say "dark" in response to "light" instead of "lamp," "bright," "sun," or "bulb." Because informal talk allows little time for careful choice of words, it depends very heavily upon the cliché, which is actually a kind of conditioned response. It is the stereotyped expression that occurs to us first.

What is true of speaking, of course, need not be true of writing. When the ready phrase presents itself, the writer without too much deliberation can decide whether it has been overworked. All of the following sentences fall into highly familiar, almost set expressions:

His comments are applicable to all walks of life.

They think they should have their lives given to them on a silver platter.

Within the past few years, a new ray of hope has shone on allergy sufferers.

If we turn back the pages of our history books, we will find the account of Seward's Folly.

One might continue to list inevitable combinations like "thick and thin," "sum and substance," "rank and file," and "good clean fun." Hackneyed expressions do not fail to communicate something, but they fail to do it with much vigor, particularly if the expressions are figurative, like "smart as a whip," "deep as the ocean," or "square peg in a round hole." If the function of figurative language in expository prose is to make the ideas and feelings more concrete, then tired expressions tend to lose effectiveness simply because their meanings are ignored. They arouse no reaction; they set up no stimulus that alerts the reader to new associations and implications. In order to keep language vigorous, therefore, a writer first has to be able to recognize what is trite; then he has to be determined to avoid ready-made language.

KINDS OF PROSE STYLES

There are six major styles of writing that we encounter constantly as readers, although we may write no more than two or three of these. They represent extremely broad categories, yet they are different enough from one another in purpose and design that they do not readily substitute for one another. Two examples of each will suggest both the range within the categories and the elements that make them typical of the particular style.

1. The Style of Legal and Technical Writing

Legal and technical writing is a special kind of practical prose designed by the specialist for the specialist. The general reader does not encounter it frequently, but if he does he is likely to find it as obscure as a foreign language.

The first example is taken from the *Canadian Journal of Biochemistry:*

> The occurrence of organophosphonic acids and their derivatives has been reported in a variety of invertebrate biological material. However, a recent report by Alam and Bishop (1) describing the presence of lipid-bound choline-phosphonate in human aortas with athero-sclerotic plaques shows that the occurrence of organophosphonic acid derivatives is not confined to the lower forms of the animal kingdom. Rouser *et al.* (2) were the first to isolate an intact phospholipid deriving from phosphonic acid. While investigating the composition of phospholipids of the sea anemone *Anthopleura elegantissima* by a combination of column and paper chromatographic methods, they obtained a sphingolipid differing from known sphingolipids in that on acid hydrolysis it gave a mixture of fatty acids, long-chain bases, and 2-aminoethyl-phosphonic acid. Examination of the long-chain bases by paper chromatography revealed the presence of *erythro-* and *threo-* sphingosine, *erythro-* and *threo-* phytosphingosine, and related compounds of different chain length (2).
>
> Erich Baer and G. Raghupati Sarma,
> "Phosphonolipids. XX."

Apart from its highly technical vocabulary, the most noticeable feature of the style is its compression. This introductory paragraph refers to two research studies and manages to summarize the relevant findings of each in a few sentences. Even though the words themselves are obscure to the general reader, we may assume that to the biochemist they are precise ones. Others would not substitute. Thus, technical language of this order is a kind of private language which merely uses the standard grammar of English.

The second example is a paragraph from the mortgagee clause of a homeowner's insurance policy:

> Whenever this Company shall pay the mortgagee (or trustee) any sum for loss or damage under this policy, and shall claim that, as to the mortgagor or owner, no liability therefor existed, this Company shall, to the extent of such payment, be thereupon legally subrogated to all the rights of the party to whom such payment shall be made, under all securities held as collateral to the mortgage debt, or may at its option pay to the mortgagee (or trustee) the whole principal due or to grow due on the mortgage, with interest and shall thereupon receive a full assignment and transfer of the mortgage and of all such other securities; but no subrogation shall impair the right of the mortgagee (or trustee) to recover the full amount of said mortgagee's (or trustee's) claim.

Even though copies of insurance policies are given to purchasers, the prose is not written for them. It is written by lawyers for lawyers in case of any disagreement about the provisions of the policy. It is a contractual agreement. The language therefore must be exact, carefully qualified to cover all possible alternatives, and punctuated so that no ambiguities occur. Like other technical writing, the prose is completely impersonal and formal, limited to bare facts. The need for complete accuracy in documents, laws, and contracts allows for no flexibility of language. The result is, therefore, a style that is rigid and all too often unreadable except as a matter of necessity.

2. The Style of Popular Reporting: The Plain Style

The style of popular reporting retains both the factual and impersonal emphasis of technical writing, but its chief difference as a style is that it is written to be read and understood by a wide audience. We encounter it in news reporting, program notes, announcements, business letters, and encyclopedia articles. It is also the style of written examinations that call for facts and analysis. It is often unsigned prose, but signed or unsigned it is anonymous in effect because the writer excludes his feelings and avoids coloring the prose by any unusual words or strategies. The style therefore includes much writing in an extremely simple and practical form.

The first example is an excerpt from a university bulletin, briefly describing a course of special interest being offered during the summer quarter:

Beginning and advanced mountain climbing have been scheduled for the full quarter in order to provide a complete summer of climbing. Evening lectures and practice sessions are combined with weekend field trips to nearby mountains. An additional fee of $25.00 will be charged for registration in either course. No auditors will be allowed.

The basic course (PE 136) includes evening lectures or practice sessions and weekend field trips. No prior experience is necessary. Two sections are offered; the first begins Tuesday, June 24, the second on Wednesday, June 25.

The advanced course (PE 137) includes instruction and practice in techniques used in high-angle rock, snow, and ice climbing. Evening lectures and weekend field trips are planned. Interested students must have successfully completed any basic nountain climbing course (or have equivalent experience) and must obtain the instructor's permission. The course will meet on Monday evenings beginning June 23.

One of the most noticeable features of the style is the consistent use of the passive voice in order to maintain an impersonal tone. This passage uses no connectives. The facts are set down in sequence in relatively brief, uncluttered sentences. The vocabulary is undemanding.

The second example is a news report:

Washington—(UPI)—President Nixon watched the Apollo 11 liftoff today on television with the Apollo 8 commander, Astronaut Frank Borman.

The President viewed the launching at Cape Kennedy on a set in a White House aide's office. Mr. Nixon has no television sets in his office.

The President originally intended to have dinner with the Apollo 11 crew last night at Cape Kennedy but called off the plan to avoid any possibility of "contaminating" the three. He telephoned them instead to wish them well on "this greatest adventure ever undertaken."

The Seattle Times. July 16, 1969

The human interest and even trivial detail of this account seem to make it less cold than the catalog description, but the style itself is completely uncolored by the writer. He is an unidentified and unidentifiable person. The use of "contaminating," which might be interpreted as a bit of sardonic comment, is actually a quotation of the word used by the agency in requesting that the President's dinner with the astronauts be cancelled. The prose uses typically short journalistic paragraphs. The statements are condensed, set down without particular concern for variety or rhythmic effect. The phrasing provides no obstacles. The prose is designed to do an efficient job. It does it.

3. The Style of Learned Discourse

Although the style of legal and technical writing treats specialized material, not all discourse of this nature needs to read as laboriously as an act of Congress or an insurance policy. Learned discourse may be described as a style also written by specialists for specialists with the broader purpose of analyzing and expanding upon a topic, as opposed to prose that sets down facts in the most abbreviated way possible. Because learned discourse may also need to argue and persuade, rhetoric becomes one of its concerns. Subjects in this style are often of limited interest to a general audience, but it is possible for the prose to be read by educated readers outside the field if they have enough knowledge of the terms and references.

The first example is taken from a paper read by Alfred North Whitehead before a meeting of the Aristotelian Society. He himself considered this writing less complex and technical than material he was writing concurrently for books on the same subject:

> I presume that the fundamental position of idealism is that all reality can be construed as an expression of mentality. For example, I suppose that Mr. Alexander is a realist because for him a mind is one among other items occurring in that evolution of complexes which is the very being of space-time. On the other hand, Mr. Wildon Carr is an idealist because he finds ultimate reality in the self-expression of monadic mentality. The test, therefore, of idealism is the refusal to conceive reality apart from explicit reference to some or all of the characteristic processes of mentality; it may be either thought, or experience, or knowledge, or the expression of valuation in the form of a historical process, the valuation being both the efficient and the final cause of the process. Now Berkeley's argument in favor of this central position of idealism is that when you examine the objects of sense-perception they are essentially personal to the observer. He enforces by a variety of illustrations the doctrine that there is nothing left when you have torn the observer out of the observation. The planet, which is no bigger than a sixpence, is the observer's planet, and he walks off with his own property.
>
> "The Philosophical Aspects of the Principle of Relativity"

Whatever difficulty there may be in reading this passage perhaps derives more from the concepts than the language. Although Whitehead uses several terms that have special meanings in philosophy, all of them are defined in a standard collegiate dictionary and are therefore accessible to the educated reader, if he is interested in capsule definitions without doing extensive background reading. But more important about the prose is that Whitehead seems interested in helping the reader follow the line of reasoning. There are markers like "on the other hand," "therefore," and "now." There is an elaboration of the definition in sentence 4 and a moving from the general to the particular in the last three sentences, ending with a comparison. These are all signs of the writer's concern for the reader, even by involving him personally by the use of "you." All in all, even though the learnedness of this writing is apparent, so also is the writer's willingness to expand upon his phrases and seek understanding.

The second example is taken from a learned periodical. The topic of the role of the American university in society could be discussed from various viewpoints by such people as the editor of a popular periodical, by a daily columnist in the newspaper, or by a university official in an alumni magazine, and the writing of each of these would probably differ in emphasis and tone. The following passage is taken from an article written by a respected professor of philosophy at New York University for fellow-colleagues in the Modern Language Association of America—a group that was widely divided in its views on the function of the university at the time of this article. Professor Hook, therefore, is treating a highly controversial topic of current interest in the style of learned discourse:

> Until now I have referred to this philosophy of social commitment as novel-sounding. It should, however, be obvious that it is novel in form alone. The logic of its position is identical with that of those Christian divines who, convinced that the end of learning was piety, censored science, art, and literature in the light of the revelations vouchsafed them. There are obvious differences, of course. The felicities of the future life for the first had its locus in the Kingdom of Heaven, whereas Marcuse hopes for them on earth. There are also differences in the nature of the anticipated felicities. In the first, there is neither marriage nor giving in marriage but only the life of the spirit. In the second, marriage is dialectally *aufgehoben:* everybody loves everybody. Nothing is repressed and no one is repressed. But for both, once the ideal is imperiled by heretical and retrogressive notions, it must be safeguarded by withdrawal of tolerance and all that this implies in the real interests of the victim as well as in the interests of the truth.
>
> Sidney Hook, "The Barbarism of Virtue"

The assumptions of the writer about the audience are clear: that they are interested in the historical relations of thought, that they have some knowledge of his references without detailed explanation, that words which a mass audience might find mystifying are here used without ostentation. Further, there is close attention to matters of coherence and emphasis. There is variety of sentence structure and strategy. This is prose carefully constructed because the writer knows it will be scrutinized by a highly critical audience. Thus, the standards of learned discourse are those that are set by a restricted audience of educated persons, who characteristically write for one another without condescension or accommodation.

4. The Style of Popular Discourse

The style of popular discourse varies as widely as the audience it is written for. What all of it seems to have in common is an interest in communicating feeling as well as fact. At times, the feeling is expressed in a direct personal way. At other times, it is implicit in the choice of words and strategies that play upon a reader's emotions. Popular discourse need not be less serious in its subject matter than learned discourse, although characteristically it is written in a more flexible and informal manner which allows the writer's voice to come through. It uses almost any device that will convince, appeal, influence, sell, amuse, or attract a reader. It turns often to description and narration for purposes of illustration. It is a prose written from a personal viewpoint for a general audience.

A passage from E. B. White's *One Man's Meat* will suggest how radically the style of popular discourse can differ from that of learned discourse:

> I keep forgetting that soldiers are so young. I keep thinking of them as my age, or Hitler's age. (Hitler and I are about the same age.) Actually, soldiers are often quite young. They haven't finished school, many of them, and their heads are full of the fragile theme of love, and underneath their bluster and swagger everything in life is coated with that strange beautiful importance that you almost forget about because it dates back so far. The other day some French soldiers on the western front sent a request to a German broadcasting studio asking the orchestra to play *"Parlez moi d'amour."* The station was glad to oblige, and all along the Maginot Line and the Siegfried Line the young men were listening to the propaganda of their own desire instead of attending to the fight. So few people speak to the young men of love any more, except the song writers and scenarists. The leaders speak always of raw materials and *Lebensraum.* But the young men in uniforms do not care much for raw materials (except tobacco) and they are thinking of *Liebestraum,* and are resolving their dream as best they can. I am trying hard to remember what it is like to be as young as a soldier.
>
> > "First World War," written
> > October 1939

This prose has all of the marks of easy informality—uncomplicated sentences of varied length (some very short), relatively simple words except for the play upon the two German words *Lebensraum* and *Liebestraum,* parenthetical asides, and a brief narration to illustrate. The writer characterizes himself in this short paragraph as a man, who twenty years after World War I, finds it hard to remember how young a young soldier is. The manner is appealing; the tone inviting.

Even though some prose written in the style of popular discourse is clearly different from the learned style, it is also true that there has been a narrowing of the differences between the two. Writers of learned discourse, particularly in the humanities, often tend toward an informal manner and pursue their subjects with a kind of easy discursiveness that makes the prose popular in its appeal. The result is simply more readable prose without the writer necessarily suggesting that the audience is being talked down to. Most student writing, in fact, seems to fall within this overlap of the two styles—what might be described basically as an informal (but not casual) treatment of a subject, which by its words and ideas still assumes that the reader has reached an advanced level of education. A student theme will illustrate this kind of writing; it was written in response to a selection from James Baldwin's *The Fire Next Time:*

James Baldwin's story is not unique. It can be told and retold in various ways by other men in other cities. Their versions may differ slightly from Baldwin's; some more shocking than others; some less involved; others more ruinous. Yet all these stories are alike. Their causes are the same and their themes identical—fear, hate, mistrust, despair, apathy, and hopelessness.

Baldwin mirrors these feelings clearly. Even though he has found his "gimmick" and has apparently escaped from the clutches of the world he discovered when he became fourteen, his essay still reveals the fear and despair that he shares with thousands like him. He attempts to portray himself as a calm, experienced man saying quietly, "Listen to me. I know. I've been there." But whether he wants to or not Baldwin says more than that. He says "hate." He says "despair." He says "mistrust"—mistrust of society, mistrust of his own community, mistrust of his father, even mistrust of his God.

As I said before, these feelings of Baldwin are not unique. In fact, in the black community they are the rule rather than the exception. Nearly all blacks in the ghettoes of this country share this attitude toward life. It is not normal. This is not just "the way the black is" or a trait of the race. Rather it is a pathological condition in which the black finds himself. It is a continuing cycle of despair and apathy. Baldwin says that "... the girls were destined to gain as much weight as their mothers, the boys, it was clear, would rise no higher then their fathers." This cycle, of course, is the result of the breakdown in the structure of the black family. The family breakdown is directly attributable to the days of slavery, the years of legal segregation as a result of the infamous Jim Crow laws, and the black migration to the northern cities in the 1940's and 1950's. Slavery removed the black male from the family picture. It took away all his pride as leader of the family and source of authority. Women naturally assumed this role and were able to continue it because they were not a threat to anyone or anything. During the Reconstruction Period, the Negro faced segregation and Jim Crow laws. The male lost all courage and ambition, for the "sassy nigger" was lynched. With his move to the North, the black was still hemmed in by unemployment and segregation; and the family condition, rather than changing, became more and more matriarchal. Statistics on crime rates, unemployment, divorce rates, and illegitimacy in the black community demonstrate vividly what this family breakdown has created.

Our society has caused this breakdown. Americans have allowed it to continue. And now—today—we must correct it.

This essay begins in the first two paragraphs with the impulse that Baldwin's prose has given the writer; in the third paragraph, it includes historical and sociological material to broaden the implications; and it ends in a short fourth paragraph on a persuasive note—a direct appeal to the reader as a part of society to correct these ills. All of this is set forth in a flexible prose that sometimes piles up words in series; sometimes interprets Baldwin by a kind of simulated direct discourse, that is, attributing words to him as if he were speaking them himself; uses repetition for emphasis; and builds the sentences to a climax. All of this is quite different from an unimpassioned factual account; yet in paragraph three the writer shows his capacity to write a basically direct style of learned discourse, which is set down factually without commentary. In other parts of the essay, however, the writer's own emotional responses remove the prose from the category of a sociological profile of the black American.

The strategies that generate feeling in the student essay are even more obvious in any prose that is written to be delivered as a speech. The style of public address, therefore, represents a more generous use of rhetorical devices for purposes of persuasion.

5. The Style of Public Address

The style of public address is shaped by the fact that the writer is present and speaking to a group of people. The presence of an audience does not necessarily mean that the prose will be more informal; it may mean only that the writer will structure his prose more loosely to take into account the fact that a listener cannot easily absorb succinctly stated ideas. Generalizations need to be elaborated upon in order to give the reader time to reflect; they need to be repeated or paraphrased so that he can absorb. Crucial words need to be put in emphatic positions; sentences need to be built to a climax to allow the speaker to use his voice effectively.

Among the kinds of public address that continue to be prepared as written statements to be read are the sermon, the occasional address, and the political speech. The first example is taken from a book of sermons by the well-known American preacher Harry Emerson Fosdick:

> Come at this matter now from another angle, and see that hidden in this truth lies the reason for some of our most unintentional, and yet most deplorable hypocrisies. It is easy to choose the good in general, and then to fail utterly in paying the price of getting it. For Kreisler to say, in general, I want to be an artist, is one thing; it is something else to be willing, day by day, to pay the cost.
>
> The nations of the world now are presenting a fearful illustration of this truth. Have we not chosen peace? Is not that what we want? If anyone should ask for war, would he not be howled down in indignation? It is peace we want, all are saying. But the price of peace—the necessary surrenders of national sovereignty, the cessation of power politics, the ending of competitive armament, the shift of our economy from self-centered nationalism to co-operative internationalism, the overcoming of racial prejudice, the building of a real world government where such suspicious remnants of the old order as the veto power in the Security Council have been overpassed—these conditions of peace, that must be fulfilled as indispensably as in a laboratory the conditions of achievement must be met, we shrink from. Give us peace! we say; but not the cost of it.

Most evident in this writing is an ordering of words and ideas for dramatic impact. There are contrasts, there are rhetorical questions, there is a building to the climactic statement "Give us peace!" and then an intentional trailing off of the thought in the final six words. The whole piece is written with the human voice and actual presentation in mind.

A readjustment of the word order and a few changes in the strategies of the second paragraph will reveal how the total effect changes:

> We have chosen peace as the course we want to pursue. If anyone asked for war, he would be howled down in indignation. But peace has its price. It involves necessary surrenders of national sovereignty, the cessation of power politics, the ending of competitive armament, the shift of our economy from self-centered nationalism to co-operative internationalism, the overcoming of racial prejudice, and the building of a real world government where such suspicious remnants of the old order as the veto power in the Security Council have been overpassed. We shrink from these conditions of peace that must be fulfilled as indispensably as the conditions for achievement must be met in a laboratory. We say we want peace, but we do not want the cost of it.

With these alterations of Fosdick's paragraph, the style of public address has reverted essentially to the style of learned discourse. The rhythms have been changed; the sentences have been given a general uniformity of tone. Everything has been moderated to such an extent that the word "howled," carried over from the original paragraph, actually seems out of place, even though it is appropriate in the more intense and dramatic version.

The second example is taken from a speech called "The Black Revolution," delivered on April 8, 1964, by Malcolm X in New York City:

> This is a real revolution. Revolution is always based on land. Revolution is never based on begging somebody for an integrated cup of coffee. Revolutions are never fought by turning the other cheek. Revolutions are never based upon love-your-enemy and pray-for-those-who-spitefully-use-you. And revolutions are never waged singing "We Shall Overcome." Revolutions are based upon bloodshed. Revolutions are never compromising. Revolutions are never based upon negotiations. Revolutions are never based upon any kind of tokenism whatsoever. Revolutions are never even based upon that which is begging a corrupt society or a corrupt system to accept us into it. Revolutions overturn systems. And there is no system on this earth which has proven itself more corrupt, more criminal, than this system that in 1964 still colonizes 22 million African-Americans, still enslaves 22 million Afro-Americans.
>
> There is no system more corrupt than a system that represents itself as the example of freedom, the example of democracy, and can go all over this earth telling other people how to straighten out their house, when you have citizens of this country who have to use bullets if they want to cast a ballot.

The force of this passage is based almost exclusively upon its use of repetition. Each short sentence, parallel in form with the one before it, adds to the cumulative effect. The words and phrases are familiar, known both to whites, who constituted almost three quarters of his audience, and also to blacks. One of the themes of the speech, that bloodless revolution in this country is still possible, is reduced to a simple alternative: bullets or ballots.

The style of public address is, of course, not consistently declamatory. In long passages, it may be expository or conversational or anecdotal, but qualities that identify it as a special style are found in those passages which are designed to give the human voice free play with words and rhythms. None of the other styles employs rhetorical strategies so generously and flamboyantly.

6. The Style of Private Discourse

The style of private discourse is a highly personal kind of writing. It may be the open, perhaps unstructured manner of personal correspondence, doing freely what the writer wants to do because at the time he is writing to an intimate friend or relative, not a public audience. It may shortcut detail because the reader and writer share a common understanding of the background.

We are all familiar with the style of personal letters we ourselves write. There are no conventions to follow. We can make the prose what we want it to be. Much of the interest in the published letters of famous people lies in the new insights that we get of them when they show themselves unmasked and writing with no sense of doing it for the general public. A letter of the well-known American poet Theodore Roethke to the critic Kenneth Burke, whom he often addressed as "Pa" or "Pop," reveals both the openness of his manner in writing to Burke and the difficulty outsiders have in understanding references the two of them share:

Saginaw, Michigan
September 6, 1949

Dear Pa: Your post-natal letter received: forwarded from Washington.

I'm delighted, of course: and pleased that you've documented my pre-human history so extensively. As to the *Sewanee:* they've announced the piece, don't forget. Palmer has been very decent: why shouldn't he be decenter? Tell him that some of the *zeit-geist,* ear-to-the-ground boys in England like John Lehmann think I'm the only bard at present operating in the U. S. of A., that everybody is tired of Tiresome Tom, the Cautious Cardinal, and wants to hear about the new jump-boy, the master of diddle-we-care-couldly. They have to be told, the goddamned sheep. Boom-boom, you gotta believe. (I don't mean Palmer but the public.)

Sure, I'd love to see it, but that isn't necessary. Anything you say is Ho-Kay mit mich mir. Just so I ain't drummed out of Christendom, or that part of it called Academia. I had to do a loathesome solo job on me & poems for an anthology. I made it in the form of a letter to make the tone less odious: lifted a page out of that letter I showed you (the one to the lady critic). The whole thing ran to 5 ½ pages, but when I got done I had the sense of not really having come to grips with the subject. But some cracks seem pertinent and I hope I wasn't puke-making.

Only when the references are annotated can the general reader begin to understand the setting and the comments. In the second sentence, Roethke expresses his delight with an essay which Burke has written about him. Tiresome Tom is T. S. Eliot, and the lady critic is Babette Deutsch. The language encompasses foreign words, playful phrases, slang, and profanity. The tone throughout is unguarded.

The same kind of prose, which often shows little concern for coherence and unity and effects calculated to influence a general audience, may also be found in some diaries, memoirs, and journals. The second example is taken from the diary of Mary Walker, who with her husband Elkanah served as missionaries among the Spokane Indians:

Saturday, September 1 [1838], Waiilatpu.

It was decided that Mr. Smith remain with Dr. Whitman; that Mr. Gray go with Mr. Spalding to assist in building a mill, that Mr. Walker and Mr. Eells go to explore, assist Mr. Spalding, etc. I find it hard to be reconciled, yet trust it is for the best. We are short-sighted creatures, and know not what a day may bring forth. All will be right in the end, although we cannot foresee how it may be. It is very trying to me to think of having my husband gone. Inclination would make me wish to be where no one else scarcely could see me. Had female prayer meeting, a very good one.

Monday, September 10 [1838], Waiilatpu.

Rose early; worked hard as I could till Mr. Walker got ready to start which was at three P.M. After crying a little picked up and found myself somewhat tired. Oh! dear how I would like to be at home about this time, and see brothers, hear from all the good folks! I wish I could have a letter from some of them.

These daily notes, clearly unintended for publication, include routine, trivial details of everyday life, but of special importance are those revelations of inner conflict and nostalgia which the writer confesses to her diary. The topics shift rapidly; the thoughts are at times put down in fragments. The manner is strictly private.

The description of the six major styles given here should suggest that no writer writes only one style. He needs to write what is appropriate to his task and his audience. A scientist who would try to give a compact technical report as a public address would be doomed to disaster, even if his audience consisted of fellow-scientists. A writer who would use the style of popular discourse for a job that required only the reporting of facts would probably appear to be trying too hard. His use of learned discourse for an informal essay or a personal letter would be no less than pompous. The expectations that people have are conventional, but they exist nevertheless. It is probably true that the style of popular discourse is becoming more and more widespread, not only because it is the most spontaneous and natural of the public modes but because we encounter it most frequently in newspapers, magazines, and books of nonfiction. Every skilled writer, however, needs some range, some capacity to adjust his words and strategies and personal manner to meet the demands of varying audiences. He can make these adjustments only if he accepts the idea that he can control stylistic effects by the choices he makes in the course of writing. The flexibility of a writer, therefore, depends upon the range of choices he has at his disposal.

10

Toward Better Writing: Revision

Attempts to define good writing are for the most part futile because once the definition has been completed it may cover good writing of one variety, but fail to take into account numerous other kinds. Yet the beginning writer who wants to improve his prose style needs guidelines. What qualities should he seek in his own writing? When is revision advisable and when actually necessary?

First, it would be well to note that some writers are more disposed to revision than others; that is, they find revision a natural part of writing. They put down their thoughts spontaneously and then revise at a later time by cutting, adding, changing, or transposing. Other writers, however, seem to be able to get their thoughts down without the need for extensive revision. It has been said that Sir Walter Scott could send manuscripts to the printer without even rereading them.

As a general rule, most writers find that revision can improve their prose as long as they know when to stop reworking it. Too much revision can erase the spontaneity of the first version and leave the writer dissatisfied with everything. It is best, therefore, to think of rereading and revising not as a testing of every word and sentence but as an attempt to get some sense of the qualities, both good and bad, that the prose reveals. If weaknesses appear, the writer can concentrate on these.

What guidelines, then, does a writer use in making decisions about his own writing and that of others? Certainly, apart from the matters of grammatical and mechanical accuracy, he will want to consider the qualities listed below. Most of these are discussed at greater length in other parts of the book, and cross references are provided.

Some of the qualities are illustrated differently from others. There are examples that cannot be revised by the change of word or phrase or sentence because they involve the personality and thinking of the writer. They are qualities of himself that are written into the prose. To insert a change here and there would not get at the heart of the problem. Even though these are more difficult kinds of qualities to illustrate because they are intangible and intuitive, to ignore them would be to dismiss an important part of style. They are not actually illusive qualities. All writers have them in varying degrees, and they can be developed further. If a writer is anxious to improve his prose, he needs to consider all matters and questions that can help him. A beginning writer in particular should remind himself that the emphasis of revision should not be simply to eliminate errors but to work constantly toward a more readable and effective prose style. To do that, he must be aware of characteristics that mark good writing. These are spelled out here in considerable detail, and the advice attempts to say what the writer should *do* rather than what he should *avoid*. Some of these qualities overlap, but they are separated in order to give due attention to each one.

CONCERNING THE WRITER

10A EFFECTIVENESS OF VOICE. Are the statements made with confidence, or are they weakly phrased or unduly qualified so that the writer's voice is ineffectual?

Voice   Related discussion: pp. 11–14

Samples	Revisions
1. I think what is considered funny now is to a certain extent the same as what was considered funny twenty or maybe even fifty years ago.	1. What is funny now is basically what was funny twenty or even fifty years ago.
2. One of the major characteristics of a Negro in a big city is that he lives in one certain area. This area is generally not the best part of the city.	2. One of the marked features of Negro life in the big city is that it is usually confined to one inferior ghetto area.

3. Throughout the book Burgett expresses the violence in the world. He shows it with very good description, giving the reader a feeling of being part of it.	3. Throughout the book, Burgett reveals violence in the world by vivid descriptions which make the reader a part of the scene.

Analysis: In Sample 1, weakness derives from a hesitancy on the part of the writer seen in such phrases as "I think what is considered . . . ," "to a certain extent," and "maybe even." Such phrases are often useful as qualifiers, but an accumulation of them expresses doubt. In Sample 2, the weakness derives from the uncertainty of such roundabout phrases as "one certain area" and "generally not the best part of the city." In the final example, the weakness is chiefly a matter of vagueness. In order to strengthen the statement, the revision substitutes more specific phrases for "very good" and "a feeling of being part of it."

Advice: Try to keep a firm and confident tone without seeming to be dogmatic.

10B DIRECTNESS. Is there a tendency to fall into passive voice constructions rather than make straightforward statements of fact? Does the writer use circumlocutions rather than a direct use of the first person pronoun?

Dir   Related discussion: pp. 18, 116–117

Samples	**Revisions**
1. It could be felt that lifting this restriction would result in loss of valuable time.	1. Many people might feel that lifting this restriction would result in loss of valuable time. *or* I feel that lifting this restriction . . . .
2. Through John, the undesirability of such a system is presented.	2. Huxley shows the undesirability of such a system by means of John. *or* John illustrates the undesirable side of this society by his reactions.
3. Ferlinghetti's poetry is best when read by himself.	3. Ferlinghetti's poetry is best when he reads it himself. *or* I like Ferlinghetti's poetry best when he reads it himself.

4. Because the protagonist is attempted to be rehabilitated by a corrupt society, it is impossible for him to know exactly what he is being rehabilitated to be.

4. Because a corrupt society attempts to rehabilitate the protagonist, he doesn't know exactly what he is being rehabilitated to be.

5. To me, the man's remark was justified.

5. I think the man's remark was justified.

Analysis: All of the sentences can be made more direct and natural by supplying the agent and changing the verb to active voice. The use of first person need not be avoided in expository writing unless the nature of the writing requires an impersonal style. However, when a writer is voicing an opinion, as in Sample 5, the use of first person is both appropriate and emphatic.

Advice: In general, prefer active voice to passive voice, unless the subject is unknown or the agent is unimportant to the emphasis of the sentence. Prefer the direct statement to the circumlocution.

10C INSIGHT. Do the sentences make worthwhile assertions or merely echo the trite and obvious?

Ins   Related discussion: pp. 131–132, 145–146

Samples

1. Each and every college girl is different; therefore, each one is amused in a different way.

2. We can now kill a great number of people at one time, whereas in the beginning we could kill only one at a time.

3. If people were more honest, the world would be a better place to live.

Analysis: The obviousness and generality of these statements need not be labored. They indicate either a lack of perception on the part of the writers or a failure to think hard about the things they are writing.

Advice: Slice out obvious statements that are self-evident to most people without being written.

10D HONESTY. Is the reader persuaded that the personal voice is sincere? Is the writer conveying what he actually feels?

Hon Related discussion: pp. 11–14, 135–146

Samples

1. I was struck by Jarrett Boone's "Poem." It's difficult for me to verbalize what this poem means to me, but it is especially descriptive of what I do at night. Sitting in bed in the dark, I think. There's a peacefulness and quietness at midnight that one rarely has access to during the day. Some of the thoughts I have then "filter through" or some float around—the others, settled or gone, return at various intervals into my consciousness. It's rather amazing how precise and clear everything becomes at these times. Maybe I've been worried about something for days, and then one night, very suddenly, the solution sort of slides into my mind, whole and so timely it *is* refreshing. Like a mint, its sweetness can be tasted.

2. Since I am from the ghetto and dropped out of school, I can agree that sometimes it seems like an impossible task to get a good education. At the high school I attended, I got with the in-crowd. That's what I wanted, but this was a wrong move because these were the most affluent students and the best dressed, who had plenty of spending money and nice cars. The other students just settled for the fancy dress, which after a period of time I couldn't keep up with. This annoyed me very much, and I kept a chip on my shoulder and got expelled for assaulting an instructor. You see, because I wasn't able to keep up with the fellows, I caused a lot of trouble and almost ended my education altogether.

3. The return to the rough and tough ways of the pioneers is good for all concerned. Father may fish for delightfully-tasting Rainbow or Eastern Brook trout; the children may wander through well-traveled trails and pick blueberries, huckleberries and blackberries; Mother may cook over an open fire and watch chipmunks, squirrels, deer and occasionally the black or brown bear wandering through the campground.
    So, for a delightfully worthwhile and relaxing experience, try camping sometime. Can't you just smell the aroma of fresh, hot coffee being perked over a crackling campfire?

4. The most essential part of being "cool" is being an individual with a compatible personality—a person who could get along with most people, even people who have nothing in common with him.

This person would have the ability to compromise and gain friendship with an intrinsic motivation. This person should have a sparkling personality that gives others a refreshing feeling. This requires a good sense of humor and skillful gregarious techniques. It would make other people wanting to be with him. Therefore, being "cool" is having an almost impeccable image that shines upon others and being a compatible individual who has the ability to cope with different types of people.

Analysis: Honesty in writing should not be identified with unpolished writing. On the other hand, polished writing need not be thought of as dishonest. Sample 1 is not less honest because it ends with a figure of speech. In fact, that comparison has an appropriateness that makes the previous thoughts wholly convincing. The writing reveals thoughtfulness and sensitivity. In Sample 2, the facts speak for themselves, but what is important about the writing is its openness, its frankness, its lack of self-pity, and the clear sense that education is now of foremost importance to the writer. What is important about Samples 3 and 4 is the impression the reader gets from the prose as it stands separated from the writers, not what the writers might tell us about their motives or sincerity if that were possible. Both passages seem as glossy and idealized as the advertisements in the latest issue of *Sunset* or *Family Circle* or *Woman's Day.* If the writer of Sample 3 thinks she describes the "rough and tumble ways of the pioneers," then she deludes herself. If the writer of Sample 4 thinks being "cool" is displaying a shining image, then she has succeeded in being cool at the expense of being forthright. Writing can be a mask, as it is in 3 and 4, but it can also be a mirror of the writer in his own person, as it is in 1 and 2.

Advice: Use personal experiences and firsthand observations whenever possible; don't invent hypothetical characters and situations. Above all, be natural in the expression of feeling.

10E CONTROL OF TONE AND FEELING. Does the unrestrained expression of feeling achieve its purpose or boomerang upon the writer? Does the channeling of feeling necessarily work against sincerity of tone?

Cont   Related discussion: pp. 135–146

Samples

1. In evaluating a professor, I place the highest importance on the three following qualities: (1) mastery of the subject, (2) enthusiasm of the instructor for his subject, (3) the warmth with which

he regards and responds to his subject. (1) Mr. H. is very able not only in understanding and explaining the material, but also in relating subject matter to other things, idealism, beliefs, etc. (2) He is apparently eager to think about further implications of literature and readily accepts different ideas with a necessary amount of disciplined thought. (3) He showed warmth by his responses to students and his interest in literature.

2.   Get every person in class to talk—not just a few. Don't give your own opinions (although they're good) because so many individuals depend on them. Even if the student is off base a mile, don't raise your voice: you'll never get another response. Suggestion: Have a minor fraction of the final grade depend on participation. I believe this would stimulate some of the "bumps on a log" and make those who participate talk more frequently.

3.   He always came to class prepared with good questions and ideas to stimulate our thinking. He respected our opinions and never embarrassed or hurt anyone. If he disagreed with a comment, he would state why. I feel that his method of teaching was very effective. Until this course I had never enjoyed English. Now it's my favorite subject. He was very easy to get along with and was much more helpful than I had expected. He was reasonable in his assignments, although he was not an easy instructor. The questions or topics we were given to write about in our themes were easy for the students to relate to.

4.   I feel Mrs. S. has done an excellent job as a teacher. Her classes were intellectually stimulating to the extent that once you got out of the classroom you remembered what was discussed and made it part of your life. Through this class I have become much more socially aware of the problems we are confronted with in the world today and am able to deal with them better. The course has opened up a whole new world for me—one in which creativity is presented as something fun as well as beneficial. Reading became meaningful and the writing became exciting. I felt like I could express myself without having to worry about what anyone else thought. Mrs. S.'s class was a beautiful, growing experience for me. Our confrontations with poetry were enlightening as well as delightful. Her attempts at drawing the class out as individuals worked fantastically to the point where as a class we became one. This has never happened before in a class, and I think this closeness between a teacher and students is essential and very important to the relationship of learning and growing. The idea of the journal

of our thoughts was a new experience for me and one which helped me understand myself as I never thought possible. Another thing which impressed me was Mrs. S.'s interest in us outside of teaching as well as in class. Many times after class or during her free moments, we talked and discussed things which I was upset about. Her time was always our time and made readily available. I appreciated the interest she showed in us as human beings and not just as students. Very rarely is a teacher sincerely concerned with his students. When a teacher is concerned, I think that says an awful lot about the teacher as a person. This class was really a joy and a fantastic experience. I only hope I can take another course from Mrs. S. or that my other encounters will be as happy.

5.   He has a thorough knowledge of the material, and he seemed interested in actually teaching the class something. He was also willing to discuss problems with students. In general, he seems to be a thoroughly devoted instructor with a good deal of knowledge to transmit to the students. His main weakness lies in the way he presents it. Instead of lecturing, he should encourage more participation. I realize this is often difficult to do when the students will not cooperate, but he seemed to jump at the chance to lecture when the students failed to show an immediate understanding of the material. When the students fail to respond at first, it would be better if he would ask more leading questions so the students can dig out the answers bit by bit. This would help the student to analyze literature himself, instead of taking notes on the instructor's ideas.

6.   For some reason undefined, it annoyed me to have Mr. K. announce one day near the middle of the quarter that we need not bother ourselves very much with satire or *Gulliver's Travels* anymore. Our future themes need not be concerned with previous material, but with opinions on overworked subjects like race problems and education. Ecch! It shook my confidence. We should have pursued a straight line through the material intended. Once when I chose not to correct a certain commonplace paper, Mr. K. assigned me another paper, after I had already received a satisfactory grade on the stupid paper. (It was a boring paper, I admit.) But the second paper was on an obscure subject, which I thought wholly unfair. If I had known the alternative, I would have gladly, even joyously rewritten the first horrendous paper.

Analysis: All of the samples are taken from survey forms of student opinion and therefore record the responses of these students to their instructors in Freshman English. Among many varied responses, which ones does an instructor take seriously? Which ones say more about the writer than about the instructor? Samples 1 and 2 contrast two students who are both orderly in their responses. The essential difference is not that one tends to be positive and the other negative but that the writer of Sample 1 seems both sensitive and reasonable, while the writer of Sample 2 makes himself appear both dogmatic and uncompromising.

Samples 3 and 4 illustrate two highly favorable responses. Sample 3 is enthusiastic but controlled; Sample 4 is exuberant. Probably no one would question the honesty of the writer of Sample 4, but one might question her judgment because everything seems so indiscriminately "fantastic," almost miraculous. In fact, the instructor of this student reported that this young lady had come from such a restricted home and school environment that everything at the university seemed great and marvelous. The prose catches that glow.

Samples 5 and 6 record negative comments. The differences are obvious. The writer of Sample 5 attempts to balance good and bad, although the remarks hint more at dissatisfaction than satisfaction. Nevertheless, the student tries to be fair. The writer of Sample 6, above all, records his own peevishness and self-indulgence. The entire blame for his reaction is placed upon the instructor. Even though the comment raises questions in the reader's mind about the instructor's actions, it gives no basis for forming a clear-cut opinion about him.

Advice: Control the tone of writing so that a worthwhile idea has its full effect.

CONCERNING THE TREATMENT OF THE SUBJECT

10F CLEARNESS. Is the meaning unambiguous? Is the structure unconfused?

Cl   Related discussion: pp. 138–140

Samples	Revisions
1. A young adult's religious beliefs will be threatened by opposition from minor details, such as the stance in praying, to strong influence of atheistic friends.	1. A young adult's beliefs can be weakened by his resistance to the trivial details of religious rites (what position to take when praying) or by his susceptibility to the influence of atheistic friends.

2. Satire has some merit in that it is able to put the subject before the people where they least expect it.

2. Satire has merit because it can involve a reader personally before he fully realizes it.

3. In order to find solutions to the problems confronting America today, it is necessary that each group be represented by one of its members. But because the individuals chosen are mere members of a whole individual group, alone the member is ineffective. For the groups form indivisible entities and its parts, when taken separately, fail to function effectively.

3. ... But one person who speaks only for himself is limited in what he can do. Progress cannot be made until that person is able to speak as the representative of a united group.

Analysis: The confusion of Sample 1 springs, first of all, from the difficulty of making the thoughts fit into a "from˙. . . to" construction following the word "opposition." The revision eliminates this problem by using the word "weakened," followed by parallel phrases beginning with the word "by." The second difficulty arises from the imprecise use of words, particularly "opposition from minor details." The revision attempts to substitute a few words that make the meaning more specific, although the revision itself would suggest that the writer would do better to cast this sentence aside altogether and start again.

The revision of Sample 2 eliminates the humorous ambiguity contained in the last clause of the original. The example illustrates that words sometimes mean what the author does not always see and does not intend. The revision of Sample 3 attempts to eliminate a jumble of words in the second sentence, particularly the confusing use of "individual." Although the revision offers a possible interpretation of the words, it would be impossible to know precisely what the original sentence meant until the writer rephrased it in different terms.

Advice: Keep in mind that the writer may know what he is thinking, but the reader knows only what the words on paper are saying.

10G CONCRETENESS. Is the prose vague because the concept and words are abstract rather than concrete?

Conc   Related discussion: pp. 131–132

Sample	**Alternate Version**

Sample

Americans have always considered the problems of education. They want a good education for their children. Sometimes, though, they weren't having a major say, or sometimes they didn't want it bad enough. For a lot of areas in American education have been hurt, better teachers for one, buildings to house our students, the best of books, all have suffered. Why blame one area, why try to correct it in just one area? Because that one area in which action is implied won't solve the problem. It would be just the first step in deciding which areas will suffer for the benefit of others. The reason it won't work is because you are not improving the total picture, just going back to what you generally had to start with. We shouldn't discriminate within but rather go outside of the system and get help. This way the total picture will be improved, not just part for the expense of another. My value judgment would be that not enough value on education as a whole is being seen, not that a minority of our school buildings are getting too much value placed upon them.

Alternate Version

I have attended more than a dozen schools in California, Nevada, and Washington. Some of them were little more than a collection of quonset huts and portables, some a sprawling maze of well-lighted classrooms and landscaped play areas. Stadium High School, which I now attend, is a huge brick edifice nicknamed "The Old Brown Castle" by generations of students admiring its castle-like architecture and decrying its falling plaster and exposed overhead pipes. I have found these schools similar in almost every respect except architecture. The administrators and financial directors have been caught up by the rising maintenance and budget expenditures of existing schools and the need for yet more school buildings and more teachers. Teachers find themselves in larger and larger classrooms, some even teaching double sessions. There is a real need for more classrooms and more teachers: we hear it over and over again from journalists and educators. The answer always seems to be the same: criticism of the extravagance and waste in American education. Nothing is really being done to ease the situation.

Analysis: Both samples are the opening paragraphs of responses written in answer to the question, "In the light of your own observation and experience, to what extent do you think the United States places more value on elaborate school buildings than on expert teaching?" The specific nature of the question throws some light upon the meaning of the first sample, but much of its vagueness grows out of the writer's failure to focus upon the topic, leading himself into a general discussion of problems of education. Undefined abstractions occur in almost every sentence: "problems of education," "good education," "major say," "areas," and "the total picture." To be revised, a paragraph of this kind has to be reconceived in new terms, with an attempt to approach the question concretely. The alternate version, written by another student, does that. It illustrates how she starts by thinking in terms of actual places and buildings in relation to education. As a result, she writes a more satisfactory response.

Advice: Try to think in terms of the specific and concrete. In revision, consider whether some abstract words can be replaced by more concrete ones. If simple changes cannot be made, rethink and rewrite the passage in different terms.

10H CREDIBILITY. Are the statements believable in terms of facts and experience that we know or that the writer supplies?

Cred   Related discussion: pp. 67–70, 77–80

Sample	Revision
The one institution today which most openly practices the discouragement of ideas is the church. Essentially it tells its members not to think. From birth to death it controls its members' intellectual environment.	[The writing itself needs no revision, but the writer might possibly revise his opinion or qualify it if he knew more about the great differences among churches.]

Analysis: If this statement were made in terms of one particular religious sect it might be credible, although it would still be difficult to conceive the implied total control of an individual's "intellectual environment." Because the writer generalizes about all churches in terms of some churches, he falls into the *all-some* fallacy (see p. 77). The third sentence of the statement is also difficult to accept as an unsupported statement, but in the theme the writer goes on to explain more precisely what he means by that sentence.

Advice: The bald statement is impressive, but not often persuasive. In writing, consider the credibility of broad generalizations, particularly those that are unsupported.

10I SUPPORT. Is sufficient detail given to support statements that are made? Does the evidence given actually support the generalizations?

Sup   Related discussion: pp. 89–96

Samples	Revisions
1. We tend to laugh at others because of their shortcomings. For instance, if we see someone hit in the face with a cream pie we see it as absurd and very unreal.	1. We sometimes laugh at others because we see some incongruity between what is happening to them and what ordinarily happens. Thus when we see someone get hit in the face with a cream pie we laugh because the action is unexpected and absurd.
2. Paul Goodman labels subject matter, especially on the college level, as abstract and barren. He says that "the lessons are only exercises, with no relation to the real world. They are never for keeps." I agree with him to some extent. I'm sure that memorizing all the presidents of the United States is something that will stick with me forever.	2. ... I'm sure that being able to identify thirty-five passages of English literature on the basis of style and content will have little or no relevance to anything I will ever do again.
3. The blacks get along fine with each other, but it is the whites who are constantly fighting, not only with the blacks, but among themselves.	3. Last year, members of the BSU on our campus got along fine with each other, but the SDS-ers fought constantly, not only with the blacks but among themselves.

Analysis: In Samples 1 and 2, the illustrations do not support the statments that the writer makes. In the revision of Sample 1, the lead statement has been changed so that the evidence is appropriate. In the revision of Sample 2, a more appropriate example has been substituted. Sample 3 illustrates a broad generalization which is insupportable in terms of all blacks and all whites. The revision provides a similar statement in terms of particular groups at a specific time and place. With added detail, the statement becomes plausible.

Advice: Provide as much relevant detail as necessary to support statements that cannot stand upon their own assertion.

CONCERNING THE AUDIENCE

10J APROPRIATENESS: Is the language appropriate to the subject and the audience, and the usage appropriate to the overall style?

Appr   Related discussion: pp. 19–25, 136–137, 376–381

Samples	Revisions
1. I think meeting and knowing Gordon would be a good experience. If a person can come right out and say that criminals should be treated real nice because they create jobs for other people, he's got to be nuts.	1. I think meeting Gordon would be a good experience. If a person can say outrightly that criminals should be treated tolerantly because they create jobs for other people, I think he's eccentric enough to be worth knowing.
2. As for the adults who wish to crack down on this younger generation and teach them some respect and manners, I would like to clobber them all. They seem to forget that most of the vandalism is caused by a few. They wish to punish us all for being young. They advocate more police and stricter laws. They assure us that they know how we should be handled. The most saddening part of this is that they have no understanding of us at all.	2. Adults, although they are more sophisticated and experienced, tend to come to solutions which they think are best without fully understanding that young people's reactions are different from theirs. Teenagers, although they are often immature, have their own ideas about solving a problem like vandalism. Neither side, however, gives in sufficiently, and in the end harsh feelings result.

Analysis: The first sample illustrates the mixture of an informal writing style with a much freer conversational style. Phrases like "right out," "real nice," and "got to be nuts" are unobjectionable as everyday expressions, but, in writing, more precise and appropriate choices can be made, as the revision shows.

The second sample is part of a student's response to a topic on a college entrance test which described a public meeting of citizens who were undecided how to solve the problem of teenage vandalism in their city. One group wanted a curfew and a larger police force; the other wanted expanded programs and facilities for the amusement of teenagers. Students were asked to discuss which group they would support and why. The directions added the statement, "You are expected to express your best thought in your best natural manner." The writer of Sample 2, like the writer of Sample 1, shows some tendency to fall into speech patterns, but the writing is basically inappropriate in a different way. The student overreacts and lets himself be carried away by sweeping and thoughtless accusations. What we read seems natural enough, but it is doubtful whether it is the best manner for the occasion or the audience who would read the test. Sample 2 cannot be revised; it needs to be rewritten. The revision is actually an alternate version written by another student, who gives a more balanced and appropriate statement of the differences between adults and teenagers.

Advice: Choose expressions and a tone of the writing appropriate both to the audience and the purpose of the writing.

CONCERNING THE STRUCTURE AND LOGIC

10K COHERENCE. Does the prose have the necessary links to hold it together closely?

Coh   Related discussion: pp. 107–109

Sample	Revision
Is higher education suited for all students? Paul Goodman feels that "lessons are only exercises, with no relation to the real world." Philip Wylie finds that to the founding fathers of higher learning universal education consisted of "teaching everyone the language, simple arithmetic, and the structure of eighteenth century society. Science was elementary. Industry was nil, as we know it. There is no such society today." Yet their higher	Is higher education suited for all students? No, it isn't, because higher education still tries to make a general program apply to all students. Classes designed for all students are irrelevant. Paul Goodman thinks that the typical lessons of higher education are only "exercises, with no relation to the real world." Philip Wylie touches upon a similar kind of irrelevance in discussing the original concept of universal education

education has practically remained the same. They both feel that there should not be just one type of college institution, but a variety of schools where advanced instruction is taught so that all knowledge is represented and each student can pick where his interest and ability lie, whether it is computer processing, ancient Greek, or dancing. No more single college degree.

envisioned by the founding fathers. "Universal education consisted, then," Wylie writes, "in teaching everybody the language, simple arithmetic, and the structure of eighteenth century society. Science was elementary. Industry was nil, as we know it. There is no such society today." In similar terms, higher education seems to hold to principles of the past. It does not address today's society. Both writers see the need for innovations in the total structure of education that will bring about relevance. If varieties of schools were created at the lower levels, then advanced instruction could not be as much one thing as it now is. There would be no such thing as a single college degree.

Analysis: The opening question of the sample is precise. A previous paragraph of the theme has asked, "Are all students suited for higher education?" The second basic question, then, reverses the emphasis: "Is higher education suited for all students?" That is, is higher education suited for those students who presumably have the potential to do college work? What follows the question, however, lacks coherence for several reasons. First, the writer gives only a vague answer. Second, he forces his illustrations to say things that the essays themselves do not say. It is not surprising, therefore, that his examples do not seem to fit together. The phrasing of the quotation from Philip Wylie indicates clearly that he is talking about education in the lower schools. The writer attempts to make the statement relevant by referring to "the founding fathers of higher learning." Wylie says simply, "The idea of universal education sounded sensible to the founding fathers," and then moves into the sentence which the student quotes.

Coherence is closely linked with clearness, logic, relevance, and unity. The revision attempts to use the same illustrations as the original, but to use them honestly and to relate them to one another by appropriate explanations. The new paragraph has both an answer to the question and a thesis of its own to develop. The revision is longer than the original because it fills in the missing links.

Advice: Consider the gaps in thoughts that keep a reader from following the line of development easily. Provide bridges and links in the prose.

10L CONSISTENCY OF PERSON. Do the personal pronouns shift needlessly?

Person   Related discussion: pp. 14–18

Samples	Revisions
1. I think if I try to succeed I can. If one has the will to try and has people who want to help, you should be able to do something with your life.	1. I think if I try to succeed I can. If anyone has the will to try and has people who want to help, he should be able to do something with his life.
2. If a person buys something from Woolworth's or Kress's and one of your friends finds out, you will be laughed at and considered "uncool."	2. If you buy something from Woolworth's or Kress's and one of your friends finds out, you will be laughed at and considered "uncool."

Analysis: In Sample 1, the writer begins from a personal point of view; in his second sentence, he generalizes but unnecessarily shifts the personal pronoun in the middle of the sentence. The second sample shifts from third person to second person; the revision uses a consistent second person.

Advice: Revise personal pronouns that alter the point of view already established in a sentence or in the essay as a whole.

10M LOGICALITY. Are the statements rationally consistent with one another? Do they make sense? Are they organized so that the development is orderly?

Log   Related discussion: pp. 55–62, 66–81

Samples

1. I defend the principle of draft deferments for college students. In fact, they should give students who want to go on further deferments. As it is now, only medical students are able to get deferments, and mechanical engineers, architects, and many other students are not able to. The students who go to college and make

it through are very few; and the number that go on further are fewer yet. Our country would not be as far as it is if it weren't for mechanical engineers and architects, etc. If this country is to keep growing and doing things like going to the moon, all students should get deferments.

People are now beginning to see that we should give students deferments. Many of the riots that have and are going to take place are because students have too much pressure from the draft, school, and life. Because of this pressure they want the vote to get this pressure off or lessened. The draft is the main problem and if students were to get total deferments riots would be a thing of the past. Other problems that occur because of the draft are broken homes, deaths, and even killings. Many soldiers have come home with killing planted into their mind. It's a shame that this mind along with many others could not have been saved for a helpful purpose.

If all students were able to work without all these pressures, the world would grow and grow. But, as it is, the world is getting smaller and smaller, as if it were a balloon deflating. Soon if students aren't relieved of pressure, the balloon will be nothing more than a raisin. If the world is going to grow, the students' minds must not be confused with all the problems of war, just the problems of how to prevent it.

2. The Selective Service System in the United States faces severe criticism from many directions. Much of this criticism is well deserved. There are built into the draft extreme irregularities which cannot be justified. Contrary to our domestic policy of helping the uneducated and downtrodden, the draft seems to pick on these groups. Those with the education and money to afford college are deferred, leaving the poor and uneducated to carry the burden of the military. This discrimination may have been insignificant when a relatively small portion of young people ever got to college, but now these inequalities are heating up an already boiling racial situation.

Other inconsistencies are present throughout the draft system. With as much bureaucracy as exists in today's military establishment, it is senseless to continue sexual discrimination, despite the emotional objections to this practice. In testimony before a senate subcommittee, military officials revealed that over half of the positions in the armed forces could be held by women.

The conscientious objectors pose another inequality inherent in the military draft. The draft recognizes service to the country only in the form of military service, not allowing credit to a dedicated American, especially the conscientious objector serving his country through work in such organizations as the Peace Corps or VISTA.

The last inconsistency is the amount of time during which a man is eligible to be drafted. From the age of eighteen through twenty-six, a man is subject to the draft. It has been shown that even with the present deferment system, an eligibility period of two years is more than enough to supply the military with the manpower it needs. No one seems to be listening.

From this point on, there must be some changes—to a volunteer army, to universal service, or perhaps to a simple lottery. This is certainly a poor time to take chances with procrastination.

Analysis: Logicality, as opposed to coherence, is difficult to illustrate in terms of a short selection because it is a quality of the writer's mind that reveals itself both in the total conception of the topic and in the working out of the parts. These two brief essays, however, suggest the difference between careless and careful thinking.

In the first and second paragraphs of Sample 1, the writer touches upon seven reasons he defends draft deferments for students. First, he says that there are very few students anyway, and then he maintains that deferments are necessary to sustain technological progress in this country, to prevent riots (mentioned twice), to reduce personal pressures upon young men, to prevent broken homes, to eliminate the deaths of young men, and to eliminate the necessity to kill. There is also mention of the agitation among young people to have the voting age lowered, but the writer's position on this question is not clear. The logical progression from point to point is not apparent, all of the facts are not self-evident, and nothing is done to consider any of these reasons from any other point of view, namely, the nonstudent who is subject to the draft. Precisely in what way the world is growing smaller and smaller until it will be "nothing more than a raisin" is not explained. The reader's total impression is that in this writing there is more illogicality than logic.

Sample 2 illustrates a logical approach to the same general topic. The brief essay in orderly fashion considers the way in which present policy discriminates between the privileged and the disadvantaged, then between men and women, and how it works injustices against conscientious objectors and men of a certain age bracket. The writer of Sample 2 makes fewer points than the first writer and develops them more fully. His brief conclusion grows logically from his previous discussion.

Advice: Attempt to formulate some notes and a plan before beginning so the ideas presented represent a logical arrangement. In revising, start over rather than try to patch up the logic.

10N PROPORTION. Are the topics given space and development in proportion to their importance? Is the reader left with a sense of completeness because the topics are adequately developed?

Prop   Related discussion: 46–65

Samples

1.   Movies are one of the worthwhile national pastimes in America. They not only can be entertainment to the people but they also can be educational as well.

   People react to the movies in one way or another, especially young people in today's society. They take the movies as their guide. Rather than thinking of this particular movie as good or bad, they will try to follow the same procedures or patterns they saw in the movie.

   Strangely enough, many people do think that movies are parallel to education today. Movies can affect the younger generation in the way they behave. Producers try to simplify the meaning of the purpose of the movies for the people as best they can. But some people do take them for granted. Why is this so? The answer will depend upon each individual's family background and his environment.

2.   Of the national pastimes available, I feel bicycling is the most worthwhile. From the standpoint of exercise, it develops many muscles not used in our relatively sedentary daily life. Stimulation to the circulatory system can be invaluable to persons of all ages. The entire family can become involved together, including the grandparents who would otherwise rarely participate or exercise.

   The most important aspect of bicycling, however, is the beneficial effect on the emotional system. In the pressured world of the executive or the busy but frequently nonstimulating world of the housewife, there are few moments to relax and simply watch things as they exist. The schoolchild can be so wrapped up in schoolwork and extracurricular activities that he becomes nearly unaware of the world about him. The suburban family typically whirls in a self-absorbed circle. Bicycling offers an escape from routine and a chance to stand apart and see oneself and things about him.

   Analysis: Sample 1 begins with two sentences which state that movies are worthwhile because they are both educational and entertaining. One might expect that each of the paragraphs following would develop one of these points. Instead, the writer writes first about the manner in which young people indiscriminately accept movies as a guide.

The second paragraph then turns to the general populace, but its point is not wholly clear. Neither paragraph is adequately developed, and nothing is said about movies as entertainment. The reader is left with a sense of disproportion and incompleteness. It is apparent that this writer has major difficulties with writing, but he needs help first in the prewriting stage; he needs to focus upon a limited topic, estimate how much or how little he has to say about it, generate more ideas, and learn to develop them as fully as he can.

The writer of the second sample treats the same topic in a modest way, but the aims are clear. Bicycling, the writer points out, benefits both young and old physically and emotionally. Since the effect upon the emotional system is a less obvious point, it receives the greater emphasis. Despite the briefness of the treatment, the reader nevertheless perceives that the topic has been developed with a sense of proportion.

Advice: Consider the size of the topic in relation to the space available, make appropriate limitations, and develop individual points to the extent of their relative importance.

10O UNITY. Do the sentences have a oneness of purpose? Do the ideas have a point?

U   Related discussion: pp. 105–107

Samples

1.   The lust for power and material values corrupts the mind. The power of oil as an implement of war is a terrible wrong to humanity. Only for peace can we find true happiness. Today we seek peace for the preservation of humanity, but progress is making this a difficult task. Modern devices are slowly taking over man's mind. No longer do they conform to us but we to them. We are slowly losing our identity and individualism, becoming just a number. With the push of a button the destruction of the earth and its life can come about. Maybe it would be better to be dead than to live in a huge machine.

2.   In rock music there is a distinct and almost overpowering beat. There is not a single beat characteristic of the music today, but each song has an easily audible rhythm. As you listen to a song, your foot usually starts to pick up the beat. Before long, your entire body seems to be moving with it. Your head bounds with the beat, and there is no room for thought. Only the music is important.

Analysis: It is impossible to know precisely what the point of Sample 1 is. It touches upon the evils of materialism, the need for peace, the dehumanization of man, and the possible destruction of the earth, but these statements do not seem to support the topic the first sentence sets forth. By contrast, Sample 2 states a precise topic in the first sentence and in four succeeding sentences sticks closely to it.

Advice: Establish a main theme for a paragraph or an essay and keep the ideas related to it.

CONCERNING THE STYLE

10P BALANCE AND PARALLELISM. Do the sentence constructions meet the expectations they themselves set up? Do they satisfy the reader's sense of uniformity, balance, and parallelism?

Bal/Par   Related discussion: pp. 120–122

Samples	Revisions
1. James, a young teenage black, experienced an exhilarating, soul-searching encounter with God which he thought was something to cling to, protecting him from the immoral clutches of the Avenue and that would relieve his feelings of despair. It didn't.	1. James, a young teenage black, experienced an exhilarating, soul-searching encounter with God which he thought was something to cling to, protecting him from the immoral clutches of the Avenue and relieving him of feelings to despair. It didn't. *or* ... something to cling to, something to protect him from the immoral clutches of the Avenue and relieve him from feelings of despair.
2. The black motorist claimed that the officer was discriminating against him in terms of racial prejudice and not only because a law had been broken.	2. The black motorist claimed that the officer was discriminating against him because of racial prejudice, not because of a traffic violation. *or* The black motorist claimed that the officer's motive in charging him was racial prejudice, not the traffic violation.

3. Not only was he seeking self-respect, which he could not have hoped to achieve in his base condition, but also for respect from the white man, who had built the cage he was trapped in.

3. He was seeking not only self-respect, which he could not have hoped to achieve in his base condition, but also respect from the white man, who had built the cage he was trapped in.

4. The cartoonist brings out the satire vividly by comparing the tragedy with the trivial.

4. The cartoonist brings out the satire vividly by comparing the tragic and the trivial.

Analysis: Each of these sentences becomes more readable and clear by a few simple changes: shifting the position of words or using parallel phrasing in balanced constructions.

Advice: Take advantage of the effects that can be gained by balanced and parallel phrasing.

10Q CONSISTENCY OF FIGURATIVE LANGUAGE. Is the figurative language consistent with the overall style and consistent in itself?

Fig   Related discussion: pp. 133–134, 247–251

Sample

Revision

Putting on the breastplate of rhetorical technique and taking up the sword of Dante and the Bible, Buckley pulls out all the stops in this paragraph.

Using a full range of rhetorical techniques and literary allusion, Buckley pulls out all the stops in this paragraph.

Analysis: This sentence is taken from a student's analysis of William F. Buckley's prose style. In context, it seemed unduly elaborate; it is the kind of metaphor that calls attention to itself, not to the thought of the sentence. The image of Buckley dressed as a warrior playing an organ at full volume is an unintentional bit of hilarity.

Advice: Strive for the expressive metaphor, not the ornamental one. Be on the alert for mixed metaphors that turn out to be more amusing than meaningful.

10R ECONOMY. Is language used without waste? Will fewer words do the same work with better effect? Are the words redundant?

Econ   Related discussion: pp. 138–140, 380–381

Samples	**Revisions**
1. The Countess is saying in this statement that she realizes such evil exists, that she opposes it, and that this evil is becoming an undesirable influence upon her surroundings. This thought leads the Countess toward some idea of stopping or exterminating the wrongdoers in some manner.	1. In this speech, the Countess seems to say that she realizes such evil exists, that it is undesirable, and that she opposes it. This decision leads her to think of a way to exterminate the wrongdoers.
2. A baron in the English noble ranking is two levels of nobility below that of a countess.	2. A baron in the English nobility is two levels below a countess.
3. In the modern world of today, it is difficult to find completely isolated places.	3. In the modern world *or* In the world today, it is difficult to find completely isolated places.

Analysis: Economy in writing is not a virtue simply because it saves space. The economical use of words is good because deadwood obscures meaning, and redundancy amounts to saying twice what can be better said once. The revisions indicate how the thoughts of the original samples can be expressed much more briefly and directly. In Sample 1, "saying in this statement" is a redundancy; in Sample 3, "the modern world of today" is a particularly common tautology.

Advice: Consider how much deadwood can be cut out without interfering with the meaning or the natural rhythms of the prose. Pare redundancies.

10S EMPHASIS. Are the words and sentences arranged to gain emphasis? Have the most appropriate words been chosen to make an emphatic statement?

Emph   Related discussion: pp. 126–128

Samples	**Revisions**
1. The statement that was written was a good one.	1. The statement was perceptive.

2. There are educated people who engage in crime on an organized scale, and I would say that their purpose would be money.

2. There are educated people who engage in crime on an organized scale to make money.

3. As history shows, with the decreased control of the aristocracy over the working class, freedom of the press developed, which is an interesting point.

3. History reveals the interesting fact that with the decreased control of the aristocracy over the working class, freedom of the press increased.

4. That man is naive in that he thinks that criminals are an asset to the economy and he doesn't realize that they are a liability to the community.

4. That man is naive if he doesn't realize that criminals are not primarily an asset to the economy, but a liability to the community.

Analysis: Emphasis is an effect related both to the choice of words and their arrangement. In some instances, like Sample 1, the sentence might be quite satisfactory in a particular context. If the writer wanted to create a more emphatic statement, however, he might eliminate "that was written" (unless those words were necessary to contrast the statement with one "that was spoken"). He might also substitute a more explicit adjective for "good." The revision uses "perceptive," but other adjectives like "original" or "purposeful" would be more precise and emphatic than "good." The revision of Sample 2 tightens the prose for emphasis. The nine words of the second sentence are easily compressed into the phrase of three words used in the revision. The final clause in Sample 3 is the author's reflection upon his own statement, but from the reader's point of view it is an afterthought tagged on ineffectually. The revision incorporates the thought into the main sentence. The balancing of "decreased" with "increased," a substitute for "developed," adds further emphasis. Sample 4 demonstrates how a perceptive idea can be weakly phrased. The revision emphasizes the contrast of the two views by using the "not primarily . . . but" construction.

Because emphasis derives from many different strategies of writing, other examples of emphatic and unemphatic writing may be studied in the sections on Balance and Parallelism, Clearness, Concreteness, Directness, Economy, Effectiveness of Voice, Freshness, and Precision.

Advice: Look at various words and constructions that can be altered to produce more emphatic effects.

10T   EUPHONY. How would the written words sound if they were read aloud? Do the words read rhythmically?

Eu   Related discussion: pp. 125–126

Samples	Revisions
1. In the first three books of *Gulliver's Travels,* Swift jests objects of his displeasure in witty and imaginative ways.	1. In the first three books of *Gulliver's Travels,* Swift attacks objects of his displeasure in witty and imaginative ways.
2. Her world is based on values that mean something—something not shallow but which you can draw a sense of fulfillment from.	2. Her world is based on values that mean something—something not shallow but fulfilling.
3. I would like to know G. P. because he seems sensible, cynical, and sincere.	3. I would like to know G. P. because he seems cynical and sincere.

Analysis: All of the samples illustrate combinations of words that make the alliteration of sounds too obvious. The revision of Sample 1 substitutes a more pleasant and idiomatic word for "jests." The revision of Sample 2 not only eliminates an awkward alliteration at the end of the sentence but improves the rhythm and emphasis as well. The revision of Sample 3, although it cuts out only one word, seems to eliminate the objectionable hissing of the original and to create a rather appealing alliteration, as well as sharpening the antithesis of "cynical and sincere," which seems to be the point of the statement.

Advice: Consider the potential sounds of words when they are combined on the page, even though they may never be read aloud.

10U FRESHNESS. Is the language stale and meaningless because it falls too easily into the familiar phrase?

Fr   Related discussion: pp. 145–146

Samples	Revisions
1. A person who stubbornly remains unaware or ignorant of the other side of a picture is usually so emotionally involved with his opinions that he refuses to envision the other side of the story.	1. A person unaware of other viewpoints is usually so emotionally involved with himself that he stubbornly refuses to listen to other opinions.

2. Living in the ideal common-wealth is not all roses.

2. Living in the ideal common-wealth is actually less than ideal.

3. Everywhere one sees nature dressed in her best attire.

3. Everywhere nature is luxu-riant and beautiful.

Analysis: "The other side of the story" and "the other side of the coin" are clichés. In Sample 1, the writer uses only one of these, but his thinking in terms of these clichés causes him to write a relatively meaningless phrase "the other side of a picture." Here he falls into an easy expression without thinking that it does not actually say anything in this context. The revisions of 2 and 3 avoid the tired phrases of the originals.

Advice: Sidestep hackneyed words and expressions. A writer does not need to invent new words to be fresh; his main job is to avoid being stale.

10V NATURALNESS. Does the prose sound like the English language? Are the expressions grammatical and idiomatic and the arrangements unforced? Are the words and phrases idiomatic?

Nat   Related discussion: pp. 360–366, 373–378

Samples	**Revisions**
1. When people cease to toler-ate themselves is the time hy-pocrisy comes about.	1. Hypocrisy comes about when people cease to tolerate themselves.
2. With physical death does not, nor cannot die the existence of the achievements of man.	2. With physical death, the achievements of man do not and cannot die. [The credibility of this statement can be ques-tioned.]
3. These people are kept at a minimum as to being able to outwardly express their opin-ions, which is wrong.	3. It is wrong that these people are discouraged from openly ex-pressing their opinions.

Analysis: In Sample 1, the awkwardness results from trying to make a "when" clause the subject of the sentence. In Sample 2, the inverted structure serves no purpose except to make the sentence difficult to read. Sample 3 simply does not sound like English. The revisions eliminate these difficulties.

Advice: Rewrite involved and obviously unidiomatic expressions. Consider whether departures from normal word order add or detract from the effect of the sentence.

10W PACE. Does the prose move? Are the sentences varied so that the pace slows or quickens to suit the meaning?

Pace   Related discussion: 105, 110–112, 138–140

Samples

1.   One criterion is obvious and of special importance for the present discussion; namely, that sets of such primitives should be comprised of *observational,* or as we shall sometimes say, *experimental,* terms (i.e., that such predicates should refer to observable features of the universe). The import of positivist, pragmatist, and operationalist philosophies of science on the thinking of methodologically self-conscious scientists has no doubt been so pervasive as to require no extended comment here on this point. But from the foregoing discussion, it should be clear that one way of meeting the demand of experimental testability on any candidate concept that we are considering introducing into a theory is to introduce it through definition by primitives which, themselves, *are known to have experimentally testable reference.* Thus, an important by-product of the experimental-testability criterion for a set of primitives lies in the fact that any set that meets this condition in a theory guarantees that all new concepts introduced through definition will, in turn, be experimentally testable concepts.

> Richard S. Rudner, *Philosophy of Social Sciences*

2.   It must be admitted that when people speak of using experimental methods in social enquiry, they are frequently using the word 'experiment' in a narrower sense. They would not, that is to say, regard mere learning by trial and error in the normal course of life as satisfying the conditions of a properly conducted experiment. For this they would require that we also have control over the conditions in which we act, and arrange these conditions so as to eliminate the influence of factors other than our action. It is this control which we have in its most developed form in a labo-

ratory, and action under 'real life conditions' rarely attains it, even when there is a merely theoretical end in view. In any discussion of experiment, therefore, the distinction between the narrower and the wider sense should be kept in mind.

Quentin Gibson, *The Logic of Social Enquiry*

Analysis: Pace involves more than a variety of sentences to produce the right rhythms. It also means eliminating obstacles that keep the reader from moving easily, with understanding, through the prose. The illustrations above are taken from comparable books by two social scientists rather than from two completely different types of writing, like narrative and definition, which ordinarily move at a different pace from one another because of the difference in purpose. In neither sample is there a striking variety of sentence length. However, the length of the sentences in Sample 2 ranges from 20 words to 34; in Sample 1, from 33 to 48. The sentences of Sample 1 therefore begin at the upper reaches of those in Sample 2. An accumulation of long sentences naturally slows the pace of prose.

More significant, however, is the difference in the diction of the two samples. The prose of Sample 1 becomes bogged down in an impenetrable jargon and a mass of polysyllables. The sentences are overloaded, making it difficult for the reader to carry the burden of the thought. The writer of Sample 2 chooses a different vocabulary altogether, even though his book is addressed to a comparable audience. The prose of Sample 2 also shows careful attention to the linking of sentences, enabling the reader to follow the thought easily. The result is well-paced, readable prose, even though the subject is specialized.

Advice: Note that almost all elements of writing—the diction, the structure, and the style—make the difference between well-paced and ponderous prose. Read prose aloud to test its sound and movement.

10X PRECISION. Are words used accurately and precisely so that the meaning is unconfused?

Prec   Related discussion: pp. 130–131

Samples	Revisions
1. The main theme of *Hamlet* can generally be summed up in the Greek work *nemesis,* meaning the weakness in a character causing disaster to that person.	1. The plot of *Hamlet* turns upon the Greek idea of *nemesis,* that is, a concept that the gods demand the punishment of those who disrupt the harmony of the moral order.

2. To use violence as a means of obtaining a goal is a far too poignant dosage of barbarism for most people to sympathize with.

2. The use of violence to obtain a goal is a stronger dose of barbarism than most people can take.

3. Bitzer would probably be a great success in business, but a man so deficit of emotion cannot be considered a whole man.

3. Bitzer would probably be a great success in business, but a man so deficient in feeling cannot be considered a whole man.

Analysis: In Sample 1, the writer reveals he does not understand what *nemesis* means because he defines it inaccurately. The second example seems to be saying that violence is a dose of medicine that is too strong for most people to tolerate. But "poignant" and "sympathize" are inaccurately used. The third example confuses "deficit" and "deficient."

Advice: Consult the dictionary for various meanings; then consider whether the words mean precisely what they should mean in a particular context.

10Y VARIETY. Are the sentences sufficiently varied, particularly in length, to avoid a monotonous effect?

Var   Related discussion: pp. 110–128

Sample

Bob Dylan's message is clear to anyone who reads or listens to the songs. He finds fault with many facets of our society. The one I have chosen to discuss is war. These three songs were written prior to 1963 before there was a great deal of outspoken opposition to the war. So I imagine one could say that these songs apply to past, present, and future wars. The first two are about his feelings toward war and injustice. The last is, I think, an explanation of why he feels the way he does.

Revision

Bob Dylan's message is clear to anyone who reads or listens to his songs. Many of them, particularly those written about war, find fault with society. I have chosen three songs on war that were written prior to 1963. Because they were written before there was a great deal of outspoken opposition to the Vietnam war, one could say that these songs pertain to past and future wars as well as the present one. The first two songs tell about Bob Dylan's feelings toward war and injustice; the third tells why he feels the way he does.

Analysis: These seven short sentences, which vary only slightly in length, have a choppy effect. The writer avoids subordination that would give the sentences variety in structure as well as length.

Advice: Test the variety of sentences by their readability in context, not by arbitrary percentages of how many are subordinated or inverted or introduced by clauses.

SPECIAL
KINDS
OF
WRITING

11

Writing on Literary Topics

THE NATURE OF LITERATURE

Today literature is most commonly understood to refer to written expression, although much of what we now preserve in written form was once perpetuated by an oral tradition. Nevertheless, literature is a verbal art; that is, it is not dance, it is not music, it is not cinematography. It has elements in common with each of these, but each has its own identity and means of expression; each must be understood in terms of its own forms, conventions, and effects. Literature must also be understood in its own terms. But one further distinction needs to be made.

The word "literature" is frequently used in a very general sense to refer to the whole body of writing in a culture, regardless of its purpose. In this sense, both informative and imaginative writing clearly belong to our literature. In a more restricted sense, however, literature has come to be identified specifically with artistic forms of verbal expression, particularly fiction, poetry, drama, and kinds of prose fiction that reveal an imaginative mind at work—some familiar essays, biographies, autobiographies, and letters. All of these may be differentiated from prose that is designed specifically for explanation and persuasion. Thus, not much journalistic prose gains literary status, and seldom does technical and scholarly writing. The distinction is not necessarily one of quality but one of purpose and method.

If a writer, in observing the current scene, viewed injustices in the exercise of law, particularly in the courts, he could take the position

that civil law is at times not in harmony with a higher order of justice—
what he might call natural law or moral law. If he used such a term
as "moral law," he would no doubt need to define it and state what
the source of moral law is and how it operates. Then, if moral law
and civil law conflicted with one another, he would have to weigh the
claims of each. Conceivably, a writer could treat this complex subject
in terms of an essay, trying to explain and illustrate what the concept
means; he would probably proceed by fairly standard kinds of reasoning,
drawing out the thought in sequence, attempting to verbalize the abstraction.

Yet the essay is only one way of conveying thought. There remains
the alternative of a different kind of writing that can be made to
substitute for the direct presentation of ideas—call it a representation.
Typically, this is the way of the storyteller, dramatist, and poet. Even
though this way may be less forthright than that of the essayist, paradoxically it is capable of promoting greater persuasion and belief.

If anyone finds it difficult to comprehend an idea such as the
appeal to higher justice beyond the laws which men make and judges
enforce or of men actually being moved to take the side of one law
against the other, then the test is to read a literary work on a theme
of this kind, for example, Melville's *Billy Budd*. Billy is a youthful
seaman, an almost unnaturally naive and innocent young man. We
seldom meet people like Billy, but we would like to believe they could
exist. Or perhaps we would like to believe that we have an element
of Billy's innocence in our own nature. We become involved with him
as a character. We see him falsely and helplessly accused of plotting
mutiny by a strangely diabolical figure named Claggert. In a climactic
confrontation between Billy and Claggert, Billy strikes Claggert with
his fist and kills him. All of the circumstances are against Billy. The
military court is obligated to call the act murder under the dictates
of military law governing a ship in time of war, but as Billy hangs
upon the gibbet, we know the sentence has been cruel and unjust, that
a higher law exonerates him.

How does one come to such a conclusion from the story? Certainly,
Melville's story gives us little rational justification for belief in a higher
justice, but it does give us a strong moral conviction of a force operating
in our thinking and influencing our decisons. Melville makes us first
feel a position, then reflect upon it. He presents a paradox of innocence
and guilt strangely reversed. Billy is sentenced to die by the decision
of the military court, and we are left to accede to the practical and
pitiless claims of human law if we also believe that every man cannot
be his own law. But Melville also lets us know that Billy is innocent.
For a short span, Melville creates a world we cannot change. It is a
world in which the central issue of justice is dramatized by characters

who involve us not only in their own dilemma but in the total human dilemma of which we are all a part.

The Fictional Universe

Characteristically, literature acts through a world of its own; it creates its own fictional universe. It may be as completely fanciful as the setting of *Alice in Wonderland* or as graphic as scenes in *Last Exit to Brooklyn*. Perhaps one of the greatest obstacles to an understanding of literature is to assume that the literary work, even when it seems most factual, is an actual transcription of real life. Even when a writer chooses to be most faithful to experience, what he writes is only an approximation of actuality. We read only a digest, a selection of details from the multitude of words and gestures and actions that are a part of everyday living. In the universe of fiction, we encounter only segments and scenes of the lives of characters. Almost all of the repetitive details of everyday living are taken for granted—bathing, taking out the garbage, washing the car, going to the grocery, writing the monthly checks. These may be included if they provide the writer an occasion to reveal something of significance about a character; otherwise they are simply omitted in the abbreviated world of fiction. The world of fiction has an existence independent of anything else; it does not need to correspond to what we see about us. It is not justified by saying that it is very much like the world we know. In fact, though fiction may at times be grotesque, it is more often less strange than truth. It has to be. If a writer included in his story the kinds of incredible accidents and deaths we read about in the daily newspaper, he would be accused of cheap sensationalism. In creating an illusion of reality, a writer is first bound to what is probable, not to what is possible.

Even though the fictional universe customarily observes natural law and circumstance, it is not necessarily bound to it as the real world is. When the ancient storyteller chooses to have the goddess Artemis seize Iphigenia from the sacrificial altar and carry her off in a cloud to a distant land, he has introduced a miraculous event that dramatizes his concern for the innocence of Iphigenia. He would have us believe that there is a force which preserves good in the world. It is his viewpoint, not universally accepted, to be sure, but one that many people believe. The narration of the ancient myth, therefore, may not correspond to the external system of logic and law in nature we know, but it does correspond to an inner psychic system within those individuals who desire to believe in a moral and purposive universe. The rescue of Iphigenia is an objectification of a way of feeling and believing which is therefore not less true because it is improbable. It may be less true literally, to be sure, but not less true metaphorically.

Misconceptions concerning the fictional universe may account for the fact that many readers find a literary work "an alien structure of imagination." The phrase is Northrup Frye's. A literary work discloses an incomplete world; it operates on unrevealed assumptions; it functions internally by its own laws; it observes its own conventions; it promotes its own values. At times, it may seem like the world of experience; it may share things with it, but then it deviates. It may be a world that the author thinks ought to be, a world that he sees variously through his characters, or a world that he imaginatively creates to move man beyond the limits of his experience. But if a work is not purely escape literature, it undoubtedly has a relationship to the nonliterary universe. As we have noted, the world of fiction may not literally imitate the world of experience, but by imaginatively transcending the limits of time and place it is capable of becoming generally and universally true. One of Oscar Wilde's characters formulates the doctrine that "Life imitates Art far more than Art imitates Life." If this is so, one need not use experience as a measuring stick for literature. Literature may well set the measures for man.

The Influence of Literature

What is literature capable of doing? What means does it use to affect the reader? An attempt to answer these questions directly forces one to see that literature shares many elements in common with other art forms, even though the total effect of each may be different; but that, finally, literature is distinct from dance or painting or music in the particular effects it can create.

How, then, does literature function and with what effects?

1. Through character, literature reveals human motives; it invites identification and reaction.
2. Through actions and situations, literature brings characters into relationships with one another or into relationships with institutions and forces beyond their control; it reveals man in conflict.
3. Through its own compressed world, it focuses upon its central concern without being distracted by other details of life; it sorts out and orders the experiences of its characters; it objectifies experience so that it can be viewed as a whole and reflected upon; it shields the reader from the intensity of actual experiences.
4. Through form, it orders the action, shapes the thought, and channels the feeling.
5. Through the word, it creates effects of beauty and ugliness; it stimulates the imagination; it moves the audience to respond.
6. Through thought, it mirrors experience, embodies wisdom, anato-

mizes the world, raises issues, and searches for solutions.
7. Through style, it embodies the uniqueness of one writer's way of looking at things and provides us the pleasure of reading him.

The Genres

Among the various kinds of literary production, three predominate: poetry, fiction, and drama. These are the major literary genres. One might add to the list or subclassify them, but these represent three distinct classes because each depends upon its own techniques and effects.

Almost anyone recognizes the differences in appearance between a story, a poem, and a play on the printed page. Yet these differences do not take us very far in differentiating among the three. Ultimately, individuals begin to use phrases like "dramatic poem" or "poetic prose" or "a reading drama," each of which suggests that essential qualities of one genre apparently have fused with the essential qualities of another: perhaps a poem has the strong qualities of a drama, or a short story has the effect of a poem, or a drama reads more like a story than a play to be acted.

One is therefore entitled to ask what the essential components of a particular genre are, what characterizes it so that a writer chooses it as opposed to another mode to express himself, and why at times he seems to fuse the modes. An examination of three skeletal examples of drama, narrative, and poetry may possibly lead the reader to see more clearly what he is less able to perceive in far more complete and sophisticated examples.

The Essential Elements of Drama

In an effort to determine what makes literary drama, one might ask himself whether the following dialogue could possibly be considered a drama in miniature.

The Question Game

No. 1 is on the stage, not doing much of anything. No. 2 enters, apparently confused.

NO. 2: Where am I?
NO. 1: What?
NO. 2: Where am I going?
NO. 1: Where did you come from?
NO. 2: What are you doing here?
NO. 1: Why do you ask?

NO. 2:	Who are you, anyway?
NO. 1:	What's it to you?
NO. 2:	Why are you here?
NO. 1:	Me?
NO. 2:	Are you mad?
NO. 1:	What do you mean?
NO. 2:	Are you?
NO. 1:	Who do you think you are?
NO. 2:	Did God put you here?
NO. 1:	What?
NO. 2:	Is there a God?
NO. 1:	What?
NO. 2:	Is there?
NO. 1:	How should I know?
NO. 2:	Don't you know?
NO. 1:	No, of course not. *Pause.*
NO. 2:	Neither do I.

No. 2 exits, leaving No. 1 on the stage, apparently confused.

The first thing we should note is that there are two different sources of information about the setting and the characters: first, in three stage directions, the author gives us a few brief notes about the location (the stage is not actually described) and about the characters ("apparently confused") and about the action (No. 1 present, a pause, No. 2 exits, leaving No. 1); then in a series of twenty-one questions and two statements, the unidentified characters reveal things about themselves and about each other. Even though characters in fiction also converse and reveal things about themselves, it is drama essentially that depends exclusively upon this technique of self-revelation.

Through stage directions, the author also tells us that a change has occurred. At the beginning, No. 2 is "apparently confused"; at the end, No. 1 is also "apparently confused." In the course of the dialogue, we can see how the change occurs. No. 1 is at first "not doing much of anything." No. 2 enters and takes the initiative. His question, "Where am I?" seems to inquire about his location, but, as the dialogue develops, all of No. 2's questions have philosophical overtones. They are inquiries about identity and purpose in life. No. 1, alone and possibly self-confident at first, grows perplexed at the questioning, seems to become irritated, then possibly indignant (Who do you think you are?). He makes only one declarative statement ("No, of course not"), which could be interpreted as an admission of agnosticism that he has been forced into. There is a pause; then No. 2 affirms that he doesn't know either. No. 1 in a changed state, is left disturbed.

The characters do not actually say enough for us to be very definite about the content, but there seems to have been a brief conflict, perhaps more internal than external, then a resolution. There seems even to have been some change in both characters as a result of the dialogue. No. 2, only at the end, can affirm something instead of asking a question. No. 1 has had his state of "not doing much of anything" upset. Even though we know nothing about No. 1 and No. 2 as people—what they look like or even whether they are male or female—we know a few of their thoughts and attitudes; and, in these, they have a representativeness.

Nothing much happens in this miniature drama. It cannot be said to have a formal plot. But in a similar way nothing much happens in a play like Samuel Beckett's *Waiting for Godot.* It is a play about waiting. This brief drama conceivably might be called a play about asking questions, as the title indicates. In its telegraphic style, it is a drama of the dilemma of modern man—his sense of uncertainty. And this skeletal drama does precisely what a far more sophisticated drama does on a larger scale. It reveals a setting in which characters speak, interact, and develop; it comments upon the human scene; it moves us to respond to the thoughts and emotions expressed. This particular combination of character, action, setting, and thought, using this dialogue form and producing this effect upon an audience, creates a drama.

Is it a good drama? Most likely not. There is actually not enough to tell. The setting is too diffuse, the characters too unearthly, the action too static, the events too limited, the conflict too suppressed, the thought too undeveloped. But it is potential drama. And it should be clear from this skeletal example that not just any conversation produces a drama. Drama develops out of a progression of events, contrasts of character and emotional conflicts, either in action or word. Drama remains even when words are stripped away, even though it then gives up its status as literature. When a play is translated into dance, for example, movement and gesture substitute for words, but the situations and the juxtaposition of characters remain unchanged. Walter Terry once described Herbert Ross's ballet *The Maids,* based upon Genet's play of the same name, as "a superb dance-drama in which attraction and repulsion, desire and abnegation, physical union and individual isolation, and Genet's belief that 'profound unreality' passes itself off 'as reality' are projected through spare and powerful and cuttingly direct choreographic action."

Drama itself is elemental in its appeal; we use the word "dramatic" to apply to experiences that are lively, striking, intense, and emotionally moving. These are the qualities drama has derived from its theatrical traditions. A student reading drama as literature needs to keep firmly in mind its tradition as a lively art.

The Essential Elements of Fiction

Just as we have considered the elements that make up a drama and have tried to examine the genre in terms of an elementary form, we can proceed in a similar way with fiction.

It is useful first to ask ourselves if we think that any narration of events represents fiction, for example, the kind of story a writer tells in an essay for purposes of illustration; whether that kind of anecdote is actually an abbreviated version of the form we ordinarily refer to as a short story or novel. In most instances, narrations of that variety are accounts of actual experience, which in the brief space allotted to them must depend upon compressed action, fragmentary characterization, abbreviated dialogue, and simplified detail to make their point. Making a point is essentially the purpose of an illustration, even though as a bonus an anecdote may help the essayist to express his thought more specifically and concretely. In this kind of expository narration, the potential for storytelling is reduced to a minimum, but the essentials may be present even in an extremely brief sample:

> They had lunch together—husband and wife. He ordered drink plentifully, food modestly. She ordered no drink, food plentifully. She soberly attacked her fare, all the while her ear glued to a portable transistor, speechless. He, with wandering eye, smiled at me.

This is an account of an actual experience. It has no beginning in a traditional sense; that is, we do not know the circumstances leading up to this moment. It has no outcome; we do not know what eventually happens to this relationship. We are introduced into the middle of a situation that suggests any number of possibilities. A storyteller or novelist might do quite different things with these spare details. He might see the episode only as the beginning of a story that would develop the possibilities of the new relationship suggested by the momentary flirtation in the last sentence. (The word "flirtation" is already an interpretation of the smile.) Or the episode could also be an unresolved and undramatic ending of a story about two people whose loveless existence together has been traced in full detail up to this moment. Or, further, this particular slice-of-life, with its beginning and ending, might be fleshed out by means of dialogue, reminiscence, and interior monologue to tell a story about the conflicts that have brought the marriage to this stage of lifelessness.

A more pragmatic mind, of course, might argue that there is no support for any of these interpretations: that it is a passing incident of no significance, that it deals only with superficial details of eating, drinking, listening to the radio, and smiling. The fact that there appears to be an estrangement between the husband and wife could be misleading. The wife might explain her preoccupation with the radio as exceptional; perhaps she had to be away from home and simply did not want to miss the interview of a close friend on a local station. The husband might also explain that his drinking and smiling were quite innocent and unextraordinary.

These diverse ways of looking at the short written experience illustrate an essential difference between fact and fiction. Once the words have been written down, even in the brief form we find here, they have created a fictional universe which is possibly quite different from the actual experiences of the two people who served as the model for the written episode. Thus, we might draw a line of distinction between the life-drama in actual experience and the writer's representation of their drama revealed through literature. The difference between the two is the way we experience them. The particular circumstances of life or of a novel or of a play may not vary greatly from one another, but the form does. In the nonliterary world, we are our own observers and interpreters. In a story, we are told about the characters; they are permitted to reveal themselves only in part, as opposed to the drama, which depends largely upon the technique of self-revelation. We are observers of stories and dramas, but we are permitted to observe only what the storyteller or dramatist shows us.

If we return to the skeletal example of the story, we will observe that we are told about the husband and wife in a limited way; we must depend upon a narrator, who in this instance is not an all-knowing author capable of telling us what is going on in the minds of his created characters but someone present in the restaurant who sees two strange people and makes inferences about their lives. Even if the husband and wife were allowed to reveal things about themselves through dialogue in an expanded version, that conversation would have to be overheard by this narrator, directed to him, or reported to him by another character. If the manner of storytelling were altered altogether, eliminating the narrator, the author himself would be freer to tell us more about the characters. Yet limited narration actually comes closer to the way we learn about other people in experience. We ourselves are creatures of limited perception; we constantly interpret experience as we see it from our point of view. Because of this we can assume that the way a narrator tells his story reveals much of his own character and experience.

Fiction is characterized chiefly by its manner of narration. In the brief restaurant episode, the narrator selects details. We have no other perspective. In this version, the husband is more sympathetically described than the wife. We would assume the narrator is a woman, but then we do not have enough story even to know whether the narrator is a man or woman. Knowing that fact would alter considerably the implications of the last sentence. The incident anticipates the perennial triangular situation—husband, wife, and rival, but the identity of the rival in this instance would change the nature of the story considerably. In all of this, the author is actually an outside agent, a fourth figure working through the narrator. Even from this story in miniature, one might infer that this writer is not so much interested in the things that happen like eating, drinking, listening to the radio, and smiling as he is in the significance of these events as a commentary upon the marriage. Words like "plentifully," "modestly," "soberly," "speechless," and "wandering" are far more important than the verbs in these few sentences because they set a tone. They influence us to respond to the characters in fairly uniform ways. Narration permits the storyteller to be in much more complete control of his effects than the dramatist, who by the restrictions of his form is unable to comment upon his characters except as he has them act or speak in particular ways. Both drama and fiction depend upon scene, characters, situations, and language, but their form and techniques give each writer different capabilities for literary expression.

Today, fiction is the storyteller's natural medium. Once it was the poem, particularly the epic. Now, however, when a poem tells a story, it is identified as a narrative poem, as if to explain that the poem has borrowed an art not its own. Of the three genres, fiction is the latest to come to full fruition in the form of the novel, dating from the eighteenth century, and the short story, dating from the nineteenth. In technique, fiction is perhaps the most expansive and least restricted of the types, allowing the writer great freedom and variety, so that narrative prose can at times create both the effects of drama and poetry. Nevertheless, fiction is basically prose narrative, and the extent to which it moves from that base invites discussion in other terms.

The Essential Elements of Poetry

Poetry is yet another form of literary expression, another vehicle of human thought and feeling—perhaps the most misunderstood of the genres because it seems to demand the most of its readers. It is not primarily an acting out of events to be observed; it is not primarily a telling about them; it is something to be experienced itself. It demands not a responding *to,* but a responding *with.* The observer-reader may be frustrated with poetry because he thinks he needs more setting to see, more details to examine, more events to react to, failing to realize that the reader often needs to bring to the poem more than the poem gives. The poem therefore acts as a catalyst of the imagination and feeling.

Because poetry is basically a compressed form of expression, its essentials can be clearly seen in skeletal form. The following poem by John Nist is not as brief as some poems are, but it is purged almost completely of dramatic situation, of narrative, of special point of view, and of argument. It permits us to see what elements work together to produce a poem.

Revolution: The Vicious Circle

John Nist

bread!

b r e a d !

B   r   e   a   d   !

B   r   e   a   d   !

B   R   E   A   D   !

dead-dead-dead-dead-dead-dead-dead-dead-dead-dead-dead.

dead-dead-dead-dead-dead-dead-dead-dead-dead-dead-dead.

dead-dead-dead-dead-dead-dead-dead-dead-dead-dead-dead.

dead-dead-dead-dead-dead-dead-dead-dead-dead-dead-dead.

dead-dead-dead-dead-dead-dead-dead-dead-dead-dead-dead.

bread!

b r e a d !

B   r   e   a   d   !

B   r   e   a   d   !

B   R   E   A   D   !

A reader who wants to be told more completely what is going on or needs to be given more clues to what the poet himself is trying to say will find little satisfaction in this particular poem. First, the reader must provide his own setting and characters and actions. The limits to supplying concrete details to this poem are those provided by the title and the two words used in the poem itself. Further, there are no sentences. Nothing is said about "bread;" nothing is said about "dead." Nothing is said explicitly. There are only utterances.

Yet the form of this poem makes a statement. Stanzas 1 and 3 repeat the word "bread" so that there is a visual image of a crescendo of sound. It is almost a cry of basic need; it is a demand unknown people are making of an unknown power structure; it is the voice of revolution in a single word.

The response to that demand is conveyed by a different word— "dead"—in a different pattern. The calm, orderly, row-by-row arrangement suggests the symmetry of crosses on the graves of masses buried together. The poet reading these lines aloud makes them sound like the rat-ta-tat-tat of a submachine gun. His reading provides a second interpretation. One is not true, the other false. Both are there. One is a visual image; the other, a sound image.

The third stanza, a repetition of the first, takes the reader back to the subtitle. The cry cannot be stilled by oppressive measures; the cycle continues.

It should be noted that an interpretation of this poem results in translating it into a story, a situation, a drama. It should also be noted that the interpretation is not the poem itself. The poem is a combination of form, image, sound, and rhythm to which the reader is able to respond. It employs rhyme, repetition, and contrast. It appeals both to the eye and to the ear and to the intellect indirectly through the imagination. The significance of it is not what it says; it is what it does. If the poem is paraphrased, one might conclude that it says very little or that it echoes only a truism. But paraphrasing is not experiencing the poem—the way as a thing in itself it expresses the tensions of suffering. Even though this may be a poem about revolution and conflict, the poem itself promotes harmony, identification, and understanding.

Poetry, more completely than the other forms of literary expression, has the capacity to move from the world of outward circumstance to the inner world of feeling. For that reason, it depends more exclusively than the other genres upon the particularity of the word and the image to evoke feeling. Poetry as a genre does not have to have character, setting, action, and ideas, but it cannot sacrifice rhythm, pattern, image, and sound without losing its identification as poetry. These are its trademarks.

The Changing Genres

To think of genres as highly prescribed forms is to lose sight of the great variety of works that fall into the classifications of drama, fiction, and poetry and to ignore the continuing evolution of these forms.

Further, if anyone has a firm and narrow preconception of what a tragedy is, or a novelette, or a lyric, then he may not be much disposed to accept what experimental writers often attempt to do. When the stage director of a recent controversial, avant-garde production in New York announced to the audience that the intermission of the play would occur if the actors and audience cleared the stage, someone was heard to shout from the audience: "What actors? What stage? What play?"

A first step in writing about a work of literature is to begin with the work on its own terms. Once asked what poetry was, Robert Frost responded, "Poetry is the kind of thing poets write." The definition may have been facetiously given, but it wisely takes into account that our understanding of what a poem is, or of any other genre for that matter, must be able to change. Nevertheless, even though one should attempt to be receptive to changing forms, readers do accumulate certain expectations about basic forms as a result of their reading. Anyone who has read Dickens, Conrad, and Dostoevsky forms notions of what a novel is. These notions actually become criteria for criticism. If a reader thinks Keats's "Ode on a Grecian Urn" is close to a perfect poem, then the qualities that that poem represents shape his thinking about other poems. The touchstone method is practically unavoidable as a method of criticism. But it should also alert us to the fact that touchstones change and need to change. Students today are more likely to hold to Hesse as a touchstone for the novel than to Conrad. These changes are in part changes in taste and fashion, but one should not be misled that the present always supplants the past. Sophocles and Shakespeare, despite their age, remain perennially popular, and the schools are not solely responsible for their endurance, even though these writers regularly find a place in the curriculum. Poets of their stature survive because their forms and substance are incomparably durable.

In the present age that seems eagerly devoted to all kinds of change, it has been observed that people may not so much be seeking new forms as they are seeking new substance in old forms. Others may hold that no wise artist puts new wine in old bottles. Others may say that no old form can persist unchanged. Even if a poet writes a modern epic, he is not likely to follow the tradition of Virgil, Dante, Spenser, and Milton. He will emulate the spirit of the epic tradition in the modes of his own time. Epics are still being written, but essentially in novel form. The novel is the contemporary counterpart of the poetic epic. What a development of this kind may suggest is that completely new forms are not so likely to emerge as that old forms shift, divide, and fuse so that more flexible categories emerge. Knowledge of the past, therefore, will continue to serve both the creative artist and the writer who is seeking to understand what the artist is doing. The writer about literature will do best first to know what the components of literature are and then see how they are treated by a particular writer in a work that has a purpose of its own. To this end, then, we will discuss each of the major elements of literature in terms of drama, fiction, and poetry, attempting to make clear how literature functions and how traditional concepts are undergoing reevaluation.

Action

When in the *Poetics* Aristotle lists the six parts of a tragedy in the order of their importance, he puts plot in first place. To him, plot was not simply the story or the action; it was the arrangement of the incidents. The same story might be told by a number of different plots. Things that happen—actions—continue to be a major factor in literature, but as one thinks about the current scene, particularly in contrast to early poems, plays, and stories, it seems that a static quality has crept in. Characters no longer do things; rather, they make speeches or reflect upon or philosophize about the things they have done. Action is no longer even the heart of narrative. The clear exception, of course, is the massive production of murder mysteries, science fiction, and western stories, which still feature adventures, searches, and chases. A modern Aristotle observing today's tragedies, however, would be hard pressed to consider plot of prime importance.

Yet some action is implicit in almost every play, story, and poem. What the modern reader has to consider is that the action sometimes derives from the world of dreams and fantasies rather than from the world of observable behavior—not the mind thinking about physical acts but the mind producing its own private kind of action. The reader's job is to recognize action from whatever source it comes, to discover what is significant in it, and to consider what relation the action has to those elements the writer seems to give greatest emphasis.

The Events   As simple as it is to ask the question, What is happening? it is by no means easy to answer it. The reader's first obligation is to be as clear as he can about the sequence of events. In long narrative poems, and novels, and plays, the events may be fairly well defined and expanded. The more compressed the form or the more oblique the point of view, however, the more difficult it may be to establish the narrative sequence. Readers accustomed to rapid narration will no doubt encounter considerable trouble with Faulkner's "Barn Burning," merely trying to establish what is happening. Or in Pirandello's *Six Characters in Search of an Author,* in which the events are fragmented as if the author tossed the pieces of a puzzle in the air to leave them where they fell, one clue to understanding the drama fully is to get the events in the order in which they happened, not the order in which they are revealed. In Marvell's "To His Coy Mistress," some readers may miss completely what is happening, because the poem itself is a lover's speech, but it is a speech made to move his coy mistress to act with him like "amorous birds of prey." To miss the seduction that is going on is to miss a good bit of the irony.

Nevertheless, merely to summarize what is happening in any work is not advisable unless one suspects that he has discovered something that no one else has perceived. Determining the events is usually the spadework that one assumes of every writer before he begins. Yet student themes too often reveal that the writer has failed to start at this most basic level. What one can observe and describe, however, are the kinds of changes in action that take place. These observations are usually closely related to character analysis because in works of adequate length characters often grow and change, not always in terms of time, but in terms of realization and understanding. One can think of the relationship between actions and thoughts in two ways. First, actions sometimes influence characters. These are essentially forces beyond their control, like work, taxes, health, interpersonal relations, whatever affects them externally. On the other hand, a character himself often determines the action. Motivated by his own needs, desires, or ambitions, he shapes the things that occur. He causes actions; he is not acted upon. Inasmuch as the things that happen in a work of literature are the writer's invention, even though they may be based upon actual fact, we are obliged to draw significance from actions, either as they happen to characters or as they are made to happen. They are clues to change and indications of the forces that are operating to cause them. What is happening or perhaps not happening is therefore one of the sources of learning what a story or play or poem is about.

The Selection of Events   The length of a work to a great extent determines what is included or omitted. Short stories ordinarily embrace a short span of time and limited situations. Poems may focus upon the detail of a single event, sometimes upon something of seemingly little importance, like the widening concentric circles caused by a pebble tossed into a pond. If a writer wants to write a short story, his choice of form may influence the scope of the action, or he may have the action in mind and choose a form appropriate to it. The epic and novel (consider Milton's *Paradise Lost* and Tolstoy's *War and Peace*) hold the greatest potential for the panoramic. The drama is less compatible to the densely populated and shifting scene. Ibsen's *Peer Gynt,* for example, suffers from diffuseness. Goethe's *Faust* is essentially a reading drama, not easily adaptable to the theater. Shakespeare's *Antony and Cleopatra* is without doubt more successful in its revelation of the intimate love scenes between Antony and Cleopatra than it is in its depiction of the political and military events involving Antony, Octavius, and Lepidus.

During two main periods in literary history—during the fifth century B.C. in Athens and the Renaissance on the Continent and in England—most dramatists restricted their plays to an observance of what are familiarly called the unities of place, time, and action, that is, limiting the action to one setting, covering a twenty-four-hour span, and using a single plot line, omitting contrasting or supporting subplots and other episodes not immediately necessary to the exposition of the drama proper. What dramas of this kind lost in their illusion of reality they often gained in the intensity of their effects through compression. In a similar way, short stories and poems that represent only a modicum of action may comment more deeply and meaningfully upon experience than novels and dramas of far broader scope.

Given the customary limits of the various forms, the writer is still left to include and omit what he wishes. The reader is left to infer that what the writer includes he includes for a purpose and what he omits he also omits by choice. Analysis of literature, therefore, involves the weighing of all details in relation to the total purpose. Why does Shakespeare have King Lear at the moment of the old man's supreme grief and tragedy concern himself with asking Albany to undo a button? Why does Browning have the Duke in "My Last Duchess" lead the envoy down the staircase and point out a particular statue done by Claus of Innsbruck? These are seemingly unimportant details of action, but the writers have included them at climactic points as touches of humanity or means of commentary. Such details of action cannot be ignored.

Focusing upon Events   Both distortion and understatement are means of drawing attention to special events. Each is possible because each is a deviation in an opposite direction from what a reader customarily expects. From everyday experience, readers know in a very general way how things usually happen and how people react. This knowledge determines what we might call ordinary expectations. This is not to say that expectations about living and thinking do not change, but they clearly prevail among the majority of people at any particular time. A distortion of action or an understatement of effect, therefore, gets a special response from readers because they consider these changes improbable or unexpected.

Shakespeare's Richard III records the desperate measures of that monarch to secure his throne by conniving, imprisonment of enemies, and murder. But his efforts cannot offset the growing rebellion of the powerful lords of the realm. These are matters of historical record. But

Shakespeare, although he was writing a play based upon history, was not writing history. In scene iv of Act IV, he has a messenger arrive from Devonshire to report to Richard that Sir Edward Courtney and the Bishop of Exeter are in arms. Almost immediately, a second messenger arrives from Kent to report that the Guildfords are in arms. A third messenger enters to report the destruction of Buckingham's army—a message favorable to Richard's cause. A fourth messenger from Yorkshire enters to report that Lovel and Dorset are also in rebellion. The distortion of the time element—the coincidence of these arrivals—becomes a dramatic means of conveying the impact of these events upon Richard, and the compression of the time permits Shakespeare to have Richard stirred to immediate action against the rebels, saying,

> While we reason here
> A royal battle might be won and lost.

Here the depiction of the action is not historically accurate, but it is dramatically valid. A similar device of messengers arriving one after the other to report disasters is used also in the Biblical story of Job and retained by Archibald MacLeish in his modern adaptation of the tale. In all three examples, the overwhelming effect of disaster becomes the test of a man.

Understatement of action also has its own shattering effect. One would be hard pressed to find a more skillful use than the ending of Katherine Anne Porter's *Pale Horse, Pale Rider,* a subtle story of young love during wartime. Miranda, snatched from death after a prolonged illness from influenza during the epidemic of 1918, turns finally to a collection of unopened letters that she has willingly left unopened on her table. Encouraged to read them, she takes them in order—"What a victory, what triumph, what happiness to be alive, sang the letters in a chorus." But one of them is a thin letter notifying her that Adam her lover has died of influenza in a camp hospital. Miranda does not collapse. There is no emotional outburst, no hysteria, no cursing of fate. Miss Porter's closing description of Miranda going about the business of telling a friend what few items she will again need—lipstick, gauntlets, stockings, and a walking stick—and then her awful sense of aloneness—these understated details of action are as overwhelming and dramatically moving as any piling up of effects. Katherine Anne Porter leaves the reader with a paralyzing sense of the irony of the story she has told:

> No more war, no more plague, only the dazed silence that follows the ceasing of the heavy guns; noiseless houses with the shades drawn, empty streets, the dead cold light of tomorrow. Now there would be time for everything.

Observations of this kind concerning action in a story or play reveal in what way a writer is influencing our thoughts and feelings. Since a literary work is not bound to fact or nature, a writer is free to alter people and circumstances to the extent that he dares. His skill in doing so may be his major claim to greatness.

A Complete Action   Like many other critical principles, the concept of what completeness is derives from Aristotle. Aristotle defined a whole as that which has a beginning, a middle, and an end; and he continued by specifying that a beginning is that which does not follow something else as a necessary result; an ending is that which naturally does follow other consequences; and a middle is something which naturally follows something else as something else in turn follows it. One may think that his definitions are too obvious to be said. Nevertheless, even though his concept is a strong, inescapable part of our thinking about wholeness, its obviousness can no longer be taken for granted. For more than a hundred years already, developments in art, music, and literature have been undermining the notion that a whole is that which has a beginning, a middle, and an end. We have come to recognize fragments as wholes, incompleteness as completeness, disorder as a kind of order, and endings as a convenience, not a necessity. The first of these new concepts is already firmly established in literature and the others continue to make themselves evident in various writings that deviate sharply from conventional norms.

One of the clearest illustrations of the adjustment in our thinking about a fragment as a whole may be observed in our acceptance of what we now familiarly call slice-of-life dramas and stories. The phrase originated in the nineteenth century and now serves as a common descriptive term for plays and stories that do not attempt to account for beginnings and endings in the Aristotelian sense, that give us only a view of the middle—a passing scene through a window, an opening of a door upon a room, only to have it closed again without explanation; figuratively, a slice from the total lives of the characters involved. Thus, middles stand as wholes unless one insists that a whole must also have a beginning and an ending.

Obviously, every work of literature has some point of starting and stopping, and every work of literature in the same line of reasoning may be said to only a segment of life. Yet these concepts of beginning and ending and the idea of slicing out a middle are quite different from the logical completeness that Aristotle speaks of. What we now read may be only a beginning or a middle or an ending, not necessarily all three. If any reader's aesthetic satisfaction depends upon having actions come to completion or complications be brought to a resolution; if his aesthetic satisfaction depends upon perceiving the shape of a beginning and a middle and an end, then he will be constantly frustrated by much of the fragmented work that he encounters in modern literature, and in art and music as well.

The interrupted or unfinished or unpolished work is now praised, because in its incompleteness it is said to communicate less but suggest more. It has greater capacity to move us emotionally. The reader or viewer or listener must participate. It is possible that Dickens' unfinished novel *The Mystery of Edwin Drood* has prompted more imaginative speculation than the carefully worked out endings of all of his other novels. If the mystery is to be solved, the reader must do it. One can consider the work unfinished, particularly since Dickens undoubtedly intended to finish it, but one can also entertain the idea that any writer might deliberately stop his work short of resolution, just as Puccini ended *Madame Butterfly* on an unresolved chord. That particular ending, even though it is not logically or aesthetically satisfying, comments upon the action that comes before it, and its failure to satisfy does not make it less complete. One might argue that a work is complete if the author says it is.

In a similar vein, the fragmented and disorderly are now highly regarded as characteristic of both man, nature, and society. Not even science as it continues to make new discoveries can cling to its former theories of an orderly universe. The question arises whether order actually does exist or whether it exists only in art or whether it represents a condition that man imposes upon the disorderliness of the world in which he lives. Perhaps disorder is the "natural order" of things—a paradox that only art can reflect. A novel by William Burroughs is no longer an easy progression from beginning to middle to end; it is a labyrinth that the reader must work his way through and out of, at the risk of being lost altogether.

Once the traditional concept of beginning, middle, and end is given over, then the well-made stories and plays, with their set incidents and coincidences and intrigues and solutions, become passé. Once the concept of beginning, middle, and end is relinquished, then the entire Western sense of time is somehow irrelevant to art. Things can continue indefinitely. The music of Messiaen and Cage is not conceived and shaped in terms of traditional time. In fact, Cage writes that music is not a set experience with a frame around it; it is constantly manifest in all of the sounds about us, including noise. It can be experienced by tuning in; formal pieces of music tend to lose the dynamic quality of life. Popular ballads no longer end; they fade out as if they continue on and on. Once the concept of beginning, middle, and end is disregarded, then the whole idea of rising action, climax, and falling action no longer holds, because this view also assumes the traditional concept of wholeness. Richard Schickel, writing in 1969 about Andy Warhol's movie *Lone-*

some Cowboys observed: "I left *Cowboys* 10 minutes before it was over, on the grounds that since it had no beginning and no middle it probably had no ending either." What is apparent is that the reviewer was operating on a different concept of wholeness from that of the director. In fact, the best of contemporary movies—particularly those popular among young people—do operate upon different assumptions. A movie is no longer fiction translated into film. The film has become an art form in its own right with its own principles of narration and characterization, its own techniques, and its own concept of what completeness is. Much of what is innovative in literature today suggests that writers are attempting to adapt cinematic techniques to writing. It is wholly possible that in the future films will be considered literature, just as drama from the time of the Renaissance on has gained the status of literature.

Point of View   One of the fascinating things about literature is to consider the action from the point of the view of the narrator. Point of view is a less significant factor in drama than in fiction or poetry because in drama many points of view may be operating at the same time. Even though the author may be speaking through one of the characters, his is not ordinarily the only viewpoint represented.

In fiction and poetry, however, the voice of the narrator is of prime importance. That voice may not be the author's own. John Donne wrote a verse epistle entitled "Sappho to Philaenis." In the poem, he adopts the thoughts and point of view of Sappho. He does it as readily as Shaw writes speeches for Eliza Doolittle in his play *Pygmalion.* Always basic to reading a poem, therefore, is considering who the speaker is, whether the speaker is identified with the author, and, if he is not, who he represents and what kind of speaker he is.

In far more intricate ways, the point of view in fiction determines what action can be narrated. If the author's point of view is omniscient, that is, if he assumes the role of all-knowingness, he can include whatever he chooses to include. But space does not usually allow the writer to penetrate and make clear the motives of all of the characters. He may therefore focus upon several of the main ones. In the following passage from Thomas Hardy's *The Mayor of Casterbridge,* the author's omniscient point of view permits him to see the entire scene, to describe sounds both outdoors and indoors, to give close details of a woman's appearance, and to know the thoughts of another woman and her daughter:

> Other clocks struck eight from time to time—one gloomily from the gaol, another from the gable of an almshouse, with a preparative creak of machinery, more audible than the note of the bell; a row of tall, varnished case-clocks from the interior of a clockmaker's shop joined in one after another just as the shutters were enclosing them, like a

row of actors delivering their final speeches before the fall of the curtain; then chimes were heard stammering out the Sicilian Mariners' Hymn; so that chronologists of the advanced school were appreciably on their way to the next hour before the whole business of the old one was satisfactorily wound up.

In an open space before the church walked a woman with her gown-sleeves rolled up so high that the edge of her under-linen was visible, and her skirt tucked up through her pocket hole. She carried a loaf under her arm from which she was pulling pieces of bread, and handing them to some other women who walked with her; which pieces they nibbled critically. The sight reminded Mrs. Henchard-Newson and her daughter that they had an appetite; and they inquired of the woman for the nearest baker's.

In a somewhat different approach to narration, the author can voluntarily place limits upon his point of view and let one of the characters within the scene narrate. As an author, he therefore limits himself only to what the character can see and hear. In the following passage from *The Sound and the Fury,* Faulkner narrates from the point of view of the thirty-three old idiot Benjy:

Through the fence, between the curling flower spaces, I could see them hitting. They were coming toward where the flag was and I went along the fence. Luster was hunting in the grass by the flower tree. They took the flag out, and they were hitting. Then they put the flag back and they went to the table, and he hit and the other hit. Then they went on, and I went along the fence. Luster came away from the flower tree and we went along the fence and they stopped and we stopped and I looked through the fence while Luster was hunting in the grass.

"Here, caddie." He hit. They went away across the pasture. I held to the fence and watched them going away.

Once an author chooses a limited point of view, any number of other options present themselves. He can turn over the narration to the main character of the story and let him relate his own story, or he can choose any other character involved in the story to narrate what he observes. Each change of focus, of course, holds the possibility of an entirely different kind of story because, obviously, no two people view the same situation in the same way. One of the fascinating demonstrations of a story told from a variety of points of view is Robert Browning's long narrative poem "The Ring and the Book." In ten of the twelve books composing this long poem, we read the contrasting views of different characters and groups concerning the story of Guido, Pompilia, and Caponsacchi. The reader is not finally given the author's definitive version; the truth is left to be interpreted as the reader wishes to view it through the character of his own choice.

Thus, the narrator may or may not be the author. If he is not the author, he may be identified closely with him or he may diverge sharply from the author's opinions, just as if he were an entirely different person. Only the investigation of point of view in terms of particular stories and poems can suggest the rich diversity that is open to the writer by this means.

Suggestions for Writing about Action   Writing about action or plot depends upon being able to answer questions of the following variety as they may apply to a particular story, poem, or play:

1. Why has the author selected certain details of action and not others which we may possibly know from another source, for example, from a different version of the same story by another author (various works based upon the Trojan war) or from actual experience (Truman Capote's *In Cold Blood*)?
2. What is gained by the particular point of view the author chooses for his narration?
3. What particular effects of suspense, irony, or discovery are gained by the arrangement of the incidents, particularly if they depart from a straight chronological scheme? Why does the story begin or end as it does?
4. What significant changes occur in the course of the action that lend themselves to interpretation?
5. What elements of foreshadowing permit the reader to foresee the eventual outcome of the action?
6. Is more than one story operating at one and the same time in the same work (subplots)? Do various lines of action comment upon one another?
7. What characters or forces determine the action?
8. What are the key events in the narration? Why are these more important than others?
9. Why are some events that may seem strange or improbable included in the action?
10. In what ways are actions shaping characters?

Setting

Setting, of course, is closely associated with the staging of drama and with descriptive passages in fiction and poetry. In drama, the scene may be served by a simple backdrop and a few props, or, even if these are dispensed with, as they frequently are in modern productions, it can be supplied by the imagination of the audience. But in either case, the physical properties creating a setting are not as important as the function of the scene in the mind of the writer and reader.

The Setting in Drama A setting can be scenery against which the characters in a play move, or it can represent a symbolic force, acting upon the characters and reinforcing the thought of the play. The setting of Ibsen's *The Wild Duck,* for example, is conceived in symbolical terms, even though in an actual stage production the setting would demand nothing more than the usual accumulation of household furniture to suggest rooms in a house. Four of the five acts of the play take place in a combination studio-sitting room in the home of Hialmar Ekdal. Constantly referred to throughout the play, however, is an adjoining garret. A producer would have the option of making part of this garret visible to the audience, but he would not need to because Ibsen supplies all of the necessary details about it in the dialogue.

Inside the garret are nest boxes for poultry, pigeons, rabbits, and a wounded wild duck which can no longer fly; four or five withered Christmas trees; a cupboard full of picture books; and a large clock that no longer runs. One of the characters says that the books belonged to an old sea captain, called "The Flying Dutchman," who used to live in the house.

All of the details and implications of the garret cannot be explored here, but the relationship of each of the main characters to the garret is a means of characterization in the play. Old Man Ekdal has come to think of the garret as a real world where he can hunt and putter about; the young girl Hedvig loves the wondrousness of the books and the otherworldliness of the room; Hialmar Ekdal, the girl's father, is constantly tempted to spend more time in the garret than at his photography in the studio. It is alternately a timeless world of illusion, romance, and escape. Some of the characters in the play prefer the garret to the studio; some never enter it; some stay outside but look in. All in all, Ibsen has translated the theme of reality and illusion that pervades the play into the very setting in which his characters move. The play cannot be fully understood without considering their actions in terms of the scene.

The Setting in Fiction In Conrad's *Heart of Darkness,* the setting of the story is literal and vivid, but it is also a means for revealing the significance of the action. Each move that Marlow makes into the interior of the Belgium Congo of the nineteenth century seeking out Mr. Kurtz—a journey Conrad himself had taken in 1890—retraces the adventures of Kurtz's soul on this earth to its final state of deepest horror and savagery. A journey to another place would not have told the same story. Only the setting in Africa provides Conrad with the symbolic implications that he needs for this commentary upon mankind. In this story, as in many others, he describes a special world, a setting removed from the familiar scene and the usual trappings of civilization—a moral island, as it were—that tests man's essential values and capacities when he is released from the ordinary pressures of everyday life. The setting of a typical Conrad story is almost as restricted as a theatrical stage, and it must almost always be taken into account in speaking of the characters and the action.

In other fiction, of course, the setting may be a less integral part of the story than it is in *Heart of Darkness;* it may be provided only as if it were a landscape in the background. Modern writers, however, tend less often to treat the setting perfunctorily. The development of the social sciences in the twentieth century has placed such strong emphasis upon the total environment, including the actual place one lives, that a corresponding school of realistic writers in the late nineteenth century and thereafter devoted new attention to the influence of environment on their characters. Thus works like Sherwood Anderson's *Winesburg, Ohio,* Sinclair Lewis' *Main Street,* and James Farrell's *Studs Lonigan* are almost as much stories about places as they are about people.

In reading and writing about fiction, it is important first to dismiss the idea that description is only pictorial filler. Once beyond that point, one can begin to consider the possible intention of the writer in providing the details he does.

The Setting in Poetry At a particularly breathtaking sight, people are often heard to say, "Words cannot describe such a scene." Yet poetry among the forms of literary expression often catches the quality of the indescribable; it often succeeds in conveying what the writer has seen and thought and felt. Reading the British poets from Chaucer to Thomas is to gain a knowledge and familiarity with the English countryside that is second only to seeing it, and what they have seen in times past can at times no longer be seen. Descriptive poetry, however, is not merely scenic. It is often the point of departure for reflection, a typical pattern in Wordsworth's poems. The description cannot be dismissed as ornamentation. It is the source of the thought; it permits the reader to have some sense of the poet's experience. In "Lines Written a Few Miles above Tintern Abbey," Wordsworth first describes the scene, then comments:

> These beauteous forms,
> Through a long absence, have not been to me
> As is a landscape to a blind man's eye:
> But oft, in lonely rooms, and 'mid the din
> Of towns and cities, I have owed to them,
> In hours of weariness, sensations sweet,
> Felt in the blood, and felt along the heart;
> And passing even into my purer mind,
> With tranquil restoration:—feelings too

Of unremembered pleasure: such, perhaps,
As have no slight or trivial influence
On that best portion of a good man's life,
His little, nameless, unremembered, acts
Of kindness and of love. Nor less, I trust,
To them I may have owed another gift,
Of aspect more sublime; that blessed mood,
In which the burthen of the mystery,
In which the heavy and the weary weight
Of all this unintelligible world,
Is lightened . . . .

The setting is the inspiration of the poem.

In other kinds of poems, more dramatic in quality, the description serves as a substitute for a stage. Often, however, the scene needs to be inferred, as in Archibald MacLeish's short poem "The End of the World:"

Quite unexpectedly as Vasserot
The armless ambidextrian was lighting
A match between his great and second toe
And Ralph the lion was engaged in biting
The neck of Madame Sossman while the drum
Pointed, and Teeny was about to cough
In waltz-time swinging Jocko by the thumb—
Quite unexpectedly the top blew off:

And there, there overhead, there, there, hung over
Those thousands of white faces, those dazed eyes,
There in the starless dark the poise, the hover,
There with vast wings across the canceled skies,
There in the sudden blackness the black pall
Of nothing, nothing, nothing—nothing at all.

In this poem, the setting itself is a metaphor: the world is a circus, a variation upon those more familiar lines from Shakespeare:

All the world's a stage
And all the men and women merely players.

MacLeish again used the particular implications of the circus metaphor years later when he wrote his drama *J.B.*, based upon the story of Job. In that play, all of the action takes place inside a circus tent—a kind of total universe that includes man and God.

In a poem entitled "Come Up from the Fields Father," Whitman describes the reactions of a family to a letter carrying word that the only son has been gravely wounded in the war. The poem begins with the lines:

> Come up from the fields father, here's a letter
> from our Pete,
> And come to the front door mother, here's
> a letter from thy dear son.

After this brief stanza with its sense of foreboding, the narrative shifts to describe the setting, but the reader learns almost immediately that Whitman is providing more than a physical setting, he is describing an emotional setting for the news that will arrive:

> Lo, 'tis autumn,
> Lo, where the trees, deeper green, yellower and redder,
> Cool and sweeten Ohio's villages with leaves fluttering in the moderate
> wind,
> Where apples ripe in the orchards hang and grapes on the trellis'd
> vines,
> (Smell you the smell of the grapes on the vines?
> Smell you the buckwheat where the bees were lately buzzing?)
> Above all, lo, the sky so calm, so transparent after the rain, and with
> wondrous clouds,
> Below too, all calm, all vital and beautiful, and the farm prospers
> well.

Into this world of calm and sensuous delicacy, the harsh news of the outside world comes as a stroke of lightning. Thereafter, we read of trembling and grief and, finally, death. The contrast the poet provides serves to intensify the feeling.

Contemporaneity of the Setting   The contemporaneity of a setting is not always a matter of its familiarity. Writers have characteristically sought parallels to the modern scene in the past. Thus, readers are permitted to look with detachment upon situations that seem removed from immediate experience, even though they realize the writer is commenting upon current issues or problems very close to them. Thus, Giraudoux sets his play *Tiger at the Gates* in ancient Troy, and the war between the Greeks and Trojans serves as the background of the dialogue. As *Tiger at the Gates* continues to enjoy revivals, it is apparent that it is a perennial commentary upon the theme of man and warfare. Yet the play, written by a man who was a member of the French government, has special relevance to the situation in France in 1935 when the play first appeared. The scene of Giraudoux's play is a strategy that actually aids the reader in gaining a perspective upon current turmoil. Of course, writers of stories, novels, and poems utilize the same technique. The revival of the past is a constant reminder not only that there is nothing much new in human affairs but also that the past holds infinite wisdom for the future.

Suggestions for Writing about Setting   To give a few examples of the uses of setting in literary works is only to suggest in this short discussion the kind of thought and emotional impact setting can convey, not to explore the full range of possibilities. The reader needs first to be aware of setting, then to look at details. These offer him an opportunity to interpret. One recalls Melville's use of a high brick wall in "Bartleby the Scrivener" to objectify the insurmountable barrier within Bartleby's mind. Or Chekhov's use of the barren cherry trees in his play *The Cherry Orchard* to comment, not without irony, upon the changing social and political scene in Russia of the early twentieth century. These are all imaginative means of involving the reader in a concrete experience, tied to a place and time, and valuable clues to the thought of the literature.

Writing about setting will first involve some description in order to provide the reader with details of the scene that will be considered. The second important step, however, is to reveal in what way the setting functions in the literary work. Questions of the following kind will provide guides for the reader:

1. In a play, how much detail do the stage directions give in describing the setting? Is the playwright explicit, or does he leave the scene to be interpreted in various ways by scene designer and stage director? Can the reader also supply an interpretation? In what way could the play be staged meaningfully?
2. If stage directions are sparse, to what extent can the setting be reconstructed from the dialogue?
3. In a story or play, to what extent is the setting literally realistic or symbolical? If it is symbolical, in what way does the setting function?
4. In a literary work, in what way does the setting relate significantly to the action?
5. In what way does a character's response to the setting reveal things about him?
6. In what way is the setting a reinforcement of the theme of the work?
7. Particularly in poems, is the setting the point of departure for the thought or emotion expressed? Does it serve as contrast? Does the

description supply commentary upon the author or the speaker in
the poem?

8. How is description narrated? Who is telling what he sees and what
is happening? What difference does the point of view make in the
nature of the description? What methods of description are used?
Does the writer depend upon precise details, lyrical suggestion,
comparisons, and allusions? What is the effect upon the reader?

9. If the scene is remote in time or place, what correspondences can
be found in the details of setting and situation that will permit
the reader to draw parallels between the past and the present? How
contemporaneous is the setting?

10. To what extent do elements of nature or of the environment become
active forces in the literary work, changing the action and determining the fate of characters?

Character

Literary characters are those creations that permit the artist to
play deity—to populate a fictional universe with people and creatures
of his own making. This power of creativity exceeds man's capacity
to reproduce, for in physical reproduction the offspring is determined
by natural law and heredity. The imagination can exceed those bounds;
it can permit man to create what his body cannot. Early mythology
is filled with hybrid beings—part woman and part serpent, part man
and goat, part woman, lion, and bird. But the imaginative power of
a writer is not measured by his capacity to create the grotesque but
by his ability to shape with words an artistic world so that readers
will view it with credibility.

If the world of a story is pure fantasy, the author must describe
it so that readers believe imaginatively what they have not seen. If
there are people who are unfamiliar, he must reveal them or let them
reveal themselves by their words and actions so that readers know them.
Unless characters say something, do something, interact, or have something happen to them, they are no more than mannequins on display.
Within the confines of a novel's length or a play's duration, the writer
causes us to identify and involve ourselves emotionally with his characters, or to withdraw ourselves from them and look at them with detachment and criticism, or to react to them indifferently. An indifferent
response by the reader is a sign that the artist has failed or that the
reader has failed to take into consideration what the writer intends
to do. At times, it is difficult to decide in modern works whether the
writer is inviting us to believe in his characters or to laugh at their
absurdities. Perhaps in a paradoxical way one can do both.

The Independent Life of Characters   One of the major misjudgments which many readers make about literature is to measure all characters by a single standard: their lifelikeness. Characters are not all alike and cannot be written about as if they were living creatures who exist in our own private surroundings. It matters little whether Macbeth would be a good or bad next-door neighbor; it does matter that he betrayed King Duncan for his own self-interest. It matters little whether the mad Ophelia would be good fun at a rock festival; it does matter that the fragile girl has understandably collapsed under the burdens which confront her in the play. In short, literary characters must be considered in their own literary environments, and the reader must consider the nature of the story before he dismisses any character as "unreal," "unbelievable," or "unlikely" because "people don't act that way." In writing about literature, one needs always to take into account different kinds of characters, the dimensions they assume, and the roles they are given in any particular story or play.

Stereotypes   A stereotype is a conventional character representing a particular group or class or occupation. Because the character is conventional, he acts according to set patterns. His appearance is familiar; his speech predictable; his actions patterned. Thus anyone who has read a story or seen an old movie knows how to impersonate a southern gentleman, a Jewish mamma, or a British lord with the aid of only a few gestures, props, and speech intonations. Imitations of this kind border upon caricature; that is, they take identifiable characteristics of people and exaggerate them. People get classified by this means.

All stereotyping, of course, is not caricature, but it is a simplified way of looking at people as representatives of a group rather than as individuals. In Giraudoux's *Madwoman of Chaillot* the cast includes characters such as The President, The Ragpicker, Prospector, Doorman, and Sewer Man, all unnamed, identified only by their rank or occupation. Yet these are not wholly wooden characters. Stereotypes often seem true to experience, not because they are exact replicas of people who walk the streets but because people whom we meet show some of the same traits of talking, dressing, and acting associated with types: hard sell with salesmen, beads with hippies, and shuffling with cowboys. Unquestionably, stereotypes in literature and other art forms have had their effect upon social attitudes, often with serious and unjust consequences. Stereotyping conditions the way we look at one another, so that we tend to see a type that may not be at all accurate. Typing is a superficial way of looking at people.

Despite the serious social and personal implications of stereotyping, it persists in literature as a quick means of characterization. The typical senator, the typical Texan, the typical evangelist—these are all characterizations that may be used by a writer for a purpose, perhaps for comedy or satire. Because background characters of a story or drama make only brief appearances, they may have to be made recognizable quickly by typing devices. Bertolt Brecht, the German playwright and producer, knowing that typing sets the audience's expectations and dulls human perception, often defied physical stereotypes by deliberately avoiding type casting: calling for cooks who were thin, statesmen who were unstately, and lovers who were ugly. He was interested in having an audience respond to the characters as presented, not in terms of preconceptions of them.

To label a literary figure as a type does not provide an individual much material for writing, but it does help as a starter if one can estimate how far beyond the typical a particular characterization moves. The Nurse in *Romeo and Juliet,* for example, could have been only a functional type, performing routine duties and making brief, innocuous responses. As it is, she does far more, but this limited conception of a servant role in other plays makes clear how far Shakespeare has gone to create an individual and colorful character who defies the conventions of her role.

Stock Characters   Closely related to stereotypes are stock characters. Even though the work "stock" has close associations with drama, stock figures occur in other genres as well. They are figures who because of their customary association with a dramatic situation have become conventions. Thus in Ovid's elegies, a young wife and a secret lover are haunted by the jealous eyes of an old and repulsive husband. These are stock figures who have been recast with variations over and over again throughout literature. The triangle situation is, of course, perennial. The philandering husband is as common as the erring young wife within the triangle.

Today we tend to identify the stock villain with a snarling, moustachioed character of nineteenth-century melodrama, but that figure is only an exaggerated portrayal of a long tradition of dark villains, including giants, misers, and magicians who pervade even the early mythology and literature. Among other stock characters, one could talk of established traditions of fools, scapegoats, sworn brothers, and fallen women. These traditions, which can be traced wherever and whenever a written literature is still extant, are a fascinating study, but they are not an indispensable condition for understanding characters in any particular story or play. To see how Falstaff is a variation of a stock comic figure of the braggart soldier in Roman comedy or how Hamlet fits into the tradition of the revenge hero helps the reader to come to a deeper understanding of Shakespeare's powers of characterization, but this knowledge is not necessary to respond to these characters as they are revealed in the play.

Stock figures need not be typically portrayed. Willy Loman in Arthur Miller's *Death of a Salesman* might be considered the stock figure of the traveling salesman, but Miller does not treat Willy Loman in stock situations. Even though the world of salesmanship has been his whole life, the play itself focuses upon Willy's private life as a husband and father. As a consequence, *Death of a Salesman* seldom permits the audience to cater to its stock responses. Willy Loman is one of the most pathetic of modern characters—a far departure from the prototype of the salesman in the common joke.

Allegorical and Symbolical Characters   In a letter to Sir Walter Raleigh, the English poet Edmund Spenser explained that he intended the long poem he was going to write to be read as an allegory. It would tell stories about knights who would represent the moral virtues set down by Aristotle, and Arthur himself would represent Magnificence, the perfection of all the other virtues. The poem he was planning became *The Faerie Queene,* written over a period of many years and never completed. The poem was not done exactly as Spenser described it to Raleigh, but his basic intention of writing an allegory did not change. Thus the incidents of the poem tell not only a story of knightly adventures but of moral and political struggles. Many of the characters in the poem have obvious counterparts in the political world of the 1500s, and they can be aligned on the side of good or evil, as Spenser sees them. His allegory was a protective cloak in an age when criticism could seldom be spoken forthrightly. John Bunyan, a prose writer of the seventeenth century, also allegorizes throughout his long work *The Pilgrim's Progress.* It is the story of a Christian man's search for salvation. Its central character is called Christian, and his travels lead him finally to the Celestial City. On his journey, he encounters figures like Giant Despair, Mrs. Diffidence, Neighbor Pliable, and Neighbor Obstinate, all of whom personify the obstacles to virtuous living.

In works as obviously allegorical as Spenser's and Bunyan's, the reader's response to the characters is shaped by the nature of the work. But it does not follow that all allegorical figures are two-dimensional, cardboard personifications. In depicting the temptations of life, for instance, Bunyan is often as incisive in his brief characterizations as early painters like Breughel were successful in depicting the sins of mankind on vast canvases populated by hundreds of allegorical figures. The characters of allegory can be as cartoonlike as Orwell's menagerie in *Animal Farm* or as lively and intense as the children in Golding's *Lord of the Flies* or as dramatic and memorable as the seamen of Melville's *Moby Dick.*

The author's allegorical intentions may at times help to explain the motivations and actions of his characters. Any character may be interpreted as symbolical when it appears that his actions and words seem designed to represent some thought or view or quality. A character is not symbolical unless he is symbolical *of* something. Thus the strange and unearthly Mélisande in Maeterlinck's play *Pelléas and Mélisande* seems to symbolize a pure innocence, a fragile quality like Mélisande herself, who cannot survive in the world she inhabits.

Yet all characters who are representative are not symbolical. Even though Holden Caulfield in *The Catcher in the Rye* may epitomize the attitudes of his age group, one cannot think of him in any way as symbolical. Ultimately, a symbolical figure is one whose accumulated actions lead the reader to see him as something more than his own person, to see him perhaps as the embodiment of pure barbarism or redemptive power or hope. In these terms, the symbolical nature of a character may at times grow beyond the author's original intentions, but an author, once he has created his characters, no longer controls them. The reader is free to see symbolical implications in a character if the evidence within the literary work itself supports such a reading. Symbolical interpretation is forced when the reader deliberately distorts to arrive at what he considers profound implications. A reader ordinarily does not need to ferret out symbolical characters. Their illusiveness and mystery usually announce them and invite explanation.

Full-Dimensional Characters   Just as individuals interest us more than masses of people representing movements, so also the full-dimensional characters of literature have attracted most of the attention to themselves. They are described at greater length and revealed in more detail; they are capable of greater individuation. No doubt, many people whom we encounter casually and see only as stereotypes—the waitress, the cab driver, the elevator operator—would be interesting subjects for study, but, just as in life, literature does not permit us to know every character equally well. Leading characters of a literary work are drawn in full; other figures are sketched in to fill out the scene. Although poetry ordinarily does not permit the same space for character development that fiction and drama do, it still manages by implication to suggest the full dimensionality of its characters. T. S. Eliot creates the memorable figure of Prufrock in only 131 lines; Chaucer uses only 32 for the Wife of Bath.

Nevertheless, the very length of fiction and drama permits the possibility of presenting characters who grow and change over a period of time. A novelist like Dickens very often accounted for the full lifespan of his characters, from birth to death, even though his story might focus mainly upon one period. The final chapter of *Oliver Twist* gives an accounting of "the fortunes of those who have figured in this tale. . . ." Yet a long novel following a character through many years, through many experiences at different ages, allows us to know him as intimately as we know only those who are closest to us. And the probing of a twentieth-century author like James Joyce into the inner mind and motivations of characters permits us to know them even more intimately than we know our friends. Literature gives us an opportunity to stop the life of a character, to turn back pages, to reread, to reflect, to examine motivations, to be involved and detached at one and the same time; and, after the story has been completed, to reconsider those thoughts and feelings we have accumulated in the course of the novel. Seldom do we think of any living person's actions in such detail, even our own. Literature is a public view of private matters; it is both open and intimate.

Yet space, detail, and full-dimensionality alone do not create a Madame Bovary, a Raskolnikov, or a Studs Lonigan. The great characters of literature are those who constantly recreate themselves in the imaginations of readers. They are not limited to durable types or perennially symbolic figures. They are individuals who can be seen coping with other men or destiny or God or themselves. They may fail, but they embody human strengths and weaknesses and man's undying impulse to be himself, even if it is not the highest self of which he is capable. Readers do not permit characters who embody man's essential nature to fade away, because the expression of true human individuality in literature and life is all too rare.

The Permanence and Universality of Character   The permanence of literary characters in their written form raises a question about their true nature. They are persistent and stable because they cannot change; only readers can change their attitudes about them. They continue to live on for centuries, whereas men die. Yet we constantly distinguish fictional characters from real men, implying that their reality is of a different nature. Indeed it is, but not necessarily of an inferior nature. Literary characters are limited by the qualities and situations and scenes given to them by the author to live over and over again, but they enjoy an earthly immortality which men achieve only by also becoming, like them, fictional characters in history books, novels, and biographies.

Nevertheless, the permanence of fictional characters is tenuous. It is dependent upon more than the durability of the manuscript on which the character is recorded. Granted that the manuscript and its contents can always be reproduced (what likelihood is it that *Huckleberry Finn* will be lost to subsequent generations?), these volumes continue to exist either as inert museum pieces or as vital creations. Literary figures must constantly experience an imaginative revival in the minds of men to gain their immortality. In this respect they are subject to the whims of men. Only those characters who continue to meet the test of future generations become the truly universal figures.

Characters are not universal in the sense that they are everybody. A character who is everyman is probably no man at all, only a symbol. A universal character is first a person whose qualities can be generalized. Not many men, like Oedipus, kill their fathers and marry their mothers. His particular circumstances are not the bond between him and us, but his reactions are. Given equally catastrophic circumstances, how does any man respond? Does he feel within himself Oedipus' stubborn resistance to fate and show his persistence to dig out the truth? Oedipus is a man of pride and guilt and grief who comes to realize the consequences of his acts and his role as a man of fate. These are dilemmas which many men have not solved for themselves. The tragedy of Oedipus teaches them and involves them in an experience that warns them to fear for themselves.

Paradoxically, a writer cannot guarantee the universality of his creations. He can only attempt to create an individual whom he hopes will continue to appeal to subsequent generations. Once separated from the author's mind in the form that he gives it, a literary character begins an independent existence. Like a Falstaff, he can assume an importance that the author probably never intended. Like a Shylock, a stereotype can undergo a complete metamorphosis. Therefore, any reader of a new day holds the capacity to see a literary figure in a new perspective. Anyone writing about literature needs to realize that the final word can never be said about the truly great figures of literature.

Functions of Characters   What also cannot change about literary characters is their relationships to each other within their own fictional universe. A new generation's attitude may change toward matters like adultery, rebellion, and pride, but it cannot alter how the author has structured his characters to reveal their qualities.

In almost any literary work, several characters receive the main focus. Accordingly, they are considered the leading characters or protagonists. When no character receives such an emphasis, as in Hauptmann's *The Weavers* or Gorky's *The Lower Depths,* it is customary to observe that the people as a whole—as a force or movement—are the author's central interest.

But given a protagonist, the conflict of a story may depend upon the existence of an antagonist. Hamlet's rivalry with King Claudius makes that drama a struggle for survival between "mighty equals." In other instances, like Stephen Crane's *The Open Boat,* the antagonist is a natural element—the unconquerable sea. With varying degrees of emphasis, the sea or the desert or the mountains or the elements can assume such a role.

A foil is a character who serves as a contrast to another, usually in such a way as to work to the advantage of the leading character. At times, the foil may also be the antagonist, as Hotspur is to Henry IV in Shakespeare's history play or even as Laertes, a foil to Hamlet, eventually becomes his antagonist. One of the most memorable of all foils is Sancho Panza, the earthy companion of the lofty-minded Don Quixote in Cervantes' novel

Familiarity with even these few examples will suggest that, even though a foil may be intended to enhance the reader's opinion of the protagonist, the reader may actually prefer the foil. His nature may be more attractive to the reader's own temperament and views. This kind of reaction can be a subject for writing, particularly if the writer examines what this personal counter-reaction does to his attitude toward the work as a whole, which has usually been constructed to gain sympathy for the protagonist.

A confidant, often used in drama, is a character to whom the protagonist reveals his inner thoughts; he becomes a convenient device for the protagonist to speak his thoughts to without addressing them to the audience in the form of a soliloquy. Thus, Hamlet, who at times does soliloquize, takes Horatio into his confidence. If the confidant himself plays an active role in the play, then his own character serves as a commentary upon the protagonist in the same way that the foil represents a contrast. In many instances, however, the confidant is only a passive character, perhaps a servant or close friend, whose main purpose is to listen, not to advise or influence the main character.

A narrator is consistently a special kind of character because, in fiction, he either shapes the entire story by his point of view or, in drama, he acts as a kind of one-man chorus commenting upon the action. The narrator may play a double role; that is, he may actually be a character in a particular set of circumstances, and he may also be the one who at some future time chooses to tell the story in which he was involved. Thus, Melville's *Moby Dick* begins with the words, "Call me Ishmael." Ishmael is the narrator. He is also a seaman who accompanies Ahab in the pursuit of the white whale and survives. Ishmael is therefore a character in the novel who is subject to analysis as any other character. On the other hand, the narrator in Thornton Wilder's *Our Town,* even though he is one of the townspeople, views the dramatic scene as if it were framed. He is identified as a stage manager and plays that role. At various times, he narrates the history of the characters; he interrupts the action to shift the scene; he communicates with the living and the dead; he philosophizes. He is a wise, interested observer, but one whose special role as stage manager and narrator and chorus makes him a unique character.

Finally, in almost all stories and plays there are background characters who populate the scene. Ordinarily these are of no special interest unless, as a mass, they assume an active role. In Ibsen's *An Enemy of the People,* the people as a group are the antagonists of Dr. Stockmann. He is the individual who has to stand up against the many. They are the composite economic society; they are the ones who want to maintain their investments even at the expense of human life. As individuals, they are not greatly differentiated. But as people in a community they can be discussed as if they were one.

Methods of Characterization   Because of the fixed nature of literary characters, writing about them depends to a great extent upon being able to seek out meaningful clues and to determine what techniques the writer uses to reveal his characters. In character analysis, it is helpful to begin with the assumption that a character is coherently developed. This assumption does not necessarily mean that the complete characterization exists in the author's mind before he ever begins, for we have the testimony of authors that characters grow in their minds as they write and, even at times, escape their control, seemingly creating their own lives. Characters may change within the course of a story or play and still be coherent. But the idea of a coherent character does assume that certain values and motives and beliefs—a kind of functional philosophy—cause a character to act and speak in a particular way; and, if he deviates, he is performing inconsistently or he has changed his value system. Interpretations about motivation and action will vary, of course. Much discussion about a complex character like Hamlet hinges to a great extent upon differences of opinion about his madness or his feigned madness and the extent to which he fully controls his words and actions, to what extent he is deliberate and purposeful, to what extent he is frenzied and impulsive.

Even though we can assume that artistic creations are coherent, a careful reader will nevertheless approach characterization inductively, beginning first with details of characterization and then coming to some conclusions about the elements of coherence: Do the causes justify the effects? Are a character's actions adequately explained? Do his responses seem consistent with the things we learn about him? Literature provides a map of character. We can trace the starting points, the directions, and the destination. The whole terrain is laid out to be viewed and examined. Intuitions about fictional characters can be trustworthy or completely misleading; character analysis itself depends upon a presentation of detailed evidence about a character with the intention of seeing him as a whole being.

The Actions of Characters   Clearly, the reader has to be alert to the actions of a character because actions are the author's way of showing, not telling what his characters are like. Yet surface appearances must be questioned. In one scene of Melville's *Benito Cereno,* Babo appears to be a faithful servant shaving Don Benito in the presence of Captain Delano, the visiting captain aboard ship. At that moment, however, Babo, with razor in hand, is actually terrorizing Don Benito in order to keep him silent. The suspense of a story like Melville's *Benito Cereno* depends upon the unsuspecting nature of the American Captain Delano, who is deceived by what he sees and through whom we as readers view the scene. Only when at the end of the story Babo jumps into a boat in an effort to kill the escaping captain is Delano's deception illuminated. In an instant, his mind moves to review all of the previous events in the light of a newly discovered truth that the slaves have mutinied and already massacred most of the Spanish crew.

Written during a period when the antislavery movement in America was strong and the reactions to slave revolts were received sometimes with sympathy and sometimes with hostility, Melville's story raises the question whether he is taking a stand on the slavery issue. Is Babo a heroic rebel or a monstrous murderer? An abolitionist would favor the first interpretation. But one answer given in terms of the literal narrative about a slave mutiny changes if Melville intended the story to be read as a moral allegory, as many of his stories are. Then the characters need to be interpreted in terms of symbols, especially the color symbols. In the story, black seems clearly symbolic of evil and white of good; in these terms, Babo becomes a depraved leader. Obviously, black readers today would find this symbolism and this interpretation distasteful, but without the historical context the work can be read in terms of itself. Critics are not in complete agreement about Melville's intentions, but what is apparent is that the reader can see Babo as either good or evil; one interpretation or the other simply emphasizes different kinds of evidence.

The Appearance of Characters   In some stories and plays, the appearance of a character may be taken as a clue to his nature if the author leads the reader to attach significance to it. Most people today tend to look upon ugliness and distortion without suspicion, but in times past outer flaws were taken as a sign of inner corruption. From early childhood, fairy tales and mythological stories have conditioned us to accept the literary fact that dwarfs and witches and monstrous creatures are servants of evil, and heroes and heroines are handsome, beautiful, and good. The world of the fairy tale is one of simple contrasts.

Yet, even when the fictional universe is not quite as simplified and stories are not told to set forth moral platitudes, writers continue to attach significance to physical appearance. The brief sketches in the

Prologue to Chaucer's *Canterbury Tales* consistently include descriptions of physical details and dress which give significant indexes to character and social station. Chaucer's description of the Squire includes the line, "Short was his gowne, with sleves longe and wyde"—usually understood to be details that indicate the Squire was dressed in the very latest fashion. Chaucer describes him as a young and lusty knight, gaily dressed, and full of spirit—a sharp contrast to the divinity student, the Clerk, whose coat is threadbare and whose horse is as lean as a rake.

Shakespeare uses appearance in a play like *Richard III* as a psychological motivation. In the opening soliloquy of the play, Richard reveals the thoughts about his deformity that prey upon his mind, finally declaring:

> And therefore, since I cannot prove a lover,
> To entertain these fair well-spoken days,
> I am determined to prove a villain
> And hate the idle pleasures of these days.

Thus, from the outset Richard's physical ugliness is announced as a motive for his monstrous actions.

In *Hedda Gabler,* Ibsen provides clues to the interpretation of character in the brief descriptions he includes in the stage directions at the first entrance of the characters. When Hedda enters, Ibsen assumes the part of a narrator: "Her steel-gray eyes express a cold, unruffled repose. Her hair is of an agreeable medium brown, but not particularly abundant." When Mrs. Tesman, Hedda's foil and rival, enters, Ibsen writes, "Her eyes are light blue, large, round, and somewhat prominent, with a startled, inquiring expression. Her hair is remarkably light, almost flaxen, and unusually abundant and wavy." If one ignores these contrasting characteristics, he ignores how Ibsen defines the relationship between the two women from the very beginning and how, in particular, the references to hair and stroking hair and pulling hair at scattered points throughout the play are intended as significant clues to Hedda's character.

The Speech of Characters   It is axiomatic that what characters speak ought to be important in learning about them. There is a tendency, however, in reading (as opposed to listening) to concentrate upon the what and the why—the substance and purpose—and to pay less attention to the when and the how—the occasion and the manner. In writing about a character's speeches, an interpreter has to attempt to project himself into the character: How would he say the words? What are his habits of speech? What is his tone? Does the occasion color the tone? Answering these questions can provide possible insights into meaning, especially extrasensory meaning, which nonverbally always represents another level of communication. When people are speaking, they are also gesturing, grimacing, inflecting the voice, stressing, and in numerous subtle ways influencing the meaning, adding to it, and, when they are being ironic, even reversing the meaning. All of these extrasensory implications have to be inferred from the reading. A fictional narrator may add a few introductory details to a speech, telling how it was spoken, but the reader is still left to interpret. In drama, the whole matter is taken over by actor and director. It is therefore not at all unusual that different readings of identical roles by different individuals can produce a totally different conception of a character. The rhythms can be slowed or quickened. The lines can be consistently twisted for humor or satire. All of the speeches can be heightened or understated. Nevertheless, the original author by his choices of words, usages, structures, and rhetorical devices builds into the speeches a core of meaning and effect which in itself cannot be altered but can be developed as the interpreter sees fit, consistent with his total interpretation of the character. Two strikingly different examples out of context will illustrate what kinds of elements are built into speeches. The first is a speech from a play; the second is a line of dialogue from a story.

Character No. 1

Mount, mount, my soul! Thy seat is up on high,
Whilst my gross flesh sinks downward, here to die.

Character No. 2

"Don't worry, darling ... I'm not a bit afraid.
It's just a dirty trick."

What is first obvious is that there is a different rhetoric operating in each speech. It is unlikely that Character 1, even in his own person, could speak Character 2's line. Not only is the meaning a part of the style—the characteristic thoughts of the character—but the manner also. The first speech seems to be a dramatic, oratorical apostrophe of the character to his soul at the moment of death. The second is calm and intimate, addressed to another person—a completely different approach to death, since these are also words spoken at the moment before dying. Having to die is the "dirty trick."

Thus, knowing the occasion throws considerable light upon the implications of the second speech, but the intimate elements are built in. It cannot be delivered in the manner of the first, because the structures and words do not lend themselves to that treatment. Yet each speech, within the limits of its language, can be interpreted to show different qualities about the characters at the moment of their death.

Character 1 could be seen as noble and high-minded or as pompous and shallow. Character 2 could be seen as casual and superficial or as brave and bitter. Or perhaps these are not the exact descriptive adjectives at all in terms of the total characterization and the occasion; they explain only possible effects. Yet we do know that the speeches identify two characters of quite different temperament, and the speeches contain clues to the characterization.

Character 1 is actually King Richard II in Shakespeare's play of that name. Richard has been forced to abdicate and has been replaced on the throne by Bolingbroke (Henry IV). He is imprisoned in Pomfret Castle, reflecting at length upon the discontent of his life, daily fearing that his food will be poisoned to end his life. Death, ironically, comes as a rude assault. Men break in, slay the guards, and strike Richard down. In his dying words, Richard damns his slayer and, in a final gesture of kingliness, cries out

> Mount, mount, my soul! Thy seat is up on high,
> Whilst my gross flesh sinks downward here to die.

His slayer is moved to speak:

> As full of valor as of royal blood.

Character 2 is Catherine Berkeley in Hemingway's *A Farewell to Arms*. She is an American nurse serving in World War I. Her lover is Frederick, a lieutenant in the United States Army. In the final scene of the novel, Frederick comes to the hospital where Catherine has given birth to his child. The baby is dead; she knows she is dying and says she hates it. She tries to reassure Frederick, kidding him a bit, vacillating between thoughts of loving and dying. When a nurse directs Frederick to go out of the room, the novel records with simplicity:

> "Don't worry darling," Catherine said. "I'm not a bit afraid. It's just a dirty trick."

They are her last words. They too are "full of valor as of royal blood," but her bravery and nobility are of a different variety.

These two brief speeches do reveal character. Because they are dying speeches, they are particularly important ones. But what each reveals, it reveals less by what it says literally than by the way the words are spoken, to whom they are addressed, when, and under what circumstances.

Almost identical words can be interpreted differently when they are considered in a total context. For example, the terrified Johnny in Sean O'Casey's *Juno and the Paycock,* about to be dragged out and killed, reverts to ritual:

> Sacred Heart of Jesus, have mercy on me! Mother o'God, pray for me—be with me now in the agonies o' death! . . . Hail, Mary, full o' grace . . . The Lord is . . . with Thee.

In Eliot's *Murder in the Cathedral,* Thomas Becket, Archbishop of England, about to be slain, speaks to those around him:

> Now to the Almighty God, to the Blessed Mary, ever Virgin, to the blessed John the Baptist, the holy apostles Peter and Paul, to the blessed martyr Denys, and to all the Saints, I commend my cause and that of the Church.

One ritualistic speech reveals misery and desperation; the other courage and affirmation; yet these are impressions that are derived from more than the meanings of the words themselves. Characters in stories and plays seldom make formal addresses about themselves; their speeches are indexes to them, but their lives need to be interpreted dramatically, for to ignore the total context may be to distort the interpretation.

The Persona of the Poet   Poems, like plays and stories, are sometimes written about people, and we show essentially the same interest in these characters as we do about other ones in fiction and drama, except that we are seldom provided with the same kind of detail which permits us to understand them as fully developed characters. These, however, are the visible and identifiable characters of a poem. But like the narrator of a story or the director of a play who remains behind the scenes, a similar kind of character frequently appears in a poem. He is the character whose voice we hear but do not see in person. He is the author in the role he chooses to assume rather than speak in his own voice. This voice is ordinarily referred to as the author's persona or the persona of the poem.

In Edwin Arlington Robinson's poem "Luke Havergal," the speaker, the "I" of the peom, is clearly not the author:

> Go to the western gate, Luke Havergal,
> There where the vines cling crimson on the wall,
> And in the twilight wait for what will come.
> The leaves will whisper there for her, and some,
> Like flying words, will strike you as they fall;
> But go, and if you listen she will call.
> Go to the western gate, Luke Havergal—
> Luke Havergal.

No, there is not a dawn in eastern skies
To rift the fiery night that's in your eyes;
But there, where western glooms are gathering,
The dark will end the dark, if anything:
God slays Himself with every leaf that flies,
And hell is more than half of paradise.
No, there is not a dawn in eastern skies—
In eastern skies.

Out of a grave I come to tell you this,
Out of a grave I come to quench the kiss
That flames upon your forehead with a glow
That blinds you to the way that you must go.
Yes, there is yet one way to where she is,
Bitter, but one that faith may never miss.
Out of a grave I come to tell you this—
To tell you this.

There is the western gate, Luke Havergal,
There are the crimson leaves upon the wall.
Go, for the winds are tearing them away,—
Nor think to riddle the dead words they say,
Nor any more to feel them as they fall;
But go, and if you trust her she will call.
There is the western gate, Luke Havergal—
Luke Havergal.

The outlines of the dramatic situation seem fairly clear: a girl whom Luke has loved has died; he is left in bewilderment, not knowing what to do. It is then that a voice both commands and lures him to "go to the western gate." Who is the figure who comes "out of a grave" to tell him this? Is it Death himself? Or Death's agent? Or is it merely an inner voice within Luke which tells him to follow her by killing himself? There are no definite answers who the voice is, but any interpretation of the poem must attempt to account for it in some way.

The importance of the persona will, of course, vary from poem to poem, but, after a first reading, one should always attempt to resolve in his own mind who the speaker is. If it is not the author, then the persona is functioning as a dramatic character, assuming a role that is integral to an understanding of the dramatic conflict and meaning of the poem.

Suggestions for Writing about Characters   Characters are the focus of almost any literary work of a dramatic nature. No one needs to direct attention to them as subjects for writing, but it is not always equally as clear what one writes about in analyzing characters. Literary analysis is not pure description or a summary of the action, although it may include elements of these. It is not gossip—the nature of much of our talk about living people. It is more in the nature of amateur psychoanalysis which concerns itself with the way a character acts and talks, with the reasons he acts as he does, or with the way parts of his life fit together to create a total impression. The writer's job, above all, is to convey to the reader his understanding of the character and the character's role in a literary work. He may want to approach the analysis diagnostically, looking at the symptoms and signs which lead to a particular conclusion. A character analysis of this kind may set out to prove a kind of thesis, such as: Nora in Ibsen's *A Doll's House* is a nineteenth-century forerunner of the twentieth-century feminist and career woman, or Henry Fleming in *The Red Badge of Courage* is a central figure in a story about Christian redemption. The first thesis would look at Nora from the perspective of a different age, but it would still be an analysis limited to what actually happens in the play. Topics of this variety indicate that it is rarely possible to write about characters without referring to numerous other elements that go to make up the literary work. The second thesis would emphasize how the novel works out a general theme through its characters—Henry's relation to Jim Conklin, for instance.

Another approach to writing about character comes close to a completely personal view, because essentially it is a reader's attempt to get at the nature of a character by an impressionistic sketch. This kind of character analysis is clearly more speculative and intuitive than the first, but it can at times be successful in delineating the emotional temperament of a character.

However varied written papers about characters may be, they ought to be true to the details that the author gives about a character in the special fictional world that has been created. Questions of the following variety will help the reader come to some understanding of literary characterization as opposed to his usual casual assessment of people in daily life:

1. Into what categories do the characters of a story or drama fall? Are they types? Are some clearly individualized and fully developed?
2. In what ways do characters comment upon one another either by their words or their actions? Are they grouped so that they form contrasting views or attitudes or values?
3. What is the author trying to do with particular characters? What is his chief intention? To reveal the variety of human nature? To use characters as mouthpieces for his own ideas? To show a certain style of living? To illustrate a theme through them?
4. Is the characterization of the protagonist coherent? Are his actions

motivated? Are some actions unexplainable in terms of the character or of the continuing story?

5. Does the time span of the action allow for a developing character? What changes take place in the thinking of a character? Why?

6. How do we learn to know the characters? How well? What typical techniques does the author use to reveal character? In what special ways do actions and appearance add to our knowledge of a character?

7. What details about a character seem to give him universal appeal? What particular elements are dated?

8. Does the reader look sympathetically or critically upon the characters? What in the literary characterization and action affects one to respond one way or the other?

9. In what way do minor characters fit into the total scheme of the story? Why couldn't they be omitted?

10. How do the characters speak?

Form and Structure

There is no question of the need for structure in the useful arts as opposed to the fine arts. An engineer who builds a bridge has to work with a design first of all and then with structural means to execute the plan. In like manner, an architect works both with external shape and interior arrangement. The function of form and structure in literature, however, is not as readily apparent as it is in construction, but it is no less basic to the art. The principles may be less mechanical, but no less functional in making a literary work what it is.

Because the external appearance of a literary work is one of the first ways to classify it as fiction, drama, or poetry, form needs to be discussed in terms of each of the genres, not as a general principle common to all. Further, of the various elements that concern the reader of literature, form is perhaps the most technical. The more knowledge he has of structural matters, the more aware he will be, no doubt, of the way form is operating to shape the literary work and increase its readability. But a brief discussion cannot make professionals out of general readers. The subject matter here, therefore, will concern itself with those matters of form and structure that are readily observable to the nonprofessional and can aid his understanding and appreciation of literature if he is more conscious of them. Sean O'Faolain, himself an accomplished short story writer, speaks of the short story as showing the "most highly perfected technique in prose-fiction" and emphasizes that we read these stories not alone for what they say but "for the joy we get out of seeing a craftsman doing a delicate job of work." Every reader should have some awareness of how a writer does his job.

Tradition and Experiment in Fiction   The novel and the short story are perhaps the least formally structured of the various kinds of literary works that are produced; that is, fiction seems to be less bound by set conventional forms than drama or poetry. Drama is linked to the theater and poetry to recitation—at least in times past—but fiction continues to be a form designed mainly to be read silently from the printed page. Characteristically, it is written in prose, and its appearance on the page is fairly uniform. Long works are divided into chapters or sections. In such relatively superficial matters, most novels are alike; but, as far as the form of the novel is concerned, there is no designated length, no set number of parts or divisions. One might note that some experiments in fiction often hinge upon trying to make the external appearance of the printed page look different, thus trying for new effects. An early experimental novel like Dos Passos' *The 42nd Parallel* included newspaper headlines and biographical sketches, so that the novel took on a multigenre effect similar to what we now familiarly experience as a multimedia effect. A recent experimental work, *Informed Sources* by Willard Bain, is called a novel, but its typography sometimes resembles verse, sometimes cartoonlike designs, often with symbols and single letters splashed on the page instead of words. Attempts such as these are designed to break down the deadening effects of habit in readers so that their customary assumptions about fiction are challenged. Readers have the option of trying to come to grips with a new approach, figuring out what serious purpose it may have, or of dismissing it as mere foolishness. Experiments always meet with detractors because the familiar is pleasant and comforting. Works that alter patterns are disturbing.

Internal Structure of Fiction   Basic to understanding structure in fiction is coming to a realization that it can be thought about in several ways. The concept of structure does not have to be limited to the most apparent one of putting parts together in an orderly way. That is one concept, but it is essentially a static notion to think of a literary work as if it were a construction. It conjures up an image of a novelist building his work as if he were a carpenter or mason and, when everything is complete, we as readers look upon his workmanship.

Literary structure, however, can also be thought of in more active terms, not so much as an assemblage of parts according to a blueprint but as an ongoing process in which characters interact and ideas, images, and themes recur and connect. A novel is most conveniently thought of as a developing form, as finding a shape as the writer writes. The fact remains that even if a writer chooses to imitate another author's form, he can do it only in the more obvious ways of using structural techniques another writer has used, like Faulkner's choice in *The Sound and the Fury* of four different narrators in four sections focused upon four days in the history of the Compson family, or Melville's miniature encyclopedia on whales in the chapter on cetology in *Moby Dick*. But the fact remains that novels do not have set forms that can be labeled and followed exactly. The terms that are used refer to specific techniques or general approaches. Thus, an epistolary novel is one like Samuel Richardson's *Pamela* that uses the letter as its chief device of revealing the characters and their story. A picaresque novel is one like Fielding's *Tom Jones* that uses a series of rambling episodes as a means of taking its rogue hero through adventures which comment upon everyday life. But these are essentially structural patterns in very broad terms; they can assume many different forms in the hands of different writers. For purposes of writing about form, several structural features are worthy of attention: time structure, space structure, character patterns, and motifs.

Time Structure in Fiction   Every novelist and short story writer has to come to terms with chronology. Given a set of circumstances that represent his story, where does he begin? If he begins his story at the culmination of events, then he transfers the attention of the reader from a concern with what will happen to a concern with how it happened and why it happened. A shift in time structure can change the primary emphasis of a story from plot to character because if the outline of the events is known in advance, then interest focuses upon the way characters respond to those happenings. And if time is not a central structural feature of a story, the major emphasis then falls upon theme or image.

Time structure obviously affects the dramatic impact of the narration. Always decisive to a particular effect is the reader's knowledge about the characters and events. If the reader knows the outcome in advance, his attention can be drawn to the ironies of circumstance because at any point in the story it is possible for the reader to know through the narrator what a character himself cannot know about his future. Rearrangement of time, therefore, can move the reader to emotional concerns about the characters that would not otherwise be possible in a straight chronological sequence. In addition to the actual chronology of events, there is also the matter of timing in a story, which is in part structural and in part stylistic. It concerns the time at which the narrator chooses to reveal details about his characters, particularly about their past. It is one technique to begin a story at the beginning and move to the end. It is another to start at a given point and then with calculation to reveal what only needs to be known at any particular time. In Fitzgerald's "Babylon Revisited," we are first told that Charles Fessenden has returned to Paris where he once spent a wild two years with his wife Helen. Then we learn that he is returning to visit his daughter Honoria, who is living under the legal guardianship of his sister-in-law Marian. These are all current circumstances in the story. Details of the past begin to unfold. We learn that Helen, his wife, is dead and only later in the story that she died of a heart attack and still later that Charlie had locked Helen out of the house during a snowstorm. Each of these details moves the story back in time and helps to explain the conflict between him and Marian and the reason she will probably not release Honoria again to her father. This structuring of the action clearly becomes a matter of interest in itself and affects the entire pace and emphasis of the story.

Space Structure   Space structure refers simply to the geographical bounds a writer limits himself to. The choice of location is usually closely allied with the time element, and the two affect the scope of the story. If a story has only one location and a brief time span, then the writer usually treats only a fairly limited set of circumstances, just as a dramatist has to adapt his action to a particular stage setting. Nevertheless, it should be added that an author can always employ narrative devices like the flashback, the interior monologue, the dream, or the vision, which will carry the story beyond its immediate geographical dimensions.

One of the remarkable things about James Joyce in *Ulysses* is that he manages to compress the epic dimensions of Homer's *Odyssey*, the model for his characters and their relationships, into a twenty-four hour period in Dublin. In linear sequence, from the time of Odysseus' departure from home to his return, Homer's epic ranges to distant places over a period of twenty years. Joyce's reduced space and time structure has altered the effect of the original completely and placed demands upon the author to achieve the scope and complexity that he does by a variety of narrative techniques. What is most obvious is that Joyce's novel is no longer a tale of adventure as Homer's epic is; *Ulysses* is a psychological exploration.

Writing about time and space structure mainly involves two things: (1) deciphering and describing it if it is sufficiently complex, as in Faulkner's "Barn Burning," and (2) discussing the effects gained by the choices the author has made. Fitzgerald's "Babylon Revisited," already discussed briefly above, treats two Parises: Paris, the Babylon-like city of young Charles Fessenden's two-year binge and the Paris of the immediate present of the story, seemingly tame, empty, and provincial. This contrast simply reflects the way the new Charles sees things and thus becomes a means also of revealing changes that have taken place in him. We see that the elements of literature are never independent of one another, but that the who, what, where, when, how, and why combine to create the organic structure of the literary work.

Character Patterns   Thinking of characters in terms of structure will often reveal that they fall into groupings which reinforce the theme of the story. The division may be as simple as that between characters who are good and those who are evil, particularly in stories like Hawthorne's, which are strongly allegorical. In other instances, the interrelationships may be more involved. To illustrate again from "Babylon Revisited." There are six main characters in Fitzgerald's story. The protagonist is Charles Fessenden, eager to gain possession of his daughter Honoria, who in turn is anxious to live with her father. They represent one group. Charles's attempt to establish this relationship permanently is the object of the action. Marian, the sister-in-law, is Charles's antagonist; she resists his effort to regain Honoria. Although her husband Lincoln is not wholly unsympathetic toward Charles, he stands by his wife and therefore represents with her a second group of characters who will determine the future of the first group. The remaining two characters are "sudden ghosts out of the past"—Duncan Schaeffer and Lorraine Quarrles. They are carry-overs from Charles's earlier experience in Paris. When they intrude into the household of Marian and Lincoln, all six characters for the first time are brought face to face with one another. It is a decisive scene in the story, and the result is that Charles's hopes to have Honoria are frustrated. The characters are forced into two groups of three. Charles is associated with Duncan and Lorraine, whether he chooses to be or not; under the circumstances, Honoria is forced to remain with her aunt and uncle. Father and daughter are together only for the duration of the story.

In a similar kind of analysis, examination of character patterns in other works can sometimes provide a means for writing about the story that might not otherwise be possible if the characters are viewed only one at a time.

Motifs   Motifs are an expressive means of repeating the same idea a number of times throughout the story. Motifs are structural in the sense that they connect parts of the story by taking the reader back to an earlier scene or reminding him of a constant feature about a character which has not changed. Fitzgerald's "Babylon Revisited" again serves as an apt illustration, indicating, of course, that a single short story depends upon any number of structural features.

The story opens in the Ritz bar in Paris. Charles Fessenden has a drink. When the barman asks him if he wants another drink, he refuses, saying that he is "going slow these days"—a reminder of the days when he was "going pretty strong." Charles later explains that he has vowed to have only one drink every afternoon. In the story, his daily whiskey becomes a motif, indicating Charles's determination not to fall back into old excesses. At the end of the story when Charles is again in the Ritz bar after he has learned that he will not be able to regain the custody of his daughter, the narrator might have indicated a change in Charles by having him take a second drink. But the motif is not broken. As the story closes, Charles once more shakes his head as the barman looks questioningly at his empty glass. It is a final touch in the story that confirms the reader's sympathies for Charles.

There is nothing particularly subtle about Fitzgerald's use of this motif. Each time it occurs the reader is fully aware that it is a test of character which Charles has set for himself and has to pass. Yet the motif also adds suspense and connective purpose to the story as a whole. Recurring themes, actions, and symbols are therefore important clues both to the meaning of the story and to its organic unity.

Freedom and Convention in Dramatic Structure   The matter of dramatic structure is so closely linked to the history of the stage and the playhouse that the one can hardly be explained except in terms of the other. Further, the active presence of the audience viewing live performances has had an additional effect upon the structure of the play. Act divisions which provide a rest for the performers, an intermission for the audience, and an opportunity to reset the stage are the formal solutions to the time and space problems of drama. Even long movies now provide an intermission for the audience, although the break seems to have affected the structure of movies very little as yet; it is merely an interruption of the running of the film at an appropriate halfway point—a matter of stopping the projector—rather than a formal division of the action into two parts.

In plays, however, act and scene divisions have had very specific effects upon the structure of a play because playwrights have characteristically seemed concerned with drawing the audience back into the theater after each break. Thus, two-, three-, four-, and five-act plays tend to break down into discrete and self-contained parts. The effect is different from a one-act play with multiple scenes which have the continuousness of a movie. The kind of theater for which an author writes also frequently determines the structure of a play.

Dramatic Structure and the Theater   Greek tragedies, which were produced in open-air amphitheaters with little scenery, belong to the tradition of continuous-action plays. The setting did not change. The scene divisions which we note in printed versions of the plays today marked the coming or going of one of the two or three actors who were available to play a larger number of roles. And scene divisions were also influenced by the role of the chorus, a conventional feature of the theater of that day. Even though Greek plays are not divided into acts, many of them fall into five formal divisions: prologos, parados, epeisodion, stasimon, and exodos. These are determined to a large extent by the entrance, function, and exit of the chorus. Playwrights therefore observed fairly rigid dramatic conventions in a theater which might have been used far more flexibly, as indeed it was on the Elizabethan stage.

The open-air Elizabethan theater, epitomized by the Globe Playhouse, provided at least three main acting areas. The projected platform, the rear stage with a curtain, and the upper stage, also provided with a curtain, were all adaptable to different purposes. The characters of the play could act as if they moved from outside to inside, or from place to place, by shifting their location on the stage or by describing the scene in the poetry of their lines. Properties and machinery were used to suggest localities, but the theater was not primarily devoted, as later theaters were, to creating an illusion of reality. The scenes could shift rapidly, and an entire play might be produced in two and one-half or three hours, broken only by convenient musical intermissions for the benefit of the actors and the audience.

Thus, to produce Shakespeare's plays today with the same effectiveness as they were in the Elizabethan theaters demands an equally adaptable stage or a vehicle as flexible as film. The act and scene divisions in texts of Shakespeare's plays are additions of early editors. The structure of these plays was influenced by the stage itself, not by arbitrary conventions as in Greek times.

Neoclassical drama of the seventeenth century in France, however, was bound strictly by rules. Playwrights like Corneille and Racine wrote plays in an effort to observe what critics of that time had established as the dramatic unities. The unities limited a play to a single line of action in one place within a twenty-four hour period. These principles were inferred from Aristotle's *Poetics,* based upon observations of plays being produced in Athens in the fifth century B.C., but no Greek dramatist presumably ever considered himself as formally bound to the unwritten unities as the dramatists of the distant future were in their attempts to imitate them. Greek dramatists observed conventions which the theater demanded; they did not have Aristotle as their mentor. Ironically, one of the purest examples of Greek tragedy in the neoclassical sense is John Milton's *Samson Agonistes* (1671), declared by Milton not to have been written for the stage at all.

Despite their differences, Greek and Roman plays, Elizabethan plays, and neoclassical plays are all strongly theatrical; that is, they do not deny the fact of the theater itself, that action takes place on a stage. They do not pretend to present an illusion of life itself. The proscenium-arch theater from 1660 on popularized the concept of illusionism. Elaborate scenery and fixed properties were designed to disguise the stage and transform it into the world of the play. Thus no longer would it have been possible for a Shakespeare of that day to write the forty-two scenes which make up *Antony and Cleopatra,* and Shakespeare's plays themselves were actually cut and adapted to be performed at all on a far less flexible stage. Drama settled into a conventional act structure, which was to dominate dramatic production until new concepts of staging in the twentieth century once again gave to dramatists a complete freedom of form.

What this brief survey of the influence of the stage and convention upon dramatic structure suggests is that uniform standards of evaluation about form cannot be applied to all plays. One reader may prefer the economical structure of a Greek play; another, the range of an Elizabethan drama; another, the disciplined unity of a neoclassical drama; and still another, the loose fragmentary quality of many contemporary plays. But without reference to stage history, the final test of the form of a play, at least from the viewpoint of a reader, is its suitability to the dramatist's theme and purpose. Dramatists in this century who have attempted to say new things in new ways and, in particular, have attempted to depict inner actions as well as outer actions have had to seek new structures. Thus, Arthur Miller explains that certain scenes in *Death of a Salesman* are not flashbacks in time but they are the past flowing into the present through the mind of Willy Loman. The structure of the play accommodates scenes of this kind because, as Miller describes it, the stage can be adapted either to the world of the moment or to the world of reverie. The fact remains, however, that a drama is not as flexible a form as the novel for purposes of psychological probing. Even though drama has found ways of escaping the immediate stage scene, the form still demands that a character's inner experiences be objectified. Thus in *Death of a Salesman,* Ben, who occupies Willy's thoughts, actually appears on the stage. This is memory objectified. It works as a device in this particular play, but having to show thought places far greater limitations upon the playwright than telling about it does upon the writer of fiction.

Internal Structure of Drama   Basically, the setting of a play and its time divisions determine the external form of a play. Its internal structure, like fiction, depends upon motifs of action, characters, themes, and symbols which run throughout the play as a whole and bridge what may be its leaps in time and place.

Chekhov's plays, for example, depend heavily upon internal structure. Externally, his longer plays, all written in four acts, show the strong influence of Greek drama. They have a compactness which is reinforced by a limited setting, a limited span of time, and limited action.

Typically, the main action occurs off stage; the onstage action concerns the indirect effects of those offstage occurrences upon the characters. Thus, in *The Cherry Orchard,* the important action is the sale of the orchard. It is the major concern of the characters throughout the play, but the auction itself finally takes place between Acts II and III. At the end of Act III, when Lopahin announces that he has purchased the orchard, the play reaches its climax. The final act reflects not only the changes that will take place in the estate but those that will occur in the lives of these people.

Throughout Chekhov's play, the cherry orchard itself is the pervading symbol, and the characters may be classified by their attitudes toward it. They belong either to the old order of Russian society which would seek to preserve the beauty of the trees or to the new order which would chop them down to make the land useful for subdividing and building. Thus the characters fall into loose patterns in relation to the main symbol of the play.

The recurring motifs—the ominous sound of a breaking harp string, Madame Ranevsky's carelessness with money, the weeping, and mournful music—are important structural features of a play of this nature, because the dialogue is often marked by incoherence. Each character seems primarily dedicated to himself, thinking his own thoughts, and speaking little monologues. Not much communication takes place in a Chekhov play in the sense of one character talking and responding to another; the dialogue does not build upon an idea, as a Shaw play does, for example. Chekhov's dialogue shapes an impression, not an argument, and the motifs are in part responsible for creating that illusive, mysterious quality that often pervades his plays.

The Range of Poetic Structure   Just as the novel seems better suited than the drama for subjects of broad scope and those of psychological depth, so the poem among the three genres seems best suited for subjects of small dimension and intimate feeling. Even though long poems on epic themes have been written, these tend to be versified dramas and narratives and vary considerably in effect from the lyric poem. Long poems are developed freely, in most instances limited only by a particular metric line but not by the kinds of stanza forms the lyric poet follows or imposes upon himself. The obvious exceptions to this statement are Dante's *Divine Comedy,* written in an interlocking rhyme pattern (*aba, bcb, cdc*), called terza rima, and Spenser's *The Faerie Queene,* written entirely in nine-line stanzas with a set rhyme scheme.

Set Forms   As soon as a poet chooses to write in a set form, the form itself exercises a control over the content, not only limiting its range but shaping it as well. The best example is the sonnet, a fourteen-line form with a set line length and rhyme scheme.

The fourteen lines of a sonnet limit the expression to a narrow range. "Narrow" in this instance does not mean that sonnets are less profound or less complex, or that they have fewer implications than other poems, but that they are merely less expansive. Whatever thought and feeling the poet has must be compressed into that space. Sonnet writing is a severe discipline.

Within the bounds of the sonnet, two rhyme patterns have become traditional; the Shakespearean and the Petrarchan. The first divides the fourteen lines into three groups of four lines and one of two lines: *abab cdcd efef gg.* The Italian form divides the fourteen lines into one group of eight lines and one group of six lines: *abba abba cdc dcd,* although the rhyme schemes in both the octave and sestet vary greatly. The effect of these divisions is that the logic of the poem is affected by the form itself. In the Shakespearean sonnet, the final couplet is always a break from the previous twelve lines, and the twelve lines may break down into four very precise logical units, as it does in Shakespeare's Sonnet XXX:

> When to the sessions of sweet silent thought
> I summon up remembrance of things past.
> I sigh the lack of many a thing I sought
> And with old woes new wail my dear time's waste.
> Then can I drown an eye (unus'd to flow)
> For precious friends hid in death's dateless night,
> And weep afresh love's long since cancell'd woe,
> And moan th' expense of many a vanish'd sight.
> Then can I grieve at grievances foregone,
> And heavily from woe to woe tell o'er
> The sad account of fore-bemoaned moan,
> Which I new pay as if not paid before.
>   But if the while I think on thee, dear friend,
>   All losses are restor'd and sorrows end.

In this poem, the parts are introduced by the key connective words "When ... Then ... Then ... But." These four words also shape the logic. The poem consists of three variations on a single theme with a final conclusion.

The Italian form achieves a different effect, which can be illustrated by Wordsworth's sonnet to John Milton, given the title "London, 1802":

> Milton! thou shouldst be living at this hour:
> England hath need of thee: she is a fen
> Of stagnant waters: altar, sword, and pen,
> Fireside, the heroic wealth of hall and bower,

Have forfeited their ancient English dower
Of inward happiness. We are selfish men;
Oh! raise us up, return to us again;
And give us manners, virtue, freedom, power.
Thy soul was like a Star, and dwelt apart;
Thou hadst a voice whose sound was like the sea:
Pure as the naked heavens, majestic, free,
So didst thou travel on life's common way,
In cheerful godliness; and yet thy heart
The lowliest duties on herself did lay.

After a brief opening invocation, the poem describes conditions in England that Wordsworth deplores. A break comes after line eight. The final six lines, then, give reasons why a man of Milton's character and spirit might again be able to help. The thought is conveniently accommodated to the form. (For discussion of other stanza forms and meter, see Chapter 33 under Stanza and Versification.)

The Effect of the Medium   Perhaps in none of the other genres does the form influence the reader as forcefully as it does in the poem. The medium has its own effect quite apart from the content—or if not "quite apart" from the content, then in conjunction with it. But the form has its own message. The sonnet speaks preciseness, logicality, and compactness. The closed couplet of two rhyming lines speaks pithiness and certainty. The limerick speaks bounciness and lightheartedness. The poet's feeling for form undoubtedly influences his choice in the first place, with the result that content and form fuse in such a way that the "message" of the form reinforces the thought of the poem.

The Paradox of Form   The paradox of self-imposed form lies in the fact that control of expression has the capacity to free it. The imagination must find ways to circumvent the restraints of form. Form encourages invention. Poetic creation is the act of making immediate the highly intangible images and sensations of the imagination. It is an act of ordering and channeling thoughts and feelings.

In an interview, Edward Villella, a distinguished ballet dancer, once referred to this paradoxical effect of form and discipline. He spoke of the highly structured nature of most ballet, the way in which each step is prescribed, and the disciplined technique necessary to perform the movements. Yet he added that when he was most in control of his technique he had the greatest experience of absolute freedom, as if he were floating on air. In a similar way, one might observe that an audience has the same liberating reaction when the artist is in full control. If he has to struggle or force himself, then the audience becomes conscious of the form and technique itself, not the total experience and expression. In a similar way, form aids the poet. A parachute in the open sky is not a burden. It is the only safe way down.

Free Forms: Rhetorical Structure   Free forms do not imply an absence of form, only a greater flexibility and a greater dependence upon internal structural features. Free verse, for example, abandons rhyme schemes, set stanzaic patterns, and regular line lengths, but it cannot escape rhythmic design, controlling images, repetitions, and a variety of rhetorical strategies which bind the parts together. Walt Whitman, who sought freedom from traditional forms and expressed themes of freedom in his poetry, was yet highly susceptible to structural patterns. His short poem "I Hear America Singing" illustrates his strong tendencies toward repetition, parallel structure, rhythmic balance, contrast, and the sustained image:

> I hear America singing, the varied carols I hear,
> Those of mechanics, each one singing his as it should be blithe and
>   strong,
> The carpenter singing his as he measures his plank or beam,
> The mason singing his as he makes ready for work, or leaves off work,
> The boatman singing what belongs to him in his boat, the deckhand
>   singing on the steamboat deck,
> The shoemaker singing as he sits on his bench, the hatter singing as
>   he stands,
> The wood-cutter's song, the ploughboy's on his way in the morning, or
>   at noon intermission or at sundown,
> The delicious singing of the mother, or of the young wife at work, or
>   of the girl sewing or washing,
> Each singing what belongs to him or her and to none else,
> The day what belongs to the day—at night the party of young fellows,
>   robust, friendly,
> Singing with open mouths their strong melodious songs.

In its irregularities, Whitman's poem seeks its own structures. Free verse represents only a different concept of what form can be.

Since Whitman's time, of course, free verse forms have become more and more common, but the popularity of free verse does not deny the importance of structure. Contemporary poetry simply confirms that the poet, with his typical inventiveness, constantly finds new ways to shape poems. After all, the imaginative fusion of words into form is the quality that continues to give poetry its uniqueness among the various modes of literary expression. (For additional discussion, see Chapter 33 under Anaphora, Free Verse, Imagism, and Sound Effects.)

Suggestions for Writing about Form   Writing about form depends, first, upon a perception of what form is doing in a particular literary work. It further requires a special way of looking in order to see what the structural basis of a composition is. One significant contribution of the cubist painters to our way of looking at things was their idea that everything is a composite of shapes and designs. Their technique demonstrated this idea; paintings emerged as combinations of triangles, rectangles, and circles. This technique helped others to see what the cubists themselves perceived with a keener eye.

Writing about structure must attempt also to demonstrate what the writer intuits about form. But vague generalizations are of no help. The demonstration must be finally reduced to hard facts—counting the parts, determining why the divisions are made as they are, seeking out the less obvious connectives, recognizing patterns, determining the way themes and motifs shape the whole, and finally verbalizing what the total effects are.

Questions of the following variety suggest possible leads for discussion of matters of form:

1. What is the total effect of the work's structure? Does it seem to be a continuum? Is it a combination of fragments? Does the whole fall into an orderly sequence of parts?
2. What is the significance of the parts? At what point is a division made? Why? What effect would be altered if the division had not occurred?
3. Beyond actual division of the work into parts, what patterns emerge either through characters, symbols, motifs, or ideas?
4. What is the time arrangement and space dimensions of the work?
5. What special effects grow out of the author's particular definitions of time and space? What effects would be lost if the time and space plan were altered?
6. What is the particular suitability of the form the author chooses to the themes and ideas of the work itself? How does the form support the content?
7. Does the choice of form in any way run contrary to the content of the work so that the form is ironic or satiric? Are all subjects appropriate to every form? Do jingles express profundities?
8. In what way can the form of the work as a whole be characterized? What is the "message of the medium"?
9. If a particular work—a poem, for example—were adapted to another form—to a story or play—what alterations would have to take place in the structure? Does consideration of these changes reflect upon the suitability of the form as it stands originally?
10. In what way is the language itself acting as a structural feature, particularly in a poem? What are the grammatical patterns? The rhetorical patterns? The metric patterns? The rhyme scheme?

Matters of Style:
Language, Symbol, and Imagery

A writer's passion for language is often his incentive for writing. Words crystallize his thoughts, realize his emotions, and bring the images of his mind to the life of literature. The vitality, the imaginativeness, the beauty of this creation depend upon words.

In one sense, the concerns of the imaginative writer are not far different from those of any other writer, whether he is an amateur or a professional. He needs to have an adequate stock of words to begin with. He has to be concerned with their meanings, both the accuracy of their literal use and their extended implications. He has to be concerned with the fact that language grows out of a variety of contexts which relate to age, occupation, education, ethnic background, social status, and a host of other factors, and that words derive associations from all of these sources. He has to be concerned with the interaction of words in any particular verbal context—what I. A. Richards calls the "interinanimation of words"—because in context the words gain a tone and meaning all their own. Words are the writer's paints, and every writer must show some capacity to use their coloration, texture, intensity, and harmony to produce an identifiable style.

Ultimately, however, there is always the distinction between the dabbler and the artist. The concerns of the literary artist characteristically do go beyond those of the ordinary writer—his desire to tap the powers of language to communicate his imaginative vision and his search for ways to push the limits of language outward in order to express the inexpressible. Because imaginative literature often accomplishes these ends, we look to it as the highest expression of man's capacity with language.

Metaphorical Language   Metaphorical or figurative language is perhaps the writer's most important single source of imaginative power. It almost always represents the writer's invasion of an alien verbal context to bring back a word or phrase or image to work into a different setting of words. Metaphorical language defies ordinary associations; it makes fresh ones by seeking out likenesses in dissimilar areas of experience.

Metaphor is possible only because our common experiences lead us to use words in familiar patterns. Words cluster around topics; certain words fit together. Thus, phrases like these are totally familiar and factual:

He was born.
He served in the air force during the war.

He was a turret gunner on a plane.
He was killed during an attack upon the enemy.

Randall Jarrell's short poem "The Death of the Ball Turret Gunner," however, shows what a complete transformation can take place
when these prosaic phrases are translated into metaphorical language.

From my mother's sleep I fell into the State,
And I hunched in its belly till my wet fur froze.
Six miles from earth, loosed from its dream of life,
I woke to black flak and the nightmare fighters.
When I died they washed me out of the turret with a hose.

What Jarrell has added is a whole new set of associations which go
beyond the simple facts of being born, fighting, and dying; these additions can be suggested by phrases such as these:

Being in the womb is like sleeping.
The rapid time between birth and army service is like a fall.
The plane is the State.
The ball turret is the plane's belly.
Being in the turret is like being in the womb.
In his furry suit, he is like an animal.
Life on earth is living in a dream.
Flying high is like being released from something.
The attack is a nightmare.
Dying is an awakening.
His bodily remains are like debris.

These paraphrases of the metaphors are not an interpretation of the
poem, but they do reveal what areas of experience the poet has explored
to bring imaginativeness and feeling to the basic experience and to make
a shocking commentary upon the life and death of a young man. Further,
only metaphorical language makes possible the compression that the
poem achieves and the intensity that grows out of that telescoping of
language. The metaphors add the feeling; the metaphors invite the extensions of meaning. They are the source of the poetry.

The one sustained metaphor of Randall Jarrell's short poem is
that of sleeping and waking. Living is sleeping; dying is waking. In
fact, the "I" of the poem is awake, telling his experience; only he is
dead. The poem therefore turns upon a paradox. We ordinarily think of living as waking; death is like a kind of sleep, a comparison invited by the
appearance of the body in sleep and in death. The effective metaphor,
however, does not always depend upon the obvious likeness but frequently upon the unexpected similarity, even though the poet might

find only one possible link between two verbal contexts. In "A Valediction: Forbidding Mourning," John Donne compares separated lovers to the legs of a compass hinged together at the top. In a sustained metaphor, he relates the movements of the compass to the movements and emotions of the lovers. It is the kind of ingenious conceit that prompted Dr. Johnson to condemn the Metaphysical poets of the seventeenth century when he said that they yoked "the most heterogeneous ideas ... by violence together."

The effect of a metaphor, of course, does not depend upon its ingeniousness but mainly upon its concreteness and meaningfulness. As a comparison, the purpose of metaphor is to clarify, not to cloud the thought. If it draws upon a subject or experience that is totally unfamiliar to most readers, it cannot succeed in illuminating the thought. If it draws upon that which is too familiar, it also fails because the reader does not respond to the overused metaphor. Nor does he ordinarily recognize the dead metaphors which are the common stock of our daily speech—"the hand of a clock," "the foot of a mountain," "a paddlewheel," or "a tubby man." A reexamination of any page of our own writing will reveal the extent to which metaphor is a natural way of thinking. The artist goes further to depend upon it as a major means of conveying his perceptions.

Symbolic Language   Like metaphor, symbol-making is a natural process. It is a way of simplifying the complexities of thought and experience by hitting upon one thing as representative of many. The symbol may be used as a reminder, a signal, a call to action. It is a means by which men seek to express the unity of their perceptions and experiences. It is a hook to hang on to.

In 1969, the "closed fist" became the symbol of a whole movement of defiance and protest among militant blacks. It was a symbol that could be dramatized, pictured, and spoken. Even though the symbol had special implications for that particular movement, it was basically a borrowing of a universal symbol. We have always recognized the clenched fist as a symbol of threat and resistance, just as we tend to recognize doves as symbols of peace, the crown as a symbol of authority, and water as a symbol of purification. Symbols such as these which have become traditional are called universal symbols. Literature draws heavily upon them, but it also creates occasional symbols, like the duck in Ibsen's *The Wild Duck,* whose significance is apparent only from the context of the work itself.

Language that employs symbols is clearly symbolical, but language that is spoken by a symbolic figure, whether or not it includes specific symbols, also becomes symbolical, by implication; that is, one seeks for general significance beyond the particular context of the words. The thought is raised to a symbolic level. Jesus' phrase "Turn the other cheek," although it might be interpreted literally, represents, more importantly, a symbolic act expressive of passive resistance. Thus, the use of the phrase is ordinarily symbolical in implication.

In a similar way, literary characters who are drawn larger than life or who are clearly set forth as symbolic figures may often speak lines that hold significance beyond their simplest level of meaning. One senses this quality in lines like the Ancient Mariner's cry of despair when his boat is calmed on the sea:

> Water, water, everywhere
> Nor any drop to drink.

The context does not demand a symbolical reading, but it invites it.

A symbol is also capable of compressing the emotional impact of an overwhelming experience into a brief descriptive passage. In Book IX of *Paradise Lost,* after Eve tells Adam that she has eaten of the forbidden fruit—the act that first marks man's fall from divine grace—Milton expresses Adam's stunned sensation by two simple lines:

> From his slack hand the Garland wreath'd for Eve
> Down dropp'd, and all the faded Roses shed.

Symbolic language of this kind has a vividness and force far beyond any kind of ordinary description.

Imagery   Images are the mental impressions that words create in such a way the mind perceives sensations without actually experiencing them. Metaphor and symbol are, of course, common sources of imagery, but other uses of words can evoke the same kind of image-making. Imagery adds sensuousness to language. The opening quatrain of an Emily Dickinson poem is tense with sensations:

> I heard a Fly buzz—when I died—
> The Stillness in the Room
> Was like the Stillness in the Air—
> Between the Heaves of Storm—

This is not a simple contrast of sound and stillness, because worked within the images of the sound of the fly and the stillness of the room are also images of the stillness of air and the sounds of the storm like the troubled breathing of a person.

A passage from James Joyce's *Araby* also represents a complex interweaving of sense images of all varieties to create a vivid description of a winter's evening:

When the short days of winter came dusk fell before we had well eaten our dinners. When we met in the street the houses had grown sombre. The space of sky above us was the colour of ever-changing violet and towards it the lamps of the street lifted their feeble lanterns. The cold air stung us and we played till our bodies glowed. Our shouts echoed in the silent street. The career of our play brought us through the dark muddy lanes behind the houses where we ran the gauntlet of the rough tribes from the cottages, to the back doors of the dark dripping gardens where odours arose from the ashpits, to the dark odorous stables where a coachman smoothed and combed the horse or shook music from the buckled harness.

One needs only to reflect upon those details that appeal to sight, touch, hearing, and smell to perceive the rich, sensuous quality of this prose.

Besides the animated effect that imagery gives to poetry and prose, it also provides a basis for analysis. Imagery serves as an index to the author's conception of his work. In fact, if it is used with consistency, it may even mirror his interests, his experiences, and his temperament. Some writers draw constantly upon images of nature or love or domestic images or religious images; in a particular work, images may be prevailingly violent or beautiful or gloomy, images may express sadness or buoyancy or sterility. It is often possible to trace threads of imagery running throughout a work—a color scheme, a concern for sounds, an interest in animals, a preoccupation with sex—patterns of images emerging from the writing as a means of setting the tone, of commenting upon a character's actions, or indicating the author's attitude toward his material. The choice of imagery may be a clue to where the author's sympathies lie.

All references to color, sound, animal life, and sex are, of course, not necessarily image-making. These can be discussed in quite abstract, unemotional, encyclopedic terms. But the simplest alteration can change the effect. Even a simple proverb can be expressed by fact or fancy. One proverb may attempt to explain:

A wise man will hear, and will increase learning; and a man of understanding shall attain unto wise counsels.

Another may attempt to express its meaning by images:

A whip for the horse, a bridle for the ass, and a rod for the fool's back.

The difference between the two is that the words in the second proverb move the imagination to perceive first, then to interpret; in the first, one need only interpret. Imagery is the link between the imagination of the writer and the imagination of the reader.

Stylized Language   What is convenient to keep in mind for purposes of analyzing language in literature is that even the most realistic work does not record speech as we ordinarily use it. The tone may seem colloquial and natural, but the dialogue we read is a conventionalized speech for literary purposes. It is highly compressed; many of the filler words are omitted. Missing also are the bland phrases that have meaning only because we speak them with a particular intonation, and absent too are the repetition and stammering that are characteristic of speech. The degree to which dialogue departs from the customary diction and rhythms of speech is the degree of its stylization. Some dialogue departs so very little from the expected patterns that we take no notice of it. It creates an illusion of conversation. However, some plays are even written in verse so that the dialogue in its total effect becomes stylized.

Stylization is relative, and dependent to a great extent upon conventions that prevail at any one particular time. Elements of an Elizabethan play that may seem highly stylized to us in the twentieth century may have seemed far less so to a sixteenth-century audience accustomed to the diction of the plays and the prevalence of verse drama at that time. In a similar way, the diction and arrangement of words of pre-twentieth-century poetry often seem highly stylized to modern ears accustomed to the words and rhythms of standard colloquial speech in the drama and poetry of today. Reading experience helps to distinguish what is customary for any particular age and what is a departure from the ordinary for special effects.

When T. S. Eliot wrote *Murder in the Cathedral* for the Canterbury Festival of 1935, he chose verse as an appropriate vehicle for the twelfth-century story of Thomas Becket. The chorus, itself a stylized device of drama, speaks in this manner:

> Here is no continuing city, here is no abiding stay.
> Ill the wind, ill the time, uncertain the profit, certain the danger.
> O late late late, late is the time, late too late, and rotten the year;
> Evil the wind, and bitter the sea, and grey the sky, grey, grey, grey.

And the Archbishop achieves high drama even in ordering the door of the cathedral to be opened:

> Unbar the doors! throw open the doors!
> I will not have the house of prayer, the church of Christ,
> The sanctuary, turned into a fortress.
> The Church shall protect her own, in her own way, not
> As oak and stone; stone and oak decay,
> Give no stay, but the Church shall endure.
> The church shall be open, even to our enemies. Open the door!

In an essay entitled "Poetry and Drama," T. S. Eliot explains that he intended this style to be "neutral" in terms of time. It is neither twelfth-century nor modern; neither Shakespearean nor nineteenth-century. In brief, we can now look upon it as highly stylized speech that is appropriate both to the tense dramatic action, the elevated nature of the characters, and a subject drawn from the past.

Stylization may, of course, take other forms. In a German play dating from 1919, Ernst Toller's *Man and the Masses,* the characters speak in a telegraphic style. The lines are frequently short elliptical phrases like the messages of a telegram:

THE WOMAN: You! Who sent you?

THE NAMELESS ONE: The masses.

THE WOMAN: They've not forgotten me?
    The message ... the message ...

THE NAMELESS ONE: My mission here is to set you free.

THE WOMAN: Freedom!
    Life!
    We escape? Is everything prepared?

THE NAMELESS ONE: Two keepers have been bribed.
    There's one more at the gate. I'll strike him down.

THE WOMAN: You'd murder him ... for me?

THE NAMELESS ONE: For the cause.

THE WOMAN: I have no right.
    To win life through a keeper's death.

THE NAMELESS ONE: The masses have a right to you.

THE WOMAN: And the rights of the keeper?
    Keepers are men.

THE NAMELESS ONE: We have no "men" as yet.
    On one side, the group belonging to the mass.
    On the other, the class belonging to the State.

THE WOMAN: Man is naked.

THE NAMELESS ONE: Mass is godlike.

THE WOMAN: Mass is not godlike.
    Force made the mass.
    Evils of property made the mass.
    Mass is the movement of distress,
    Is meek devotion ...
    Is terrible vengeance ...
    Is blinded slavery ...
    Is holy purpose ...
    Mass is a fertile field that has been trampled;
    Mass is the choked-up, inarticulate people.

                        Tr. Louis Untermeyer

The stylization is Toller's way of trying to write a completely abstract and colorless dialogue which will communicate the intellectual substance and nothing else. The emotion arises out of the circumstances.

In a contemporary play like Ionesco's *The Bald Soprano,* stylization takes yet another form. In this play, the characters speak with
deliberate absurdity to express the lack of communication between
people and the triviality of their concerns when they do speak. The
following lines are only a brief excerpt from a scene between a husband
and his wife as they sit facing each other:

> MR. MARTIN [*musing*]: How curious it is, how curious it is, how curious
> it is, and what a coincidence! You know, in my bedroom there
> is a bed, and it is covered with a green eiderdown. This room, with
> the bed and the green eiderdown, is at the end of the corridor
> between the w.c. and the bookcase, dear lady!
>
> MRS. MARTIN: What a coincidence, good Lord, what a coincidence! My
> bedroom, too, has a bed with a green eiderdown and is at the end
> of the corridor, between the w.c., dear sir, and the bookcase!
>
> MR. MARTIN: How bizarre, curious, strange! Then, madam, we live in
> the same room and we sleep in the same bed, dear lady. It is perhaps
> there that we have met!
>
> MRS. MARTIN: How curious it is and what a coincidence! It is indeed
> possible that we have met there, and perhaps even last night. But
> I do not recall it, dear sir!
>
> MR. MARTIN: I have a little girl, my little daughter, she lives with me,
> dear lady. She is two years old, she's blonde, she has a white eye
> and a red eye, she is very pretty, her name is Alice, dear lady.
>
> MRS. MARTIN: What a bizarre coincidence! I, too, have a little girl. She
> is two years old, has a white eye and a red eye, she is very pretty,
> and her name is Alice, too, dear sir!
>
> MR. MARTIN [*In the same drawling, montonous voice*]: How curious it
> is and what a coincidence! And bizarre! Perhaps they are the same,
> dear lady!
>
> MRS. MARTIN: How curious it is! It is indeed possible, dear sir. [*A rather
> long moment of silence. The clock strikes 29 times.*]

Stylization, therefore, represents a deliberate distortion of language for
a particular effect.

Paradox, Dramatic Irony, and Verbal Irony   Paradox and verbal irony
work essentially on a common principle of apparent contradiction and,
therefore, often arise from the same context. Paradox treats opposites
in such a way that both elements of the contradiction seem to be true
but in different contexts. Because a statement of this kind works contrary to what we ordinarily expect, the effect is also ironic. Irony is based
upon a sense of some difference: things are not as they seem; they do
not turn out as they should; or there is a discrepancy between intention
and effect. The irony of drama and fiction frequently depends upon a

situation, hence the term "dramatic irony." But irony may also be a figure of speech; hence the term "verbal irony," in which the meaning of the words is simply reversed by the ironic tone. Popular phrases like "the home of the brave," "the land of the free," or "America the beautiful" can be easily twisted to mean just their opposite.

Dramatic irony and verbal irony are at times not completely separable. Complex circumstances which are themselves paradoxical and ironic often produce language of a similar variety. Sophocles' *Oedipus the King* has become almost the standard example of the way in which dramatic irony works. The play itself is based upon a series of paradoxical situations:

> Oedipus the king, the savior of Thebes, is also its destroyer.
> The curse he places upon the killer of Laios he places upon himself.
> The tracker of the criminal is the criminal himself.
> Teiresias, who is blind, can see; Oedipus, who can see, is blind.

Each element of these paradoxes holds true because Oedipus, the savior and king of Thebes, is also without his own knowledge the slayer of his father Laios. Separated from his father as a child, he later unknowingly kills him. Thus, the lines of the play are constant sources of irony and paradox. When Oedipus prays that the guilty man waste his life away, he concludes his speech with highly ironic words:

> In my house, I knowing it, he dwells,
> May every curse I spake on my head fall.

Without knowing it, he is the one in his own house on whom the curse has fallen.

A later speech turns upon the paradox of seeing and not seeing. After the blind Teiresias has told Oedipus that he is the murderer of his father and the scourge of the land, Oedipus speaks:

> In one long night thou liv'st, and can'st not hurt,
> Or me, or any man who sees the light.

Oedipus' mocking of Teiresias as one who cannot hurt him because he cannot see produces irony because all that Teiresias speaks is true and will bring about Oedipus' grief and tragedy.

Irony, however, does not always strike a serious note. The unexpected turn of events that Marvell describes in a short couplet from "To His Coy Mistress" produces a touch of ironic humor:

> The Grave's a fine and private place,
> But none I think do there embrace.

Likewise, the paradox may be comic as well as serious. A short poem by John Donne gives this effect:

Antiquary

If in his study he hath so much care
To hang all old, strange things, let his wife beware.

Irony and paradox can be sought out in almost any literary work, because their concern with self-contradiction is implicit in almost all experience, if one will choose to see it. They can be easily missed unless one reads with an eye and ear for them. They demand that the reader be able to think from more than one point of view. They ask him to flip a coin to see what is on the other side. They demonstrate that the literary artist typically does not see everyday life with a single and simple aim. If he does so, he risks superficiality or dogmatism. Paradox and irony are both literary ways of coping with many of the seemingly unresolvable complexities of experience. As expression, they do not offer solutions. They merely reflect the nature of things to help us understand.

Ambiguity and Punning   Ambiguity and punning, like irony and paradox, turn upon double meanings. Words are used so that they have more than one implication. Punning is basically a twist of a familiar expression ("There's method in his gladness"); a play upon words that are spelled differently but sound alike (Max Beerbohm, asked to hike to the top of a Swiss mountain, declined by saying, "I am an anti-climb Max"); a play upon a single word that may have several possible meanings (HAMLET:'T is for the dead, not for the quick, therefore thou liest. FIRST CLOWN: 'T is a quick lie, sir; 't will away again, from me to you.).

Punning is most commonly written for a comic effect, but when the situation is a serious one the effect is gently ironic. The literature of the past indicates that writers did not consider it amiss to pun in serious situations. Dylan Thomas seems to follow that tradition in these lines from "Do Not Go Gentle into That Good Night":

Grave men, near death, who see the blinding sight
Blind eyes could blaze like meteors and be gay,
Rage, rage against the dying of the light.

The opening line is reminiscent of the speech of the dying Mercutio in *Romeo and Juliet*:

. . . ask for me tomorrow, and you shall find me a grave man.

Ambiguity, however, has broader possibilities than punning alone. Generally to be avoided in expository prose because of the uncertainty of meaning that arises, it is intentionally used in literature as a way of revealing the paradoxes and ironies of life which plague thoughtful men. In this sense, ambiguity adds richness of suggestion to the language.

In particular scenes of *Hamlet,* the ambiguity of Hamlet's remarks is appropriate to the character, for one can never be wholly certain when the frenzy of his emotions has carried his feigned madness into true madness. One such scene is his conversation with Ophelia, which follows immediately his thoughts of suicide in the soliloquy "To be or not to be." He taunts Ophelia with questions that are deliberately ambiguous, that seem to doubt her chastity but on the surface could mean something else:

HAMLET: Ha, ha! Are you honest?
OPHELIA: My lord?
HAMLET: Are you fair?
OPHELIA: What means your lordship?

The ambiguity carries over into his phrase "Get thee to a nunnery. Why would'st thou be a breeder of sinners?" A nunnery is a place of refuge from the world, but Elizabethan audiences would also have known the word as a cant term for a bawdy house. The ambiguity in these lines suggests Hamlet's divided thinking and complicated state of mind, both his concern for Ophelia in this scene and his bitterness toward her.

Ambiguity frequently results when feelings are mixed. At times, the writer may not convey with certainty and clarity what he feels or thinks. In a short poem "Dust of Snow," Robert Frost leaves his "change of mood" unexplained:

The way a crow
Shook down on me
The dust of snow
From a hemlock tree

Has given my heart
A change of mood
And saved some part
Of a day I had rued.

It is clear that the falling snow has changed his spirits for the good, but the precise nature of his new mood remains ambiguous. What realization has the experience brought about? Should one place emphasis upon *the way* the crow shook down the dust of snow? In this instance, the vagueness of situation and feeling makes the miniature poem a source of wonder and suggestiveness. Ambiguity, like many other effects of language, demands of a reader the kind of imaginative participation that ultimately draws him into the experience so that he must weigh what he, as well as the writer, understands by the language he reads.

Verbal Humor   Verbal humor is itself an ambiguous effect because it depends upon a reader's responding to an incongruity between the statement and the writer's intention. If the incongruity is lost upon the reader, the effect is lost. Some people do not see humor where others do.

Incongruity can exist only in terms of some norm. If incongruity means that something is out of keeping, it is logical to ask in terms of what. Verbal humor has direct reference to ordinary communicable speech, which maintains a semblance of reasonable tone, uniform usage, and orderliness. Any departures from these general norms are capable of producing something comical. Verbal humor has three main sources: disproportion, surprise, and confusion.

Disproportion is the incongruity that arises between the way something is said and what has actually happened. It is therefore the stock and trade of the braggart, the bluffer, and the teller of tall tales. Falstaff's speeches are funny because he is all three of these. In Henry IV, Part 1, in the scene at the Boar's Head Tavern in Eastcheap, Falstaff makes a fool of himself by boasting how he overcame a dozen rogues on the road near Gadshill:

> I am a rogue if I were not at half-sword with a dozen of them two hours together. I have 'scaped by miracle. I am eight times thrust through the doublet, four through the hose; my buckler cut through and through; my sword hacked like a handsaw—*ecce signum!* I never dealt better since I was a man. All would not do. A plague of all cowards! Let them speak. If they speak more or less than truth, they are villains and the sons of darkness.

Falstaff speaks more than truth, because from an earlier scene the audience knows that Falstaff and his three companions were set upon as a prank by Poins and Prince Hal and that, when attacked, all of them ran, leaving behind them the money they themselves had robbed from pilgrims on the road. As Falstaff is later prodded into telling the incident, the numbers grow from 12 to 16 to 22 or 23 and finally to the climactic figure:

> If there were not two or three and fifty upon old Jack, than am I no two-legged creature.

Falstaff's story is amusing, not only in the exaggeration with which he tells it but in the way he draws it out. It is disproportionate in its hyperbole and its length.

The second source of verbal humor, surprise, is the incongruity that arises between what is said and what is expected to be said. This kind of humor almost always shifts the tone the author has established, so that a sudden contrast produces a comic effect. One amusing scene of Bernard Shaw's *Pygmalion* is when Eliza Doolittle, who has been taught to speak the King's English with propriety, shocks a small group of socialites by letting a vulgarism slip into her speech. Asked by Freddy if she is going to walk across the park, she responds: "Walk! Not bloody likely. I am going in a taxi." The humor is often lost on American audiences because they fail to respond in the same way that proper Englishmen would to the word "bloody." In the musical *My Fair Lady,* based upon this play, the device is repeated, but the scene is shifted to a race track and a phrase used that American audiences would immediately recognize as an outrageous breech of language etiquette. Saying the unexpected is a common source of humor and one that Shaw commonly used in his writing.

A third source of verbal humor is confusion. It is the incongruity between the disorderliness of what is said and the coherence of what is expected. It is the humor of nonsense. Since the device is more common in spoken than written humor, it is more likely to be found in drama. The fools in Shakespeare's plays are often given confusing word-play and absurd non-sequiturs. In *Twelfth Night,* a short dialogue occurs between Viola, disguised as a young man, and a clown, carrying his tabor, a small drum:

> VIOLA: Save thee, friend, and thy music! Dost thou live by thy tabor?
> CLOWN: No, sir, I live by the church.
> VIOLA: Art thou a churchman?
> CLOWN: No such matter, sir. I do live by the church; for I do live at my house, and my house doth stand by the church.
> VIOLA: So thou mayst say, the king lies by a beggar, if a beggar dwell near him; or, the church stands by thy tabor, if thy tabor stand by the church.
>
> III, i

This is a way, as the Clown himself says, of showing "how quickly the wrong side may be turned outward."

In Eugene Ionesco's farce *The Lesson,* the Professor tutoring his young pupil walks up and down the room as he delivers a nonsensical lecture on the neo-Spanish languages:

> That which distinguishes the neo-Spanish languages from each other and their idioms from the other linguistic groups, such as the group of languages called Austrian and neo-Austrian or Hapsburgian, as well as the Esperanto, Helvetian, Monacan, Swiss, Andorran, Basque, and jai alai

groups, and also the groups of diplomatic and technical languages—that which distinguishes them, I repeat, is their striking resemblance which makes it so hard to distinguish them from each other—I'm speaking of the neo-Spanish languages which one is able to distinguish from each other, however, only thanks to their distinctive characteristics, absolutely indisputable proofs of their extraordinary resemblance, which renders indisputable their common origin, and which, at the same time, differentiates them profoundly—through the continuation of the distinctive traits which I've just cited.

Variations of this kind of humor occur in any repartee in which word-play predominates.

Satire   When humor is given a target, it becomes satire. Satire mixes humor with criticism. Yet not all satire balances the elements of humor and criticism equally. Two traditions have continued since Roman times: one of satire written with geniality and urbanity in the manner of Horace; one of anger and violent lashing out against evil in the manner of Juvenal. The proportion of humor or criticism produces literary works of a quite different nature. If the element of criticism is lost altogether, the work becomes empty farce. If the humor is lost altogether, the work degenerates into invective. Ideally, satire may be said to lie somewhere between the extremes of buffoonery and verbal abuse. Yet since satirists are not of one temperament, the English language offers a generous supply of words to suggest various tones and forms of satire: derision, invective, vituperation, jeremiad, raillery, ridicule, mockery, *reductio ad absurdum,* sarcasm, irony, caricature, parody, burlesque, comedy of manners, mock-epic, *commedia dell' arte,* clownishness, farce. In each of these, satire exists to a greater or lesser degree; the scale ranges from bitter scorn to gentle irony to sidesplitting laughter.

Since satire is actually a mode of perception—a predisposition—which shapes the writer's thought and language, it needs to be discussed in terms of a work as a whole. Unless the reader catches the writer's intention at an early stage, the effect can be lost or misinterpreted. Even the grotesquerie of Swift's "A Modest Proposal" was read straight by members of the eighteenth-century audience, and in our own time some readers fail to perceive the satire of some of their favorite nursery rhymes.

The twist the satiric manner represents may be illustrated by the first stanzas of a series of poems that use Marlowe's "The Passionate Shepherd to His Love" as a point of departure. Marlowe's poem is an effervescent expression of love in an idyllic scene:

> Come live with me and be my love,
> And we will all the pleasures prove,

> That valleys, groves, hills and fields,
> And all the craggy mountains yields.

In response, Sir Walter Raleigh wrote "The Nymph's Reply to the Shepherd":

> If all the world and love were young
> And truth in every shepherd's tongue,
> These pretty pleasures might me move,
> To live with thee, and be thy love.

Here the note of skepticism in the opening lines gives the poem a gentle satiric edge.

Some thirty or more years later, John Donne wrote another version entitled "The Bait":

> Come live with me, and be my love,
> And we will some new pleasures prove,
> Of golden sands, and crystal brooks,
> With silken lines, and silver hooks.

Donne's switch of the scene throughout his poem from valleys and mountains to sands and streams to pursue a metaphor of his love swimming in the river as bait for "enamoured fish" adds a touch of absurdity that makes the poem virtually a parody of the delicate sentiments of Marlowe's poem.

Yet another poem of the twentieth century, C. Day Lewis' "Come, Live With Me and Be My Love," adds the strongest hint of satire by again imitating the poem that extols pastoral delights that are no more:

> Come, live with me and be my love,
> And we will all the pleasures prove
> Of peace and plenty, bed and board,
> That chance employment may afford.

These are examples of genial satire, a mockery of Marlowe's starry-eyed but charming view of young love.

In hard-hitting satire, the laugh fades quickly or the pleasantry takes the shape of a sardonic grin. E. E. Cummings, however, is one of the contemporary writers who maintained a firm grip on humor even when he was being most devastating in his comment. His poem "my sweet old etcetera" represents the art of satire at its best; the criticism and the humor come through equally clear:

> my sweet old etcetera
> aunt lucy during the recent

war could and what
is more did tell you just
what everybody was fighting

for,
my sister

isabel created hundreds
(and
hundreds) of socks not to
mention shirts fleaproof earwarmers

etcetera wristers etcetera, my
mother hoped that

i would die etcetera
bravely of course my father used
to become hoarse talking about how it was
a privilege and if only he
could meanwhile my

self etcetera lay quietly
in the deep mud et

cetera
(dreaming,
et
     cetera, of
Your smile
eyes knees and of your Etcetera)

Suggestions for Writing about Language   Since literature is a verbal art, it is the word that makes possible all of its effects—not the isolated word but the word set down appropriately with other words; the words shaped in forms that reveal the author's plan; the words arranged with timing so that the pace and tone are varied; the words chosen imaginatively so that the writer's intentions and feelings are implicit in the style as well as the thought and characters and actions. The language of a literary work can be examined as an end in itself, but ordinarily the language is studied as a source of tone, atmosphere, pacing, characterization, and the implied thoughts of the writer as well as his explicit statements.

Questions of the following variety will therefore suggest possible leads for the discussion of language in literature:

1. Is the language appropriate to the narrator? Does his dialect and style differentiate him from the author?

2. Is the speech of characters in the work differentiated? Does a major part of the characterization spring from the way a character speaks, as opposed to the way he acts? To what extent does the dialogue create an illusion of reality? To what extent is it conventionalized? Does the author depend upon certain techniques for recording speech?

3. Is the language stylized? To what degree? For what purpose? Does stylization seem to draw attention away from the matter of the work to the manner?

4. Are images and symbols natural or contrived? Universal or occasional? To what extent do they seem forcibly imposed upon the material? What is gained by images that hit upon extremely unlikely comparisons?

5. What are the consistent mental and emotional impressions that emerge from reading the work? What areas of experience are drawn from? Do these follow a pattern? Do the sources and patterns comment upon the characters? Upon the author? Do they create a special tone or atmosphere?

6. What explanations can be given that will resolve a paradox? What relations does paradoxical language have to the action and the characters? What relation does paradox have to the author's state of mind?

7. What different meanings grow out of a particular example of verbal ambiguity? What are the implications of any one of them? From what source does ambiguity arise? From the words? From the syntax? From general vagueness? From the tone? Does the thought and structure of the work as a whole help to settle upon one interpretation in preference to another?

8. In what terms can the author's language be characterized? Highly figurative or symbolical? Abstract? Colloquial? Mixed? What is the general appropriateness of the language to the theme of the work?

9. What is the source of verbal humor? What is its purpose? Is it used for contrast, diversion, satire? If it is satiric, what is being mocked?

10. What manner does the writer assume to satirize? Is anger evident, moral indignation, geniality, fun? How do these qualities promote criticism?

Matters of Style:
Strategies and Nonverbal Effects

Literary style can refer to a number of different things: the style of a writer, the style of a particular work, the style of a period. These obviously are not independent of one another: writers produce the works that establish the characteristic manner of a movement. Yet the range of emphasis between the man and the period is great enough to cause confusion about what style actually is. Where does it exist? In the writer? In the product? In the mind of the reader?

In this discussion, style will be used as a term to refer to the effect which grows out of a writer's ways of working with elements that combine to make up a literary work. Style can be discussed in terms of any one of the components: the arrangement of the plot, the details of the setting, the manner of characterization, the effects of form, the choice and arrangement of language, the modes of thoughts and feeling. Almost all writing about literature is in some way a discussion of style. Yet beyond particular focuses of this kind, style can also be discussed as a cumulative effect of the various strategies used, as a total impression gained by the reader as he reads and reacts. Style is therefore not infrequently discussed in highly impressionistic and metaphorical terms. Upon occasion, these generalizations are diverse enough that one wonders if critics have read the same writer. In fact, writers do not always maintain a consistent and invariable style, so that the generalizations may legitimately vary. Writers experiment; they come under new influences; they change with age. Even though we think of their minds and personalities as relatively constant, even they may change in philosophy and temperament with age.

Meaningful discussions of style, therefore, are those that are most specific at the same time they attempt to explain what effects grow out of the writing. The effect of style cannot be dismissed as an illusion, because even after all of the strategies have been explained, the structures analyzed, and the words diagnosed, the dimensions of style extend further into areas of sensory and extrasensory perception. These effects are often contextual; they can be explained only in terms of the whole, as the effect of the parts interacting together. In these terms, a number of stylistic features contribute to the readability of literature.

Climax and Suspense   Climax is a part of the dynamics of a literary work. It is a point of culmination, a moment of high tension and involvement. In these terms, a work might possibly have a number of climactic incidents, but the main one is usually apparent—the confrontation, the discovery, the revelation, the realization, the final struggle—whatever may be the high point of interest on which the story turns. Tracing the action to a point of climax is a way of recognizing how the writer has built his story and involved the reader in the process.

Suspense is a tension caused by looking forward. It is the anticipation that accumulates before the climax is reached and is generally limited to works that withhold crucial information from the reader. If the entire story is known to the reader in advance, suspense is minimized. Both Greek and modern works based on familiar myths have little suspense because the outcome of the events is known from the beginning. The primary interest lies in the writer's way of working out the narrative and his interpretation of the characters and actions. The interest in such works is, therefore, focused upon different aspects of style.

Works in which the outcome of the action is unknown generate a strong element of suspense. Thus, the courtroom and trial by jury are a natural setting and situation for suspense. Detective fiction and adventure stories depend heavily upon suspense as a main source of interest.

Pace   All writing is based on motion. It is not a static art as the words on the printed page might lead one to believe. We not uncommonly speak of the pace of a work. Pace is the matter of timing, both the writer's own sense of movement in developing his ideas and the reader's sense of how it moves. A slow pace encourages reflection; it also risks boredom. A rapid pace magnetizes the reader; it also risks superficiality. Long works will, therefore, be paced so that the movement is sometimes slowed, sometimes quickened. The novelist's sense of timing may not be unlike the strategy of a long distance runner; he cannot go the whole distance at the same speed.

Pace is often a matter of the relation between action, description, and dialogue, but it is also a matter of specific technique. In poetry, for example, the metrical line has the effect of moving the verse more quickly or slowly. A regular line which runs smoothly and uninterruptedly tends to move quickly. A metrical variation usually tends to slow the rhythm. In a long work like *Paradise Lost,* consisting of more than 10,000 lines of blank verse, Milton depends upon deviations from the regular line to vary the effects. In two succeeding lines from Book IV, the pace changes noticeably:

> So farewell Hope, and with Hope farewell Fear,
> Farewell Remorse: all Good to me is lost.

In the second regular line, the pace quickens.

Frequently, the pace of a line suits the thought. The description of Satan's journey through the realms of Chaos and Night reflects his changing progress, sometimes fast, sometimes slow:

> So eagerly the fiend
> O'er bog or steep, through strait, rough, dense, or rare,
> With heads, bands, wings, or feet pursues his way,
> And swims or sinks, or wades, or creeps, or flies:

II, 947–950

In another description of motion, the final line of eight stressed syllables reflects the arduous progress against obstacles:

> Through many a dark and dreary Vale
> They pass'd, and many a Region dolorous,
> O'er many a Frozen, many a Fiery Alp,
> Rocks, Caves, Lakes, Fens, Bogs, Dens, and shades of death.
>
> II, 618–621

These, of course, are variations only within the pattern of blank verse. They do not take into account the variety of pace that can be achieved by different metrical patterns, short and long lines, and the variations within those patterns. Versification is the poet's special way of controlling the pace of his words.

The prose style of fiction can also strongly affect the pace of a work. There is little doubt that the characteristic sentence patterns of Melville, James, or Faulkner cause their prose to move at a slower pace than that of Lawrence, Hemingway, or Sherwood Anderson. But, in general, the pace of fiction is much more a matter of the rate at which the narrative moves forward. The action can move ahead rapidly in a linear sense or hesitate and move in a vertical direction, so that the writer or his characters in a sense stop the action to probe, reflect, or philosophize. In long works, there are alternate horizontal and vertical movements. A story of little action in which most of the movement is vertical may well be highly static, not dull as a consequence, but interesting in terms of other than straight storytelling.

The narrative technique of a story may also affect its pace. A cinematic technique, basically one in which fragments are projected before the reader without obvious transitions between them, is designed as a kind of economical narration. It is less concerned with the linear quality of narration and more with the gestalt. It operates like a collage. On the other hand, a story in which the transitions are carefully drawn so that all of the parts are linked and interfused to make a continuous whole may move with a less obvious sense of speed, but the logic of its narration may make it read more easily so that it seems to move at an equally rapid pace. Pace is a matter of intuitive perception in fiction, not unrelated to the technique the writer is using.

In drama, pace is largely a matter of the relation between action and dialogue. The drama is not a form that invites large-scale action. If the background is war, the action ordinarily takes place offstage or between acts. The clashes of rival forces onstage in some of Shakespeare's history plays inevitably fail to convey a sense of intense conflict. Drama is primarily a form for talking about action, not showing it. Yet it is quite another matter if there is no action at all and only talk remains. Then the movement must depend entirely upon the pace of the dialogue.

One noticeable development in twentieth-century drama has been writers' interest in discursive plays—plays in which the characters drawn together in a common crisis simply talk. Nothing of significance happens; the reader's interest must be in the characters as speakers, or there is no interest. Many of Shaw's plays, particularly one like *St. Joan,* fall into this category. Plays by Giraudoux, Beckett, and Ionesco are similarly discursive. Plays of this kind differ from others in that they lack a strong narrative base. All drama is composed of speaking, and in none is language more important than in Greek tragedies, which traditionally relegated violent action to offstage. Yet these plays were not without violent action. The tragedies were tragedies of dying, not the modern tragedies of living and talking about it. The pace of drama, therefore, seems to relate primarily to the kinds of things characters talk about and the length at which they expound. Drama that utilizes the natural pace of conversation with a strong sense of a developing action is likely to move at a far brisker pace than one in which characters make speeches and only wait for their fate.

Tone and Atmosphere   The tone of a literary work derives primarily from the choices and combinations of words that writers use, and we identify these stylistic effects as irony, satire, humor, understatement, hyperbole, or ambiguity. These verbal qualities were discussed in the previous section on Language, Symbol, and Imagery. Tone, however, may also result from the reader's response to form and rhetorical design, like orderliness or balance. What impresses us as a tone of eloquence in a work may be largely a result of emphasis or repetition or parallelism. Or what impresses us as unpleasant may be a writer's deliberate attempt to avoid the euphony of liquid sounds, appealing alliterations, or rhymes. All of these are tone qualities with which every writer has to be concerned if he is at all interested in more than the simple act of communication. In literature, tone is more than the tone of the language. It also depends upon other effects which are essentially nonverbal in nature. These can be grouped as typographical and theatrical.

Typographical Effects   Typographical effects include both the use of various kinds of type styles for dramatic effect and the arrangement of words on a page for a rhetorical effect. Both devices are deliberate attempts to escape the most routine form of presentation on the printed page. They force a reader to respond because they deviate from customary practices. The now familiar appearance of the name of e e cummings without capital letters and punctuation reminds us of the kind of awareness we have of changes from conventional practice. Cummings' own poems are familiar examples of rearrangements of words which will not permit the reader to view them thoughtlessly. They are a visual attempt to get away from the routine, just as a fresh image is an attempt to escape the cliché. Or they may be an attempt to get beyond the medium of words—to suggest motion or to appeal to the visual image. Any alteration of type, mechanics, line length, form, or spacing needs to be considered for the purpose the author had in mind.

Many typographical variations, particularly in fiction, may be best characterized as nonbook effects. They imitate the more spectacular appeals of newspaper and magazine techniques, or they seem to borrow from the movie script or television commercial. Even though some readers may dismiss these as cheap and superficial effects, the conclusion cannot be avoided that they are operating in their own nonverbal way to contribute to the tone of a work.

Theatrical Effects   Aristotle, one of the earliest writers on dramatic theory, recognized both music and spectacle as parts of dramatic effect, even though he spoke of them as accessories rather than as essential components. Any overemphasis upon them he would have considered a distraction from a tragedy's purpose. The history of dramatic production indicates that the elaborateness of staging has varied with fashion and the availability of resources. Yet prior to the modern period, the resources of the stage seem to have been looked upon as supplemental to the writer's script—something added to give the play dramatic life on the stage. The play could be seen with the additions, but it could also with equal force be read without them. Its meaning was in the language, not in the acting, the lights, and the sounds.

Many modern dramatists, however, have experimented with theatrical resources in an effort to establish tone and atmosphere as a new dimension of meaning. Thus a language of pantomime, light, and sound at times substitutes for the language of words. The result is that meaning becomes more and more implicit rather than explicit, expressive rather than reasoned, sensuous rather than discursive. These are plays written to be experienced; reading them requires a special kind of imaginative interpretation.

The final stage direction of Ionesco's *Exit the King* will serve as an example:

> *Sudden disappearance of* QUEEN MARGUERITE *on the left. The* KING *is seated on his throne. During this final scene, the doors, windows and walls of the throne room will have slowly disappeared. This part of the action is very important.*

> *Now there is nothing on the stage except the* KING *on his throne in a grayish light. Then the* KING *and his throne also disappear.*

> *Finally, there is nothing but the gray light.*

This disappearance of the windows, the doors and the walls, the KING
and the throne must be very marked, but happen slowly and gradually.
The KING *sitting on his throne should remain visible for a short time*
before fading into a kind of mist.

This particular ending is a tableau in which the most important commentary is made by the language of silence and light. The fade-out
is more than a representation of lights going off or night coming on;
it is a vehicle that depicts emotionally and symbolically the experience
of death and man's disappearance into the unknown darkness.

Many effects of lighting and sound and mime that the dramatist
writes into his directions are not intended to create an illusion. In fact,
they may work directly to the contrary. They make the audience aware
that the theater is a theater; that characters are actors playing roles;
that real life is not being enacted on the stage. At the end of Edward
Albee's *The American Dream,* Grandma interrupts the dialogue to speak
directly to the audience:

> GRANDMA: (*Interrupting . . . to audience*)
>
> Well, I guess that just about wraps it up. I mean, for better or worse,
> this is a comedy, and I don't think we'd better go any further. No,
> definitely not. So, let's leave things as they are right now . . . while
> everybody's happy . . . while everybody's got what he wants . . . or every-
> body's got what he thinks he wants. Good night, dears.

In its effect, the speech functions somewhat like the ancient Greek
chorus, which remained on stage as an observer and commented upon
the action.

The stage has definite limitations, but the nonverbal effects are
definite attempts to transcend the limitations and to use them to advantage. At the beginning of Tennessee Williams' *The Glass Menagerie,*
Tom, the narrator and also a character in the play, addresses the
audience. After speaking of the social background of the play, he says:

> The play is memory. Being a memory play, it is dimly lighted, it is
> sentimental, it is not realistic. In memory everything seems to happen
> to music. That explains the fiddle in the wings.

These few remarks indicate the extent to which the music and the
lighting are an integral part of this play. They must be taken into
account not only for production purposes but for reading purposes as
well.

In this same play, Williams planned to use a slide projector which
would cast titles and images on one of the walls of the stage. The device

was not actually used in the original Broadway production, but is written into the published manuscript. Williams explains the use of the slides as a structural device—as a means of giving a narrative line to an episodic play, and as a way of accenting values in particular scenes. Some of the legends read, "After the fiasco," "You think I'm in love with continental shoemakers?" "Things have a way of turning out so badly." The images include "Amanda as a girl on a porch, greeting callers," "Sailing vessel with jolly roger," "Blue Roses," and a "Glamor magazine cover." The screen images, therefore, serve additional purposes: they act as a memory device, they comment on the action, and they create atmosphere.

Theatrical effects of this kind cannot be ignored in reading a play. In fact, stage directions from the time of Ibsen on become increasingly important as explanations of the writer's intentions. They are not exit-and-entrance instructions; they are interpretations. A reader and interpreter of drama, particularly of modern drama, must therefore assume the mental role of director, scenic designer, and choreographer in an effort to determine fully the implications of the dramatist's directions. In this way, he must try to interpret the way nonverbal effects have been made an essential part of the style of the work.

Suggestions for Writing about Strategies and Nonverbal Effects   In order to avoid the pitfall of writing only vague generalizations about style, a reader needs to focus his attention upon specific strategies that the writer is using to create his effects. The reader's impressions and emotional responses are by no means to be ignored, although they should be only the starting point. The reader has to ask himself why he responds as he does. Why is he interested? Why must he read to the end without stopping? Why is he moved to pause and reflect? What makes the style compelling?

In order to get at particular strategies that often make a writer's style what it is, questions of the following variety will provide leads for the discussion of style in understandable and concrete terms:

1. What words best characterize the style of a particular work? Does this manner of style seem to predominate in other works by the same writer? Is there one style of the writer that seems to include many different manners?
2. What are identifiable strategies the writer is using? What are they accomplishing stylistically?
3. What are the climactic points in a novel or play? Do these seem to build to one main climax? Do these seem to set up a rhythmic pattern of stress and lack of stress, like the meter of a poem?
4. Where does the main climax occur in relation to the end? Is there

an abrupt denouement after the climax or a continuation of the story? What is the effect of either strategy?

5. What are the main elements that sustain the reader's interest in the literary work? What anticipations are set up? Are there other kinds of suspense than the one that depends upon withheld information or wondering what will happen? Can the emotional effects of the literary work upon the reader be explained in terms of suspense?

6. What elements can be identified which affect the pace of a long work? In fiction, what is the balance of action, description, and dialogue? What makes a drama static or fast moving? Is pace also related to climax and suspense?

7. In what way are the metrics of a poem suitable to its thought? What are the effects that derive almost completely from the versification? What is the degree of irregularity in the meter? Are the lines long or short or alternating?

8. What is the predominant tone of a work? Do the words that best describe the tone tend to be highly metaphorical? Can the impressions be supported by direct reference to particular incidents, scenes, and speeches?

9. What nonverbal resources does the writer utilize? What human senses are responding to these strategies? How many are being used simultaneously? To what effect?

10. Does the use of music, symbolic action, or light tend to support the general tone of the work and act in conjunction with the thought? Or do they tend to be accessories? Or do they serve as an ironic commentary upon the characters and actions? What are nonverbal effects doing? What would change if they were omitted? In what different ways could a play be produced to get different effects?

Thought and Meaning

The previous elements of literature we have discussed—the action, the setting, the characters, the structure, the language, and the strategies—all go to make up the literary vehicle. They are the elements that in special ways make a poem a poem or a story a story. The remaining element hinges upon the writer's purpose. Why did he write what he did in the first place? What is he saying?

John Ciardi has a book entitled *How Does a Poem Mean?* He explains that an alternate title might have been "How to talk about a poem without paraphrasing." The title of his book can readily be extended to the other forms: How does a novel mean? How does a short story mean? How does a play mean? The answers may begin to shape themselves if we ask, by contrast, How does an essay mean?

How does a telegram mean? In every instance, the form itself is a part of the meaning because the author has deliberately chosen it as his way of expressing his meaning in preference to some other way.

From Literal to Metaphorical   Readers who are intent upon finding "messages" in literature are applying the principles of the telegram to works that are not operating on those same principles. This is not to say that many poems, stories, and plays do not have explicit statements to make; but it is to say that they do not usually make them with the directness and literalness of the expository statement. In "Song of Myself," Walt Whitman writes:

> I find letters from God dropt in the street,
>   and every one is sign'd by God's name.

Paradoxically, this line uses the letter, a literal form of communication, as a metaphor. In the three preceding lines, Whitman says much more literally what he means:

> Why should I wish to see God better than this day?
> I see something of God each hour of the twenty-four, and each moment
>   then,
> In the faces of men and women I see God, and in my own face in the
>   glass.

To be quite explicit: the letters Whitman refers to are not written ones; they are implied in everything around us; they are metaphors of God. In a similar way, an author does not write letters to his readers in stories, poems, and plays; he communicates by everything he creates, sometimes by simply holding up a glass for us to see ourselves.

The Availability of Meaning   The obliqueness of the author's technique does not preclude writing about his thought, although it may be impossible to reduce everything to one generalization which accounts for the work as a whole. Occasionally, a summary can be made in terms of a thesis statement; for example, Turgenev's *Fathers and Sons* reveals the clash that occurs between the old and the young when the values of the older generation can no longer be accepted as the values of the younger. At other times, the meaning may be stated in terms of the commanding image: the thought and tone of Sartre's *No Exit* are expressed by the metaphor of its own title: life is a room with no escape; hell is other people. When the author has come to an understanding about life, when he has formed attitudes, when he has opinions and possibly even solutions to problems, his own convictions come through clearly, so that a reader can reduce the thought to a simple statement.

This is not to imply that the thought is simple or superficial, only that it is clear and inferable.

All works, however, are not reducible in these terms. The author may claim to have no understanding of what he sees and knows, but by revealing his thoughts he may bring about awareness and understanding in others. Some literary works, particularly poems, are only observations; others are explorations with no discoveries; others are conjectures, grasping for balance and hope. To say precisely what the author's thought is in works of this kind may be impossible. He may have only a view. He may have an idea only in the sense that an idea is a predication of some kind, however diffuse: life is a lunatic asylum or a circus or a brothel. His sights may be set upon fragmentation, dislocation, and discontent, not unity, order, and stability. Those who want answers in literature may not find them in writers who see their role primarily as recorders of experience, not as seers and teachers.

The important thing in writing about the thought of a literary work is not to begin with a single expectation: that the thought is there to be read as it is in an essay, open and available. The reader must expect to reach for the thought, not to have it handed to him. In works in which the meaning must be inferred, the thoughts are not hidden in the sense that they are removed from view or that they are deliberately secluded to make understanding difficult. Most authors write to be read and understood, but the most thoughtful ones are seldom reductionists. They do not find platitudes and clichés adequate expressions for their insights. They may find it necessary to work out the meaning of a story or a poem in complex ways. It is certainly a legitimate question to ask what a writer is driving at as long as we do not always expect to be able to come up with a quick and easy answer.

Intrinsic Sources of Thought   Even though the total meaning may be a matter of putting together the parts or drawing out inferences, particular ideas can be derived from a number of different sources within the work itself. These are intrinsic sources of thought as opposed to those which are imposed upon the work from without. These are built into the structure itself and, like all meaning, vary from the literal to the metaphorical. Clues to thought and meaning come from a number of different sources:

1. Titles

The title ought always to be taken into account; it may hold a key to the author's emphasis and tone. Ibsen's play *Hedda Gabler* is named after the protagonist. It could be a quite literal title like Flaubert's *Madame Bovary* or Tolstoy's *Anna Karenina. Hedda Gabler* is different, however, because in the play Hedda Gabler is married; her name has been changed to Hedda Tesman. In the title, therefore, Ibsen hints at an idea about the main character which is developed throughout the play.

Shaw's title *Arms and the Man* provides a humorous ambiguity; the play concerns both war and romance. In addition, the title is an echo of the opening lines of Virgil's *Aeneid,* another tale of war and romance, but Shaw's play is a satire. Its title therefore suggests its mock-heroic tone. On the other hand, Hemingway's title *Farewell to Arms,* also a story of war and romance, contains the same ambiguity, but in its combination with *Farewell* suggests a tone of serious irony rather than light mockery.

A standard trick question is to ask who the Merchant of Venice is in Shakespeare's play of that name. Why does the title place the emphasis upon Antonio when many people think the play is about Shylock? The title invites another way of looking at the play. Joyce's *Ulysses* and Shaw's *Pgymalion* direct the reader's attention to sources outside the works as keys to their understanding. Dickens' *Bleak House,* a novel about people's entanglements with the law, and Whitman's *Drum-Taps,* his collection of poems about the Civil War, establish a tone. Jane Austen's titles *Pride and Prejudice* and *Sense and Sensibility* give the key themes for interpreting these works. Titles like Thomas Wolfe's *Look Homeward, Angel* and Faulkner's *The Sound and the Fury* are literary allusions and therefore metaphorical in their implications. O'Neill's *The Hairy Ape* and Ibsen's *Ghosts* are also metaphorical titles which provide a commanding image for the play's meaning as a whole. Titles need to be carefully examined.

2. Names

The names of characters and places may have special appropriateness or irony. At times, they may actually mean something significant in terms of the play, as the name of Oedipus means "swollen feet." Or the names may invite an extended interpretation of the work, as George and Martha in Albee's *Who's Afraid of Virginia Woolf* may be seen as the primal husband and wife of the nation. The main characters in Shaw's *Man and Superman* parallel characters in Mozart's opera *Don Giovanni,* so that a comparison between the two works is necessary for a full insight into Shaw's intentions. Other names like those of Blanche Du Bois and Stanley Kowalski in *Streetcar Named Desire* are associative. Others are suggestive like the array of humorous names in Dickens' novels, which include Mr. Gradgrind, Mr. Bounderby, Mr. Murdstone, Mr. Pumblechook, Mr. Skimpole, and the Hon. Samuel

Slumkey. Place names may take on the same qualities—*Streetcar* is set in a slum area of New Orleans called Elysian Fields—but names of this kind are usually not plentiful unless the work is clearly an allegory.

Equally important as the names chosen is the omission of names. Most of the soldiers in Stephen Crane's *The Red Badge of Courage* are nameless. It makes them as anonymous as soldiers become in a war; it also makes them universal. In a similar way, characters in Strindberg's *The Dream Play* are identified simply by their sex or occupation: He, She, The Daughter, The Officer, The Lawyer, The Poet. These are dreamlike figures; they are also universal types.

3. Allusions

Allusions represent the intricate interweaving of the author's reading and experience into his own writing. They are therefore a source of interest about the writer, but they may prove to be essential to a complete understanding of the work. An allusion like "Jonah's Moby" in a sonnet by Dylan Thomas is a kind of puzzle, but an entire poem based upon an allusion, like Yeats's "Leda and the Swan," cannot be understood without knowing the mythological story. Frequently, a poet may give almost all of the facts one needs to know about an allusion, as Wallace Stevens in his poem "Peter Quince at the Clavier" tells the story of Susanna, taken from *The Apochrypha;* yet knowledge of the original story provides a base for knowing how Stevens uses the allusion for his own purposes. Literary references of this kind are clearcut; they can even be footnoted. But they do not cover all of the subtle echoes of phrase and line in a poem that may give clues to the author's thinking and meaning. In Eliot's *Murder in the Cathedral,* when the Second Priest expresses joy at the impending return of Archbishop Becket, the Third Priest says:

> For good or ill, let the wheel turn.
> The wheel has been still, these seven years, and no good.
> For ill or good, let the wheel turn.
> For who knows the end of good or evil?
> Until the grinders cease
> And the door shall be shut in the street,
> And all the daughters of music shall be brought low.

The last three lines are almost the exact words of Ecclesiastes 12:3-4, and the first four lines suggest the spirit of Chapter 3 of the same book of the Bible. In this instance, the allusion is the meaning.

Allusions are obviously not limited to literary references. A major portion of Auden's "Musée des Beaux Arts" is based upon a reference to Breughel's painting of the fall of Icarus. His poem "September 1, 1939" is a topical allusion to the invasion of Poland by Hitler's troops. The allusion becomes the point of departure for the thoughts of the poem. It cannot be fully understood without that historical background. Allusions in writing are so very numerous that one can only conclude that the more one reads and knows, the more likely he will be able to come to grips with subtleties of meaning in an author's work.

4. Dialogue

One obvious source of ideas occurs in the dialogue of the characters. At times, when an author is interested in particular issues, he introduces a discussion among his characters. There seem to be no bounds—from general topics about morality, politics, and women's rights to more specific theories and ideas. Samuel Butler concerns himself with Darwinianism in *The Way of All Flesh,* Dickens with Utilitarianism in *Hard Times,* and Shaw with the Bergsonian Life Force in *Man and Superman.* These sometimes take the form of actual intellectual discussion or may influence the conception of the characters.

What one needs to guard against is to identify the views of a character in a novel or play with the author unless there is reason to do so. In a time when authors as self-advertisers are given to writing about their own ideas and their own works, identifications are often possible to make. Inevitably, a character who is a freethinker or reformer becomes the author's mouthpiece. Some playwrights see themselves primarily as teachers or preachers. In the Epistle Dedicatory to *Man and Superman,* Shaw writes:

> . . . it annoys me to see people comfortable when they ought to be uncomfortable: and I insist on making them think in order to bring them to conviction of sin. If you don't like my preaching you must lump it. I really cannot help it.

The ideas of a play, therefore, may be its main reason for its existence, and it becomes the interpreter's job to sort out opinions among the characters to see precisely how the ideas develop and how the action comments upon them.

How Literature Means   To consider how a story or a poem or a play means is to go beyond what the words say. Meaning is not limited strictly to ideas, to its intellectual substance and sense. Meaning cannot always be summarized in a sentence because works of literature have other varieties of meaning. They mean by the feelings they convey; they mean by the attitudes they create; they mean by the style they assume; they mean in terms of the author's intentions and the time and occasion of his writing. Accordingly, new meanings emerge constantly with the passage of time and with the investigations of new readers. Thus, writing about the meaning of a work is always justified because it can never be set down definitively at one particular time. An old work in a new time may be a revelation to its readers. A new reader is capable of seeing new meanings.

Extrinsic Sources of Thought   Thus far we have discussed the analysis of a literary work in terms of itself, in terms of the elements that combine to express meanings. This emphasis is sometimes referred to as formalistic; it has been more popularly labeled the New Criticism. What was new about New Criticism in the 1930s and 1940s has in one sense grown old, but it has now become established as an indispensable approach, particularly for the nonprofessional. What it does is to assert the primacy of the text, to ask the reader to look at it as material contained between the covers of the book and to consider it without reference to all of the other knowledge in the world that can be brought to bear upon it.

However, the growing sterility of New Criticism, the social rebellion of the second part of this century, and a new spirit of Romanticism have brought about a shift in critical emphasis—from a consideration of the work as an isolated text, severed even from its author, to a consideration of a work in a variety of contexts. Thus, outside knowledge can be brought to bear upon a literary work in such a way as to enlighten its meaning. These are extrinsic considerations. They are critical frames of reference that require specialized knowledge and are therefore less available to the amateur reader. Yet the perspectives which these approaches represent should be briefly considered.

Biographical Considerations   The biographical approach to literature is a standard one of long duration. Its value lies in the extent to which facts about the author's life help to enlighten the content of his works. Its value is also relative. Some works contain more of their writer's immediate thoughts and experiences than others. If we had no outside sources of information about John Milton, for example, we would know most of the things we need to know about him from his own works. He constantly reflects upon his own experiences in the prose and poetry and sometimes records them quite literally in personal digressions. On the other hand, the person of Shakespeare, about whom we know surprisingly little despite the fact that he is a major figure, cannot be inferred from the plays and poems. Biographies of him which exist are based upon a few facts and a mass of inference; they are largely speculative.

Biographical facts should not be absolutely necessary for reading a poem or story or play, but certainly all of the possible meanings have not been explored until they have been investigated. Once a work has been written, it is severed from its author, but the fact that it was derived from the source of his thought and experience may account for many things. The writer of biographical criticism needs one major caution: to keep the biographical facts and the critical interpretation in balance. When the life and works are discussed together, all too often the works are forgotten, and the study becomes a biographical sketch. Biography is valuable as a study in its own right; it is not the same, however, as the critical application of biography to a work of literature.

Historical-Social-Political Considerations   Every literary work also springs from the context of its times. Yet, like the personal experiences of an author's life, these must be weighed more heavily in some works than in others for the obvious reason that some writers are more socially and politically conscious than others. The slavery issue and the Civil War are hardly reflected at all in the poetry of Longfellow; they are everywhere apparent in the poetry of Whitman. The French dramatist Giraudoux served in the Ministry of Foreign Affairs of France for a major portion of his life, eventually becoming the Minister of Propaganda, a post he held until the German occupation of France. His plays clearly show his interests in political matters.

Most writers at one point or another, however, make allusions to the times in which they live. What the writer does and what the critic does are two different things, however. What criticism of this variety tends to do is to read a particular work with a bias, to consider it as a political or social document, and to consider it from the one view of history which the critic has adopted. Steinbeck's *The Grapes of Wrath* is a moving novel of human interest which can be read in terms of its own intrinsic values as a literary work; it is also an important social commentary upon the plight of dispossessed farmers during the depression of the 1930s. In its sympathy with the farmer and its denunciation of the businessman, the work invites the attention of Marxian critics. For them, the analysis of the novel and its values therefore hinge upon the extent to which it is good or bad Marxian doctrine, upon the extent to which the author seems to show attitudes of acceptance or rejection. The author's own intentions are in this case irrelevant. It is possible to read any author's work as Marxian if it is critical of materialism, religion, and traditional social values, although the author's own interests may not at all be political. Criticism of this nature often begins with presuppositions and then measures the literary work in terms of them. It may not let a literary work speak for itself by imposing a framework upon it.

Psychological Considerations   The difference between intrinsic and extrinsic considerations needs to be stressed constantly. It is one thing to examine the motivations of the characters in a novel; it is another to begin with a theory and to view all characters in terms of it. Or to take all of the outward signs of a character as symptoms of inner psychic drives so that a psychologist-critic can offer explanations not apparent to the nonspecialist. Criticism of this variety in a sense subjects literary characters or the author to psychoanalysis in terms of a particular school of thought. Freudianism is commonly represented.

As fascinating as psychological criticism can be at times, its shortcomings should be apparent. The critic is limited only to what the literary work reveals—a selection of outward signs that cannot be expanded; he is unable to elicit more information from the subject. It is not surprising, therefore, that criticism of this kind tends to speculate, to fill in the gaps, to extend the meanings beyond those the work invites. The more complex a character is, the more likely he is to attract the attention of psychological critics. One of the standard works of this kind is Ernest Jones's study of Hamlet in terms of the Oedipus complex. Any writer whose works tend to dwell upon introspection, sex, the macabre, the occult, the visionary, and the dreamlike—Poe, Kafka, Coleridge, and D. H. Lawrence come quickly to mind—is an especially fruitful source for this kind of critical analysis. Above all, however, criticism of this variety requires knowledge.

Archetypal and Mythic Considerations   Closely related to psychological criticism is an approach that views literature in terms of archetypal patterns and myths. This kind of criticism draws heavily upon anthropology, religion, and mythology. It is an exploration of the communal response of all men to certain patterns of experience and phenomena of nature. They are inescapably a part of basic human behavior. For example, one of the archetypal experiences of all men is growth from childhood to manhood, from immaturity to maturity, from innocence to knowledge. The pattern applies not only to individual experience but to collective experience as well. Thus, one of the best known of all myths, which like all myths may or may not have basis in fact, is the story of Adam and Eve in the Garden of Eden. Adam and Eve become primal father and mother. They are individuals; they are also all mankind. They pass from their state of innocence to a state of knowledge. As a result, they are expelled from Eden. Thus arises another deep subconscious drive in all men: the desire to return to the Edenic experience and the quest for a means, often a savior, to achieve it. In turn, other kinds of experience follow: suffering, sacrifice, and death, with the idea that these will achieve redemption, purification, and immortality. All of these human manifestations are reflected in the cycles of nature: all things spring to life, grow, die, and revive again. These patterns of nature and experience all men seem to know and understand and believe.

In ancient times, the archetypal patterns were embodied in simple but powerful stories. Today we call them myths. They are present in almost all cultures. Common motifs run throughout them, and they share symbols that are only variations upon one another. Men are still fascinated with the simple stories of the sun, moon, water, and the garden; or of a hero's search against obstacles for the answer to a riddle or a sword or a chalice which will make him a savior, or of a hero's willingness to die to deliver his people or remove the blight of sterility from the land.

These archetypal and mythic patterns continue to emerge in both the structure and imagery of contemporary writers. Critics interested in this approach are sometimes able to demonstrate convincingly that an author, whether intentionally or not, has once again recast one of the ancient myths in a new garb. These strains seem to demonstrate that beneath all of the knowledge and sophistication of modern man, he still cannot escape the most elemental concerns of his nature.

Like most of the extrinsic approaches, archetypal and mythic criticism requires an acquaintance with a vast body of knowledge on the subject. We may all know instinctually more than we think we know, but anthropology and cultural history provide a rich source of organized knowledge with which to begin.

Philosophical Considerations   It is not uncommon for authors to turn to philosophical works for clarification of their own thinking about the universe and to reflect this reading in their own works, sometimes superficially, sometimes profoundly. Therefore, an investigation of an author's own reading has been a fairly standard kind of project among scholars and critics interested in the influence of outside thought upon a writer. One comes to understand Dante better by knowing Aquinas; Alexander Pope by knowing Deistic thought which he got from his friend Bolingbroke; Wordsworth by knowing John Locke and David Hartley; John Stuart Mill by knowing Auguste Comte; and Shaw by knowing Henri Bergson. In more general terms, certain concepts occur over and over again in literature. Platonic ideas are pervasive in the writings of the Renaissance. The concept of the Great Chain of Being, which had its genesis in Greek philosophy, occurs again and again, as Arthur Lovejoy has shown, in philosophy and literature.

Knowing the philosophical backgrounds of a literary work can add immeasurably to one's understanding of it. The general reader should be aware, however, that this kind of outside knowledge does not necessarily present an insurmountable barrier toward understanding a writer. Authors also take on the role of informants. They often explain what they are talking about through one character or another. The purpose of criticism of this variety is finally to verify the accuracy of the writer's ideas and to see what adaptation he makes of other people's ideas for his own purposes. This type of analysis is a specialized approach which requires more than the capacity to name sources. If it is of value, it should add to the completeness of the work's meaning.

Considerations of Literary History   Criticism that involves literary history amounts to placing a writer or a particular work he has written into any number of literary contexts. An author can be considered in relation to a literary movement, or he can be considered as influencing other writers or being influenced by them. A work can be considered as employing literary conventions or rebelling against them. A particular writer may be more important historically than the quality of his works justify. Emile Zola is significant for his leadership of the Naturalistic movement in the late nineteenth century. His novels are still read, but they do not equal the reputation of those of Stephen Crane, who followed later in the movement. John Lyly's *Euphues,* written in a highly inflated and affected style popular in the sixteenth century, gave the English language a new word, but the work ordinarily is known only through brief excerpts which appear in anthologies to illustrate "euphuism." Sarah Arne Jewett is an important writer of regionalist literature in America, but she has not achieved major stature as a literary figure. Gertrude Stein exercised a powerful influence upon a whole group of writers and artists emerging in the 1920s, but many people find her own works largely unreadable. Thus, one can multiply the examples of literary figures and particular literary works that loom large in literary history, although they are not of major interest from other critical viewpoints. It is obvious that only an acquaintance with literary history can do justice to this form of criticism.

Creative Critical Responses   This kind of critical response as an extrinsic source of thought may best be described as a bringing of the self to the literary work. It is creative rather than analytical; it is often an emotional response rather than an intellectual one. It requires only that the writer react in some way to the work he has read. He may want to imitate it; he may want to write a poem; he may be moved to give a personal testimonial how he has responded to the work; he may want to speak to one of the characters. After reading Arna Bontemps' "A Summer Tragedy," one student wrote:

I became so involved in the story that Bontemps could take me anywhere, have me see the story through any eyes. I could see where the people's outlook stopped and where the living situation began. Bontemps could inject any sensation into the story and I could feel it immediately.

I am—no, it doesn't matter what I am except that I am a reader. Arna Bontemps is a writer. He reached me. He said his thing to me, I listened to him through my own patterns, and I saw things his way all of a sudden. He made my world larger.

These are only the concluding remarks of a critical response which gives specific examples why the writer was moved as she was. This is affective criticism, that is, criticism concerned with feeling. Like all highly personal criticism, it may say more about the critic than about the work itself, but it does testify to the vital effect literature can have upon the individual. Criticism does not need to be considered a purely diagnostic art; it can itself be a creative activity which seeks out its own forms and modes.

Suggestions for Writing about Thought and Meaning   Since thought and meaning emerge from almost all things that an author does in his composition, a few questions of the following variety will help to bring into focus a large and involved topic:

1. To what extent is the author's meaning literal or metaphorical? Can the author's meaning be reduced to a sentence, or can it only be hinted at?
2. Is the author firmly committed to a point of view, or does he seem only to raise questions? Does he seem to express a particular philosophy or set of ideas which are peculiarly his own? Are the ideas derivative? Does the uncertainty about the author's meaning comment upon the complexity of the work or upon its purpose only to observe, not to give answers?
3. Does the title give a clue to the work's major emphasis? Does the work seem to be about other things than the title suggests? Is the title ambiguous? Is it derived from another source which will comment upon the meaning of this work?
4. Do the names of characters and places seem to have special significance? Are they metaphorical? Associative? Allegorical? Are characters nameless for a particular purpose? Is any character an embodiment of an idea?
5. Are allusions a key to the author's meaning? Of what nature are they? Topical? Literary? Mythological? Natural? Is the allusion a passing reference or an integral part of the structure? What does a comparison with the source reveal about the author's use of it?

6. Do particular ideas dominate the dialogue? Are particular ideas countered by opposite views? What characters speak particular ideas? Are they sympathetic characters? Do they seem to speak for the author?

7. Are the ideas of a particular work dated? Have they been discredited by later findings and developments? Is the work therefore dated because its ideas are outmoded? Do some ideas seem to be perennial, unchanging?

8. What outside sources of knowledge does a particular work seem to invite? Is the work highly autobiographical so that the facts of the author's life are particularly relevant? Is it a work that concerns itself with a special body of knowledge so that full understanding depends upon turning to outside sources? Is a special knowledge of psychology, philosophy, myth, or literary history especially valuable?

9. What are the social and historical issues that will enlighten the meaning? Are they still vital considerations? Has the work transcended its own times?

10. What are the affective qualities of the meaning? How does the reader respond? What is he moved to do? Does the literary work touch him in a personal way? Does it cause him to react? What is the vital force of the work?

GENERAL APPROACHES TO WRITING ABOUT LITERATURE

The discussion up to this point has concentrated mainly upon the nature of literature and the way it functions as an art form, indicating the kinds of things a reader can focus upon. With this as background, then, what can he do in actually writing about literature?

1. He can summarize

Summary statements are close to exercises that merely test the reader's capacity to paraphrase the content accurately. Anyone who writes a lengthy synopsis as a substitute for an essay should realize that he has done little more than given evidence that he has read closely enough to be able to reproduce the details.

Summary may be considered the most elementary and least demanding approach to writing about literature. It does become important, however, when the presentation demands any kind of illustration. Even though the writer may assume that his audience knows the work under discussion, it is necessary to give brief summaries from time to time to refresh their memories and to establish a common base for understanding. When summary predominates over all other approaches, however, the reader knows that the writer has failed to take an additional step of lending his own thought to the material.

2. He can interpret

Interpreting is seeing the implications of what is going on or what is being said in a literary work. It goes beyond retelling the story; it says what it is about. It may consist of any number of different approaches. It may mean deciphering the difficult syntax of a poem; it may mean recognizing that the reading of a poem is intentionally ambiguous and that it therefore has several implications. It may mean filling in the details of a story or play which are left implicit. By leaving some things unexplained, imaginative literature differs rather consistently from discursive prose. The essayist characteristically wants to supply as much detail as possible so that his meanings are direct and clear. But the writer of literature leaves much for the reader to conjecture and imagine. It is a part of the appeal of literature.

Interpretation may also be described as a translation as opposed to a transcription. Nietzsche once wrote, "There are no facts, only interpretations." Once a work of literature is written, all kinds of private, representative, and universal implications may emerge. If a work by its obviousness or superficiality stimulates little thought, then there is little need for interpreting it. Interpretation may consist of working within the framework of the work itself—intrinsic considerations—in order to dig down into the core of meaning. Interpretation may also consist of extending outward—extrinsic considerations—in order to build upon suggestions the literary work contains. In either instance, interpretation amounts to bringing thought and feeling to the act of reading and then verbalizing those thoughts.

Interpretation is seldom objective, but its subjectivity does not mean that it can be deliberately wrongheaded. When interpretation seems no longer to have any connection with the facts of the literary work, then surely it can be dismissed as farfetched. Interpretation consists of saying what one thinks, but saying what one thinks is one thing; saying what one thinks the writer is saying is another. The interpreter should be like an orchestral conductor who takes the score of a musical work. He can make it his own composition by ignoring completely the author's intentions, or he can put the composer first and let his own interpretation bring out the fullest intentions of the composer.

The best criticism makes the work primary; it begins with the work and keeps it always in focus. It is the critic's purpose to provide a number of access routes to understanding. If an interpretation leads the reader *to* the work, it provides a service. If it leads the reader completely *away* from the work, it has surely lost sight of its purpose as criticism.

3. He can analyze

Analysis is a kind of internal dissection that permits the reader to come to some understanding about the work as a whole. John Ruskin once defined artistic composition as "the help of everything in the picture by everything else." Analysis does assume that a literary work is organic, its parts working together to produce a total effect. It does not imply that the examination of the parts, like an exploratory operation of the human body, is done to discover what the flaws are. Analysis reveals weaknesses at times, but it may also increase the reader's understanding of how intricately the parts conjoin to create responses in a reader. Analysis is simply a way of seeking understanding.

Very often the secret of understanding is being able to ask good questions. The suggestions for writing about each of the components of literature given in the sections above furnish an array of questions for purposes of analysis and interpretation. One question—an obvious one—may provide an obvious answer. Some readers know only obvious questions. If they ask a different question, a less obvious one, the answer may provide new insights.

The best criticism asks many questions, although some critics who associate themselves with a particular school of thought may ask only a limited few. Thus, they tend to see every literary work in the same terms. Their remarks become monotonous, pat, and often forced. Certainly the student-critic needs all of the resources he can find, not only to be able to write about literature, but to form his own standards of critical judgment.

4. He can evaluate

To say of a literary work only "I like it" or "I don't like it" is not actually an evaluation; it is a dismissal. The personal response is an important beginning, but in some way it must be pushed further to say what the worth of a literary work is or what is lacking to make it valuable. Evaluations, therefore, extend over a range of possibilities from formal considerations to private ones.

First, a work may be considered in terms of itself, as this chapter has emphasized. Evaluation of this kind assumes something about what a work of art should do, namely, that all of its parts should be working toward the total effect. Therefore, evaluation of this kind asks what the relation of each part is to the whole. And, equally important, what the relation of the parts are to each other. Why do they follow one another? What are the principles of arrangement? To say that a literary work is "all of a piece" is in some way to account for almost all of its details.

Although some literary works are not structurally flawless, they are nevertheless impressive. Their worth may rest on other grounds, perhaps on their plausibility: the plausibility of the action, of the characters, of the thought. If the actions are contrived and improbable under the pretense of being lifelike, then the illusion fails. If the characters are appealing but superficial, then they may be wholly forgettable. If the thought is fragmentary but penetrating, the work may still have merit. Yet the elements of literature are not ordinarily isolated from one another. Evaluation is simply a way of considering the merits and limitations of a work in separate terms.

A literary work may have worth in still other ways. Its value may be judged in terms of its stylistic effectiveness—its use of the language and strategies the writer uses. Criticism of this kind depends to a great extent upon reading experience, and comparison may be the way of arriving at a decision about effectiveness. In one of his critical essays on poetry, Matthew Arnold proposed that the best way to determine excellence was "to have always in one's mind lines and expressions of the great masters, and to apply them as a touchstone to other poetry." He goes on to explain that other poetry will not have to resemble these touchstones closely, but they will serve as the means of determining the presence or absence of quality. They are in a sense, then, reminders of what quality is.

Arnold's touchstone method can be easily discredited as too intuitive, too limited, or too backward looking. Yet it does cause us to ask ourselves what criteria we are using when we are moved to praise. Some critics have no outside criteria; their decision about worth depends upon themselves alone.

Evaluation that depends wholly upon one's personal engagement is, of course, a private kind of criticism. Its writer cannot expect others to share his response unless he explains why he feels as he does. That explanation may involve narrating a personal experience which reveals why he has identified with a literary work. He may reveal his involvement by recording his reactions in a journal. The form of the creative critical response may be as varied as the individual who responds. Susan Sontag has written, "What a few people know now is that there are ways of thinking we don't yet know about. Nothing could be more important or precious than that knowledge, however unborn." Expressive criticism may also be a source of thoughts yet unknown.

Formal considerations are essentially irrelevant to the final judgments that expressive criticism makes, although an individual who permits himself honestly to respond to literature may in time become interested enough to ask himself what sources of value are in the work itself when many other individuals find it equally meaningful. Writing about literature is one way of discovering what one's own and other people's values are.

What Literary Criticism Is and Is Not

Criticism, then, is a kind of orderly way of looking at a literary work—asking questions about it—what Reuben Brower calls "Discovery of Design." His phrase might also be made to read "Discovery *by* Design." For criticism is discovery. It is not a deathblow to the literary work. It is not necessarily a negative judgment. Criticism can be both positive and negative. It is not necessarily a tearing apart, a way of spoiling enjoyment. It is most meaningful when it provides a way of seeing together—a new view and a new kind of communication.

In its approaches, criticism is not summary alone. It is interpretation, analysis, and evaluation. It is exploring, probing, playing with possibilities, gambling and usually winning, if only a little, seeking what is memorable and engaging. It always demands thought and involvement. Criticism does not have to be strictly writing *about* literature; it can also be writing *through* literature, *with* literature, *by means of* literature, and always, one hopes, *for* literature.

The Topic as an Aid to Writing

Writing about literature in the classroom often depends upon the topics assigned. In most instances, these are designed to help rather than hinder the student and to focus his attention upon matters that may not have occurred to him on his own. If the topic is completely free choice, the demand is even greater upon the student because on his own he must then know how to avoid the completely obvious.

In order to demonstrate the expectations and range of topics— either those assigned or self-designed—a number of English instructors independently wrote assignments on a single literary work, a modern one-act play by Dennis Jasudowicz, entitled *Blood Money,* described by the author as a play "on the value of money stretching." The play is skeletal in form. It has only three characters: D. H., a Negro man (the initials are those of D. H. Lawrence), Lady C., a Negro woman (the name suggests Lady Chatterley, the main character of D. H. Lawrence's most famous novel), and Oil Magnate, unnamed, but described as an overfat white man. The scene takes place in the mountains in a highly grotesque cabin painted black with black window shutters. Recently, the Oil Magnate has sent a man to the slums to buy a beautiful woman to bring to his mountain retreat, but when Lady C. arrives he pays no attention to her. He has also brought a man, D. H., to paint his cabin. D. H. and Lady C. are physically attracted to one another. When the Oil Magnate appears on the scene, he speaks only the words "Gosh! Gosh!" and obscenely stuffs dollar bills into his nostrils. D. H. and Lady C. defy Oil Magnate by making love together outside the cabin as he listens inside. When he will not readmit them to the warm cabin from the freezing outside, they taunt him. In the cold, they grow desperate. D. H. first abuses Lady C. and then kills her in order to take for himself her warm clothes against the freezing weather. D. H. perishes in an avalanche of snow when he tries to sit on the roof of the cabin warming himself by the chimney. Oil Magnate remains inside, pinning two signs to the wall. One reads "HOMECOMING, I HAVE ARRIVED"; the other says "MESSIAH."

Each of the following topics was written by a different instructor. In almost every instance it is impossible to write about only one element of this play as if it were completely isolated from all of the other ones. If the topic focuses upon character, it asks for the relationship between characters and thought; or if the topic focuses upon language, it then speaks about language and strategy and purpose. The notation after each topic suggests what the instructor is trying to get the student to see and to do.

1. In *No Exit,* Sartre argues that "Hell is other people." A person's scheme of values is alien to others, and their schemes are alien to him. What causes the hell portrayed in *Blood Money?* Is it a conflict between white and black, rich and poor, man and man (i.e. the "eternal triangle"), between individual schemes of value, or some combination? In other words, describe what seems to you to be the most significant cause for conflict. You would do well to make reference to actual statements in the play.

[The topic begins with a definition drawn from another literary source and asks the student to apply it to the situations in this play. This topic demands essentially an interpretation of the action, which, of course, cannot be separated from the characters who are involved in the conflict.]

2. Which character in this play triumphs? You may take the position that in such a drama no one "triumphs," that "triumph" is a contradictory term. Whatever position you take, support it with evidence from the play. Keep in mind that the last figure on stage is not necessarily victorious, that the most interesting characters are not necessarily going to come out on top, that death is occasionally a triumph of sorts, and that your own sympathies, attitudes, and preferences have nothing to do with the outcome of the play.

[This topic also deals with the conflict and its resolution. It asks who wins, if anyone does at all. In the assignment, the instructor tries to help his students avoid obvious thinking on the subject and, finally, encourages them in this instance not to let their preconceptions get in the way of letting the play speak for itself.]

3.   The characters in this play form a triangle, a common device in many stories of love and romance. Do the characters and the kinds of love they exhibit differ from those in other works with "love triangles" you have read? If so, in what ways?

[This topic points to the pattern of characters in the play and then asks how the working out of the traditional triangle is different in this play from others of a more conventional nature. This topic, therefore, asks for internal analysis and the application of some outside information for purposes of comparison.]

4.   To the extent that these characters are not "real people," what do you suppose Jasudowicz's purposes are in working with "unreal people"?

[This is a topic that actually asks about the nature and purpose of the special fictional universe that Jasudowicz has created. Since the play does not attempt to give an illusion of reality, the student is asked to consider how this kind of approach comments significantly upon life.]

5.   The Oil Magnate has no lines in the play. What other means does Jasudowicz use to characterize him?

[This topic focuses upon one character who is not revealed, as characters usually are, through spoken lines. The Oil Magnate says only the words "Gosh! Gosh!" but he does not engage in dialogue. The topic therefore asks the student to consider other ways in which the nature of this character is made known.]

6.   Discuss the power and limitations of money in human relationships as suggested by the characters in *Blood Money*.

[This topic asks for a discussion of the general idea of the play in terms of specific characters. The very fact that this topic is less focused than the others places a greater demand upon the student to limit it. He further has to caution himself whether he is writing about how important money is in general or about how important money is as a factor in this play.]

7.   Does the play seem to present only a problem, or does it offer a solution; *i.e.,* does the play go anywhere?

[This topic calls for an interpretation of the play as a whole, not in terms of the characters and actions but in terms of the general problem it treats. The student must first decide what he considers to be the central thesis of the play and then consider whether the play merely makes observations or offers solutions and criticism.]

8.   There are several important threads in *Blood Money*. Choose one (*e.g.,* race, capitalism, Christianity, sex). Trace it through the play, and explore it in relation to what you see as the central theme.

[This topic indicates that the previous question in number 7 does not necessarily ask for one right answer. There are several themes; this topic asks the student to choose one and examine it as it is developed throughout the play. The assignment does not ask whether the play comes to solutions, but if the student thought it did, he might appropriately discuss the ending.]

9.   Does the play submit to interpretation as a moral allegory? Consider especially whether good and evil are discussed in the play and, if so, what they embody.

[This topic invites the student to consider the play as moral allegory. The characters, therefore, must be considered as embodiments of ideas and the conflict as a struggle between good and evil. The student may find that the play does not fit such a simple pattern of moral allegory and argue accordingly.]

10.   Identify the elements in *Blood Money* that may be termed "absurd." How does the absurd function in the play? What effect does this absurdity have? Compare the use of absurdity in *Blood Money* with its function in "The Wrecker."

[This topic focuses upon dramatic strategy. The student must consider why the playwright has chosen to introduce the obviously absurd elements. The assignment asks for interpretation and then for comparison with another work he has read as a way of suggesting that the element of the absurd may not always have the same function.]

11.   Color—not only of skin—is used by the playwright, sometimes expressly, other times by implication, in developing his ideas. Focus on one major idea in the play and discuss how the colors help develop that idea.

[This topic focuses upon a different kind of strategy—the use of colors in the play as symbolical. The student is asked to relate the color symbolism to the development of a particular idea. The theme, therefore, should not become merely a catalog or description; it must also be an interpretation.]

12.   Do you feel that the play's obscenity is overdone? Or do you feel that it bears a legitimate functional relationship to Jasudowicz's central concerns? Why or why not?

[This topic asks the student whether he thinks the play's language and situations accomplish what the playwright intends them to. As in most of the other topics, the student has to come to some understanding of

the play's meaning and then decide whether all things are working together to accomplish the writer's purpose.]

13.   There is an abundance of blood in this little drama. There is also
a rich oil magnate who stuffs money in his nose. Comment on the possible
significance of this action, and try to develop an argument that relates
the ideas of blood and money in the play. In other words why is *Blood
Money* a good title, if it is?

[This topic assumes that the two key words of the title are especially
important; it asks the student to consider the action and ideas in terms
of them and then to decide whether they are an adequate index to the
action and thought in the play.]

14.   Study the language each person uses in the play and show how
the speech of each helps to characterize him. Do their names and histories
reinforce or conflict with your conclusions about their characters? If
they conflict, what is the function of the contrast?

[This topic asks for an analysis of the language as a device of characterization. If the student chooses to develop the question about the names
and histories of the characters, he would have to turn to sources outside
the play for information about D. H. Lawrence and Lady Chatterley.
Without this knowledge, the student would not be able to perceive a
contrast.]

15.   Can you find a parallel between the ill-fated affair of D. H. and
Lady C. and the biblical story of Adam and Eve in the Garden of Eden?
How does the recognition of such a similarity add to your understanding
of the play?

[This topic explores the possible mythic significance of the play. The
whole issue would be whether this parallel adds significantly to the
writer's insight. If it did not, he obviously could not write at length on
a topic like this one.]

16.   Discuss the Oil Magnate in terms of his Messianic complex. In what
ways is he or is he not a Messiah?

[This topic also explores the mythic and psychological significance of
the play in somewhat different terms. It also invites the possibility of
considering the play as satire, since the play is clearly a distortion of
any traditional myth.]

17.   Although most plays are written and produced either on stage or
in films, some are termed "closet dramas" because they are most suited
for private reading and for some reason would not "come off" in production. Decide the category in which you think *Blood Money* belongs.
Develop your argument with specific illustrations from the play.

[This topic asks the student to consider the actual theatrical possibilities of the play. Although some knowledge of the tradition of "closet drama" might be useful, it would not be absolutely necessary in order to indicate whether this play could be produced effectively or not.]

18.   One former student of this course complained that some of the anthology selections exhibited a "hang-up on sex a little outdated for today's young college student." He asked for selections which would express instead youth's "search for relationship and friendship with each other." Do you think this student would object to *Blood Money* on these grounds, or do you think the play expresses his concern for human relationship and friendship? Defend your opinion.

[This is a topic that asks for a reaction to someone else's opinion about the play's relevance to current thinking. It involves an evaluation of the play not in terms of itself but in terms of personal standards.]

19.   Is this a moral play? If so, what moral lesson are we to learn and why? If it is not, why not?

[This is a topic that also asks for an evaluation, but not in literary terms. The discussion would depend upon the student's concept of what is moral and what isn't and his own response to this particular drama.

20.   It could be claimed perhaps that the play with its violent language and simple plot works only because of its topical approach. But is the play purely topical, or does it appear to have some lasting value?

[This is another kind of evaluation that is purely speculative: Does the play seem to have durable values? In a discussion of this kind, some knowledge of the literary tradition would be helpful, for example, a knowledge of what kind of work tends to fade and what kind tends to survive. The discussion demands a judgment and an opinion. If the writer is able to weigh the play's values, then he may also be able to estimate whether it has potential to transcend the change of time.]

These topics on one short play—and they could be multiplied many times—suggest the range of emphasis that is possible in writing about literature. Of special importance is the fact that each topic has been phrased by someone who has already given the play careful thought. Each question hints, leads, or directs in some way. None forbids the student from exploring new possibilities, but each is urging, shoving, luring him to think what possibly he has not thought about before.

SPECIFIC APPROACHES TO WRITING ABOUT LITERATURE

One of the main problems every writer has to solve is how to talk about a literary work as a whole without falling into vacuous generalizations. The problem increases as the length of the work increases, for the accumulation of detail seems always to invite a statement that will include the whole work. What happens can be illustrated by a sentence one student wrote in an attempt to embrace three stories by D. H. Lawrence:

> In his three short stories, Lawrence deals with love relationships. He reveals the participants' feelings, needs and desires—both conscious and unconscious—and their resulting behavior—emotional and often irrational—when these needs and desires are not fulfilled.

The weight of the generalization is almost more than one sentence can bear. But, more to the point, it is a high-level generalization that might apply to three stories by three other writers. It is not specifically a meaningful statement about the stories of D. H. Lawrence. How then does one avoid generalizing about all literature and all life so that an essay seems clearly related to the work it is discussing? How does one organize his thoughts so that in a relatively brief space he can indicate his grasp of the whole? Several approaches suggest themselves:

1. He can carefully select a speech or passage or detail that brings many elements of the work into focus. The discussion can then move outward to illustrate the central importance of this passage and its representativeness.
2. Instead of the familiar summary that begins with the beginning, he can begin with the end of the work and explain the outcome in terms of the earlier development. This approach invites selection of detail for purposes of illustration.
3. He can attempt to see the major characters from the point of view of one of the secondary characters. This provides a means of selective analysis and demands an interpretation from a point of view other than the writer's own.
4. He can collect small clues and signs that set the tone and create an atmosphere for the whole work.
5. He can select one theme for discussion rather than the full breadth of the literary work.
6. He can attempt to relate selected details of the story to a single emotional effect: one work as a study in horror, another as a study in the grotesque.
7. He can examine particular literary devices as a way of discovering how the author creates his effects.
8. He can begin with what interests him most about the work and then try to account for this reaction in terms of other things that have receded in his attention.
9. He can begin with an interpretation or critical evaluation written

by someone else and then agree or disagree, support or refute, expand or offer an alternate interpretation.

10. He can begin with any kind of preconception or idea or impression and then examine the work carefully to see if it holds up under special scrutiny.

Once a writer has determined his approach, writing about literature is essentially the same as writing about anything else—determining a purpose, making it clear, providing evidence, illustrating, narrating, describing, defining, comparing, arguing—doing anything that will make the writing persuasive. These ways can best be made clear in terms of specific examples.

Writing about Drama: Analysis and Interpretation

▶ STUDENT THEME

The Hope of Man

"Think of living up there in the top flat, with a beautiful young wife, two pretty little children and an income of twenty thousand crowns a year," yearns The Student in the first scene of Strindberg's *The Ghost Sonata*. To live in a house like that would be the answer to his hopes for happiness. His hope is for a life of sweet, innocent love, of sunshine-filled rooms with pink draperies, of his own children's bubbling laughter, and of money enough to insulate himself from the common worries of existence. This is his personal interpretation of the basic hope of man—that somewhere there is something beautiful and true to make the suffering of life worthwhile. The question asked by The Girl—so often asked but so seldom answered—is therefore central: "Is life worth so much hardship?"

Strindberg's *The Ghost Sonata* is not a play written to fill one's heart with hope for human triumph over the "labor of keeping the dirt of life at a distance," as the girl aptly phrases the problem. Instead, Strindberg destroys the false dreams of the romantic and, through a horror-filled nightmare, shows the blackness of reality that is hidden so securely behind a well-scrubbed facade of deceit. This is shown symbolically by the house—modern, pleasant-appearing, so seemingly filled with "beauty and elegance." It is a mansion. To the passerby it is the home of virtuous and high-minded aristocrats: the wealthy colonel, the benevolent consul, the aged spinster, the baron, the beautiful daughter, and the well-mannered servants. But what are these people after Mr. Hummel, the most flagrant deceiver of them all, disrupts their stagnating existence, and "the deepest secret is divulged—the mask torn from the imposter, the villain exposed ..."? All of these people are tortured by the sins of their past; all live on in the horrid loneliness of a hell full of "crime and deceit and falseness of every kind," in which payment is painfully wrung from their condemned souls.

In this symbolic house of lies, what is more a paradox of appearance and reality than the Hyacinth Room, full of the splendor of nature. The Student extols hyacinths of many colors: "the snow-white, pure as innocence, the yellow honey-sweet, the youthful pink, the ripe red, but best of all the blue—the dewy blue, deep-eyed and full of faith." But The Girl shows the other side of the picture: "This room is called the room of ordeals. It looks beautiful, but it is full of defects." The chimney smokes, the desk wobbles, the pen leaks, the maid makes more work for the girl, the cook gives her no nutrition. "Living is hard work, and sometimes I grow tired," laments The Girl. Finally, she grows tired from her labors and dies. Her whole life is a hopeless situation; for, as the student explains, "The very lifespring within you is sick."

There is no hope here for The Girl, or for man in general. But is there hope in the patient Buddha, waiting endlessly for the time when "this poor earth will become a heaven"? I think not. The Student explains, "Buddha sits holding the earthbulb, his eyes brooding as he watches it grow, outward and upward, transforming itself into a heaven." This symbol of man's hopes seems to be contradicted by the meaningless death of the girl, killed by the world's cruel deceit. Buddha's shallot, blooming beautifully out of the ugly earth, is the hope of man. Yet it may be contrasted with another flower, the girl, the flower of reality, who withers and dies in this vale of tears we call life.

To end the play, The Student soliloquizes on the hopelessness of finding anything in life worth living for. He hopes that death will liberate, that the girl will eventually find the hopes of man fulfilled "by a sun that does not burn, in a home without dust, by friends without stain, by a love without flaw."

Comment: The clarity and orderliness of this analysis belie what a remarkable accomplishment this short essay is. The student takes a highly complex, symbolical drama and by focusing upon selected details of the setting and dialogue by two of the main characters manages to get at the substance of Strindberg's thought. At no point does he summarize the action, although he does suggest in paragraph two what the general situation is. He is primarily concerned with the strategies that Strindberg uses: the house, the Hyacinth Room in particular, the Buddha. All of these he interprets so that their significance is made known. But the essay is not all formalistic analysis. When the major topic of the paper—the hope of man—is introduced in the fourth paragraph, the writer expresses his personal opinion. He shares the doubts of the student in the play. He makes clear which character he identifies with.

Writing about Drama: A Mythic Interpretation and Personal Assessment

▶ STUDENT THEME

Blood Money

Often in modern plays the author creates characters that are concerned with a major problem, but, unlike plays from past centuries that conclude with a moral being learned or a lesson taught, these modern plays generally leave the reader in a state of wonder, not knowing answers, forced to decide for himself. One such play is *Blood Money* by Dennis Jasudowicz. The author presents a problem, but has left the decision-making to the reader: which character is the hero, which is right in his actions, which to believe, what to think.

The love between D. H. and Lady C. resembles the biblical story of Adam and Eve—lovers in the ideal state who have sinned and are forced to face the consequences of their sin. D. H. and Lady C. willingly sin and realize too late that it means the loss of their re-entry to the paradise of safety, warmth, and shelter. The god they have spurned, the power above them (represented by the Oil Magnate) now spurns them and is deaf to their cries and pleadings. Their faith in each other is destroyed as they realize their situation—that they have caused their own downfall in mistakenly believing and having faith that they will be forgiven.

Faith, here, is an extremely important issue. Do I trust and have faith in those I love, in those who have power over me, or only in myself? In *Blood Money* all these possibilities seem to be ridiculous, since we must watch as Lady C. is murdered by her trusted lover, as the powerful Oil Magnate shows no mercy toward the lesser beings, and as D. H.'s faith in himself is destroyed.

The author has touched on the timeless search of every age. Is it enough to have myself, have faith that I can survive and succeed? Or is it necessary to find another to love, to rely on someone else besides myself for security, happiness, and success? Or are these relationships too concrete and too earthly? By this I mean, does man have to go out of his own personal realm towards faith in and love for a superior being with power over him? Man in himself is so small, but added to another is twice again in size. D. H. and Lady C. could have had so much strength and beauty in their love and unity, but the weak basic nature of man allowed fear and desperation to take the upper hand. Man can add nothing to himself with false relationships; only through honesty and truth can strength and success in friendship and love grow. Perhaps man's belief in a superior being is his only hope, perhaps it is his major downfall. I have yet to come to a decision....

Comment: This essay begins by stating that *Blood Money* is the kind of play that leaves moral decisions to the reader. This student does not have moral preconceptions which will simplify looking at the play. The essay is an attempt to consider the possibilities, to ask questions.

The interpretation begins by rather remarkably condensing into one paragraph a parallel between the Garden of Eden story and the situation in *Blood Money.* This comparison then invites the possible solutions to man's plight: faith and love. A kind of self-examination follows, but the answers are prompted by details from the play. At this point, the student has not abandoned the drama to write a personal narrative. The essay reveals the student's mind at work in interaction with the play. The essay concerns itself primarily with the plot and the ideas that grow out of it.

Writing about Fiction: An Impressionistic Comparison

▶ STUDENT THEME

On Seeing a Blind Bird

There is something about seeing the blind that wrenches horror out of the viewer. Perhaps it is an innate fear in us that we, too, may be blind one day. Or maybe it is an instinctive aversion to weakness. Certainly our immediate reaction to blindness is not sympathy. Every fiber in us resists the humane attitude.

This horrified fascination hits a viewer of "Blind Bird," a black-and-white ink painting by Morris Graves. Graves's bird, black and huddled, clings flightless to a rock, its feet bound down by a tangle of white cobwebs. The bird's eyes are either dark voids or nonexistent. It crouches alone; it touches nothing but its rock, the tangle holding it there, gray mists around it, and whatever its mind contains. The bird looks totally vulnerable, yet somehow utterly impenetrable.

The main character in Dostoevsky's "Notes from Underground" draws from the reader that same "Blind Bird" horror. We may ultimately wring a drop of pity from our hearts over the underground man's plight if we feel no identity with him, yet immediately we feel a revulsion over his condition. The underground man seems to huddle bitterly in his shell as the bird does on its rock, bound to his spot with a web of uncontrollable thought patterns. He broods like the bird; what else can a vulnerable flightless hulk do?

Something about blindness urges us to ask, "How did this happen?" The question is usually not derived from kind concern but rather from a certain morbid curiosity. There is more than a hint of lingering Puritanism in our unvoiced suspicion that somehow the blindness is a result of the afflicted creature's actions: perhaps the bird might still see if it had been a good bird; perhaps the underground man would be a social success if he did not cling so obstinately to his bizarre reflections.

The lingering quality of the "Blind Bird" is a certainty of unalterable isolation. The bird will not enjoy voluntary solitude; the webby tangles imprisoning its feet will keep it on its rock in a most involuntary manner. Yet if the bird had a chance to fly, we can suspect it would react just as the underground man says:

> Come, try, give any one of us . . . a little more independence, untie our hands, . . . relax the control and we . . . yes, I assure you . . . we should be begging to be under control again at once.

Comment: This essay is an attempt to solve the very difficult matter of expressing one's feelings about a work of literature in such a way that another reader will understand what the effect has been upon the writer. With an opening paragraph about human reactions to blindness in general, the writer turns immediately to a picture by Morris Graves. Not until the third paragraph do we come to the literary work under discussion, but the previous remarks have prepared the reader for a meaningful comparison. From that point on, the thought vacillates back and forth from bird to man and from man to bird. The writer has made the two one.

Writing about Fiction: A Critical Evaluation

▶ STUDENT THEME

"Go Down Moses"—The Old versus The New

The most successful story in Faulkner's *Go Down, Moses* is the final episode entitled "Go Down, Moses." This story is successful because it achieves, in a simple way, the presentation of the attitudes and misunderstandings which are part of the southern heritage. The story revolves around Mollie Beauchamp, a post-Civil War Negro, and Gavin Stevens, the county attorney. Mollie represents the old order of Negro society which is incapable of handling its own affairs after two centuries of slavery, and Gavin Stevens represents a segment of the modern white society that knows it must live with the Negroes and senses an obligation toward them. This obligation is unusual, or perhaps it may be said to be traditional in the same sense that the pre-Civil War plantation owner had an obligation to his slaves. Yet, Gavin Stevens does feel a respect and compassion for the downtrodden Negroes. This story attempts to determine the extent of the obligation of one race to the other, at least as it is resolved in one man's mind.

The story also probes the questions, How much is a "dead nigger" worth to the white race and ultimately how much is the entire Negro race worth to the white race? The story is successful because of the way Faulkner arrives at his answers. He sets up a situation in which Mollie's boy has disappeared. She believes that he is in trouble and goes to the county attorney for help. The bulk of the story is concerned with the county attorney's efforts to ease Mollie's burden. In the course of the action, the reader draws several conclusions relevant to southern life and thinking:

1. Mollie and a majority of the southern Negroes do not and probably will not understand completely the system of white domination in which they must function.
2. The white race still does not understand the Negro's thinking and emotional patterns.
3. The Negro is still treated as a child by the white race as a result of the two races' misunderstandings.
4. There is no immediate solution to the problems between the races.

Yet, why is this story unique? True, Faulkner has explored these same conflicts in other stories, but he has nowhere else crystallized them as he does in the final story of *Go Down, Moses.* He has gotten away from the plantation, where white domination is traditionally expected; he has gotten away from the hunt, where all men tend to be equal in the chase; and in this story he has situated himself in the city, the new center of southern life in the years after the Civil War as Negroes drifted from the plantations. He has shown how the same attitudes, prejudices, and misunderstandings that he has so carefully explored in the earlier stories now function in the city, in the new restructured social system.

This story, with the possible exception of "The Bear," is the most vital in the entire collection, as Faulkner is pitting the old social order against modern society and new situations. He is not simply explaining life on the plantation with its predictable patterns of behavior, but life in the modern world where action does not allow a predictable pattern. It is this unpredictable pattern—that Stevens goes so far out of his way to please the mother of a dead Negro, who to him is only a criminal—that makes this story unique.

Stevens realizes that the whites have an obligation to the Negroes, not as the McCaslins did because they owned them as slaves but because the Negroes are people with desires and feelings the same as any member of the white race. Faulkner's characters do not reach this point of understanding in any of the other stories. "Go Down, Moses" is successful because it explores the old relationships in contrast with the new and thus gives us a new perspective on southern life that none of the other stories can provide.

   Comment: The essay begins with an evaluation: the writer's judgment that one particular story in a collection is the most successful of the group because it accomplishes effectively what it sets out to do. The writer immediately begins summary details as a way of supplying the conclusions that follow. The summary naturally involves the characters, action, and setting; the conclusions are the emerging ideas. In an effort to establish the uniqueness and success of this particular story, the writer then turns to comparison. He says that the setting of this story makes it unique. He refers also to its special vitality and to the depth of its understanding and penetration. Each of these points he attempts to support.
   In the course of the analysis, the writer has touched upon most of the elements of fiction except possibly the style. Even then, there is some concern with tone. The essay indicates clearly how summary, analysis, interpretation, and evaluation depend upon one another and how the various components of this story cannot be rigidly separated from one another for purposes of writing.

Writing about a Poem: Analysis and Interpretation

▶ STUDENT THEME

Organization: A Definition

Anecdote of the Jar

I placed a jar in Tennessee,
And round it was, upon a hill.
It made the slovenly wilderness
Surround that hill.

The wilderness rose up to it,
And sprawled around, no longer wild.
The jar was round upon the ground
And tall and of a port in air.

It took dominion everywhere.
The jar was gray and bare.
It did not give of bird or bush,
Like nothing else in Tennessee.

                                                        Wallace Stevens

   If there were no black, would white have meaning? If there were no night, what would day mean? It is this basic premise that a concept has no meaning, or substance, until it is contrasted with an opposite concept—that seems to prompt Wallace Stevens to write "Anecdote of the Jar." The poem is a contrast between jar and wilderness, exemplifying a dependency of jar and wilderness on each other for definition. The jar lends substance to the wilderness, just as the wilderness defines the jar.

Consider the man who, traveling through a presumably unexplored region, comes upon a beer bottle in the midst of it. Not only does he feel a sense of depression at discovering that the region is not unknown but he also is struck by the contrast between bottle and wilderness, or in a broader sense, between that which is man-made and that which is not. In "Anecdote of the Jar" the jar is placed deliberately upon nature by man, perhaps as an experiment, to judge the effect of art on nature. The poem itself is an account, an observation of the contrast it creates.

The jar is "round," suggesting a sense of structured order, but the wilderness is "slovenly" and "sprawled around," portraying a lack of neatness and organization. The jar assumes superiority over the wilderness. It "made" the wilderness surround the hill. It causes the wilderness to "rise" up to it, an image which also supports the idea that the jar is above the wilderness, not only physically but hierarchically. It tames the wilderness until it is "no longer wild"; it is "sprawled around," implying a sense of subservience. The jar is "tall and of a port in air," a note of the jar's height and an observation of its noticeability.

The jar stands out in an unnoticed wilderness, and in this way, the jar grants dimension to the wilderness. Without the jar there is no criterion for judging any aspect of the wilderness. By providing contrast, it is also defining the area, as black defines white.

The idea of the jar's superiority is repeated in the third stanza: "It took dominion everywhere." Man claims no dominion over nature, because he himself is created as wilderness is. But, by means of the jar, man is able to organize wilderness, and in this way, wilderness falls into the order of man. This organized, ordered structure causes wilderness to appear "slovenly" and unstructured, through force of contrast, creating a similar effect to that which one obtains from pondering the question of life's meaning in the absence of death.

The jar is an artifact—a man-made product. It is a functional thing, but it is also unproductive. It is "gray and bare" and does not "give of bird or bush." And so, though the jar can organize and grant definition to wilderness, it cannot produce life. To me, in brief, the poem contrasts man's creativity and nature's. The jar, being man-made, follows a human organization. The wilderness does not; yet it can produce "bird and bush"—life, the most organized structure of all. The jar cannot.

Comment: Since the Stevens poem is short, the paper attempts to deal with the complete meaning and purpose; it does not touch upon other elements of the poem at all. The first paragraph states the basic premise that the essay will develop. It is the student's interpretation of the meaning; it is the conclusion he has come to after his careful reading, which the remainder of the essay suggests. Paragraph 2 offers an analogy. If the experience of the poem seems somewhat abstract and remote, this example makes it familiar. Paragraphs 3 and 4 of the essay proceed line by line through the first two stanzas of the poem, selecting details and relating them to the main idea of the poem. Paragraphs 5 and 6 develop the thought further in terms of the third stanza, constantly phrasing and rephrasing the basic premise. Interpretation throughout is the product of analysis. It is the kind of poem that can be defined in this way.

Writing about a Popular Song Lyric: Personal Response as Evaluation

▶ STUDENT THEME

Silence

Often—and it is becoming a pretty regular thing these days—when I become depressed and tired of the silence of people I step out into the darkness of night to relax and think. I can take people only for so long, and then I want to scream. I find myself asking: "What in the hell is going on here?" I get tired of the usual escapes: drugs, drinking, or talking to my parents or a priest. After a while these human escapes from humanity put me right back where I started. I sometimes find consolation in just being aware of the situation Man is in, but after trying to get action and finding only the silence—it brings me down pretty fast. I'm not sure whether it is better to live with questions unanswered or with answers to questions that no one cares to ask. So I take a walk in the darkness of the night, trying to understand how some people can feel satisfied.

There are several forms of silence: the silence of people who are unaware; the silence of people who are aware; and the silence of those who won't allow themselves the self-education that is required to become aware of the faults that are in need of correction. From "The Sound of Silence" by Paul Simon, I receive the impression that he was trying to break through the silence of aware people—people who talk day after day without saying or hearing a thing; fools who are creating a guiding system of life which is not to be questioned, just accepted as it is now until the end of time. But time is running out for such silence. Today more than ever the silence is being shattered—but time may still run out.

I feel very strongly about the plight of the American Indian and Negro. It makes me very sad to see so many satisfied people walking around, when there is so little to be satisfied with today. I know life cannot really be described in words, but I feel that whatever it is it is an individual thing. By living every day of our lives honestly, trying to seek out the corruption that must be corrected and to find love instead of quick, unjust hate, perhaps we can manage to create a satisfactory environment for ourselves and each other.

Comment: The student's essay reveals a thorough understanding of the song lyrics, even though it does not deal directly with the verses. What is written in the first paragraph parallels the experience narrated in the poem, but it is the student's own. The second paragraph paraphrases several of the ideas in stanza 3 of the song. The details of the third paragraph grow out of the previous one and take the reader back to the sense of discontent expressed at the beginning of the essay. The ending reflects the spirit of the original lyrics, although the student expresses a stronger sense of hope and idealism than the composer.

The student's response to the song—being able to express a parallel experience and similar thoughts—comments upon the validity of the poem. This is a private, nonformal kind of evaluation, but it is meaningful because one knows that the student has been involved with the verses.

The Individual as His Own Model

The six examples of writing—all done by college freshmen—indicate a range of excellence, of literary sophistication, of detachment and involvement, of varying interests in the effects of literature. What they should by all means suggest is that there is no stereotype for the theme about literature. In fact, any kind of model would defeat the idea that the individual himself must come to some realization about the world of literature and its effects upon men. Given some understanding of the elements that go to make up a literary performance, the student must then try to find the best way he possibly can to make clear his own understandings and feelings. In fact, in writing about literature, he may find that he has come to know himself in a more meaningful way.

12

Writing a Reference Paper

The term "reference paper" includes what is familiarly called a library paper or a research paper. It also includes any paper that makes repeated references to primary sources or to a manual that includes collected materials on a specific topic. Whether the researcher collects his own materials or has them made available to him in a book, his task as a researcher and writer does not change essentially.

In recent times, the word "research" has been closely associated with scientific research and laboratory experimentation, and the emphasis has been placed upon finding new knowledge. What this emphasis overlooks, of course, is much routine research that does not result in dramatic discoveries and inventions. Occasionally the etymology of a word lends insight into the lost meaning of a word or one that has faded because a more popular one has prevailed. The word "research" comes from a French word *rechercher.* There is first the prefix *re-,* which occurs frequently in words borrowed from Latin; it means "again" or "again and again." The *chercher,* meaning "to seek or to search," was derived from the Latin word *circāre,* meaning "to go round or about" or "to explore."

In these original terms of the words, much undergraduate research has meaning and value. It is going the rounds again; it is seeking again and again to see what more may be found; it is taking another look. And often in this kind of review one is able to see what someone else has not seen or to see things in new relationships. To the extent that a reinvestigation of a topic brings new insight, it is original, although it may discover no new facts. The main purpose of most undergraduate research, therefore, would seem to be to learn how to find materials, how to evaluate them, and finally how to integrate them into a new set of relationships. These are the basic research skills; taking notes and documenting are only incidental to them. The basic skills are fundamental to what education is all about—first, looking at what was and is as a means of looking ahead.

FINDING MATERIALS

The most resourceful person is not necessarily the one who carries around the greatest amount of information in his head but the one who knows where to go to find the answers to his questions. Unfortunately, libraries are either museums or labyrinths to many people. They walk through awed by what they see on display, afraid to touch, or they get lost because they do not know the intricacies of the way through. Libraries are not museums; all materials are there to be used. And they do not have to be labyrinths; there are guides that solve the complexities. Every researcher needs some basic knowledge about getting around a major library.

THE CARD CATALOG AS AN AID TO RESEARCH

The card catalog is the "open sesame" of the library. Without it, the books would be almost completely inaccessible to the average user. The card catalog also permits one to learn a great number of facts about a book without ever actually seeing it. In fact, the card catalog may be a great time-saver, revealing to the researcher that a particular book is not what he thought it was; but, more important, the card catalog may open up leads to books he would not otherwise have encountered on his own. By its system of cross-referencing, the card catalog sometimes sends the user from drawer to drawer. But following through on these leads can turn up the exact sources one may be seeking.

The representative cards in the illustration indicate the kinds of information available in the card catalog (see page 306).

STANDARD BIBLIOGRAPHICAL SOURCES

Even though the card catalog is an index to the books in a particular library, it is limited as a subject guide, particularly as a source of information to material within periodicals. For that reason, the library includes a number of standard guides which are available as aids to the researcher, at whatever level he is working. These are often located in the reference section.

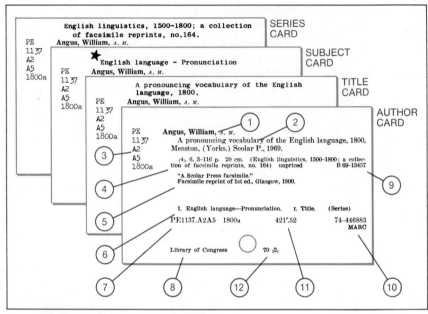

(1) The author's name and title.

(2) The title of the book, place of publication (Menston, Yorkshire, England), publisher (The Scolar Press, Ltd.), and date.

(3) Call number in the library being used.

(4) Collation, including the preliminary pages (10, of which 4 are used and 6 are blank), and the pages in the book proper, the height of the book in centimeters, and the title of the series.

(5) Contents of the book.

(6) Subject entries in the card catalog. These other cards are shown.

(7) Call number in the Library of Congress.

(8) Designation that the book is in the library of Congress.

(9) Number in *The British National Bibliography.*

(10) Order number of the card from the Library of Congress.

(11) Call number under the Dewey Decimal System.

(12) Librarian's information concerning the date of the card and the number of hundreds printed.

General Encyclopedias

General encyclopedias are a good starting point for the beginning researcher. Since they provide concise summaries of information and scholarly viewpoints, they are useful as an overview which will open up possible topics for detailed investigation. One of the main things to note about an encyclopedia is its date, particularly if current information is vital to the subject being studied. No dates are given here because revisions of some encyclopedias occur frequently.

Chamber's Encyclopaedia
Produced in England and reflects European viewpoints. Gives standard references on a topic.

Collier's Encyclopaedia
Bibliography is included in Volume 24.

Columbia Encyclopedia
Available in one volume or five. More useful for quick information than for survey of a topic. Brief bibliographies.

Encyclopedia Americana
Contains references to source materials.

Encyclopaedia Britannica
Provides brief, selected bibliographies. In addition to the current edition, most libraries keep the 11th ed. (1910–1911) available. Some of its fine long articles are books in brief.

New International Encyclopedia
No longer revised under this title, but yearbook continues. Not to be confused with *Encyclopedia International* (1963–1964).

Note: Some encyclopedias attempt to keep current between major revisions by means of yearbooks. These are more useful as collections of information than as comprehensive statements on certain subjects. For yearbooks in specialized fields, see the references listed under Other Standard Reference Works.

Americana Annual, 1923 –

Britannica Book of the Year, 1938 –

Collier's Year Book, 1938 –

New International Yearbook, 1907 –
Formerly *International Yearbook* from 1898.

Special Encyclopedias, Comprehensive Histories, and Handbooks

The main limitation of special encyclopedias and reference works of this kind is that they are not consistently kept current by revisions or yearbooks. But they can be of value to the beginning researcher who may see how bringing one of the topics up to date can be his subject for special study and who will find the selective bibliographies in most of these works an appropriate starting point. The list here is not intended to be comprehensive, only to suggest the wide variety of these aids.

Art and Architecture

Encyclopedia of Painting, 1955.
Encyclopedia of World Art, 1959.
Larousse Encyclopedia of Prehistoric and Ancient Art (1962), Byzantine and Medieval Art (1963), *Modern Art* 1965.

Economics and Business

Encyclopaedia of Banking and Finance, 6th ed. 1962.
The McGraw-Hill Dictionary of Modern Economics, 1965.

Folklore and Mythology

Frazer, Sir James G. *The Golden Bough: A Study in Magic and Religion.* 12 vols., 1907–1915; Supplement, 1936; 1955.
Funk and Wagnalls Standard Dictionary of Folklore, Mythology, and Legend. 2 vols., 1949–1950.
Larousse Encyclopedia of Mythology, rev. ed., 1968.
Larousse World Mythology, 1965.
The Mythology of All Races, 13 vols., 1916–1932.

History

The Cambridge Ancient History, ed. John B. Bury *et al.,* 12 vols., 1923–1939; rev. eds., 1961 —.
The Cambridge Medieval History, ed. Henry M. Gwatkin *et al.,* 8 vols., 1911–1936.
Encyclopedia of American History, ed. Richard B. Morris, rev. ed., 1965.
An Encyclopedia of World History, ed. William L. Langer, 4th rev. ed., 1968.
McGraw-Hill Encyclopedia of Russia and the Soviet Union, ed. Michael T. Florinsky, 1961.
The New Cambridge Modern History, ed. George N. Clark *et al.,* 14 vols., 1957 —.

Literature

The Cambridge History of English Literature, ed. A. W. Ward and A. R. Waller, 15 vols., 1907–1916; 1933.
Cassell's Encyclopaedia of World Literature, ed. S. H. Steinberg, 2 vols., 1953.
Encyclopedia of Poetry and Poetics, ed. Alex Preminger *et al.,* 1965.
A Literary History of England, ed. A. C. Baugh *et al.,* 2nd ed., 1967.
Literary History of the United States, ed. Robert E. Spiller *et al.,* 2 vols., 3rd ed., 1963.
The Oxford History of English Literature, ed. Frank P. Wilson and Bonamy Dobrée, 12 vols., 1945–1963.
The Reader's Encyclopedia, ed. William Rose Benet, 2 vols., 2nd ed., 1965.

Music

Grove's Dictionary of Music and Musicians, ed. Eric Blom, 10 vols.,
   5th ed., 1955, 1961.
International Cyclopedia of Music and Musicians, 9th ed., 1964.
The New Oxford History of Music, 10 vols., 1954 –.
The Oxford History of Music, 8 vols., 2nd ed., 1929–1938.

Philosophy

Copleston, Frederick C. A History of Philosophy, 8 vols. New York:
   Image Books, Doubleday and Co., 1947–1966.
The Encyclopaedia of Philosophy, ed. Paul Edwards, 8 vols., 1967.

Religion

Encyclopaedia of Religion and Ethics, ed. James Hastings, 13 vols.,
   1908–1927.
Jewish Encyclopedia, ed. Isidore Singer et al., 12 vols., 1901–1906.
The New Catholic Encyclopedia, 15 vols., 1967.
The New Schaff-Herzog Encyclopedia of Religious Knowledge,
   13 vols., 1908–1912; 1950.
Universal Jewish Encyclopedia, ed. Isaac Landman et al., 11 vols.,
   1939–1944.

Science and Mathematics

The Encyclopedia of the Biological Sciences, ed. Peter Gray, 1961.
International Encyclopedia of Chemical Sciences, 1964.
McGraw-Hill Encyclopedia of Science and Technology, 15 vols.,
   rev. ed., 1966.
Universal Encyclopedia of Mathematics, 1964.
Van Nostrand's Scientific Encyclopedia, 3rd ed., 1958.

Social Sciences and Education

A Cyclopedia of Education, ed. Paul Monroe, 5 vols., 1911–1913.
Encyclopedia of Educational Research, 3rd ed., 1960.
Encyclopedia of the Social Sciences, 15 vols., 1930–1935.
International Encyclopedia of the Social Sciences, 17 vols., 1967.
International Yearbook of Education, 1948 –.
World Survey of Education, UNESCO, 1955 –.

OTHER STANDARD REFERENCE WORKS

Almanacs and Yearbooks

Information Please Almanac, 1947 –
Complements The World Almanac.

The New York Times Encyclopedic Almanac, 1970 –
All inclusive in scope.

The Statesman's Yearbook, 1864 –
Historical on an international scale.

The World Almanac and Book of Facts, 1868 –
Comprehensive in its coverage.

Yearbook of the United Nations, 1947 –
Covers activities of the organization.

Yearbook of World Affairs, 1947 –
Important in the social sciences.

Atlases and Gazetteers

Columbia Lippincott Gazetteer of the World, 1962
Encyclopaedia Britannica World Atlas, 1964 (frequently revised)
Historical Atlas, ed. William R. Shepherd, 9th ed., 1964
National Geographic Atlas of the World, 2nd ed., 1966
The Time Atlas of the World, rev. ed., 1967

Biography

Current Biography: Who's News and Why, 1940 –
Features biographies of living newsworthy figures.

Dictionary of American Biography, 22 vols., 1928–1958
Main volumes include people who died before 1927. The supplements
update the work to 1940.

Dictionary of National Biography, 1885 –
Includes biographies of notable, deceased British figures.

International Who's Who, 1935 –
Reissued annually. Includes people of current international reputation.

National Cyclopaedia of American Biography, 1892 –
Includes lesser known figures, both living and dead.

Webster's Biographical Dictionary, 1962 –
Frequently revised. Sketches of world figures, living and dead.

Who's Who in America, 1899 –
Reissued every two years. Brief sketches of prominent living Americans.

Dictionaries (See pp. 416–419)

Indexes

The single most important index for the beginning researcher is
Reader's Guide to Periodical Literature. It indexes approximately 135
of the most widely read popular magazines in contrast to the more spe-

cialized indexes that concern themselves with scholarly and less well-known periodicals.

Because *Reader's Guide* indexes articles by author and subject and lists literary works and movies by title, it makes available a vast amount of information from widely scattered sources.

The sample entry illustrated makes clear exactly how works are indexed in *Reader's Guide.*

UNIVERSITY professors. See College professors and instructors
UNIVERSITY research. See Colleges and universities—Research
UNIVERSITY students. See College students
UNIVERSITY study tours. See Travel study courses
UNMARRIED men. See Single men
UNMARRIED mothers. See Mothers, Unmarried
UNMARRIED women. See Single women
UNRUH, Glenys G.
Parents can help their children succeed in school. NEA J 55:14-16 D '66
UNTERMEYER, Louis
Fates defied the muse. Sat R 49:32-3 N 5 '66
Person first, a poet second. Sat R 49:54+ D 3 '66
To each man his own metaphor. Sat R 49:45 F 19 '66
UPDIKE, John
Air show; poem. New Repub 155:25 D 17 '66
Amoeba; poem. New Repub 154:23 Je 25 '66
Bech in Rumania; story. New Yorker 42:54-63 O 8 '66
Books (cont) New Yorker 42:115-18+ F 26 '66
Harv is plowing now; story. New Yorker 42:46-8 Ap 23 '66
Marching through Boston; story. New Yorker 41:34-8 Ja 22 '66
Mastery of Miss Warner. New Repub 154:23-5 Mr 5 '66; Correction. 154:40 Mr 26 '66
Nabokov's look back: a national loss. Life 62:9+ Ja 13 '67
Pro; story. New Yorker 42:53-4 S 17 '66
Seal in nature; poem. New Repub 155:16 O 15 '66
Witnesses; story. New Yorker 42:27-9 Ag 13 '66
Your lover just called; story. Harper 234:48-51 Ja '67
about
Can a nice novelist finish first? J. Howard. il pors Life 61:74-74A+ N 4 '66
Domestic felicity? G. Hicks. Sat R 49:31 S 24 '66
John and Bruce. por Newsweek 68:116 S 26 '66
Language, myth and Mr Updike. A. Burgess. Commonweal 83:557-9 F 11 '66
Onward with Updike. S. Kauffmann. New Repub 155:15-17 S 24 '66

(1) Cross-indexing by subject. Articles are listed under subject headings by title, and bibliographical information is given.

(2) Author entries. Under Glenys G. Unruh, the information following the title

means that the article appeared in the *NEA Journal* [National Education Association Journal] volume 55, pages 14–16, in the December 1966 issue. Abbreviations are explained at the beginning of each issue of *Reader's Guide*.
(3) Articles, stories, and poems *by* John Updike.
(4) Articles *about* John Updike.

Other valuable indexes include:

Agricultural Index, 1916 —(subject index).
Applied Science and Technology Index, 1958 —(subject index).
Art Index (subject and author index).
Biography Index, 1946 —(indexes books and articles on the living and dead).
Biological and Agricultural Index, 1964 —(subject index).
Books in Print, 1948 —(indexes books by author, title, and series; appears annually).
Book Review Index, 1905 —(indexes current reviews of books mainly in the humanities and social sciences).
Business Periodical Index, 1958 —(subject index).
Cumulative Book Index, 1898 —(lists almost every book printed in the United States).
Dramatic Index, 1909 —(concerns articles on drama and theater, English and American).
Education Index, 1929 —(author and subject index).
Engineering Index, 1929 —(author and subject index).
International Index to Periodicals, 1907 —(indexes scholarly periodicals in the humanities and social sciences).
London Times Official Index, 1906 —(besides *New York Times Index,* only other major newspaper index available in most libraries).
Music Index: The Key to Current Periodical Literature, 1949 —(author and subject index).
New York Times Index, 1913 —(Since most newspapers are not indexed, this one serves as a general index to the dates of events, which can then be read about in other newspapers.)
Poole's Index to Periodical Literature, 1802–1881; supplements through 1906 (subject index for nineteenth-century articles on a wide variety of topics of general interest).
United States Government Publications: Monthly Catalog, 1895—(invaluable because it covers every department of the government).
United States Library of Congress: A Catalog of Books Represented by Library of Congress Printed Cards (kept current; indexes available also for motion pictures and filmstrips).

Bibliographies of Bibliographies and Guides to Libraries

The accumulation of special bibliographies, catalogs, records, and indexes has now made necessary another kind of publication: the bibliography of bibliographies. One of the best known is Theodore Besterman's *A World Bibliography of Bibliographies,* in five volumes, now in its fourth edition. *The Bibliographic Index,* which appears semi-annually, includes bibliographies which are included in books and periodicals. But these are bibliographical aids beyond the needs of most beginning researchers. Of use, however, are several general guides:

> Galin, Saul, and Peter Spielberg. *Reference Books: How to Select and Use Them,* 1969.
> Gates, Jean Key. *Guide to the Use of Books and Libraries,* 2nd ed., 1969.
> Russell, Harold G., *et al. The Use of Books and Libraries,* 10th ed., 1963.
> Winchell, Constance M. *Guide to Reference Books,* 8th ed., 1967.

Of particular value to the student of language and literature are two books, both available in paperback editions:

> Altick, Richard D., and Andrew Wright. *Bibliography for the Study of English and American Literature,* 3rd ed., 1967.
> Bond, Donald F. *A Reference Guide to English Studies,* 1962.

Bibliographies in English studies are numerous, but among the annual bibliographies four are of special importance:

> *Essay and General Literature Index,* 1900 —(author and subject guide to essays and articles in collections).
> MHRA (Modern Humanities Research Association). *Annual Bibliography of English Language and Literature,* 1921 —.
> *MLA International Bibliography* in *Publications of the Modern Language Association of America,* 1922 —(the single most important index to literary and linguistic studies).
> *Year's Work in English Studies,* 1921 —.

Quotations

> *Familiar Quotations,* eds. John Bartlett and E. M. Beck, 14th ed., 1968.
> *The Home Book of American Quotations,* ed. Bruce Bohle, 1967.
> *The Home Book of Quotations, Classical and Modern,* ed. Burton E. Stevenson, 10th ed., 1967.
> *The Oxford Dictionary of English Proverbs,* rev. Paul Harvey, 2nd ed., 1966.

EVALUATING MATERIALS

Books and magazines are designed for different purposes and audiences; they are therefore not of equal value to the researcher. It may be difficult for beginners to know the reputation of writers on a particular topic or the trustworthiness of their opinions, but there are several general considerations that are important in choosing materials that one will use:

The Audience: The nature of a publication comments generally upon its audience. Encyclopedias, for example, address themselves to a broader and more varied audience than scholarly books. Popular magazines treating many topics are different from specialized periodicals addressed to experts. Textbooks for lower-division courses are different from those designed for graduate courses. The most specialized work is not necessarily the best for the beginning researcher (it may be too detailed), but he should recognize that his choice of sources will determine to a great extent the level and style of his own paper.

Length and Documentation: The length of a work does not alone determine the thoroughness of its coverage because a big book may treat a very broad topic. But given two works of approximately the same scope, it follows that the longer one will probably include more detail than the shorter one. The short one may in its outlines include as much support, but not as much elaboration. An article in a scholarly periodical is often an extended, thoroughly documented treatment of a very limited topic and valuable for that very purpose. What the researcher needs to seek, therefore, is not long works as opposed to short ones but inclusion of works that are adequately detailed and documented as well as general ones.

Primary and Secondary Sources: The authoritativeness of a work will often depend upon its sources of information. A primary source is an original record, statement, or document; a secondary source is something written about it. These two terms, however, are relative. If we consider a speech given by the President of the United States as a primary source, the newspaper commentary written about it is secondary. But if one's topic is public opinion at the time of that speech, the newspaper commentary would then be considered primary. If a novel by a writer is the primary source, criticism of it is secondary. But if a student's topic is a writer's reputation at a particular period, the criticism would then become primary.

    If a book derives its material only from what has already been written about primary sources and is wholly derivative, it may be valuable as a summary work but not as a source of new information. Returning to primary sources is a way of reinvestigating and reevaluating what already has been written. Works that ignore primary sources and depend entirely upon secondary ones may be limited by the dependence they show upon other people's findings.

Publisher: The reputation of a publishing house, press, or periodical may often be taken as a general factor in evaluating books and periodicals. Over a period of time one learns which publishers are noted for carefully edited, definitive editions and which periodicals screen and check carefully the soundness of the material they publish. The name of a vanity press, which requires the author to pay the cost of his own publication, may suggest that the author was unable to have his book published under other circumstances.

Author: A famous name is not consistently a sure guide to the soundness of the author. Some writers are well known because they are controversial. In this respect, they are interesting and stimulating thinkers, but their opinions should be checked against well-documented scholarship. The title of a writer may also be a clue to his qualifications. A full professorship at Harvard is an impressive recommendation; long experience in the field or other publications may also be additional proofs. The researcher should be alert to any special interest that enters as a factor in the writer's judgment. On particular topics, it may make a considerable difference whether the writer is a southerner or a northerner, a Mormon or a Catholic, a black or a WASP, a Democrat or a Republican. If a writer reveals strong prejudices of one kind or another, these must be considered as representing a special point of view.

Value: All of the factors that have been noted here—the degree of the author's objectivity, the length and documentation of the work, the use of primary and secondary sources, the audience, the date of the writing, and the publisher—will combine to create an effect that either inspires confidence in the work or a general wariness about it. Everything in print is not of equal value. The researcher must be able to make discriminations.

TAKING NOTES

Perhaps everyone has to go through the experience of writing a reference paper without using notes, with only books on hand, to know how difficult and frustrating it is. Notes are simple means of excerpting information from books so that the facts are easily available when the writer needs them. A hundred cards drawing information from ten books can be sorted and shuffled; the pages of ten books cannot. In fact, it may not even be possible to have the ten books available. Notes therefore are a simple expedient.

Notes are also personal working cards; that is, there is no special reason why they have to follow a prescribed form. By the same token, there is no reason why every beginner should have to learn the pitfalls of note-taking the hard way. There are a few obvious facts that are often repeated for a good reason:

1. The first thing to do is to make up a bibliography card for each source used and include *all* of the necessary data so that it is not necessary to return to the book. Choose some kind of label or slug, usually the author's last name, that can be used on note cards, since it is a waste of time to report all of the information on every note card (see sample bibliography card below).
2. Notes from a book or article should be taken according to subject headings so that they can be later sorted by topics. Cards 4 by 6 inches are a good size to use for notes.
3. Between the time of reading and the time of writing, note cards cool off—or the mind cools off. Notes therefore should not be too cryptic. It is also better to take too many notes than too few. Some can always be discarded.
4. The memory plays tricks. It forgets, but it also remembers exactly. It is therefore advisable to put in quotation marks the phrases that seem worthy of quotation or that are likely to stick in one's mind. It is embarrassing to come up with a fine phrase that actually belongs to someone else. In general, however, notes should be a paraphrase of the original, avoiding as many of the author's own words as possible.

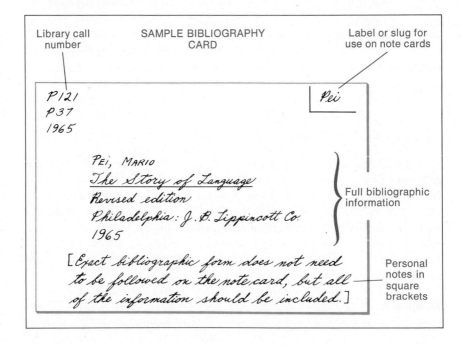

Library call number | SAMPLE BIBLIOGRAPHY CARD | Label or slug for use on note cards

P121
P37
1965

Pei

PEI, MARIO
The Story of Language
Revised edition
Philadelphia: J. B. Lippincott Co.
1965

Full bibliographic information

[Exact bibliographic form does not need to be followed on the note card, but all of the information should be included.]

Personal notes in square brackets

5. Any immediate reaction the reader has can be included in square brackets. Notes to oneself are often useful when the time to write arrives.
6. The page numbers must be included so that all of the information for writing a footnote is accessible. If a direct quotation occurs on two pages, it is advisable to use a slash to indicate where the information on one page ends and the information on another begins: pp. 295–296 "We are left with the impression of a painful sincerity and of a nobility that expresses itself only in definitions, not / in the activity of the imagination."[1]
7. If it takes three cards to jot down the notes on one topic, it is good to mark these as 1 of 3, 2 of 3, and 3 of 3 so that it is clear that one card has not been misplaced (see sample note card below).

THE NATURE OF THE REFERENCE PAPER

In one sense, writing a reference paper is no different from writing any other expository theme. However, because the reference paper is ordinarily a more sustained piece of writing based upon an extended project of several weeks or months, it sets its own requirements for the writer:

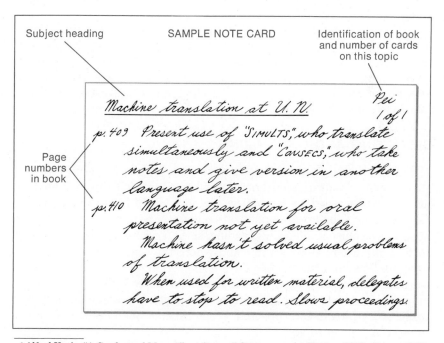

Subject heading   SAMPLE NOTE CARD   Identification of book and number of cards on this topic

Page numbers in book

Machine translation at U. N.   Pei 1 of 1

p. 409 Present use of "SIMULTS," who translate simultaneously and "CONSECS," who take notes and give version in another language later.

p. 410 Machine translation for oral presentation not yet available. Machine hasn't solved usual problems of translation. When used for written material, delegates have to stop to read. Slows proceedings.

---

[1] Alfred Kazin, "A Condemned Man: Albert Camus," *Contemporaries* (Boston: Little, Brown, 1962).

1. It requires more information, more facts, more variety of opinion than the ordinary essay.
2. It requires an ability to synthesize material into a larger frame of organization than a paper of lesser scope.
3. It requires more control on the part of the writer, more attention to orderliness and transition than he might ordinarily show in other kinds of writing.
4. It requires objectivity to differentiate clearly between one's own opinions and the opinions of others, between matters of fact and matters of opinion. A reference paper need not be impersonal.
5. It requires support for its assertions and specific documentation.

These requirements, therefore, focus attention upon a series of steps which are important to writing a successful reference paper. The remaining sections of this chapter comment upon each of these.

LIMITING THE SUBJECT

The subject must be adaptable to the length of the paper so that it can be treated in some depth. Three thousand words are not adequate for a topic on the position of women from Roman times to the present. By a judicious selection of material, a student might possibly write about attitudes toward women in the Old Testament of the Bible, with a few added reflections upon the influence of Hebraic concepts upon later times.

Some topics are too broad and vague for anything except book length; others are too narrow and specialized because they require primary sources or original investigation beyond the beginning student. Even though extremes of broadness or narrowness are usually self-evident, no one knows precisely what the limits of a topic are until he has done considerable reading and sees clearly the dimensions.

SELECTING AND ORGANIZING

It is wise to think of the organization of a long paper in terms of stages: first, a tentative outline of main topics which can be added to, developed, discarded, or regrouped. No one should try to settle upon a plan too soon. The precise organization usually becomes more and more apparent as one completes his reading, sorts his notes, reexamines them to find out where they are full and where they are sparse, where one has found his interests turning during the period of investigation, where the paper must place its emphasis to use the notes available, and what must be discarded. One big pitfall of the beginning researcher is to try to use everything he has collected. When the final plan becomes evident, some things have to go.

PARAPHRASING, QUOTING, AND PLAGIARIZING

Plagiarism is the act of passing off someone else's ideas or words as one's own. Some plagiarism represents deliberate dishonesty: a student copies material word for word from a book and submits it without the use of quotation marks or documentation. Perhaps a greater source of plagiarism, however, derives from carelessness—failure to take adequate notes which use quotation marks, failure to paraphrase in words sufficiently different from the original, failure to get far enough away from the notes in writing the paper.

If a writer looks upon his notes as reminders of the material he has read and absorbs them into the pattern of his own thinking, he will avoid the kind of research paper that is mere patchwork, a collection of other people's words in cut-and-paste style. A reference paper should be written in the student's own manner with occasional direct quotations, and each of those should have a justification.

Direct quotations are justified

—if the original phrasing is particularly striking and memorable;
—if the special feeling or style of the writer would be lost by paraphrasing it;
—if the original phrasing is so well known that a paraphrase would be a distortion;
—if the quotation itself is an example of proof of what is being discussed, for example, the print-out response of a computer grading a student theme;
—if the quotation is used to typify a writer or a character in a work of literature.

It should be emphasized that the reference paper does not give the writer more license to quote than any other theme. It is a paper, however, that ordinarily demands full proof and may therefore invite more quotation than usual. Nevertheless, other people's words cannot be made a substitute for the writer's own.

REVISING AND POLISHING

Because the reference paper holds the writer accountable for his sources as well as his own ideas, it may be a paper that can be less spontaneously written. The writer often has to consult his notes at the same time that he is writing. A series of drafts may actually be necessary to get a final paper that reads smoothly. Matters that often require particular attention include:

—using adequate transitional words and phrases between sections that may have been written at different times;

—varying the comments leading up to direct quotations so that they do not all read: "Bertrand Russell says";

—paring down the prose or expanding it, whichever may be necessary to get a clear, accurate statement;

—reordering material to get more coherent, effective discourse;

—supplying a detail or checking an item for accuracy.

SUPPORTING AND DOCUMENTING

Footnotes are the means commonly used to document specific statements within the main body of a reference work. These can be given at the bottom of the page on which they appear, separated from the main text by a rule across the page; grouped at the end of the paper in one continuous list; or, as some disciplines prefer, placed immediately after the citation in parentheses or immediately below the citation, separated by rules from the rest of the text in the manner illustrated here:[1]

---

[1] Some footnotes are purely information notes as opposed to others which are references. Writers, however, should avoid lengthy digressions in footnotes. If comments are too long, they are best omitted.

Even though footnote forms often monopolize the attention of the beginning researcher, a far more substantive problem is to know when to footnote. A ten-page paper with a hundred footnotes is a parody of a reference paper, not necessarily a well-documented one. The writer must be able to discriminate between material that is considered common knowledge and material that is clearly identified with one particular writer or source. Facts and opinions that are recognized as general knowledge need not be footnoted. All others should be attributed to their source. The obvious example of material to be footnoted is the direct quotation, but the ideas of another person, even if they are freely paraphrased, are also to be footnoted.

What is and what is not general knowledge on any particular subject usually becomes apparent during the time of reading and note-taking. The researcher will encounter the same basic information again and again. He may take notes on these facts one or two times and then come to the realization that information of this kind is common knowledge among those who write on this subject. He too can make the same assumption, even though he considers himself far less knowledgeable. General knowledge may be characterized as encyclopedic knowledge. On the other hand, special findings, opinions, and interpretations need to be accounted for.

The bibliography is a different kind of documentation; it is a list of books, periodicals, and any other source materials, either complete or selected, that the writer has used in preparing his paper. Ordinarily, if works like a dictionary or the Bible are referred to in the text, these are not listed. But all other works referred to in the footnotes should be included.

FOOTNOTES

Footnote forms are a conventional system, and they vary from discipline to discipline. Any writer, therefore, submitting a paper to his sociology professor or to his engineering professor should consult a style manual in that discipline or refer to one of the established periodicals in that field. The forms given in this section are those ordinarily used in English studies and other related studies in the humanities.

The following practices are standard for typewritten papers:

1. A footnote is signaled by a number, slightly raised and placed after the material being cited.
2. Footnotes are most commonly numbered consecutively from 1 to — throughout the paper, whether they are put at the bottom of the page, in the text, or at the end.
3. Footnotes do not repeat any information given in the text. If the author's name is given in the comment leading up to a quotation, the note will supply only the title, place of publication, and date.
4. Although the name of the publisher may be omitted in the footnote, the latest style sheet of the Modern Language Association of America includes it. See footnote 6a for alternate form without publisher's name.
5. Footnotes are indented and typed single-spaced with a double space between them, separated from the text by a rule if they are placed at the bottom of the page.
6. All citations made on a particular page are included on the same page if the footnotes are placed at the bottom. If the last note is lengthy, it may be continued on the next page.
7. Footnotes should be as specific as possible. A reference like "pp. 101–132" is not particularly helpful unless the writer is intentionally making a recommendation for additional reading.
8. In footnotes, the first name of the author comes first.

12A   SAMPLE FOOTNOTE FORMS

Articles in a magazine or periodical

> [1] Archibald A. Hill, "The Tainted *Ain't* Once More," *College English,* 26 (1965), 301.

> If the volume of a periodical is numbered consecutively throughout, it is not necessary to list the month. The month, however, may be given as a convenience to individuals who have unbound issues.

> When a volume number is not given, the symbol for page, as in footnote 4, is used.

> [2] Archibald A. Hill, "Grammaticality," *Word,* 17 (April 1961), 9.

> [3] L. M. Myers, "Generation and Deviation," *CCC,* 18 (1967), 217.

> For a briefer note, long titles of periodicals are abbreviated. The full title is given in the bibliography.

Articles in weeklies with no volume number

> [4] Rand McNally: More Than a Mapmaker," *Business Week,* November 22, 1969, p. 66.

Bible

> [5] John 1:1.

> Books of the Bible are not italicized.

> The translation and edition are not given unless the differences in phrasing are a significant point in the paper.

Books with a single author

> [6] James Sledd, *A Short Introduction to English Grammar* (Chicago: Scott, Foresman, 1959), p. 5.

> If the publisher's name is not included in the footnote, the form changes slightly:

[6a] James Sledd, *A Short Introduction to English Grammar* (Chicago, 1959), p. 5.

If the author is unknown, the note begins with the title of the book.

If the date is not given, n.d. [no date] should be used.

If the publisher's name is not listed, n.p. [no publisher] should be used.

Books with two authors

[7] Donald A. Lloyd and Harry R. Warfel, *American English in Its Cultural Setting* (New York: Knopf, 1956), p. 279.

As many as three authors are usually listed by name.

Books with more than three authors

[8] Alfred J. Ayer *et al., Studies in Communication* (London: Secker & Warburg, 1955), p. 34.

The words "and others" can be used instead of the Latin equivalent.

Books with an editor

[9] *Readings in Applied Transformational Grammar,* ed. Mark Lester (New York: Holt, Rinehart and Winston, 1970), p. 60, n. 5.

This is a collection of essays by various authors. The reference is to a note by the editor on p. 60.

Books with a translator

[10] Karl Vossler, *The Spirit of Language in Civilization,* tr. Oscar Oeser (London: Routledge & Kegan Paul, 1932), p. 15.

Books in later revised editions

[11] C. K. Ogden and I. A. Richards, *The Meaning of Meaning,* 8th ed., Harvest Book (New York: Harcourt, Brace and World, 1946), p. 140.

Books published in several volumes

    [12] George P. Krapp, *The English Language in America* (New York: Ungar, 1925), II, 147.

Books published in a series

    [13] James T. Hatfield *et al.,* eds., *Curme Volume of Linguistic Studies,* Language Monograph, No. 7, Linguistic Society of America (Washington, D.C., 1930), p. 4.

Dissertations (See Unpublished Material)

Dramas

    [14] *Macbeth* V. i. 39.

If variant texts are available, the edition should be indicated in the first footnote and listed in the bibliography; for example: All references to *Macbeth* are taken from *Shakespeare: Twenty-three Plays and the Sonnets,* ed. Thomas Marc Parrott, rev. ed. (New York: Scribner's, 1953).

Encyclopedia article

    [15] "Language," *Encyclopaedia Britannica,* 14th ed., 13, p. 700.

Essays in an edited collection

    [16] James D. McCawley, "The Role of Semantics in a Grammar," in Emmon Bach and Robert T. Harms, eds., *Universals in Linguistic Theory* (New York: Holt, Rinehart and Winston, 1968), pp. 168–169.

Government documents

    [17] U. S., Department of State, *Language and Area Study Programs in American Universities,* compiled by Larry Moses in cooperation with the Language Development Branch of Health, Education and Welfare Department (Washington, D.C.: External Research Staff, 1964), p. 105.

Interview

[18] Senator Henry M. Jackson, personal interview on student activism, Washington, D.C., May 7, 1970.

Introductory materials written by another author

[19] Samuel R. Levin, Foreword to Otto Jespersen, *Analytic Syntax,* Transatlantic Series in Linguistics (New York: Holt, Rinehart and Winston, 1969), p. vii.

Newspaper articles

[20] *The Seattle Times,* June 3, 1970, Section C, p. 1.

If author and title are given, they can be indicated as in footnote 1.

Quotations from a secondary source

[21] William of Nassyngton, *Speculum Vitae* as quoted in A. C. Baugh, *A History of the English Language,* 2nd ed. (New York: Appleton-Century-Crofts, 1957), p. 172.

This is a work dated 1325 and not easily available in any other source. In general, quotations from secondary sources should be avoided.

Reviews

[22] Noam Chomsky, rev. of *Verbal Behavior* by B. F. Skinner, *Language* 35 (1959), 29.

Unpublished material

[23] James E. Hoard, "On the Foundations of Phonological Theory," Diss. University of Washington, 1967, p. 120.

Second References to Footnotes

Subsequent references to the same work differ from the first. Instead of the abbreviations of the Latin words *ibidem, opere citato,* and *loco citato,* commonly used in the past, current practice favors the use of the author's name or, if two works by the same author are used, his name and a short title. *Ibid.* is still widely used but not the other abbreviations. Every reader, however, should understand their meaning.

Ibid., meaning "in the same place." *Ibid.* is used to refer only to the citation immediately preceding it, although it may be used several times in succession. It is usually combined with a page number, for example, *Ibid.,* p. 20, but if it is used without a number, the reference means the same source and the same page.

op. cit., meaning "in the work cited." *Op. cit.* is used together with the author's name and the page reference, for example, Vossler, *op. cit.,* p. 18. Its use refers to a work previously cited but not immediately preceding.

loc. cit., meaning "in the place cited." *Loc. cit.* is used with the author's name but no page reference, for example, Goodlad, *loc. cit.* It refers to an exact passage previously cited but not immediately preceding.

The following citations illustrate subsequent references to books and periodicals cited in the sample footnote forms above.

[24] Hoard, p. 121. [reference to work immediately preceding]
[25] Hoard, p. 119. [reference immediately preceding]
[26] "Language," *Britannica,* p. 689. [reference to n. 15]
[27] Hill, "Grammaticality," pp. 7–8. [reference to n. 2, but two works by same author]
[28] Hill, "Tainted *Ain't,*" p. 301. [reference to other work by Hill in n. 1]
[29] Hill, "Tainted *Ain't,*" p. 302. [title repeated to avoid confusion with n. 27]
[30] Krapp, I, 43. [same work in n. 12, different volume]
[31] Krapp, II, 149. [same work, different volume]

The same notes using *Ibid.* would read:

[24] *Ibid.,* p. 121.
[25] *Ibid.,* p. 119.
[26] "Language," *Britannica,* p. 689.
[27] Hill, "Grammaticality," pp. 7–8.
[28] Hill, "Tainted *Ain't,*" p. 301.
[29] *Ibid.,* p. 302 [no confusion here because *Ibid.* refers to citation immediately preceding]
[30] Krapp, I, 43.
[31] *Ibid.,* II, 149.

BIBLIOGRAPHY

The bibliography is usually the last portion of a reference paper, if it is used at all. If all of the footnotes contain full bibliographical information, the bibliography is superfluous except as a convenience to the reader. Articles in the humanities customarily do not use bibliographies.

The following practices are standard for preparing bibliographies:

1. Books are listed alphabetically by the author's last name. If no author is given, the book or article is listed by its title.
2. The author's name is given last name first—a reversal of footnote form.
3. Full publishing information is given for books. If the name of a publishing house has been changed in recent years, the name given on the title page should be used.
4. The main parts of a bibliographical entry are punctuated differently from footnotes. See models in 12B.
5. Several works by the same author are listed in alphabetical order by their titles. A long dash substitutes for the author's name after the first reference.
6. Inclusive page numbers of articles and parts of books are listed. The page numbers of complete books are not given.
7. Items in a bibliography are not numbered.
8. Items are single-spaced, with the second line slightly indented so that the author's name is prominent. Double spacing is used between items.
9. Books and periodicals may be grouped together or listed separately.

12B SAMPLE BIBLIOGRAPHY FORMS The items included in the footnotes above are listed here in bibliographical form.

Ayer, Alfred J., *et al. Studies in Communication.* Longon: Secker & Warburg, 1955.

Baugh, Albert C., *A History of the English Language.* 2nd ed. New York: Appleton-Century-Crofts, Inc., 1957.

Chomsky, Noam. Review of B. F. Skinner, *Verbal Behavior. Language,* 35 (1959), 26–58.

Hatfield, James T., *et al.,* eds. *Curme Volume of Linguistic Studies.* Language Monograph, No. 7. Washington, D.C.: Linguistic Society of America, 1930.

Hill, Archibald A. "Grammaticality." *Word,* 17 (April 1961), 1–10.
————. "The Tainted *Ain't* Once More." *College English,* 26 (1965), 298–303.

Hoard, James E. "On the Foundations of Phonological Theory." Ph.D. dissertation, University of Washington, 1967.

Jackson, Henry M., Senator. Personal interview on student activism. Washington, D.C., May 7, 1970.

Krapp, George P. *The English Language in America.* Vol. I. New York: Frederick Ungar Publishing Co., 1925. [If both volumes were used, the entry would read "2 vols."]

"Language." *Encyclopaedia Britannica,* 14th ed., 13, pp. 696–704.

Lester, Mark, ed. *Readings in Applied Transformational Grammar.* New York: Holt, Rinehart and Winston, Inc., 1970.

Levin, Samuel R. Foreword to Otto Jespersen, *Analytic Syntax.* Transatlantic Series in Linguistics. New York: Holt, Rinehart and Winston, Inc., 1969.

Lloyd, Donald A., and Harry R. Warfel. *American English in Its Cultural Setting.* New York: Alfred A. Knopf, 1956.

McCawley, James D. "The Role of Semantics in a Grammar," in *Universals in Linguistic Theory.* Ed. Emmon Bach and Robert T. Harms. New York: Holt, Rinehart and Winston, Inc., 1968, pp. 124–169.

Myers, L. M. "Generation and Deviation." *College Composition and Communication,* 18 (1967), 217.

Ogden, C. K., and I. A. Richards. *The Meaning of Meaning.* 8th ed. Harvest Book. New York: Harcourt, Brace & World, Inc., 1946.

"Rand McNally: More Than a Mapmaker." *Business Week,* November 22, 1969, pp. 66–68.

The Seattle Times, June 3, 1970, Section C, p. 1.

Shakespeare: Twenty-three Plays and the Sonnets. Ed. Thomas Marc Parrott. Rev. ed. New York: Charles Scribner's Sons, 1953.

Sledd, James. *A Short Introduction to English Grammar*. Chicago: Scott, Foresman and Co., 1959.

U.S., Department of State. *Language and Area Study Programs in American Universities*. Compiled by Larry Moses in cooperation with the Language Development Branch of Health, Education and Welfare Department. Washington, D.C.: External Research Staff, 1964.

Vossler, Karl. *The Spirit of Language in Civilization*. Trans. Oscar Oeser. London: Routledge & Kegan Paul, Ltd., 1932.

12C COMMON ABBREVIATIONS USED IN NOTES

c., ca. (*circa*)	about, approximately (*ca.* 1450)
cf. (*confer*), cp.	compare
ch., chs., chap., chaps.	chapter, chapters
diss.	dissertation
ed., eds.	edited by, editor, editors
e.g. (*exempli gratia*)	for example
et al. (*et alii*)	and others
f., ff	the following page(s) or line(s)
fl. (*floriut*)	flourished
ibid. (*ibidem*)	in the same place
i.e. (*id est*)	that is
il.	illustrated
l., ll.	line(s)
loc. cit. (*loco citato*)	in the place cited
ms., mss.	manuscript(s)
n.	note
n.d.	no date of publication
n.p.	no place of publication
n.s.	new series
op. cit (*opere citato*)	in the work cited
o.s.	old series
p., pp.	page(s)
pass. (*passim*)	throughout, here and there
q.v. (*quod vide*)	which see
rev.	revised
tr., trans.	translated by
v. (*vide*)	see, consult
viz. (*videlicet*)	namely
vol., vols.	volume(s)

12D SAMPLE PAGES FROM REFERENCE PAPERS

SAMPLE TITLE PAGE

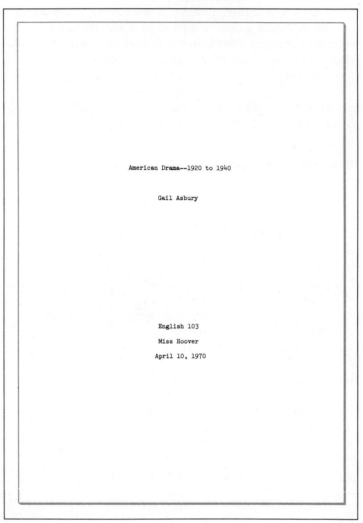

American Drama--1920 to 1940

Gail Asbury

English 103
Miss Hoover
April 10, 1970

Comments

Many departments or individual instructors have their own requirements for the information to be included on the title page. Those instructions should be followed as prescribed.

When a title page is used, the title is not repeated on page 1 of the essay.

The title page is customarily followed by one blank page. It is not a numbered page if used.

SAMPLE OUTLINE FOR PAPER

```
Thesis:  The era of the 1920's and 1930's brought new ideas and new concepts
         to the stage and marked a significant advance in the American theater.

    I.  The setting and spirit of the 1920's and 1930's

        A.  The spirit of rebellion in Eugene O'Neill

        B.  Other playwrights of the 1930's:  George S. Kaufman and Elmer Rice

   II.  Threats to the success of the theater at the end of the '20's

        A.  The talkies

        B.  The depression

            1.  Change in mood from the gay, nose-thumbing revolt of the '20's

            2.  Low economic ebb of the theater

            3.  Increase in spiritual values depicted on the stage

  III.  Spurs to the growth of the theater in the 1930's

        A.  Influence of the Theatre Guild

            1.  Movement toward a permanent theater group

            2.  Emergence of Clifford Odets as group's playwright

        B.  Influence of federal funds upon theater:  Federal Theatre Project

            1.  Jobs for the unemployed

            2.  Spread of live theater to forty states

            3.  Termination in 1939 because of suspected Communist influence

   IV.  Variety of theatrical productions during the period indicated by the
        works of significant playwrights

        A.  Marc Connelly

        B.  George S. Kaufman and Moss Hart

        C.  James Thurber and Elliot Nugent

        D.  Robert Sherwood

        E.  Thornton Wilder

        F.  Lillian Hellman
```

Comments

If an outline is required by an instructor, it should be inserted following the blank page. It is considered preliminary material. The pages of preliminary materials are usually unnumbered, or they may be numbered with small Roman numerals, as prefatory materials to books frequently are.

Outlines are never submitted unless they are part of an academic assignment.

SAMPLE FIRST PAGE

The atmosphere of the changing 1920's and 1930's provided an ideal setting for advances in American drama. The American people were questioning
many of the traditional values in the post-war (World War I) society, and
their quest for new ideals is apparent in the plays of the time. This was a
time for experiments, and many new playwrights with fresh, bright ideas produced some plays that are still considered great today.

The 1920's and 1930's were both decades of revolt, but in the twenties
the mood was gay and festive. Emory Lewis characterizes the spirit: "Following the follies and brutalities of World War I, hedonism, disillusion with
the Establishment's proprieties, religious skepticism, and a general thumbing
of the nose at inflated misleaders were the values--or non-values, if you
prefer--of the Lost Generation, The Flaming Youth of the Jazz Age."[1] Their
rebellion was not violent, but rather a general feeling of distrust of society's
values. The playwrights of this time, as I will discuss later, branched out
in their subject matter and made the play an effective tool with which to mold
public opinion.

The most noteworthy playwright of the twenties, as my sources agree, was
Eugene O'Neill. He was the first major playwright to emerge from what is now
a familiar movement, the theater groups "off Broadway." In 1920, he presented
The Emperor Jones, which quickly drew crowds away from Broadway and down to
Greenwich Village.[2] His most significant achievement during these early years
was Beyond the Horizon, his first full-length play to be produced. Compared
with today's uncompromising frankness of language and unsparing probing of
character, it is tame. In the context of its own time, however, its honesty
was "like a refreshing breeze in a stale front parlor, grandly and excessively

[1] Stages (Englewood Cliffs, N.J.: Prentice-Hall, 1969), p. 31.

[2] Lewis, p. 36.

Comments

The material in the first two paragraphs illustrates what might be considered general knowledge. A particular description by one writer is footnoted.

The use of "I" and "my" in lines 14 and 17 is easy and unobtrusive. These first person references avoid clumsy phrases like "as will be discussed later" and "as the sources consulted."

The comparison between *Beyond the Horizon* and contemporary plays may be considered the writer's own.

The quotation in the last line is worked smoothly into the main text.

Both footnotes refer to the same book. Lewis' name appears in the main text in n. 1. The writer is using short titles instead of *Ibid*.

Page 1 is characteristically not numbered, although it is counted in the total number of pages.

SAMPLE PAGE FROM A DIFFERENT PAPER ON THE POETRY OF THEODORE ROETHKE

-4-

In "Root Celler" the last two lines of the poem add to the idea conveyed in "Cuttings":

> Nothing would give up life:
> Even the dirt kept breathing a small breath.[11]

Here again is the struggle to be born and to exist "hunting for chinks" or dangling "like tropical snakes" or "lolling obscenely."[12] In this smelly cellar, "a congress of stinks," all the things making up this awful stench are working to remain alive. These minor things in life, the roots, stems, bulb shoots and even the dirt, are no different from man. They illustrate that there is simple beauty in living, and one finds it not only in man but also in the workings of nature. Perhaps it is seen a great deal clearer in nature, for nature is simple, true and above all real.

Then comes the "Old Florist," "Frau Bauman, Frau Schmidt, and Frau Schwartze," and "Transplanting," poems about the tenders of greenhouses, the so-called "manipulators of the vegetable world," from whom god-like images are developed.[13] In "Old Florist" we have a gardener who

> . . . could flick and pick
> Rotten leaves or yellowy petals,
> Or scoop out a weak close to flourishing roots,
> Or make the dust buzz with a light spray,
> Or drown a bug in one spit of tobacco juice,
> Or fan life into wilted sweet-peas with his hat,
> Or stand all night watering roses, his feet blue
>   in rubber boots.[14]

He is one who determines, as much as God does for man, who is to live or die. The poem is also the first representation by Roethke of his father as a type of a god. This refers back to Roethke's idea of the importance of childhood and illustrates the "awe and respect" with which Roethke held his father.[15]

---

[11]*Ibid.*, p. 39.

[12]*Ibid.*

[13]Malkoff, p. 54.

[14]*Words for the Wind*, p. 46.

[15]Malkoff, p. 3.

Comments'

Pages are numbered at the top unless the page has a special heading, in which case the number is placed at the bottom of the page.

Quotations set off by special indentation do not require quotation marks. Phrases quoted in the text use them.

N. 11 illustrates that *Ibid.* can be used as the first note on a new page. In this case, it refers to a book of poems by Theodore Roethke cited in n. 10 on the previous page. N. 13 is the same book, but *Ibid.* can be used to refer only to the previous entry.

With many quotations from a single text, *Ibid.* is more economical than short titles.

SAMPLE PAGE FROM A PAPER BASED ON PRIMARY SOURCES:
THREE STORIES BY WILLIAM FAULKNER

-6-

Under the circumstances, Molly reveals a great tolerance for the conditions under which she lives.

Molly's marriage to Lucus is symbolic of the fact that she accepts her condition in life as being inferior. Lucus, just as the white man, dictates to her as she faithfully performs the duties of a wife--the cooking, house work, and caring for the children. He ignores her when she tells him that he should get his planting done like Mister Roth wants.[28] Thus, when Lucus no longer gives her the strength she needs, she turns to Roth in pursuit of a divorce. With no money or land or any material objects of her own, Molly who "felt no larger than a reed stem of the pipe she smoked," depended entirely on her husband, but in a larger sense looked to the white man for fulfilling her inadequacies.[29]

Consequently, it is apparent that in the marriage of these two Negro characters William Faulkner has combined two qualities of life that enable them to endure. At one extreme is Molly who accepts humbly her inferior position as black bound to the white world, and at the opposite extreme is Lucus who shows through imitation of the white man that, although he is black, he is a man too. Even though they are mortal beings, those qualities which predominate to give them strength and purpose in life will remain alive in the generations to succeed them. As a young boy, their son Henry asserts "I ain't shamed of nobody, not even me."[30] Already his father's quality is beginning to be a part of him. Out of the humility to bear the bondage of a white man's world, yet with the pride as a black man to live as a man, Faulkner shows that the Negroes' spirit will not only endure, but will prevail.

[28]"The Fire and the Hearth," p. 42.

[29]Ibid., p. 100.

[30]Ibid., p. 114.

Comments

This paper accumulates thirty footnotes in six pages because it draws frequently upon short phrases from the three stories being discussed. Full bibliographical information for the story cited in n. 28 was given in n. 3. The writer could also repeat the title, but *Ibid.* is simpler in this case.

The final paragraph—the ending of the paper—draws together various points made throughout the discussion.

Since this paper uses three stories by Faulkner taken from one collection, a bibliography is unnecessary.

SAMPLE BIBLIOGRAPHY PAGE FROM A BRIEF FIVE-PAGE PAPER ON THE ENGLISH CYCLE PLAYS

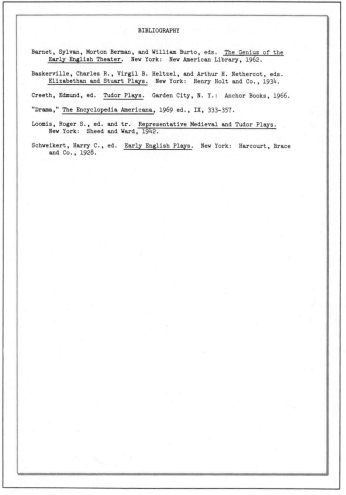

BIBLIOGRAPHY

Barnet, Sylvan, Morton Berman, and William Burto, eds. <u>The Genius of the Early English Theater.</u> New York: New American Library, 1962.

Baskerville, Charles R., Virgil B. Heltzel, and Arthur H. Nethercot, eds. <u>Elizabethan and Stuart Plays.</u> New York: Henry Holt and Co., 1934.

Creeth, Edmund, ed. <u>Tudor Plays.</u> Garden City, N. Y.: Anchor Books, 1966.

"Drama," <u>The Encyclopedia Americana,</u> 1969 ed., IX, 333-357.

Loomis, Roger S., ed. and tr. <u>Representative Medieval and Tudor Plays.</u> New York: Sheed and Ward, 1942.

Schweikert, Harry C., ed. <u>Early English Plays.</u> New York: Harcourt, Brace and Co., 1928.

Comments

The bibliography includes no periodical material, suggesting that the writer probably did not consult periodical guides. If she consulted *Reader's Guide,* she probably found no material on this particular topic.

It would have been necessary to consult specialized bibliographies listed in books like Altick and Bond (see p. 313).

The bibliography includes several recent sources. Since the writer depends almost exclusively upon the introductions of edited anthologies, which are usually brief and general, it might be questioned whether the sources for this paper are adequately varied.

Because of the heading at the top, the page number goes to the bottom.

EVALUATING THE REFERENCE PAPER

As a completed project, the reference paper is subject to the same criteria a researcher uses in evaluating the sources he has used. In brief, a reference paper is good

—if the author has adequately canvassed his topic and carefully weighed his sources;
—if the material is up to date;
—if the material is authoritative and accurate;
—if the material is fully and accurately documented;
—if the paper is properly limited so that particular points can be handled with adequate detail;
—if the paper inspires in the reader a sense of confidence by its objectivity and persuasiveness of its style.

THE
ENGLISH
LANGUAGE:
ORIGINS,
GROWTH,
AND
CHANGE

13

The Heritage of Language

The English language is our heritage, but we do not preserve it as a museum piece. We use it daily. We refurbish it. We discard parts of it that no longer seem suitable for our times. The language experiences a constant renewal through its speakers. No one is born with the capacity to speak a language; he grows up with it, he absorbs it, he learns it, he practices it. By the time he goes to school, he has mastered the fundamentals. From that point on, education attempts to develop his capacities with language and to familiarize him with the best of the heritage that has been preserved in the literature.

Language, therefore, is one form of human behavior. It is mainly social behavior, because it is our means of communication with one another, either spoken or written. Interaction between speakers keeps the language vital and flexible. Languages like Sanskrit and Gothic are known as dead languages because they no longer have an active history of living speakers. They are preserved only in a written literature. Nothing is altered, and nothing is added. Because the history of a language is largely an account of its changes, its history ends when change is no longer possible.

English is a relatively young language. Its history extends over a period of approximately 1500 years, although its origins may be traced back to a more distant past. But its development as a separate language coincides with the movement of tribes from the continent of Europe to the British Isles about the middle of the fifth century. The people already living in Britain were by no means without languages. Numerous dialects of Celtic were spoken, and surely Latin survived as a remnant from the earlier Roman occupation. But the native people of Britain could not resist the force of the invading tribes. English, the new language, predominated. The other languages died or managed to survive only because their speakers retired to isolated and remote parts of the island. In the years following, English underwent a natural course of development, but the facts of its origins and early development were lost. Not until the sixteenth century did the English show an interest in the study of Old English, and not until the nineteenth century did scholars throughout the world provide the evidence that established the concept of the Indo-European family of languages and the ties of English with that family (see Table 1).

ORIGINS OF ENGLISH

The visit of Sir William Jones to India in the 1780s assumes special importance in tracing the origins of the English language because that visit brought him for the first time in touch with Sanskrit writings dating back to as early as 2000 B.C. Sir William, a man learned in many languages, was impressed by the resemblances between ancient Sanskrit and the more familiar ancient languages of Latin and Greek. Sir William was not the first to notice these similarities, but he was the first to state with emphasis that the resemblances were surely not accidental and that languages of both the Western and Eastern worlds must have sprung from a common source.

Thus, the hypothesis of a parent for languages as widely separated in time and place as Sanskrit, Latin, and English was set down in 1786. The findings of men like Franz Bopp, Jacob Grimm, Rasmus Rask, and Karl Verner in the following century represent a remarkable feat of scholarship. What the first three of these men did was to tabulate corresponding words in widely scattered languages and to conclude that their differences could be explained in terms of regular and predictable sound changes. The work of the fourth, Karl Verner, conclusively established the principle of the orderly development of languages because he was able to explain changes that seemed to be exceptions to the principles of Grimm and the others. These principles of sound change are familiarly known today as Grimm's Law and Verner's Law (see Glossary 33).

Indo-European

The hypothesis of Indo-European as the original tongue may be stated briefly: enough evidence exists to conclude that Indo-European was a language spoken by a tribe probably in north central Europe, in the late Stone Age. No written documents exist in the language because it was spoken before the invention of writing. About 2500 B.C., possibly earlier, the members of the tribe dispersed both to the west and to the east, moving eventually as far west as Cornwall and as far

Table 1 _____

INDO-EUROPEAN FAMILY OF LANGUAGES

I. SATEM GROUP*
  A. Indo-Iranian Branch
    1. Indic (Sanskrit, Pakrit, Pali, Hindi, Urdu, Hindustani, Bengali, Gujarati, Marathi, Panjabi, Singhalese, Romany)
    2. Iranian (Avestan, Old Persian, Pahlavi, Sogdian, Scythian, Balochi, Pashtu, Persian, Kurdesh, Ossetic)
  B. Armenian Branch (Classical Armenian, Eastern and Western Armenian)
  C. Albanian Branch (Thracian, Illyrian, Albanian)
  D. Balto-Slavic
    1. Slavic (Old Bulgarian, Bulgarian, Serbo-Croatian, Slovenian, Czech, Slovak, Polish, Wendish, Great Russian, White Russian, Ukrainian
    2. Baltic (Old Prussian, Lithuanian, Latvian)
II. CENTUM GROUP
  A. Hellenic (Mycenean Greek, Attic, Ionic, Doric, Aeolic, Cyprian, Modern Greek)
  B. Italic
    1. Oscan
    2. Umbrian
    3. Latin (Faliscan, Latin, Italian, Provençal, French, Spanish, Catalan, Portuguese, Rumanian)
  C. Celtic (Gaulish, Welsh, Cornish, Breton, Irish, Manx, Gaelic)
  D. Germanic
    1. East Germanic (Gothic)
    2. North Germanic
      a. East Norse (Swedish, Danish, Gutnish)
      b. West Norse (Norwegian, Faroese, Icelandic)
    3. West Germanic
      a. High German (Alemannic, Bavarian, Yiddish)
      b. Franconian (Dutch, Flemish)
      c. Low German or Plattdeutsch
      d. Old Frisian, Modern Frisian
      e. English (Old English, Middle English, Modern)

---

* *Satem* is the word in Avestan for "hundred." Languages are grouped according to the initial consonant used in the word for "hundred." They are either *satem* or *centum*, the Latin word for "hundred." Tocharian and Hittite are sometimes considered third and fourth major classifications because they do not fit the *satem-centum* groupings.

east as Chinese Turkestan, carrying with them a common language which was to undergo different kinds of change in scattered places of the world. Certain words, however, especially the numerals and terms for family relationships, did not completely lose signs of their origin. The study of these clues in the earliest written documents of many ancient languages has made possible the reconstruction of a lost language and its grammar.

Comparison of variant forms in many languages suggests that some languages have undergone more changes than others. Among modern languages, Lithuanian is considered closest to the parent language. Modern English represents a wide divergence. In the relatively brief period of its history, English has undergone vast changes, so that what we now recognize as English is quite different from English of a thousand years ago.

THE STAGES OF DEVELOPMENT

The history of the English language is customarily divided into three periods: Old English, 450–1100, Middle English, 1100–1500, and Modern English, 1500 to the present. Some histories choose to distinguish between Early Modern from 1500 to 1800 and Modern, a later development from 1800 on. But all of these divisions are arbitrary. The dates vary slightly from history to history, but the breaks in this gradual and continuous evolution reflect events which had a strong impact upon the development of the language. The earliest invasion of Germanic tribes that we know was A.D. 449; the Norman conquest of England occurred in 1066; William Caxton set up the first printing press in England in 1477; by 1800, England's political and social structure was remolded by the Industrial Revolution. These are only a selection of the external conditions that affected the conditions under which people lived and influenced the way they used the language.

Because a full account of the development of the English language would involve a detailed discussion of its grammar, vocabulary, and pronunciation in each of the periods, a handbook of this kind can give only an overview and some suggestion of the kinds of change that occurred.

Old English (450–1100)

The overall change that has occurred in English from its earliest period to the present may be summarized as a gradual shift from a synthetic language to an analytic language. A synthetic language is one that depends chiefly upon a well-developed inflectional system for its operation; an analytic one depends mainly upon word order. Indo-European itself was a synthetic language, and many of the branch languages, like Modern German and Russian, still utilize inflections extensively. The fact that Old English was a synthetic language causes it to resemble Modern German more closely than it does Modern English.

A quotation from an Old English translation of the Bible will quickly suggest some of the features of the language:

> Ðās þing se Hǣlend sprǣc, and āhōf ūpp his ēagan tō heofenum, and
> Those things the Saviour spoke, and lifted up his eyes to [the] heavens and
>
> cwæð; 'Fæder, tīd ys cumen; geswutela þinne Sunu, þæt þīn Sunu geswutelige
> said: Father, time is come; glorify thy Son, that thy Son may glorify
>
> þē; and swā þū him sealdest anweald ǣlces mannes, þæt he sylle ēce līf
> thee; and as thou to him gavest power of each man, that he might give eternal life
>
> eallum þām þe þū him sealdest. Ðis ys sōþlice ēce līf, þæt hī oncnāwon
> to all those whom thou him gavest. This is truly eternal life, that they know
>
> þæt þū eart ān sōþ God, and se þe þū sendest, Hǣlynde Crīst.'
> that thou art the one true God, and he whom thou sendest, Saviour Christ.'
>
> John 17:1–3

The strangeness of Old English is in part due to symbols we no longer use, like the þ (thorn) and ð (edh), used indifferently in Old English for either the *th*-sound in *thin* or the *th*-sound in *thine*. The symbol *æ* in the word *sprǣc,* the past tense of *sprecan* ("to speak"), stands for a sound like the *a* in *at*. These early forms of the verb "to speak" may be compared with Modern German *sprechen* and *sprach*. The *um*-ending on *heofenum* indicates a dative plural, no longer used in Modern English. *Ēagan* is an old plural form still recognizable in a word like *oxen*. The case of Ðas in Ðas þing shows that the noun is accusative plural, and the case of *þinne* in *þinne Sunu* shows that it is accusative singular. *Geswutela* is the imperative mood of *geswutelian,* a Class II weak verb; *geswutelige* is the same verb in the optative mood, expressing wish or desire. *Tīd* is an archaic word for *time* that we retain in the expression "Time and tide wait for no man." *Ðū him sealdest* ("thou to him gavest") represents a word order we no longer follow, but the words can be understood in Old English because the inflected form of *him* indicates that it is dative after the verb *sealdest* and should be read "to him." These are only a few details that give a clue to the highly complex system of noun, pronoun, and adjective declensions, complicated verb classes and conjugations, and a spelling and sound system quite different from Modern English.

Middle English (1100–1500)

John 17:1–3 in John Wycliffe's translation in Middle English, about 1388, shows to what extent the language had evolved over a period of several centuries:

> These thingis Jesus spak, and whanne he hadde cast up hise iȝen into hevene, he seide: 'Fadir, the our cometh; clarifie thi sone, that thi sone clarifie thee; as thou has ȝovun to hym power on ech fleisch, that al thing that thou hast ȝovun to hym, he ȝyve to hem everlastynge liif. And this is everlastynge liif, that thei knowe thee very God aloone, and whom thou hast sent, Jesu Crist.'

Even though the spellings and forms of this passage continue to have a strange appearance, they have enough resemblance to Modern English that an interlinear translation is no longer necessary. The pronunciations of Middle English words differ from those of both Old English and Modern English. Vowel sounds in Middle English had basically the values of what are now referred to as continental vowels; that is, they were pronounced like vowels in Modern French, German, or Italian. Through the centuries, vowel sounds have shifted, so that a word like *stan* in Old English, which was pronounced with an *a* as in *father,* changed to Middle English *ston* or *stoon,* pronounced with an *o* as in *bought,* and finally reached its present fully rounded sound. Sound shifting is a complete history in itself.

The most significant change that took place in the Middle English period was a gradual erosion of the inflectional system. *Thingis* in the passage above has a plural ending that has been retained and become standard in Modern English (compare OE Ðas þing in the earlier passage); *iȝen* (eyes) is one of the irregular plurals that have been almost completely dropped except for *children* and *oxen,* although we retain a few other irregular forms. The most frequent ending in Middle English is the final *e,* but it no longer serves a grammatical function. The numerous inflections of Old English which distinguished case and number and gender of nouns and adjectives were gradually leveled to a single form *e.* No longer serving their former purpose, however, the ending was doomed to be dropped—first in pronunciation and later in spelling. With the decay of the inflectional system, English had to depend upon word order. By the end of the Middle English period, English had already become essentially an analytic language.

The invasion of the Normans in 1066 exercised a major influence upon the English language because French became an invading language, as Old English had at an earlier period. As the language of the aristocracy and of almost all official bodies, French might conceivably have replaced English. Or Latin, as the language of the church, may have undermined the importance of English in high places. But English always remained the speech of the common people and, in its struggle for survival, strengthened its resources by absorbing approximately 10,000 words from French and innumerable other words from Latin.

By the end of the thirteenth century, political and social conditions in England had dulled the prestige of French. The military struggle during the long Hundred Years' War in the fourteenth and fifteenth centuries brought about a growth of national feeling. By 1400, it was necessary for everyone in England—king, judge, professor, churchman, and common man alike—to know English. A flourishing literature at the end of the fourteenth century, particularly the work of Chaucer, seems to testify that English, as the language of its people, deserved survival.

Modern English (1500 to Present)

By 1500, the English language had established the principles of operation we recognize as modern. Spelling, however, was to remain unstandardized for at least another two hundred years, and forms that we now recognize as obsolete were still in use. The pronunciations of the sixteenth century, vastly changed again from Middle English values, may have sounded more like Modern Irish than Modern English. Nevertheless, the language of 1500 was essentially the language of today. Tyndale's translation of John 17:1-3, given above in Old English and Middle English, will indicate exactly how the printed language appeared in 1534:

> These wordes spake Jesus, and lifte uppe his eyes to heven, and sayde: 'Father, the houre is come; glorify thy Sonne, that thy Sonne maye glorify the; as thou hast geven hym power over all fleshe, that he shulde geve eternall life to as many as thou hast geven him. This is life eternall, that they myght knowe the, that only very God, and whom thou has sent, Jesus Christ.'

The forms *thou, thee,* and *thy,* commonly used in speech, not just in poetry and formal address as they are today, fell into disuse during this period. *Ye,* as a distinguishing nominative plural of *you,* was dropped, although the King James version of the Bible (1611) continues to make the distinction: "For the Father himself loveth you, because ye have loved me . . ." (John 16:27). Impersonal constructions like "it dislikes me that . . ." also disappeared. *Its* as the possessive of *it* makes its appearance about 1600 instead of the former *his,* although Shakespeare does not use *its* in his plays. *Who* and *which* were added to *that* as relative pronouns.

Printing had its effect upon the language, not only as a standardizing force but as a means of introducing new words. Words no longer had to be imported by mouth; books could serve the purpose. The sixteenth and seventeenth centuries were periods of extensive borrowing, particularly from Latin and Greek. At times, borrowings even displaced English words. The influx of strange words and their use in English sentences caused a reaction of distaste among writers of the seventeenth century. They denounced "inkhorn terms," their phrase for obscure and pedantic words like *accersited* for *brought* and *adjuvate* for *aid,* both derived from Latin. They expressed the view that the English language had to be kept pure—a theme that has been repeated at various times in various places throughout the ages and continues to have its spokesmen at the present.

The past four hundred years have produced unquestionable evidence of the force of analogy upon language, both upon pronunciations and forms, but particularly upon forms. Analogy works as a leveler, a force to make things the same. Thus, the irregular forms of nouns and verbs and adjectives that carried over from Middle English have been regularized. *Shoon* has become *shoes* like most plurals; *holpen* has become *helped* like most participles; *doth* has become *does* like most third person singulars. Of course, irregular forms remain in current English, but analogy continues to wear away at their nonconformity. *Indexes* is now a common substitute for *indices, syllabuses* for *syllabi,* and *hoofs* for *hooves.* Even the plural of *mongoose,* a much later addition than *goose,* reads *mongooses,* not *mongeese.*

Thus, time has changed English radically. Not much of Old English remains today in the active language. Eighty-five percent of Old English words have been lost, but those that have survived are among words that we use most frequently. Less than half of the Old English irregular strong verbs survive, and some of those, like *dive* and *thrive,* have been regularized. But, in the process of alteration, English has become a simpler language and a cosmopolitan one. Today, it is spoken by more than 300,000,000 people throughout the world. It is no longer exclusively the language of England and the United States. English has become an international language.

14

Sources
of Words

The total stock of words in the English language is its lexicon, not just those that appear in standard dictionaries but all words that are used in speech or writing. In fact, the bound dictionary with its label "unabridged" creates an illusion that the verbal resources of the language are contained within its covers. The truth is that only the more stable words are recorded there—words that have been established by use and words that for the most part fall within the category of standard English, essentially the words that are appropriate for writing. The nonstandard, dialectal, obscene, and archaic words are numerous enough to supply material for many other dictionaries. Even though supplementary dictionaries of this kind do exist, dictionary makers cannot possibly keep up with a living language that permits its users to invent new words constantly and to reinterpret old words in new contexts. New words in the language originate in four main ways: by borrowing, combining, inventing, and shifting.

BORROWING

The vocabulary of Old English was relatively stable, forming new words by joining native words. *Wīs,* meaning "wise," was combined with *dōm,* meaning "judgment" to make *wīsdōm,* the word for "wisdom" and "learning." English, however, was not always able to supply equivalent words for new ideas and situations. For example, when Christianity was adopted in A.D. 597, English borrowed words like *mass* and *alms* from Latin.

From the twelfth century on, English resorted more and more to borrowing from foreign languages to supply its needs, at first mainly from Latin, French, and the Scandinavian languages, but eventually from the languages of many nations, particularly as transportation and communication brought the far-flung people of the world in touch with one another. A selected list of borrowed words in English reads like an inventory of languages, both ancient and modern:

African dialects	gumbo, banjo, voodoo
Algonquin	moccasin, toboggan, wigwam
Arabic	coffee, harem, zero
Assyrian	ziggurat
Australian	boomerang, kangeroo
Celtic	down [hill], vassal, Avon
Chinese	silk, tea, yen
Czech	polka, robot
Dutch	buoy, easel, sleigh
Eskimo	igloo, kayak
Finnish	sauna
French	bourgeois, cabaret, resumé
Gaelic	bard, bog, whiskey
German	delicatessen, nickel, wanderlust
Greek	academy, catastrophe, stoic
Hawaiian	hula, luau, ukulele
Hebrew	amen, cherub, jubilee
Hindu	punch, shampoo, thug
Irish	colleen, leprechan, shamrock
Italian	bankrupt, confetti, soprano
Japanese	haiku, jujitsu, tycoon
Latin	appendix, interim, prospectus
Malyan	bamboo, gingham, orangutan
Mexican	enchilada, mesquite, taco
Norwegian	fiord, ski, slalom
Persian	lilac, shawl, turban
Polish	mazurka, polonaise
Polynesian	taboo, tapa, tattoo
Portuguese	cuspidor, flamingo, tank
Russian	boyar, tundra, vampire
Sanskrit	ginger, jute, swastika
Scotch	kale, plaid, skulduggery
Spanish	adobe, canyon, sombrero
Swedish	ombudsman, troll, smorgasbord

Tibetan	polo, yak
Turkish	odalisque, seraglio, tulip
Yiddish	schnozzle, schlemiel, bagel

Even though it is obvious that many of these words are native terms for products, activities associated with a foreign country, or cultural, commercial, and political words for which English has no equivalent, it is also true that all of these words are fully Anglicized; that is, we think of them as English words, not as foreign words. In print, they are not italicized as unadopted words characteristically are. They have full status in our own language.

In the history of borrowing, foreign words have upon many occasions displaced words of Old English origin. Thus, today we use the Latin importation *library* instead of a modern version of Old English *bōchord,* meaning "book treasure." The oft-repeated generalization that all of the short, vivid words of the English language are of Old English origin does not hold consistently. *Mount, firm,* and *flame* were borrowed from Latin through French (compare *ascend, secure,* and *conflagration* borrowed directly from Latin). *They, die, egg,* and *sky* were borrowed from the early Scandinavian dialects. At times, words have entered the language by different routes at different periods, so that two English words that have the same meaning may have different forms, like *cipher* and *zero.* Both are derived from Arabic. The first entered the language about the sixteenth century through Old French. The second entered about one hundred years later through Italian. The two forms are called doublets. *Regal* and *royal* and *compute* and *count* illustrate the same phenomenon. Other doublets, deriving from a common source, sometimes take on completely different meanings. Thus, pairs like *cruise* and *cross* and *dainty* and *dignity* are related to one another by a common parentage, although they are quite unlike in their implications.

The examples of borrowing already cited indicate that some foreign words are adopted ready-made into the language with no change in form or spelling, whereas others are adapted to English. Among French borrowings in the first category that have become common English words are *apropos, cliché, devotee, etiquette, prestige,* and *souvenir.* Among other words less obviously French in form are *government, attorney, jury, estate, soldier,* and *vestment.*

Needless to say, the English language makes use of a number of purely foreign words and phrases for which it has no equivalent. These keep their foreign spellings, and we usually think of them as foreign. Many of them are professional and technical terms like *doppelgänger, pas de chat,* and *medulla oblongata.* Others are highly useful phrases like *sine qua non* and *raison d'être.* Despite the indispensable nature of foreign words in some contexts, their overuse continues to be looked upon as either affectation or exhibitionism. Their use always requires discretion on the part of a speaker or writer.

COMBINING: DERIVATION, COMPOUNDING, BLENDING

Combining as a source of new English words occurs by means of derivation, compounding, and blending. The forming of words by adding prefixes and suffixes to word stems is called derivation. Foreign influence is particularly strong in this kind of word-making. The word *translation,* for example, combines the Latin prefix *trans-* ("across") with the Latin participle *latus* ("carried") and adds a typical noun suffix *-ion.* At other times, Latin or Greek prefixes and suffixes are attached to familiar words, thus *atypical.* The Greek prefix *a-* means *not,* similar to the Latin prefix *in-* (insane) and the English *un-* (unjust). Knowledge of word elements, therefore, often provides a quick clue to the meaning of words derived by this process.

Latin Prefixes Used in English

ab-, abs-	from, away	*abstain*
ad-	to, toward	*address*
ante-	before	*antebellum*
bene-	well	*benefactor*
bi-	two	*bimanual*
circum-	around	*circumnavigate*
con-	with	*concurrent*
contra-	against	*contradistinction*
de-	down	*depress*
dis-	apart, opposite of	*distrust*
ex-	out, from	*excavate*
extra-	beyond	*extracurricular*
in-, il- im-, ir-	not	*inapt, illicit, immature, irrational*
in-, im-	in	*infringe, impress*
inter-	between	*intercede*
intra-	within	*intramural*
intro-	within	*introspection*
juxta-	near	*juxtapose*
non-	not	*nonconformist*
per-	through	*perforate*
post-	after	*postdoctorate*
pre-	before	*premature*
re-	again, back	*reclaim, recoil*
retro-	backward	*retroflex*

sub-	under	*subside*
super-	over	*supersonic*
trans-	across	*transplant*
ultra-	beyond, extremely	*ultraconservative*

Greek Prefixes Used in English

a-, an-	not	*amorphous, anhydrous*
ambi, amphi-	around, both	*ambidexterous, amphibious*
ana-	back, opposite	*anaphase*
anti-	against	*antibody*
cata-	down	*cataclysm*
dia-	through	*diatribe*
dys-	bad	*dysfunction*
epi-	upon	*epigraph*
eu-	good	*euphony*
hyper-	beyond, excess	*hyperthyroid*
hypo-	under	*hypotension*
meta-	beyond, denoting change	*metalinguistics, metamorphosis*
para-	side by side, near	*paraphrase*
peri-	around	*perimeter*
proto-	first	*prototype*
syn-, sym-	together	*synchronize, symphony*

Prefixes of Native Origin

a-	in, on, of	*ashore, akin*
be-	near, about	*bemoan*
for-	off, to the uttermost	*forswear, forbear*
mis-	wrong, bad	*misconduct*
out-	beyond	*outlaw*
over-	too much	*overeat*
un-	not	*unbeaten*
with-	against	*withstand*

In addition to the lists above, English adverbs and prepositions have the force of prefixes when they combine with other words, like *backhand* and *uphill.*

English words are also derived by adding suffixes. The suffixes are of special importance because they permit the words of the language to shift from one part of speech to another. Thus, *emotion* can be changed to *emotional* and, in turn, to *emotionalize, emotionally, emotionalist,* and *emotionality.* The suffix in each case marks the change and varies the meaning. Thus, suffixes are best grouped in terms of the parts of speech they ordinarily identify.

> *Suffixes marking nouns:* -acy, -age, -an, -ance, -ancy, -ant, -ar, -ard, -ary, -ate, -cy, -dom, -ee, -eer, -ence, -ency, -ent, -er, -ery, -ess, -ette, -hood, -ice, -ie, -ier, -ite, -ism, -ist, -ity, -ive, -kin, -let, -ment, -mony, -ness, -or, -ory, -ship, -ster, -teen, -tion, -tude, -ty, -ure, -y, -yer
>
> *Suffixes marking verbs;* -ate, -en, -fy, -ify, -ise, -ize
>
> *Suffixes marking adjectives:* -able, -ac, -aceous, -al, -am, -ar, -ary, -ate, -ble, -ent, -er, -ern, -escent, -ful, -ible, -ic, -ical, -id, -ile, -ine, -ish, -less, -like, -ly, -ory, -ose, -ous, -some, -ty, ulent, -wise, -y
>
> *Suffixes marking adverbs:* -ally, -fold, -like, -ly, -ward, -ways, -wise

Even though derivation is one of the common means of forming words, English also uses compounding, that is, joining together stems of words to form new ones. The process is by no means limited to native words. Recent additions to the language, like *television, telethon, astronaut, neutrosphere, bathosphere,* and *helicopter* show the tendency to combine Latin and Greek roots to supply our contemporary needs, particularly in science and technology.

The meanings of native compounds are sometimes self-explanatory when two elements are combined, like *newsworthy, teenage, lackluster,* and *flowerpot.* In other instances, however, they assume meanings beyond the literal addition of the two parts, like *henpeck, ladykiller, browbeat,* and *handbook.*

Compounding is particularly common in popular speech. One form will often spawn numerous others. By analogy with established words like *manpower* and *horsepower,* the late 1960s coined *black-power, white-power, flower-power, green-power,* and *boy-power.* Other popular compounds were *sit-in, stand-in, camp-in, love-in,* and *be-in,* possibly by analogy with *drive-in.* Many compounds of this kind are colorful and expressive, but almost always shortlived.

Blending is a third means of combining words; the resulting forms are called portmanteau words. Some of these are long established words, like *flare* (a combination of *flame* and *glare*), *glimmer* (*gleam* and *shimmer*), and *smash* (*smack* and *mash*). More recent ones like *motel* (*motor* and *hotel*) and *smog* (*smoke* and *fog*) are relatively self-explanatory. *Napalm* makes a short pronounceable blend of its two main ingredients, naphthenic and palmitic acids. Some blends are informal, like *josh* (*joke* and *bosh*) and *chortle* (*chuckle* and *snort*). Others are puns or deliberately humorous combinations, like *sexretary* or *grifty* (*groovy* and *nifty*).

SHIFTING

The discussion of derivational suffixes above has shown how words of one part of speech can be made to serve as another part of speech by actually changing the form of the word. The English language, however, also permits a functional shift of a word without an actual change of form. A word need only be moved from its accustomed position to a position usually occupied by another part of speech. Thus, the space-age phrase "All systems are go" changes *go* from a verb to an adjective. In the sentence "She won't believe in you hereafter," *hereafter* functions as an adverbial modifier. In "She believes in the hereafter," the placement of *hereafter* in an object position after the preposition *in* indicates that it is used as a noun in this sentence. Thus, by a constant process of shifting, words of the language assume new functions and meanings. The basic reason, of course, is economy. No new word needs to be created if an old one will serve.

Economy operates also in two other forms of shifting: clipping and back formations. Clipped words are essentially only shortened forms of other words, like *quote* for *quotation, mod* for *modern, exam* for *examination.* In these instances, both forms are retained, the shortened form usually associated with informal speech and the longer one with more formal occasions of speaking or writing. In other instances, however, the shortened form has become as firmly established as the standard form, and both are used interchangeably. We do not ordinarily think of *fan* as short for *fanatic* or of *pants* as short for *pantaloons.* Clipped forms like *gas* (for *gasoline*), *flu, phone,* and *gym* have a similar independence from their sources and are used freely in writing as well as speech. The most extreme form of clipping, of course, occurs when a word or phrase is reduced to its initials, like *TV, U. S., DDT,* and P.M.

Back formations are another kind of shifting and shortening to make current words do additional work. Some back formations have been accepted for so long that the only way to determine whether they were created by back formation or by derivation is to consult an historical dictionary. For example, the *Oxford English Dictionary* indicates that *commune* is a back formation from *communion, educate* from *education,* and *edit* from *editor.* At the time back formations are introduced, they are almost always condemned as gaucheries and continue to have that reputation until such time as usage has established the back formation and no one knows any longer which word preceded the other. Back formations of relatively recent origin, like *enthuse* from *enthusiasm* and *destruct* from *destruction,* are still in that period of transition when favor and disfavor counterbalance one another.

INVENTING

Combining words and shifting them are actually forms of inventing, in that new words are created as a result. But invention often takes a more ingenious twist. Existing elements are sometimes combined in highly unusual ways, or new words are created without reference to existing forms. Trade names, echoic words, nonce words, acronyms, and folk etymologies are the clearest signs of inventiveness at work.

Trade names would be no more important than any other proper names which are invented except that they often change their status as patented trademarks to become a class name for all other products of the same kind. *Zipper, nylon, kleenex, xerox,* and *escalator* have now discarded their trade identifications to become utility words of the language.

Echoic words are combinations of letters that are invented to approximate sounds. Some like *whew, whoa,* and *boom* are conventional sound words recorded in the dictionary, but others like *shh, psst,* and *hmm* continue to be used only as symbols of sounds rather than words. Closely related to the imitative words are reduplicating words that seem to play with sound for the sake of sound. Some of these words are slangy, like *super-duper, helter-skelter,* and *wishy-washy,* but others like *knicknack, humdrum,* and *zigzag* have lost most of their colloquial flavor.

Nonce words, or neologisms, are words and phrases invented for a particular context or occasion. In one sense, all new words might be considered nonce words when they first appear, but the fate of some words seems clearer than that of others. The limited usefulness of a nonce word frequently dooms it to a short life. A few like *boondoggle* and *gobbledygook* have become established; Winston Churchill's phrase "iron curtain" also survives. But blends like *psychedelicatessen* (a store to buy psychedelic posters), *archeolatry* (reverence of the past), *magnicide* (murder of an important man), and *numbskulduggerous* are not likely to find many users. They are left to perish in their newborn state.

Acronyms are words whose individual letters are telescoped from a series of several words. *Snafu* (situation normal, all fouled up), a popular word of World War II, has been cleaned up and finds general acceptance in the language. Organizations with long titles provide one of the most common sources of acronyms; UNESCO (United Nations Educational, Scientific, and Cultural Organization, NASA (The National Aeronautics and Space Administration), and PAWS (Progressive Animal Welfare Society) are only three among thousands of examples. Acronyms are either pronounced as words or, when unpronounceable, are sounded as individual letters, like SOS.

Folk etymologies are inventions in that they are usually popular translations of difficult words or phrases that people do not understand. *Varicose veins* is first heard and then written as *very close veins; cole slaw* becomes *cold slaw.* Foreign terms are given the same treatment: *cucaracha* is simplified to *cockroach,* and *coquetier* to *cocktail.* The unfamiliar in general is made familiar. Thus, *crayfish* becomes *crawfish* and *groseberry, gooseberry.* Comparable to these are simplified spellings of difficult words, like *pigeon English* for *pidgin English* and *shammy* for *chamois.* The interesting thing about many folk etymologies and simplified spellings is that their use sometimes prevails, so that in time we wonder why they are called what they are. A primrose, for example, looks nothing like a rose. The word is actually a folk version of the Middle English and Old French word *primerole,* which was the early word for the flower that we recognize as a primrose.

15

Changing Meanings
and Values
of Words

Etymology, the study of the history of words, satisfies man's perennial fascination with detection and his delight in narrative. It seeks out the origins of words and traces the changes that have occurred during the period of their use. New words constantly emerge; others, like *olden* and *bestow,* grow obsolescent; innumerable others are obsolete. Apart from being born and dying, however, words represent other kinds of changes. They move in and out of fashion or up and down the social ladder. Seldom do they retain absolute meanings, because meaning is a property that exists in the minds of men, not in the words themselves. Words are being constantly reinterpreted by their use. Their meanings may be extended or narrowed, improved in their connotations or debased. These four changes are customarily referred to as generalization, specialization, amelioration, and pejoration or by an alternate set of terms—extension, limitation, regeneration, and degeneration.

GENERALIZATION

Extensions of meaning are almost always gradual and may be either logical or figurative extensions. The change a word undergoes is not always limited to a single language. If the word has been borrowed, its meaning in another language is a part of its history. The word *governor,* borrowed from French, comes from a Latin word which originally meant "the steersman of a boat." The fact that "ship of state" persists as a cliché in the language today seems to relate to the shift that *gover-nor* underwent from a specialized and literal usage to a general and figurative one.

Words as unlike in meaning as *assassin* and *hashish* are related by their history. *Assassins* were originally members of a Mohammedan sect who ate hashish to fire up their zeal to kill Christians during the time of the crusades. *Assassin,* of course, is now a general term for murderer, not specifically one who had taken hashish to inspire his act.

Extensions of meaning frequently result from a change whereby some common usage displaces the particular meaning of a word. For example, in the sixteenth century, *Bedlam* was the popular word for a madhouse in London named the Hospital of St. Mary of Bethlehem. *Bedlam* now means "confusion," only an association with the original place and clearly an extended meaning.

Almost all words derived from proper names necessarily show an extension of meaning. *Sadism, silhouette,* and *dunce* are derived from the names of men; *maudlin, georgette,* and *marijuana* from the names of women; *utopia, serendipity,* and *quixotic* from the titles of books; and *wiener, paisley,* and *bourbon* from place names. To these might be added countless others drawn from mythology. The qualities associated with the original person, book, or place are universalized and made generally useful.

Synecdoche and metonymy are figures of speech that ordinarily represent extensions of meaning. Synecdoche involves the substitution of a part for the whole—*boards* for "the stage," *hands* for "workers," *mouths* for "persons to feed." In each instance, the part stands for the meaning of the whole. Metonymy describes a similar kind of association by which one term loosely substitutes for another related one, thus, *sweat* for "energy," the *press* for "newspapers" or "newspapermen," *tongue* for "languages," *Milton* for "Milton's works." The close relation between metonymy and synecdoche has blurred a hard and fast distinction between them.

Words are also capable of taking on metaphorical extensions at the same time that they retain their basic meanings. This transfer of association is no more obvious than in the use of the names of animals, fish, and birds to describe people, either in a complimentary or insulting way. Most of the terms are highly colloquial. *Chicken, pigeon,* and *quail* are complimentary terms for females; *crow, cat,* and *vixen* are of another order. Men seem to inspire consistently negative terms like *wolf, goat, rat,* and *worm.* Anyone, male or female, can be a *beaver, shark, louse, pig,* or *dodo.* All kinds of popular usages seem to tend toward generalization. *Guy,* originally a term used only for males, now includes both sexes. *Great* and *fantastic* take on more and more burdens of meaning, and the list of words could be extended to great length. The ultimate fate of a word subject to endless extension, however, is that it finally signifies almost nothing at all (See *counter word,* Glossary 18). But the fact remains that the language seems to need such words as well as more precise ones.

SPECIALIZATION

Specialization denotes a narrowing of meaning rather than an extension. Usage alone is responsible for the change. Outside the United States, *corn* refers to grain in general rather than to the one we identify with the word. *Vest* originally meant any garment; now it is one particular article of clothing. *Undertaker* was a general term for anyone undertaking a job; now it is used only for a mortician. *Computer* now refers almost exclusively to an electronic computer. The monopoly of the medical profession on the word *doctor* has tended to obscure its more general meaning as one highly skilled to teach. A professor now has to identify himself to a stranger as a "teaching doctor," not a "doctor doctor." *Doctor* has been specialized.

The continued narrowing of a word's meaning over a period of time ultimately places its lifespan in jeopardy. A word may possibly become a purely technical term used in very limited contexts; and, in rapidly changing times, it may disappear when the specialty has faded. Innumerable terms associated with early sciences and heraldry died out when those pursuits were no longer viable, although a few like *quintessence, chevron, humor,* and *tincture* took on extended meanings and have survived.

AMELIORATION

Amelioration, a word derived from the Latin word *melior,* meaning "better," identifies the kind of change that occurs when the meaning of a particular word improves. A word itself does not become better or worse because of changes, but its associations do. The word *nice* has made a complete shift. Its original negative connotations of "foolish," "stupid," and "wanton" have changed to current meanings that are consistently agreeable. A *brave* in the sense of a warrior was used in the sixteenth century as a term for a bully or hired assassin. *Enthrall* originally meant "to enslave." By a transfer of meaning from literal enslavement to a captivation of the senses, it has come to have its present meaning of "to charm." It is not unusual to find that the fine print of historical dictionaries hides the skeleton origins of many reputable words.

PEJORATION

Pejoration is a process that attaches negative connotations to a word. Often it occurs simultaneously with changes in specialization or generalization. *Spit* once referred to anything spewed from the mouth. We retain that sense of the word when we say something like "He spits out bitter reproaches." When *spit* became more specialized to refer mainly to ejecting saliva, it underwent pejoration. It usually carries unpleasant associations. *Idiot* originally referred to a private citizen who preferred not to hold public office. The transition from "an educated private citizen who prefers not to hold office" to "one totally incapable of holding office" accounts for the negative associations that the word now has.

The reputation of words is sometimes relative. Among people of liberal, nonauthoritarian thought, words like *reactionary, fundamentalist,* and *purist* are used pejoratively. Among ultraconservative thinkers, *liberal, left,* and *intellectual* are used with scorn. Over a long period of time, negative connotations that spring up may at times stick. *Pontificate* is almost exclusively used today in a negative, uncomplimentary sense. In-groups frequently borrow words of the standard vocabulary and give them private associations for their own purposes. These secondary meanings, compared with their usual ones, are often pejorative. One might list *acid, lid, gay,* and *powder* as only a few examples. Private associations are capable of beginning the downfall of a word's reputation, but unless those associations are widely understood, devaluation is not likely to occur.

16

Grammar

In popular usage, *linguistics* and *grammar* are overlapping terms. *Linguistics* is a collective term for historical and descriptive studies in the phonology, morphology, syntax, and semantics of the language. Grammar is a covering term for morphology and syntax, at times also for phonology, but it is most often used as a synonym for syntax alone. As a word, *linguistics* has connotations that relate it closely to science and theory. In the popular mind, *grammar* remains firmly associated with teaching and the practical matters of speaking and writing the language. Misunderstanding of the true nature of grammar often accounts for the unpleasant response that the word gets.

THE MEANING OF GRAMMAR

Many people associate grammar so closely with rules about what should be said and should not be said that they fail to recognize what grammar actually is and how it operates. It may be well, first, to make a distinction between *grammar,* which can be called the working plan of our language, and *usage,* which is the way we put language to work for whatever personal, social, economic, or cultural reasons we might have. Grammar is therefore more concerned with meaningful communication than it is with socially approved communication.

Grammar is an inescapable fact of a language system, because it is the set of operating principles that permit orderly speaking and writing. A grunt may be expression, but it has little to do with grammar. The fact is that grammar would exist even if there were no books about grammar because it is essentially the unwritten agreement among speakers of the language about the ways they will express ideas most efficiently. Even children subscribe to the code of grammar before they ever learn about it in school, although at early ages they very frequently use a grammar characteristically their own. All native speakers are so accustomed to set patterns of expression that grammar might be referred to as an imprint upon their minds. Thus, grammar is the structure of speaking and writing that we accept—an internalized set of principles that enable us to use the language—whether or not we are students of grammar. Once we are students of grammar, we then concern ourselves with explicit descriptions of those operating principles.

If someone began to read words from the dictionary randomly, each word might convey some element of meaning, but the list as a whole would be essentially meaningless. We can illustrate briefly by considering just six words:

desk his pencils my on lay.

This series is obviously not without meaning because we recognize the six words. In fact, the associations among them are so close that we instinctively find ourselves trying to arrange them into a meaningful statement. We are first tempted by a combination that makes sense: *his pencils.* From that point on, we have no great difficulty in combining *on my desk* and then arranging all six words into a complete pattern: *his pencils lay on my desk.* This arrangement, however, is only the most obvious one. The series might be combined to read *my pencils lay on his desk* or, less likely but still possible, *my desk lay on his pencils,* if we thought of the desk as overturned and lying on the pencils. *His* and *my* might also be interchanged to produce another version: *his desk lay on my pencils.* In some particular context, the cluster beginning with *on* might be put in first position (*on his desk lay my pencils*), but this transposition would not alter the basic pattern or meaning.

Each of these meaningful sentences is a structured arrangement as opposed to the first chaotic and senseless one. Further, each represents a precise statement which is different from each of the others. The six words have not changed, but their relationships have. The basic grammar of the language reduces all of the possible combinations of these six words to four orderly and understandable ones. Because grammar has the capacity to place limitations upon meaning, it has the capacity to make clear communication possible.

The devices that grammar uses to limit meaning are its operating principles. The chief ones in the written language are (1) word order, (2) the addition of suffixes, including inflections, and (3) the use of function words. The suprasegmentals, discussed below (see pp. 369–370), are an additional feature of the spoken language. All are illustrated in the six-word sentences above.

THE OPERATING PRINCIPLES OF GRAMMAR

The most important operating principle in the English language is word order. Our sense of grammar as native speakers leads us immediately to seek out words that combine with one another, like *his pencils, on my desk,* and *his pencils lay on my desk.* The last arrangement breaks down into two parts—first, a subject (*his pencils*) and then a predicate (*lay on my desk*). Until the subject-predicate relationship is established, the pattern is neither complete nor fully meaningful. Until that arrangement is arrived at, transposing part of the sentence to another position for a different effect is impossible.

Four words in the series show grammatical features by inflection. *My* and *his,* as opposed to *I* and *he,* show possession. The form *lay* signals the simple past tense form of the verb *lie,* and the *s* of *pencils* shows that this word is plural.

Finally, the word *on,* a function word, signals a relationship between *lie* and *desk;* namely, the phrase *on my desk* tells where the pencils are lying.

In similar ways, all grammatical sentences in English depend upon these three devices to express basic meanings and variations of meaning. Coherent meaning is not possible without grammar. A grammarless language would be only a discord of sounds.

THE MEANING OF GRAMMATICAL

In practice, grammar permits us to (1) analyze what has been expressed and (2) understand our own expressions. In either case, grammatical expression represents a norm. A writer or speaker either holds to the standard or deviates from it.

Deciding what is grammatical and what is not depends, of course, upon a common definition of "grammatical." Grammarians themselves are by no means agreed on a definition, and native speakers of the language, when tested whether particular sentences in their opinion are grammatical or ungrammatical, will express doubts and often disagree widely. But the doubts and disagreements ordinarily concern sentences that seem to fall between examples that are unquestionably grammatical and ones that are obviously ungrammatical. Everyone will agree, for example, that *desk his pencils my on lay* is totally ungrammatical and that *my pencils lay on his desk* is fully grammatical. But there might be strong doubt about the opening of Lewis Carroll's famous poem:

'Twas brillig, and the slithy toves
Did gyre and gimble in the wabe. . . .

This sentence shows conventional grammatical features and order-liness, but it does not make sense. The same doubts might be expressed about a grammarian's well-known test sentence:

Colorless green ideas sleep furiously.

With such a sentence, we might compare lines from a poem by Andrew Marvell:

Annihilating all that's made
To a green thought in a green shade.

The difficulty with the last two examples is that they violate our usual expectations of acceptable combinations in a literal sense: green is not colorless and not ordinarily an attribute of ideas or thought, although we might attempt to figure out a metaphoric association. Nor does sleep relate literally and sensibly with ideas. Yet in each of these examples, we react to the structure and try to impose meaning upon the words. Carroll's poem and the grammarian's nonsense sentence are both well formed but uninformative. If we change *colorless green ideas sleep furiously* to *formless dull ideas die easily,* we see that the transition from one sentence to the other is not great, and some idea of what is fully grammatical begins to be apparent.

What we have to recognize is some intermediate degree between sentences that are fully grammatical, which are both well formed and informative, and sentences that are fully ungrammatical, which are both chaotic and meaningless. Such an intermediate degree might be called semigrammatical. Semigrammatical sentences, therefore, might be de-fined as well-formed sentences that are deviant in the way they combine words.

It is not surprising that two of the semigrammatical examples given above are excerpts from poems. Poets have traditionally been inventors of original expression. The imaginativeness of their work often springs from the departures they make from the ordinary. Yet their departures are structurally based. In one sense, poetic expression is an extension of the grammatical system. The grammar of our language is sufficiently flexible to allow deviations without falling into chaos. Thus, when Dylan Thomas writes *a grief ago,* we associate his phrase with time expressions like *a month ago* and *a while back* and proceed from that point on to interpret. Thomas' phrase is poetic, not conventionally factual. But only an analogy with a fully grammatical phrase makes an interpretation possible.

GRAMMAR OR GRAMMARS

The term "grammar," as we have noted, is used in different senses, sometimes as the equivalent of what is called usage, sometimes as a broad term for the formal features and fundamental principles of a language, and sometimes in a more limited sense as a description of the structure and operation of a language. If grammar is considered a description of the structure and operation of a language, it then follows that descriptions may vary. A description of the grammar of German will differ from a description of the grammar of Chinese, and a description of Latin grammar will differ from a description of English grammar, although Latin and English grammar may have more features in common than German and Chinese grammar. It is also possible that descriptions of the same language will vary. Even though each language operates in its characteristic way, each description is a particular interpretation, a way of looking at it. Before the invention of the camera, painters depicted horses in full gallop with their fore limbs and hind limbs stretched out simultaneously before and behind the body of the horse. The invention of the camera, and particularly the evidence of still shots of movie sequences, revealed that horses gallop with their hoofs following one another in an orderly sequence. It is perfectly obvious that horses had not changed their way of running before and after the invention of the camera, but the camera altered man's way of seeing how they ran.

A similar situation has occurred in the history of grammar. In the last two hundred years, the operation of the language has not changed radically, but our views of how it operates have changed. As a result, we now have several descriptions, some based upon verifiable evidence of a scientific nature. We no longer have *one* grammar, that is, one description, but several. The three main and most complete descriptions at the present time are those usually identified as traditional, structural, and transformational-generative. Their differences can be overestimated. One linguist has estimated that the three coincide in at least 95 percent of their facts. These three grammars merely represent different viewpoints and therefore emphasize different features of the language. They need not be thought of as competing with one another, although exponents of each have certainly competed for attention in the scholarly world. It is preferable to think of these three descriptions as phases of the development of grammar, and this book, therefore, emphasizes in what ways the three grammars supplement one another in order to give us a clearer notion of how the language operates.

Traditional grammar had its roots in the thinking and attitudes of eighteenth-century grammarians. It began with the assumption that Latin was superior to English and that English grammar should therefore use Latin as a model. Thus, the case of the pronoun *her* in a strongly Latinate construction like *I knew her to be an actress* (compare *I knew that she was an actress*) was explained in the same terms that Latin grammar would explain it—as the subject of an infinitive in the accusative case. In this example, *her* might also be explained as an object form because it is the object of the verb *knew*. If the sentence is broken down into two parts, it reads: *I knew her. She was an actress.* But traditional grammar has chosen to follow the Latin model.

Eagerness for a fixed language, logical consistency, and uniform practice led early grammarians to be highly prescriptive about matters of usage. Their injunctions about double negatives and the use of *shall* and *will* still survive, because many individuals, including some teachers, think that these principles, having been set down once, remain inviolable. But all of the assumptions of traditional grammar need not be considered outmoded. In its coupling of form, function, and meaning and in its recognition of intuition as a strong factor in the functioning of a grammar, traditional grammar has by no means been displaced. In fact, it has evolved and continues to thrive. Many of its terms, definitions, and explanations of the grammatical process survive in current descriptions of the language.

Structural grammar, primarily a twentieth-century description, was an outgrowth of the historical and comparative studies of language in the second half of the nineteenth century. These studies reinforced the idea that language operates systematically and that the system can best be determined by describing exactly what occurs in the language, both in speaking and in writing. Structural grammar begins with the assumption that English is English and Latin is Latin. English is an analytical language; Latin is a synthetic language. English, therefore, has to be described in its own terms without reference to Latin grammar.

Structural grammar is basically a descriptive grammar. Historically it served as a methodical inventory of English after a long period of failure to assess what the resources of our own language actually were. It established the priority of the spoken language over written language as a major influence upon grammar. By confining their description of the language to the observation of forms and patterns, divorced from meaning and logic and usage, books on structural grammar necessarily limited themselves to the products of language—the written and spoken utterances—rather than to the process of language or the generation of language. At the present time, structural grammar survives alongside traditional grammar, and its objective descriptions have added immensely to our total knowledge of the language system.

The newest grammar, which is a product of the second half of this century, is transformational-generative, commonly referred to simply as transformational grammar. Taking advantage of the spadework performed by the structuralists, transformational grammarians have begun to build a structure they hope will ultimately account for all of the well-formed sentences of the English language, not just those that have already been produced but all those that are yet to be produced. Transformational grammar thus shifts its major emphasis from matters of form isolated from meaning to matters of function. It is interested in the way native speakers are intuitively capable of producing complex structures that are seemingly combinations of many simple basic patterns of meaning. The breakdown of a sentence in these layers or kernels reveals what is called its deep structure (see also pp. 496–500). Thus, transformational grammar has added a new dimension to grammar—the deep structure of a sentence as well as its surface structure. Deep structure and the transformational process are theoretical concepts, but they help to explain how form and meaning are connected in the grammatical process. In emphasizing the role of intuition and meaning in grammar, the transformationalist has returned to some of the concerns of the traditional grammarian. He is not merely interested in describing what has happened but what can happen. Within the bounds of its own rules for the formation of grammatical sentences, transformational grammar has assumed a highly prescriptive attitude, but that prescriptivism does not extend further to matters of usage. Usage seems to be a concern beyond the interest and consideration of the theoretical grammarian.

The possible limitation of transformational grammar at this stage of its development is the scope of the task it has set for itself. In attempting to explain logically and completely everything that native speakers do naturally, transformational grammar has assumed a monumental task. Because most grammars never succeed in accounting for all of the irregularities of the English language, it is not uncommon to hear grammarians console themselves with the assertion that "all grammars leak." (See Chapters 20–31 for a microgrammar.)

THE SOUND SYSTEM

Grammar is concerned with both written and spoken discourse, but the spoken language shows some grammatical features that writing does not. One of the simplest of these characteristics is the contrast that a speaker is able to make between words like *cónflict* and *conflíct* with the sound of his voice. The written word has to add accent marks or put the words into a context to make the same distinction. Thus, the sound system of English functions grammatically and, as the history of the language reveals, speech has acted consistently as a major influence upon change.

Speech is possible because the mouth of the human being is extremely flexible; the human muscular system permits free movement of the lips, tongue, palate, and uvula. Each adjustment inside the mouth allows a speaker to block the flow of air that comes from the lungs through the vocal cords. The way that air is interrupted and the kind of resonance that is produced by the mouth or the nose determines the identity of a sound. Sounds like /b/ and /p/ are called stops; the air is stopped and then exploded with the lips (labial). Sounds like /t/ and /d/ are also stops, but they are produced with the tongue against the front ridge of the palate (alveolar). Sounds like /f/, /v/, /th/, /s/, and /z/ are interrupted in such a way that the breath escapes between the lips and the teeth with the sound of air leaking out of a balloon (fricatives). /w/, /j/, and /r/ (glides) prolong the escape of air in a slightly different way. /m/, /n/, and /l/ (continuants) also prolong the escape of air, but when /m/ and /n/ are sounded, air resonates in the nose instead of in the mouth to produce a different effect (nasals). Producing each of these sounds aloud with a particular awareness of the movements of the tongue in relation to the other parts of the mouth will indicate quickly the significant differences of the phonetic terms. All sounds produced by some kind of stop action in the mouth are called consonants.

All sounds interrupted or modified by the mouth, however, are first affected by the vocal cords, which seem to operate on the same principle as a reed in an oboe. If the membranes of the vocal cords are relaxed so that air passing through them causes no vibration, the sound produced is said to be voiceless. If, on the other hand, the cords are tensed and closed so that the air must pass through a very small opening, the result is a vibration and a voiced sound. Any speaker may actually feel this vibration by holding his fingers on his neck in the general vicinity of the larynx and producing a series of sounds in full voice; all whispered sounds are voiceless. Consonants are either voiced or voiceless, but all vowels are voiced.

Vowels differ from consonants in that there is no noticeable blocking of the sound within the mouth. Air is simply allowed to resonate freely in the mouth cavity, and changes in sound are made primarily by the position of the tongue and lips. The mouth is opened widely to produce an *a*, as in *father;* the lips are rounded to produce an *o* in *rose;* and the mouth is considerably readjusted again to sound the vowel in *beet.* Vowels are classified as high, mid, or low and as front, central, and back, depending upon the position of the tongue in producing the sound. There are nine simple vowels in English. When they are combined with /y/, /w/, and /h/ to form dipthongs, the total number of vowel sounds increases to thirty-six. Including the simple vowels and consonants, English may have as many as forty-six identifiable sounds. Linguists do not agree on the exact number, and all sounds are not present in the speech of every person. Linguists are in agreement, however, that a phonemic alphabet is necessary to record sounds accurately. What is apparent is that the letters of the alphabet do not provide a particularly good index to the sound system of the language. Twenty-six letters of an alphabet borrowed from Latin are made to serve almost twice that number of sounds. Without doubt, the spelling system of English continues to be one of the most difficult features of the language, because the correspondence between sounds and letters follows no regular patterns. The *sh*-sound, for example, can be represented by as many as fourteen different letters or combinations of letters.

A complete analysis of the sounds of English would require a more technical discussion than is possible here. Table 2 identifies the most basic sounds of the English language and gives guide words to interpret the symbols.

Table 2

THE SOUNDS OF ENGLISH

CONSONANTS		VOWELS	
Phonemic Symbol	Key to Pronunciation	Phonemic Symbol	Key to Pronunciation
/p/	pat	/i/	beat
/b/	bat	/e/	bait
/m/	mat	/æ/	bat
/f/	fat	/a/	balm
/v/	vat	/u/	boot
/Θ/	moth	/o/	boat
/ð/	mother	/ɔ/	bawdy
/t/	tat	/i/ or /ɪ/	minute (unstressed)
/d/	dad		bit (stressed)
/n/	nag	/ə/	above (unstressed)
/l/	late		
/s/	sat	/ə/ or /ʌ/	but (stressed)
/z/	zero		
/ʃ/ or /š/	shame		
/ʒ/ or /ž/	vision	COMMON DIPTHONGS	
/tʃ/ or /č/	choke		
/dz/ or /ǰ/	joke	/ai/	bite
/k/	coke	/au/	bowwow
/g/	go	/ɔi/	boy
/ŋ/	rang	/iu/ or /ju/	beauty
/h/	hat		
		SEMIVOWELS	
		/r/	rat
		/w/	woke
		/j/	yoke

SEGMENTALS AND SUPRASEGMENTALS

In linguistic terms, the vowels and consonants of the language make up a group of sounds referred to as segmentals. Combined, they form words. Speech, however, permits an individual to vary the sound of segmentals by adjusting the stress with which they are spoken, altering the pitch of his voice, and making pauses of different degrees between words or parts of words. These three devices—stress, pitch, and juncture—are called suprasegmentals.

The suprasegmentals are not the same in all languages. It is frequently difficult for a nonnative speaker to catch the intonation that is characteristic of another language. For example, pitch is a much more important feature in Chinese than it is in English, and what we sometimes refer to as a foreign accent may result from a foreigner's attempt to use the suprasegmentals of his own language when he speaks another one.

Because stress, pitch, and juncture occur simultaneously in speech, it is virtually impossible to speak of one without reference to the others. Linguists, however, generally recognize four degrees of stress, four levels of pitch, and four types of juncture in English. The degrees of stress are marked from heavy to weak as primary / ´ /, secondary / ˆ /, tertiary / ` /, and weak / ˘ /. Pitch, of course, is relative to the speaker and what is ordinarily his normal speaking tone. The norm is identified as /2/. One level below is marked as /1/; the levels above are designated as /3/ and /4/. Level-four pitch is characteristically the kind of sound produced by a speaker during high excitement. Juncture is marked as internal / + /, level /|/ or /→/, rising /‖/ or /↗/, and falling / # / or /↘/.

The only thing the writing system can do to indicate the suprasegmentals is to use punctuation and a few conventional mechanical devices like italics and ellipses. A phrase like "It is with ..." would be spoken with one kind of pitch, stress, and juncture if it were part of the familiar phrase "It is with great pleasure. . . ." It would be spoken quite differently if it were a part of the following dialogue:

Can you read this word?
Yes, it is *with.*

In this reply, what appears to be a fragment in writing can be made a sentence in speech by giving the words the appropriate stress, pitch, and final juncture.

Furthermore, variations of the suprasegmentals determine the differences between statements, questions, and exclamations. These are grammatical differences. The writing system must use a question mark to indicate that "You really mean it?" is a question, not a statement or an exclamation. The rising intonation pattern of speech makes the distinction quite easily.

The stresses, pitches, and junctures of words are by no means constant. In a word like *primary,* the first syllable clearly gets the heaviest stress if the word is spoken by itself. When the form of the word is changed to *primarily,* the heavy stress shifts. When words are combined, other changes take place. In the phrase *primary goal, goal* gets the heaviest stress, and the stress on the first syllable of *primary* is reduced in relation to the heaviest.

Native speakers of the language ordinarily have no problem with suprasegmentals. They know how to make contrasts between *the White House* and *a white house.* If their pronunciation has not made clear whether they have said *a nice chest* or *an ice chest,* all that needs to be done is to exaggerate stress, pitch, and juncture to make the contrast. Therefore, the suprasegmentals are natural means of making ourselves understood, and they are the devices that give expressiveness to our speech. In fact, the whole rhythmic structure of the English language is based upon them. The suprasegmentals are particularly important in teaching English to children and to foreigners. It is also highly likely that animals respond not so much to the words that we say to them as to the suprasegmentals we use in saying those words.

17

Usage

Usage is the active force of a living language upon words and current structures, at times working contrary to established grammar and standard practices. Usage is the way people, both educated and uneducated, use the language, not necessarily how books say it should be used. Sometimes users of the language conform to prevailing practices; sometimes they deviate. In the use of language, there are individual, occupational, and regional differences, varying social patterns, degrees of formality and informality, and differences between speaking and writing. Every speaker and writer is faced with choices. Over a period of time, if the differences get obscured so that people no longer know that a choice exists, then the more popular form simply prevails. Thus we can assume that as long as a language is used, it will change.

Those who express a perennial longing for a pure and stable language look upon change as corrosion. But resistance to change does not alter the fact that human beings today show the same tendencies in their speech habits as they did a thousand years ago. The present dependence of English upon word order as opposed to inflection grew out of man's sense of economy with sound. Inflections occurring in syllables of weak stress were lost because persons obscured them in speaking. Even today sounds in similar positions are highly susceptible to change. Speakers of some dialects characteristically drop *ed*'s and *s*'s when the strong stress falls on a preceding syllable. Thus, *exercised* becomes *exercise; teacher* is reduced to *teach*. The final syllable, which requires an extra effort to pronounce, tends to get lost. Even though dialects that operate on a reduced grammar are generally considered nonstandard, they illustrate the kinds of changes that usage has forced upon grammar in the past and that have now become standard.

The Middle English construction *Charles, his day* now reads *Charles's day,* because over a period of time speakers of the language bridged the sounds of *Charles* and *his* in order to make two sounds only one. Every speaker shows the same inclination when he says "gonna" instead of "going to" or "would've" instead of a clearly enunciated "would have." The written language still acts as a restraint upon the changes that speech makes, but, in the past, oral usage has tended to prevail unless the literary tradition has been very strong. Today, publishing companies and editors of periodicals often act as a control over innovations that a writer may want to include in his writing.

The now established word order of the language acts constantly as a force for the change of traditional forms. A strict observance of grammatical principles would demand expressions like *It is I* and *Whom are you talking to?* In the first example, the pronoun *I* occupies a position normally reserved for the object of a verb; and, in the second example, the pronoun *whom* occupies a position ordinarily reserved for the subject of the sentence. Thus, usage has established the expressions *It's me* and *Who are you talking to?* Whether expressions such as these continue to function merely as idioms of the language or will in time affect the whole grammatical system of pronoun use cannot be predicted. Pronouns have been considerably altered in the past, and since they still remain one of the most complex parts of speech in the language, usage may well act in its characteristic way to simplify and regularize them.

The regularization typical of usage acts also upon verbs and noun plurals. Irregular verb forms like *awoke, proven,* and *clad* now commonly appear with regular verb endings: *awaked, proved,* and *clothed.* Usage also provides regular plural forms for words borrowed from foreign languages. Thus, *libretti* changes to *librettos, stadia* to *stadiums,* and *châteaux* to *châteaus.*

Usage has by no means acted as a chaotic influence upon the language. In most instances, it has worked for greater efficiency and clarity. But recognition of change in language does not by any means condone permissiveness. Usage at any one period tends to be highly stable, although controversies always exist about particular usages and innovations. However, speakers of the language who are concerned about acceptable usage will usually find agreement among educated speakers upon most matters of importance. Familiarizing oneself with the backgrounds of English to see what has happened in the past is one means of gaining confidence in the use of the language in the present.

IDIOM

Idiom may be used in two senses. First, it may refer to a characteristic manner of English expression, as opposed to the way of saying something in another language. English idiom in this sense is almost synonymous with grammatical expression. In the second sense, however, idiom may be used to refer to any expression that does not quite fit the customary grammatical or logical expectations of English, but has become established as a way of saying something in our own language. In this sense, idiom is a stereotyped expression. Thus, a sentence like *The protesters were riding high* is wholly idiomatic, although in a literal sense it is illogical (compare *The protesters were having great success*). Likewise, idiom establishes the differences in meaning between phrases like *make away with, make out, make over, make up,* and *make up to.* Because idioms are a vernacular feature of language, native speakers have little difficulty with them. Usage alone establishes an idiom.

IDIOLECT AND DIALECT

The way a person uses the language—his choice of words, his pronunciations, and his grammar—is his idiolect. One person's speech, however, does not ordinarily differ so greatly from another's that he cannot be understood at all. The common features of language that certain speakers share with one another represent their dialect. The elements that dialects share with one another establish a language.

Dialects in the United States differ from one another mainly in the pronunciation of certain sounds and in the selection of words for fairly common things. All of them share a common grammar and a large stock of words which everyone understands, even though the words may be pronounced with variations.

Language almost always operates within a community, either large or small. The community may be groups like the family, a circle of friends, a business organization, or a lodge. The language of these groups is shaped further by the locality, either the neighborhood, the city, or the region. Local characteristics are deeply rooted, so that persons moving from one part of the country to another usually carry with them the marks of their former communities. Because dialectal features are transferable in this way, dialectologists are particularly interested in population shifts. The speech traits of Negroes in some black ghettos of the North, for example, may be traced to patterns of speech in particular rural areas of the South. Big cities can usually be subdivided into local communities whose members share a common dialect.

Dialects thrive in isolation, but in an age in which transportation and communication have erased almost all natural geographical divisions, dialect differences tend to be diminished. Nevertheless, two opposite forces operate constantly on language. On the one hand, schools, the military, the press, radio, and television act as leveling influences, tending to iron out dialectal differences. On the other hand, local pride, racial consciousness, individualism, and the exclusiveness of tight groups with common interests tend to preserve these differences. Absolute uniformity in the use of language, even if it were possible, would scarcely be a virtue, because nonconformists in language have always acted as a stimulus to the growth of the language.

Dialects, therefore, may be studied in terms of regional differences, social patterns, or group functions such as an occupation, hobby, or sport.

REGIONAL AMERICAN DIALECTS

Regional dialects are identified by attempting to determine boundaries, called isoglosses, where distinct pronunciations or the use of particular words and forms is divided. An expert linguist can place a speaker within fifty miles of his home by hearing him pronounce a series of test words and phrases like *merry, marry, Mary; wash, water, Washington; on, off, dog, oft, lot, log, sorry; about the house; greasy; park the car; first, bird; fur, four; horse, hoarse,* and others. These words provide a few of the clues to differences between speakers of the major dialect areas: northern, midland, and southern and, within those areas, regions like eastern Virginia, eastern New England, and New York City (see map, p. 375).

In addition to pronunciation differences, the regions also represent certain other types of local characteristics that set off one dialect from others. A northerner, for example, may refer to a *pail* or *faucet* instead of a *bucket* or *spigot,* used predominantly by midlanders and southerners. *Polecat* for *skunk* is a southernism. A northerner characteristically uses *chipmunk* for *ground squirrel. Might can, might could,* and *used to could* are markedly southern expressions, even among educated speakers.

The massive task of mapping the linguistic geography of the United States has not yet been completed, but studies that have been published mark off boundaries on the basis of regional features, and they include maps showing the direction of migrations (see map, p. 376). Dialects, of course, are no respecters of state lines. At one time, mountains and rivers may have determined the major isoglosses, but today the existence or absence of a road may be the main factor that determines the degree of a region's isolation. Some dialects spoken today in isolated parts of the Appalachians and Ozarks preserve features of English that were common in seventeenth-century England.

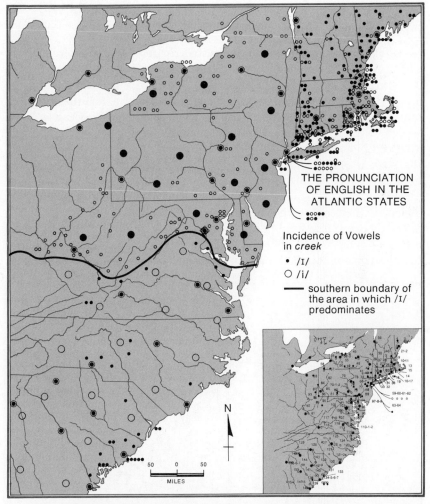

THE PRONUNCIATION
OF ENGLISH IN THE
ATLANTIC STATES

Incidence of Vowels
in *creek*

• /ɪ/

○ /i/

—— southern boundary of
the area in which /ɪ/
predominates

The map indicates that the pronunciation of *creek* with an I as in *pick*
predominates in the North except in southern New England and metropolitan New York. Pronunciation with an /i/ as in *peak* predominates
in the South except for the coast of South Carolina. Since /i/ is used
as a prestige pronunciation among educated speakers, the insert shows
how their usage differs from that of the general populace.

The history of early settlement in a region is also an important
part of the field work in dialect study, mainly because patterns of speech
and usage in an area can often be traced to foreign influences. Thus,
stoop for *front porch* or *steps* is used in northern areas where the Dutch
settled; *smear-case,* common in midland areas, is a clear sign of German
borrowing.

SOCIAL PATTERNS: STANDARD AND NONSTANDARD ENGLISH

The social patterns of the United States are closely related to education and economics. Ours is not so much a class society as it is a status society, and it is a society divided to a great extent by the use of language. An uneducated man may make a fortune, but find himself excluded from the society of the educated rich because of his speech. On the other hand, an educated man may sometimes find himself accepted in social circles that he cannot well afford. Standard English, the speech of the majority of educated Americans, has become the prestige dialect of this country.

In a nation as diverse as this one, the existence of a standard dialect is inevitable. One dialect becomes the official language of the nation because it is used in official documents, in formal public gatherings, and in all serious deliberations. Knowledge of it is therefore helpful to anyone who intends to participate in the serious affairs of this nation.

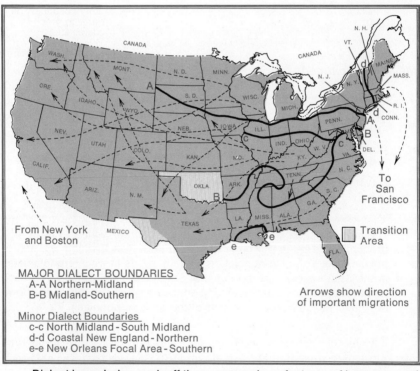

To San Francisco

From New York and Boston

Transition Area

MAJOR DIALECT BOUNDARIES
A-A Northern-Midland
B-B Midland-Southern

Arrows show direction of important migrations

Minor Dialect Boundaries
c-c North Midland - South Midland
d-d Coastal New England - Northern
e-e New Orleans Focal Area - Southern

Dialect boundaries mark off those areas where features of language and pronunciation clearly identify the speakers. The West is mainly a mixture of various groups.

Standard English, however, is by no means one thing. It represents a wide range of formal and informal uses, particularly in the choice of words, although it should be stressed again that media, education, and transportation work much more strongly toward the uniformity of our language than toward its diversity. One of the usual characteristics of standard English is its adherence to the regular grammatical features of the language. An obvious sign of nonstandard English is a speaker's consistent and unaffected deviations. An uneducated speaker may say "I done it" because he is unaware of the standard models of the grammar, or he may impose a regular pattern upon the grammar when irregularity exists so that he says, "He say he is in trouble" instead of "He says he is in trouble."

Educated speakers also show lapses, particularly in matters of usage, but often their choices, like the use of *ain't,* are quite deliberate, even affected. Often an individual's attitude toward the prevailing order of society influences the kind of language he uses. Some speakers show a strong desire to conform. They may even know that there are guidelines for choices between *who-whom, I-me,* and *bad-badly,* but lack confidence or experience to apply them correctly. It is highly unlikely that an uneducated speaker would fall into the unnaturalness and incorrectness of sentences like *Whom do you think you are? They gave the present to him and I,* or *I felt badly about the error.* Ungrammatical uses of this kind represent an "educated nonstandard" English. It is quite unrelated to the typical unaffected characteristics of nonstandard speech.

The generations of young people born after 1950 have expressed clear protests against an inflexible standard for English, just as they have protested against other established structures. No doubt, these protests will influence attitudes toward language in the future, especially in minimizing the concept of language as etiquette and in breaking down the rigid social barriers that language is capable of erecting. But it is doubtful that any movement will wholly destroy the basic concept of a standard dialect that promotes efficient communication and common understanding. The concept of a standard dialect was established in England as early as the fourteenth century. It would have to be reinvented today if it did not exist.

GROUP DIALECTS

Every occupation, hobby, and sport—in fact, every possible pursuit—gives rise to a certain number of terms that have special meaning in that activity. The language that identifies a trade or profession is referred to as its argot or jargon or shoptalk. It may even vary from place to place or from business to business. For example, a waitress changing jobs may have to learn a new set of terms for placing orders in a different restaurant.

If the purpose among speakers of any group is to exclude outsiders, that is, to carry on a kind of private or secret communication, then the language is referred to as cant. Slang is a common collective term which may include all of the occupational dialects, but more commonly refers to rapidly changing words of popular speech that are deliberately invented to give language new vigor. Because slang is associated with every speaker's most casual and lighthearted way of talking, it is generally considered inappropriate for truly serious occasions. Also because most slang dies quickly, it is generally considered inappropriate for any written work that hopes for survival. Using slang in writing may be a way of being in vogue, but it is also the fastest way of being out of vogue six months or six years later.

Despite these reservations, however, slang continues to create new words and phrases and to extend the meanings of old ones. Even though slang is sometimes invented by professional gag writers and advertisers, it is more likely to spring up at any time or place in any situation without intention. Slang invites inventiveness. Without doubt, it is one of the most powerful influences upon the living language.

FORMAL AND INFORMAL USAGE

A newspaper account recently quoted the words of a judge, who in censuring an attorney appearing in his court, said, "It is the opinion of the court that you are under the influence of alcohol." It is difficult to think of any other situation in which this particular phrasing might be appropriately used. The sentence is impersonal, guarded in tone, and stiffly formal as compared with any of the following alternatives:

1. You appear to the judge of this court to be intoxicated.
2. You appear to me to be intoxicated [his position as judge implied by the courtroom setting].
3. I think you're drunk.
4. You're boozed.

The test of any of these usages, including the judge's original statement, is not whether one is good English and another bad or whether one is correct and another incorrect but whether the statement is appropriate to the speaker and his relation to the listener at a particular time and place. A standard of appropriateness implies a concern for the opinions and reactions of others. In the courtroom, the judge might possibly have used alternatives 1 and 2 without jeopardizing the dignity of his position or the seriousness of his tone. Or, if he had been primarily interested in giving greater directness and emphasis to his remarks in that formal situation, he might also have chosen alternative 3 for purposes of contrast. In any formal situation, alternative 4 would be clearly out of place, although it is conceivable that the same judge might have said this to the attorney in private if the two of them were on close speaking terms.

The varieties of English account for confusion in the minds of many people about the actual use of the language. They want to know precisely what is correct and what is incorrect. They think of rules. They are perplexed by degrees of formality and intimacy, the differences between writing and speaking, and the various accommodations of language that a speaker can make for differing audiences and differing

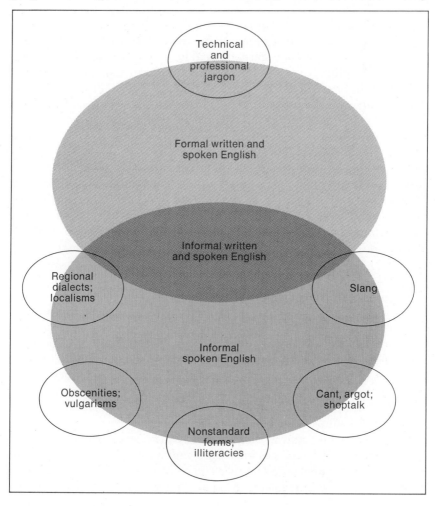

purposes. They are perplexed because they want choices to be clear-cut. Actually, there is considerable overlapping in the speech habits of any one individual. In terms of society as a whole, there is an intermingling and borrowing among the various dialects, as the diagram on page 379 suggests.

The discriminations we make in the use of language are therefore more relative and involved than any dictionary or glossary of usage can cover. At most, usage guides can suggest the formal or highly colloquial implications of certain words and phrases, but their prescriptions are almost always subject to exception. Good taste and judgment will help a speaker more than a whole stack of dictionaries.

USAGE AS ETIQUETTE

The regard for appropriateness in the use of language is often referred to as the etiquette of language—the adjustment of our speaking to different occasions and gatherings. The concept of language as etiquette is helpful if it clarifies the notion that an individual does not have to talk one way all the time any more than he dresses one way all the time. The analogy is misleading, however, if it suggests that a person is ill-mannered at any time that he fails to use the language in most precise terms. Almost any variety of English is acceptable under certain circumstances. Overly polite usage in an informal situation is as unsuitable as crudity on a somber occasion. The best manners in any form of behavior are those that a person follows intuitively in consideration of others. Those that do not arise spontaneously among persons who have not been taught good manners tend to be empty conventions. Some long-standing prescriptions about usage, like the distinction between *different from* and *different than,* belong to this category.

SPEAKING AND WRITING

Writing is rather consistently a more highly conventionalized form of expression than speaking. Even dialogue set down in writing tends to be more abbreviated, controlled, and orderly than conversation ordinarily is. Because writing is a slower process than speaking, the writer can reflect upon his remarks, make decisions about phrasing, and edit and polish his remarks. Speaking in an informal situation does not allow the same degree of control.

Both speaking and writing may vary in their degree of formality, but the basic difference between the conditions under which the two are produced ordinarily affect the choice of usage. Speaking assumes that an audience is immediately present. The reading audience of written prose is removed in time and place. In fact, a writer may create his own audience by the way he writes, because a reading audience chooses what it will read or not read. A listener, on the other hand, is captive, unless he intentionally leaves or refuses to listen.

The immediacy of an audience gives a characteristic directness and simplicity to colloquial expression. Almost every technical term and learned phrase has a colloquial equivalent that permits speakers to talk about such things in an easy way. It is also true that colloquial expressions infiltrate written prose. If they do to a great extent, the writing merely takes on an increasingly informal quality. Twentieth-century writing has shown a marked preference for informality, so that hard and fast divisions between expressions appropriate to speaking or to writing are now being constantly obscured. The fact remains, nevertheless, that the nature and conditions of writing seem always to place greater restraints upon the writer, no matter how deliberately rebellious he may try to be.

18

A Glossary of Usage

A

Above, below *Above* is a standard way of referring to material that precedes a particular passage on a printed page. *Below* is the counterterm for something that follows: *The diagram above* [or *below*] *shows population growth in terms of individual countries.*

Accept, except Verbs easily confused. *Accept* means "to receive." *Except,* derived from the preposition, means "to take or leave out."

He *accepted* the award.
Freshmen were *excepted* from the regulation.

Affect, effect Words easily confused. *Affect* as a verb means "to influence": *His ideas affected future generations. Effect* as a verb means "to bring something about": *We will see if we can effect a workable plan.* The noun usage is almost always *effect,* meaning "result": *The effect of the storm was disastrous. Affect* is used as a noun by psychologists, but the usage has not become common.

Aggravate *Aggravate* means "to intensify" or "to make worse": *The rigid attitude of the President only aggravated the political situation.* In an extended, informal sense, *aggravate* means "to annoy": *The people were aggravated by the President's manner.*

Ain't   Still a highly controversial usage. Generally characteristic of nonstandard speech, but clearly used by educated speakers in an effort to be casual or funny, particularly in tag questions like *ain't I?* The word is inappropriate in expository prose unless dialogue is a part of the writing.

Alibi   A word that has undergone extension of meaning so that it is now commonly used to mean any kind of excuse. The original legal sense of the word remains. An alibi is an attempt to establish one's innocence by explaining that he could not have committed a crime because he was elsewhere at the time.

All, all of   In many constructions, the *of* is optional and may be dropped. As a predeterminer, particularly in constructions with pronouns, it cannot be dropped: *all of them, all of Hemingway,* but *all the dignitaries, all this confusion.*

All the farther, all the further   Dialectal variants in certain regions of the country for *as far as: This is all the further I'm going. As far as* is preferred as a standard form in writing.

Almost, most   See **Most.**

Alot, a lot   Although pronounced as one word, *a lot* should be written as two words.

Already, all ready   Forms sometimes confused. *Already* is an adverb meaning "prior to some designated time": *He has already gone. All ready* is an adjective phrase expressing preparedness: *We're all ready to start.*

Alright, all right   *Alright* has not yet been fully established as an acceptable substitute for *all right.* Dictionaries reflect the divided usage. *Webster's Seventh* lists it without a usage label; *New World* identifies it as a spelling much used, but still considered nonstandard; *Random House* labels it as nonstandard.

Although, though   See **Though.**

Alumnus, alumna   The endings of these Latin borrowings show that *alumnus* pertains to a male graduate and *alumna* to a female graduate. *Alumnus* and its plural *alumni* are now commonly used to refer to anyone, either male or female, who attended or graduated from a school.

Amidst, amongst   Acceptable variants of *amid* and *among,* but words that clearly sound like a kind of poetic diction now outmoded.

Among, between   See **Between.**

Amount of, number of   Many writers make a careful distinction between the use of *amount of* with mass nouns expressing bulk and the use of *number of* with count nouns expressing a collection of particulars: *a small amount of pepper, a large number of boxes.* The use of *amount of* with count nouns, however, is increasingly common in speech: *The amount of people who came in was amazing.*

Anyplace, anywhere   Standard usage no longer makes a distinction between the two, but *anyplace* has only recently established itself as an acceptable form. It is therefore subject to the usual lingering prejudice against new usages. *Anyplace* tends to be less formal than *anywhere.*

Anywheres, somewheres   Dialectal forms of *anywhere* and *somewhere.*

Apt, liable, likely   See **Liable.**

As   In speech, *as* has become a general utility word. When a word of this kind is made to serve many purposes, it loses its capacity to make fine distinctions of meaning. Writers therefore need to be aware of the extended and sometimes nonstandard uses of the word:

1.   Because it expresses manner, time, and cause, *as* substitutes for *when, while, since,* and *because.* Those words might preferably be used to emphasize cause or time:

Lacking emphasis:	As we are the only two who enrolled, the class has to be dropped.
More emphasis:	Because we are the only two who enrolled, the class has to be dropped.

2.   *As* acts as an obviously folksy substitute for *who, that,* and *whether: Anybody as tries can succeed; I am not sure as I know; I don't know as I can go.*
Among the many uses of *as,* several are particularly important:

As a preposition, meaning "in the function or part of": *He was excellent as Romeo.*
As a conjunction expressing simultaneous action: *As I was leaving, visitors arrived.*
As an adverb in comparisons, meaning "equally": *as stately as a steeple.*

As . . . as, so . . . as   Traditionally, *as . . . as* makes a positive comparison; *so . . . as* makes a negative comparison: *He is as skillful as*

John; he is not so skillful as Don. In current usage, *as . . . as* is acceptable for both purposes.

As, like   See **Like.**

Awake, awaken   See **Wake.**

Awful, awfully   *Awful* is seldom used in the sense of "inspiring awe or reverence." It is now a colloquial synonym for "very bad" or "disagreeable": *an awful book, an awful person. Awfully* is used as an intensifier in expressions like *awfully good* or *awfully pretty.* Both usages are highly informal, common in speech but for the most part inappropriate in formal prose.

Awhile, a while   Two separate but acceptable usages. *Awhile* is an adverb: *we waited awhile,* which might also be phrased *we waited for a while.* In the second sentence, *while* is used as a noun.

B

Bad, badly   The grammar of the language calls for a predicate adjective after sense verbs. Thus, the choice between the adjective *bad* and the adverb *badly* after these special verbs is clear: *I feel bad, the corn tastes bad,* but *the saw cuts badly.* Speech, however, tends to follow the usual pattern of making adverbs modify verbs: *I feel badly, the corn tastes badly.* Even though usage is divided, a careful writer will observe the grammatical distinction. *Badly* in the sense of "very much" is colloquial: *I need a rest badly.*

Barely   See **Hardly.**

Because of   See **Due to.**

Being as, being that   Both nonstandard phrases for *since* or *because:*

Nonstandard: Being as I am here, I'll eat dinner.
Standard: Since I am here, I'll eat dinner.

Below   See **Above.**

Beside, besides   Both *beside* and *besides* act as prepositions, but their meanings are different:

The runner-up stood beside the winner. [at the side of]
There was a runner-up trophy besides the winning trophy. [in additon to]

Besides in the same sense of "in addition to" is also used as an adverb: *Campaigning is fun besides.*

Better   See **Had better.**

Between, among   *Between* is ordinarily used to express a relation between two things: *between you and me, between France and England. Among* is used to express a relation involving more than two: *among the nations, among the fish.* However, *between* is also used to express an interrelation between several things when they are considered individually rather than as a group:

We worked between Boston, New York, and Chicago.
There is an obvious difference between the three composers.

Bi-, semi-   *Bi-* is a prefix which usually means "multiplied by two." *Semi-* is a prefix which means "divided by two." But *bi-* is not consistently used. *Bimonthly* means occurring every two months, but *biennial* means occurring twice a year. Confusion can be avoided by substituting *semiannual* for *biennial.*

Bunch   A word referring to a cluster of things, usually growing together or tied together: *a bunch of bananas, a bunch of asparagus.* Colloquially and informally, it is much more loosely used to refer to any mass: *a bunch of kids, a bunch of nonsense.*

Bust, busted, burst   *Bust* was originally a dialectal variant of *burst.* Its principal parts are *bust, busted, busted. Burst,* the standard form, is invariable: *burst, burst, burst. Bust* has proved to be an adaptable word; it is used as a noun, adjective, or verb—all with different meanings:

The show was a bust. [failure]
He is busted. [without money]
He busted out. [escaped]
He busted chemistry. [failed]

These uses, of course, are either slang or strictly informal.

But that, but what   Both constructions are now considered standard, occurring usually in negative statements of doubt or concern:

I am not certain but that he is guilty.
I don't doubt but what he was disappointed.

In either sentence, however, a simple *that* serves just as well.

C

Calculate   *Calculate* is a mathematical term meaning "to compute" or "to reason." The extended usage meaning "to suppose," "to guess," or "to plan" is dialectal: *He calculated there were about a hundred people there.*

Can, may   Formal usage observes a distinction between the two words—*can* expressing ability or power (*I can do it*) and *may* expressing permission or chance (*May I do it? I may do it*). Speakers tend to use *can* for both meanings, depending upon the tone of the voice to convey the idea of request.

Cannot, can not   Both forms are acceptable. If writing is published, the choice between them is usually the editor's.

Can't help but   An acceptable American idiom: *I can't help but sympathize with him.* Many writers, however, still prefer the British usage: *I can't help sympathizing with him.*

Censor, censure   Two verbs easily confused because they are often pronounced very much alike. *Censor* means "to examine in order to delete or suppress objectionable material." *Censure* means "to criticize or blame." *Censure* is a much more general term than *censor.*

Center around, center about   A common idiom, even in writing, but one that easily offends some people who insist that the expression is illogical. Things ordinarily revolve around a center, not the opposite.

> *Informal:*   Our discussion was centered around the idea of civil disobedience.
> *Alternatives:* Our discussion was centered on . . .
>   Our discussion focused upon . . .

Colloquial, colloquialism   Not terms of condemnation but ways of describing words and expressions that we ordinarily say but seldom write, either because of their informality or because of their dialectal nature.

Come and   See **Try and.**

Common   See **Mutual.**

Compare, contrast   Although *contrast* means "to show differences," *compare* may mean "to consider in such a way as to show likenesses and differences." Joining the two terms, as professors often do on examinations, is a way of emphasizing that two things should be done: *Compare and contrast Pope's style and Wordsworth's style.*

Compare to, compare with   *Compare to* is used to emphasize the resemblance between two things: *He compared the surface of the pond to a mirror. Compare with* is used to show relative values, whether they are alike or different: *He compared the use of alcohol with the use of drugs.* The distinction is difficult to hold to, particularly since either *to* or *with* is used with the past participle: *Compared with [to] any other novel, this one is sensational.*

Complected   The awkwardness of the standard form *complexioned,* as in *dark-complexioned,* no doubt accounts for the currency of the colloquial form *dark complected.* The usage is probably better evaded than debated by saying *Her complexion was dark.*

Consensus of opinion   Now an idiomatic and acceptable phrase, even though it is redundant. *Consensus* means "a general harmony of opinion."

Considerable, considerably   The adjective *considerable* is used colloquially as a noun or an adverb:

Colloquial:	I had considerable to do.
Standard:	I had a considerable amount of work to do.
Colloquial:	His tax was considerable more than mine.
Standard:	His tax was considerably more than mine.

Contact   Widely used as a verb to mean "to get in touch with" without reference to a specific means of communication: *Mr. Smith should be contacted.* Many people object to the usage as a brand of commercial jargon. Without doubt, the word has already been disassociated from the world of salesmanship so that more and more it can be freely used.

Continual, continuous   A useful distinction exists between the two words, although it is not always observed. *Continual* refers to happenings that recur with sufficient frequency to be considered a series: *There has been continual warfare for the last one hundred years. Continuous* refers to something that occurs without interruption: *My electric clock has a continuous hum.*

Contractions   Contractions are abbreviated forms in writing that reflect speech habits: *I'm* for *I am; would've* for *would have; John's been sick* for *John has been sick.* Because contractions reflect the informality of speech, they are appropriate in writing when the situation and occasion are informal enough to justify them. Otherwise, they are out of place. Writers who are sensitive to the rhythm of their prose treat the use of contractions flexibly.

Contrast   See **Compare.**

Could of, would of   See **Of.**

Counter word   A particular word that accumulates so many different meanings that in time it becomes vague. *Cute, nice, great, cool,* and *tough* have become only general expressions of approval and disapproval. Slang and nonstandard dialects are responsible for a great number of counter words. It has been estimated that *mess* as one part of speech or another has more than fifty meanings. Because counter words are "umbrella" terms, their impreciseness makes them inappropriate to most kinds of writing.

Couple   In an exact sense, *couple* mean "two." In speech, however, it is loosely used to mean "several": *a couple of minutes ago.* The difference in meaning may cause a writer to choose "two" if he needs to be absolutely precise. The tendency to drop words in unaccented syllables accounts for expressions like *a couple times* and *a couple doughnuts* instead of *a couple of times* and *a couple of doughnuts.* These shortened expressions, like contractions, are informal and appropriate to writing only if they are consistent with the general tone of the whole.

Credible, creditable, credulous   Three words sufficiently similar in sound that they are confused in usage. *Credible* means "capable of being believed": *His story was credible. Creditable* means "worthy of recognition": *His writing is creditable. Credulous* means "gullible, too willing to believe without evidence": *Children are often credulous.*

Cuss, cussed   *Cuss* is an informal variant of *curse.* Its uses as a noun to mean "a particularly annoying person" *(she is an old cuss)* and as an adjective to mean "stubborn" *(cussed mule)* are slangy.

D

Different from, different than   *Different from* has traditionally been the preferred form in America; however, *different than,* the British usage, has become more and more common and acceptable in this country because it avoids the piling up of words that the use of *different from* sometimes requires. Two groups of sentences will illustrate:

The spirit of Franz Hals's painting is considerably different from that of Rembrandt's.
The spirit of Franz Hals's painting is considerably different than Rembrandt's.
It's different from what you think.
It's different than you think.

Dinner, supper   Inasmuch as *dinner* is defined as the main meal of the day and *supper* as the evening meal, *dinner* may be substituted for *supper* or, of course, refer to the noon meal if that is the principal meal.

Discreet, discrete   Words easily confused. *Discreet* means "prudent" or "careful": *He was discreet in what he said. Discrete* means "separate" or "discontinuous": *The naval research laboratory was a discrete unit of the campus.*

Disinterested, uninterested   Two words that allow a useful discrimination of meaning, but now used interchangeably to mean "having no interest." *Disinterested,* however, is still often used to mean "impartial": *What the dispute needs is a disinterested mediator.* The person who knows the difference between *uninterested* and *disinterested* will understand such a sentence; the uninformed will remain confused.

Due to, because of   Although both of these phrases are now used as prepositions in both speech and writing, it is useful to know the traditional distinction which many educated people still observe. They classify *due to* as an adjective and use it following the verb *to be: His success was due to years of hard work.* They reserve *because of* for prepositional phrases used as adverbs: *He was recognized because of his hard work.* Since the choice depends upon some knowledge of grammar, it is easy to see why the distinction has been blurred.

E

Effect   See **Affect.**

E.g.   See **Viz.**

Enthuse, enthused   A back-formation from *enthusiasm,* giving rise also to the participial form *enthused.* Characteristically, back-formations tend to be scorned until their usage is so established that no one remembers why scorn was necessary. Our reactions to *peddle* and *reminisce,* also scorned at one time as back-formations, are now completely neutral. *Enthuse* and *enthused* are now widely used, but they are not yet so firmly established in standard English as to find general acceptance.

-ese   A suffix used to refer to a language or literary style, used in words coined especially to designate special kinds of jargon: *officialese, commercialese, journalese.*

Etc.   Abbreviation for the Latin phrase *et cetera,* meaning "and other things." To say "and *et cetera*" is to show ignorance of the Latin. Although *etc.* sometimes serves a useful purpose in technical writing to indicate an indefinite list of items, it is a lazy substitute in other kinds of prose for a fairly selective list. If the list is an unduly long one, the English words *and so forth* and *and so on* serve better than the Latin.

Ever so often, every so often   Often pronounced alike, but their meanings are different. *Ever so often* means "very often": *We go to the theater ever so often. Every so often* means "now and then": *He writes a note every so often.*

Everyplace, everywhere   Traditionally, *everywhere* has been the preferred form, but *everyplace* is now so commonly used that it must be recognized as standard English. *Everyplace* continues to be more informal than *everywhere.*

Except   See **Accept.**

Expect   Colloquial usage in the sense of "suppose": *I expect he'll be coming soon.* In standard usage, *expect* means "to anticipate something": *I expect him soon.*

Exceptional   In educational jargon, the usual meaning is often reversed. An exceptional child is not necessarily a superior child but one who is exceptional because he is below average or has some special problem that hinders his educational development.

F

Farther, further   Originally, *farther* was a variant of the adverb *further;* the comparative form of the adjective *far* was *farrer.* In time, *farther* displaced *farrer* and became associated with distance: *Portland is farther from here than Vancouver. Further* expressed other ideas of advancement: *He went further in school than Al.* Current usage has blurred the former distinction. Perhaps the most accurate statement that can be made is that *further* is now a variant of *farther.* The difference between them is mainly a matter of regional variation.

Faze   In most dictionaries, *faze* still carries some kind of usage label, either colloquial or informal. Since synonyms like *discomfit, disconcert, daunt, perturb,* and *abash* all seem to be much more formal in tone than *faze,* it is understandable why the word is being more and more used in both speaking and writing.

Fewer, less   *Fewer* is used with count nouns expressing a collection of particulars, and *less* with abstract nouns and mass nouns expressing bulk: *fewer errors, less excitement, less salt.* However, *less* is popularly used with count nouns, so that it is not uncommon to hear expressions like *less voters* and *less words.* Careful writers tend to make a distinction between the two forms.

Field   A standard and acceptable word in the language, but frequently overused, so that it ends up as deadwood in the sentence:

Deadwood: I have increased in the *field* of understanding.
Rephrased: I have increased in understanding.

Flaunt, flout   Words easily confused. *Flaunt* means "to make a showy display": *He flaunted his defiant attitude. Flout* means "to show scorn for": *He flouted conventional manners.*

Folks   The formal plural of *folk* is *folk. Folks* is a popular plural, often used informally to refer to relatives.

Former, latter   *The former* and *the latter* are relatively formal ways of referring to two things already mentioned. For a series of more than two, *first* and *last* are the appropriate terms for referring to the beginning and end.

Freshman, freshmen   Although *freshmen* is the plural form of *freshman,* only *freshman* is used as the adjective form: *a freshman theme, a freshman meeting.*

Further   See **Farther.**

G

Get   One of the utility words of the language which has a variety of idiomatic uses, both standard and colloquial. *The Random House Dictionary,* College Edition, lists fifty-one subheadings under the word. Of particular interest is the use of *get* as an auxiliary verb: *I get to go soon,* signifying future; *I have got to finish,* emphatic use; *I got to thinking,* progressive implication; *I got caught,* passive sense. In questions, *got* serves as a filler: *What have you got to say?* The use of *got* by itself in sentences like *You got good sense* is colloquial. A writer would include *have: you've got good sense* or *you have good sense.*

Go and   See **Try and.**

Good, well   Interchangeable words in certain constructions when they are both adjectives meaning "in a sound state of health." *I feel good* means the same as *I feel well.* But *He is well* is quite different from *He is good.* When *well* is an adverb (*He plays the flute well*), the substitution of *good* is nonstandard.

Good and, good many   Colloquial uses to mean "exceedingly": *I was good and mad. I had a good many complaints.*

Gotten   An acceptable past participle of *get* in addition to *got.* The choice between *got* and *gotten* is largely a matter of rhythmic preference. *Gotten* is probably more common:

The flowers *were gotten* this morning.
I *have gotten* many compliments on the decorations.

H

Had better, had best, you'd better   All acceptable idioms in standard English for *should* or *ought: You had [you'd] better report to the man in charge. I had best do it myself.* Any further shortening is strictly colloquial: *You better go.*

Have got   See **Get.**

Had of   A pronunciation spelling of *had've.* Either form is nonstandard.

Nonstandard: I wish I had of gone.
Standard: I wish I had gone.

Had ought, hadn't ought   Nonstandard forms. *Ought* is an obsolete participle of the verb *owe.* Today it is used only as an invariable form, combined with infinitives: *I ought to speak up; he ought to be elected.*

Half a, half an, a half, a half a   The first three are acceptable variants: *He worked half a day; We chatted for half an hour; I will take a half dozen. A half a* (*a half a piece*) is colloquial.

Hanged, hung   When *hang* means "to execute," *hanged* is the preferred past form and past participle: *He was hanged at 10:00 a.m.* In other senses of "suspend," *hung* is used: *The decorator hung the picture.*

Hardly, barely, scarcely Since the meaning of all three adverbs is "not quite," the negative does not need to be reexpressed. Phrases such as *hardly didn't know* and *scarcely never went* are considered nonstandard.

He or she, his or her The word *man* may be used in a generic sense to mean "all mankind," including males and females. In like manner, *he* may be used in a generic sense to refer to both males and females. *He or she* is an unnecessary and clumsy construction:

> *Awkward:* If anybody expressed his or her opinion, he or she would be penalized.

> *Rephrased:* If anybody expressed his opinion, he would be penalized.

Help but See **Can't help but.**

Honorable, reverend In strictly formal written address, the words are capitalized and spelled out fully, preceded by *the,* usually capitalized, and followed by the full name of the person:

> The Honorable William L. Taylor
> The Reverend Arthur C. Holman.

In less formal situations, *the* may be dropped and the titles abbreviated:

> Hon. William L. Taylor,   Rev. Arthur C. Holman.

Human, humans Now acceptably used as nouns, although *human beings, people,* and *persons* seem to predominate in formal writing as alternate ways of expression.

Hung See **Hanged.**

I

I.e. See **Viz.**

If, whether After verbs like *ask, doubt, know, remember, see* and *wonder,* the two conjunctions are used interchangeably: *I'll see if* [*whether*] *I can go. I wonder if* [*whether*] *it'll rain.* If an alternative is expressed, *whether* is the preferred form in standard usage: *I don't know whether you can use the typewriter or not.*

In-, un-, il-, im- All negative prefixes, but not often used interchangeably. Dictionaries indicate which words use *in-* (*incoherent,* *inartistic*), *un-* (*unlikely, unnecessary*), *il-* (*illiterate, illegitimate*), and *im-* (*immoral, impractical*). *In-* sometimes appears to mean "not" when it is actually an intensifier, for example, *invaluable* (very valuable) or *inflammable* (very flammable).

Imply, infer   The traditional distinction between the two words is worth preserving. *Imply* is concerned with sending out a suggestion; *infer,* with receiving it or drawing it out: *His actions implied a sense of doubt. I inferred a sense of doubt from his actions.* Nevertheless, in practice, the distinction is fading. *Infer* is often used in the sense of *imply: I presume that anarchy was not inferred by your remarks.*

In regards to, with regards to   Nonstandard forms for the standard phrases *in regard to* and *with regard to.*

Incredible, incredulous   Words easily confused. *Incredible* means "unbelievable": *It was an incredible feat of strength. Incredulous* means "skeptical": *He looked at me with an incredulous smile.*

Individual, person, party   Of the three, *person* is the most common and general term for the human being: *an average person. Individual* emphasizes the person is one of a group: *the rights of the individual. Party* refers to a group and is jargon when used to refer to an individual: *Your party is on the line.*

Ingenious, ingenuous   Two words easily confused. *Ingenious* means "clever" or "resourceful": *an ingenious composer. Ingenuous* means "frank" or "straightforward": *an ingenuous remark.*

Inside of, outside of   When used as prepositional phrases, the *of* can be dispensed with: *We walked inside* [*of*] *the vault. We lived outside* [*of*] *the city.* When *inside* and *outside* are used as nouns, the *of* is necessary: *The inside of* [*outside of*] *the door is scratched.*

Intent, intention   Both mean "determination to do something." *Intent* is the more formal and restricted term, often legal in its implications: *with intent to kill. Intention* is a more general, all-purpose word: *His intentions were good.*

Intermural, intramural   The prefix *inter-* means "between" or "among." Intermural athletics, therefore, occur between different colleges. *Intra-* means "within." Intramural athletics, therefore, occur between groups within a particular college.

Invite   As a shortened form of *invitation,* pronounced with the accent on the first syllable, *invite* is dialectal: *We got an invite to the party.*

Irregardless A nonstandard variant of *regardless*. Since *-less* expresses the negative idea, the negative prefix *-ir* is unnecessary.

Is when, is where *When* and *where* may sometimes introduce noun clauses after the verb *to be: The big decision is when we should start.* If the speaker is defining, however, a *when* clause or *where* clause usually supplies an example instead of a definition.

Awkward: A libation is when wine is spilled in honor of the deity.
Rephrased: A libation is an act of spilling wine in honor of the deity.

Awkward: The chancel of a church is where the clergy and the choir are.
Rephrased: The chancel of a church is that part reserved for the clergy and the choir.

Its, it's Two forms frequently confused. *Its* is the possessive form of *it. It's* is a contraction of *it is.* The two are not interchangeable.

J

Judgment, judgement *Judgement* is a British spelling; *judgment,* the common American form.

K

Kind of, sort of Strictly colloquial when used an an adverb to mean "rather" or "somewhat":

Colloquial: He was kind of [kinda] peeved at what I said.
Standard: He was rather peeved at what I said.

L

Laid, lain See **Lie.**

Latter See **Former.**

Lay See **Lie.**

Lead, led The verb *lead* (to conduct) and the noun *lead* (a metal) are spelled alike but pronounced differently. *Led,* the past tense and participle of the verb, rhymes with the noun. The confusion often leads to the misspelling of one of the forms.

Leave, let Easily confused because their meanings overlap. When *leave* clearly means "depart" and *let* means "allow," no confusion occurs. But when both words mean "permit to remain," the choice between the two is difficult. Both *Leave me alone* and *Let me alone* are accepted as standard usage.

In many instances, *let* is followed by an infinitive; *Let the rope go. Let it stay.* In these constructions, *leave* cannot substitute.

Lend, loan   For a period of time, *lend* was a verb only and *loan* a noun only. *Loan,* however, has come to be used as a verb. Today, the two words are used interchangeably as verbs. *Loan* remains the only noun.

Less   See **Fewer.**

Lest   A conjunction meaning "for fear that": *The government took unusual precautions lest the peace negotiations be endangered.* Because *lest* is very often followed by a verb in the subjunctive, it has become associated with formal expression, even a slightly archaic tone.

Let's   Since *let's* is a contraction of *let us,* it should not be used with *us:*

Colloquial: Let's us get together for lunch.
Standard: Let's get together for lunch.

Liable, likely, apt   *Likely* implies strong probability that something will happen: *It is likely to snow.* In speech, *liable* and *apt* might substitute in the same sentence. In its own right, *liable* implies susceptibility to something unpleasant (*The machine is liable to error*) or, in a legal sense, responsibility for damages (*He is liable for the damage*). *Apt,* in its own right, implies a natural tendency or inclination: (*She is apt at sewing*).

Lie, lay   Words easily confused because their principal parts overlap: *lie, lay, lain* (an intransitive verb meaning "to recline") and *lay, laid, laid* (a transitive verb meaning "to place"):

I lay down an hour ago.
If I lay the key on the table, will you pick it up?
The hen laid an egg.

The past tense of *lie* is the source of most of the trouble.

Lighted, lit   Both acceptable past tense and participial forms of *light.* Because *lighted* is a two-syllable word, it is usually preferred in combinations like *a beautifully lighted tree* or *could have been lighted earlier.*

Like   In informal speech, *like* has become a popular, all-purpose word, often merely serving as a filler in almost any position. In many instances, it seems to be a loose substitute for "for example":

Colloquial:	Like our first lesson, most of us didn't know the first thing about poetry.
Standard rephrasing:	During our first lesson, for example, most of us didn't know the first thing about poetry.
Colloquial:	When you have your first introduction, they should like give meanings.
Standard rephrasing:	When you have your first introduction, they should give meanings, for example.
Colloquial:	like lots of times; like when they were kids
Standard rephrasing:	many times, for instance; when they were kids, for example.

Like, as   The traditional distinction between *like* as a preposition and *as* as a conjunction is being rapidly worn away. *Like* is more and more commonly used as a conjunction, although that usage predominates in speech rather than in writing:

Informal:	Few tenors can sing top notes like he does.
Formal:	Few tenors can sing top notes as he does.

Writers should be aware that the use of *like* as a conjunction remains controversial; *as* as a conjunction remains the safe choice.

Likely   See **Liable.**

Lit   See **Lighted.**

Literally   When *literally* means "in a strict accurate sense; without exaggeration," it represents the opposite of *figuratively,* which means "in an imaginative or metaphorical sense." In speech, however, *literally* is often used as an intensifier in contexts that are clearly figurative: *He literally split his sides laughing* or *He literally sailed across the room.* Since these are not literal statements, the use of *literally* seems not only unnecessary but confusing.

Loan   See **Lend.**

Loose, lose, loosen   *Loose* is either a verb meaning "to unfasten" or an adjective meaning "unrestrained." *Lose* is always a verb, meaning "to be deprived of something." Confusion between the two is a common cause of misspelling. *Loosen* is a common substitute for *loose: He loosened the knot for me.*

Lots, lots of Colloquial substitutes for *much, many, a large number,* or *a great amount: a lot of courage* for *a great amount of courage; lots of times* for *many times; I resent that a lot* for *I resent that very much.*

M

Majority, plurality In elections, *majority* means "more than one half of the total votes cast." *Plurality,* ordinarily used when three or more candidates are involved, refers to "the excess of votes received by one candidate over those received by the next highest candidate." Since *plurality* is not often used, majority is sometimes extended to include its meaning.

May be, maybe *May be* is a verb phrase; *maybe* is an adverb meaning "perhaps":

I *may be* late.
Maybe I'll be late.

May See **Can.**

May of, might of See **Of.**

Mighty Although *mighty* occurs in standard written English, it is highly informal when it is used as an intensifier meaning "very" or "extremely": *mighty useful, mighty good.*

Most, almost *Most* is commonly used as an adverb to form the superlative degree of adjectives and adverbs: *most helpful, most strikingly.* Shortening *almost* to *most* is a common colloquialism:

Colloquial: A good night's sleep will help most anything.
Standard: A good night's sleep will help almost anything.

Muchly *Much* is both an adjective and adverb form. The *-ly* is unnecessary.

Must Ordinarily an auxiliary verb expressing obligation. New usages indicate that the word is undergoing a functional shift: as a noun *The film at the Uptown is really a must* and as an adjective *This is a must proposal.* These usages are essentially colloquial.

Mutual, common *Mutual* implies "having the same relation to one another": *a mutual agreement, a mutual exchange of gifts. Common* means "sharing something equally with each other or with others": *a common cause, common property. Common* is often substituted for *mutual:*

Misuse:	They have a common admiration for one another.
Properly used:	They have a mutual admiration for one another, a common respect for Faulkner.

N

Need, needs   Both third person singular forms of the auxiliary verb. *Need* is used in negative statements: *He needs to go. He need not go.*

Nice   The history of the word *nice* is long and varied. At various times among other definitions it has meant "foolish," "wanton," "strange," "tender," "coy," "thin," "appetizing," and "trivial." It now expresses only a very general and mild approval, little used by writers who are interested in precise words.

No place, nowhere, nowheres   Of the three, *nowhere* is the most formal usage; *no place* tends to be colloquial; *nowheres* is nonstandard.

Nowhere near   Colloquial expression for "not nearly" or "not by a wide margin": *He was nowhere near right.*

Nowheres   See **No place.**

Number of   See **Amount of.**

O

O, oh   Two acceptable interjections varying in usage. *O* almost always combines with other words, usually in formal address or apostrophe: *O lord our Lord; O moon of my delight!* It is capitalized and not followed by punctuation. *Oh* acts independently: *Oh, that isn't so; Oh! That's terrible!* It is not capitalized unless it begins a sentence; it is usually followed by a comma or exclamation point.

Of   *Have* in unstressed syllables sounds very much like *of,* particularly when *have* is contracted in forms like *could've, would've, may've, might've,* and *must've.* The tendency to transcribe the neutral sound as *of* instead of *have* accounts for such nonstandard forms as *could of, would of, may of, might of,* and *must of.*

Off of   A colloquialism. The *of* can be dispensed with in writing: *He fell off* [*of*] *the fence.*

O.K., OK, okay   Perhaps the most popular of all Americanisms, but clearly a colloquialism. All three transcriptions are acceptable in informal writing. The expression is made to serve as several parts of speech: *get an O.K.* (noun), *he OK'd it* (verb), *an OK-guy* (adjective), *he ran O.K.* (adverb), *Okay!* (interjection).

Olden   A Middle English inflected form of *old*. Clearly archaic and inappropriate in contemporary prose: *the olden days*.

Oldster   The aged counterpart of *youngster*. Potentially a useful word, but usually considered an unflattering usage by elderly people, who think of it as a synonym for *ancient*.

Only   As a modifier, *only* tends to move forward in a sentence. Thus, three versions of the same sentence may be quite acceptable:

> You have to do *only* the first problem.
> You have *only* to do the first problem.
> You *only* have to do the first problem.

In other instances, however, the placement may directly affect the implication and tone:

> A telescreen fell from a box to the audience below. Fortunately it injured *only* a standee [not a regular subscriber].
>
> Fortunately it *only* injured a standee [did not kill him].
>
> Fortunately it injured *only* one standee [not many].

Ought   See **Had ought.**

Out loud   Colloquial for *aloud* or *very loudly.*

Outside of.   See **Inside of.**

P

Party   See **Individual.**

Per   Standard in set Latin phrases like *per annum, per capita,* and *per diem.* When the Latin noun is translated and *per* is kept, the phrases become typical business jargon: *per year, per head, per day.* In these and other phrases like *per yard* and *per week,* the article can be substituted very naturally: *$12 a day, $7 a yard, 25 cents a head. Per* in the sense of "according to" (*per your instructions, per agreement*) is a carryover of business jargon into speech.

Per cent, percent, percentage   *Percent* may be written as one word or two and does not require a period, even though *cent* is an abbreviation of Latin *centum.* The word is ordinarily used after numbers: *10 percent.* The symbol % is used only in technical and business contexts. In speech, *per cent* and *percentage* have become synonymous, but some editors still insist upon the distinction between *per cent* with numbers and *percentage* in other contexts: *a large percentage of the population.*

Person See **Individual.**

Phase Not to be confused with *faze* (see p. 392).

Playwrite, playwright *Playwrite* is a logical but incorrect word for the writer of a play. The spelling *wright* is derived from an Old and Middle English word meaning "maker" or "creator."

Plenty Its uses as an adverb meaning "very" or "fully" are colloquial: *plenty sore, plenty hot enough.*

Plurality See **Majority.**

Practical, practicable Words easily confused, but not interchangeable. *Practical* means "tested by experience," "concerned with applications," or "useful": *a practical method, a practical mind, a practical invention. Practicable* means "potentially useful" or "feasible" and does not apply to persons: *practicable material, the proposal is not practicable.*

Presently *Presently* is most frequently used to mean "in a little while, soon." It is also used informally to mean "at the present time, now." The context will usually decide which meaning the speaker intends, but most listeners expect the first meaning.

Pretty Overused as an adverb meaning "moderately," "somewhat," or "in good condition": *pretty bad, pretty clever, sitting pretty.* Even though *pretty* is well established in this sense, the usage remains basically colloquial.

Principal, principle Words commonly confused. As a noun, *principal* refers to the head of a school, a leading performer, or to a sum of money (*principal and interest*). As an adjective, it means "main": *principal idea, principal stockholder. Principle* means "theory, concept, or rule": *the principles that determine our conduct. Principle* has no adjective use.

Proved, proven Both acceptable past participles of *prove.* The choice between them is usually the writer's preference for a one- or two-syllable word in a particular context: *a proven proverb, a claim that has been proved again.*

Provided, providing   Equally acceptable as subordinating conjunctions: *I will accept, providing [provided] the terms are favorable. Provided* is more commonly used in formal legal and business contexts.

Q

Qua   Adverb meaning "in the function of," "in the character of," or "as," used to designate in which of several roles a person acts: *He cannot act* qua *governor as he did* qua *private citizen.* Essentially a pretentious usage.

Quite, quiet   Words easily confused in spelling. The adjective *quiet* means "calm." The adverb *quite* means "completely" or "positively": *They are quite mistaken.* Colloquially, the adverb is used to mean "rather" or "somewhat": *We live quite close to the center of town.*

Quotes   Used colloquially as a shortened form for "quotation marks" and "quotations." Even though the usage grows increasingly, it is still casual in tone and should be used only in informal writing.

R

Raise, rear   See **Rear**. Also **rise**.

Rarely ever   Now as established idiom for *rarely if ever.* The *ever* is unnecessary and may be dropped in more formal writing: *I rarely* [ever] *pretend to be what I'm not.*

Re   Strictly business or legal jargon for "in the matter of" or "regarding": *Re your letter of the 15th ....*

Real, really   *Real* is the acceptable adjective form: *a real triumph, real trees. Really* is the acceptable adverb form: *a really enthusiastic crowd, things as they really are.* Colloquially, *real* is also used as an adverb: *a real nice conversation, a real good story.*

Rear, raise   It is no longer true that one "raises cattle" but "rears children." *Raise* is now standard usage for "bringing up children."

Reason is because, reason is that   Traditionally, a writer of formal prose used a noun clause introduced by *that* following the verb *to be: The reason he didn't vote is that he was out of town.* The common use of *because* constructions in speech, however, has influenced the accepted standard for written prose. *Reason is because* may be found in the prose of established persons writing for reputable journals.

Regardless   See **Irregardless.**

Reverend   See **Honorable.**

Right   Colloquial as an adverb meaning "very" except in formal titles:

> *Formal:*   The Right Reverend Thomas Henrikson
> *Colloquial:*   right cute

Rise, raise   Verbs sometimes confused. The principal parts of *rise,* an intransitive verb, are *rise, rose, risen: The audience rose to applaud.* The principal parts of *raise,* a transitive verb, are *raise, raised, raised: The flag was raised. He raised his family well.* See **Rear.**

S

Said, same   The use of *said* and *same* to mean "the foregoing" or "above-mentioned" is strictly legal or business jargon and inappropriate to other kinds of prose: *The said motor is one of the best. I would like credit for same.*

Scarcely   See **Hardly.**

Seldom ever   A colloquial expression for *hardly ever. Seldom,* of course, may be used alone: *I seldom go to the concerts any more.*

Semi-   See **Bi-.**

Set   See **Sit.**

Shall, will   *Will* is rapidly replacing *shall* to express the future. In fact, the almost exclusive use of *will* now gives *shall* a special formal tone. The old device of using *shall* in the second and third persons (*You shall go, He shall go*) and *will* in the first person (*I will go*) for special emphasis is a strategy that depends upon the reader's knowing what the writer is doing. Linguistics has made clear that emphasis is not a matter of choosing one word or the other but of arranging words so that they fall into stressed positions: *They were told that they couldn't appeal. But they will.* The choice of *shall* in this sentence would not add to the emphasis that *will* naturally gets because of the rhythm of the sentence.

Shan't   An acceptable contraction of *shall not,* but even more formal in tone, possibly archaic, than the use of *shall* itself.

Should of   See **Of.**

Sit, set   Words easily confused. *Sit* is almost always used intransitively; its principal parts are *sit, sat, sat.* The principal parts of *set* are *set, set, set. Set* is sometimes used transitively: *I set it down. I set the trap. Set* is also used intransitively: *Cement sets, Chickens set,* and *The sun sets.*

Smart   A highly adaptable word that tends to be overused. It has a variety of meanings in phrases like *a smart person, a smart pace, a smart blow, smart talk, smartly dressed.*

So, so that   *So* has become an all-purpose word. It substitutes for other conjunctive adverbs like *accordingly, consequently, hence,* and *therefore;* it acts as a subordinating conjunction in place of *so that;* and it serves colloquially as an intensifier: *so lovely.* The problem is mainly one of overuse, particularly when subordination would be more effective:

Informal: This sketch is only a rough copy, so it lacks detail.
Rephrased: This sketch lacks details because it is only a rough copy.

Some   Lends itself to colloquial uses in such sentences as:

That was some game! [unusual]
You will have to go some to beat that. [to a great extent]
He is some better. [somewhat]

Someplace, somewhere   See **Anyplace** and **everyplace.**

Somewheres   See **Anywheres.**

Sort of   See **Kind of.**

Such, such as   The use of *such* as an intensifier is informal: *He was such an effective speaker.* In written prose, *such* is ordinarily followed by a clause of result: *He was such an effective speaker that no one in the audience seemed to move at all.*

Supper   See **Dinner.**

Sure and   See **Try and.**

Sure, surely   *Sure* is the adjective form; *surely,* the adverb. The use of *sure* as an adverb is common in speech mainly because *surely* manages to sound pompous in some contexts:

Colloquial: He sure can throw the ball far. [Cp. He surely can throw the ball far.]
Standard: We would surely discourage any kind of interference.

Swell   Colloquial in many of its uses: *a swell head* (short for *a swelled head,* a conceited person); *a swell show* (excellent); *a swell house* (fashionable).

T

Therefor, therefore   Used interchangeably by some persons. In a strict sense, *therefor* is an adverb, with the stress on the second syllable, meaning "for this" or "for it": *The company gave a new play; the setting therefor was Rome. Therefore* is also an adverb, with stress on the first syllable, and can be used as a conjunction to mean "as a result" or "consequently": *The setting was Rome; therefore, the stage director attempted to make it authentic.*

Though, although   Two acceptable subordinating conjunctions with no difference in meaning. Since one is a two-syllable word and the other a one-syllable word, the choice between them often depends upon the rhythmic pattern of a clause. *Though* seems to be more frequently used, particularly in clauses following a verb: *He spoke hesitatingly, though he was not actually reluctant to tell his story. Though* is also used colloquially as a synonym of *however: He kept going to the meeting, though. I decided, though, that I wouldn't. Tho* and *tho'* are variant spellings, but should be recognized as inappropriate to serious writing.

Thusly   *Thus* is an adverb. The *-ly* is unnecessary.

Toward, towards   *Toward* is the American form, *towards* the British. Usage in this country, however, is divided.

Try and, come and, go and, be sure and   All well-established usages in conversation: *Try and stop me, come and get me, go and see, be sure and do it.* All, however, are colloquial equivalents of the more accepted idioms for formal writing: *try to, come to, go to,* and *be sure to,* which more clearly express an element of purpose.

Type   Colloquial for *type of:*

Colloquial: He's not that type student.
Standard: He's not that type of student.

U

Un-   See **In-**.

V

Very, very much   Traditionally, glossaries of usage have held that *very* should be used to modify an adjective and *very much* to modify a verb or past participle: *very rich, very much inclined.* The main difficulty with such a usage is that it is not always possible to say with certainty what is a participle and what is an adjective: *I was very much [very] concerned about the matter.* General usage is rapidly wearing away the old distinction.

Viz., i.e., e.g.   Latin abbreviations with separate meanings and uses. *Viz.,* now also acceptable without a period, is derived from *videlicet* and means "namely." It is the most formal of the three and is used to particularize: *The major sources of the play,* viz, 1.____, 2.____, 3.____. *I.e.* is an abbreviation of *id est,* meaning "that is." It is commonly used to interpret: *He was Faulknerized;* i.e., *he was mesmerized by Faulkner's novels. E.g.* is an abbreviation for *exempli gratia,* meaning literally "for the sake of the example." It is used to introduce an illustration: *Shortened spelling forms exist for a number of conjunctions,* e.g., *"thru," "tho," and "til."*

W

Wake, awake, waken, awaken   The principal parts of these verbs cause uncertainty. Since all of them have overlapping meanings, they may often be used interchangeably:

[a]wake   [a]wake or [a]waked   [a]woke or [a]waked
[a]waken   [a]wakened   [a]wakened

Want, want that, want for   The standard usage after *want* is an infinitive: *I want you to help me.* The other idioms are nonstandard: *I want that you should help me* or *I want for you to help me.*

Well   See **Good.**

Well-nigh   An acceptable adverbial form, but noticeably archaic in tone.

What with   *What* combined with *with* is a very old but still acceptable expression, meaning "with the attending circumstances of": *What with the threat of a recession, we had better not sell our house.*

Whereas   The use of *whereas* as a subordinating conjunction meaning "while on the contrary" often goes unrecognized: *Three of the five girls made a perfect score, whereas only one of the ten boys did. Whereas* is often treated only as a conjunctive adverb.

Whether   See **If.**

Whilst   The British equivalent of *while.* Sometimes used in poetry for a special effect, usually to suggest antiquity.

Will   See **Shall.**

Win   In the sense of "defeat," *win* is colloquial: *I won him at tennis.*

-wise   A suffix for forming adverbs, found in certain established usages such as *lengthwise, otherwise, counterclockwise,* and *likewise.* In recent years, however, nonce words ending in *-wise* have flourished, so that coinages of this kind have become associated with bad jargon: *examination-wise, weather-wise, car-wise, distance-wise.* Undoubtedly, a number of useful words will survive out of this language fad; but, for the present, careful writers proceed with caution.

Wist, wot   *Wot* is the present tense form of the archaic verb *wit,* meaning "to know." *Wist* is the past tense and past participial form. The words appear commonly in Shakespearean plays and in biblical passages:

Wist ye not that I must be about my Father's business?

Luke 2:49

Would of   See **Of.**

Writ   Archaic past participial form of *write.* Still survives in familiar phrases and quotations: *writ large, writ in water, The Moving Finger writes, and having writ, Moves on.* (Fitzgerald). As a noun, *writ* is an established legal term and occurs also in a phrase like *Holy Writ.*

X

Xmas   Commercial spelling of Christmas, but not a modern form. *X* is the first letter of the Greek spelling of *Christ.* The form was used in ancient times, and the *OED* records a usage in English as early as 1551.

X-ray, x ray   Variant forms. Also appears with an initial capital. *X* was used by Roentgen, the discoverer of X-ray, to indicate the unknown nature of the ray.

Y

Ye   Old English for *the.* The form is a survival of early printing practices when a *y* was substituted for the Old English thorn. Thus þe was written as *ye* and still appears in deliberately contrived antique names like Ye Olde Coffee Shoppe. Not to be confused with *ye,* an archaic form of *you.*

You all   A familiar southern dialect form, often shortened to *y'all.* Most commonly used by southerners as a means of distinguishing *you* singular from *you* plural. Poor imitators of southerners use *you all* in the singular.

Youth, youths   *Youth* may be used in a collective plural sense to mean young people in general: *Youth have always been restless. Youths* emphasizes individuals in a plural sense: *Six youths were injured in the bus accident.*

19

The Dictionary

Using a dictionary is an old and established custom, but the earliest word lists, called glosses, in no way resembled what we now think of as a dictionary. They were chiefly lists of difficult foreign words, with simple explanations sometimes in the same language as the foreign words, sometimes in English. The first dictionaries of English words date from the beginning of the seventeenth century, but they remained lists of hard words and still concentrated upon foreign borrowings.

As the words of the language continued to increase, dictionaries became more and more a necessity, and their contents were expanded to include information about spelling, pronunciation, etymology, and usage. One of the most influential of early dictionaries was Samuel Johnson's *A Dictionary of the English Language* (1755), which continued to be used in various revisions until 1900. Johnson fully recognized the changing nature of the language, but he also thought it was the duty of the lexicographer to "retard what we cannot repel." Further, recognizing what he considered the "improprieties and absurdities" of the English language, he set out "to correct or proscribe."

No modern editors claim that a dictionary proscribes or prescribes. With consistency, they assert that a dictionary describes. It becomes an authority only insofar as it is a faithful and complete recorder of language as it is used. In this sense, the dictionary assumes only the role of adviser, what the editors of *Webster's New World Dictionary* call "a friendly guide, pointing out the safe, well-travelled roads."

THE RELIABLE DICTIONARY

In what sense is a dictionary either good or unreliable?

First, no one dictionary is a definitive reference. Each is an interpretation of the language. Some modern editors assert that lexicography is now a linguistic science; others, like Philip B. Gove, the editor of *Webster's Third New International Dictionary,* say that it never will be a science, because the interpretation of words requires "subjective analysis, arbitrary decisions, and intuitive reasoning." In whatever sense we think of dictionary making, the editors and staff are chiefly responsible for its reliability. The contributors and consultants must be specialists in language study. No modern dictionary is a one-man job. The staff may involve hundreds of scholars, and the total production represent more than a million dollar investment.

Whatever is the degree of its authority at any one time, a dictionary does not continue to be a reliable current reference unless it is kept up to date. Desk dictionaries, because of their relatively small size, are frequently supplemented or revised. Unabridged dictionaries may undergo major revisions only every twenty or thirty years. Many inexpensive dictionaries on the market today are only reprints of old editions, sold by a previous publisher to be retitled and distributed by another one.

The size of a dictionary is a clue to its coverage. The more information it contains, the more likely it will be able to serve the needs of its users. Since every dictionary must of necessity select certain words to be included and compress its definitions into the smallest possible space, the large dictionary naturally gains an advantage because of its size. *Webster's Third New International* lists more than 450,000 words. The popular collegiate dictionaries list from 100,000 to 150,000 words. These are ordinarily complete enough for the purposes of most college studies.

Every dictionary gives details about its coverage and arrangement in its prefatory materials. These sections, although usually printed in a forbiddingly small type, are the clearest guides to the reliability of the book.

INFORMATION INCLUDED IN A DICTIONARY

Dictionaries, of course, vary in their emphasis. Besides basic definitions of words, some contain more encyclopedic information than others, some more etymological data, some more illustrations. But to varying degrees, all reliable dictionaries provide users with information of the following kind:

Spelling and Capitalization

Words that have variant spellings, like *catalog* or *catalogue,* are frequently given separate entries, although definitions are given only under one form. If a variant is not standard American, it is labeled. Thus, *defense* as a spelling for *defence* is labeled as a typical British spelling. If no label is attached, all variants may be considered acceptable in American usage.

Capitalization of proper nouns is indicated.

Syllabication

Since the American system of dividing words by syllables in typed and printed copy involves numerous complicated principles, the simplest thing to do is to refer to the divisions made in the dictionary for every entry of more than one syllable.

Pronunciation

Each dictionary explains its own system for describing the sounds of words. Key symbols are given in the Preface and at the bottom of pages for convenient reference.

In matters of pronunciation, the editors usually emphasize that they are not the arbiters of correct pronunciation. They merely record what pronunciations are used by educated native speakers. If one or more variants are accepted by a sufficiently large number of persons, these are listed. Each dictionary has its own way of indicating which pronunciation may be more common, if it is possible to make a judgment. In general, however, dictionaries do not label preferred pronunciations beyond suggesting how widespread a pronunciation may be. Any pronunciation that is entered may generally be considered standard unless it is given a special label.

What dictionaries cannot record, of course, are all of the changes in pronunciation that occur when words are used in context and subject to variations of pitch and stress. Therefore, what is listed as acceptable is at best only an approximation of the sounds we usually hear in conversation.

Parts of Speech and Inflected Forms

The definitions of words are grouped in terms of the parts of speech. If a word is commonly used in several ways, the forms are given and labeled. A change in the part of speech sometimes requires additional definition. For example, *ideal* is defined separately as an adjective and as a noun.

Forms of the past tense and participles of verbs, the plurals of nouns, and the comparative and superlative forms of adjectives are given when these are irregular in form or spelling.

Etymology

A dictionary's own explanation of its symbols and abbreviations is the key to interpreting the etymological information, which is ordinarily placed either before or after the definitions. If the source of a word is obvious, like *mailman,* no etymology is given. In addition, the sources of many words are uncertain. If an explanation is speculative or controversial, the word *probably* is often used as a qualifier.

The premium upon space in a dictionary requires that all of the above information be condensed into a small space in the most abbreviated terms.

Sep·tu·a·gint \sep-'t(y)ü-ə-jənt, 'sep-tə-wə-,jint\ *n* [LL *Septua-ginta,* fr. L, seventy, irreg. fr. *septem* seven + *-ginta* (akin to L *viginti* twenty); fr. the approximate number of its translators — more at SEVEN, VIGESIMAL] : a pre-Christian Greek version of the Old Testament used by Greek-speaking Christians

From *Webster's Seventh Collegiate*

Definition

The definitions of a dictionary attempt to cover as many meanings of a word as it commonly carries. The dictionary, however, cannot begin to explore all of the implications of a word or to concern itself with personal connotations. The extended and figurative meanings of words are not listed unless they have become established by frequent use. Dictionaries, therefore, seek as broad a coverage as possible in terms of most common usages. It is left to the user to select a particular meaning in terms of the context in which he finds or uses a word.

Each dictionary describes its own arrangement of definitions. Some begin with the etymology and earliest meaning and progress historically to current senses of the word. Others begin with the most frequently used definition and proceed in turn to more specialized and rare uses. Two citations will illustrate:

in·spire (in spīr′) *vt.* **-spired′, -spir′ing** [ME. *inspiren* < OFr. *inspirer* < L. *inspirare* < *in-*, in, on + *spirare*, to breathe] **1.** orig., *a*) to breathe or blow upon or into *b*) to infuse (life, etc. *into*) by breathing **2.** to draw (air) into the lungs; inhale **3.** to have an animating effect upon; influence or impel; esp., to stimulate or impel to some creative or effective effort **4.** to cause, guide, communicate, or motivate as by divine or supernatural influence **5.** to arouse or produce (a thought or feeling) [kindness *inspires* love] **6.** to affect with a specified feeling or thought [to *inspire* someone with fear] **7.** to occasion, cause, or produce **8.** to prompt, or cause to be written or said, by influence [to *inspire* a rumor] —*vi.* **1.** to inhale **2.** to give inspiration —**in·spir′a·ble** *adj.* —**in·spir′er** *n.*

From *Webster's New World*

in·spire (in spī³r′), *v.*, **-spired, -spir·ing.** —*v.t.* **1.** to infuse an animating, quickening, or exalting influence into. **2.** to produce or arouse (a feeling, thought, etc.): *to inspire confidence.* **3.** to influence or impel: *opposition inspired him to a greater effort.* **4.** to animate, as an influence, feeling, thought, or the like does. **5.** to communicate or suggest by a divine or supernatural influence. **6.** to guide or control by divine influence. **7.** to give rise to, bring about, cause, etc.: *to inspire revolution.* **8.** to take (air, gases, etc.) into the lungs; inhale. **9.** *Archaic.* to infuse (breath, life, etc.) by breathing. **10.** *Archaic.* to breathe into or upon. —*v.i.* **11.** to inhale. **12.** to give inspiration. [ME *inspire(n)* < L *inspīr(āre)* (to) breathe upon or into = *in-* IN-² + *spīrāre* to breathe] —**in·spir′a·ble,** *adj.* —**in·spir·a·tive** (in-spī³r′/ə tiv, in′spə rā′tiv), *adj.* —**in·spir′er,** *n.* —**in·spir′ing·ly,** *adv.*

From *Random House Dictionary*

Synonyms, Antonyms, and Idioms

The listing of synonyms and antonyms aid the user in finding a variety of similar or opposite terms. For many words, dictionaries sometimes add a short section in which they discriminate between the meanings of closely related words and illustrate by a quotation or citation.

beau·ti·ful (bū′tə fəl), *adj.* having beauty; delighting the eye; admirable to the taste or the mind. —**beau′- ti·ful·ly,** *adv.* —**beau′ti·ful·ness,** *n.*
—**Syn.** BEAUTIFUL, HANDSOME, LOVELY, PRETTY refer to a pleasing appearance. That is BEAUTIFUL which has perfection of form, color, etc., or noble and spiritual qualities: *a beautiful landscape, girl* (not *man*). HANDSOME often implies stateliness or pleasing proportion and symmetry: *a handsome man.* That which is LOVELY is beautiful but in a warm and endearing way: *a lovely smile.* PRETTY implies a moderate but noticeable beauty, esp. in that which is small or of minor importance: *a pretty child.* —**Ant.** ugly.

From *American College Dictionary*

In a similar way, the oftentimes special meanings of idiomatic phrases are added to a main entry. Thus, to the main entry of the verb *fall* are added phrases like *fall away* (withdraw support), *fall back* (retreat), *fall back on* (depend), *fall behind* (lag), *fall down* (disappoint), *fall for* (be deceived), and *fall in with* (meet by chance).

Labels

The special labels used in dictionaries help the user to understand what limitations particular words and meanings have. Some of these labels indicate usage in terms of region (*British, Southwest*), in terms of time (*archaic, obsolete*), in terms of subject (*Philosophy, Anatomy*), or in terms of style (*poetic, dialectal, nonstandard*). When the labels involve value judgments, as dialect or colloquial labels frequently do, they may vary from dictionary to dictionary. For controversial items of usage, *The American Heritage Dictionary* offers extended discussions, referring to the opinions of a special panel of more than a hundred prominent writers, educators, and public figures, selected by the editors:

> **ain't** (änt). *Nonstandard.* Contraction of *am not.* Also extended in use to mean *are not, is not, has not,* and *have not.*
>   ***Usage:*** *Ain't,* with few exceptions, is strongly condemned by the Usage Panel when it occurs in writing and speech that is not deliberately colloquial or that does not employ the contraction to provide humor, shock, or other special effect. The first person singular interrogative form *ain't I* (for *am I not* or *amn't I*), considered as a special case, has somewhat more acceptance than *ain't* employed with other pronouns or with nouns. (*Ain't I* has at least the virtue of agreement between *am* and *I.* With other pronouns, or nouns, *ain't* takes the place of *isn't* and *aren't* and sometimes of *hasn't* and *haven't.*) But *ain't I* is unacceptable in writing other than that which is deliberately colloquial, according to 99 per cent of the Panel, and unacceptable in speech to 84 per cent. The example *It ain't likely* is unacceptable to 99 per cent in both writing and speech. *Aren't I* (as a variant of the interrogative *ain't I*) is acceptable in writing to only 27 per cent of the Panel, but approved in speech by 60 per cent. Louis Kronenberger has, this typical reaction: "A genteelism, and much worse than *ain't I.*"

From *The American Heritage*

Encyclopedic Information and Illustrations

Dictionaries vary widely in their encyclopedic information, that is, the extent to which they include miscellaneous biographical, historical, scientific, and literary information, foreign words and phrases, as well as pictures, diagrams, tables, and maps. Some dictionaries include information of this kind in the main alphabetical listing; others relegate some of this information to separate sections or exclude it altogether. Many dictionaries also provide basic handbook information on grammar and mechanics.

COLLEGIATE DICTIONARIES

The following list represents a sampling of responsibly edited dictionaries which are kept current between major editions by minor revisions at the time of reprinting:

The American College Dictionary. New York: Random House.
The American Heritage Dictionary of the English Language. Boston: Houghton Mifflin Co.
Funk & Wagnalls Standard College Dictionary. New York: Harcourt, Brace & Co.
The Random House Dictionary of the English Language. College Edition. New York: Random House.

Webster's New World Dictionary of the American Language. Second
College Edition. New York and Cleveland: The World Publishing Co.
Webster's Seventh New Collegiate Dictionary. Springfield, Mass.: G. &
C. Merriam Co.

UNABRIDGED DICTIONARIES

Besides the greater number of entries in an unabridged dictionary,
one of its significant advantages is the fuller use of quotations or phrases
to support particular meanings and usages. These dictionaries will also
vary in the amount of encyclopedic information they include.

One or more of the following unabridged dictionaries will be found
in most public or college libraries:

Funk & Wagnalls New "Standard" Dictionary of the English Language.
The Random House Dictionary of the English Language.
Webster's New Twentieth Century Dictionary.
Webster's Third New International Dictionary.

ENCYCLOPEDIC DICTIONARY

*The Century Dictionary: An Encyclopedic Lexicon of the English
Language.* 12 vols.

Since *The Century Dictionary* has not been revised in more than
fifty years, many of its entries are out-of-date. It is not completely
useless, however. For words of historical rather than current interest,
the dictionary still provides a wealth of information.

SCHOLARLY DICTIONARIES

Scholarly dictionaries are primarily for students of the English
language who are interested in the progressive history of meanings and
in the various forms that English words have had in the past. One
of the monumental projects of dictionary making in any language is
The Oxford English Dictionary in twelve volumes and one supplement,
originally published in ten volumes under the title *A New English
Dictionary on Historical Principles.* Thus, it is familiarly referred to
as the *OED* or the *NED,* and at times as *Murray's Dictionary,* because
the name of Sir James Murray, the general editor, appeared prominently
on the spine of the original volumes.

The project, which was first conceived as early as 1850, was in
motion by 1879, when preparation in its present form began. The first

volume appeared in 1884; the last in 1928. *The Supplement and Biblio-graphy* was issued in 1933. The exhaustive entries in this dictionary are based on more than 5 million quotations, contributed by hundreds of teachers and scholars in Great Britain and America. The *OED* is now available in three abridgments: a two-volume edition entitled *The Shorter Oxford English Dictionary,* a large one-volume edition called *The Oxford Universal Dictionary on Historical Principles,* and an essentially different one-volume, updated edition entitled *The Concise Oxford Dictionary of Current English.*

A comparable historical study of words as they have been used in the United States is *A Dictionary of American English on Historical Principles* in four volumes (1938–1944), edited by Sir William Craigie and J. R. Hulbert. Mitford Mathews' *A Dictionary of Americanisms* in two volumes (1951) adds further material to the total body of knowl-edge about English and American words.

Besides these dictionaries for specialists, there is a variety of other dictionaries that define words in Old English, Middle English, and Early Modern English. A number of dialect dictionaries also exist. A lengthy list of these by period is included in *A Bibliography of Writings on the English Language from the Beginning of Printing to the End of 1922* by Arthur G. Kennedy (1967). More recent additions may be found in Harold B. Allen's bibliography entitled *Linguistics and English Linguistics* (1966).

OTHER DICTIONARIES

In addition to the standard dictionaries, innumerable other vol-umes have been compiled on almost any specialty that one can think of. Such dictionaries, of course, provide more thorough coverage than any general dictionary of the language is able to. A selection of those that are especially helpful to the reader and writer of English are listed below:

Dictionaries of Usage

Bryant, Margaret M. *Current American Usage* (1962).

Evans, Bergen and Cornelia. *A Dictionary of Contemporary American Usage* (1957).

Follett, Wilson. *Modern American Usage* (1966).

Fowler, H. W. *A Dictionary of Modern English Usage* (2nd ed. rev., 1965).

Nicholson, Margaret. *A Dictionary of American-English Usage* (1957). Based on Fowler's Dictionary.

Dictionaries of Synonyms, Antonyms, Acronyms, and Abbreviations

Dutch, Robert A., reviser of *The Original Roget's Thesaurus of English Words and Phrases* (1965).

Goldstein, Milton. *Dictionary of Modern Acronyms & Abbreviations* (1963).

Hayakawa, S. I. *Modern Guide to Synonyms and Related Words* (1968).

Mayberry, George. *A Concise Dictionary of Abbreviations* (1961).

Webster's New Dictionary of Synonyms (1968).

Dictionaries of Etymologies

Klein, Ernest. *A Comprehensive Etymological Dictionary of the English Language*. 2 vols. (1966).

Morris, William and Mary. *Dictionary of Word and Phrase Origins*. 2 vols. (1962).

Onions, C. T. *The Oxford Dictionary of English Etymology* (1966).

Partridge, Eric. *Origins: A Short Etymological Dictionary of Modern English* (1963).

Shipley, Joseph T. *Dictionary of Word Origins* (1945).

Dictionaries of Slang, Idioms, and Clichés

Freeman, William. *A Concise Dictionary of English Idioms* (1952).

Partridge, Eric. *Dictionary of Clichés* (1950).

————. *A Dictionary of Slang and Unconventional English* (1961).

Weingarten, Joseph A. *An American Dictionary of Slang and Colloquial Speech* (1954).

Wentworth, Harold, and Stuart B. Flexner. *Dictionary of American Slang* (1967).

Whitford, Harold C., and Robert J. Dixson. *Handbook of American Idioms and Idiomatic Usage* (1953).

Wood, Frederick T. *English Prepositional Idioms* (1967).

————. *English Verbal Idioms* (1964).

Dictionaries of Foreign and Difficult Terms

Bliss, A. J. *A Dictionary of Foreign Words and Phrases* (1966).

Newmark, Maxim. *Dictionary of Foreign Words* (1962).

Pei, Mario. *Glossary of Linguistic Terminology* (1966).

————. *Language of the Specialists* (1966).

Trench, Richard C. *Dictionary of Obsolete English* (1958).

REFERENCE
RESOURCES

20

Units
of Discourse:
A Microgrammar

Discourse is a general term in the language for the communication of thought. No analysis of discourse would be possible without convenient terms for referring to elements of language that join together to form wholes. Such parts or divisions are the working terms of the language, not absolute truths, and therefore subject to different definitions and interpretations.

The most useful units for the discussion of discourse are the word, the phrase, the clause, the sentence, the paragraph, and the paragraph bloc. Each of these is a means of expressing some concept, each an increasingly larger unit. For everyday purposes, it is seldom necessary to refer to units smaller than the word, although the linguist is particularly interested in the subcategories and is seldom concerned about units larger than the sentence.

Words, because of their great number and variety, have been traditionally classified into groups called parts of speech. The categories are determined mainly in terms of inflectional features, the positions words ordinarily take in a sentence, and the functions they perform. Because some words are capable of assuming various positions and of doing different things, the parts of speech do not represent inflexible categories. Rather, they are concepts that help us understand the working of the language.

The eight parts of speech are the noun, pronoun, verb, adjective, adverb, preposition, conjunction, and interjection. These terms, closely associated with traditional grammar, have been retained for the most part by modern grammarians, although they have tended to group them under two broad and meaningful headings. The first group includes the form words, those identified by the inflections they show and the positions they take (nouns, pronouns, verbs, adjectives, and adverbs). The second group includes function words, those that are uninflected and therefore are mainly identified by their particular use and characterisic position (conjunctions and prepositions). Interjections are anomalous.

These two groups may be further contrasted by the exclusiveness they show. The form words are an open category; the function words are a relatively closed class. "Closed" means that all of the words may be cataloged, and users of the language show little tendency to add new ones to the list. On the other hand, "open" means that the category is undergoing constant change by the addition of new words and the shift of words from one part of speech to another. *Run,* for example, may be classified as a verb because it shows features of a verb and occupies typical verb positions, but it can also act like a noun if it assumes noun characteristics (*a run, running*) or occupies the position of a noun (*A run is invigorating*).

Modern grammarians have tried to define parts of speech exclusively in terms of form and function; nevertheless, usage tends to associate meaning with the words of particular categories—nouns with things, verbs with action, adjectives with qualities, adverbs with manner, and prepositions with direction, to mention only a few selected associations.

One of the most difficult tasks is to provide definitions for the working terms of the language because they often need to be explained in terms of one another. It is almost impossible to define the sentence usefully without reference to subject and predicate and to define these terms without reference to noun and verb. The following list of terms, therefore, is intended to provide only capsule definitions that depend mainly upon obvious examples to make their meaning clear, just as a mechanic might say, "This is a box wrench," without trying to define it or explaining its complications; or as a botanist might say, "Examine a leaf," without bothering to explain a term familiar to everyone. The following definitions do not take into account numerous irregularities and exceptions.

BASIC WORKING TERMS

Noun   A noun is a word like *car* or *class* that indicates its plural and possessive forms by inflection: (*cars, classes, car's class's; cars', classes'*).

Nominal   A nominal is a noun or any other word, phrase, or clause that can assume its position: the *cars* collided; *they* collided; *to push* is impolite; *what we thought* was trivial.

Pronoun   All pronouns are nominals: *I, you, he, we, they.*

Verb   A verb is a word like *collide* or *run* that shows differences between present and past time by inflection: *collide, collided; run, ran.*

Verbal   A verbal is a form of the verb that functions as another part of speech: The *driving* is strenuous (gerund as noun); *composed* a century ago, the song ... (participle as adjective); *to enter* was impossible (infinitive as noun).

Adjective   An adjective is a word that may be compared by inflection (*big, bigger, biggest*) or any other word that can occupy a typical adjective position: *beautiful* day, time *immemorial,* he is *famous.*

Adverb   An adverb is a word that is often marked by the suffix *-ly* (*confidently*), often compared by using *more* and *most* (*more confidently, most confidently*), but, not showing these characteristics, it can be tested in one of several typical adverb positions (we returned the books [*promptly*] or [*to the library*]).

Preposition   A preposition is a structure word or phrase like *to, from, at, across from, in front of.*

Conjunction   A conjunction is a connective like *and, but, when, because,* and *either ... or.*

Interjection   An interjection is an independent word or construction which has no special features or special grammatical function: *ouch, oh goodness, hi.*

Subject   A subject consists of a nominal and its modifiers placed in special relation to a verb, usually as its topic:

> *The two cars* / collided.
>
> *A steady rain* / fell.

Predicate   A predicate consists of a verb and its modifiers which act together as a commentary upon the subject:

> The two cars / *collided at the intersection.*
>
> A steady rain / *fell throughout the state.*

Sentence   A grammatical sentence is a group of words that divide into a subject and predicate:

> *The houses* / *showed signs of weathering.*
>
> *I* / *didn't give the idea much thought.*

Clause A clause is any combination of words that contains a subject and predicate. Some are independent, called sentences. Others are dependent, usually called subordinate clauses: *when he broke his glasses; if they were free.*

Phrase A phrase is a combination of words that acts as a single part of speech but does not contain both a subject and predicate as clauses do: *this envelope* (noun phrase), *on the floor* (prepositional phrase), *have been sleeping* (verb phrase).

Marker A marker is a word that helps to identify the words following it: *this* world (noun marker), *have been* helped (verb markers), *at* the circus (phrase marker), *if* he in doubt (clause marker).

Modifier A modifier is a general term for words like adjectives and adverbs that qualify in some way the meaning of other words: *a narrow* street; have been helped *significantly.* Or modifiers may take the form of phrases or clauses or other parts of speech that act like adjectives and adverbs (*adjectivals* and *adverbials*): ran *with determination;* a street *that was made of brick;* a *stone* fence.

Headword A headword is the word in any larger group that is modified: blue *sky,* exactly *two,* very *fiercely, drove* cautiously.

Antecedent An antecedent is an explanatory reference for another word: The freshmen read *Gulliver's Travels.* They found it more relevant than many current works. [*Freshmen* is the antecedent of *they; Gulliver's Travels* is the antecedent of *it.*]

Object An object is a noun or other nominal that completes the actor-action relationship of the subject and verb (The crowd gave a *cheer*) or serves as the goal indicated by a preposition (in *town,* at a *minimum*).

Complement A complement is a collective term to include (1) the object of a verb: I told a *joke;* (2) a noun in the predicate after the verb *to be* or other linking verbs: he was an *officer;* and (3) an adjective in the predicate after the verb *to be* or other linking verbs: he was *brave;* he seemed *modest.*

Appositive An appositive is a word or phrase that extends the meaning of another word of the same part of speech immediately preceding it and may act as its substitute: The orchestra played his favorite song, *"Tea for Two."*

Absolute construction An absolute construction is a collective term for any sentence modifier that is attached to a sentence but has no grammatical ties to any particular word in the sentence: *The tributes having been given,* the crowd dispersed.

For the paragraph and paragraph bloc, see pages 87–109.

21

Nouns

FEATURES OF NOUNS

1. Case

   Nouns show only one case by inflection. The genitive is commonly called the possessive case, but it also includes connections of various other kinds:

   Possession: my aunt's picture [one belonging to her]
   my aunt's picture [a likeness of her]
   Other relations: the committee's chairman
   a month's duration
   the film's perspective
   a lady's man

2. Number

   Nouns are either singular or plural in form. The most common way to show plural is to add *-s* or *-es* to the base words, but certain words have irregular plurals:

   Regular plurals: brick, bricks; church, churches
   Irregular plurals of
      Old English origin: mouse, mice; goose, geese
   Irregular foreign plurals: hypothesis, hypotheses;
   alumnus, alumni
   Singular and plural the same: Japanese, barracks,
   zebra, salmon

3.   Gender
Although gender is ordinarily associated with sex, grammatical gender has no necessary connection with it. In Old English, the word for *queen* was feminine, the word for *womanhood* masculine, and the word for *wife* neuter. Modern English nouns show no grammatical gender except for a few words referring to men that also have a corresponding feminine form in *-ess: host, hostess; actor, actress.*

Modern English may be said to follow natural gender in choosing pronouns to refer to nouns: *he* for *man* and *she* for *woman.* The exceptions are conventional: the tendency to refer to nature, boats, and countries as *she* or to refer to animals and babies as either *it, he,* or *she* when the sex is unknown.

4.   Markers
a. Function words: Nouns are preceded by determiners like *all, ten, his, a, an, the, this, these, that,* and *those.* The use of a determiner is in many cases optional. (See p. 429.)
b. Suffixes: Nouns are frequently marked by a characteristic group of suffixes, like *-ance, -ist, -ness,* and *-tion.* (See p. 352 for full list.)

KINDS OF NOUNS

1. Common and proper nouns
Common nouns are words that identify general categories of things without reference to a particular one: *river, university, philosopher.*

Proper nouns identify a particular member of a group by a name given especially to it: *Mississippi River, University of Washington, Nietzsche.* Proper nouns are capitalized.

The distinction between the two categories determines how they are customarily used. Proper nouns are almost never used in the plural and may often be used in the singular without determiners.

2. Mass nouns and count nouns
Mass nouns are general collective words like *fruit, water,* and *wheat,* not usually thought of in terms of numbered parts. In this sense, mass nouns are usually singular, although certain contexts may invite plural references, like *All wools are not sheep wool.* Mass nouns do not require determiners; thus, *Pepper is expensive.*

Count nouns are nouns that are thought of as separate units and can therefore be numbered when they are plural: *a staple, staples, five hundred staples.* In the singular, count nouns require determiners, thus *a desk, the desk,* but in the plural the use is optional: *Desks are scarce. The maple desks are particularly scarce.*

The way we interpret a noun affects the way we use determiners with it. Some words can be used either as count nouns or mass nouns. The use of the determiner changes accordingly.

Mass noun: We are studying film [art form].
Count noun: We saw a new film [a separate item].
Mass noun: Cereal builds muscles [collective sense as food].
Count noun: This cereal tastes good [a particular one].

3. Abstract nouns and concrete nouns
In terms of meaning, abstract nouns name qualities or ideas, like *interest, initiative,* or *justice,* which have no physical substance and therefore cannot be perceived by the senses.

Concrete nouns, in the same terms, name animate and inanimate objects, like *elephant, road,* and *flour,* which can be perceived by the senses.

Some words, like *man* or *animal,* can be used in either a generic sense (*Man is mortal*) or in a concrete sense (*That man is thin*). Many concrete nouns, like *treasure,* may also be used in a figurative abstract sense: *His book is a treasure of odd facts.* Transformational grammarians note that abstract nouns usually act as mass nouns and therefore use the determiner differently from concrete nouns, which usually act as count nouns.

4. Collective nouns
Collective nouns are plural in meaning but singular in form, like *audience, flock,* and *committee.* The inflection of the verb in a sentence can suggest whether a group acts as a single unit or as individuals within a group:

The jury votes as one [singular concept].
The jury were unable to agree [as individuals among themselves].

Since groups can be thought of in a plural sense, some collective nouns have plural forms, like *fleets* and *orchestras.*

Some like *corps* and *grouse* have the same form for the singular and plural. Words like *politics, data, people,* and *athletics* are plural in form, but may be singular or plural in use.

5. Nominals
    Nominals are words and structures that fill noun slots, but do not ordinarily show the characteristic features of individual nouns. Besides pronouns, treated in Section 22, nominals include infinitives, gerunds, phrases, clauses, and other parts of speech shifting from their usual function. All of these noun substitutes are evidence of the flexibility of the grammatical categories to accommodate expression. A selection of examples will illustrate:

As subject:
  1. The *best* didn't win. [adjective]
  2. *Running* is good exercise. [gerund]
  3. *Spading the ground* is hard work. [gerund phrase]
  4. *To run a mile* is tiring. [infinitive phrase]
  5. *From New York to Los Angeles* is a long drive. [prepositional phrase]
  6. *That we finish on time* was crucial. [clause]

As direct object of verb:
  1. They had their *ups* and *downs.* [prepositions or adverbs]
  2. I will teach *whatever book is available.* [clause]

As object of preposition:
  1. He went from *here* to *there.* [adverbs]
  2. He did everything except *wreck the car.* [infinitive phrase without the *to* expressed]
  3. He injured his shoulder by *swinging too hard.* [gerund phrase]

As indirect object:
  1. Tell *whoever arrives late* that we have gone. [clause]

As retained object:
  1. They were not told *what they should do.* [clause]

As subjective complement:
  1. The decision of the hearing was *that he was negligent.* [clause]

As appositive:
  1. The main point, *that he refused to come,* has been ignored. [clause]

USES OF NOUNS

1. Subject
    A noun is the model word for the subject of a sentence:

    The *tornado/* struck violently.

2. Direct object
    A noun may be used as the direct object of a verb or preposition:

    The tornado destroyed *homes* in its *course.*
    He led *them* a merry *chase* [double object].

3. Indirect object
    A noun may be used as indirect object after verbs like *give, make,* and *send.* The indirect object ordinarily precedes the direct object, with *to* or *for* implied after the verb:

    He sent [to] his *friend* a gift.

    When a sentence of this kind is transformed to passive voice, the object is retained:

    His friend was sent a *gift.*

4. Subjective complement (also called predicate noun or predicate nominative)
    A noun may be used in the predicate following the verb *to be,* certain intransitive verbs like *become,* or the passive construction of transitive verbs:

    Mr. Wilson is the *chairman.*
    Mr. Wilson became *chairman.*
    Mr. Wilson was elected *chairman.*

5. Objective complement
    A noun may be used to refer to the direct object as a way of completing the meaning of the predicate. The objective complement occurs only with certain verbs like *appoint, call, choose, elect, make, find, judge, keep, prove,* and *think.*

    We elected Mr. Wilson *chairman.*
    We considered him a fine *choice.*

6. Appositive
A noun may be used to complement the meaning of another noun immediately preceding it:

Mr. Wilson, *the chairman,* called a meeting.

7. Direct address
A noun may be used as a form of address:

Mr. Wilson, did you call a meeting?

USAGE NOTES

21A COLLECTIVE NOUNS Collective nouns are an exception to the general principle that a verb agrees with its grammatical subject (the form of a particular word), not its logical subject (the general idea). Deciding whether to use a singular or plural verb with nouns like *means, Cherokee,* and *sheep* is a logical decision. The choice will vary with the interpretation of the sentence:

The Cherokee were a people originally from the mountains of Tennessee and North Carolina.

The Cherokee was a tribe originally from the mountains of Tennessee and North Carolina.

21B PLURALS OF COMPOUND NOUNS Usage is divided on the plural forms of compound nouns: *mothers-in-law* and *maids-of-honor,* but *cat's-eyes* [the gems], and either *courts-martial* or *court-martials*. The dictionary gives all irregular plurals.

21C HYPHEN WITH COMPOUNDS Usage is divided on the use of the hyphen with compound nouns: *major general,* but *major-domo.* An up-to-date dictionary is the best source of information about the use of the hyphen or whether compounds of this kind are now written as one word, like *mousetrap.*

21D IRREGULAR PLURALS WITH NUMBERS Even though words like *foot, inch, gallon,* and *pair* have regular plurals, these plurals are frequently not used in idiomatic expressions with numbers: *a ten-foot ladder, a two-inch margin, a three-gallon bucket, four pair of socks,* but also the regular *four pairs of socks.*

21E PLURAL POSSESSIVES OF COMPOUNDS The possessive form of compounds in the plural is written by adding the apostrophe

and inflection to the end of the compound: *mothers-in-law's,
cat's-eyes',* and *courts-martial's.*

21F POSSESSIVES WITH -*ING* FORMS The use of the possessive with
-ing forms in the subject position causes no problem: *The President's coming is a special event.* The use of the possessive with
-ing forms in the object position, however, may be easily confused
with a construction consisting of a noun and a participle. The
two constructions are capable of different meanings:

> *Possessive with gerund:* We saw the boy's whipping [being
> whipped].
>
> *Noun plus participle:* We saw the boy whipping [doing
> the whipping].
>
> *Possessive with gerund:* We expected the President's com-
> ing [the event].
>
> *Noun plus participle:* We saw the President coming [the
> action].

Other uses, however, cannot be decided on the basis of meaning,
but only in terms of emphasis or rhythm:

> *Either:* The hope of man ending war is dim.
> *Or:* The hope of man's ending war is dim.

21G PERIPHRASTIC GENITIVES English shows the genitive relation
either by inflection or by a phrase beginning with *of,* called a
periphrastic genitive: *the story's end* or *the end of the story.* Some
idiomatic expressions combine both means: *a story of Poe's.* Awkward double possessives like *my sister's husband's brother* may
be rephrased more simply and clearly: *the brother of my sister's
husband.* Nonstandard dialects often omit the characteristic sign
of the genitive: *That's Nick boy* or *John old lady house.*

21H ABSOLUTE CONSTRUCTIONS A noun stands in the same relation to an absolute construction as the subject does to a sentence.
In fact, some absolute constructions may be considered transformed sentences, the noun of the phrase corresponding to the
subject of a sentence:

> *Two sentences:* The *car* stalled. We walked.
>
> *Transformation to
> a nominative absolute:* The *car* having stalled, we walked.

21I   CAPITALIZATION OF NOUNS Usage is often divided on the capitalization of nouns. Although proper nouns are capitalized and common nouns are not, usage is often divided because the distinction between the two is not always clear-cut. A few principles seem to operate, however:

   a.   When a word is used in a restricted sense, it is capitalized: *China, the country;* when its meaning is extended, it is not capitalized: *china, the pottery.*
   b.   The descriptive references of geographical names and organizations are usually capitalized: *Black Canyon, Howard Street, Democratic Party.* Informal usage, however, may drop the capital: *Black canyon, Howard street, Democratic party.*
   c.   Points of the compass when used as nouns are capitalized: *he grew up in the West.* When used as adverbs, they are not: *We drove west.*
   d.   University ranks are capitalized: *Freshman year, Senior standing.* The member of a class is not: *a sophomore* or *a junior.*
   e.   The names of specific courses are capitalized: *History 214, Introduction to Biology;* the names of the subjects are not: *history, biology.* The names of languages are capitalized, however, because they are proper nouns.
   f.   Second references to titles and names are capitalized only if the context makes the reference specific and clear:

   The Governor spoke.   [Previous reference would make
   We go to the University.   clear which governor and which
   university are meant.]

   References to the President and Constitution of the United States are customarily capitalized.
   g.   Capitalization of a noun to attach special meaning or effect to it is an optional matter of style, not one of established usage: *He believed in the idea of Universal Grammar.*

22

Pronouns

FEATURES OF PRONOUNS

1. Case
   Personal pronouns and the relative pronoun *who* show three cases by inflection: subjective, objective, and two different forms of the possessive or genitive. (See the paradigm on page 436.)

2. Number
   Most of the personal pronouns and the demonstratives (*this, these, that, those*) show singular and plural number by change of form. Other pronouns do not, although they may be singular or plural by implication, like *everyone, anyone,* and *none.*

3. Person
   Personal pronouns vary their forms by person, a feature that nouns do not show. Person indicates whether someone is speaking (first person, *I, we*), whether someone is spoken to (second person, *you*), or whether someone is spoken about (third person, *he, she, it, they*).

4. Gender
   The three forms of the personal pronoun in the third person singular distinguish between masculine, feminine, and neuter (*he, she, it*).

PARADIGM OF PERSONAL PRONOUNS

	SUBJECTIVE	OBJECTIVE	POSSESSIVE, FIRST FORM	POSSESSIVE SECOND FORM*
Singular				
1st person	I	me	my	mine
2d person	you	you	your	yours
3d person	he	him	his	his
	she	her	her	hers
	it	it	its	its
Plural				
1st person	we		our	ours
2d person	you		your	yours
3d person	they		their	theirs

RELATIVE PRONOUN WHO

who	whom	whose

ARCHAIC FORMS OF PERSONAL PRONOUN

thou	thee	thy	thine

ye (singular and plural, both subjective and objective)

---

* The second possessive form of pronouns is used both as a subject and as a complement in the predicate:

> *His* is the one on top.
> The coat on top is *mine*.

KINDS OF PRONOUNS

1. Personal pronouns
    Since pronouns have no independent meaning of their own, personal pronouns refer to beings and objects and assume the person and gender of the antecedent. Personal pronouns are a stable category; that is, it is not likely that new ones will be added, although a look at the history of the English language shows that the pronoun system has undergone a number of changes.

2. Reflexive pronouns and intensifiers
    Reflexive pronouns are combinations of the personal pronouns with *-self* or *-selves*. They are used to express a reflex action upon the subject:

He cut *himself.*
They blamed *themselves* for the accident.

The same forms are also used to intensify. The intensifiers are more movable within the sentence than the simple reflexives:

The topic *itself* is impossible.
I did it *myself.*

3. Indefinite pronouns
    Indefinite pronouns are indistinguishable by gender. They are consistently used for third person references: *all, another, any, anybody, anyone, anything, both, each, each one, either, everybody, everyone, everything, few, many, many a, much, neither, nobody, none, no one, one, other, several, some, somebody, someone, something.*
    Indefinite pronouns combined with *else* add *'s* to the end of the compound to form the possessive case: *anybody else's, everyone else's.*

4. Reciprocal pronouns
    Reciprocal pronouns combine various indefinite pronouns to suggest an interaction: *each other, one another.* Possessive forms: *each other's, one another's.*

5. Demonstrative pronouns
    Demonstrative pronouns have the special function of focusing upon something or pointing out. They show number: Singular forms: *this, that;* Plural forms: *these, those.* Their possessive must be expressed by a phrase with *of: The point of that is clear.*

6. Relative pronouns
    Relative pronouns introduce clauses that act as nouns or as modifiers. *Who, whom, whose, which, that,* and *what* are the simple relatives. All of these forms except *that* combine with *ever* to form additional relatives: *whoever, whosever, whichever, whatever.* The forms *whosoever, whichsoever,* and *whatsoever* are archaic.

7. Interrogative pronouns
    The interrogative pronouns *who, which,* and *what* and the

combinations with *ever* are identical with relative pronouns in form, but different in function. Interrogatives phrase direct questions:

> *What* is his name?
> *Whom* did the newspapers mention?
> *Whatever* could he have meant?

8. Numerals
   Both the cardinals (*one, two, three*) and the ordinals (*first, second, third*) may be considered pronouns in certain uses:

> *Two* are enough for me.
> The *sixth* was the hardest.

USES OF PRONOUNS

The personal, indefinite, and demonstrative pronouns share with nouns most of their uses as subject, direct object, indirect object, retained object, subjective complement, objective complement, appositive, and direct address:

> *Someone* must act quickly. [Subject]
> Did the fire cause *that?* [Direct object of verb]
> Most of *them* responded. [Object of preposition]
> He owes *me* money. [Indirect object]
> Thanks were given *us.* [Retained object]
> I know *who* you are. [Subjective complement]
> We made him *one.* [Objective complement]
> *Otello,* the *one* by Rossini, is less well known. [Appositive]
> Hey, *you!* Come here. [Direct address]

The reflexives, relatives, interrogatives, numerals, and reciprocal pronouns serve only a limited number of these uses.

USAGE NOTES

22A GUIDELINES FOR USE OF PERSONAL PRONOUNS

a. Personal pronouns agree with their antecedents in number, gender, and person, but their case is determined by their own function in a sentence:

Everybody had a locker to *himself.*
Everybody had *his* own lock.

b. Self-consciousness about correctness often leads to the mistaken notion that *I* is categorically more proper than *me,* whereas the object form may be both correct and natural, particularly when the object of a verb or preposition is compound:

Misuse: She told my secretary and *I* to take the day off.
Rephrased: She told my secretary and *me* to take the day off.

Misuse: Between you and *I,* I think he's wrong.
Rephrased: Between you and *me,* I think he's wrong.

c. The use of the subject form after the verb of being continues to be standard in written prose and is applied particularly when writing is edited. Thus, *it is I, it is he, it is we,* and *it is they* may be used quite unpretentiously when the context tends to be formal. However, the position of the subjective complement in the object position causes the object forms like *it's me* and *it's them* to predominate in speaking. These also now commonly appear in informal prose. Most people who are aware of the differences adjust their usage to suit the purpose and occasion of speaking or writing.

d. The use of *they, you,* and *it* as indefinite pronouns leads either to vagueness or redundancy in writing, although the pattern of expression is common in speech.

Vague: When I was in Paris, they said that hemlines were going to change again.
               In school, you weren't permitted to wear slacks.

*More
precise:*   When I was in Paris, dress designers said that hemlines were going to change again.
               In school, girls weren't permitted to wear slacks.

Redundant: On the form it says that the bill is due now.
More direct: The form says that the bill is due now.

e. Mentioning others before oneself is considered a form of polite expression: *Jim and I went fishing* instead of *I and Jim went fishing* or *Me and Jim went fishing.*

f. Constructions with *than* and *as* are sometimes shortened so that the case of the pronoun depends upon elements that are understood:

> He got a bigger raise than *I* [did].
> We like him better than [we like] *her*.
> She is as old as *I* [am].

g. *His* is accepted and preferred as a substitute for *his or her* when the sense is generic. *Their* is less often used.

> *Awkward:* Every person should sign *his or her* form.
> *Preferred:* Every person should sign *his* form.
> *Optional:* Every person should sign *their* form.

22B AGREEMENT WITH INDEFINITE PRONOUNS Indefinite pronouns cause considerable difficulty in agreement because their number may be doubtful, or usage may be changing. The following guidelines reflect common practices in making pronouns agree with antecedents and verbs with their subjects:

a. Clearly singular: *another, anything, each one, either, everything, many a, much, neither, nobody, no one, one, other, someone, something.*
b. Clearly plural: *both, few, many, several.*
c. Singular or plural depending upon the implication and depending whether they are used with mass nouns or count nouns: *all, any, each, none, some.*

> All of the land is ... [mass noun]
> All of the boxes are ... [count noun]

d. Changing usage: *Anybody, anyone, everybody, everyone,* and *somebody* are singular in form and take singular verbs, but because of their plural sense, informal usage has established the use of plural pronoun references to them: *Everybody took their seats.* The traditional usage, however, is no less natural: *Everybody took his seat.*

e. The number of pronoun phrases like *each of you, none of us, either of them, some one of you* depends upon the number of the head word:
> Either of them is an acceptable choice.
> None of us are going.

22C GUIDELINES FOR USE OF DEMONSTRATIVE PRONOUNS

a. Demonstratives are commonly used to refer to the entire idea of a previous sentence rather than to a specific word in that sentence. The use is acceptable when the meaning is unambiguous:

> *Ambiguous:*   Everyone has to work hard if we are not going to fail in this venture. This is what we really want.
>
> *Unambiguous:* Germany lost World War I. That explains much of the history of the next fifty years.

b. *This* and *that* are sometimes used as synonyms for *the former* and *the latter.*

c. *So* and *such* at times serve as demonstratives in the sense of *that:*

> I will be glad to do *so.*
> *Such* are the circumstances.

22D GUIDELINES FOR USE OF RELATIVE PRONOUNS

a. A relative pronoun does not itself show number, gender, or person, but, by connecting a relative clause to its antecedent, it determines the number, gender, and person of elements that follow it:

> *Pl.*   *Pl.*   *Pl.*
> Those *who* are willing to donate their services should sign now.

b. When the antecedent of a relative pronoun is either of two words, one singular and one plural, the number of the verb may vary with the writer's choice:

> He is one of those who are [is] constantly complaining.

Although the singular use appears in the writing of reputable authors, the weight of evidence favors the conservative use of a plural verb in a construction of this kind. The plural usage might be interpreted as follows: There are people who are complaining [a group classification]. He is one of them [the individual in relation to the classification]. The use of the singular verb might be considered more a matter of emphasis than of logic.

c. *Who* is characteristically used to refer to people and some animals, *which* to things and animals, and *that* to both beings and things. *Which* to refer to people (*Joe which was here*) occurs in nonstandard dialects.

d. Since *which* has no possessive form, *whose* has been established as an acceptable substitute for awkward constructions beginning *of which:*

> *Awkward:* The mountain, the top peak *of which* you can see now, is Mt. Rainier.
> *Preferred:* The mountain *whose* top peak you can see now is Mt. Rainier.

e. The relative pronoun may be often omitted:

> The car *which* I bought recently was stolen.
> *Omitted relative:* The car I bought recently was stolen.

f. *What* is frequently a simple substitute for more involved constructions like *that which, that of which,* or *the thing which:*

> *Stilted:* He was held at fault for *that of which* he knew nothing.
> *Rephrased:* He was held at fault for *what* he didn't know.

g. *Who* and *whom* hold more pitfalls for misuse than any of the other relative forms. Standard written English observes the distinction between subjective and objective cases when the pronouns are used as relatives or as interrogatives:

> *Who* is he?
> *Who* does he think he is?
> He is one person *who* should be invited.
> He is one pérson *who* I think should be invited.
> List the ones *who* you think should come.
> To *whom* did he refer?
> *Whom* did he refer to?
> He is a man *whom* everyone should know.

However, the subject position which the relative pronoun occupies has the force in speech of dulling case distinctions. In speaking, usage favors the general substitute of *who* for all uses of *whom* except in highly conventional phrases like *to whom it may concern.* This common practice now affects writing, even by respected authors, so that it is possible to observe a change going on now that may result in the ultimate reduction of *who-whom* to one form only.

h. *Than whom* is ungrammatical, but acceptable in such an idiomatic expression as *than whom none lived longer.* The phrase usually creates an awkward construction and is better avoided altogether.

22E NONSTANDARD FORMS

a. *-Self* and *-selves* combine with the first possessive form of first person and second person pronouns (*myself, yourself, yourselves*) and with the objective form of third person pronouns (*himself, herself, itself, themselves*). For this reason, forms like *hisself* and *theirselves,* which do not follow this pattern, are considered nonstandard.

b. The nonstandard forms *ourn, yourn, hisn, hern,* and *theirn* are formed by analogy with *mine.* The second possessive forms of these pronouns end in *s: ours, yours, hers, theirs. His* remains unchanged.

23

Verbs
and Verbals

FEATURES OF VERBS

1. Inflection
   Regular verbs show four forms: *help, helps, helping,* and *helped.* Irregular verbs like *sing* show five: *sing, sings, singing, sang, sung.* Other verbs like *can, ought, spread,* and *cut* may show fewer than four forms. The verb *be* shows eight. These forms differentiate the various uses of the verb.

2. Suffixes
   Some verbs are marked by typical suffixes like *-ate, -en, -ify, -ise,* and *-ze.*

3. Position
   Verbs have characteristic positions. A test of a verb is its ability to fill one or more slots in sentences patterned like the following:

   The novel ____ long. [*is, seems*]
   John ____ my brother. [*is, struck*]
   A man ____ the window. [*shut, washed*]
   The men ____ promptly. [*arrived, began*]

4. Person and number
    With the exception of the verb *to be,* verbs show person and number by inflection in the third person singular of the present and present perfect tenses only (*sees, is seeing, has seen*).

5. Tense
    Verbs have only two grammatical forms for showing tense: the simple present (*see*) and the simple past (*saw*). However, since the most characteristic way of thinking about time is in terms of present, past, and future, English expresses future time by means of phrases like *shall see* and *will see* or by the present or progressive forms of the verb: *I leave shortly; I am going tomorrow.*

6. Aspect
    Aspect is the property of verbs that extends their capacity to express many other time relations besides simple present, past, and future. These additional meanings include action occurring in the past and continuing (*has seen*), action completed at some past time (*had seen*), action to be completed by some future time (*will have seen*), action occurring in the present (*is seeing*), action repeatedly occurring (*keep singing*). All of these concepts are expressed by phrase structures. For convenience, *has seen, had seen,* and *will have seen* are called the perfect tenses (present perfect, past perfect, and future perfect). English, therefore, may be said to have six tenses. The *-ing* forms with a helping verb (*is seeing*) are called the progressive forms.

7. Voice
    Voice is a property of verbs that permits the verb to show whether the subject is acting (*he hates*) or is acted upon (*he is hated*). These are called active voice and passive voice. Since Modern English has no specific forms for expressing voice as Latin does, it depends upon verb phrases.

8. Mood or mode
    Mood is the capacity of verbs to indicate the manner of the speaker's expression. A verb may be indicative (expressing fact or inquiring about it), subjunctive (expressing condition, wish, or possibility), or imperative (expressing request or command). With the exception of the verb *to be,* subjunctive forms are identical with indicative forms except in the third person singular of the present tense of a verb (*if he see* instead of *if he sees*).

The changes of the verb by number, person, tense, aspect, voice, and mood may be set down in a complete arrangement called a *conjugation*. However, the same material can be indicated by a *synopsis,* that is, a conjugation in one or more persons. The following synopsis of the verb *to see* in the third person singular and plural summarizes the verb system:

<table>
<tr><td colspan="2" align="center">ACTIVE VOICE,
INDICATIVE MOOD</td><td align="center">PASSIVE VOICE,
INDICATIVE MOOD</td></tr>
<tr><td>Present</td><td>He sees</td><td>He is seen</td></tr>
<tr><td>Past</td><td>He saw</td><td>He was seen</td></tr>
<tr><td>Future</td><td>He will see</td><td>He will be seen</td></tr>
<tr><td>Present Perfect</td><td>He has seen</td><td>He has been seen</td></tr>
<tr><td>Past Perfect</td><td>He had seen</td><td>He had been seen</td></tr>
<tr><td>Future Perfect</td><td>He will have seen</td><td>He will have been seen</td></tr>
</table>

PROGRESSIVE FORMS

<table>
<tr><td>Present</td><td>He is seeing</td><td>He is being seen</td></tr>
<tr><td>Past</td><td>He was seeing</td><td>He was being seen</td></tr>
<tr><td>Future</td><td>He will be seeing</td><td>*He will be being seen</td></tr>
<tr><td>Present Perfect</td><td>He has been seeing</td><td>*He has been being seen</td></tr>
<tr><td>Past Perfect</td><td>He had been seeing</td><td>*He had been being seen</td></tr>
<tr><td>Future Perfect</td><td>He will have been seeing</td><td>*He will have been being seen</td></tr>
</table>

EMPHATIC FORMS

[Necessary for the formation of questions and negative constructions]

| Present | He does see [*Does he see? He does not see.*] |
| Past | He did see [*Did he see? He did not see.*] |

IMPERATIVE FORMS

See [*See what he is doing!*] Be seen [*Be seen less often here.*]

SUBJUNCTIVE FORMS

[If] he see   [If] he be seen

---

* Although the paradigm invites these constructions, they would be extremely rare in use, if at all possible.

KINDS OF VERBS

1. Finite and nonfinite

   Finite verbs are primary verb forms that show distinctions of person, number, tense, aspect, and mood. They therefore act as the focal word of the predicate. Nonfinite verbs include the gerund, participle, and infinitive, which show only some of the distinctions of finite verbs and cannot therefore stand alone as the verb of a predicate. (See verbals, pp. 453–454.)

2. Linking verbs or copulas
    Linking verbs are those that serve as a connection between a nominal in the subject and a nominal in the predicate (*He is a leader*) or between a nominal in the subject and an adjective in the predicate (*He is strong*). The verb *to be* is the most common linking verb, but a number of others can substitute for it: the sense verbs like *feel, look, smell, sound,* and *taste* and others like *appear, become, continue, grow, prove, remain, seem, stand,* and *turn.*

    > He *became* the leader.
    > The weather *continues* bad.
    > The future *looks* hopeful.

3. Transitive and intransitive
    Transitive verbs are those that have direct objects (She *gave* a dollar); intransitive verbs are those that do not (She *cried*). Most verbs can be used either transitively or intransitively:

    > They *produced* automatic weapons. [transitive use]
    > *The fields produced* heavily. [intransitive use]

    A few verbs like *arrive* and *lie* (to recline) are always intransitive. Transitive verbs are sometimes referred to as action verbs. The term is a technical one because some verbs in this category like *possess, receive,* and *owe* do not necessarily imply physical action. These verbs, however, like other transitive verbs, may take direct objects: *He possesses talent, He received a medal, He owes money.*

4. Auxiliary or helping verbs
    Auxiliaries are verbs that combine with other verbs to show tense, aspect, mood, voice, and various other degrees and manner of action. These include *be, can, could, dare, do, have, may, might, must, need, ought, shall, should, will,* and *would.*

    > *Expressing possibility:*   I can go.
    >   I may go.
    >   I would go.
    >   I could be going.
    >   I might be going.

Expressing obligation: I must go.
                                        I have to go.
                                        I ought to go.
                                        I have got to go.
                                        I should have gone.

Expressing emphasis: I did go.
                                        I dared to go.
                                        I do need to go.
                                        I will be going.

As these representative examples suggest, the auxiliaries and progressive forms permit the English verb to express a great number of highly refined and often subtle meanings beyond simple time relationships.

5. Regular and irregular verbs
    Regular verbs contrast the past tense and past participle from the base of the verb by adding *-ed* (*engage, engaged, engaged*). These three forms—the base, the past tense form, and the past participle—are called the *principal parts of a verb*. Irregular verbs are those that show variations, which have usually evolved from the earlier forms of these verbs in Old English. The irregular verbs fall into four main categories:

    a. Verbs whose past tense shows a change from the base but whose past participle is the same as the past form:

BASE	PAST TENSE	PAST PARTICIPLE
bend	bent	bent
bind	bound	bound
bleed	bled	bled
breed	bred	bred
bring	brought	brought
build	built	built
buy	bought	bought
catch	caught	caught
cling	clung	clung
creep	crept	crept
deal	dealt	dealt
dig	dug	dug

BASE	PAST TENSE	PAST PARTICIPLE
feed	fed	fed
feel	felt	felt
fight	fought	fought
find	found	found
flee	fled	fled
fling	flung	flung
grind	ground	ground
hang [a painting]	hung	hung
have	had	had
hear	heard	heard
hold	held	held
keep	kept	kept
lay	laid	laid
lead	led	led
leave	left	left
lend	lent	lent
lose	lost	lost
make	made	made
mean	meant	meant
meet	met	met
read	read [vowel change]	read
rend	rent	rent
say	said	said
seek	sought	sought
sell	sold	sold
send	sent	sent
shoe	shod	shod
shoot	shot	shot
sit	sat	sat
sleep	slept	slept
slink	slunk	slunk
speed	sped	sped
spend	spent	spent
spin	spun	spun
stand	stood	stood
stick	stuck	stuck
sting	stung	stung
string	strung	strung
sweep	swept	swept
swing	swung	swung
teach	taught	taught
tell	told	told
think	thought	thought
weep	wept	wept
win	won	won
wind	wound	wound

b. Verbs whose past participles add *n* or *en* either to the base or to the past tense form, at times with a slight variation in spelling:

BASE	PAST TENSE	PAST PARTICIPLE
be	was	been
bear	bore	borne
bite	bit	bitten
blow	blew	blown
break	broke	broken
choose	chose	chosen
do	did	done
draw	drew	drawn
drive	drove	driven
eat	ate	eaten
fall	fell	fallen
forsake	forsook	forsaken
freeze	froze	frozen
give	gave	given
go	went	gone
grow	grew	grown
know	knew	known
ride	rode	ridden
rise	rose	risen
see	saw	seen
shake	shook	shaken
speak	spoke	spoken
slay	slew	slain
steal	stole	stolen
stride	strode	stridden
swear	swore	sworn
take	took	taken
tear	tore	torn
throw	threw	thrown
wear	wore	worn
weave	wove	woven
write	wrote	written

Two verbs show a unique pattern. Like other verbs in lists a and b, they are derived from Old English strong verbs, but have evolved differently.

come	came	come
run	ran	run

c. Verbs that show a change of vowel in both the past tense and past participle. The short list below includes verbs that at present have no alternate forms in standard

usage. Additional verbs in this category that are undergoing change are listed under e:

begin	began	begun
fly	flew	flown
lie	lay	lain
ring	rang	rung
swim	swam	swum

d. Verbs that show no change in any of the principal
parts. They are called invariables: *bet, bid* [at auction],
*burst, cast, cost, cut, hit, hurt, let, put, set, shed, shut,
split, spread,* and *thrust.*

e. Most important is the list of verbs that are currently
undergoing change so that alternate forms are in use.
An examination of the list will suggest the kinds of
changes that typically occur. Naturally, a tendency
exists to regularize any verb that is irregular. Therefore, *ed* forms appear for the invariables (*rid, sweat*) and
for verbs that change vowels (*awake, thrive*). A second
kind of change by analogy is to make a regular verb irregular (*dove* for *dived* to correspond to *drive-drove*) or
to reduce the changes of vowel in the principal parts
from two to one (*sink, spring*). A number of the participial forms listed appear to be antiquated. Although
they may not be ordinarily used in forming the perfect
tenses, they are used in passive-voice constructions (*was
stricken, was shrunken*) and particularly as adjectives in
such expressions as *thinly clad waif, rough-hewn board,
badly swollen hand,* and *a sunken boat.* Other alternate
forms like *spat* and *bade* seem clearly dated and little
used. Up-to-date dictionaries attempt to record the
changes that usage has established over a period of time.
In many instances, it is difficult to estimate which form
might be more common.

BASE	PAST TENSE	PAST PARTICIPLE
abide	abode (abided)	abode (abided)
awake	awoke (awaked)	awoke (awaked, awoken)
beat	beat	beaten (beat)
bereave	bereaved (bereft)	bereaved (bereft)
beseech	beseeched (besought)	beseeched (besought)
bid [command]	bade (bid)	bidden (bid, bade)
bide	bode (bided)	bided
broadcast	broadcast (broadcasted)	broadcast (broadcasted)

BASE	PAST TENSE	PAST PARTICIPLE
chide	chid (chided)	chidden (chided, chid)
cleave [adhere]	cleaved (clove)	cleaved (clove)
cleave [split]	cleaved (cleft, clove)	cleaved (cleft, cloven)
clothe	clothed (clad)	clothed (clad)
crow	crowed (crew [Brit.])	crowed
dive	dived (dove)	dived
drink	drank	drunk (drank)
fit	fitted (fit)	fitted (fit)
forget	forgot	forgotten (forgot)
forecast	forecast (forecasted)	forecast (forecasted)
get	got	got (gotten)
heave	heaved (hove)	heaved (hove)
hew	hewed	hewed (hewn)
hide	hid	hidden (hid)
kneel	knelt (kneeled)	knelt (kneeled)
knit	knitted (knit)	knitted (knit)
light	lighted (lit)	lighted (lit)
mow	mowed	mowed (mown)
quit	quit (quitted)	quit (quitted)
prove	proved	proved (proven)
rid	rid (ridded)	rid (ridded)
saw	sawed	sawed (sawn)
seethe	seethed	seethed (sodden)
sew	sewed	sewed (sewn)
shave	shaved	shaved (shaven)
shear	sheared	sheared (shorn)
shine	shone (shined)	shone (shined)
show	showed	showed (shown)
shrink	shrank (shrunk)	shrunk (shrunken)
sing	sang (sung)	sung
smite	smote	smitten (smote)
sow	sowed	sowed (sown)
speed	sped (speeded)	sped (speeded)
spit	spit (spat)	spit (spat)
spring	sprang (sprung)	sprung
stink	stank (stunk)	stunk
strew	strewed	strewed (strewn)
strike	struck	struck (stricken)
strive	strove (strived)	striven (strived)
sweat	sweat (sweated)	sweat (sweated)
swell	swelled	swelled (swollen)
thrive	throve (thrived)	thriven (thrived)
tread	trod	trodden (trod)
wake	waked (woke)	waked (woke, woken)
wed	wedded (wed)	wedded (wed)
wet	wet (wetted)	wet (wetted)
work	worked	worked (wrought)

Other kinds of variants reflect the substitution of a *t* sound for the *ed* sound that we often make in speaking: *blent, blest, burnt, dreamt, swelt, gilt, girt, leapt, learnt, split,* and *spoilt.*

6. Verbals
   Gerunds, participles, and infinitives
   a. Gerunds: A gerund is an *-ing* form of the verb used mainly as a noun. It has both active and passive forms (*seeing, being seen*). It is identical with the present participle in form, but different in function. Even though a gerund functions as a noun, it retains characteristics of a verb: it conveys the notion of a verb; it can take an object; and it can be modified by adverbs:

   Gerund   Obj.   Adv.
   Counting money daily is a tedious job.

   Gerund Obj. Adv.
   He liked *driving* cars fast.

   b. Participles: Participles have a variety of forms in both active and passive voice:

ACTIVE VOICE		PASSIVE VOICE	
seeing	viewing	being seen	being viewed
seen	viewed		
having seen	having viewed	having been seen	having been viewed

   Participles function mainly as adjectives, either as single words (a *broken* glass) or as phrases (*Having given a toast,* he broke his glass.) Like gerunds, participles retain their characteristics as verbs: they also express the verb idea, take any kind of complement, and are modified by adverbs:

   Part.   Obj. Adv. Phrase
   Having no money at the time, he was forced to hitch-hike.

   The participal phrase *having no money at the time* modifies *he.* Participles also function within absolute phrases as modifiers of the noun:
   The argument *having ended suddenly,* we walked away.
   I turned sharply, my face *confronting his.*

c. Infinitives: Infinitives have active and passive forms:

ACTIVE VOICE	PASSIVE VOICE
to see	to be seen
to be seeing	
to have seen	to have been seen
to have been seeing	

Infinitives retain verb characteristics by taking complements and adverbial modifiers. They often combine with other verbs to form verb phrases: *decided to go, was said to have been recommended.* Infinitives may function as nouns, adjectives, or adverbs:

> *To be known* is *to be doubted.* [as noun, used as subject and subjective complement]
> They tried all forms of appeal except *to go* in person. [as noun, object of a preposition]
> They agreed upon a plan *to end the war.* [infinitive phrase as adjective]
> She was too angry *to object.* [as adverb]

Although *to* is the mark of the infinitive, it is omitted in some constructions:

> He helped [to] lift the piano. [optional omission]
> He need not [to] come. [obligatory omission]

USES OF VERBS

1. A finite verb acts as a predicate to the subject; that is, it indicates the speaker's intention to write a fully grammatical sentence. As the focal word of the predicate, all the thought of the sentence turns upon the verb. Without it, no comment could be made about the subject.
2. As the principal word of the predicate, the finite verb governs the kind of complements used in the predicate. If the verb is transitive, for example, it takes a direct object; if it is a linking verb, it takes a subjective complement.

USAGE NOTES

23A NEW VERBS Irregular verbs are a closed class; that is, the ones in the language can be listed and no new ones are being added. Regular verbs are an open class. Therefore, new verbs coming into the language form their principal parts by adding *-ed,* like *computerized, remediated,* and *dognapped.*

23B GRAMMATICAL LIMITATIONS OF VERBS Transformational grammar has been successful in demonstrating that verbs have performance limits, particularly in forming questions and negative statements with or without auxiliary verbs. The grammar allows only certain combinations, for example,

Does he understand?	*but not*	Understands he?
Is he sure?	*but not*	Does he be sure?
He does not understand the question.	*but not*	He understands not the question.
He is not here.	*but not*	He does not be here.

23C VERBS WITH SEPARABLE PARTICLES Verb constructions that on the surface appear to be the same may be quite different in the way they behave; for example, the two following sentences appear to be basically the same:

> He shouted down the stairs.
> He shouted down the crowd.

Yet, these two sentences divide differently:

> He shouted   down the stairs
> He shouted down   the crowd.

The second division indicates that *down* is a part of the verb and acts as a separable suffix that can be moved to another position in the sentence:

> He shouted the crowd down.

The verb in the first sentence, however, is intransitive; the prepositional phrase *down the stairs* is adverbial, telling where he shouted. The *down* cannot be moved to final position, and the sentence cannot be converted to passive. The second sentence, however, can be made passive:

> The crowd was shouted down [by him].

The passive transformation shows that the separable suffix stays with the verb. In the first sentence, *down the stairs* is a unit; in the second sentence, *down the crowd* is not.

Particles that are bound to verbs create new verbs with meanings of their own. The particles, however, are separable and movable. *Keep back* [restrain] has a meaning quite separate from the base word *keep,* and the particle is separate and movable. Combinations like *argue for, argue with, argue about,* and *argue against* are closely related in meaning to *argue,* and their particles are not separable or movable. In the first instance, the particle may be considered part of the verb itself.

23D NONSTANDARD USES OF THE VERB Many of the nonstandard forms of verbs may be accounted for by the tendency to regularize verb forms or to form them after the pattern of other verbs. Thus, the participle *swollen* gives rise to *swoll* as the past tense of *swell; snuck* as the past tense of *sneak* and *tuck* as the past tense of *take* are related to forms like *struck* and *stuck. Flang, swang,* and *wrang* as the past tenses of *fling, swing,* and *wring* imitate *sing-sang.* Irregular verbs treated as regular ones result in *knowed, blowed, runned, stinked, taked,* and *throwed,* common also in children's speech.

Other nonstandard forms of verbs, however, are less a matter of following a pattern as of following no pattern, giving rise to uses like *I sees, we was, he do, I taken it,* and *they boughten that.* Still other nonstandard uses result from the tendency to reduce the inflectional forms common to standard grammar. Thus, *s*'s, *es*'s, *ed*'s and other verb endings are omitted. Auxiliaries may be dropped from both statements and questions: *he goin' now* or *you do that?* In other instances, *been, done, done been,* and *ain't* are made to do general service for *has* and *have: done been finished, ain't been finished.* In like manner, *used to* substitutes for *formerly* in expressions like *used to couldn't* and *used to wasn't.* The use of auxiliaries as main verbs gives rise to *hadn't ought, might can,* and *might could.* Even though *might could, used to could,* and *ought to could* are generally considered nonstandard, they do appear commonly in the speech of educated southerners as dialect forms.

23E THE SUBJUNCTIVE It is common to say that the subjunctive is disappearing from English and that it remains only in set expressions like *Long live the king* and *Peace be with you.* This is true as far as it goes because the subjunctive has only a few forms that distinguish it from the indicative, and some of these like *if I be* and *though he were* sound archaic. It might be more accurate to say that the use of the subjunctive to express wish, condition, and doubt has been largely assumed by the auxiliaries *may, might,* *shall, should, will,* and *would* and by adverbial modifiers of the verb like *hopefully* or *perhaps.* In modern prose, *though he live* becomes *though he may live* and *if he go* becomes *if he should go.*

Despite this shift of function, the subjunctive still crops up naturally in a few sentences, particularly with verbs of saying, asking, and wishing and those that express condition contrary to fact:

> I asked that he *be excused* from gym.
> It is important that he not *be given* special consideration.
> I wish I *were* you.
> Even if she *were* to come now, she couldn't participate.

23F SEQUENCE OF TENSES The sequence of verb tenses within a sentence of some complexity is largely a matter of the speaker's natural sense of time. If the main verb is present tense, for example, any tense may logically follow:

> I realize that you are going.
> that you were going.
> that you will be going.
> that you have been going.
> that you had been going.
> that you will have been going.
> that you can be going.
> that you may be going.

If the main verb is past tense, past time imposes limits upon the sequence that follows:

> I realized that you were going.
> that you had been going.
> that you would be going.
> that you could be going.
> that you might be going.

If the main verb is future tense, the past forms are logically excluded:

> I will see you because I am going.
> because I will be going.
> because I have been going.
> because I will have been going.

The tense of participles is also governed by the verb of the main clause:

> *Present:* Now realizing what the problem is, we offer this solution.
>
> *Past:* Having realized what the problem was, we offered a solution.

23G CONSISTENCY OF TENSES In units of discourse beyond the sentence, writers ordinarily maintain an order of tenses consistent with natural time; that is, they use present tense forms for matters of the present and past tense forms for matters of the past. The writer's point of view establishes a time base for a series of sentences. If this base is present tense, he will maintain a sequence of tenses consistent with the present unless the thought recalls an event from the past. Then, logically, he turns to the past tense to narrate the past, only to return to the original present-tense base when the narration has ended.

Two exceptions are conventional. First, it is customary to write about any published document, particularly literary works, in the present tense, for example: *The Constitution says* ... or *In Walden,* Thoreau *writes.* ... Second, any writer may narrate past events in the present tense in order to add immediacy and color to his prose. This adjustment of point of view is referred to as the historical present.

23H DANGLING PARTICIPLES AND INFINITIVES Dangling participles supposedly violate a fundamental grammatical principle that adjectives or words that function like adjectives should modify specific nominals. Danglers either modify nothing or modify the wrong word. More important than the grammatical sin, however, is the uncertainty of meaning and the unintended humor that usually arises from the implied actor-action relation. The misuses can be corrected by simple rephrasing:

> *Dangling:* Getting into the car, the motor wouldn't start.
> *Rephrased:* Getting into the car, he couldn't start the motor.
> *Or:* When he got into the car, the motor wouldn't start.

> *Dangling:* Caught in the act, his excuses meant nothing.
> *Rephrased:* As he was caught in the act, his excuses meant nothing.
> *Or:* Caught in the act, he could not make his excuses convincing.

Dangling:	Having been told that he was out of order, the judge held the attorney in contempt of court.
Rephrased:	Having told the attorney that he was out of order, the judge held him in contempt of court.
Or:	Having been told that he was out of order, the attorney was held in contempt of court by the judge.

Since participial and infinitive phrases are transformed sentences, the best test of the dangler is to phrase it as a complete sentence supplying the proper agent. The test may reveal that the agent is not expressed. A sentence like

Feeling the tension strongly, a fight broke out

consists of two sentences:

He felt the tension strongly.
A fight broke out.

But *he* does not appear in the original sentence; the one who *feels* is unidentified. An analysis of this kind suggests two possible rephrasings:

Feeling the tension strongly, he started a fight.
A fight broke out because he felt the tension strongly.

It should be noted, further, that words like *considering, according, providing,* and *speaking* take on the function of prepositions rather than participles when they introduce phrases of a general or impersonal nature:

Considering the complications, the decision was the only one that could be made.
Speaking of fashion, a show is going to be held soon.

These particular phrases act as absolutes. Since mentioning the specific agent is not crucial to the meaning, they are not ordinarily considered dangling modifiers. Infinitive phrases also function in the same way as absolutes in highly idiomatic constructions that state generalizations:

To tell the truth, the boat should never have sailed.
To do this, it is necessary to have a strong rope.

Despite the existence of "acceptable" danglers, careful writers keep alert to those that are clearly unacceptable.

23I SPLIT INFINITIVES A firm denunciation of the split infinitive is a carryover of the grammatical tradition that consistently looked to Latin for models. The infinitive in Latin (*amāre*) cannot be split. The infinitive in English, however, must at times be split to express the writer's exact intentions:

> The agency was determined to deliberately spread subtle propaganda.

This sentence with a split infinitive is different in meaning and emphasis from any of the following:

> The agency was deliberately determined to spread subtle propaganda.

> The agency was determined deliberately to spread subtle propaganda. [ambiguous modifier in this sentence]

> The agency was determined to spread deliberately subtle propaganda.

Widely split infinitives, with several words inserted in between, appear to be forcing the issue of the split infinitive:

> He was inclined *to* sometimes but not always *tell* the truth.

The writer who splits all infinitives as a sign of rebellion shows as little good sense as the writer who avoids all split infinitives as a mark of virtue.

23J DOUBLE NEGATIVES The double negative is a construction with a respectable history, but no longer accepted in standard English as a device of emphasis. The tendency to attach the negative to the verb is strong. However, the usage is clearly nonstandard in a sentence like *Nobody won't do nothin'*. Expressions like *can't hardly, couldn't scarcely,* and *won't barely,* although commonly heard in speech, are inappropriate in writing. A combination of a negative with an adjective or adverb as a device of understatement is, however, an acceptable usage: *not infrequently, not wholly unsuccessful, not impoverished.*

23K AGREEMENT OF VERB AND SUBJECT Verbs agree with the grammatical subject of the sentence in number and person. At times, the grammatical subject may be singular, even though the thought is logically plural. A few constructions cause most of the problems in agreement:

a. Compound subjects take plural verbs whether or not the subject is inverted:

Music, theater, and art *are* grouped as the fine arts.
Both men and women *are* included.
On top of the buildings *were* TV antennas.

b. Compound subjects or plural subjects that express a unit idea take singular verbs:

Sears, Roebuck and Company *is* an established store.
My friend and neighbor *comes* over often.
Ten dollars *is* a good price.

c. Compound subjects expressing mathematical relations may be singular or plural:

One and one *makes* [*make*] two.
Six from twenty-one *leaves* [*leave*] fifteen.

d. Singular subjects joined by *or* or *nor* take singular verbs; plural subjects joined by the same words take plural verbs:

A freshman or sophomore *is* eligible.
Either freshmen or sophomores *are* eligible.

If one subject is singular and the other plural, the verb agrees with the nearer form:

Either the seniors or John *has* to do it.
Neither he nor other parents *want* the job.

e. Singular subjects joined by *and,* but introduced by *many a, such a, no, every,* or *each* take a singular verb.

Many an actor and actress *has* triumphed here.
No student and no faculty member *is* expected.
Every chair, table, and lamp *has* to be moved.

f. The agreement of the verb with a singular subject is not affected by any intervening phrase, even though the phrase seems to make the meaning plural:

One of my reasons *is* purely personal.

The scout leader, as well as the whole troop, *is* being honored.

He, not any of the substitues, *has* to be present.

The representative from the Soviet Union, together with the delegates from the satellite countries, usually *votes* negative on this issue.

g. The number of the verb may vary with the meaning of collective nouns (see p. 432) or of pronouns that are sometimes singular and sometimes plural (see p. 440).

The brood of chickens *were* scattered in the yard.
A brood of pigeons *tends* to be small.
None *is* correct.
None *are* more successful than he.

h. A verb of being agrees with its subject, not the complement following it, unless the subject is a *what* clause followed by a plural subject:

His mania *was* cameras.

Diplomatic relations between the United States and Japan *are* an interesting topic for discussion.

What concerns me most *are* the conditions they have to endure.

i. A verb of being introduced by *there* agrees with the subject following it:

There *are* many problems to be met.
There *is* no reason to be upset.

24

Adjectives

FEATURES OF ADJECTIVES

1. Comparison
   Some adjectives show three degrees of comparison—positive, comparative, and superlative—in either of three ways:

   a. By adding *-er* and *-est* to the positive stem: *heavy, heavier, heaviest; short, shorter, shortest.*
   b. By forming phrases with *more* and *most: meaningful, more meaningful, most meaningful; famous, more famous, most famous.*
   c. By using irregular forms:

bad	worse	worst
far	farther, further	farthest, furthest
good	better	best
little	littler, less, lesser	littlest, least
many, much	more	most
near	nearer	nearest, next
old	older, elder	oldest, eldest

   Some adjectives may be compared in two ways: *true, truer, (more true), truest, (most true). Common, bitter, happy,* and *lovely* also have double forms. Other adjectives like *optimum, foremost, innermost, main,* and *chief* are ordinarily used in only one degree.

2. Suffixes
    Adjectives may often be identified by typical suffixes like *-able, -ful, -ic, -less, -like, -ous, -some,* and *-wise* (see p. 352 for a more complete list).

3. Position
    Adjectives and words that function like adjectives may be tested by their ability to fill the typical adjective position between a *determiner* and a *noun:*

    > the *tall* building
    > a *bright* day
    > a *Tuesday* afternoon

    Adjectives, but not those words that function like them, may be modified by an intensifier like *very:* "very *tall,*" "very *bright*" but *not* "very *Tuesday.*" Most adjectives that fill the slot between the determiner and the noun will also complete the pattern of *determiner/noun/be/* ____: *the pretty house* or *the house is pretty.* A few adjectives like *main* and *chief* cannot be used in the second pattern: *the main reason,* but not *the reason is main.*

KINDS OF ADJECTIVES

The categories of adjectives are particularly important because some words function quite differently from others. The wide variety of words included under the general heading of adjective has prompted structural and transformational grammarians to discuss determiners as a separate part of speech, not as a subcategory of adjectives. When most people refer to the adjective, they commonly mean the descriptive adjective.

1. Descriptive adjectives
    Descriptive adjectives include all those words that represent the qualities of nominals: *ripe* peaches, *ingenious* writing, *comparative* literature.

2. Proper adjectives
    Proper adjectives are derived from proper nouns and retain

their capital letters: *Afro-American* movement, *Shake-spearean* glossary.

3. Adjectivals
   Adjectivals are those words and structures that fill adjective positions, but do not ordinarily show the characteristic features of individual adjectives. See also phrases, pages 489–490 and clauses, pages 491–492.

   > The room had a *brick* fireplace.
   > It was an *above-board* agreement.
   > Theirs was a *going* affair.
   > We had to attend a *morning* meeting.
   > The dog was particularly *high-strung*.
   > The spirit of the group was *you-name-it-we'll-do-it*.

4. Interrogative adjectives
   An interrogative pronoun in an adjective position functions as an adjective:

   > *Which* question are you answering?
   > *Whose* belongings are these?

5. Relative adjectives
   A relative pronoun in an adjective position functions as an adjective:

   > He will do *whatever* job has to be done.
   > He witnessed for the man *whose* wallet had been stolen.

6. Determiners
   The determiners are modifiers that do not show regular adjective features and tend to limit nouns rather than describe them. They may be classified by the manner in which they combine with other determiners and adjectives:

   a. Regular determiners, including

      > Articles: *a, an, the*
      > Demonstratives: *this, these, that, those*
      > Genitives: *my, your, his, her, its, our, their, car's, John's*
      > Indefinite adjectives: *all, another, any, both, each, either, every, neither, no, some*
      > Only one regular determiner may precede a noun.

b. Postdeterminers, including

Ordinals: *first, second, next, last*
Cardinals: *one, two, three*
Comparatives and superlatives: *more, most, fewer, fewest, less, least*
Indefinite adjectives: *few, little, many, much, other, own, several*

More than one postdeterminer may occur with a noun, but usually in a fixed order:

The *second most* admired athlete; *one last* man.

c. Predeterminers, including

Prearticles: *all, only, both, just*
  all the people
  both the keys
  just a joke

Regular determiners and postdeterminers plus *of: all of, some of, most of, the first of, just the last of*

Nouns of quantity plus *of: a slice of, a quart of, a piece of, a gallon of*

Predeterminers precede both regular determiners and postdeterminers when there are a number of modifiers:
  a gallon of that most delicious wine
  all the hundred other possible versions
  not one of her own three ancient Egyptian coins.

USES OF ADJECTIVES

1. General modifier
    The primary function of adjectives and other words, phrases, and clauses acting like them is to describe or limit nouns and pronouns. Besides their most typical position preceding the noun, adjectives may also follow immediately after the noun:

    Cherries jubilee is a treat *supreme.*
    The crowd, *noisy* and *milling,* shoved forward.
    The clerk *at the desk* apologized. [phrase modifying *clerk*]

The man *who could not stop coughing* finally left. [adjective clause, modifying *man*]

2. Appositive
   One adjective may be used to interpret another adjective, for which it can also act as a substitute:

   He assumed a paternal, that is, *authoritative* manner.

3. Predicate adjective
   Adjectives in the predicate which modify nouns or pronouns in the subject occur with three types of verbs:

   a. Verbs of being:

      He is *honest.*
      His check will be *good.*
      The photographs were especially *clear.*

   b. Other linking verbs:

      He looks *healthy.*
      The milk tastes *rancid.*
      She remains *inflexible* in her opinion.

   c. Certain transitive verbs in passive voice:

      The ceiling was painted *beige.*
      The game was played *fair.*
      The crew of the plane was found *dead.*

4. Objective complement:
   When sentences like those in 3c above are converted to active voice, the adjective becomes an objective complement, modifying the direct object:

   I painted the ceiling *beige.*
   He played the fame *fair.*
   The rescue party found the crew of the plane *dead.*

USAGE NOTES

24A ARTICLES The old school rule which says, "Use *a* before consonant sounds, and *an* before vowel sounds" is still the surest guide to the use of *a* and *an: a sweater, a jacket, an onion, an African.*

The distinction, however, is made upon *sound,* not spelling. In certain contexts, the degree of stress or the degree of elision may alter the choice of *a* or *an.* Certain speakers say *a history course,* but *an historical event; a humiliating experience,* but *an humble man.* Words like *usury* and *eugenics* that are spelled with beginning vowels are actually pronounced with consonant sounds.

Both *a* and *an* come from an Old English word meaning *one* and are still used only with singular nouns. *The* was originally a form of the Old English demonstrative pronoun and combines with both singular and plural words. In current usage, *the* still retains its demonstrative quality. Compare *the man,* for example, with *any man. A* and *an* are called indefinite articles; *the* is a definite article. The distinction between them determines their use with certain kinds of nouns (see p. 429).

Articles are sometimes used irregularly with proper nouns for special effects:

We are fortunate to have the Mr. Nixon present.
A Mr. Jones is here.

24B AGREEMENT OF DEMONSTRATIVE AND NOUN Words like *kind, sort,* and *type* invite errors in agreement between the number of the demonstrative and the number of the noun, particularly if the noun is followed by a prepositional phrase. Expressions like *these kind of conductors* and *those sort of games* are commonly heard in speech. Standard English holds to an exact agreement: *that kind* and *those kinds; this type* and *those types.*

24C NONSTANDARD USES OF THE ADJECTIVE The use of *this here* and *them there* in nonstandard dialects as substitutes for *this* and *those* shows a tendency to invent a kind of emphatic demonstrative. Double comparisons (*more better, most ugliest*) are now considered strictly nonstandard, in the same category as inflected adjectives that are usually compared with *more* and *most* (*wonderfullest* time, *dancingest* kid, *lovinger* child) or irregular forms that are compared regularly (*worser*). Expressions like *Give me chair* for *Give me a chair* or *Give me some cashes* for *Give me some cash* show departures from the standard use of determiners with count nouns and mass nouns.

24D ABSOLUTE ADJECTIVES An absolute adjective is one that does not lend itself to comparison. Adjectives like *prior, daily,* and *principal* present no problem, but words like *equal, essential, unique, round, perfect,* and *black* are subject to divided usage.

Phrases like *more nearly perfect* or *almost round* are precise ways of preserving the absolute meaning of these terms, but usage among reputable writers has established *more perfect, more round,* and *blackest black* as acceptable ways of expressing relative degrees that are less than absolute. Nevertheless, the comparison of absolutes remains a taboo among many persons. The writer, therefore, has to consider his audience and the formality of his writing in deciding upon usage.

24E COMPARISONS Some comparisons are left incomplete because the context makes clear what the implication is and completing it would only add unnecessary words. An advertisement that reads "Oldsmobiles cost less at Richie Center" means that they cost less there than at any other Oldsmobile dealer in town. The full statement would sound pedantic. Phrases like *better stores* and *higher prices* are commonly used without completing the comparisons.

The use of *any other* indicates that things of the same class are being compared; the use of *any,* that things of a different class are being compared:

> My aunt thinks she can cook better than any other woman.
> My nephew thinks he can cook better than any woman.

The doubling of a comparison may be expressed in either of two ways:

> He is as old as, if not older, than I am.
> He is as old as I am, if not older.

A third version occurs in standard English, but shows less regard for exactness:

> He is as old if not older than I am.

24F COORDINATE ADJECTIVES Adjectives that show an equal relation to the noun they modify are considered coordinate and are separated from one another by commas:

> a perceptive, concise, interestingly presented speech.

In a phrase like *the warped kitchen cabinet,* however, *warped* and *kitchen* are not coordinate. *Kitchen cabinet* is the equivalent of a single word, modified by *warped.* The most common test is to see whether *and* can be inserted between coordinate adjectives and still have a natural sounding phrase: *a perceptive* and *concise* and *interestingly presented speech,* but not *the warped* and *kitchen cabinet.* Similar phrases also illustrate that the modifiers are not coordinate:

> an elegant walking stick
> a fast running jump
> an irritating old man.

The ability to distinguish between adjectives that are coordinate and those that are not solves a number of punctuation problems.

24G DANGLING MODIFIERS Adjective phrases attached to a misleading reference need rephrasing:

> *Misleading:* Grateful for any favor, a wave showed his appreciation.
> *Rephrased:* Grateful for any favor, he showed his appreciation with a wave.

> *Misleading:* At the age of three, my father taught me to swim.
> *Rephrased:* When I was three years old, my father taught me to swim.

See also Dangling Participles, page 458.

25

Adverbs

FEATURES OF ADVERBS

1. Inflection
    Adverbs do not show identifiable features of inflection as do
    nouns, pronouns, verbs, and adjectives. They are identifiable
    mainly by their position in a sentence.

2. Comparison
    Many adverbs, like adjectives, show three degrees of compari-
    son, formed by the use of *more* and *most: promptly, more
    promptly, most promptly.* A few adverbs like *slow, fast, quick,
    loud, early, right,* and *deep* have two forms, one of them iden-
    tical with the adjective form: *slowly, more slowly, most slowly*
    or *slow, slower, slowest. Soon* also compares in two ways, but
    it is always an adverb.

3. Suffixes
    The most characteristic adverb suffix is *-ly,* although every
    word ending in *-ly* is by no means an adverb (see p. 352 for
    a more complete list).

4. Position
    The adverb is the most movable part of speech, even though
    it has constraints upon its placement. An adverb may come

before the subject, after the subject, after the verb, or occupy a number of other positions depending upon the word it modifies:

> *Then* I made an announcement.
> I *then* made an announcement.
> I made an announcement *then.*
> I *also* made an *equally* important announcement.
> I adjourned the meeting *very abruptly.*

A phrase, clause, or another part of speech that can fill an adverb position is referred to as an adverbial.

KINDS OF ADVERBS AND ADVERBIALS AND THEIR USES

Because of the great variety of adverbs, they are best grouped by meaning and by use. The two categories, of course, overlap.

1. Classified by meaning:

   a. Adverbs of time: *immediately, today, ago, now, again, always, by and by, forever,* and other words and phrases answering "when."

   b. Adverbs of place: *here, there, everywhere, inside, forward, downward,* and other words and phrases answering "where" or "in what direction."

   c. Adverbs of manner: *maybe, possibly, apart, happily, particularly, not, never, only,* and other words and phrases answering "how" or "to what degree." *Extremely, quite, rather, somewhat, too,* and *very* serve as special intensifiers of the words they modify.

2. Classified by use:

   a. As modifiers of verbs, adjectives, and other adverbs:

      > He read *thoughtfully.* [modifies the verb *read*]
      > He read *very* thoughtfully. [modifies the adverb *thoughtfully*]
      > His *particularly* thoughtful reading drew applause. [modifies the adjective *thoughtful*]

b. As sentence modifiers:

> *Yes,* I know what is wrong.
> *Conceivably,* the policies of the government may change.
> *Arm in arm,* they paraded through the streets.
> *Several hours ago,* we would have welcomed the chance.

c. As sentence connectors (see list of conjunctive adverbs, p. 484):

> You can cross the border; *however,* you have to be checked.
> We had extra money; we *therefore* stayed longer.
> He enjoyed himself. *In fact,* he acted without restraint.

d. As appositives:

> They came home extremely late, *at 3:00* A.M.
> The job was done accurately—*with utmost precision.*

e. As interrogatives:

> *How* did you get along?
> *Where* is the game?

f. As clause markers (relative adverbs)

> I didn't know *when* to get off.
> This is *where* the battle was fought.

g. As correlatives:

> *The harder* we tried, *the less* we accomplished.
> *The sooner* we know, *the better.*

h. As idiomatic particles with verbs:

> We looked *over* [scanned] the document.
> He is going to try to hold *out* [endure].

Nearly all one-word prepositions like *in, to, up, down,* and *beneath* may also be used as adverbs. The forms are the same, but the function and often the meaning are different:

She / jumped *at* / the chance. [adverb, combining with *jump* to mean "accept eagerly"]

She / jumped / *at* the Olympics. [preposition, introducing phrase]

He / was driven *to* / madness. [adverb]

He / was driven / *to* the city. [preposition]

i. As adverbials: Nouns in adverb positions that express ideas of time, place, manner, or degree function as adverbs:

One *year* we had rain continuously for two days.
He went *home*.
The sweater costs ten *dollars*.

USAGE NOTES

25A PLACEMENT OF ADVERBS The placement of the adverb is often a device for giving emphasis to a particular word or thought in a sentence. The writer, therefore, has to be aware of interpretations differing from his own and varying degrees of emphasis that are possible. Compare the differences of the following sentences:

He *just* nodded to me as I was about to get up. [emphasis upon the manner, possibly suggesting that the nod was given in a grudging way]

He nodded to me *just* as I was about to get up. [emphasis upon the timing and simultaneous action]

He stopped *only* to say hello. [emphasis upon the shortness of the greeting]

He *only* stopped to say hello. [emphasis of above sentence lost, no new emphasis gained]

As a general principle, adverbs should be put as close as possible to the words they modify. In certain contexts, however, adverbs may seem to modify either of two constructions. Because they look in two directions, they are called squinting modifiers:

Squinting: The new play that we hoped to support *completely* disappointed us.

Moving the adverb clarifies either of two meanings:

> The new play that we hoped to *completely* support disappointed us.

> The new play that we hoped to support disappointed us *completely*.

In speech, adverbs tend to move forward in sentences. Thus, we commonly hear:

> He *just* plays golf on Tuesday.
> The boss *only* fired two men.

These sentences would be more emphatic, particularly in writing, if they read:

> He plays golf *just* on Tuesday.
> The boss fired *only* two men.

The same tendency to move the negative *not* forward in the sentence is acceptable in both speaking and writing. *I don't believe he is honest* is the equivalent of *I believe he isn't honest.* Compare also the greater naturalness of *He is not interested in painting but in sketching* as opposed to *He is interested not in painting but in sketching.*

25B CONFUSION OF ADVERBS AND ADJECTIVES Ordinarily a word ending in *-ly* can be identified as an adjective instead of an adverb if it can be compared by inflection. Thus, *homely, homelier, homeliest* and *lowly, lowlier, lowliest* are adjectives, but *merely* and *badly,* which cannot be compared in this way, are adverbs. Confusion, however, occurs in actual usage. Adjectives and adverbs have separate uses in the following sentences:

a. Adverbs, not adjectives, modify verbs:

> I was driving along pretty *steady.* [colloquial use of adjective]
> I was driving along pretty *steadily.* [standard use of adverb]

b. Adverbs, not adjectives, modify adjectives and other adverbs:

> She seemed *terrible* upset. [colloquial use of adjective]
> She seemed *terribly* upset. [standard use of adverb]

He acted *awful* strange. [colloquial use of adjective]
He acted *awfully* strange. [standard use of adverb]

Most always we go on Mondays. [colloquial use of adjective]
Almost always we go on Mondays. [standard use of adverb]

c. Complements referring to the subject after special linking verbs take adjectives, not adverbs (see also predicate adjective, p. 467):

I feel *badly*. [misuse of adverb after *feel*]
I feel *bad*. [correct use of adjective]

He looks *good*. [correct use of adjective after *looks*]
He looks *well*. [correct use. *Well* is both an adjective and an adverb; here it is used in its adjective sense of "in good health."]

26

Prepositions

FEATURES OF PREPOSITIONS

1. Forms
   Prepositions show no identifiable features of form. They are uninflected. They have no characteristic suffixes. The simple prepositions may be listed, but some of these are identical with adverbs and conjunctions. Prepositions therefore may be identified primarily by their position and function. Some grammarians have stressed the functional features of prepositions completely at the expense of their meaning. If prepositions had no meaning, any one of them might logically substitute for any other. Those that express spatial relations most clearly have meaning. *Above* means something quite different from *below* and *around;* and *in, on,* and *by* express relative positions. A failure to recognize the meaning of prepositions is a failure to recognize the subtle differences they are capable of expressing.

2. Position
   The most typical position of the preposition occurs before a nominal which is its object: *of* distant places, *beneath* the surface, *except* two, *by* him. Prepositions are also used idiomatically with adjectives.

477

Following adjectives: antagonistic to
                          deficient in
                          symbolic of

In almost all instances, prepositions occupy positions that receive weak stress in speech, unless they are deliberately distorted for emphasis.

KINDS OF PREPOSITIONS

1. Simple forms
   The most commonly used prepositions are *of, on, to, at, by, for, from, in,* and *with.* Other familiar prepositions are *about, above, across, after, against, around, before, behind, below, beneath, beside, between, beyond, down, during, except, following, like, near, off, opposite, out, over, through, toward, under, until,* and *without.* The total list numbers about sixty.

2. Compound forms
   The simple forms combine with each other and with other words to form various other possibilities: *according to, because of, by means of, due to, except for, in addition to, in front of, in spite of, instead of, on account of, with regard to.*

USES OF PREPOSITIONS

1. The preposition is a structure word. It usually introduces a phrase, which acts as a single part of speech, usually an adjective or adverb, and connects the phrase with another word in the sentence:

   > He demonstrated the differences *between individual and group thinking.* [adjective use of phrase, modifying *differences*]

   > The cities are full *of people.* [adverbial use, modifying *full*]

   > The budget has been reduced *to its minimum.* [adverbial use, modifying *has been reduced*]

2. The prepositional phrase with *of* is an alternate way of expressing genitive relations: a third *of the group,* the top *of the building,* the collar *of my shirt.*

USAGE NOTES

26A IDIOMATIC USE OF PREPOSITIONS The choice of idiomatic prepositions with nouns, adjectives, and verbs causes considerable difficulty even for native speakers, and the dictionary provides no help in interpreting the differences between *resemblance between, resemblance of,* and *resemblance to* or *agree to* and *agree with.* In most instances, a context will help; but, in stubborn cases, dictionaries of prepositional and verbal idioms are available (see p. 419).

26B IDIOMATIC USE OF PREPOSITIONS IN COMPOUND EXPRES-SIONS In compound expressions with a suspended object, one of the prepositions is often dropped, particularly in speaking:

> *Omitted* We were interested and anxious for a change.
> *preposition:* [*for* is not an idiomatic preposition with *interested*]

> *Rephrased:* We were interested in and anxious for a change.

> *Or:* We were interested in a change, and anxious for it.

If two words combine with the same preposition, the preposition does not have to be repeated.

> *Acceptable:* We were anxious and agitating for a change.

26C CONFUSION OF PREPOSITIONS AND CONJUNCTIONS *But, for, after, since,* and *before* function as prepositions and also as conjunctions. Even though the forms are identical, the uses and positions make clear the differences. Conjunctions, for example, are seldom used at the end of a sentence unless the sentence is elliptical.

> I was vaguely hopeful, *but* not optimistic. [conjunction connecting two adjectives]

> I could do nothing *but* hope. [preposition in the sense of *except* with the infinitive [*to*] *hope* as object]

> Here is a new collar *for* the dog. [preposition]

> He protested, *for* it was the thing to do. [conjunction]

Even though *for* is very close in meaning to *because,* the part of the sentence beginning with *for* cannot be moved to first position as it could be if *because* were substituted.

26D USES IN SPEAKING AND WRITING Two opposite tendencies occur in speaking. One is to add more prepositions than are absolutely necessary. The other is to omit them when they occur in positions of light stress. It is easy in speech to pile up prepositions in expressions like *get off of into* or *lying outside down underneath.* Revised versions of these in writing would omit at least one of the prepositions without any sacrifice of meaning.

The omission of the preposition in speech is particularly common in certain expressions: *a quart milk* instead of *a quart of milk; a slice bacon* instead of *a slice of bacon.* An expression like *What size shoe do you wear?* is completely idiomatic, and *a couple minutes ago* is wholly as acceptable as *a couple of minutes ago. He came Monday* is also standard for *He came on Monday.* Clearly, many of the common prepositional structures are undergoing change. Omitting the preposition in writing except for the clearly idiomatic expressions is always a questionable usage. Certainly, using the preposition would be playing safe.

26E PREPOSITION AT THE END OF A SENTENCE One of the most carefully preserved bits of folklore in usage is the old taboo about not putting a preposition at the end of a sentence. Normally, because prepositions introduce phrases, they don't come at the end of a sentence anyway. But what does come at the end of a sentence very naturally is a preposition used with a verb (or it may be an adverb form identical with it), particularly if the sentence is a question:

What are you waiting for?

To say or even write "For what are you waiting?" is an affectation. And this kind of cultivated usage often leads to worse blundering—saying the same thing twice:

Here is the place *to* which he was going *to.*
This is a matter *of* which I was speaking *of.*

Of course, thinking that the preposition at the end is always a virtue is as wrongheaded as believing that it is a sin. At times, a preposition is left dangling ineffectually at the end:

It is one of the things which he was willing to give his faithful and undying attention *to*.

This particular sentence might possibly be strengthened by moving the particle forward:

It is one of the things *to* which he was willing to give his faithful and undying attention.

In most instances, a writer will do best to follow his natural sense of word order and then revise only if there is a change he really cares about.

27

Conjunctions

FEATURES OF CONJUNCTIONS

1. Forms

   Conjunctions, like prepositions, show no identifiable features of form. They are uninflected. They have no characteristic suffixes. A complete list of conjunctions would be a relatively short one, and the language shows little tendency to add new ones. Although the definition of a conjunction as a structure word duplicates that of the preposition, the two perform quite different structural functions.

2. Position

   Their position depends both upon the kind of conjunction they are and upon their function in relation to other words in the sentence. Conjunctions that introduce, like subordinating conjunctions, obviously occupy an initial position in a phrase or clause (*because* we are leaving). Conjunctions that join are ordinarily medial (brown *and* white), although some writers as a stylistic choice prefer to use a conjunction joining two sentences as the first word of a new sentence:

   We could give up. *Or* we could die fighting.

   Conjunctions may therefore occur at variously defined positions in a sentence except the final position, unless the conjunction is left as the final word in an elliptical sentence.

KINDS OF CONJUNCTIONS

1. Coordinating conjunctions
   Coordinating conjunctions connect words, phrases, dependent clauses, and complete sentences. The most commonly used coordinators are *and, but, or,* and *nor.* A few others, like *for, yet,* and *so,* may also be considered coordinating conjunctions. Each of the four main connectives acts differently: *and* is the only conjunction that joins in the sense of "adding to"; *but* excludes or contrasts; *or* and *nor* provide alternatives.

2. Subordinating conjunctions
   Subordinating conjunctions introduce dependent clauses. Even if the clause stands in first position, the subordinating conjunction acts as a connective by defining the relationship between the clause and the remainder of the sentence. Several categories suggest the range of these relationships:

   Cause: because, in that, since
   Condition: if, although, unless
   Manner: as, as though
   Result: in order that, so that
   Time: after, before, since, until, when, whenever, while

3. Correlative conjunctions
   Correlative conjunctions are connectives that are typically used in pairs. The common ones are *either ... or, neither ... nor, both ... and, not only ... but also, so ... as,* and *whether ... or.*

4. Conjunctive adverbs
   Conjunctive adverbs are transitional adverbs and phrases used to express relations between two units of discourse. They are most commonly used between complete sentences, although they may also be used to join paragraphs. In joining sentences, the conjunctive adverb does not need to be placed at the exact point of transition; it may be moved to other positions in the sentence:

   Joe is stubborn; therefore, he hears only what he wants to hear.

   Joe is stubborn; he therefore hears only what he wants to hear.

   Joe is stubborn; he hears only what he wants to hear, therefore.

Conjunctive adverbs may be grouped in terms of their function:

Addition: also, too, furthermore, likewise, moreover, besides, in fact, likewise

Emphasis: indeed, that is to say, to be sure

Discrimination: however, nevertheless, anyway, on the contrary, on the other hand

Illustration: namely, that is, for example, for instance, by way of illustration

Conclusion and result: accordingly, consequently, hence, so, therefore, thus, as a result

Time and space: first, second, then, later, finally, in conclusion, at the top, further on.

5. Other connectives
The classification of conjunctions could be extended greatly by including all other words that act as phrase and clause markers and thus also as connectives. In this collective sense, relative pronouns, relative adjectives, relative adverbs, and prepositions might be included.

USES OF CONJUNCTIONS

As connectors and transitionals, conjunctions serve as one of the major devices for order and coherence in prose. The relations they signal provide a structure for clear communication. The way they are used, misused, or overused influences the whole matter of style.

USAGE NOTES

27A GUIDELINES FOR USE OF COORDINATING CONJUNCTIONS
Coordinating conjunctions imply a principle of use by their name. They connect units of the same rank—pronouns with pronouns, participles with participles, clauses with clauses. Mixtures result in sloppy prose:

Lacking coordination: Having been harangued and because we were tired of fighting, we came to a compromise.

Rephrased: Because we had been harangued and because we were tired of fighting, we came to a compromise.

More concise phrasing, but still coordinate: Because we were tired and harangued, we came to a compromise.

Careful choice of the conjunction may be a way of adding emphasis or a special discrimination of meaning. Compare the differences between the following pairs of sentences:

He studies *and* he doesn't get good grades.
He studies, *but* he doesn't get good grades.

She is never quiet, always talking *and* singing.
She is never quiet, *either* talking *or* singing.

27B GUIDELINES FOR USE OF CORRELATIVES Correlative conjunctions, like coordinating conjunctions, join elements of equal rank. A basic principle of use is to place the correlatives as close to the words they join as possible:

Misplaced: Either I must *send* a telegram or *make* a long distance call.
Rephrased: I must either *send* a telegram or *make* a long distance call.

Misplaced: Not only is she *bright,* but *pretty* too.
Rephrased: She is not only *bright* but *pretty* too.

Neither ... nor is the negative equivalent of *either ... or. Or* is not an acceptable substitute for *nor* after *neither,* although it may follow other negatives:

I got *neither* money *nor* glory.
I got *no* money *or* glory.

27C OMISSION OF CONJUNCTIONS The use or omission of conjunctions in a series is a stylistic difference, not a matter of grammar:

Omission of connectives: The garden was an array of spring flowers—crocuses, daisies, peonies, carnations, iris, lilies-of-the-valley, lilac.

Varied use of connectives: The garden was an array of spring flowers—crocuses and daisies and peonies, carnations, iris, lilies-of-the-valley, and lilac.

27D AMBIGUITY WITH "AS WELL AS" and "WHILE" Constructions with *as well as* invite ambiguity. *Lily sang the role as well as Joan* means either that the singing of one soprano is as good as that of the other or simply that they both sang a particular part. Rephrasing resolves the ambiguity:

Lily sang the role equally as well as Joan.
Lily and Joan sang the role equally well.
Lily sang the role; Joan did too.
Both Lily and Joan sang the role.

While may express concession or time. The ambiguity that results can be resolved by substituting other words:

Ambiguous: While the grass dies, the weeds flourish.
Concession expressed: Even though the grass dies, the weeds flourish.
Time expressed: At the same time that the grass dies, the weeds flourish.

For ambiguous uses of *as,* see page 384.

28

Interjections

FEATURES OF INTERJECTIONS

As a group, interjections have no identifiable features of form. They are utterances used to attract attention or to express various degrees of feeling. They function as independent elements without grammatical connections with the rest of a sentence. They frequently stand alone as separate fragments or sentences. In speaking, their effect depends more upon the pitch and stress of the voice than upon the meaning of the words.

KINDS OF INTERJECTIONS

1. Sound words
   Most interjections are expressive sounds. Some are relatively spontaneous and instinctive sounds without specific meaning, like *oh* and *ah;* others are conventional or cultivated sounds with implications established by usage, like *ouch* [pain], *eureka* [discovery], *shh* [be quiet], *psst* [pay attention]. Included in this category also are a great number of swear words.

2. Other parts of speech
   Any word, phrase, or short clause spoken with a stress or marked with an exclamation point can be made to serve as an interjection:

[noun]	Mercy!
[pronoun]	Oh me!
[adjective]	Outrageous!
[verb]	Watch out!
[phrase]	Not on your life!
[sentence]	You don't say!

USES OF INTERJECTIONS

1. Interjections are used as means of address: *Hi! Hey there! Come on! John, hurry up! O Lord, maker of us all!*
2. Interjections express feelings, either mild or strong ones.

USAGE NOTES

28A LIMITED USE OF INTERJECTIONS The most important thing to observe about written prose is that an exclamation point is only an arbitrary device for creating interjections. An experienced writer will learn to depend upon the total effect of his words for expressing feeling rather than a conventional, mechanical symbol.

29

Phrases

DEFINITION

The word "phrase" is often used loosely to mean any brief expression. Grammatically, it is a meaningful unit of more than one word which acts as a single part of speech. It differs from a clause in that it does not have both a subject and a finite verb, although it may have one or the other.

KINDS OF PHRASES

1. Noun phrase
    Prepositional, gerund, and infinitive phrases used as nouns are called noun phrases, but in transformational-generative grammar, a noun phrase consists of a noun and its modifiers: *the paper, a very indignant old gentleman, time immemorial.*

2. Verb phrase
    A finite verb phrase consists of a verb and any other words that help it or complete its meaning: *have been going, have to study, put up with.*

3. Gerund phrase
    A gerund phrase is a verbal phrase, nonfinite in nature, which acts as a noun:

We were interested in *gathering the facts.* [object of preposition]

Living the remainder of his life in isolation will be punishment enough. [subject of verb]

4. Participial phrase
   A participial phrase is a verbal phrase, nonfinite in nature, which acts as an adjective:

   The snow *piled high on the curb* was a barrier.
   Acting with unusual intensity, the cast surpassed itself.

5. Infinitive phrase
   An infinitive phrase is a verbal phrase, nonfinite in nature, which acts as a noun, adjective, or adverb:

   To hear him is a treat. [as a noun]
   It was a drink *to be sipped.* [as an adjective]
   It would be appropriate *to send a card.* [as an adverb]

6. Prepositional phrase
   A prepositional phrase consists of a preposition and its object. It acts as an adjective or adverb and occasionally as a noun:

   We missed the sign *with a blinking light.* [as an adjective]
   He did it *without thinking.* [as an adverb]

7. Absolute phrase or nominative absolute
   A nominative absolute consists of a noun and some portion of a predicate, often a participle. The phrase acts independently; it modifies no particular word in the main clause:

   She stood up, *her hands on her hips.*
   The light of day just beginning to show, we started out.
   He failed to respond, *his face impassive.*

USES OF PHRASES

As the examples above indicate, prepositional phrases and the three nonfinite verbal phrases are used as nouns, adjectives, or adverbs; that is, they occupy positions typical of these parts of speech and perform their functions. Absolute phrases, more closely related to a complete sentence than to the typical phrase, function independently.

30

Subordinate Clauses

DEFINITION

A subordinate clause is a sentence changed from independent status to dependent status by the addition of a subordinating conjunction for the purpose of expressing a relation between it and some part of the main clause.

> *Two independent clauses:* It is raining. We won't go.
> *One clause subordinated to express a new relation:* If it is raining, we won't go.

KINDS OF CLAUSES

1. Noun clause
   A noun clause is one that occupies the position of a noun and serves its functions:

   Whoever is going should sign up. [subject of verb]
   I don't know *what his name is.* [object of verb]
   Give it to *whatever organization you choose.* [object of preposition]
   The complaint was *that he was constantly late.* [subjective complement]

2.   Adjective clause
An adjective clause functions as an adjective by modifying nouns and pronouns. Typically, it follows the word it modifies:

> The secretary, *who also had to double as treasurer,* was overworked. [modifying the subject]

> I see no reason *why we should be excluded.* [modifying the object of the verb]

> This is a book *that I like.* [modifying a subjective complement]

> Anybody *who denies what he can't see* is foolish. [modifying a pronoun as subject]

Adjective clauses introduced by a relative pronoun, relative adjective, or relative adverb are called relative clauses. In these constructions, the relative may substitute for the subject of the clause.

> *who* confessed his involvement [the relative pronoun is the subject]
> *whom* I was expecting [the relative pronoun is the object]
> *whose* talents we know
> *where* I was heading

3.   Adverb clause
An adverbial clause functions as an adverb by modifying verbs, adjectives, and other adverbs:

> They made the attempt, *although the risk was great.* [modifying the verb *made*]

> I am confident *that they'll succeed.* [modifying the adjective *confident*]

> We accomplished considerably more *than we did yesterday.* [modifying the adverb *more*]

USAGE NOTES

30A ELLIPTICAL CLAUSES It is not uncommon to omit some portion of a clause if the understood element is perfectly clear from the context:

> I remember the first time [that] we met.

When [he is] on the job, he's usually sober.

This flour is a better quality than that [flour is].

Some of the revelers had on masks, others [had on] massive heads, and a few [had on] almost nothing at all.

30B MISPLACED CLAUSES A sure way to avoid ambiguity is to put a clause as close as possible to the word it modifies. If intervening words confuse the meaning, the only solution is to rephrase or rearrange the words:

Ambiguous: A short story is a form of fiction, briefer than a novel, which often has the emotional effect of a poem.

Rephrased: A short story, much briefer than a novel, is a form of fiction which often has the emotional effect of a poem.

30C RESTRICTIVE AND NONRESTRICTIVE The principle of restrictive and nonrestrictive applies to the use of all modifiers, including single words, phrases, and clauses. It has particular application to clauses and direct bearing upon their punctuation.

Nonrestrictive elements are basically free modifiers; that is, they are not bound to the antecedents they modify and, if they were omitted, the meaning of the antecedent would not change.

Old Nick, *which is a common term for the devil,* continues to be used as a way of saying that someone is mischievous.

The relative clause, set off by commas and thus marked by the writer as nonrestrictive, undoubtedly adds a fact that the reader may not know; but if the information in this clause is dropped from the sentence, the meaning of the subject is not affected. Thus, the nonrestrictive clause is not binding grammatically.

Restrictive elements, on the other hand, are bound modifiers. They are essential to the meaning of the antecedent and cannot be dropped without altering the meaning of a sentence radically. Compare *Men who hate women should stay single* with *Men should stay single.* The meaning has changed radically. Either sentence might represent someone's viewpoint, but they are two entirely different views. The relative clause *who hate women* places a necessary restriction upon the subject. A restrictive clause is a means of limiting the general classification of *men* to a narrower classification of *men who hate women.* If the clause in this particular sentence were punctuated as if it were nonrestrictive—*Men, who hate women, should stay single*—it becomes apparent that the incidental comment would be both gratuitous and false, because obviously all men don't hate women.

Restriction or nonrestriction, therefore, is an interpretation placed upon the material by the writer and controlled by him. It is his responsibility not to mislead the reader by incorrect punctuation.

30D TAGGED-ON CLAUSES The addition of a *which* clause to refer to the complete idea of a sentence is a questionable usage. This kind of tagged-on thought is better rephrased:

> *Tagged-on:* The union is going to strike, which I thought was the only solution.

> *Rephrased:* The decision of the union to strike seemed to me the only solution.

31

Sentences

DEFINITION

The sentence is a means of dividing discourse into finite and separable parts. In speech, any group of words signaled by some kind of final juncture is a sentence. In writing, words beginning with capitals and ending with a terminal mark of punctuation are called sentences. But all units spoken or written as sentences are not grammatical sentences. *A grammatical sentence is a unit that has a subject and a predicate which contains a finite verb* and is not made a subordinate structure by an introductory relative pronoun or subordinating conjunction. A sentence with a subject and predicate is grammatically complete, but the completeness of its thought may depend upon sentences preceding or following it.

KINDS OF SENTENCES

In grammatical terms, sentences are classified as simple, compound, and complex. The three, of course, may be combined in various ways:

1. Simple sentence
    A simple sentence is a complete grammatical unit that has one subject and one predicate, either or both of which may be compound:

    Fruit is often expensive.

Nectarines and pineapples are particularly high.

Apples and oranges tend to be plentiful and at times may even be cheap.

2. Compound sentence
    A compound sentence is a combination of two or more independent clauses:

    I could arrange to come late, or I could send a substitute.

    The drive takes twenty minutes with no traffic, but we should allow at least forty minutes at the rush hour.

    In typical fashion, a few members were strongly in favor of the motion, a few were violently opposed, but the majority seemed to be generally indifferent.

3. Complex sentence
    A complex sentence combines one independent clause and at least one dependent clause:

    Even though the government took action, the measures were too few and too late.

    The audience applauded enthusiastically when the new choral group sang Bach.

In rhetorical terms, sentences have been traditionally classified as *declarative,* stating facts, *interrogative,* asking questions, *imperative,* giving commands, and *exclamatory,* expressing feeling. The terms merely explain the effect of the sentences:

    My notes are lost. [Declarative]
    Did you misplace my notes? [Interrogative]
    Look for the notes as soon as possible. [Imperative]
    What luck that we found the notes quickly! [Exclamatory]

For the rhetoric of the sentence, see pages 110–128.

SENTENCE PATTERNS

Transformational grammarians hold to the general idea that all sentences, including the most complicated ones, are formed from a number of kernel sentences, which reduce themselves to a limited number of patterns. Because the groupings of sentence patterns have not been standardized, lists of these patterns may vary from three to nine. They are here arranged in five groups. All kernels are simple declarative statements in active voice.

PATTERN 1

SUBJECT	INTRANSITIVE VERB	[OPTIONAL ADVERB]
Paper	tears	[easily].
The leaflets	scattered	[everywhere].
The stream	was flowing	[smoothly].

PATTERN 2

SUBJECT	TRANSITIVE VERB	DIRECT OBJECT	[OBJECTIVE COMPLEMENT]
Flowers	produce	seeds.	
The plumber	repaired	the pipe.	

With special verbs:

We	considered	him	an example.
They	made	him	angry.

PATTERN 3

SUBJECT	TRANSITIVE VERB	INDIRECT OBJECT	DIRECT OBJECT
The principal	gave	Sam	a chance.
I	wrote	him	a note.
The agency	found	me	a job.
He	brought	England	fame.

PATTERN 4

SUBJECT	LINKING VERB	SUBJECTIVE COMPLEMENT
Donald	is	a child.
He	will be	an inspiration.
People	become	victims.
The examination	remained	a hurdle.

PATTERN 5

SUBJECT	LINKING VERB	PREDICATE ADJECTIVE
He	is	energetic.
Jobs	were	scarce.
I	felt	good.
The berries	tasted	sweet.

TRANSFORMATIONS

Basic sentence patterns provide the grammarian with a means of describing all other sentences that can be generated. The basic patterns can be added to, reduced, combined, or rearranged to produce an infinite number of possible sentences. Transformational theory does not necessarily describe how the mind operates to produce complex structures; to be sure, a speaker does not consciously begin with kernels and then proceed to transform and combine them. His sentences emerge whole. What transformational theory does do, however, is to advance an hypothesis that provides an orderly way of describing and analyzing the relations within sentences.

A kernel sentence may be submitted to some, but not necessarily to all, of the following transformations:

1. Passive Transformation [limited to transitive verbs with objects]:

Kernel: The church supported the movement.

Passive transformation: The movement was supported by the church.

2. Negative Transformation:
Kernel: He objects.
Negative transformation: He does not object.

3. Emphatic Transformation:
Kernel: Sarah wrote the poem.
Emphatic transformation: Sarah did write the poem.

4. Question Transformation:
Kernel: They plan to leave.
They are planning to leave.

Question Transformations:
Yes-no questions: Do they plan to leave?
Are they planning to leave?
They plan to leave, don't they?
They are planning to leave, aren't they?

Information questions: When do they plan to leave?
How do they plan to leave?

Intonation question: They plan to leave?

5. Imperative Transformation:

Kernel:	You will see me later.
Imperative transformations:	See me later.
	You see me later. [informal]

The imperative sentence meets the test of a fully grammatical sentence only if we consider its subject understood.

6. Exclamation Transformation:

Kernel:	We had luck.
Exclamation transformation:	What luck we had!

7. *"There"* and *"it"* Transformations:

Kernel:	Rumors were numerous.
	[It] is true.
"There" transformation:	There were numerous rumors.
Further transformations:	That there were numerous rumors is true.
	It is true that there were numerous rumors.

8. Subordination Transformation:

Kernel:	We have differences.
	We get along well.
Subordination transformation (adverbial clause):	Although we have differences, we get along well.
Kernel:	The man lives down the street.
	The man stopped to talk.
Subordination transformation (relative clause):	The man who lives down the street stopped to talk.
Kernel:	We know [something].
	Many people are not interested.
Subordination transformation (noun clause):	We know that many people are not interested.

9. Modification Transformation:

Kernel:	The architecture is modern.
Modification transformation:	modern architecture
Kernel:	The pages are uncut.
	The pages are ragged.
Modification transformation:	the ragged and uncut pages

Kernel:	The girls wore red berets.
	The girls paraded.
Modification transformation:	The girls wearing red berets paraded.
Kernel:	The movie was a delight.
	Someone sees the movie.
Modification transformation:	The movie was a delight to see.
Kernel:	He turned. He jerked.
Modification transformation:	He turned with a jerk.

10. Combination:

Kernels:	Paul went fishing. Grant went fishing.
Combination:	Paul and Grant went fishing.

11. Transposition:

Kernel:	I threw out that old junk.
Transposition:	I threw that old junk out.

These transformations represent only a selection of numerous other possibilities. The analysis of transformations in terms of the kernel sentences from which they originate is a means of revealing what the transformational grammarian calls the deep structure of a sentence as opposed to its surface structure; that is, deep structure is a description of the sources of all constructions in a sentence in terms of the basic patterns from which they originated. It should be noted also that the study of transformations is actually a study of the abstract structures that underlie actual styles of speaking and writing, for all of the variety of the language depends upon the infinite arrangements and combinations that can be produced from basic units.

IMMEDIATE CONSTITUENT ANALYSIS

Immediate constituent analysis is based upon the assumption that a sentence can be broken down successively into component parts by proceeding in terms of twos until no further division is possible. Subject (noun phrase) and predicate (verb phrase) are only the first and most obvious divisions that can be made. Full analysis of the phrase structure of a sentence is a means of fully understanding the relationship between its parts. The analysis in the diagram suggests some of the possibilities in a simple sentence.

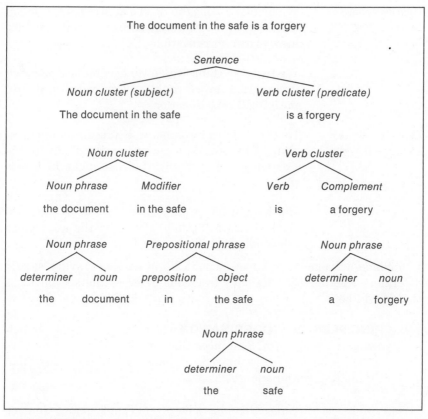

IC analysis may be extended even further to the component parts of words themselves.

USAGE NOTES

31A USE OF FRAGMENTS A fragment is a word or any group of words short of a complete sentence, set down as a thought and punctuated as a sentence. There is a distinct difference between a fragment written for special effect and one that results from the writer's inability to find punctuation that adequately suits his purposes. The use of a fragment may be a deliberate and emphatic device:

> The community was liberal, but that does not imply that it was permissive, disorderly, or immoral. Quite the contrary.

Less effective fragments are better attached to the main clause by punctuation or incorporated into it:

Infinitive phrase as fragment:	We had two things to do. To accumulate as much information as we could and to organize it into meaningful classifications.
Better:	We had two things to do: to accumulate as much information as we could and to organize it into meaningful classifications.
Dependent clause as fragment:	He thought his insomnia was a result of a general state of nerves. Which was brought about by the excitement of spending the first night in a new place.
Better:	He thought his insomnia was a result of a general state of nerves brought about by the excitement of spending the first night in a new place.

Since a fragment is an attention-calling device, a writer should determine whether the idea in a fragment deserves the special focus that it will get.

31B PRINCIPLES OF COORDINATION Coordination implies a balancing of equal parts. Sentences that are clearly not coordinate are better separated, rephrased, or joined by words other than coordinating conjunctions:

Faulty coordination; parts seemingly unrelated:	James Bond has a helper and guide named Quarrel. Quarrel has a wife and two children, who are never shown in the movie but mentioned, and he has qualms about murdering his fellow man.
Rephrased with parts regrouped and relation between them shown by a transitional phrase:	James Bond has a helper and guide named Quarrel, a man with a wife and two children, who are never shown in the movie but are mentioned. Unlike Bond, Quarrel has qualms about murdering his fellow man.
Faulty coordination; parts related but disconnected because writer makes a leap in his thinking:	There are some people who seem to have their world so well organized that they need no extra support beyond themselves, and these atheists are frequently scientists who have been trained to think in terms of absolute facts and proofs.
Rephrased with the parts separated and the gap bridged:	There are some people who seem to have their world so well organized that they need no extra support beyond themselves. This kind of self-suf-

ficiency sometimes leads to atheism. Scientists who have been trained to think in terms of absolute facts and believe only what they can prove are frequently atheists.

Faulty coordination: I was standing there minding my own business, and a man came up and insulted me.

Rephrased with one sentence subordinated: I was standing there minding my own business when a man came up and insulted me.

Separated with a transitional phrase: I was standing there minding my own business. Without warning, a man came up and insulted me.

Faulty coordination; loosely connected: By his explanation, this writer strikes me as a person who wouldn't listen to reason, and I don't like that kind of person.

Rephrased with greater emphasis: By his explanation, this writer strikes me as a person who wouldn't listen to reason. That's the kind of person I don't like.

Faulty coordination; superfluous use of coordinating conjunction: My ideals are not his ideals, and therefore I don't believe we would get along together.

Rephrased with coordinating conjunction eliminated: My ideals are not his ideals; therefore, I don't believe we would get along together.

Rephrased with one sentence subordinated: Because my ideals are not his ideals, I don't believe we would get along together.

Faulty coordination; related but not parallel: The poem expresses a great struggle, but he talks about life in the ghetto as if he were just passing through.

Rephrased with parallel subjects: The poem expresses a great struggle, but the poet talks about life in the ghetto as if he were just passing through.

Faulty coordination; excessive use with loss of effect: I think that this person had a rough time getting through life and then trying to get through the pressures of college. I think when this girl was writing this poem she was a little depressed but I also think that she had the desire and will to make it to the top and nothing was going to stop her.

Rephrased with the thoughts compressed, subordinated, and separated: I think that this girl had a rough time getting through life and surviving college. Although she seems depressed when she writes this poem, I think she shows the desire and will to make it to the top. Nothing is going to stop her.

Faulty coordination; phrasing weakened by unnecessary linking: The student's statement is completely true and I believe life will be hard for him, but if he tries he'll succeed.

Rephrased with unrelated parts separated: The student's statement is completely true. Life will be hard for him, but I believe if he tries he'll succeed.

Excessive coordination in writing tends to be amateurish, unless it can be used with a special stylistic effect (see p. 116). Transformations of short kernel sentences permit the writer to bring the segments of his thought into more suitable and meaningful relations with one another.

31C PRINCIPLES OF SUBORDINATION It should be noted that some phrases and clauses which are subordinate in structure are not necessarily subordinate in meaning. In fact, the subject of a sentence may be expressed in a noun clause, and sentences beginning with expressions like *it is true that* or *it is questionable whether* put the important thought into the dependent clause that follows. In most instances, however, subordination is a way of giving secondary emphasis to a thought, even though it may be the more important fact. The following sentence, for example, is clearly designed to emphasize a personal detail rather than the world event:

I was stationed in Marseilles, France in 1945 when the first atom bomb was dropped.

Nevertheless, most writers place the principal idea in the main clause, although the writer often determines which is the principal idea. The following sentences illustrate how a reversal of subordination shifts the emphasis from the deed in the first example to the time of the deed in the second example:

> When John Kennedy was in the third year of his administration, he was assassinated.

> When John Kennedy was assassinated, he was in the third year of his administration.

In the matter of subordination, the writer must also consider what a reader's normal expectations will be. Adverbial clauses, for example, are sometimes subject to upside-down subordination; that is, the main focus of the sentence seems to be misplaced in a dependent clause. Reading the following sentences aloud will indicate that their intonation patterns are quite different:

Upside-down subordination:	The wrecking ball swung forward again, when the last wall collapsed.
Rephrased with emphasis more appropriate to the meaning:	As the wrecking ball swung forward again, the last wall collapsed.

Excessive subordination consists in piling up clauses to the detrimental effect of the sentence as a whole:

> I was reading about Pieter Bruegel, a Flemish artist, who painted in the seventeenth century when it was common to treat Biblical subjects in terms of contemporary thought, which consistently sought out moral parallels between the Bible and the times and which did not hesitate to satirize what was immoral.

Improved phrasing:

> I was reading about Pieter Bruegel, a seventeenth-century Flemish artist, who followed the current fashion of treating Biblical subjects in terms of contemporary thought. Artists of his day consistently sought out moral parallels between the Bible and the times and did not hesitate to satirize what they considered immoral.

31D SEPARATION OF RELATED PARTS OF A SENTENCE Since readers expect related structures to be as close to one another as possible, intervening material often causes confusion:

> It was a not-to-be-forgotten and not-too-pleasantly remembered incident. [wide separation of determiner and noun]
>
> *Rephrased:* It was an incident not to be forgotten and not too pleasantly remembered.

> A ballpoint pen, formerly bright blue but now faded by the weather and at the moment I saw it covered with raindrops, was lying under a bush. [wide separation of subject and verb]
>
> *Rephrased:* Lying under a bush was a ballpoint pen, formerly bright blue but now faded by the weather, covered the moment I saw it with raindrops.

> I requested, even though I knew the deadline was past, permission to submit my application. [wide separation of verb and object]
>
> *Rephrased:* Even though I knew the deadline was past, I requested permission to submit my application.

32

Manuscript Form

PUNCTUATION

On a sheet of music, rests and dynamic markings would be meaningless without the notes, but the rhythm and style of the music would be less apparent without these notations. In a similar way, punctuation has no value except as it reveals the writer's intentions about the meaning and effect of the words he has set down on paper. Punctuation is a way of doing in writing what the speaker can do by variations of pitch, stress, and pause. But the writer does not do what the speaker does to the same degree. Anyone who merely transcribes all of the pauses of his speech will end up with superfluous punctuation marks. It should be emphasized that punctuation is designed for *readers*. There is not an exact equivalent among these marks for everything that a speaker does with his voice for listeners.

Nevertheless, all punctuation has a phonological dimension. A period, for example, is the equivalent in writing of a falling pitch that we use to indicate the end of a sentence, and commas and other internal marks of punctuation mark pauses of varying degrees. If they do not mark all of the pauses that occur in speech, we can remind ourselves that spaces between words, sentences, and paragraphs may also be considered punctuation devices in the sense that they also clarify the author's meanings and intentions.

Punctuation is always closely related to the syntactic structure of the language, and its importance increases as sentences become more **507** complex and sophisticated. A basic sentence pattern requires no internal punctuation. There is no need for it, because the simple sentence is a single unit. But as soon as the kernel sentence is added to, transformed, reordered, or interrupted—any change that alters the simple structure or invites misreading—then punctuation becomes necessary. Some marks are indispensable to prevent misreading; others are optional and therefore dependent upon the writer's sense of his own rhetoric and style.

As soon as the element of choice enters, punctuation takes on a stylistic dimension. Some writers make spare use of marks of punctuation; others try scrupulously to avoid all ambiguity by punctuating as precisely as possible. These tendencies produce two general styles of punctuation: open and close. The choice between them is not always the writer's own. Legal and technical writings clearly cannot risk possible misreading and therefore demand close punctuation. Some newspapers and publishing houses establish their own practices. Yet in most informal personal prose, the writer is free to deviate from conventional practices if he finds punctuation a way to gain emphasis or add variation to the rhythms.

Conventions of punctuations are merely practices that cover the most typical and predictable strategies which writers use. They are not inviolable rules, but they are in most instances sound guidelines. The principles they follow are simple: they mark end breaks; they separate various words and structures within a sentence; they enclose others; they serve a variety of conventional purposes that simplify the transcription of thoughts on paper. For each of these functions, several marks of punctuation are most commonly used:

1. End breaks: period, question mark, exclamation point
2. Separating within the sentence: comma, semicolon, colon, dash, hyphen
3. Enclosing: commas, dashes, parentheses, square brackets, quotation marks
4. Conventional uses: period, comma, dash, ellipsis points, quotation marks, hyphen, apostrophe

In many instances, a writer can be quite versatile about his use of punctuation as long as he understands the range that is possible. As freely as the dash can be substituted for commas, colons, and parentheses, it cannot substitute for an apostrophe. The limitations and open possibilities of marks of punctuation become fully known only after a writer becomes familiar with established practices. These are set down in the sections that follow.

32A USES OF THE PERIOD

1. To mark a full end stop, whether the break comes at the end
    of a sentence or at the end of a fragment intended as a state-
    ment or assertion:

Complete Sentences

> Fom time to time, he would glance at his notes to regain
> his confidence.

> What I see happening is a constant threat to our physical
> environment and welfare.

> Think about it. Many people have. It's not right.

Fragments

> Any number of eloquent tributes were made to Eleanor Roo-
> sevelt at her death. The most eloquent by Adlai Stevenson,
> a former Democratic candidate for President, her friend, and
> admirer.

> I think we must set up priorities among values. Human beings
> first. Yes. No doubt about the first priority.

> The radical left. There's a group that may change the whole
> structure of things if they have the staying power.

Questions: When the period substitutes for a question mark, the
question may be interpreted as a polite directive:

> Would you please make the changes and return the manu-
> script to us by June 15.

Exclamations: When the period substitutes for the exclamation
point, the force of the remark depends upon the phrasing:

> What a disastrous conclusion.

2. To indicate abbreviations:

Mr.—Mister	D.A.—Doctor of Arts
Mme.—Madame	S.J.—Society of Jesus
Esq.—Esquire	A.D.—Anno Domini

Abbreviations that tend to be pronounced as words or sounded as letters are often written without periods:

> AAUP–American Association of University Professors
> USSR–Union of Soviet Socialist Republics
> YMCA–Young Men's Christian Association
> WAVES–Women's Appointed Volunteer Emergency Service
> VIP [informal]–very important person
> BMOC [informal]–big man on campus

For the use of abbreviations, see 31AC below.

3. To indicate dollars and cents ($7.10), percentages (5.3%), divisions by act, scene, and line (*Hamlet* I.i. 5-6), and other divided numbers in itemized lists (14.17, 14.18); to serve as a typographical aid in enumerated lists:

> 1. Matthew
> 2. Mark
> 3. Luke
> 4. John

Periods are omitted following the topics.

Usage Notes

32AA Periods with Other Marks

1. Periods are placed inside quotation marks:

> The title was an allusion to a phrase in Goethe's "Erl-King."
>
> He said, "One example can be found in Whitman's 'Song of Myself.' "

2. When a quotation comes at the end of a question, the period is dropped:

> Who said "I think, therefore I am"?

3. If a sentence ends with an abbreviation, no second period is necessary:

> I attended a professional meeting in Washington, D.C.

4. Periods and commas are commonly used together:

    Whenever he encountered John, Jr., he was sure to have an argument.

5. When parentheses or brackets are used, the period may be placed inside or outside the parentheses depending upon the context or dropped altogether, depending upon the context and the placement of the parenthetical matter:

    His ten years in Rome were unhappy ones (the decade discussed in Chapter 3).

    His ten years in Rome were unhappy ones. (See the discussion in Chapter 3.)

    His ten years in Rome (see the discussion in Chapter 3) were unhappy ones.

32AB Run-on Sentence or Fused Sentence The run-on sentence represents a writer's failure to punctuate sentences properly, even though they may be well formed:

> *Run-on:* You are probably wondering why I am writing you I am angry.
>
> *Corrected:* You are probably wondering why I am writing you. I am angry.
>
> *Run-on:* I have had four years of college (without a degree) maybe I am foolish not to go back.
>
> *Corrected:* I have had four years of college (without a degree). Maybe I am foolish not to go back.

32AC Use of Abbreviations As a general principle, the use of abbreviations varies with the formality of the writing: the more formal, the fewer abbreviations. Yet, even in the most formal contexts, abbreviations may be required to avoid the unnecessary repetition of long names and involved titles. They are, of course, standard in footnote forms, lists, tables, and so on. A few are commonly required in prose of almost any variety:

Titles:	Mr., Mrs., Dr., Sr., St. (saint)
Degrees:	B.A., Ph.D., D.D.
Time:	P.M., A.M., B.C., A.D.

Foreign terms: *i.e., e.g., viz., cf.*
Names: AP (Associated Press), IPA (International Phonetic Alphabet), IRBM (intermediate-range ballistic missile).

Two guidelines will serve almost all situations:

1. Follow with consistency throughout a work whatever practice is initially adopted.
2. If in serious doubt about the appropriateness of any abbreviation, spell it out.

32B USES OF ELLIPSIS POINTS

1. To mark an omission from a direct quotation. Three points indicate that one or more words have been deleted; four points indicate that one or more sentences have been deleted. When four points appear at the end of a quotation, the fourth may be considered the period marking the end of a sentence.

> *Original:* Starting then with the being of a God (which, as I have said, is as certain to me as the certainty of my own existence, though when I try to put the grounds of that certainty into logical shape I find a difficulty in doing so in mood and figure to my satisfaction), I look out of myself into the world of men, and there I see a sight which fills me with unspeakable distress.
>
> John Henry Newman,
> from *Apologia*
> *Pro Vita Sua*

> *With omission:* Starting then with the being of a God ..., I look out of myself into the world of men, and there I see a sight which fills me with unspeakable distress.

> *Original:* You can vitiate the air by your manner of life and of death, to any extent. You might easily vitiate it so as to bring such a pestilence on the globe as would end all of you. You, or your fellows, German and French, are at present vitiating it to the best of your power in every direction; chiefly at this moment with corpses, and animal and vegetable ruin in war, changing men, horses, and garden stuff into noxious gas. But everywhere, and all day long, you are vitiating it with foul chemical exhalations; and the horrible nests, which you call towns, are little more than laboratories for the

distillation into heaven of venomous smokes and smells, mixed with effluvia from decaying animal matter, and infectious miasmata from purulent disease.

John Ruskin,
from *Fors Clavigera*

With omissions: You can vitiate the air by your manner of life and of death, to any extent. You might easily vitiate it so as to bring such a pestilence on the globe as would end all of you .... you are vitiating it with foul chemical exhalations; and the horrible nests, which you call towns, are little more than laboratories for the distillation into heaven of venomous smokes and smells ....

It should be noted that the overuse of ellipsis points is likely to create suspicion because too much omission may well distort the exact intention of the original.

2. To indicate an interruption or an unfinished sentence, particularly in spoken dialogue:

    "There is one thing I want to ...," but the mumbled words were lost in a final effort to take one last deep breath.

3. To indicate the omission of one or more lines of poetry or one or more paragraphs of prose by the use of a full line of spaced ellipsis points:

These beauteous forms,

Through a long absence, have not been to me
As is a landscape to a blind man's eye:
But oft, in lonely rooms, and mid the din
Of towns and cities, I have owed to them,
In hours of weariness, sensations sweet,
Felt in the blood, and felt along the heart;
. . . .

For I have learned

To look on nature, not as in the hour
Of thoughtless youth; but hearing oftentimes
The still, sad music of humanity,
Nor harsh nor grating, though of ample power
To chasten and subdue.

William Wordsworth, "Lines Composed a Few Miles above Tintern Abbey ..."

NOTE: The ellipsis represents the omission of sixty lines.

32C USES OF THE QUESTION MARK

1. To terminate a question:

Regular questions:	Do you know about the new policies? Is it not possible that you may be wrong and she right?
Intonation questions:	She failed? I am the one to blame for this mess?

2. To indicate questions inserted parenthetically for rhetorial effect:

He was cocksure—is it so bad to be cocksure?—that he was going to win.

3. To indicate the uncertainty of facts:

The comedies of Aristophanes (445?–385? B.C.) provide glimpses of what Athenian life was actually like.

Usage Notes

32CA With Quoted Material The question mark is placed inside quotation marks if the question is a part of the quoted material, outside if the question is being asked by the writer.

I am certain I heard him ask, "What do you want me to do?"

Have you read Francis Thompson's "The Hound of Heaven"?

32CB Indirect Question The indirect question requires no question mark:

I asked what was required of me.

One student inquired whether he could write on an alternate topic.

Compare the equivalent direct questions of these indirect ones. Tense, phrasing, punctuation, and capitalization are changed:

I asked, "What is required of me?"

One student inquired, "Can I write on an alternate topic?"

32CC For Purposes of Irony The use of the question mark to make an ironic commentary is generally considered obvious and amateurish:

> The newspaper reported that unarmed (?) policemen were present at the gathering.

> One critic wrote that much of the delight (?) we take in reading *Gulliver's Travels* derives from the prose style.

32D USE OF EXCLAMATION POINT

1. To add force or agitation to almost any kind of emotional expression or interjection:

> Please! Give the man air!
> O Lord our Lord, how excellent is thy name in all the earth!
> > Psalm 8:1

> Oh, but you are wrong!
> What a bore!

Usage Notes

32DA With Quoted Material The exclamation point is placed inside quotation marks if the statement is a part of the quoted material, outside if the emphasis is being added by the writer:

> He ended his remarks with a cynical mumble, "What's the use!"
> Every English major should certainly know Chidiock Tichborne's "Elegy"!

32DB Intensification The exclamation point is actually an intensifier. The solution to adding greater intensity to a remark, however, does not lie in multiplying the number of exclamation points (!!!) but in choosing words that will convey the writer's sense of stress and tension.

32E USES OF THE COMMA

1. To join sentences of certain kinds:

> *Compound sentences linked by the coordinating conjunctions* and, but, or, for, nor, yet, *and sometimes* so:

The whole matter is beyond our control, and it is now so confused that we have little hope of saving any lives.

The effect of his alienation was not liberating, but it forced him to become more and more hostile.

The more we earn, the less we seem to care, for money does not bring the satisfaction we thought it would.

He was persuaded that he wanted to visit Mexico, so he went.

In most of these examples, the main break is clear because there is no internal punctuation in either main clause. If internal punctuation blurs the main clause, the comma can be raised to a semicolon:

Mass media include printed materials, radio, and television; and they, after all, must bear some responsibility for the consequences of their productions.

Compound sentences with short, closely connected clauses, but not joined by a coordinating conjunction:

The newspaper came up with a theory, anyone could.

It's too bad, he could have stayed here.

The people shouted, the people booed.

Short sentences in series, usually with parallel or balanced phrasing:

I know, I was there, I saw him.

Cats shrieked, dogs barked, horses neighed.

We can, we will, we must.

War is hell, I know what I say, war is hell.

2. To separate introductory words, phrases, and clauses from the remainder of the sentence:

Introductory words:

Yes, I agree with you.

Nevertheless, we have to proceed with caution.

Hey, you could be the one I'm looking for.

Introductory phrases:

By this summer, the city will have made good progress toward eliminating air pollution.

Best of all, we got new skis for Christmas.

Of course, Tel Aviv is a modern city.

Convinced that we followed the wrong sign, we turned around.

Striking out against all kinds of abuses, he delivered a forceful tirade.

A book about the hippie subculture from a sociological point of view, the study should create new understanding.

To get recognized, we had to shout.

His fist clenched in defiance, he cursed.

When an introductory phrase is followed by inverted word order, no comma is used:

From the wings of the stage stepped a completely dazzling female.

Introductory clauses:

When people have been saying for years that vaudeville is dead, it is surprising how its ghost continues to appear in many places.

If the circus disappeared, we would lose one of the "greatest shows on earth."

Because the nation is slow in grappling with accumulated problems, a new era of peace escapes our grasp.

If an introductory clause is short and allows no misreading, the comma is sometimes omitted:

As soon as he arrived he began to cause trouble.

If a clause is the subject of a sentence, the comma is omitted:

Whoever is responsible should be arrested.

3.   To separate words, phrases, and dependent clauses in series:

Coordinate adjectives (see 24F):

He acted the role of a lost, searching, anguished youth.

We counted ten small blue boats. [not coordinate]

Series of words:

There are A, B, and C series and A, B, C series; then there are also A and B and C series.

The needs, interests, and dignity of these people must be respected.

We had to consider the time, place, occasion.

In A, B, and C series, the comma before the final *and* is optional unless misreading results from its omission. If all of the items of a series are separated by conjunctions, commas are not ordinarily used except for special emphasis:

Give him a tie or a shirt or a belt.

Compare: Give him a tie, or a shirt, or a belt.

Series of phrases:

The movie continued boringly without change of pace, without variation of tone, or without particularly interesting technique.

He was received enthusiastically wherever he went: in Milan, in Bayreuth, in Munich, and in London.

Series of dependent clauses:

If there are no good hotels, if there are no outstanding

restaurants, if there are no sports activities, what is the attraction of the place?

We should stress that one out of four marriages ends in divorce, that a large majority of divorced couples marry again within four years after their split, and that being remarried will soon be a more common phenomenon than being married only once.

4. To separate words, phrases, or clauses added to the end of a sentence:

Direct address:

I compliment you, ladies and gentlemen.

Tag question:

I would like to go, wouldn't you?

Direct quotation:

"I can't, I can't," he reported.

Nonrestrictive phrase or clause (see 30C):

We can leave, depending on the weather.

I will support your program, although I don't agree with all of its details.

We should agree on the basic costs, such as travel, meals, and lodging.

Absolute phrase:

There was nothing else to do, the celebration having ended.

Transitional words:

We ought to listen, nevertheless.

Suspended elements:

My reading speed is as slow as yours, if not slower.

He was proficient as a business executive, and as well paid.

5. To separate the parts of a cumulative sentence (see p. 113):

    The two children faced each other, eye to eye, on the play-field, the one white and oblivious, but forced to react, the other black, looking as if without warning he might explode with power, so young and abused, from a lifetime of suppression.

6. To enclose parenthetical, explanatory, or interruptive words, phrases, and clauses:

    Nonrestrictive appositives:

    The captain of the ship, Joe Delano, was only thirty-five years old.

    The play was praised by those who could best understand its meaning, namely, the ordinary people.

    My job, to post signs, was given to someone else.

    Some of Shakespeare's plays, such as *Hamlet, Othello, Macbeth,* and *The Merry Wives of Windsor,* have been made into operas.

    The prestige schools, namely, Harvard, Princeton, and Yale, are beginning to have strong competitors.

    Note: The restrictive appositive requires no comma:

    The director Antonioni was mainly responsible for the failure of the movie.

    William the Conqueror became William I of England.

    Inserted phrases and clauses:

    Cheryl, being one of those naturally impulsive people, dived in with her clothes on.

    John Cook, who was the editor for six years, finally bought the company.

The new car is as heavy as, if not heavier than, the previous model.

Companies, like ours, must keep growing.

We had to consider him, so to speak, a newcomer.

He will speak, if he speaks at all, for no fee.

A good example of a self-destructive person, if ever I saw one, was Joe.

In ordinary circumstances, when they are not playing a game, the team still sticks together.

His student, no more talented than him to be found, was still lazy.

Transitional words and phrases:

I would, however, like to try.

One of the more interesting varieties, for example, is the Golden Retriever.

The state government, as a matter of fact, is duplicating the function of the city.

The people, as a consequence, need to protest.

Direct address:

One of the purposes of this meeting, ladies and gentlemen, is to enlist volunteers for the campaign.

You know, George, that you can't take on another job.

Split quotation:

"The manpower programs," he began his address, "are classic examples of waste."

"I am going," she said with determination, "even if you don't think I should."

7. To emphasize a contrast or to give added emphasis to a particular word, phrase, or clause:

This was our first attempt, though by no means our last.

Critics in the United States, not European critics, have tended to intellectualize literature.

The more hand stitching on a dress, the higher the price.

We weren't hurrying, just flying.

The student body, rather than the faculty, ought to make that particular decision.

Milton was satisfied that he, too, would be among the great English poets.

8. To prevent misreading or to accommodate the reader when rephrasing does not seem to be the best solution:

As soon as he got in, the car pulled away.
[Cp. As soon as he got in the car pulled away.]

Ever since, the performance has run smoothly.

To Mary, Anne was very special.

He spoke with remarkable ease, and wit was his trademark.

What will be, will be.

Whoever comes, comes of his own accord.

9. To increase the readability of addresses, place names, dates, statistics, and measurements and to serve other conventional purposes:

Addresses and place names:

His new address is 117 Shiga Lane, San Francisco, California.

He is now visiting in Tulsa, Oklahoma.

Mail to: University of Washington, Seattle, Washington 98105

Note: Zip codes are not separated by commas.

Dates:

Pike's Peak was discovered by Zebulon Pike, born January 5, 1779.

In December, 1941, the United States made a formal declaration of war.

Note: Open style omits the comma when only the month and year are used:

In December 1941, the United States made a formal declaration of war.

Or the date reversed:

On 7 December 1941, Pearl Harbor was attacked.

Statistics:

By 1900, Pennsylvania's population had already reached 6,000,000.

He was six feet, five inches tall.

Note: The comma is sometimes omitted in numbers of four digits (2000 people), but it is always used in numbers ranging from 10,000 up.

Titles and degrees:

General George S. Patton, Jr., was better known as "Old Blood and Guts."

Henry Webster, Vice-Provost, was chairman.

He always signed his name George Miller, M.D.

Names reversed:

Shakespeare, William

Patton, George S., Jr.

Salutation and complimentary close in informal letters:

Dear Esther,

Sincerely,

Regards as always,

References: (see footnote and bibliographical forms, pp. 321–329.)

10. To indicate an ellipsis in sentences where the parallel structure makes clear what the omission is:

> We were leaving for Europe; they, for Mexico.

> I began to remind myself that the race was almost over; he, that it had to be won.

Usage Notes

32EA With Quoted Material The comma is always placed inside quotation marks.

> He was an exponent of "art for art's sake," a true aesthete.

When direct quotation invites the combination of the comma with the exclamation point or question mark, the comma is usually dropped in favor of the more expressive mark:

> "Quiet!" he shouted with a sense of desperation.

> "Do you know why?" Ethel inquired.

When the direct quotation ends with a dash, the comma is retained to separate the quoted material from the words that follow:

> "This is one of those–," but he was not able to continue.

32EB With Parentheses, Square Brackets, and Dashes The comma is not used before parenthetical material; it is held until the parenthesis is closed:

> I was idling along at 30 miles per hour, looking at the scenery (the mountains were snow-capped), listening to the radio (B. J. Thomas was singing "Raindrops Keep Falling on My Head"), not paying attention to the old hay wagon in front (going slower than I was).

> Thomas Campbell's *The Pleasures of Hope* (1799), a long poem, is now virtually forgotten.

The comma is not added to dashes that set off parenthetical material:

He had fallen in love again—one of his weaknesses—but this time the affair was to last.

32EC Comma Splice or Comma Fault The comma splice or comma fault represents the writer's failure to see that a comma used to join certain sentences will not suffice, because a semicolon or period is clearly demanded. The seriousness of the comma splice, therefore, is that it invites misreading, not that it is a mortal sin of punctuation.

1. One group was pushing Congress to enact a law that would permit federal authorities to fingerprint, photograph, and run identification checks on people who had no criminal charge placed against them, that would be unprecedented and probably unconstitutional.

Comma splice eliminated:

One group was pushing Congress to enact a law that would permit federal authorities to fingerprint, photograph, and run identification checks on people who had no criminal charge placed against them. That would be unprecedented and probably unconstitutional.

2. The commune had no written rules, however the members were morally obligated to share all of their earned income.

Comma splice eliminated:

The commune had no written rules; however, the members were morally obligated to share all of their earned income.

Alternate reading:

The commune had no written rules, however; the members were morally obligated to share all of their earned income.

See 32 F, Sections 1 and 2, for uses of the semicolon with and without the use of conjunctive adverbs.

32F USES OF THE SEMICOLON

1. To separate two closely related sentences joined without a connective or to separate more than two sentences of considerable length arranged as a series:

    > Practice to him came easy; he did it routinely and ungrudgingly like all of the other things in his life.

    > This is the major portion of the manuscript; the rest will be finished in another month.

    > Daniel Webster spoke of government "made for the people, made by the people, and answerable to the people"; Lincoln, of course, spoke the more familiar phrases "of the people, by the people, and for the people."

    > He considered the policies of his company objective and fair; he never questioned the reasons they were adopted; he never concerned himself with their consequences.

    > The tornado was disastrous: at least ten people were killed; property damage amounted to more than $10,000,000; the entire tourist season was jeopardized.

    > In Florida, the membership was strong; in Tennessee, less strong; and in Kentucky, negligible.

2. To separate sentences joined by conjunctive adverbs (*e.g., however, moreover, therefore*) or other transitional expressions (*e.g., in brief, by the way*):

    > Winter lasted on into May; therefore, no one could begin early spring planting.

    > First, we went to the Smithsonian Institute; then we took the trip out to Mt. Vernon.

    Note: The comma following the connecting adverb is frequently optional.

    > There are a number of things he could do to improve his writing; for example, he could try to learn how to work several ideas into one sentence rather than stringing them out in primer sentences.

The total amount is high; therefore we will have to eliminate the padding in the budget.

For an extended list of conjunctive adverbs, see p. 484.

3. To clarify the main break when sentences joined by coordinating conjunctions, which are ordinarily separated by commas, contain enough internal punctuation to obscure the main break:

>   Some of the streets ran north and south, others east and west, and yet others diagonally; but the whole city was so well plotted that it was practically impossible to get lost.

>   The professor encouraged students to collect samples of water from dormitory water taps, coffee urns, the stream that runs through the campus, which is heavily polluted; and he then had them do water analysis as a laboratory exercise.

4. To act as a strong substitute for the comma when internal punctuation obscures the main divisions of any series:

>   The sights in Venice continue to attract tourists: the Rialto Bridge, always a place of great activity; the Cathedral of Saint Mark, which is perhaps second only to Santa Sophia in Istanbul; and, of course, the Grand Canal, with its array of interesting buildings.

>   He quoted a number of Biblical passages: Job 1:21; Psalms 61:1–3; Proverbs 8:13–14.

Usage Notes

32FA With Quoted Material The semicolon is ordinarily placed outside quotation marks, unless in rare instances it is used as a substitute for a comma:

>   He was very fond of using "and what not"; it was a part of every other sentence.

>   Thoreau wrote, "I heartily accept the motto, 'That government is best which governs least'; and I should like to see it acted up to more rapidly and systematically."

>   *Rare:* A rave review is the kind that talks about a "funny furious narrative;" the kind that says the story is "tearfully

humorous, triumphantly sad;" and the kind that closes with the remark that the book "has added something fine and important to the literature of our age."

When a direct quotation ends in a semicolon, the semicolon is dropped.

32FB With Other Marks of Punctuation The semicolon is placed after parentheses, not before:

He was a strong young man (the second child in a family of five); he was unbeatable.

The semicolon does not combine with the comma or the end marks of punctuation unless the period marks an abbreviation:

The package came C.O.D.; it was clearly something Mandy had bought.

32G USES OF THE COLON

1. To introduce a list or an enumeration of items or examples:

The axial skeleton is made up of the bones of the head, neck, and trunk: the skull, the spinal column or backbone, vertebrae, the sacrum, and coccyx.

Here is a checklist for the camping trip: food, utensils, canteen, bedroll, personal necessities.

Their mission was actually to introduce Western products to the natives: transistor radios, cameras, binoculars, and rifles.

2. To indicate that an explanation, example, elaboration, or correlation will follow:

The redwood tree is matchless: it has antiquity, great size, and hardihood.

I have one major reservation: five-year-old children cannot be left unsupervised for that long.

We should consider what some of the major reasons are: first, unstable economic conditions; second, long-standing grievances; and, third, newfound strategies for protest.

There is one thing above all he lusted for: an original Cezanne.

The book deserved the praise it got: it was readable, it was substantive, it was moving.

This is the dilemma: can an honest man be found anywhere anymore?

Note: When a complete sentence follows a colon, the capital letter at the beginning of the sentence is optional.

3. To introduce quotations or formal statements, with or without a verb of saying:

With an old-style prophet's indignation, he burst out: "Evil has come upon the nation."

Pascal's observation on atheism is thought-provoking: "Atheism is a sign of mental strength, but only up to a certain point."

The relevant points from the Constitution are these: [*followed by an extended quotation*].

4. To mark conventional separations:

Formal salutation:
Dear Sir:
Gentlemen:

Hours from minutes:
9:45 P.M.
6:30 A.M.

Rhymes and related terms:
room:doom, black:white

Chapter from verse:
Micah 6:8

Volume from page:
English Journal 58: 1307–1315

Title from subtitle:
Phantoms: A Collection of Stories

Introductory tags:
   From left to right: Stalin, Truman, Atlee
   SPEAKER NO. 1: What's your name?
   SPEAKER NO. 2: Norman.

Numerals in ratio:
   3:6::4:8

Place from publisher:
   New York: Holt, Rinehart and Winston

Usage Notes

32GA With Quoted Material and Parentheses The colon is placed outside quotation marks and parentheses. If a quotation ends in a colon, the colon is dropped.

32GB Combined with Dash The practice of combining the colon and the dash ("the line goes as follows:—"), common in earlier typography, is now considered outmoded.

32H USES OF THE DASH

1. To introduce a summary statement following a series of words or phrases:

   Literature, philosophy, religion—these are disciplines which overlap.

   1918 and 1945—the dates mark the end of two world conflicts.

2. To indicate a break, shift, or interruption in the writer's thought:

   No, not again—surely we cannot repeat the same mistakes over and over.

   He was born six hundred years too late—a truly chivalrous knight if there ever was one.

   He survived the experience—but what I have been saying is obvious.

   I liked it—but then *chacun à son goût,* wouldn't you say?

3. To indicate an unfinished remark or to simulate faltering, broken, or confused speech:

> "And it's just—" but the voice was stifled.
>
> I—I—no, I can't tell you—but I must!

4. To add a sharpened emphasis to parenthetical material which might otherwise be separated by commas or parentheses:

> Most men—and I'm not far different from many others—would refuse to hit a raving woman.
>
> The scholastic record—at first good and then deplorably bad—could not be ignored.
>
> He was a man of firm conviction—I suppose he would be typical of the Silent Majority—but he was not inclined to sign petitions.

5. To expand upon an idea, often going back to pick up a word or phrase already used:

> This was an ailment that had bothered him for years—an ailment that was not going to be easily cured now.
>
> His book is clearly distinguished—distinguished in the sense that it represents not only a fair reflection of accumulated knowledge but a significant addition to it.

6. To serve as a less formal substitute for the colon in introducing an explanatory statement, list, or quotation:

> There were only two things to do—run or jump.
>
> Three patients are ready for release—the one in the first bed, the one in the second, and the one in the fifth.
>
> The committee should place special emphasis upon—
> 1. The requirements for admission
> 2. The program of studies
> 3. The implementation of the program.

7.   To serve conventional purposes:

Omission of a word or letters:

> When I look at _____, I think of _____.
> The story identifies her only as Madame G___d.

Inclusive dates, time, references:

> April 11–13, 1971
> 5:30–7:30 P.M.
> pp. 38–45

Note: In printing, inclusiveness is shown by en dashes, longer than the hyphen and shorter than em dashes. Em dashes are used to show omission of letters. On the typewriter, a hyphen is used for an en dash, two hyphens for an em dash, and occasionally four hyphens for a long dash.

Before citations of author or source:

> "The vanquished have no friends."
> > —Mussolini

Usage Notes

32HA With Quoted Material The dash is used inside or outside quotation marks, depending upon the context. Ordinarily, the period, comma, semicolon, and colon are dropped when the sentence seems to invite double punctuation. The question mark and exclamation point may be retained.

> The whole scene—what an outrage!—was shown on television.

> The question—what do we do now?—simply can't be answered at the moment.

32I USES OF THE HYPHEN

1.   To form familiar compounds:

brother-in-law	ill-concerned
cross-examine	Johnny-on-the-spot
double-jeopardy	single-breasted
heavy-handed	storm-swept

how-to-do-it   well-dressed
light-footed   well-seasoned

Note: Since over a period of time the hyphen may be dropped and the hyphenated compound become one word, the writer should always check the dictionary if he is in doubt.

2. To form one-time-only compounds and special coinages:

an I-don't-care-what-you-think-of-me type
the beep-beep-beep of the horns
a motorcycle's pb-pb-b-b-b!

3. To form coined words with a prefix or suffix:

pro-Communist   president-elect
trans-Asian   stand-in
ex-husband   shell-like

4. To form numbers, fractions, ratios, and compounds with numbers:

twenty-two   three-day pass
seven-eighths   twelve-year-old
20-20-20 soluble fetilizer   thirty-story building

Note: When fractions are used as nouns, the hyphen is sometimes omitted:

We completed one fourth of the assignment.

5. To divide a word into syllables:

re-tort   tem-po-ral
sep-tu-ple   tran-spire
spon-ta-ne-ous   vac-ci-nate

Usage Notes

32IA Word Division at End of Line The hyphen is used to divide a word at the end of a line, but dividing should be done by syllables and then with certain limitations. Not all breaks are appropriate or clear:

1. Words should not be divided if only one letter (*man-y*) or two letters (*mon-ey*) carry over to the next line.
2. Words should not be divided if the syllable leaves only one letter remaining at the end of a line (*e-ject*).
3. Hyphenated words should be divided only at the hyphen, not at other syllables (*self-deceit,* not *self-de-/ceit*).
4. Monosyllables cannot be divided.
5. Contractions should not be divided (*they're, weren't*).
6. Numbers stated in figures should not be divided (5,000,000).
7. Words that would have a misleading appearance when divided should not be hyphenated (*wom-an, oft-en*).

The dictionary is an indispensable source of information concerning syllabication, although all dictionaries do not share common principles of word division. *Webster's Seventh,* for example, divides *English* as *En-glish;* Webster's *New World* gives *Eng-lish.* Hundreds of examples might be cited, indicating, of course, that English syllabication has not been completely standardized. These variations suggest two useful guidelines for writers:

1. If possible, avoid word divisions at the end of a line.
2. If a word division is necessary, use one dictionary with consistency as a reference.

32IB Suspended Hyphen The hyphen can be used to transcribe on paper the kind of suspended expression that might be spoken. The spacing differs slightly from regular hyphenation:

> This was a three- to five-thousand-year-old vase.
>
> He was informed in both socio- and psycho-linguistics.

32J USES OF THE APOSTROPHE

1. To indicate the posessive case of nouns and indefinite pronouns:

Singular possessive

a father's devotion	anybody's privilege
an animal's instincts	everybody's concern
The New Yorker's wit	another's interests
my brother-in-law's car	everyone else's ideas
a master's degree	each one's turn

Note: Singular possessive is formed by adding an *'s*. The use of the apostrophe with words ending in sounds of *s* or *z* ordinarily depends upon the pronounceability of the syllable. If the syllable is pronounced, the *'s* is kept (*class's*); if the syllable is not pronounced, the apostrophe is kept and the *s* dropped (*Degas'*). Usage will therefore vary with the individual, who may or may not want to indicate the extra sound.

Pronounced addition	**Unpronounced addition**
Marx's doctrine	for righteousness' sake
Mr. Gomez's store	Oliver Wendell Holmes'
his mistress's apartment	writing
the grass's color	Aristophanes' plays
Brutus's betrayal	Ulysses' journey
Mars's strength or Mars'	Achilles' heel
strength	Socrates' wisdom or
	Socrates's wisdom

Plural possessive

his sisters' devotion	ten years' time
the instructors' combined skill	the Browns' cooperation.
two cents' worth	

Note: Plural possessive is formed by adding an apostrophe to the plurals of words that end in *s*. If the plural is irregular, an *'s* is added to the plural form:

men's courage	a children's book
the geese's pond	the alumni's success

Joint or collective possessive

Beaumont and Fletcher's dramas
Simon and Garfunkel's songs
Lerner and Lowe's musicals
University of London's location
fathers and sons' banquet

Note: When the writer does not wish to indicate a joint effort, he can make a distinction:

Donne's and Marvell's poetry is Metaphysical in style.
Or rephrase: The poetry of Donne and Marvell is Metaphysical in style.

2. To indicate contractions or the omissions of numbers:

isn't	we'd
haven't	OK'd
would've	Xerox'd
the class of '36	ma'am
in the '20's	reck'n

e. To form plurals of numbers, letters, signs, abbreviations, dates, and words used as words:

6's and 7's	78 rpm's
p's and q's	GI's
+'s and —'s	the 1930's (or 1930s)

He had difficulty pronouncing his *this*'s.

32K USES OF PARENTHESES

1. To enclose explanations, digressions, and interruptions to the main thought of the sentence.

The selling price is twenty-four thousand, five hundred dollars ($24,500).

The trend indicates (see Table 2) that unemployment is increasing.

Many composers (for example, Mozart, Verdi, and Saint-Saëns) have used the fugue for dramatic purposes.

The idea of consubstantiation (Burke discusses it in *A Rhetoric of Motives*) makes possible a different concept of rhetoric.

He spoke in a restrained way (totally unlike him) so that we knew something was wrong.

2. To enclose numbers and letters marking divisions included in the main text:

The two writers might be compared in terms of (1) their similar background, (2) their preoccupation with psychology, and (3) their tendencies toward the macabre.

The geological changes can be observed in (a) Siberia, (b) China, and (c) Northern India.

Usage Notes

32KA With Other Marks of Punctuation

Commas, semicolons, and colons follow a closed parenthesis. Terminal marks may be included within the parenthesis depending upon the context.

We observed one main rule (with appropriate flexibility, of course): everybody had to get at least seven hours of sleep.

He cited innumerable examples of oxymoron (most of them from Elizabethan sonneteers).

A global language seems more and more a necessity. (There are at least three thousand spoken languages in the world today.)

32L USES OF SQUARE BRACKETS

1. To insert editorial comment or explanations within a direct quotation:

   Persons of genius are, *ex vi termini* [by definition], more individual than any other people. . . .

   John Stuart Mill

   "They [the Athenians] were the most religious of the Greeks."

   Lord Acton

   Arnold demonstrated his classical spirit in his long narrative poem *Sohrab and Rustrum* [*sic*].

2. To serve as parentheses with parentheses:

   In the edition of 1890, Thomas Wentworth Higginson had made changes in Emily Dickinson's poems. (For the original and unreconstructed texts, see *The Complete Poems of Emily Dickinson,* ed. Thomas H. Johnson [Boston: Little, Brown and Company, 1960].)

3. To enclose phonetic transcriptions:

   He had visited Jaffa [jaf′ə].

Note: Angle brackets < > are sometimes used for this same purpose.

32M USES OF QUOTATION MARKS

1. To identify direct quotations:

    > G. K. Chesterton wrote: "To say that a man is an idealist is merely to say that he is a man."

    > Coleridge wrote: "Love is flower-like; / Friendship is a sheltering tree."

    > One definition of *moral* is "sanctioned by or operative on one's conscience or ethical judgment."

2. To identify spoken dialogue:

    > We were standing around. "You know what?" one fellow blurted out as if he had the world's greatest idea. "Naw, we don't know what," Snoopy sneered.

Note: Conventionally, a new paragraph marks the words of a new speaker. Narrative and descriptive detail may be included in the same paragraph.

3. To enclose titles of newspapers and magazine articles, essays, stories, poems, and parts of books as differentiated from the title of the book as a whole:

    > "Out of Place in America: Confessions of a Chauvinist" by Peter Schrag in *Saturday Review*

    > "Pulvis et Umbra" by Robert Louis Stevenson

    > "My Oedipus Complex" by Frank O'Connor from *The Stories of Frank O'Connor*

    > "As I Grew Older" by Langston Hughes from *Collected Poems* (1954)

    > Chapter II, "Humanistic Ethics: The Applied Science of the Art of Living" from Erich Fromm's *Man for Himself*

Note: Quotation marks are not used to set off the title of a student theme at the beginning of the paper.

4. To set off the names of songs, short musical compositions (not symphonies or operas), and radio and TV programs.

Grieg's *"Ich liebe dich"*
"Sympathy for the Devil" performed by The Rolling Stones
Ravel's "Bolero"
NBC's "Tonight Show"

5. To set off a particular word under discussion:

    The popular music of the 1940s was called "Swing."

    If we consider what Plato meant by "realism," we will have some insight into the basis of his philosophy.

    "Disinterested" and "uninterested" can mean quite different things.

    See also Italics pp. 543–544.

6. To indicate awareness of an obvious shift in usage or to suggest irony:

    If all he wants to do is "cool it," then let him stay where he is.

    It's one thing to use "people's talk"; it's another to be obscene.

    Marlowe might have been the "hip kid" of the sixteenth century.

7. To indicate italics within italics:

    The title of his book was *A Modern Guide to James Joyce's "Ulysses."*

Usage Notes

32MA With Other Marks of Punctuation As a general principle, periods and commas are always placed inside quotation marks; semicolons and colons, almost always outside; and other marks, inside or outside, depending upon the context. If the quotation comes at the end of a sentence, only one terminal mark is necessary, not double punctuation.

    I know what he meant when he was talking about the "dandelion."

32MB **Single Quotation Marks** Single quotation marks are most commonly used for quotations within quotations:

> She had very clearly said, "I am going to sing 'Jesu Joy of Man's Desiring.'"

British usage frequently follows the reverse pattern of American usage: single marks first, then double.

32MC **Indirect and Direct Discourse** The distinction between indirect and direct discourse should be kept clear: no quotation marks are necessary in indirect discourse.

> *Direct discourse:* I said, "I will help if I can."
> *Indirect discourse:* I said I would help if I could.
>
> *Direct discourse:* He said, "Reason must prevail."
> *Indirect discourse:* He said that reason must prevail.

32MD **Block Style for Quotations** Quotations of approximately fifty words of prose or two or more lines of poetry are most conveniently set off by special indentation in typewritten papers and by special typography in printing. When block style is used, the opening and closing quotation marks are dropped and any single quotation marks in the text are raised to double quotation marks.

> The essence of Wordsworth's poetic manifesto is contained in one sentence of the "Preface to *Lyrical Ballads*":
>
> > The principal object, then, proposed in these Poems, was to choose incidents and situations from common life, and to relate or describe them throughout, as far as was possible, in a selection of language really used by men, and, at the same time, to throw over them a certain coloring of imagination, whereby ordinary things should be presented to the mind in an unusual aspect, and further, and above all, to make these incidents and situations interesting by tracing in them, truly though not ostentatiously, the primary laws of our nature: chiefly, as far as regards the manner in which we associate ideas in a state of excitement.

The opening lines of Wordsworth's sonnet "The World Is Too Much with Us" seems to describe the twentieth century as well as his own:

The world is too much with us; late and soon,
Getting and spending, we lay waste our powers:
Little we see in Nature that is ours;
We have given our hearts away, a sordid boon!

32N USES OF THE SLANT OR VIRGULE (also called the slash, solidus, and diagonal)

1. To indicate alternatives:

    The tour included England/France and Germany/Italy.

    Traditional Africa was—and can/must/will become again—a continent of Life and Art.

2. To act as a dividing line between a period of time extending over successive years (academic year 1972/73), shillings and pence (8s/3d), fractions set into a line of type ($y/b = 1$), and run-in lines of poetry ("Oh, lift me from the grass!/I die, I faint, I fail!").

3. To stand for *per* in abbreviations like 6 ft./sec. (feet per second) or km/hr (kilometers per hour).

4. To set off phonemes and phonemic transcriptions (see p. 368): /p/ as in *pat*

5. To suggest a kind of jazz rhythm or syncopation, as used in black poetry:

    the Jess B. Semple hip sneer
    the bassist/drummer/pianist/guitarist/rhythm on top of Caldonia

    > From Ted Joans's "Passed on Blues: Homage to a Poet," in *Black Pow-wow: Jazz Poems*

CAPITALIZATION

Capitalization, like the spacing of words, is a purely conventional typographical device for increasing the readability of prose. Because conventions have been established, meaning can be very definitely affected. We readily recognize that *Turkey* and *turkey* or *Polish* and *polish* do not mean one and the same thing. Capitalization is a convenient and simple device for keeping prose orderly and unambiguous.

32O USE OF CAPITAL LETTERS

1. To begin the first word of a sentence, line of poetry, or a fragment following another sentence:

    Books surrounded me to the point of suffocation.

    How do I love thee? Let me count the ways.
    I love thee to the depth and breadth and height
    My soul can reach, when feeling out of sight
    For the ends of Being and ideal Grace.
    Elizabeth Barrett Browning

    The state decided to close the express lane of the freeway. A completely arbitrary decision.

2. To identify proper nouns, words derived from proper nouns, and the initials and abbreviations of those words (see 21I):

    Don Phillips has expressed the Afro-American point of view more forcefully than anyone else in Washington, D.C.

3. To set off references to the deity, titles, the pronoun *I* and the interjection *O:*

    Let my cry come near before thee, O Lord: give me understanding according to thy word.
    Psalm 119:169

    The committee elected Professor Lichter as its chairman.

4. To mark the first word and all principal words of a title:

    Have you read "Who Has Poisoned the Sea?"

    Helmut Nickel's *Warriors and Worthies: Arms and Armor*

Through the Ages is a fine book for both information and browsing.

Roger van der Weyden's *Descent from the Cross* is a remarkably moving painting.

Note: All words of a title are capitalized except the articles *a, an,* and *the,* conjunctions, and prepositions of five or fewer letters.

5.   To indicate that a word is personified:

As our Religion, our Education, our Art look abroad, so does our spirit of society.

Ralph Waldo Emerson

Return, return, O eager Hope,
   And face man's latter fall.

Herman Melville

6.   To set off words typographically for unusual emphasis:

There was the sign in all of its blatant defiance: NO WOMEN ADMITTED OR EVEN WANTED.

ITALICS

Italic is actually a type style, used in contrast to the kind of roman type most commonly used for ordinary reading matter. There are numerous other type styles, but their uses are more specialized— for titles and for special printing like announcements, stationery, and advertisements. Italic, however, is designed to match all roman typefaces and is considered an indispensable part of routine printing. Because of the common use of italics, single underlining has been adopted as the way to show on a typewriter and in handwriting what would appear in print as italic. Italics and underlining are therefore one and the same.

32P USES OF ITALICS

1.   To indicate foreign words and phrases not yet fully assimilated into the English language:

After disagreeing for an hour about the merits of the performance, we could only fall back upon the inevitable saying: *de gustibus non est disputandum.*

The incident became the *cause célèbre* on campus.

Note: At some point in time, doubt may exist whether a word or phrase is fully Anglicized. Usage will therefore vary with writers, depending upon their education and cosmopolitanism. The foreign words in the following sentences might well be italicized by some individuals:

He was an expert on avant-garde art.

We had a good old-fashioned kaffeeklatsch.

2. To designate titles of books, periodicals, newspapers, dramas, operas, symphonic works, paintings, movies, ships, and aircraft:

Dickens' *Great Expectations*

Harper's Magazine

The Seattle Times

Hansberry's *A Raisin in the Sun*

Verdi's *Aida*

R. Strauss's *Tod und Verklärung*

da Vinci's *Last Supper*

Midnight Cowboy

Titanic

Apollo 13

3. To add emphasis to a word or phrase:

It is not *what* you said; it's *how* you said it.

I am interested in *people,* not their clothes.

Note: A device of this kind remains effective only if it is used sparingly and then with good cause.

4. To refer to letters as letters, numbers as numbers, and words as words:

My name has a *c* in it.

The sign had a large *5* on it.

The word *affect* as a noun is seldom used except by psychologists.

The quatrain rhymed *abab.*

See also Quotation Marks, pages 538–539.

NUMBERS

Transcribed numbers fall into two major categories, Arabic and Roman. Roman numerals, of course, are less familiar than Arabic ones.

	CARDINAL NUMBERS		**ORDINAL NUMBERS**
SPELLED OUT	ARABIC	ROMAN	
zero	0	—	
one	1	I	1st
two	2	II	2nd or 2d
three	3	III	3rd or 3d
four	4	IV	4th
five	5	V	5th
six	6	VI	6th
seven	7	VII	7th
eight	8	VIII	8th
nine	9	IX	9th
ten	10	X	10th
eleven	11	XI	11th
twelve	12	XII	12th
thirteen	13	XIII	13th
fourteen	14	XIV	14th
fifteen	15	XV	15th
twenty	20	XX	20th
twenty-five	25	XXV	25th
thirty	30	XXX	30th
forty	40	XL	40th
fifty	50	L	50th
sixty	60	LX	60th
seventy	70	LXX	70th
eighty	80	LXXX	80th
ninety	90	XC	90th
one hundred	100	C	100th
one hundred and one	101	CI	101st
two hundred	200	CC	200th
three hundred	300	CCC	300th
four hundred	400	CD	400th
five hundred	500	D	500th
six hundred	600	DC	600th
seven hundred	700	DCC	700th
eight hundred	800	DCCC	800th
nine hundred	900	CM	900th
one thousand	1000	$\overline{\text{M}}$	1000th
five thousand	5000	$\overline{\text{V}}$	5000th
one hundred thousand	100,000	$\overline{\text{C}}$	100,000th
one million	1,000,000	$\overline{\text{M}}$	1,000,000th

NOTES A bar over a letter multiplies its value by one thousand. In early printed words, I⊃ is sometimes seen instead of D and ⊂I⊃ for M.

DATES EXPRESSED IN ROMAN NUMERALS

1300 MCCC	1900 MCM
1500 MD	1910 MCMX
1700 MDCC	1940 MCMXL
1800 MDCCC	1972 MCMLXXII

The representation of numbers by figures or by written words varies widely with the nature of a work. Business, scientific, technical, and legal writings tend to prefer figures to written forms. In general prose, however, numbers are frequently written out. A few specific guidelines will reflect the most common practices for prose in standard English:

32Q USES OF FIGURES

1. To represent numbers that require more than one or two words when written out:

   875 people, but ten men
   $1,365,748, but a million dollars
   1953, but the twentieth century or the 20th century
   1940s or 1940's, but the forties

Note: If various statistics are included in one sentence, all are given in figures for the sake of consistency:

   The attendance at the workshops varied from 125 at Language and Composition to 75 at Rhetoric and Composition, to 35 at Literature and Composition.

2. To represent:

   Dates: May 11, 1970 or 11 May 1970
   Addresses: 1823 West Kentucky Street, Apt. 4
   Time: 4:30 P.M., but half-past four
   8:00 A.M., but eight o'clock in the morning
   2315 (11:15 P.M. in military time)
   Dollars and cents: $3.55, but $5 per person and 15 cents each
   Decimals: 3.1416
   Measurements: 4 by 6 inch cards
   5′ 11″ tall, but six feet tall
   Code numbers: Army serial number—35481990
   Telephone number—area code 206—543-2190

Social Security number—410-17-8404
Zip code number—98105
Percentages: 6%, but 6½ percent or 4 percent
one-fourth of 1 percent
*Set forms of reference:*4-H Club, 35 mm lens, 50 mph, 7-Up,
pp. 104–105, Flight 107, Gate 3,
Channel 7

3. To prevent misreading or to serve as a greater convenience
in reading:

$8.5 billion deficit   ten 6-foot stakes or 10 six-foot stakes

Note: Numbers at the beginning of a sentence are ordinarily written
out. If such a number requires several words, the dilemma can
be avoided by a simple rephrasing:

To be avoided: 4300 students participated in the drive.
Rephrased: A total of 4300 students participated in the
drive.
Approximately 4300 students participated
in the drive.

SPELLING

Anyone who has written the English language knows why misspellings occur. Some difficulties are rooted in the spelling system itself,
others in the people who try to use the system. These are two separate
issues.

First, English spelling is not strictly phonetic. To make this observation is not to say that phonics do not help in learning to spell. Phonics
will help as long as an individual realizes that particular sounds are
not always spelled consistently and that only twenty-six letters are
available to transcribe almost twice that number of sounds in the
language. People who are interested in establishing the chaos of the
English spelling system will point out that the *sh*-sound can be represented by at least fourteen different spellings. What they do not add
is that at least nine of these transcriptions tend to be rare, used in
such words as *schist, fuchsia,* and *pshaw.* Most *sh*-sounds are spelled
in five fairly common ways, like the spellings of *shoe, mansion, nation,
suspicion,* and *conscious.*

It is true that the English spelling system in a very conservative
way retains the remnants of older spellings, for example, in the silent
letters in *governor* and *descend.* It is also true that orthography changes
much more slowly than the sound system. For that laggardness, the

speller ought to be grateful. What he learns today is likely to hold true tomorrow. If the system changed as rapidly as sounds, spelling would be chaos. If the campaigns for spelling reform and simplification consistently succeeded, every book in our libraries would soon be archaic.

At the present time, variation between British and American spelling causes some confusion. An awareness of these differences permits one to avoid the dilemma of writing perfectly acceptable British spellings to have them rejected as incorrect American ones. A comparison of these variants also demonstrates how easily a written language can be made to appear foreign by very minor changes:

BRITISH	AMERICAN
axe	ax
colour	color
cosy	cozy
defence	defense
draught	draft
encyclopaedia	encyclopedia
endorse	indorse
inflexion	inflection
judgement	judgment
milage	mileage
risque	risk
theatre	theater
travelled	traveled

Spelling reformers from Benjamin Franklin to Bernard Shaw have given most of the reasons why English words are difficult to spell. Yet, despite whatever difficulties exist, the system we have is in general use, masses of people accept the ability to spell correctly as one of the marks of an educated man, and most people, accordingly, learn to spell—not perfectly but adequately. Everyone misspells occasionally, usually because of carelessness or simple failure to observe closely. Good spelling requires an eye for detail.

An individual's attitude toward spelling often correlates directly with his performance. If he thinks good spelling is important for whatever reason—social, economic, or academic—he usually goes to some trouble to see that his words are right. If he dismisses spelling as a trivial matter and rationalizes his own inadequacies by dumping the blame on the spelling system, he is likely to be indifferent to correctness. Good spelling requires concern. Those who believe it makes a difference whether a word is spelled correctly or incorrectly have acquired a basic attitude which will permit them to go further in analyzing and understanding their own particular problems in spelling.

How Do People Misspell

Familiar lists of spelling demons include words that are most commonly misspelled. They sometimes divide the words into syllables; they sometimes identify spelling traps. But they never show exactly *how* words are misspelled. Of course, two individuals are capable of misspelling a word in different ways. One may fail to double a consonant, and the other may use a wrong vowel in an unaccented syllable. Yet for all of these potential differences, misspelling is not as erratic as it sometimes appears. Particular words are misspelled in characteristic ways, but very seldom do the misspellings of one individual fit all of the patterns. In many instances, he may repeatedly do only one thing wrong. The only sensible approach to spelling, therefore, is for every individual to list the words he personally misspells and then over a period of time see if his misspellings group themselves. In most cases, one predominant pattern will emerge. That pattern, then, can be studied and worked on.

In order to determine typical patterns of misspelling among college students, 225 misspelled words from the themes of approximately 100 students were listed and then grouped. The study produced eleven categories, although most of the misspellings fell into three of these. These categories, therefore, provide comparisons for anyone who wants to analyze his own misspellings to find out what he needs to do to become a better speller.

Misspellings Categorized

1. In the total number of 225 misspellings, almost no one, even the worst spellers, missed the first letter. There were six misspellings involving the first letter, and they fell into two categories:

UNACCENTED FIRST SYLLABLE		SUBSTITUTION OF *S* FOR *C*	
incourage	(encourage)	sensuring	(censuring)
indeavor	(endeavor)	synical	(cynical)
enevitably	(inevitably)		
enialate	(annihilate)		

What this observation suggests is that even the poor speller is not completely handicapped in looking up a word in the dictionary. If he becomes aware that syllables like *in-* and *en-* are easily confused in unaccented positions or that *s* and *c* spellings may actually sound alike, he should not have undue difficulty in finding a word.

2. By far the greatest number of spelling errors were made by missing only one vowel in an unaccented syllable. There were only three errors in the vowels of accented syllables: *complecency* for *complacency*,

combersome for *cumbersome,* and *curtesy* for *courtesy.* Some of the words misspelled were fairly difficult ones, but all of the letters were exact except for the one representing a neutral sound (the schwa). The following lists show that the error occurred most commonly in a middle or final syllable:

ERROR IN UNACCENTED FIRST SYLLABLE

discribe	(describe)
dispise	(despise)
distroy	(destroy)
granade	(grenade)
rediculously	(ridiculously

ERROR IN UNACCENTED MEDIAL SYLLABLE

catagories	(categories)
emphisis	(emphasis)
emphisize	(emphasize)
exhilerating	(exhilarating)
exhileration	(exhilaration)
gallary	(gallery)
hypicritical	(hypocritical)
imaginitive	(imaginative)
incapibility	(incapability)
instramental	(instrumental)
jealosy	(jealousy)
manditory	(mandatory)
oppertunity	(opportunity)
oppurtunity	(opportunity)
prevelant	(prevalent)
princepals	(principals)
seperate	(separate)
simularly	(similarly)

ERROR IN UNACCENTED FINAL SYLLABLE

e–a

allience	(alliance)
challange	(challenge)
competant	(competent)
existance	(existence)
guidence	(guidance)
importence	(importance)
panal	(panel)
personel	(personal)
privilage	(privilege)
relevence	(relevance)
speciman	(specimen)
vengence	(vengeance)

e–i

tangeble	(tangible)

e–o

ancester	(ancestor)
poisen	(poison)
prospor	(prosper)
rotton	(rotten)

3. The next greatest number of errors were made by adding an unnecessary letter, either by doubling a consonant, inserting a syllable which the writer used in his own speech, or spelling the word like another one.

UNNECESSARY DOUBLING OF CONSONANT

aggreement	(agreement)	impartiallity	(impartiality)
arrises	(arises)	impersonnally	(impersonally)
arroussing	(arousing)	laggs	(lags)
assett	(asset)	neccessary	(necessary)
ballance	(balance)	oppinion	(opinion)

beautifull	(beautiful)	parrallel	(parallel)
begginning	(beginning)	proffesional	(professional)
controll	(control)	reffer	(refer)
derrogatory	(derogatory)	stiffles	(stifles)
dissadvantage	(disadvantage)	symbollic	(symbolic)
donnate	(donate)	truthfull	(truthful)
exposses	(exposes)	untill	(until)
illussions	(illusions)		

ADDED LETTER,
PROBABLY PRONOUNCED

athelete	(athlete)
barbarious	(barbarous)
monsterous	(monstrous)

ADDED LETTER, PROBABLY
INFLUENCED BY ANOTHER
WORD OR THE SAME WORD
IN ANOTHER FORM

amoung	(among)
arguement	(argument)
beyound	(beyond)
confrounts	(confronts)
develope	(develop)
eleveating	(elevating)
loyality	(loyalty)
predjudices	(prejudices)
proceedures	(procedures)
scence	(scene)
truely	(truly)

4. An almost equal number of errors were made by dropping a letter, a syllable, or parts of two syllables from a word. Many of these misspellings involve unaccented or silent consonants and vowels; others reflect the writer's own pronunciation of these words; still others reflect the tendency to look at the beginning and end of a word, not its middle.

OMISSION OF ONE
CONSONANT WHICH
SHOULD BE DOUBLED

accomodate	(accommodate)
aparent	(apparent)
begining	(beginning)
dilema	(dilemma)
disatisfied	(dissatisfied)
exagerated	(exaggerated)
folies	(follies)
sadest	(saddest)
supressed	(suppressed)
totaly	(totally)
unoticed	(unnoticed)
writen	(written)

OMISSION OF ONE
VOWEL WHICH
SHOULD BE DOUBLED

smothest	(smoothest)

OMISSION OF ONE LETTER,
OFTEN SILENT OR ELIDED
IN PRONUNCIATION

accidently	(accidentally)
adultry	(adultery)
aquired	(acquired)
backwars	(backwards)
choclate	(chocolate)
cleary	(clearly)
convenieces	(conveniences)
curisity	(curiosity)
delt	(dealt)
diagoses	(diagnoses)
envirnment	(environment)
futher	(further)
impetous	(impetuous)
mathmatics	(mathematics)
minature	(miniature)
obviosly	(obviously)
pobable	(probable)
realty	(reality)
temperture	(temperature)

OMISSION OF A SILENT *E*

completly	(completely)
creats	(creates)
definitly	(definitely)
involvment	(involvement)
severly	(severely)

5. The next greatest number of misspellings involved the confusion of two words. At times, the word used was correctly spelled, but it was the wrong word. At other times, the misspelling represented an integration of two words:

TWO CORRECT SPELLINGS
  INTERCHANGED
cloths for clothes
course for coarse
deep-seeded for deep-seated
isle for aisle
local for locale
loose for lose
loosing for losing
site for sight
their for they're
they're for their

TWO WORDS CONFUSED IN
ONE SPELLING
boarder for border
cann't for can't (*compare* cannot)
characture for character (*compare* caricature)
choosen for chosen
desserted for deserted
idealogies for ideologies
incidences for incidents
layed for laid
numberous for numerous
planely for plainly
realitively for relatively
sqwiggles for squiggles (*compare* wiggles)
wheather for weather
wheren't for weren't

6. A number of words were misspelled by transposing two letters, immediately following one another or in two key syllables.

TRANSPOSITION OF *I* AND *E*		TRANSPOSITION OF OTHER LETTERS	
beleifs	(beliefs)	chruch	(church)
nieghborhood	(neighborhood)	gagued	(gauged)
peice	(piece)	enviornment	(environment)
percieve	(perceive)	irrevelant	(irrelevant)
recieve	(receive)	niave	(naive)
sieze	(seize)	perscribe	(prescribe)
soceity	(society)	plauge	(plague)
wierd	(weird)	prespiration	(perspiration)

7. Another group of words was misspelled by interchanging two letters that have the same sound value:

SUBSTITUTION OF *S* FOR *Z*		SUBSTITUTION OF *Z* FOR *S*	
characterisation	(characterization)	raized	(raised; *compare* razed)
realised	(realized)		
recognise	(recognize)	suprize	(surprise)
satirising	(satirizing)	surprized	(surprised)

SUBSTITUTION OF *S* FOR *C*		SUBSTITUTION OF *C* FOR *S*	
consentrate	(concentrate)	fantacy	(fantasy)
consise	(concise)	inconciderate	(inconsiderate)
devises	(devices)		
sensuring	(censuring)		
synical	(cynical)		
vises	(vices)		

SUBSTITUTION OF *CIOUS* FOR *TIOUS*	
ficticious	(fictitious)

8. Several words were misspelled by failing to substitute *i* for *y* when the basic word was changed:

PLURAL:	berrys	(berries)
THIRD PERSON SINGULAR:	exemplifys	(exemplifies)
SUFFIX:	livelyhood	(livelihood)
	uglyness	(ugliness)

9. Several words ending in *o* were misspelled in either the singular or the plural.

heroe	(hero)
heros	(heroes)
negroe	(Negro)
negreo	(Negro)
Negros	(Negroes)
negores	(Negroes)

10. Spelling difficulties increase, of course, when the writer makes two or more mistakes: transposing letters and using the wrong letter in an unaccented syllable, omitting a syllable and adding an unnecessary one, failing to double a consonant and using the wrong vowel, and so on. These words when misspelled often appear highly distorted:

ciriculum	(curriculum)	occurances	(occurrences)
distory	(destroy)	remencsent	(reminiscent)
groes	(grows)	tradgety	(tragedy)
inconvieniant	(inconvenient)		

11. The final group of misspellings are those that might be identified as phonetic spellings. A few patterns emerge, like the use of *ee* for any *e* sound, but for the most part these are inventions the writer substitutes to approximate what he says:

connisuer	(connoisseur)	rightchusness	(righteousness)
definetly	(definitely)	sargeant	(sergeant)
enialate	(annihilate)	squeemish	(squeamish)
extreemly	(extremely)	sumething	(something)
journees	(journeys)	venir	(veneer)
metemorphius	(metamorphosis)		

How to Remedy Misspellings

One obvious but important conclusion to be drawn from the spelling study just described is that most spelling errors occur inside a word (medially), not at the beginning or the end. This observation reflects our tendency to recognize words quickly as we read without ever stopping to examine exactly how the letters are arranged. The first and main job a poor speller has, therefore, is to look at words and see what he is looking at. If dividing a word into syllables helps him to look at each letter, then he should divide words in that way. If closing his eyes helps him obtain a clear mental picture of the word, then he should try that device. If enunciating precisely and exaggerating some sounds helps him get a sound image, then he should try the oral approach. If writing certain letters large (temperAment) helps him visualize a trap in a word, then he should dramatize it in that way. There are many useful aids for the poor speller, but whatever he does should be designed to get at the proper arrangement of letters, either by sight or sound.

The analysis of one's own spelling errors represents a kind of amateur psychotherapy. If someone becomes aware of a particular spelling problem, and especially if he learns that it may not be as severe a problem as he thinks it is, then he can direct his attention to certain helpful principles of spelling. Of course, there are exceptions to all of these principles, but one can always cope with the exceptions if he first learns the mass of words that follow the pattern.

Some kinds of spellings must be simply memorized. For example, there is no useful guideline for differentiating between words that add -*able* and those that add -*ible* or those that end in -*ance* and those that end in -*ence*. Yet where guidelines do exist, these are useful. The following twelve sections illustrate how common spelling difficulties can be eliminated by keeping in mind certain model words which illustrate a fundamental spelling guideline. Any particular individual may have to concentrate upon only one or two of these. The others he has already mastered, whether he is aware of it or not.

32R MODEL WORDS As a remedy for particular spelling problems, model words can serve as reminders of basic spelling principles.

1. The *achieve-deceive* model:

Ordinarily, *i* comes before *e* except after *c* when the pronunciation sounds like the *e* in *be*.

WORDS LIKE *ACHIEVE*		WORDS LIKE *DECEIVE*	
believe	relieve	ceiling	perceive
chief	reprieve	conceit	receive
field	siege		
fierce	thief		
niece	wield		
piece	yield		

EXCEPTIONS		OTHER SOUNDS
either	leisure	eighty
neither	seize	freight
financier	weird	sleigh
		vein
		weight

2. The *alley-ally* model:

When a word ends in *y*, preceded by a vowel, the *y* is kept and *s* added to form the plural (*alley, alleys*).

When a word ends in *y*, preceded by a consonant, the *y* is dropped and *ies* added to form the plural (*ally, allies*).

WORDS LIKE *ALLEY*		WORDS LIKE *ALLY*	
attorney	attorneys	army	armies
boy	boys	baby	babies
day	days	body	bodies
chimney	chimneys	city	cities
donkey	donkeys	copy	copies
key	keys	fly	flies
monkey	monkeys	library	libraries
turkey	turkeys	sky	skies
valley	valleys	study	studies

EXCEPTIONS: PROPER NAMES
Sherrys
Marys
Overburys
Emorys

Application of the *y* to *i* principle can be made to other formations: the third-person singular of verbs, comparatives, and changes from nouns to adjectives, adjectives to nouns, adjectives to adverbs, and verbs to nouns.

THIRD PERSON SINGULAR		ADJECTIVES TO NOUNS	
bury	buries	fiery	fieriness
marry	marries	lovely	loveliness

COMPARATIVES		ADJECTIVES TO ADVERBS	
easy	easier	crafty	craftily
empty	emptier	mighty	mightily

NOUNS TO ADJECTIVES		VERBS TO NOUNS	
beauty	beautiful	carry	carrier
mercy	merciless	fly	flier

3. The *drop-dropped-dropping* model:

Monosyllables ending in a single consonant, preceded by a vowel, double the consonant when a suffix begins with a vowel.

WORDS LIKE
DROP-DROPPED-DROPPING

brag	bragged	bragging
can	canned	canning
plan	planned	planning
ship	shipped	shipping
rob	robbed	robbing
sin	sinned	sinning
snap	snapped	snapping
stab	stabbed	stabbing
stop	stopped	stopping
whip	whipped	whipping

WORDS LIKE
DROP-DROPPING

bet	betting
cut	cutting
bid	bidding
get	getting
put	putting
run	running
sit	sitting
spin	spinning
swim	swimming
win	winning

SAME PRINCIPLE APPLIED TO OTHER FORMATIONS

big	bigger
clan	clannish
gun	gunner
mad	madder
man	mannish
pig	piggish
red	reddish

4. The *referred-reference* model:

Words of more than one syllable ending in a single consonant, preceded by a vowel, with the accent on the final syllable (*refer*), double the consonant when a suffix begins with a vowel (*referred*). If these conditions do not hold, the consonant is not doubled (*reference*).

WORDS LIKE *REFERRED*

admit	admitted	admittance
allot	allotted	
compel	compelled	
control	controlled	
concur	concurred	concurrence
occur	occurred	occurrence
omit	omitted	
permit	permitted	

WORDS LIKE *REFERENCE*

confer	conference
defer	deference
prefer	preference

SAME PRINCIPLE APPLIED TO OTHER FORMATIONS:

bevel	beveled	(*alternate:*	bevelled)
benefit	benefited	(*alternate:*	benefitted)
counsel	counseled	(*alternate:*	counselled)
kidnap	kidnaped	(*alternate:*	kidnapped)

5. The *amusing-amusement* model:

Words ending in a silent *e* (*amuse*) drop the *e* when a suffix beginning with a vowel is added (*amusing*). They retain the *e* when a suffix beginning with a consonant is added (*amusement*).

WORDS LIKE *AMUSE-AMUSING*

argue	arguing
arrange	arranging
come	coming
dine	dining
have	having
hope	hoping
judge	judging
sacrifice	sacrificing
shine	shining
write	writing

APPLICATION EXTENDED

arrive	arrival
assure	assurance
bride	bridal
force	forcible
guide	guidance
imagine	imaginary
live	livable
move	movable
use	usage
value	valuable

EXCEPTIONS

dye	dyeing	(*compare:* die, dying)
hoe	hoeing	
singe	singeing	(*compare:* sing, singing)

WORDS LIKE *AMUSE-AMUSEMENT*

achieve	achievement
arrange	arrangement
encourage	encouragement
require	requirement

APPLICATION EXTENDED

entire	entirely
sincere	sincerely
hate	hateful
use	useful
care	careless
hope	hopeless

EXCEPTIONS

acknowledge	acknowledgment
argue	argument
awe	awful
judge	judgment
nine	ninth
true	truly

6. The *outrageous* model:

Words ending in silent *e* preceded by *ce* or *ge* retain the *e* before a suffix beginning with *a* or *o,* if the sound of the consonant is soft.

advantageous	courageous	noticeable	pronounceable
changeable	manageable	peaceable	serviceable

7. The *frolic-frolicking* model:

Words ending in *c* add a *k* when a suffix beginning with *e, i,* or *y* is added.

WORDS LIKE *FROLIC, FROLICKED, FROLICKING* (*compare* frolicsome):

mimic	mimicked	mimicking	(*compare* mimicry)
panic	panicked	panicking	panicky
picnic	picnicked	picnicking	picnicker
traffic	trafficked	trafficking	trafficky

8. The *illiterate-soulless-roommate* model:

When a prefix ends in the same letter that begins the main stem, both letters are retained. When a word ends with the same letter of a suffix or a combined word, both letters are retained.

WORDS LIKE *ILLITERATE*	WORDS LIKE *SOULLESS*	WORDS LIKE *ROOMMATE*
dissatisfied	accidentally	barroom
dissimilar	critically	bathhouse
dissuade	commonness	beachhead
illogical	drunkenness	bookkeeping
irrational	finally	cannot
irresponsible	formally	cattail
misshapen	meanness	cutthroat
misspelled	morally	glowworm
override	occasionally	penname
overrule	physically	rattrap
unnamed	stubbornness	yellowwood
unneeded	suddenness	
unnoticed	totally	*EXCEPTION*
		wherever

9. The *maintenance* model:

Certain words show a significant change of spelling when the part of speech changes, like the difference between *maintain* and *maintenance*.

WORDS CHANGING LIKE *MAINTAIN–MAINTENANCE*

concede	concession	pertain	pertinence
curious	curiosity	proceed	procedure
describe	description	pronounce	pronunciation
explain	explanation	recede	recession
omit	omission	repeat	repetition

10. The *sede-ceed-cede* words:

Only one word ends with *sede,* three with *ceed;* all of the others are spelled with *cede.*

-sede	*-ceed*	*-cede*	
supersede	exceed	accede	precede
	proceed	cede	recede
	succeed	concede	secede
		intercede	

11. The *raspberry* model:

The raspberry model involves silent letters which reflect the origin of the word and its early spelling in English: *raspis* (wine) + *berry.* These are consistently tricky words to spell:

WORDS LIKE *RASPBERRY*

Silent *b*
climb
debt
doubt
dumb
lamb
subtle
thumb

Silent *c, ch*
indict
muscle
scene
schism
yacht

Silent *d*
handsome
Wednesday

Silent *e*
eagle
manure

Silent *g*
gnat
gneiss
gnome
sign

Silent *h*
ghaunt
ghetto
ghost

Silent *k*
knife
knight
knot
know

Silent *l*
calm
could
palm
salmon

Silent *m*
mnemonic

Silent *n*
condemn
hymn
solemn

Silent *o*
courtesy

Silent *p*
comptroller
pneumonia
psychology

Silent *r*
February

Silent *s*
aisle
island

Silent *t*
listen
mortgage
often

Silent *u*
guess

Silent *w*
answer
grow
snow
write

12. The *echo-solo* model:

Some words ending in *o* form their plurals by adding *es* (*echoes*); others, including a large number of musical terms, add only *s*. A few have optional spellings.

WORDS LIKE *ECHO*		WORDS LIKE *SOLO*	
hero	heroes	alto	altos
mosquito	mosquitoes	canto	cantos
mulatto	mulattoes	Eskimo	Eskimos
Negro	Negroes	folio	folios
potato	potatoes	piano	pianos
tomato	tomatoes	ratio	ratios
tornado	tornadoes	soprano	sopranos
veto	vetoes	studio	studios

WORDS WITH OPTIONAL PLURALS (THE MORE COMMON FORM IS GIVEN FIRST)

buffalo	buffaloes	(buffalos)
ghetto	ghettos	(ghettoes)
halo	haloes	(halos)
motto	mottoes	(mottos)
no	noes	(nos)
volcano	volcanoes	(volcanos)
zero	zeros	(zeroes)

32S HOMOPHONES Words that sound alike but have different spellings and meanings, homophones are a common source of spelling errors.

air, heir	blew, blue	chord, cord
aisle, isle	boar, bore	cite, sight, site
allowed, aloud	board, bored	climb, clime
altar, alter	bough, bow	colonel, kernel
ascent, assent	brake, break	complement, compliment
	bread, bred	council, counsel
bail, bale	bridal, bridle	creak, creek
ball, bawl	but, butt	currant, current
bare, bear	buy, by	cymbal, symbol
base, bass		
beach, beech	cannon, canon	days, daze
beat, beet	capital, capitol	dear, deer
beau, bow	cast, caste	dew, do, due
bell, belle	cell, sell	die, dye
berry, bury	cent, scent, sent	discreet, discrete
berth, birth	cereal, serial	done, dun

dual, duel
dyeing, dying

earn, urn
earnest, Ernest

faint, feint
fair, fare
fate, fete
flea, flee
flew, flue
flour, flower
fore, four
forth, fourth
foul, fowl

gait, gate
gamble, gambol
gild, guild
gorilla, guerilla
grate, great
gray, grey
grisly, grizzly
groan, grown

hail, hale
hair, hare
hall, haul
hart, heart
heal, heel
hear, here
heard, herd
him, hymn
hole, whole

idle, idol
in, inn
it's, its

knead, need
knew, new
knight, night
knot, not
know, no

lain, lane
lead, led
lessen, lesson

lie, lye
load, lode
loan, lone

made, maid
mail, male
main, mane
manner, manor
meat, meet
medal, meddle
mussel, muscle

naval, navel
nay, neigh

pain, pane
pair, pare, pear
pale, pail
patience, patients
peace, piece
peak, pique
peal, peel
pearl, purl
pedal, peddle
peer, pier
plain, plane
pray, prey
pride, pried
principal, principle

rain, reign, rein
raise, raze
rap, wrap
read, red
real, reel
right, write, rite
road, rode, rowed
role, roll
root, route
rote, wrote
rye, wry

sail, sale
scene, seen
sea, see
seam, seem
serf, surf
serge, surge

sew, so, sow
shear, sheer
shone, shown
sign, sine
slay, sleigh
sleight, slight
soar, sore
soared, sword
sole, soul
some, sum
son, sun
staid, stayed
stair, stare
stake, steak
stationary, stationery
steal, steel
step, steppe
stile, style
straight, strait

tail, tale
taught, taut
team, teem
tear, tier
there, they're, their
threw, through
throne, thrown
tied, tide
to, two, too
toe, tow

vain, vane, vein
vale, veil
vial, vile

wail, whale
waist, waste
wait, weight
waive, wave
ware, wear, where
way, weigh
weak, week
weather, whether
wet, whet
which, witch
while, wile
whine, wine

yoke, yolk

32T SIMILAR WORDS Words that look alike or sound somewhat alike are a common source of spelling confusion.

> advice, advise
> angel, angle
> biding, bidding
> breath, breathe
> choose, chose
> cloths, clothes
> counsel, council, consul
> dairy, diary
> decent, descent
> desert, dessert
> elicit, illicit
> ever, every
> formally, formerly
> hoping, hopping
> human, humane
> later, latter
> local, locale
> loose, lose
> medal, metal
> moral, morale
> personal, personnel
> quiet, quite, quit
> statue, statute, stature
> thorough, through, trough, through, thought
> were, where

32U THE DICTIONARY AS AN AID Knowing how to spell is, of course, an economy measure. It saves time; it saves embarrassment. But to answer the questions that crop up in everyone's mind, the dictionary is the best source of information concerning common spellings and possible variants. Among the variants, most dictionaries will suggest which is preferred or at least which is more common. A writer who cares about the way he spells cannot afford to be without a dictionary.

MECHANICS OF LETTER FORM

Upon occasion, everyone must write a business letter, perhaps a letter of application, a letter of recommendation, a letter of inquiry, or a letter of complaint. Communications of this kind make a far better impression if they are typed on 8½ by 11 inch paper and follow a standard form. Two common models are included here for those people who would not ordinarily have engraved stationery for this kind of occasional letter.

32V BLOCK STYLE, OPEN PUNCTUATION

2638 Landor Avenue
Louisville, Kentucky
April 11, 1971

Central State Insurance Company
347 Michigan Avenue
Peoria, Illinois 61614

Gentlemen:

Re: Group Policy 2-A-5217

I have recently received my hospitalization policy from your company,
effective May 1, 1971. Included was a statement asking for an
advance payment of $65.50.

At the time I sent in my application for this policy, I included my
check in the amount of $65.50, and the canceled check has been
returned. Would you please see that my account is credited with
this payment?

Sincerely yours,

John F. Gerhardt

John F. Gerhardt

32W MODIFIED BLOCK STYLE, CLOSE PUNCTUATION

2638 Landor Avenue,
Louisville, Kentucky,
April 11, 1971.

Professor Chauncey Black,
Department of English,
University of Washington,
Seattle, Washington 98105.

Dear Professor Black:

I was enrolled in your course English 347 during the fall quarter of 1970. At that time, you will recall, I was forced to take an Incomplete because I was involved in a serious automobile accident.

At a later time, you told me that if I were not returning to the University it might be possible for me to take the final examination in absentia and receive credit for the course. I have spoken to Professor Edward Johnson of the Department of English of the University of Louisville, who has indicated that he would be willing to administer the test and return it to you. He and I can be available on either May 5 or May 12.

Would you please inform me if one of these dates and these arrangements are satisfactory? I am grateful for your interest and cooperation.

Very truly yours,

Simon Gerhardt

Simon Gerhardt

32X GUIDELINES FOR WRITING BUSINESS LETTERS

1. Even though the names of streets and states are usually spelled out, abbreviations may be used depending upon the formality of the letter.

2. Some title should always be used before a person's name as a part of the inside address:

   Mrs. J. P. Braker
   16 Fifth Street
   Honolulu, Hawaii 96822

3. If the letter is not addressed to a known person, salutations like "Gentlemen:" or "Dear Sir:" may be used.

4. Complimentary closes vary in their formality:

Highly formal:	Respectfully yours, Respectfully,
Formal:	Very truly yours, Yours truly,
Less formal:	Sincerely yours, Yours sincerely,
Personal:	Cordially, Sincerely,

5. Letters should always be signed, even though the name is typed for purposes of clarity.

33

Glossary of Additional Linguistic, Literary, and Rhetorical Terms

For terms not included here, consult the general index.

A

Ablaut   A linguistic process that varies the root vowel of some verbs and related forms to indicate a change in function and meaning: *sing, sang, sung, song.*

Accent   A means of using pitch and stress to highlight certain sounds. Every language has characteristic patterns of accent. Part of what we recognize as a foreign accent is a foreigner's tendency to use the accents of his native language in speaking another language. See *Versification.*

Accusative case   A term for the objective case, derived from Latin and used in the study of Old English and other Indo-European languages.

Affective fallacy   A phrase that implies that the tendency to judge the merit of a work by its emotional effect upon the reader is misleading. By such a standard, sentimental works might consistently be rated superior.

Affix   A covering term for any addition to the root of a word to form a new word. It includes prefixes (added before the base), suffixes (added after the base), infixes (added within the base), and reduplication (repeating part of the base form). Infixes and reduplication are not characteristic of Modern English words.

Alliteration   See *Sound effects.*

Allomorph   Allomorphs are variants of a single morpheme. The sounds of *s, z,* and *es* in *books, zoos,* and *matches* may all be considered variants of the plural morpheme.

Allophone   If a dozen speakers were asked to pronounce the word *bat,* they would all produce sounds represented by the common phonemes /b/, /æ/, and /t/. Yet the difference in their voices and the differences of pitch and stress would give these sounds slight variations. The phonetic variations of a phoneme are called allophones. See also *Phoneme.*

Anacolouthon   A rhetorical device by which a writer accidentally or deliberately breaks off his line of thought and then begins again. The strategy may be used intentionally to suggest hesitation, to insinuate, or to create a dramatic effect:

The opposition must be—whatever we do, we must do it decisively and quickly.

Analogy   The tendency to make things alike—a strong force in language change. A leveling out of inflectional differences in the past accounts largely for the dependence of Modern English upon word order. Analogy continues to act upon the language both in the grammar and in pronunciation, but many forms like *he don't* for *he doesn't* and *teeths* for *teeth,* which result from regularization by analogy, are nonstandard. For literary analogy, see pages 247–251.

Anaphora   A rhetorical figure in which one or more words are repeated at the beginning of successive sentences or lines of poetry. A similar repetition at the end is called epistrophe.

Where the city of the faithfulest friends stands,
Where the city of the cleanliness of the sexes stands,
Where the city of the healthiest fathers stands,
Where the city of the best-bodied mothers stands,
There the great city stands.

Walt Whitman, "Song of the Broad-Axe"

When the two devices are combined, as in the Whitman poem, the figure is called symploche.

Antistrophe   See *Ode.*

Antonym   The common definition of an antonym as one word meaning the opposite of another is not sufficiently broad. Antonyms are more accurately described as counterterms, including relative terms that are not necessarily opposites, like *stimulus-response, parent-child, compare-contrast,* and *careful-reckless.*

Apostrophe   A rhetorical trope in which the writer turns away from his subject to address directly an object, abstraction, or person, usually dead or absent. The shift is both emotional and dignified, therefore most appropriate in serious and stately contexts:

> So when this corruptible shall have put on incorruption, and this mortal shall have put on immortality, then shall be brought to pass the saying that is written, Death is swallowed up in victory.
> O death, where is thy sting? O grave, where is thy victory?
>
> I Cor. 15:54–55

Assonance   See *Sound effects.*

Asterisk   See *Starred form.*

Asyndeton   A rhetorical figure which omits conjunctions between a series of words, phrases, or clauses:

> I am alone, I am lost, I am abandoned.

The opposite figure of deliberately including conjunctions for a special stylistic effect is called polysyndeton:

> Then Job arose, and rent his mantle, and shaved his head, and fell down upon the ground, and worshipped, and said; Naked came I out of my mother's womb, and naked shall I return thither: the Lord gave, and the Lord hath taken away; blessed be the name of the Lord.
>
> Job 1:20–21

Augustan   Originally a reference to the remarkable literary age of Horace, Ovid, and Virgil under the Roman emperor Augustus (27 B.C. to A.D. 14). English writers in the first half of the eighteenth century appropriated the label for their own period because they considered the political stability of Augustus' reign a model for English government and sought to recapture the symmetry, precision, and decorous bearing of the Latin poetry of that same age. The term is used to name neoclassical resurgences in the literature of other nations, most notably France's *le grand siècle* of Corneille and Racine. See *Classicism.*

B

Ballad   Originally a folk form with its roots in oral tradition, the ballad is distinguished by a simple stanzaic pattern readily chanted or sung (see *ballad stanza*), often with a refrain. A ballad characteristically tells a story, using abrupt transitions, terse dialogue, and supernatural elements. Its themes are traditional ones—love failed, escape from danger, a great feat. The oldest English ballads date from the thirteenth to the fifteenth centuries. "Broadside ballads" in the eighteenth century gave up traditional folk themes but exploited the ballad's popularity with a mass audience by indulging in satire. The ballad's tie with folk literature loosened even more as its treatment became more literary and personal in examples such as Coleridge's *The Rime of the Ancient Mariner* and Ezra Pound's "The Ballad of the Goodly Frere."

Ballade   A poem consisting of three stanzas and an envoy, with the last line of the first stanza reoccurring as a refrain at the end of each of the other stanzas and the envoy. The stanzas may vary from eight to ten lines in length, but the eight-line rime royal is commonly used. The envoy is usually half the length of the stanzas and in substance dedicated to a person or personification. The form is French in origin and popular in medieval poetry. Chaucer wrote a "Ballade of Good Counsel"; Swinburne's "A Ballad of Dreamland" is an eight-line ballade. The form continues to be popular today.

Ballad opera   A development in eighteenth-century England as a reaction among English authors and critics to the invasion of the English theater by Italian opera. The most successful of these satiric song-dramas was John Gay's *The Beggar's Opera* (1728), which often travesties the artificiality and excesses of the Italian style.

Ballad stanza   A four-line stanza with alternating tetrameter and trimeter lines. The rhyme scheme is ordinarily *abcb,* with the shorter lines rhyming. Other ballads, however, use different rhyme schemes. Coleridge's *The Rime of the Ancient Mariner* is written in ballad stanzas.

Baroque   A literary style which attempts to achieve with words what artists of the baroque manner accomplished in painting, sculpture, and architecture. In art, the style is marked by a restlessness, dynamism, emotionalism, and ornateness. In literature, the style is characterized by sensuous appeal, metrical dissonance, paradoxes, extravagant conceits, and asymmetricality. The manner is represented by Luis de Góngora in Spain, Giambattista Marino in Italy, and the Metaphysical poets, particularly Richard Crashaw, in England.

Bathos   From the Greek word meaning "depth," perhaps best defined by Alexander Pope in the subtitle to his mock treatise *On Bathos* as "the art of sinking in poetry." Bathos is frequently an unintentional effect of "sinking" when a poet's Pegasus forgets how to fly. The effect is therefore either humorous or pedestrian or both. Even the best poets are capable of bathetic effects, as in Wordsworth's poem "Simon Lee":

Few months of life has he in store
As he to you will tell,
For still, the more he works, the more
Do his weak ankles swell.

Belles-lettres   Translated, the French term means "fine letters." It is used by the French to describe the serious pursuit of literary studies. As appropriated to English usage, however, its connotations of nice elegance and genteel quality have emphasized the subjective, sometimes precious, quality of individual taste; and the term and its adjective form "belletristic" have assumed a pejorative cast. The words are therefore used to describe writing that may be polished but thin in substance or those persons whose appreciation of literature is wholly idiosyncratic and whimsical rather than analytical and studied.

Bildungsroman   A term borrowed from the German, meaning literally "a novel of education." A *bildungsroman* is typically a novel in which a young man grows and matures and comes to some realization about life and himself. Goethe's *Wilhelm Meister's Apprenticeship* is an early example; Dickens' *David Copperfield* and Maugham's *Of Human Bondage* are later ones.

Bombast   A form of pretentious, overly inflated diction intended for a grandiose effect, but resulting often in general windiness. Bombast is therefore at times used intentionally for comic effect, as in a speech by Pistol in Shakespeare's *Henry IV, Part Two:*

Shall dunghill curs confront the Helicons?
And shall good news be baffled?
Then Pistol lay thy head in Furies' lap.

Bound form   Bound forms, as opposed to free forms, are those that are usually attached to the word base, and they change the meaning of the root. Most prefixes and suffixes are bound forms, although a few like *pro* and *con* may be either bound or free.

Bucolic   See *Pastoral.*

Burlesque   A literary technique which mocks persons, acts, or a particular kind of style by exaggerating, demeaning, or otherwise distorting the manner. When a trivial subject is treated in an elevated manner, like Pope's mock epic "The Rape of the Lock," the result is "high burlesque." When a serious subject is trivialized, like the judgment of the dead in Byron's "The Vision of Judgment," the result is "low burlesque."

Parody differs from burlesque in that it is based upon a particular work, using words and structures from the original to reduce it to absurdity. Joyce Kilmer's "Trees" has been frequently parodied. Burlesques satirize a general manner, as Cervantes' *Don Quixote* is in part a burlesque of the chivalric tradition as recorded in the medieval romances.

C

Caesura   See *Versification.*

Caricature   A device of deliberate distortion by taking the most obtrusive traits of a person or fictional character and exaggerating them. The strategy is common in satiric cartoons, but it is equally common in literature as a means of making particular characters absurd or simply as a means of heightening their identity, as Dickens often does with his characters.

Carpe diem   A phrase from Horace meaning "seize the day," used to describe a motif in poetry which emphasizes living for the pleasure of the moment, for tomorrow may never arrive. Robert Herrick's poem "To the Virgins to Make Much of Time," which begins with the line "Gather ye rose-buds while ye may," epitomizes the theme.

Catharsis   Originally a Greek medical term meaning a purgation, especially of the bowels. In the *Poetics,* Aristotle uses the term metaphorically to describe how pity and fear are diminished by the effects of tragedy. Whether he meant that the purging of pity and fear occurs in the viewer, who leaves the theater with a sense of release from having vicariously experienced the suffering of a worthy hero, or whether the purging is a trait of the tragic plot itself, in which the hero learns to see himself more deeply, has been a source of continued debate.

Chaucerian stanza   See *Rime royal.*

Cinquain   An American version of the Japanese haiku, consisting of five lines of varying length. The first line must be two syllables, followed by lines of four, six, eight, and two syllables, respectively.

Classicism   An attitude or frame of mind that holds that the established, orderly principles of conduct epitomized by Greek and Roman traditions are superior to the anti-traditionalism and emotional spontaneity associated with romantic habits of mind (see *Romanticism*). Although the distinction between classical and romantic attitudes is never firm, classicism in literature is generally taken to imply rational control, traditional thinking, and decorous restraint in style as opposed to private insight and the liberated spirit.

In the seventeenth and eighteenth centuries throughout Western Europe, a large number of writers deliberately looked back to ancient models, attempting to restore authority, discipline, and clarity to literature. This impulse, whenever it surfaces, is known as neoclassicism.

Prominent among the writers of neoclassical temperament were Corneille, Racine, and Molière in France; Dryden, Swift, Pope, Addison, and Johnson in England; and Benjamin Franklin in America.

Cluster   A general term covering any succession of sounds, words, or sentences. It is often a convenient term to substitute for phrase, clause, paragraph, or a group of phonemes.

Cognates   Words in different languages that are related to one another because of their common ancestry, thus Modern English, *sister;* German, *schwester;* Latin, *soror;* Italian, *suor;* Sanskrit, *svasar;* and Russian, *sestra*—all from Indo-European *swesor*. See *Starred form.*

Comedy   Like tragedy, comedy is a way of viewing life; it is not exclusively a literary term. Essentially, it is a way of looking at life that invites tolerance for the follies and weaknesses of men. If tragedy tends to elevate man, showing us the strength of man in his capacity to endure the trials of life, causing us to look up to him, comedy changes the perspective. We are not looking up at figures larger than life or identifying with them on an equal level. Comedy tends to place characters in such roles that the audience views detachedly, or the audience is able to assume a superior stance that causes it to make observations on the action; it is led to comment, criticize, and find amusement in the follies of everyday affairs.

Comedy lacks the inevitableness of tragedy. Man is not trapped. In comedy, characters are permitted to emerge from complex situations and continue on their way in good spirits. It is a part of poetic justice and the spirit of comedy that offenders of good sense, good humor, and proportion will be punished. Living must go on. Even though comedy is an antidote to tragedy, it does not ignore the sadness of life, but it does show man's capacity to jump back from the edge of disaster, to cope with living. It is a positive view.

The outside world itself tends to be the arena of comedy, not the universe or the inner being. It often deals with everyday affairs, with nonheroic characters, with manners in the broad sense of the word, with the absurd and petty nature of man, with foibles, with the playful side of serious subjects like love, ambition, and corruption. Because comedy is a detached view, it can even make disaster funny. The hijinks of farce would be only calamities if we identified with the victims and felt that they were being seriously injured. Comedy does not permit a preoccupation with grief.

Comedy is didactic in a number of ways. Its view of life may be instructive to those who see only gloom and catastrophe in human affairs. Its tendency to highlight incongruity can sensitize viewers to the humor of situations; its frankness provides an antidote to self-deception. Its pronouncements about vice and folly may be forthrightly moral. Its wit may be a corrective. All in all, it is a glorification of man's love of living, despite the problems and adversities of everyday affairs.

Literary history includes a number of different labels identifying comedies with particular themes and conventions: romantic comedy, *commedia dell'arte,* comedy of humours, comedy of manners, sentimental comedy, and tragicomedy. But these can be meaningfully explained only in terms of the times during which they thrive and in terms of specific conventions that differentiate them. See separate entries for each.

Comedy of humours   Plays in which characters are shaped to illustrate one of the prevailing humours of medieval physiology. The predominance of one kind of liquid in the body, either blood, phlegm, yellow bile, or black bile, was supposed to produce a corresponding sanguine, phlegmatic, choleric, or melancholic disposition in the person. Even though a play like Ben Jonson's *Every Man in His Humour* (1598) utilizes the device freely, other comedies include characters, like Jacques in *As You Like It,* who owe their eccentricity to a particular humour. Even a serious character like the melancholic Hamlet may be viewed as a humour character.

Comedy of manners   Basically a sophisticated kind of comedy concerned with social manners in the broad sense of the term. The characters are usually drawn from high society; the dialogue is witty; the satire sharp. William Congreve's *The Way of the World* (1700) is often cited as a prototype. The form was popular in Restoration England and eighteenth-century France, but Oscar Wilde and Bernard Shaw gave the type new vigor in modern times.

Commedia dell'arte   A highly stylized form of comedy originating in Italy in the sixteenth century and popularized throughout Europe by traveling companies. The actors of the company improvised the dialogue consistent with the outline of a plot and appropriate to the stock characters, some of whom wore masks. The most familiar figures were a foolish merchant Pantalone; a pompous and pedantic man of learning called the Doctor; a boastful but cowardly captain Scaramuccia; the youthful Arlecchino or Harlequin, famous for his tight, multicolored costume; Pulcinella, a long-nosed buffoon (later the Punch of Punch and Judy puppet shows); Columbine, the sweetheart of Harlequin; and Pierrot and Pierrette, clown lovers. These same characters are still commonly seen in the circus, ballet, opera, and painting and are often made into dolls, puppets, and marionettes.

Common measure   See *Hymn stanza.*

Conceit   A word derived from "conceive," which originally described an image or comparison, but which is now almost exclusively associated with exaggerated, far-fetched metaphors, commonly found in poems written in the Petrarchan or Metaphysical manner. In Elegy XIX, John Donne addresses his mistress:

My mine of precious stones, my empery,
How blest am I in this discovering thee!

In a humorous twist upon the traditional inflated praise of the mistress in the Petrarchan manner, Shakespeare wrote:

My mistress' eyes are nothing like the sun;
Coral is far more red than her lips' red;
If snow be white, why then her breasts are dun;
If hairs be wires, black wires grow on her head.

The Metaphysical conceit is also common in the twentieth century among poets who have found new values in seventeenth-century poetry:

Dear love, these fingers that had known your touch,
And tied our separate forces first together,
Were ten poor idiot fingers not worth much,
Ten frozen parsnips hanging in the weather.

John Crowe Ransom,
"Winter Remembered"

Consonance See *Sound effects*.

Copula A grammatical term borrowed from the Latin and applied to linking verbs (see p. 447). The term is retained by some new grammarians.

Counterpoint See *Versification*.

Couplet Two rhyming lines, usually of the same meter. Couplets are called end-stopped if each line is a complete grammatical unit:

Those oft are stratagems which errors seem,
Nor is it Homer nods, but we that dream.

Alexander Pope, *An Essay
on Criticism*

Run-on couplets are those in which the sense of one line is carried over to the text. The blending of two lines is called enjambment:

Whan Zephirus eek with his swete breeth
Inspiréd hath in every holt and heeth
The tendre croppes, and the yonge sonne
Hath in the Ram his halve cours y-ronne,

Chaucer, "Prologue,"
The Canterbury Tales

Courtly love A literary tradition of love-making that flourished in the Middle Ages and continued to find expression in various forms throughout the Renaissance. The concepts of courtly love grew out of the socio-economic conditions that prevailed in feudal times. The first and most important principle of the courtly tradition was that love and marriage were irreconcilable because desire as a matter of free choice could not exist in a relationship in which duty and necessity were the compelling factors. Secrecy was an essential condition of beginning love; fear was a stimulus. Lyrics in which poet-lovers express their adulation for remote and cold mistresses and their own frustration at their inaccessibility were actually disguises for adulterous and illicit relations, although at times a lover expresses his desire for a requited love quite unambiguously. Love is an art concerned with vows, oaths, and complaints. The lover weeps, sighs, sorrows, and dies; the mistress refuses to love or is inconstant. The outward expression of love was formal, polished, and elegant.

This art of love first became a system in the north of France. The themes were crystallized in the narrative poems of Chrétien de Troyes and set down as a code in *The Art of Courtly Love* (1170) by Andreas Capellanus. By the middle of the twelfth century, the tradition had become a mock religion. It may have died with the decline of the troubadour in the thirteenth century if it had not been given new inspiration and refinement by poets like Guinicelli, Cavalcanti, Dante, and Petrarch. See *Petrarchanism* and *Neo-Platonic love.*

Creole   A term used to characterize a pidgin language that becomes the mother tongue of a subordinate group. Louisiana Creole originated among African slaves on French-owned plantations. Gullah is a creolized language from English, originally spoken by African slaves and found on the sea islands off South Carolina and Georgia. See also *Pidgin.*

D

Dative   A term borrowed from Latin to apply to one of the inflected cases in Old and Middle English and other Indo-European languages. The case of the indirect object in Modern English, formerly the dative case, is identical in form with the objective case (they gave *me* the money). The idea of the dative is now expressed by prepositional phrases: *to him, for her.*

Declension   A system of showing nouns, pronouns, and adjectives in all of their inflectional varieties. Since nouns and adjectives in Modern English have so few changes, declension is useful mainly in presenting the forms of the pronoun (see p. 436).

Decorum   Attention to propriety and appropriateness, a notion most popular in periods marked by a classical belief in right order and "everything in its place." The term is used generally to suggest a code of behavior based on tastefulness and restraint. Its literary use more specifically applies to the suitability of language to the thought of a particular work. Dryden explained decorum as "appropriateness of words to action"; Jonathan Swift wrote, "Proper words in proper places makes the true definition of a style."

Dénouement   A French term meaning "an untying," referring to that part of a play in which the complications of the plot are unraveled or in which the characters come to some realization about themselves. Dénouement is therefore the culmination of the action following the rising action and climax.

Deus ex machina   Literally meaning "God out of a machine." The term originally had reference to the act of lowering a character to the stage by means of a machine to represent the intervention of some supernatural being in the affairs of men. By extension, *deus ex machina* refers to any sudden appearance, miraculous event, or improbable device which extricates characters from dilemmas.

Diagramming   A visual means of sentence analysis by indicating on a diagram the relations among words in a sentence. The patterns of diagramming vary greatly, both in traditional grammar and in modern systems. The method and models are a complete study in themselves.

Dialectic   A philosophical term with varying implications. It frequently refers to the pursuit of truth by a question and answer method, as exemplified by the Socratic dialogue. In Plato's program of studies for the preparation of the philosopher-king as set forth in *The Republic,* dialectic represents the highest level of education, to be undertaken only between the ages of 30 and 35; it leads directly to the perception of the ultimate, pure reality in the Platonic epistemology. At a later period, the Stoics clearly differentiated dialectic from rhetoric. The first was a form of wisdom; the second, a form of eloquence. In the nineteenth century, Hegel considered dialectic a kind of logical progression proceeding from thesis to antithesis to synthesis. The Hegelian formula was adapted by Marx to economic and historical change.

Digraph   A group of two letters representing a single speech sound (*ea* in *head, th* in *both*). The word is often confused with a ligature, which in printing is a character that combines two or more letters (Æēlfric), or with a dipthong, which is a combination of vowel sounds pronounced as one.

Doggerel   A term used to describe uninspired and inferior verse. Sometimes used deliberately for comic effect by distorting meters and rhyme, as in Samuel Butler's mock-heroic poem *Hudibras:*

> Besides, he was a shrewd philosopher,
> And had read every text and gloss over;
> Whate'er the crabbed'st author hath,
> He understood b' implicit faith,

Dramatic monologue A form of dramatic poetry in which one character's spoken lines and, at times, his private thoughts are set down as a means of self-characterization. The poem also includes an awareness of setting and other characters to whom words may be spoken. Robert Browning's "My Last Duchess" is perhaps the single most famous poem of this type, although Edgar Lee Masters and Edwin Arlington Robinson among American poets have produced equally fine character portraits.

E

Eclogue See *Pastoral.*

Elegy In Greek and Roman poetry, the elegy was not bound by a particular subject matter but by an exclusive use of the elegiac couplet. Love was a predominant theme. In the Augustan age, the elegy reflected the cosmopolitan spirit of a sophisticated age, treating the lighter aspects of contemporary life and a love *à la mode.* In English poetry, the convention of a prescribed meter was abandoned. Even though love elegies continued to be written by poets like Marlowe and Donne in imitation of Ovid, Catullus, and Propertius, the form since the time of the Renaissance has become almost exclusively associated with a poem written upon the death of a particular person. Among noteworthy examples are Milton's "Lycidas," Shelley's *Adonais,* and Arnold's "Thyrsis," all written in the pastoral manner; Tennyson's *In Memoriam,* an extended series of lyrics written over a period of seventeen years in memory of Arthur Henry Hallam, has been called the greatest elegy of the nineteenth century.

Enjambment See *Couplet.*

Epanalepsis A rhetorical figure which produces an echo effect by repeating the beginning word at the end of the sentence:

When wilt thou save the people? O God of mercy, when?
Josiah Booth

Epic A long narrative poem consisting of numerous episodes and adventures, drawn together by a central heroic figure and the poet's own purpose. Epics frequently represent a glorification of a race or nation, although poems like Milton's *Paradise Lost* or Dante's *The Divine Comedy* may treat the ultimate destiny of all mankind. Milton states that his theme is to "assert Eternal Providence,/And justify the ways of God to men."

Because of the themes of high importance and the grand scale of epics, the style is characteristically elevated and dignified. Homer's *Iliad* and *Odyssey* became the models for all subsequent literary epics of the Western world, although the conventions that grow out of them were more and more formalized by the tradition. Thus the stylization of later epics can be best understood in terms of earlier examples. Epics characteristically begin with an invocation to a muse for inspiration and the recital of a question and answer, which often set the theme of the epic. The action then follows a set formula. It begins in the middle of things (*in medias res*), followed by a section during which the hero narrates antecedent events (retrospective narration); the major action then continues to the end. In the course of the narration, the epic usually includes descriptions of battles and tests of strength, catalogs of characters or ships or arms, a visit to the underworld, the intervention of the gods to protect the hero, and long debates about actions to be taken. The description is frequently interspersed with extended comparisons, usually referred to as epic similes.

Among the great literary epics in this tradition are Virgil's *Aeneid,* Tasso's *Jerusalem Delivered,* Spenser's *The Faerie Queene,* and Milton's *Paradise Lost.* Among the so-called folk epics, probably written without knowledge of the literary tradition described above but reflecting the same spirit of an heroic age, are the Anglo-Saxon *Beowulf,* the French *Song of Roland,* the Finnish *Kalevala,* and the German *Nibelungenlied.*

Epigram   Now a pithy statement, in prose or verse, marked by humor and wit, often turning upon a twist of thought or play upon words. The form, originally an epitaph in the Greek, later developed into a short polished poem on almost any topic. In Latin literature, it was cultivated by Martial; in English literature, it is particularly associated with Donne, Jonson, and Pope. The two-line epigram is particularly common:

Thy flattering picture, Phryne, is like thee
Only in this, that you both painted be.
Donne, "Phryne"

Epilogue   The counterpart of the prologue at the ending of a play, in which one of the actors usually remains on the stage to reflect upon the action, to philosophize or moralize, and to send the audience on its way. Shakespeare's *As You Like It* ends in this fashion.

Epistrophe   See *Anaphora.*

Epithalamion, also **epithalamium**   A wedding song, a kind of occasional poem, usually of lyric beauty, popular when it was customary to escort the bride and bridegroom to the wedding chamber. The poem is therefore a song in honor of the couple, including praise of them, a description of the wedding and the wedding feast, and blessings upon their future. Examples may be found among the works of the classical poets, including Pindar, Theocritus, and Catullus; among English poets, Sidney, Donne, Jonson, and Herrick may be included. Perhaps the most celebrated poem of this kind is Edmund Spenser's "Epithalamion," written on the occasion of his own wedding to Elizabeth Boyle (1594).

Epode   See *Ode.*

Existentialism   A philosophical mode of thought whose starting point is that we can know things only as they are, not as they are in essence. This position is summarized in the familiar expression: "Existence precedes essence." Existentialism therefore operates in a human setting; it depends upon human consciousness as its means of perception. It is concerned with the actual, the human, and the possible. It offers no guarantees of success or ultimate salvation, as science and traditional religion tend to do. It urges the individual to act, because he *is* what he makes of himself. Man defines himself.

   The diversity of thinkers who are labeled existentialists, both atheists and religious theologians, can be explained mainly by the fact that existentialism, in its preoccupation with the human situation, focuses mainly upon the analysis of possibilities open to man in his relation to other men and conditions. It therefore embraces many positions and attitudes. In 1947, Jean-Paul Sartre asserted that existentialism was positive and optimistic, not negative and despairing. As a philosophy, of course, it can be either.

   In the post-World War II period, in the aftermath of mass destruction and killing, existentialism became associated with all that was painful, dreadful, hopeless, and unstable about the human condition. Existentialism seemed to explain the desperate situation in which man found himself. The spiritual climate of post-World War II Europe did not create existentialism; it illustrated the negativism implicit in it and set the tone of the movement for decades to follow. Existentialism became faddish as an expression of the meaninglessness and absurdity of life. Its themes found expression in literature and art; its anti-authoritarianism led to protest against established values and institutions, even to mannerisms of dress which reflected individual contempt for bourgeois respectability.

In philosophy, the movement is associated with Karl Jaspers, Martin Heidegger, Soren Kierkegaard, and Jean-Paul Sartre. In literature, its spirit is reflected in the works of Sartre, Simone de Beauvoir, Albert Camus, and André Malraux.

Expletive   A general term in grammar meaning "filler." It is most commonly used to refer to *it* and *there* when they are used to fill in the subject position as a means of moving the subject ahead: *There was no reason to stay. It was his responsibility to call.* Expletive may also be used to refer to any kind of absolute construction that is added to a sentence for effect:

Confound it, that isn't right.

Expressionism   A literary movement with its origins in Germany in the pre-World War I period, but strongly influencing later writers, particularly dramatists. Expressionism converted the skepticism and malaise of the *fin-de-siècle* writers into an aggressive activism, directed against bourgeois values, industrial materialism, and social injustice. At the same time that writers realistically appraised the conditions of life around them, they assumed a messianic role, calling for a regeneration of all human values, a new purity and serenity in men, and a return to the values of primitive Christianity. Prominent among expressionist dramatists were Georg Kaiser, Ernst Toller, and Fritz von Unruh.

The lasting influence of expressionism, however, was its effect upon structure, stagecraft, and acting in the drama. In order to express their ideas fully, expressionist dramatists, using Strindberg as their model, abandoned the illusionism of the realistic stage and exploited any theatrical device which would convey both idea and feeling. Thus lighting, music, stylized acting, and distorted scenery gained new emphasis; the apron stage and revolving stage facilitated a different kind of action made up mainly of short scenes. These techniques have continued to be developed in the drama of the second half of the twentieth century. Even though expressionism is closely associated with drama, the fiction of Franz Kafka and James Joyce employs techniques that can be called expressionistic.

F

Fable   A story told for a specific moral or allegorical purpose, commonly represented in literature by the beast fable, which uses animals acting and speaking like human beings. In essence, the fable instructs about human affairs, but depends upon the power of the writer to keep the reader simultaneously aware of animal traits and human tendencies. The fables of Aesop and LaFontaine are successful in this way. More extended and sophisticated uses of the beast fable for satiric purposes include Chaucer's *Nun's Priest's Tale,* Spenser's *Mother Hubberds Tale,* John Dryden's *The Hind and the Panther,* and George Orwell's *Animal Farm.*

Fabliau A short tale, in verse or prose, usually bawdy and humorous in its details, particularly associated with the Middle Ages, although parallel examples may be found in early Latin and Oriental literature. The emphasis in these stories is upon practical jokes and lively action, although considerable interest also arises from the satire directed toward the clergy, marriage, and hypocrisy. Chaucer gives fabliaux to the Miller and the Reeve in *The Canterbury Tales.* Others are included in Boccaccio's *Decameron.*

Figure A covering term used to refer to any kind of metaphorical, symbolical, or rhetorical variation of ordinary words and speech patterns. See *Trope* and *Scheme.*

Folio A bibliographical term used to designate the size of a book. Folio refers to a sheet of paper folded once to make two leaves or four pages; quarto is a sheet folded twice to make four leaves or eight pages; and octavo is a sheet folded three times to make eight leaves or sixteen pages. The First Folio of Shakespeare's plays (1623) therefore refers to the format in which they appeared. Many of the plays also appeared originally in quarto editions.

Fin de siècle A French term meaning "end of the century," now signifying a general spirit of decadence, but more specifically referring to the "art for art's sake" movement at the end of the nineteenth century associated with the work of Walter Pater, Oscar Wilde, and Aubrey Beardsley. Their interest in aesthetics, polish, and refinement contrasted sharply with the strong bourgeois values of the age, suggesting an idea of effeteness and elitism among the exponents of the movement.

Frame See *Slot.*

Free form A language form that can stand alone, in contrast to a bound form that must be attached to a word base. In the word *unmentionable, mention* is a free form; *-able* is a bound form in this word, but could also be used as a free form; *un-* is a bound form only.

Free verse Free verse is free only in the sense that it abandons the rules of traditional prosody. It is often a verse that sets up its own rhythmic patterns based upon a principle of cadences rather than regular accents. Lines of free verse might be thought to fall into arcs rather than feet, suggesting the effect of a musical phrase. Two lines of Whitman's "Out of the Cradle Endlessly Rocking" shows the wavelike surging and ebbing of his verse:

From your memories sad brother,

from the fitful risings and fallings I heard;

From under that yellow half-moon late-risen and swollen as if with tears.

Each of the arcs has from two to four major stresses; these key words are pulses, but they do not come at regular intervals. They are determined by the sense of the line and the rhetorical devices the poet chooses to use. Free verse depends strongly upon repetition, parallelism, recurring images, and sound effects other than rhyme. The lines may vary in length, often determined by the sense, the rhythmic arcs, the emphasis, and rhetorical devices such as anaphora. Stanzas are flexible in form like those of the ode. Free verse accommodates itself to natural speech patterns, to the logic of the writer's thoughts, and to his desire to evolve the shape of his own peom. It need not be expansive form, as it often is in poems by Whitman and D. H. Lawrence. It can also convey concise, tight thoughts, as it does in poems by Wallace Stevens, William Carlos Williams, and E. E. Cummings.

A strong precedent for free verse in English comes from Hebrew poetry, particularly as it is translated in the King James version of the Bible. Passages from Job, Isaiah, Song of Solomon, and particularly the Psalms illustrate the dependence of this verse upon principles of symmetry:

I am come into my garden, my sister, my spouse:
I have gathered my myrrh with my spice;
I have eaten my honeycomb with my honey;
I have drunk my wine with my milk:
Eat, O friends; drink, yea drink abundantly, O beloved.

Song of Solomon, 5:1

The principles of free verse are also inherent in Old English poetry. The lines are irregular in length, with stresses falling upon the words demanded by the sense. Each line consists of two halves divided by a well-defined caesura, with two stresses in each half and an unspecified number of unstressed syllables. The two parts

are joined by the alliteration of two or three of the stressed syllables:

Oft Scýld Scéfing   scéaþena þréatum,
mónegum mægþum   méodo-sètla oftéah

Beowulf

Despite these requirements, the lines are flexible and clearly
rhythmical in the spirit of free verse.

One other variety of the free metrical line is called sprung
rhythm, invented by Gerard Manley Hopkins. Its most marked
feature is the juxtaposition of stressed syllables without intervening
unstressed ones. It is therefore sometimes called an accent meter.
A line of sprung rhythm is measured by the number of strong
accents, not the number of feet or syllables. Like Old English verse,
with which it shares common principles, sprung rhythm also depends heavily upon alliteration and other sound effects:

I caught this morning morning's minion, kingdom of daylight's dauphin,
dapple-dawn-drawn Falcon, in his riding

Hopkins,
"The Windhover"

Unlike other free verse poets, Hopkins frequently wrote in traditional stanza forms and used rhyme. See pages 242–245.

G

Gothic novel   A form of horror story which arose in the eighteenth
century as an early manifestation of the romantic spirit. Gothic
was descriptive of the pervasive gloomy atmosphere and grotesquerie suggested by medieval cathedrals. Novels and romances
written in the manner featured an abundance of villainous characters, sensational events, secret passageways and dungeons, macabre
effects, and supernatural happenings. The prototype of the Gothic
novel was Horace Walpole's *Castle of Otranto* (1764), although
the best known one is probably *Frankenstein* (1817) by Mary
Wollstonecraft Shelley. Modern writers continue to elaborate upon
the basic type.

Grapheme   A term sometimes used to differentiate the letters of the
writing system from the phonemes of the language. One phoneme
may be represented by several graphemes. Thus the phoneme /f/
appears as *f* in *fox,* as *ff* in *muffin,* as *gh* in *rough,* and as *ph*
in *physics.*

Grimm's Law   A complex principle of language change which explains in what way the consonants of Indo-European words shifted in the Germanic languages and did not shift in others. The changes that took place over a period of several hundred years between 500 and 200 B.C. may be summarized as follows:

SOUNDS IN INDO-EUROPEAN	BECAME	SOUNDS IN GERMANIC
bh, dh, gh (voiced)	→	b, d, g, (voiced)
p, t, k (voiced)	→	f, th, h (voiceless)
b, d, g (voiced)	→	p, t, k (voiceless)

Grimm's law therefore explains the difference between such cognates as Latin *piscis,* English *fish;* Latin *dentum,* English *tooth;* Latin *granum,* English *corn.*

H

Haiku   A Japanese form, consisting of three lines designed to give a sharp image. The lines consist of five, seven, and five syllables, respectively.

Harmartia   See *Tragic flaw.*

Heroic drama   A kind of grandiose drama popular in England after the opening of the theaters in 1660 following the Puritan interregnum. The plays emphasized themes of honor and love, featuring heroes of noble valor and heroines of unexceptional purity. The plots were involved and marked by stirring scenes of action and violence, inflated speeches, and the inevitable triumph of the hero in war and love. John Dryden's *The Conquest of Granada by the Spaniards* (1670) represents the type; it is mocked by George Villiers in his play *The Rehearsal* (1671).

Heteronym   Words of the same language that have identical written forms but different pronunciations and meaning: *dove* (the bird), *dove* (variant of *dived*); to shed a *tear,* to *tear* a page.

Homonym   Words of the same language that have identical spelling and pronunciation but different meanings: *pool* of water, play *pool;* pole, Pole. *Homonym* is sometimes defined to include homophones.

Homophone   Words of the same language that sound alike but have different spellings and different meanings. They are a common source of puns and of spelling errors: *bear, bare; meat, meet; to, two, too; they're, their, threw, through.* See *Homonym.*

Horatian ode   See *Ode.*

Hubris or **Hybris**   See *Tragic flaw.*

Humanism   An intellectual movement throughout Europe in the fourteenth, fifteenth, and sixteenth centuries, marking a shift in emphasis from a preoccupation with metaphysical issues and other-worldliness in the Middle Ages to a new concern with man and his problems in this life. The change in intellectual climate identifies the beginnings of the Renaissance with its glorification of human potentiality, the importance of the individual, and the spirit of inquiry and discovery. One of the important manifestations of Humanism was its revival of ancient classics in order to seek out models for human conduct and thinking in the ancient writers. New emphasis was placed upon learning the original languages (Erasmus taught Greek at Cambridge), and translations of early works were made available in England for the first time. Among the distinguished English Humanists and scholars were William Grocyn, Sir Thomas More, Thomas Linacre, John Colet, and William Lyly.

Hymn stanza or **Common measure**   A four-line stanza with alternating lines of iambic tetrameter and iambic trimeter, rhyming *abab* or *abcb.* The hymn stanza is similar to the ballad stanza but much more strictly measured.

I

Idyll   See *Pastoral.*

Imagism   A literary movement in poetry during the first quarter of the twentieth century, strongly influenced by the ideals of literary impressionism—the experience as seen and felt by the poet, but set down in sharp, concentrated visual images, like one from Ezra Pound's "Dance Figure":

White as an almond are thy shoulders;
As new almonds stripped from the husk.

The aims of the movement were set down in the preface to an anthology entitled *Some Imagist Poets* (1915). The basic principles were (1) to use exact words from common speech rather than decorative ones; (2) to avoid echoing old rhythms as a way of finding new ways of expression; (3) to place no limits upon the subject matter of poetry; (4) to write in precise images; (5) to avoid the "blurred and indefinite" in favor of the "hard and clear";

(6) to assert the belief that "concentration is of the very essence of poetry."

Besides Pound, the leader of the movement, and Amy Lowell, one of its chief advocates, Imagist poets included Hilda Doolittle, John Gould Fletcher, Richard Aldington, T. E. Hulme, F. S. Flint, and D. H. Lawrence. Even though these poets soon abandoned the purely imagistic poem because of its narrow range of expression, the movement was to influence twentieth-century poetry strongly in its move toward freer rhythms and more inclusive subject matter.

Impressionism   Less well defined as a literary movement than as an art movement, but associated with the principle that the artist considers the way he feels about characters and scenes more significant artistically than facts about them. Impressionism therefore emphasizes a highly personal view of art, in which the writer's own temperament, experiences, and moods predominate. In German literature, the movement included the plays of Arthur Schnitzler and Hugo von Hofmannsthal and the early fiction of Thomas Mann, often reflecting a bittersweet skepticism and a general *fin-de-siècle* atmosphere. Impressionism marked a transition from the realistic and naturalistic emphasis of the nineteenth century to a neoromantic, symbolic tradition of the twentieth century. See *Expressionism* and *Imagism*.

Intentional fallacy   A critical phrase that holds that the success of a literary work need not be judged in terms of the author's own design or intentions concerning it. They might be unknown or extremely limited. The work can be viewed as an object in itself.

Interlude   See *Morality play*.

International Phonetic Alphabet   Commonly referred to as the IPA. The IPA was designed by the International Phonetic Association to provide symbols by which the sounds of any language could be transcribed and understood by the speakers of another language. The phonemic alphabet of English given on page 368 uses many of the IPA symbols.

Invocation   A formal address to the deity, a muse, or to some other source of inspiration for the poet. The invocation traditionally marks the beginning of an epic, but many other poems, like Shelley's "Ode to the West Wind," begin in a similar way:

O wild West Wind, thou breath of Autumn's being,

. . . .

Wild Spirit, which art moving everywhere;
Destroyer and preserver; hear, oh, hear!

K

Kenning A type of abbreviated metaphor particularly characteristic of Old English poetry. Kennings tend to be circumlocutions; they describe persons or things in a picturesque way: "heath-stalker" for stag, "whale-road" for ocean, and "jewel of the heavens" for the sun.

Kinesics Kinesics is the study of all facial expressions, body movements, and gestures used for communication. It is sometimes lightly referred to as "body English."

L

Ligature See *Digraph*.

Limerick A catchy five-line stanza, rhyming *aabba*. The third and fourth lines are shorter than one, two, and five.

Lingua franca During the Middle Ages, a group of West Europeans known as the Franks traveled as crusaders to the eastern end of the Mediterranean. The language they used among the Levantines, called *lingua franca,* is the earliest record of a pidgin in use. By extension, the term is now applied to any hybrid language that is used, ordinarily for commercial purposes, between people who do not share a common tongue. See *Pidgin*.

Litotes A rhetorical term for understatement which gains its particular effect by phrasing in the negative what it wishes to say positively. "This is no small accomplishment" means "This is an accomplishment of considerable magnitude"; or "That is not at all unpleasant" means "It is pleasant."

Lyric Originally, a poem to be sung by an individual to the accompaniment of the lyre and differentiated in Greek times from choric odes. Although lyrics are no longer written necessarily to be sung, they do remain the expression of feeling by a single voice, whether the poet's own or that of a persona. The lyric is unspecified in form or theme, although it is usually a brief poem. Poems that are narrative, dramatic, or discursive tend to be classified differently and are referred to as lyrics only if the verse is sufficiently moving and musical to justify the epithet "lyrical."

M

Malapropism A term used to describe the kind of humorous blundering with language typical of Mrs. Malaprop in Sheridan's play *The Rivals* (1775). A malapropism ordinarily confuses two words resembling one another in sound: *supercilious knowledge* for *superficial knowledge; psychosemantic illness* for *psychosomatic illness; prostrate gland* for *prostate gland.*

Masque   A highly stylized form of dramatic entertainment, particularly popular in the sixteenth and seventeenth centuries. Masques were usually commissioned for a special celebration and were performed both indoors and outdoors on the estates of wealthy nobles. Masques were therefore often performed only once because they were written for a particular person or occasion. The host and members of his family were frequently given parts. The productions were lavish, including elaborate costumes, singing, dancing, and pageantry, at times involving machinery which allowed the spectacular effect of supernatural figures entering "from above." The plots were thin, but highly moral in tone, often casting mythological and allegorical characters in key roles. The poetry was lyrical. One of the popular features of the entertainment was the anti-masque or antic-masque, which featured animals or men in animal disguise, and usually represented a counterforce, like the deadly sins, to the good characters of the main plot. The names of Ben Jonson and Inigo Jones are intimately associated with the period during which the masque flourished.

Melodrama   Melodrama bears a close relation to tragedy in that it concerns itself with the calamities and afflictions of human experience, but it does so with a different effect. Melodrama appeals to the passions and sympathies of an audience without necessarily producing the catharsis associated with tragedy. Melodrama tends to be less complex than tragedy; it views the issues of life as clearly right and wrong, not as ambiguous and paradoxical as tragedy views them. It emphasizes plot and situation rather than depth of character. The tendency of melodrama to make clear-cut distinctions has made it a suitable literary form for presenting political and moral problems. In serious melodrama, virtue does not always win; in popular melodrama, of course, virtue always triumphs.

The implications of the word *melodramatic* are those drawn from melodramas concerned with sensational effects, exciting action, and flamboyant characters. It suggests extravagance and intrigue. Yet one need not associate all melodrama with plays like *Uncle Tom's Cabin* and *Ten Nights in a Bar-room,* designed for their propaganda value and famous for their stock characters and elements of suspense. The term might also usefully describe many Renaissance and Jacobean plays, which exploit intrigue and shock, yet whose characters fall short of tragic suffering and realization.

Metaphor   See pages 247–249.

Metaphysical conceit   See *Conceit.*

Meter   See *Versification.*

Miracle play   A form of medieval religious drama popular in the fourteenth and fifteenth centuries. The term *mystery play* is sometimes used to designate those plays based exclusively on Biblical material as opposed to the *miracle play,* concerned with the lives of saints and the conversion of pagan characters. Only a very few plays of the second variety are extant. More commonly, however, *miracle play* is used to include the far more numerous plays based on scripture.

   The miracle plays were at first performed in the church, then in the churchyard, and finally were divorced altogether from the church when the responsibility for their staging and cost were assumed by the town guilds. The guilds often vied with one another in the elaborateness and ingenuity of the staging. Two types of performances were common: the stationary, in which the platforms were built in the town square and the audience moved from one to another to view a different play; and processional, in which the audience remained stationary and the plays were mounted on wagons and rotated among the assembled groups. Miracle plays were often called Corpus Christi plays because the Thursday following the eighth Sunday after Easter was the main occasion for the performance of entire cycles of plays.

   Four cycles of miracle plays are extant in English and one in Cornish: the Chester cycle, consisting of 25 plays; the York cycle, consisting of 48 plays; the Coventry cycle, consisting of 42 plays, and the Wakefield cycle, consisting of 32 plays and including *The Second Shepherds' Play,* perhaps the best known of these dramas. The Cornish cycle consists of 50 episodes divided into three main parts. All of these plays draw upon Biblical themes extending from the story of Creation to the Day of Judgment. It has been estimated that they cover eighty-nine different episodes from the Bible.

   Despite the religious nature of the plays and their design to instruct and bolster the faith of the laity, the plays were not without their humor. Among the early humorous characters were the devil himself, Noah's wife, depicted as a nag and husband-beater, and Herod, a raving tyrant, whose ranting behavior became the norm for the expression "to out-herod Herod." Cycle plays continued to be produced well into the sixteenth century. They represent a strong, continuous tradition of dramatic production from the Middle Ages to the Renaissance that prepared England for the full flowering of its drama during the Age of Elizabeth.

Morality play   A later development of the medieval play, abandoning scriptural characters and stories as the basis for action and substituting allegorical characters and personifications. The plays were written to enforce a moral, sometimes ethical in nature, sometimes doctrinal, and sometimes political. One of the best examples is the *Castle of Perseverance* (1471), in which the central figure representing all mankind is attacked by the seven deadly sins, defended by the cardinal virtues, and forced to take refuge in the Castle of Perseverance. In the final judgment scene, his many sins are forgiven him and he is saved by Christ's mercy. An equally famous morality play is *Everyman* (ca. 1500), which still enjoys performances today.

The weightiness of these allegorical dramas was balanced by the introduction of humorous characters, particularly the devil and Vice, whose amusing scenes together added variety and anticipated the kind of brief humorous interlude which became popular in the fifteenth century.

Morpheme   The linguist's basic term for the smallest unit of language that conveys specific meaning. A morpheme may be free or bound; it may be a part of a word or a word itself. It is not to be confused with a syllable. *Incurable* is four syllables but three morphemes: (1) the root *cur*[*e*], (2) *in-* meaning "not," and (3) *-able* meaning "capable of." *Kentucky* is three syllables but one morpheme. *Chairs* is one syllable but two morphemes: *chair* and the plural morpheme *s*.

Morphology   The study of the structure of words. It concerns their derivation and inflection as contrasted with syntax, the study of their arrangement.

Mystery play   See *Miracle play*.

N

Naturalism   Naturalism is sometimes differentiated from realism in time and in degree. It was a continuation of the realistic view into the late nineteenth and twentieth centuries; it was also an intensification of that view. Emile Zola was the progenitor of the school, although he preferred to call it a method. Zola maintained that literature would have to apply the methods of science to the understanding of human nature and behavior. Thus, ideal naturalism would be a kind of clinical reporting; men would be natural organisms under observation. Naturalism did not put limits upon subject matter; the German naturalistic dramatist Gerhart Hauptmann was labeled "the painter of the putrid."

Besides its detached objectivity and harsh realism, naturalism emphasized a deterministic view of life, based upon the natural laws of heredity and environment. The tendency to see man as a victim of a purposeless universe and vast social and economic forces working against him leads to a prevailing mood of pessimism in naturalistic works.

Besides Zola and Hauptmann, naturalistic writers include Georg Büchner, a forerunner of the movement in Germany; Stephen Crane, Frank Norris, and Jack London in America.

Neoclassicism   See *Classicism.*

Neo-Platonic love   New impetus was given to the fashionableness of Petrarchanism in the sixteenth century by Pietro Bembo and his followers, who combined Platonism with this popular tradition. The doctrines of Platonism coincided admirably with the Petrarchan conventions and in many instances served as a philosophical commentary on a previously unexplained love. As Marsilio Ficino interpreted Platonic love, the souls of true lovers departed from heaven under the same astral influence; true love in this world was merely a recognition of like soul quality and the fusion of those souls. Passion emanated from the soul, not the senses. Love itself was contemplative in nature. The lover's praise of his mistress' beauty was not a cataloging of her physical charms but, refined from sensuousness, an expression of the idea of woman. This kind of love ennobled the lover and moved him to excel in virtue in order to be deserving of his mistress. With its emphasis upon love as a matter of mind and soul, Neo-Platonism moved the literary expression of love to a higher plane of thought but often left the lyrics themselves highly formal and empty of feeling.

Neoromantic   See *Romanticism.*

Nominative   A term for the subjective case, used in Latin and in the study of Indo-European languages, but also used at times by modern grammarians.

Novella   A term borrowed from the Italian, originally used to designate short narratives in prose, like those in Boccaccio's *Decameron,* popular during the Middle Ages and Renaissance. Since the development of the short story in the nineteenth century, novella is used to designate a story of approximately 30,000 or 40,000 words, between the typical length of the short story and the minimum length of the novel of approximately 60,000 words. The intermediate length of the novella permits the writer to achieve effects different from either the short story or the novel so that the difference is not strictly one of length. Melville's *Bartleby,* Conrad's *Heart of Darkness,* and Faulkner's *The Bear* may be cited as examples.

O

Objective correlative A means of objectifying and expressing emotion by finding a set of equivalent circumstances or objects which will evoke the same feeling as the one the writer wishes to express. Thus, T. S. Eliot illustrates, the state of Lady Macbeth's mind during the sleepwalking scene is conveyed by a series of sensory impressions.

Obscenity What is considered obscene in language at one particular time is not invariably obscene, primarily because a word itself is not indecent or offensive, only its associations in the mind of the user or listener. Many words in common use have obscene implications in private circles. Obscenity is an attitude of mind. It is also a way of responding. The differences of viewpoint and reaction among people give obscenities their shock value. If an obscene word loses its capacity to offend, it is no longer obscene.

Octavo See *Folio.*

Ode A stanza of unspecified number of lines and rhyme scheme, given to the praise of a person or a particular subject, such as Emerson's "Ode: Inscribed to W. H. Channing" or Keats's "Ode on Melancholy." Two traditions exist, the Pindaric and the Horatian.

The Pindaric ode follows the pattern of odes composed by Pindar for choral recitation. The form consists of three stanzas called the strophe, antistrophe, and epode. Strophe means "turn" and refers to the movement of the chorus as it chanted the ode up one side of the orchestra; the antistrophe was the second stanza as the chorus moved down the other side. The epode was the final stationary song, sometimes called the stand, as the chorus faced the audience.

The Horatian ode, in imitation of the poems of Horace, is an ode in which subsequent stanzas of the poem follow the pattern of the first stanza, like Keats's "To a Nightingale." An irregular ode is one like Wordsworth's "Ode on Intimations of Immortality" or Coleridge's "Ode on Dejection" in which the stanzas vary both in length and pattern.

Onomatopoeia   See *Sound effects.*

Oration   At the present time, any formal speech, but in ancient times an address which followed a prescribed form set down by Quintilian and embodied in the orations of Demosthenes and Cicero. Traditionally, the oration had seven parts, although some of them were at times varied or combined: (1) exordium, introducing the subject; (2) narration, presentation of the circumstances and background of the issue; (3) proposition, a brief statement of the point to be established; (4) division, a definition of terms and an outline of the parts; (5) confirmation and proof, the main part of the speech including the arguments; (6) refutation, the anticipation of objections; and (7) peroration, a summarization and final impassioned plea. Milton's *Areopagitica* (1644) is a notable example of the classical oration in English.

Ottava rima   A stanza consisting of eight lines of iambic pentameter, rhyming *abababcc,* used by Byron in *Don Juan* and "The Vision of Judgment."

Oxymoron   A rhetorical trope that links together two sharply contrasting terms. Instances are particularly common in poetry: "darkness visible" (Milton); "living deaths, dear wounds, fair storms, and freezing fires" (Sidney); "By this good wicked spirit, sweet angel devil" (Drayton); "Let the rich wine within the goblet boil,/ Cold as a bubbling well" (Keats).

P

Paradigm   A grammatical term for the arrangement of all of the forms of a word into an established pattern. It includes the declensions of nouns and pronouns and the conjugation of verbs.

Parody   See *Burlesque.*

Parsing   An outmoded method of grammatical analysis designed to explain the relationships of all words in a sentence and the rules governing the relationships. A model of parsing from Volume I of Lindley Murray's *An English Grammar* (2d ed., 1809) will suggest why the technique in this form has died:

"Vice produces misery."

Vice is a common substantive, of the third person, the singular number, and in the nominative case. *Produces* is a regular verb active, indicative mood, present tense, in the third person singular, agreeing with its nominative "vice," according to RULE 1. which says: (*here repeat the rule*.) *Misery* is a common substantive, of the third person, the singular number, and the objective case governed by the active verb "produces," according to RULE XI, which says, &c.

Particle   A rather loosely defined, inclusive term for uninflected parts of speech, including articles, prepositions, conjunctions, interjections, and adverbs used with verbs.

Pastoral   A tradition of literary expression using the rural life of shepherds and shepherdesses as the model for a kind of idyllic existence. The term *bucolic,* derived from the Greek word meaning "herdsman" or "rustic," designates the same tradition. Pastoral poems were frequently written as eclogues, taking the form of a dialogue between two shepherds.

Pastoral poetry has its origins in the poems of Theocritus, a Greek poet of the third century B.C., whose idylls, as they were called, depicted simple scenes of life in Sicily. To a Roman citizen like Virgil, pastoral life was a contrast to the complexities of cosmopolitan life and an ideal escape. It also became a convenient way of commenting indirectly upon a corrupt society and thus a suitable vehicle for satire and allegory (Virgil's *Fourth Eclogue* was long interpreted as a pagan anticipation of the birth of Jesus). As a sophisticated literary mode, pastoralism was popular among English writers of the Renaissance, including Sidney, Spenser, Shakespeare, Milton, and Marvell.

Pathetic fallacy   A phrase used by John Ruskin in *Modern Painters* to describe the tendency of poets to ascribe human attributes to inanimate objects, particularly to manifestations of nature. Although Ruskin disapproved of what he considered the untruth of phrases like "cruel, crawling foam" and "the spendthrift crocus," the phrase is now used in a neutral sense to characterize the poetic illusion that objects of nature feel and react as men do. Compare *Personification.*

Pathos   From a Greek word meaning "suffering," often a part of tragedy but not synonymous with true tragedy. Pathos is an effect produced by literature and other art forms which arouse feelings of pity and compassion and often grow out of scenes of misfortune, misery, death, or separation. Pathos appeals directly to the feelings. The difference between pathos and sentimentality is at times only one of degree.

Periphrastic construction   An alternate way of expressing the meaning of inflections by using particles and auxiliaries:

Periphrastic genitive: *the beauty of Seattle* instead of *Seattle's beauty*

Periphrastic comparison: *more clean* instead of *cleaner*
Periphrastic indirect object: *gave to him* instead of *gave him*
Periphrastic verb form: *he does go* instead of *he goes.*

Personification or **prosopopoeia**   A rhetorical and poetic way of describing abstractions or inanimate objects in human terms. Personification is common in poetry, as in lines by Sir Philip Sidney:

But words came halting forth, wanting Invention's stay;
Invention, Nature's child, fled step-dame Study's blows.

Petrarchanism   The Italian poet Petrarch (1304–1374) was to exercise a major influence upon the love lyric because he was accepted by later Renaissance writers as their master. Their model was his poetry to Laura in the *Canzoniere,* expressing his unattainable but ennobling love over a period of twenty-one years for a married woman whom scholars now believe may not have existed at all. Petrarch's poetry embodied not only an idealistic concept of chaste devotion but also an essentially human passion. His imitators at least presumed to follow these ideals and the elegance of his style, but hit mainly upon the eccentricities of his verses—the antitheses, the puns, the conceits, and the exaggerations. These devices became the marks of the Petrarchan manner, which in the fifteenth and sixteenth centuries moved more and more toward extravagance.

Phoneme   A phoneme is a working term in linguistics to cover a range of sounds that we recognize as separate from any other range. In this sense, a phoneme is comparable to a primary color. Yellow, for example, includes hues of differing brightness and saturation, but we call them by a common name and recognize them as distinct from red, blue, and green. Similarly, we recognize fine differences of pronunciation, pitch, and stress among speakers, but we give their various contrasting sounds a common name. A phoneme is the smallest unit of contrasting sound that makes meaning and understanding possible. If we could not hear the differences between /k/, /b/, and /m/, we would not be able to understand *cat, bat,* and *mat,* which differ only in the first phoneme.

   The English language has approximately thirty-three distinct vowels and consonants, called segmental phonemes, and approximately twelve different degrees of pitch, stress, and juncture, called suprasegmentals. Linguists are not agreed upon a uniform phonemic alphabet for English, and all speakers do not necessarily have all of the phonemes in their speech. (See p. 368 for a phonemic alphabet.) Other languages have their own systems of phonemes, which may vary in number from thirteen to seventy-five. A phonemic alphabet therefore pertains to only one language. A phonetic alphabet may be international in scope. See also *International Phonetic Alphabet.*

Phonemics The study of the sounds of a language in terms of its phonemes and phonemic system. Phonemics is important to the study of the grammar and meaning of a language and thus to the learning of a new language.

Phonetics The study of actual speech sounds and the way in which they are produced. Phonetics is important in acoustics, speech theory, the physiology of hearing, and other matters of sound production.

Phonics A method of teaching reading and spelling by emphasizing the sound value of letters.

Phonology An inclusive term for the study of sound, including both phonemics and phonetics. Phonology may direct its attention to the description of sounds at a given time or to the history of sound changes over a period of time.

Pidgin By folk etymology, also spelled *pigeon.* Pidgin is a utility language spoken by two groups which do not have a language in common. It ordinarily operates with a reduced grammatical system and a vocabulary drawn mainly from words of various languages. For example, the 1500 words of Melanesian pidgin include approximately 75 percent from English, 20 percent from native languages, and 5 percent from German, Malay, and others. Pidgin is not to be confused with pig Latin or the standard version of an American trying to communicate with an Italian or a Chinese. Various pidgins exist, of which pidgin English is only one. Pidgin is often ingenious in combining words to express different concepts. The following phrases from Melanesian pidgin suggest how a pidgin language functions:

gras bilong hed (hair)
gras bilong maus (beard)
yu brokim barat, nau yu go go go go (you cross a ditch, and then you keep going)

Pindaric ode See *Ode.*

Polysyndeton See *Asyndeton.*

Prefix A combining form attached to the beginning of a root or word base so as to change its meaning: *un*prepared (not prepared), *anti*social (averse to society).

Preterit   Alternate term for past tense, commonly used in the study of Old and Middle English.

Prologue   In drama, a brief introductory statement by one of the actors, sometimes designated as the Chorus, to set the action, to summarize the theme of the play, or to offer the author's apologies or comments. The Prologue to *Romeo and Juliet* may be accepted as fairly typical. See *Epilogue*.

Prosody   See *Versification*.

Prosopopoeia   See *Personification*.

Purple passage   A familiar phrase used in criticism to designate a particularly quotable passage, especially if it is characterized by elaborateness, eloquence, or colorfulness. The phrase was first used by Horace in *The Art of Poetry* when he described "one or two purple patches . . . sewed on to make a fine display in the distance." The phrase is frequently used in a pejorative sense to describe a passage that seems to strive too hard for its effect.

Q

Quadrivium   See *Trivium*.

Quarto   See *Folio*.

Quatrain   A flexible stanza of four lines, sometimes of equal length and sometimes not (see *Ballad stanza* and *Hymn*), with rhyme schemes of considerable variety. The heroic quatrain or elegiac quatrain consists of lines of iambic pentameter, rhyming *abab*. Blake uses it in "The Little Black Boy" and "The Chimney Sweep." The four-line stanza used by Fitzgerald in *The Rubaiyat of Omar Khayyam* is iambic pentameter, rhyming *aaba*. The quatrain of Tennyson's *In Memoriam* is iambic tetrameter, rhyming *abba*. Frost uses tetrameter lines rhyming *aaba* in "Stopping by Woods on a Snowy Evening," but the final stanza is *aaaa*. The quatrain is a highly flexible and popular form among English and American poets.

R

Realism   A way of looking at life and writing about it without illusion or without an imaginative transformation of the facts, recording what is with as much objectivity as the writer is capable of assuming. A realistic view also tends to take a certain focus: it is more likely to be preoccupied with the middle class rather than the nobility, with hardship rather than ease, with commonplaces rather than extravagances, with humanitarian values rather than aesthetic ones, with materialism rather than idealism, with the ordinary and everyday rather than the exotic and unique. By its selection of details it tries to be representative of the whole of daily living.

Realism, of course, has prevailed in all literature at all periods. Upon occasion, however, usually in reaction to the excesses of a previous age, it serves as a substantial bread-and-butter diet for the literary artist. Modern realism had its roots in the movement that began in France in the 1830s with the efforts of Honoré de Balzac to set down a complete picture of the social life of contemporary France in a monumental project entitled *The Human Comedy.* In twenty years, Balzac produced more than 95 novels, novelettes, and short stories in an effort to complete his depiction of contemporary manners. By midcentury, realism had taken hold through the added efforts of Gustav Flaubert and the brothers Goncourt and was being denounced as immoral and ugly. But the movement was to move to further extremes of verisimilitude in the work of Guy de Maupassant and Emile Zola. See *Naturalism.*

Associated with realism in English literature to varying degrees were Daniel Defoe, sometimes referred to as the father of English realism, Henry Fielding, George Eliot, William Makepeace Thackeray, Anthony Trollope, and Thomas Hardy. American realists include William Dean Howells, Mark Twain, Henry James, Theodore Dreiser, and Sinclair Lewis. The Russian scene of the nineteenth century was particularly conducive to the realistic temperament and produced two of the world's greatest realists, Tolstoy and Dostoevsky.

Refrain   See *Sound effects.*

Repetition   See *Sound effects.*

Rhyme   See *Sound effects.*

Rime royal or **Chaucerian stanza**   A stanza consisting of seven lines of iambic pentameter, rhyming *ababbcc,* so named because James I of Scotland wrote a poem in this form. Chaucer uses it in *Troilus and Criseyde* and other poems.

Romance   From a Latin adverb *romanice,* meaning "in the Latin manner," used to refer to early French dialects, later specifically to Old French, and finally to anything written in French. Languages derived from Latin are commonly referred to as Romance languages.

Today, romance suggests a love story. The emphasis probably derives from those medieval romances which involve some of the

most famous lovers of all times—Tristan and Iseult, Launcelot and Guinevere, Aucassin and Nicolette, and Floris and Blanchefleur. Although a love interest was often included in the romances, it was not an indispensable ingredient. The basic material was knightly activity. The romance may therefore be defined as a story of adventure, often based on historical characters but narrating fictitious incidents, frequently involving the miraculous and supernatural, written in verse or prose. The earlier romances dating from as early as the twelfth century are in verse; the later ones extending through the fourteenth century tend to be in prose. Romances are frequently classified under three headings, indicating the source of their materials: the matter of Greece and Rome, stories about Troilus and Criseyde, Aeneas, and Alexander; the matter of France, stories about Charlemagne and his knights; the matter of England, stories about Arthur and the familiar Knights of the Round Table.

Although the romance as a story of adventure shares elements with the epic, the romance tends to be a more superficial form, less concerned with character development, organic unity, and lofty purpose. The romance, however, does reflect a chivalric age and is a source of information about social status, mores, and interests during the Middle Ages.

Romantic comedy   A term that refers specifically to Renaissance comedies about lovers in an idyllic, pastoral, or woodland setting rather than to any comedy about love. The comedy depends strongly upon disguised characters and the intrigue and laughter that grow out of the deception. Shakespeare's *As You Like It* is one of the best examples.

Romanticism   A spirit or attitude that prevails at any period when the claims of the individual, his feelings, and his freedom to act and respond without the restraints of the past are given first priority. Romanticism as a manifestation of literature is almost always a part of a cycle, a breaking away from the established traditions of a previous age that honors moderation, restraint, and decorum. The great Romantic era of Western literature occurred in Europe and America during the nineteenth century, following the period of Neoclassicism in the seventeenth and eighteenth centuries. In Germany, the chief exponents were Goethe, Heine, and Schiller; in France, Dumas, de Musset, Hugo, and George Sand; in Russia, Pushkin and Lermontov; in England, Wordsworth, Coleridge, Keats, Byron, Shelley, and Sir Walter Scott; in America, Poe, Emerson, Thoreau, and Whitman. In Germany and England, the movement was early (Goethe and Scott died in 1832); in France and America the movement was delayed.

Because Romanticism typically represents a regeneration of individual values, it is difficult to generalize about its particular manifestations. Among individual writers, however, the nineteenth-century movement marked a new interest in the freedom of the common man, a concern for natural genius, intuition, spontaneity, and sensation, a belief in nature as a source of inspiration and goodness, a preoccupation with the mystical, exotic, and supernatural, a revival of interest in the Middle Ages, popular ballads, and ancient folk legends, a glorification of the natural and primitive as opposed to the ordered and civilized, a distaste for imitation, rules, and elegance, a disapproval of traditional forms and artifices, and a special trust in the powers of the imagination. Romanticism was a literary expression of the spirit of revolution that had already occurred in the political life of France and the American colonies.

Any period that marks a revival of those qualities which are peculiarly Romantic is usually referred to as a period of Neoromanticism. The abstract and symbolic plays of William Butler Yeats may be considered Neoromantic.

Root The base of a word without prefixes, suffixes, or inflections: *seg* (meaning "to cut") is the root of *suprasegmentals,* which includes the prefix *supra-,* the suffixes *-ment* and *-al,* and the plural inflection *s.*

S

Scansion See *Versification.*

Scheme A rhetorical figure of speech used to refer to any arrangement of word patterns for special effects, like those of alliteration, parallelism, and climax. In this sense, schemes may be differentiated from tropes, but the terms are sometimes used interchangeably.

Schwa Term used to describe the neutral sound given to vowels in unaccented syllables, whether in first, medial, or final position: *a*bove, hab*er*dasher, off*i*ce, lett*u*ce, Cub*a*. The symbol for schwa is /ə/.

Semantics The branch of linguistics concerned with the meanings of words, particularly the changes of meaning throughout history, variations of meaning in different contexts, extensions of meaning by connotation, confusions of meaning, social implications of meaning, and practical problems of meaning in occupations like advertising and law.

Sentimental comedy A development in comic drama during the eighteenth century as a reaction to the indecency of comedies of manners during the Restoration period. The emphasis of these plays falls upon characters who confess their faults, repent their erring ways, and thus demonstrate the perfectability of human nature. Excessive feelings, pathetic scenes, and moral sentiments abound, although the plays are not without satiric purpose. Sir Richard Steele's four comedies, including *The Conscious Lovers* (1722), represent the type.

Sentimentality An exploitation of the tender feelings in such a way that the reader reacts negatively to the oversensitization. Sentimentality is consistently used as a term condemning a surfeit of sweetness, an excess of tenderness, an overdisplay of gentleness, or a melodrama of tears. Recognition of sentimentality is, of course, relative. Some readers like to indulge their feelings; others are far more protective of their soft spots.

Sermon In medieval times, the form of the sermon often followed the model of the classical oration. It fell into six parts: (1) theme, the announcement of the text and translation of it into the vernacular; (2) pro-theme, an expression of humility on the part of the preacher and an invocation for God's help; (3) dilation, an expansion upon the text; (4) exemplum, an illustration in the form of a story drawn from life or literature; (5) peroration, the application of the lesson; and (6) a closing epilogue, usually in Latin.

Seven cardinal virtues See *Seven deadly sins.*

Seven deadly sins According to medieval theology, the cardinal sins were pride, envy, wrath, sloth, avarice, gluttony, and lust. These were considered "deadly" because they were punished by spiritual death unless the offender underwent true penitence. The sins are widely referred to and personified throughout the literature of the Middle Ages and Renaissance. The corresponding seven cardinal virtues were faith, hope, and love (the Christian virtues) and prudence, justice, fortitude, and temperance (the temporal virtues derived from Plato).

Shibboleth In the sense of a test word or phrase, the term is derived from the story in Judges 12:4–6 in which the Gileadites are able to discover their enemies, the Ephraimites, by asking them to pronounce *shibboleth,* the word for "an ear of grain." Because the Ephraimites spoke a different dialect of Hebrew, they were unable to pronounce the *sh* sound. Any peculiarity of pronunciation that marks a group or nationality is considered a shibboleth.

Simile A particular kind of comparison, marked by the use of the words *like* or *as:*

> Yet in these thoughts myself almost despising,
> Haply I think on thee, and then my state,
> Like to the lark at break of day arising
> From sullen earth, sings hymns at heaven's gate.
>
> Shakespeare, "Sonnet XXIX"

The term metaphor is often used to include the simile.

Slot Part of a sentence pattern that can be filled in various ways. A subject slot, for example, may be filled by a noun, a pronoun, a verbal, a noun clause, or a prepositional phrase. Paragraph patterns also provide slots, according to the new rhetoricians. Many paragraphs are written in a TRI pattern, consisting of a topic, restriction, and illustration. Each slot may be filled by one or more sentences or be omitted altogether.

Solecism A formal term designating the mixture of nonstandard usage in standard written or spoken English; therefore, an impropriety or incongruity in the use of language.

Sonnet See pages 242–244.

Sound effects One of the chief delights of poetry is its sound, sometimes its melodiousness, sometimes its suggestion of actual sounds, sometimes the appropriateness of sound to meaning. Word choice is, of course, the most important factor in the creation of sound in a poem, but the choices themselves are often determined by devices that poets use. Seven of these are a part of the poet's repertory of techniques.

ALLITERATION

Sometimes referred to as beginning rhyme and limited as a principle to the repetition of beginning consonant sounds, although hidden alliteration often occurs in internal and end syllables. In lines like those from Shakespeare's "Sonnet XXX," both the alliteration of *s*'s and *w*'s and the repetition of the *s* in medial and final positions are working together to produce the total sound effect:

> When to the sessions of sweet silent thought
> I summon up remembrance of things past,
> I sigh the lack of many a thing I sought,
> And with old woes new wail my dear time's waste.

Alliteration has operated as a major poetic technique in English poetry from Anglo-Saxon times to the present.

ASSONANCE

Repetition of vowel sounds throughout a poem, either exact duplications or resemblances. The device is frequently used to establish a tone appropriate to the thought of the line. Compare the opening lines of Milton's companion pieces on joy and melancholy:

Hence loathed Melancholy
  Of Cerberus and blackest midnight born,
In Stygian Cave forlorn
  'Mongst horrid shapes, and shrieks, and sights unholy.

"L'Allegro"

Hence vain deluding joys,
  The brood of folly without father bred,
How little you bested,
  Or fill the fixed mind with all your toys.

"Il Penseroso"

Melancholy is described in rounded, back vowels, low-pitched in sound; joy is described in opened, front vowels, high-pitched in sound.

Assonance can also be used as a variation upon exact rhyme when a word falls in a final stressed position, as in lines from Thomas' "And Death Shall Have No Dominion":

And death shall have no dominion.
Dead men naked they shall be one
With the man in the wind and the west moon;
When their bones are picked clean and the clean bones gone,

CONSONANCE

A kind of half-rhyme or consonantal rhyme in which the consonants are parallel but the vowels are different. Wilfred Owen uses consonance instead of exact rhyme in "Arms and the Boy":

Let the boy try along this bayonet-blade
How cold steel is, and keen with hunger of blood;
Blue with all malice, like a madman's flash;
And thinly drawn with famishing for flesh.

Consonance is sometimes used synonymously with alliteration or as a term to describe the reoccurrence of consonant sounds at the end of words.

ONOMATOPOEIA

An attempt to reinforce the meaning by using words that suggest the sounds they describe. The device can be used imitatively, as in Kipling's "The Song of the Banjo":

With my *"Tumpa-tumpa-tum-pa tump!"*

Or it can be used suggestively with varying degrees of subtlety:

Over the cobbles he clattered and clashed in the dark inn-yard,
And he tapped with his whip on the shutters, but all was
      locked and barred.

Alfred Noyes,
"The Highwayman"

The ice was all around:
It cracked and growled, and reared and howled.

Coleridge,
The Rime of the Ancient Mariner

The curfew tolls the knell of parting day,
The lowing herd winds slowly o'er the lea,

Gray,
"Elegy Written in a Country Churchyard"

The lark, that tirra-lirra chants,
   With hey! with hey! the thrush and the jay,

Shakespeare,
The Winter's Tale

REPETITION

The repetition of single words is a common technique and done almost always with a dramatic effect:

Blow, bugle, blow, set the wild echoes flying,
And answer, echoes, answer, dying, dying, dying.

Tennyson,
The Princess

We're foot—slog—slog—slog-sloggin' over Africa—
Foot—foot—foot—foot—sloggin' over Africa—
(Boots—boots—boots—boots—movin' up an' down again!)
　　There's no discharge in the war!

Kipling,
"Boots"

Lisp'd to me the low and delicious word death,
And again death, death, death, death,

Whitman,
"Out of the Cradle Endlessly Rocking"

REFRAIN

Repetition of a complete line at the end of a stanza, often with a musical effect or an intensification of the meaning of the words. It is commonly used in French stanza forms like the ballade and villanelle. Henley's "Ballade of Dead Actors" repeats the line "Into the night go one and all" at the end of each of three stanzas and the envoy.

RHYME

The identity of two words with one another because of the resemblance of their sounds. If the repetition of sounds is close, like *eyes* and *sighs,* the rhyme is said to be exact or perfect. But many rhymes are suggestive rather than exact, like John Crowe Ransom's rhyme of *drunkard* and *conquered* or C. Day Lewis' *womb* and *home* or Emily Dickinson's rhyme of *shown* and *cocoon.* These are sometimes referred to as half-rhymes, slant rhymes, off-rhymes, or various other terms which suggest their approximate nature. See also *Consonance* and *Assonance.*

The most familiar rhyme, of course, is that which occurs at the end of a line in a stressed syllable, called end-rhyme. Other rhyme, however, may occur internally, tending to divide a long line into two definite parts if it occurs at the caesura, as in Poe's well-known line from "The Raven":

Once upon a midnight dreary, while I pondered, weak and weary.

Rhymes like *dreary* and *weary,* with the stressed syllable followed by an unstressed one, are called feminine rhymes. Rhymes of single stressed syllables are masculine. Rhymes are designated as double (*bolder, shoulder*) or triple (*intuition, erudition*) in terms of the number of rhyming syllables. Some rhymes appear to be only eye-rhymes, like Marvell's

> And yonder all before us lie
> Deserts of vast eternity.

Although some modern writers use eye-rhymes intentionally, their presence in earlier poems often testifies to changes in pronunciation that have taken place. In fact, rhymes are one of the important sources of knowledge concerning the pronunciation of sounds in the past.

Rhyme can be used as a source of humor by matching unexpected words, as in Gilbert's lyrics for *The Mikado*. The rhyme for *exist* turns out to be *philanthropist*. One of Ogden Nash's favorite devices for humor is to force words into a pattern of rhyme:

> One kind of sin is called a sin of commission, and that
>   is very important,
> And it is what you are doing when you are doing something
>   you ortant.
>
> "Portrait of the Artist as a
Prematurely Old Man"

Functionally, the use of rhyme goes beyond its sound qualities. Its occurrence interlocks the parts of a poem, it gives emphasis, it reinforces the meaning, it establishes the tone of a poem. In these ways, it operates as one of the poet's most effective resources.

Spenserian stanza A nine-line stanza, eight lines of which are iambic pentameter and the final line a hexameter. The rhyme scheme is *ababbcbcc*. It is, of course, the stanza form of Spenser's *The Faerie Queene,* but other poets have used it also in major works— Byron in *Childe Harold,* Shelley in *Adonais,* and Keats in "The Eve of St. Agnes."

Spoonerism A garbling of words by accident, usually by transposing the initial sounds of two words: *Sheats and Kelly* for *Keats and Shelley.*

Stanza A grouping of lines of verse in a particular pattern. The stanza may sometimes coincide with a complete sentence; at other times, it is comparable to a paragraph representing the longer development of an idea. A stanza may be a logical unit, or it may be a strictly formal unit defined in terms of line length, meter, and rhyme scheme. See *Versification.*

Separate entries on stanza forms include:

Ballade	*Ottava Rima*
Ballad stanza	*Quatrain*
Cinquain	*Rime royal*
Couplet	*Sonnet*
Haiku	*Spenserian stanza*
Hymn stanza	*Tail-rime stanza*
Limerick	*Tercet*
Ode	*Villanelle*

Starred form   A word or construction marked with an asterisk indicates that it is a hypothetical form, reconstructed on the basis of verifiable principles of sound change: **kei,* an Indo-European word meaning "to lie" or "to remain," is the base for words like *heim* in German and *home* in English. The starred form is also used at times to identify an unacceptable or ungrammatical construction.

Stream of consciousness   A narrative technique by which the writer attempts to reproduce the timeless flow and free association of the inner thoughts of a character. The disconnectedness, irrelevance, lack of structure, and uncensored thoughts are successful in revealing the subconscious mind and allowing a psychological probing not possible by traditional narrative devices. Molly Bloom's interior monologue at the end of James Joyce's *Ulysses,* transcribed without any punctuation, is one of the most sustained uses of the technique in literature.

Strophe   See *Ode.*

Stylistics   Sometimes used interchangeably with *style,* but more specifically refers to the application of linguistics to the study of style. Stylistics is therefore primarily descriptive, placing emphasis upon measurable, quantitative data, for example, word frequency, average sentence length, characteristic use of grammatical forms, and transformations.

Suffix   A combining form added after the root or word base so as to change its meaning and often its grammatical classification. Suffixes are either derivational (consider*able,* improper*ly*) or inflectional (pillbox*es,* soft*er*).

Superfix   The symbol written above a word to indicate stress, pitch, and juncture (see p. 369). Also used as a term to describe the interworking of stress, pitch, and juncture in a single pattern.

Syllable   A division of a word based upon pronunciation. A syllable consists of at least one sound, usually a vowel: *syc-a-more, sen-sa-tion.*

Symploche   See *Anaphora.*

Synaesthesia   A special metaphorical effect in which one of the senses is used to describe the perception of another sense:

> But the creaking empty light
> Will never harden into sight . . .
>
> Edith Sitwell

Synonym   A word that means essentially the same thing as another word in the language. Even though some synonyms can be used interchangeably, others may differ in their connotation, tone, and idiomatic use. *Instance, example,* and *illustration* are relatively close synonyms; *object, remonstrate,* and *kick about* are sharply divided in tone.

T

Taboo, verbal   Modern taboos against words result from an attitude of purism about language or from moral bias. These modern taboos are scarcely more rational than primitive taboos, but they often make sense in terms of the sensibilities of people who are offended by specific words under certain circumstances. Needless to say, there are far fewer taboos in the 1970s than there were in the 1870s or even in the 1920s, but taboos are not necessarily limited to matters of sex or obscenity. It is equally important what words we use to address Italians, Jews, or the man who collects the garbage or the one who cleans our office building. All inappropriate terms become taboo. Glossaries of usage are filled with taboos, often disguised by soft phrases that nevertheless threaten the offender with some evil, usually social disapproval. Modern English has a plentiful supply of euphemisms to ease the sting of harsh words. All supposedly is good that sounds good.

Tagmeme   A term from tagmemic grammar, associated chiefly with the work of Kenneth L. Pike. Tagmemic grammar, basically a slot-filler grammar, is one grammar that has concerned itself with units beyond the sentence. A tagmeme refers to a slot like the subject of a sentence and to the class of words, like a noun phrase, that can fill it. A tagmeme comprehends both the slot (subject) and the filler (NP); it therefore marks the intersection of function and form. A tagmeme may also refer to a slot like the P-slot or S-slot in a paragraph pattern, where P stands for a Problem and S for a Solution. See *Slot.*

Tail-rime stanza A six-line stanza in which longer lines, usually tetrameter couplets, are alternated with a shorter line, called "the tail," usually a trimeter. The rhyme scheme is *aabccb.* Many variants of the stanza occur, however, chief among which is Robert Burns' use of the tail-rime in various familiar poems like "To a Mountain Daisy," "To a Mouse," and "To a Louse." His form is three tetrameters, followed by a two-foot "tail," another tetrameter, and a final "tail." The rhyme scheme is *aaabab.*

Tenor and **Vehicle** Useful critical terms from I. A. Richards' *The Philosophy of Rhetoric* for discussing metaphor. The vehicle refers to the figure of speech itself, the tenor to the underlying idea. The metaphor embraces both. The opening lines of Milton's "Lycidas" will serve as an example:

Yet once more, O ye Laurels, and once more
Ye Myrtles brown, with Ivy never sere,
I come to pluck your Berries harsh and crude,
And with forc'd fingers rude,
Shatter your leaves before the mellowing year.

The vehicle concerns the picking of berries prematurely from the trees. The tenor has to do with the poet's writing before he considers himself fully mature. Since laurel, myrtle, and ivy are traditionally associated with the poet, their choice in the vehicle suggests that the tenor is actually about poetic inspiration.

Tercet A three-line stanza, used with variations. It can stand as an independent unit, rhyming *aaa,* as Robert Frost does frequently in short one-stanza lyrics, or *aba,* as Browning does in "The Statue and the Bust." The tercet is also used with an interlocking rhyme scheme. See *terza rima,* page 242, and *villanelle.*

Terminal In linguistic terms, a terminal is the boundary of a phrase, usually indicated by a pause, but not necessarily a complete stop. Terminals are indicated in speech by features of pitch and juncture and in writing by punctuation.

Threnody A lyric lamentation, written as an expression of grief upon the death of someone whom the poet loves or admires. Ralph Waldo Emerson's "Threnody" is a personal poem written upon the death of his son; Walt Whitman's "When Lilacs Last in the Dooryard Bloom'd" mourns the passing of Abraham Lincoln.

Tragedy   The concept of tragedy is not limited to drama; it is a serious way of looking at life. But, despite its dark side, tragedy is optimistic. It shows man in his moments of greatest adversity, but also reveals his fullest capacity to endure. His spirit is not easily broken. Tragedy testifies to man's dignity even when the odds are weighed heavily against him.

Because the term *tragedy* is often loosely used to refer to any disastrous event, it is well to consider what elements characterize it, particularly as it is used in literature. True tragedy, despite its variations throughout the history of literature, always seems to involve several factors:

1.   An inevitable force. In tragedy, man cannot escape the force of destiny. In ancient dramas, the element of necessity is almost always one beyond man's control. One can describe it in different ways as fate, the will of the gods, the force of the moral universe, or predestination, but whatever form it assumes man finds himself in conflict with a fixed and noncontrovertible force. Because death is the most unyielding fact of man's experience, tragedies usually concern themselves with men facing the hour of death.

Modern writers, however, less concerned with man's relation with metaphysical forces, have tended to write tragedies of living rather than tragedies of dying, to show man in relation to different kinds of shaping forces: his heredity, his environment, his own psychic nature, society in general. Because some of these have less inevitable influence upon man and, unlike the universal will, cannot be conceived of as good, modern writers are sometimes said to have a diminished sense of the tragic. Whether diminished or not, the basic conflicts are different, and our reactions to the circumstances are therefore different. Existing conditions are seldom altered in a tragedy: the gods prevail, fate is accomplished, the harmony of the universe is restored, heredity is inescapable, society works its way. But if one believes that the gods are just, then good prevails, and man loses in the struggle. Seldom, however, do writers reveal society or environment as good. If man is a victim of environmental forces, no universal harmony prevails. Only evil conditions persist. The basic conflict in most general terms—and conflict is central to the tragic effect—is therefore between good and evil. In an ancient tragedy like *Oedipus,* the flaw in man leads him to upset the moral order. In a modern tragedy like Ibsen's *The Enemy of the People,* the flaw is in society; the individual is often seen as justified. This shifting view of the deterministic force is therefore one of the important differences in reading modern tragedy as opposed to classical tragedy.

2.   A protagonist with whom we can identify. The protagonist
of tragedy is commonly called the tragic hero. In ancient and
Renaissance tragedies, he was inevitably a man of elevated station
in life, but Aristotle had established that the hero should not be
completely blameless. He is usually shown to be responsible for
the consequences that fall to him. By some error or flaw in his
nature, he himself sets into motion a chain of circumstances which
must work themselves inevitably to their end. If man only curses
his fate and dies, if he does not have the integrity and strength
to struggle, then tragedy cannot work its effects. Tragedy, therefore, deals with a change in man's fortune from good to bad. But
the turn in fortune's wheel is only a change of outward circumstance. Tragedy concerns itself with conflict and changes in the
inner man—the way in which he meets his fate, the way in which
he struggles against it.

Modern tragedies, less concerned with the fate of kings and
warriors, have introduced unheroic heroes and heroines like Willy
in Arthur Miller's *Death of a Salesman* and Maurya, the mother
in Synge's *Riders to the Sea,* not necessarily less heroic in spirit
but less elevated in station. Their fall may be less catastrophic
but not less meaningful in the total scheme of things. In fact,
our own capacity to identify with them may be greater because
of their lower status. Rich man or poor, king or peasant, man
is capable of revealing tragic conflict.

3.   Tragic conflict and the outcome. Tragic conflict is basically any struggle of man's will against some fate from which he
cannot escape. The situation can vary from Antigone's determination to bury the body of her dead brother in defiance of the
law of the state to Job's insistence upon his own righteousness
before God. Man is put to the test; man suffers. Tragedy reveals
man in his weakness and in his strength. From the experience,
he learns. He matures, he gains in wisdom, he sees more clearly
his place in the scheme of things. His downfall and death may
be his triumph. Tragedy brings about realizations of different kinds:
that man is not totally self-sufficient, that man is vulnerable, that
human existence is precarious, that man's spirit is indomitable,
that man suffers retribution for his pride, that goodness prevails,
that man will survive despite all odds. The experience of tragedy
through literature keeps each man's life from being tragic. Tragedy
inspires both pity and fear—pity for the sufferer and, by identification, fear for ourselves. Aristotle described this human response
to tragedy as a catharsis, leaving us calmer and wiser for having
emotionally experienced the conflict and destiny of a man less
fortunate than we.

Tragic flaw or **harmartia**   A concept derived from the *Poetics* where Aristotle describes the tragic hero as a person not entirely blameless or completely despicable but as a worthy man or woman whose character is marked by some flaw, which is ultimately responsible for his downfall. The flaw commonly depicted in Greek tragedy is *hubris* or *hybris,* a sense of overweening pride which causes man to think himself the equal of the gods. The "flaw" may also be interpreted as an error in judgment which results in direful consequences disproportionate to the act itself.

Tragicomedy   The term *tragicomedy* arose as a critical expedient during the time when tragedy and comedy were rigidly defined. From the classical period through the Renaissance, tragedy was supposed to deal with the affairs of noble men; comedy with men of lesser breed. Tragedy ended in death; comedy in joyful resolution of circumstances. Tragicomedy was particularly useful to describe plays about noblemen whose destiny seemed to lead them to disaster but whose fortunes were happily transformed at the end. Shakespeare's *The Winter's Tale* fits the classification or many of the dramas written by Francis Beaumont and John Fletcher in the seventeenth century.

Trivium   Grammar, logic, and rhetoric, the three key studies of the traditional medieval curriculum leading to the degree of bachelor of arts. Combined with the quadrivium, consisting of arithmetic, geometry, astronomy, and music and leading to the master of arts, they represented the seven liberal arts.

Trope   A rhetorical figure of speech in which the literal meaning of words is altered in some way as to convey a new or added meaning. Metaphor and simile are common tropes, although any variation of irony, hyperbole, understatement, ambiguity, or paradox falls into this classification.

In a more specialized sense, trope has reference to the elaborations upon the liturgy which were permitted in medieval churches. The early ones were antiphonal variations by the choir or exchanges between a soloist and the chorus. The *Quem quaeritis in sepulchro, o christicolae* (whom seek ye in the tomb, O followers of Christ?), the words of the angels to the three Marys inserted into the Easter mass, possibly dating from the ninth century, is usually cited as the trope marking the revival of drama in Western Europe, for medieval morality and mystery plays were a direct outgrowth of these church presentations.

U

Ubi sunt A Latin phrase meaning "where are they?" It is often used as an opening line or a refrain of a poem. A question of this kind is a lament for the passing of fame, beauty, youth, or life itself. Each stanza of François Villon's "The Ballad of Dead Ladies," as translated by Dante Gabriel Rossetti, ends with the query: "But where are the snows of yesteryear?" The theme is the evanescence of beauty.

Umlaut A form of predictable language change by which an internal vowel is affected by the syllables preceding or usually following it. The differences between *long* and *length, gold* and *gild,* and *fall* and *fell* illustrate umlaut changes at an earlier period.

Ur A German prefix meaning "original," used as in *Urfaust* or *Ur-Hamlet* to refer to early versions or sources of more famous works or as in *Ursprache,* a hypothetical reconstruction of a primitive language.

Utopia Derived from two Greek words meaning "no place" and punning upon two other Greek words meaning "good place." The "nowhere" of the literary utopia is the vision of an ideal world or state held by the writer. The utopia may be set forth in direct terms, as it is in Plato's *Republic* and Sir Thomas More's *Utopia* (1516), or it may be described satirically in terms of the opposite of what is ideal, as in George Orwell's *1984* and Aldous Huxley's *Brave New World.*

V

Vehicle See *Tenor.*

Verner's Law By explaining the influence of a stressed syllable upon another syllable immediately following it, Verner's Law accounted for sound changes in words that appeared to be exceptions to Grimm's Law. According to Grimm's Law, for example, the sounds *k, t,* and *p* in Indo-European became *h, θ,* and *f* in Germanic. Verner demonstrated that these same sounds under the influence of stress of certain syllables would change to *g, d,* and *b,* explaining many of the changes in English irregular verbs. Verner's findings gave strong support to the thesis of orderly sound change in language as opposed to a concept of pure chance. The predictable elements of change became the basis of comparative linguistics in the nineteenth century and made possible the reconstruction of hypothetical Indo-European words.

Versification   When words are combined with one another, a rhythmic effect is inevitable, simply because words themselves have accented and unaccented syllables. Any combination of words set up a rising and falling movement. If the movement is regular and repeated, it is called meter. Meter is measured rhythm. The metrical form of a group of words is the chief distinction between prose and verse. Both are rhythmical, but verse is frequently written in a set pattern. Even though twentieth-century poets have veered away from strictly measured verse to freer rhythmic patterns, many poems may still be marked by means of traditional units. The measurement of a line in terms of accents is called scansion. (See *Free verse.*)

SCANSION

The basic measuring unit of verse is a foot. In the English language, a foot consists of one stressed syllable and one or more unstressed syllables in a particular arrangement producing a definable meter. This is a scansion based upon accents. Other languages use a meter based upon the principle of long and short sounds, but accent is a more suitable system for English.

Traditional scansion makes no distinction between degrees of stress. Theoretically, all stressed syllables are of equal length. Unstressed syllables are also theoretically equal. Thus the marking system is reduced to two symbols: ′ for a stressed syllable, ˘ for an unstressed one.

The common metric feet of English verse are four:

1. iambus, producing iambic meter, consisting of an unstressed syllable followed by a stressed one:
    before, delight, inspire, serene.
2. trochee, producing trochaic meter, consisting of a stressed syllable followed by an unstressed one:
    after, picture, gather, recent.
3. anapest, producing anapestic meter, consisting of two unstressed syllables followed by a stressed syllable:
    underneath, Lebanese, entertain, indirect.
4. dactyl, producing dactylic meter, consisting of one stressed syllable followed by two unstressed ones:
    equally, iciness, obligate, glamorous.

The other possible combinations of stress and lack of stress are used primarily as substitute feet in order to vary the rhythm of regular metric lines:

1. spondee, consisting of two stressed syllables:
    hymn book, lifeboat
2. pyrrhic, consisting of two unaccented syllables:
    the supernatural
3. amphibrach, consisting of an unaccented syllable, an accented, and another unacccented one in that order.
    however, elation.

Other variations, of course, are possible. For example, an anapest can substitue for an iambic foot or a dactyl for a trochaic foot; or, in the first foot of an iambic line, a trochee or a spondee is commonly substituted for the regular foot:

Fair is my love, and cruel as she's fair.

> Daniel,
> *Delia,* VI

Look Delia, how we 'steem the half-blown rose

> Daniel,
> *Delia,* XXI

The second line from *Delia* XXI illustrates the tendency sometimes for the poet to truncate a word (*esteem* to *'steem*) in order to keep a regular meter. This may also be done by elision:

Thus policy in love, t'anticipate
The ills that were not, grew to faults assured.

> Shakespeare,
> "Sonnet 118"

Or by giving value to a syllable that is usually unpronounced:

O Prince, O Chief of many thronèd Powers

> Milton,
> *Paradise Lost,* I, 128

Lines of verse sometimes end with an extra unstressed syllable, called a weak or feminine ending:

A thing of beauty is a joy forever

Keats,
"Endymion"

If the final extra syllable is stressed, it is called a masculine ending, which may occur when the final foot of a trochaic line is incomplete:

Russet lawns and fallows grey,
Where the nibbling flocks do stray;

Milton,
"L'Allegro"

At times, the regular running meter of a line can be sustained, yet natural speech intonations will impose a different accentual pattern upon the line, resulting in a kind of counterpoint:

_____   (Speech emphasis)
Wilt thou then antedate some new made vow?   (Running meter)
          Or say that now
_____   (Speech emphasis)
We are not just those persons, which we were?   (Running meter)

Donne,
"Woman's Constancy"

COMMON METERS

The versification of a poem is described in terms of its predominant meter and the length of its line determined by the number of feet. The counting system of prosody is monometer (1), dimeter (2), trimeter (3), tetrameter (4), pentameter (5), hexameter (6), heptameter (7), octometer (8). The meter of a poem therefore may be identified as iambic pentameter, trochaic tirmeter, dactylic hexameter, or various other combinations.

Iambic monometer:

A line consisting of a single foot is frequently used in combination with longer lines for a special effect:

And last, till you write your letter,

Yet she

Will be

False, ere I come, to two or three.

Donne,
"Go and Catch a Falling Star"

Iambic dimeter and trimeter:

Bianca, let

Me pay the debt

I owe thee for a kiss

Thou lend'st to me,

And I to thee

Will render ten for this:

Herrick,
"Kissing Usury"

Iambic tetrameter:

Those cherries fairly do enclose

Of orient pearl a double row;

Which when her lovely laughter shows,

They look like rosebuds filled with snow.

Campion,
"There Is a Garden in Her Face"

Iambic pentameter:

When iambic pentameter is used for epic poetry in English,
it is called heroic verse:

Of Man's First Disobedience, and the Fruit

Of that Forbidden Tree, whose mortal taste

Brought Death into the World, and all our woe,

With loss of Eden, till one greater Man

Restore us, and regain the blissful Seat,

Sing, Heav'nly Muse . . .

Milton,
Paradise Lost

When verse is written in rhyming lines of iambic pentameter, the form is called the heroic couplet:

Some truth there was, but dashed and brewed with lies,
To please the fools, and puzzle all the wise:
Succeeding times did equal folly call,
Believing nothing, or believing all.

Dryden,
"Absalom and Achitophel"

When poetry is written in unrhymed iambic pentameter, the form is called blank verse:

Something there is that doesn't love a wall,
That sends the frozen-ground-swell under it,
And spills the upper boulders in the sun;
And makes gaps even two can pass abreast.

Frost,
"Mending Wall"

Iambic hexameter, or Alexandrine:

And streams of purple blood new dies the verdant fields.

Spenser,
The Faerie Queene

Trochaic tetrameter:

Up, lad, up, 'tis late for lying:
Hear the drums of morning play;

Housman,
"Reveille"

A line which lacks part of its last foot is called catalectic.

Trochaic octometer:

Many a night from yonder ivied casement, ere I went to rest,
Did I look on great Orion sloping slowly to the West.

Tennyson,
"Locksley Hall"

Anapestic tetrameter:

> And the widows of Asshur are loud in their wail,
> And the idols are broke in the temple of Baal;

Byron,
"The Destruction of Sennacherib"

Anapestic hexameter:

> Of the maiden thy mother men sing as a goddess with grace clad around;
> Thou art throned where another was king; where another was queen
> she is crowned.

Swinburne,
"Hymn to Proserpine"

Dactylic dimeter:

> Cannon to right of them,
> Cannon to left of them,
> Cannon in front of them
> Volley'd and thunder'd;

Tennyson,
"The Charge of the Light Brigade"

Dactyllic hexameter:

> Over two shadowless waters, adrift as a pinnace in peril

Swinburne,
"Evening on the Broads"

CAESURA

The caesura of a line is the natural pause that results from the grammar or logic of the words. The caesura commonly occurs after the fourth, fifth, or sixth syllable in a ten-syllable line, but it is by no means limited to those junctures. If the caesura occurs after a stressed syllable, it is called masculine; if it occurs after an unstressed syllable, it is called feminine:

> Of all this servile herd ‖ the worst is he   [masculine]
> That in proud dullness ‖ joins with quality,   [feminine]

Pope,
An Essay on Criticism

Shifting the caesura is a means poets use to avoid a metro-nome-like effect.

Villanelle A poem of nineteen lines, consisting of five tercets rhyming *aba,* ending with a quatrain rhyming *abaa* and featuring the repetition of lines in a set pattern. The first and third lines of the first tercet, here indicated as A^1 and A^2, are repeated alternately throughout the remaining stanzas in the following manner: A^1bA^2, abA^1; abA^2, abA^1, abA^2, aba^1A^2. Dylan Thomas' "Do Not Go Gentle into That Good Night" is a well-known example. Theodore Roethke's "The Waking" is a villanelle with slight variations in the repeated lines.

Vocative The case of a noun used in direct address. In some languages, like Latin, the case has its own inflection. The term is applicable to modern grammar as far as grammatical function goes, but there is no special form for it. We regularly use direct address in uninflected forms: *Harry, don't always tease.*

W

Wit The current implications of the word *wit* have their source in a variety of meanings attributed to the word throughout its long history. The present conception of wit as an intellectual brand of humor retains a remnant of its oldest meanings as "knowledge" or "the seat of knowledge," derived from the Anglo-Saxon *witan,* meaning "to know." Its present association with swift perception and cleverness bears something in common with the seventeenth-century use of the term to designate the "fancy" or "creative imagination"—the power of conceiving. Its modern implication of aptness, even patness, has something in common with its eighteenth-century use as the excercise of judgment, resulting in propriety and good sense. In most ages, the word has been linked with verbal ingenuity, quickness, and conciseness—the products of a bright mind—but mainly since the eighteenth century it has taken on an implication of laughableness. See *Epigram.*

Z

Zero Term used for the sake of regularity to explain the omission of an expected feature. Thus, because the plural of *sheep* does not add an ending, *sheep* is said to have a zero plural. In like manner, *James'* is said to be a zero form of the possessive. The subject of an imperative may also be described as a zero subject. [*you*] *Stand still.*

Zeugma A rhetorical trope, usually of a humorous nature, producing a shift in verbal context by having one part of speech, usually a preposition or a verb, function with two subjects or two objects, which are in themselves disproportionate:

Hear thou, great Anna! whom three realms obey,
Dost sometimes counsel take—and sometimes tea.

Pope,
"The Rape of the Lock"

Index